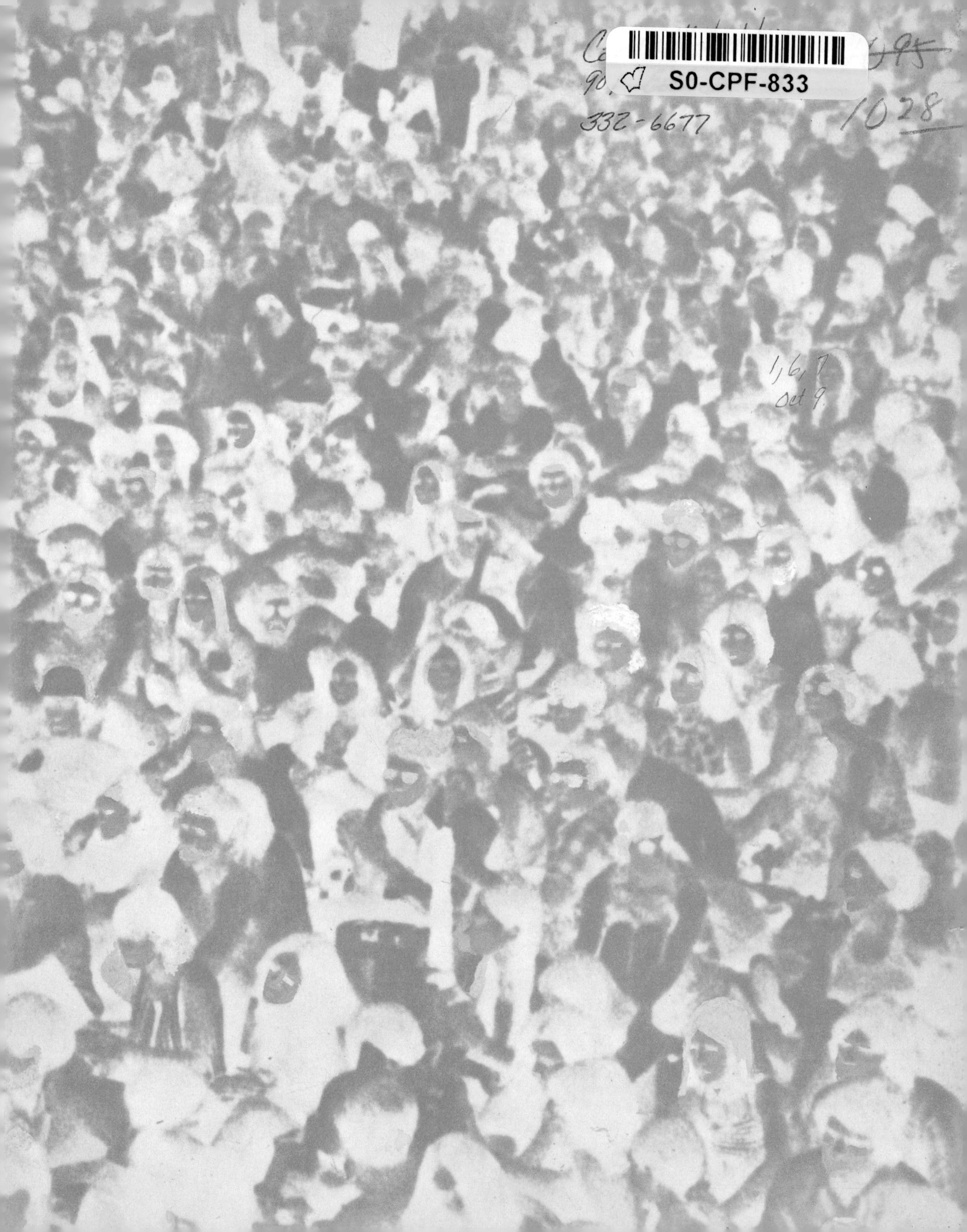

THE RIDDLE OF MAN

AN INTRODUCTION TO PSYCHOLOGY

Richard S. Lazarus

Department of Psychology, University of California, Berkeley

Prentice-Hall, Inc., Englewood Cliffs, New Jersey

To my dear family:

Bunny; David and Mary; Nancy and Rick

Library of Congress Cataloging in Publication Data

Lazarus, Richard S
   The riddle of man.

   Bibliography: p.
   1. Psychology. 2. Social psychology.
I. Title. [DNLM: 1. Psychology.   BF121 L431r 1974]
BF121.L29   150   73-13614
ISBN 0-13-781088-1

This book has been composed on film in Baskerville, with headings and margin notes in Helvetica. Photo consultant: Frances L. Orkin. Illustrator: Felix Cooper. Production by Bert N. Zelman and Norma T. Karlin. Typographical design by John J. Dunleavy.

10 9 8 7 6 5 4 3 2 1

Prentice-Hall International, Inc., London
Prentice-Hall of Australia, Pty. Ltd., Sydney
Prentice-Hall of Canada, Ltd., Toronto
Prentice-Hall of India Private Ltd., New Delhi
Prentice-Hall of Japan, Inc., Tokyo

Contents

v

Students nowadays flock to psychology courses with intrinsically positive attitudes; but many of them show little real enthusiasm for the first (and often last) such course that they take. They soon come to believe that there is a systematic plot to underplay the very things that interest them most and to teach what no one besides professors cares to know.

In this text my solution to this difficulty is to present psychology in the context of the great and classic problems of mankind, problems that are as weighty, unresolved, and poignant today as they were at the dawn of civilization. Among these are man's struggle for adaptation to his changing physical and social environment, his outbursts of destructive violence and aggression, his attitudes of prejudice tied to fear and hatred of his fellow man, and his painful efforts to master the inner and outer pressures to which he is constantly exposed.

In the search for answers to highly complex questions raised by these issues, it is my opinion that a multidisciplinary approach is often helpful. I have therefore ventured at times to cross departmental boundaries that separate psychology from physiology, biochemistry, ecology, sociology, anthropology, and other disciplines involved in the study of man.

The outlook of this book is biosocial and adaptational: man is placed in an evolutionary context. Although there are no chapters entitled *Perception, Learning,* or *Physiological psychology* per se, these topics are well examined along the way. Perception is treated in the discussion of environmental impact on the individual (Chapter 2). Analyses of conditioning and learning are brought to bear on the question of how society shapes our lives (Chapters 4, 7, and 11). Physiological psychology is represented in the treatment of biological aspects of aggression (Chapter 6). As it turns out, a surprising amount of basic psychology can be learned in this way. (The interested reader is advised to glance through the listing of basic psychological topics printed in the margin of pages x and xi. He is also invited to peruse the Prologue, pages 3 to 13, wherein are introduced the main themes of this book.)

Consistent with my feeling that students commonly feel cheated out of substantive discussion of clinical issues in the usual introductory potpourri, I have given these matters due weight in Part IV, *Adaptation versus alienation*. Here, in Chapters 11 and 12 particularly, there is considerable emphasis on Freudian thought, both as an approach to treatment and a theory of mind. Though I do not embrace the Freudian system *in toto*, and take pains to pinpoint its limitations and defects, it is my considered view that this emphasis is advantageous in a basic textbook. Freudian and neo-Freudian concepts pervade our everyday professional and lay thinking, even though their influence is often unacknowledged, and students can benefit by examining these ideas and evaluating their effects on the modern world.

It is also my opinion that the best way to foster an appreciation of sound psychological research is to show how it works in particular instances. I have therefore peppered the margins of this book with Notes commenting on methodological issues alongside of actual research observations. Thus, correlation as a concept is discussed in Notes 5.1, 6.3, and 6.4, beside discussions of correlation in the text proper. (A listing of these Notes, indicating the topics discussed, is given on page xii.)

There is an unhappy trend in recent texts to present findings of psychological research and analysis without citation of references. This is done in the desire, perhaps, to avoid intimidating the reader with names and dates having no meaning for him. It is my belief that it is undesirable and anti-intellectual to encourage dependency on unsupported statements from an august authority. We do not need any more anti-intellectualism than we already have. A fairly extensive bibliography is therefore presented at the end of this book, and text citations to it are made in such a way as to disturb the reading flow as little as possible. In addition, a brief annotated list of suggested readings appears at the end of each chapter. Occasionally, quotations from important works of science, scholarship, or literature, as well as interesting items from the press, may be found adjacent to relevant text discussions. I hope some of these quotes will entice the ambitious reader to dig more deeply into primary source material.

Unlike most texts, this is a personal book, its contents determined in part by those things I have a keen feeling about and based on my judgment about the close relationship between psychology and human problems. My personal values will undoubtedly emerge quite clearly in the treatment of the subject matter, though I have striven as much as possible to offer balanced discussions of controversial issues. But I have resisted the stultifying tradition that equates scholarship and science with cold objectivity in the face of human suffering. I think it is time for a change; indeed, it is long overdue.

If I have been successful in my efforts, students reading this problem-centered book will find the material meaningful because it is tied to their real-life concerns. The democratization of education should not mean that we must lower our standards of intellectual analysis, but it does make it urgent to strive for clarity and the absence of jargon and pedantry. It has been my aim to challenge the reader without overwhelming him, to give him a sophisticated grasp of the key issues and concepts of modern psychology—but not to leave him confused.

A considerable group of friends, associates, students, and professional persons have added importantly to this book in many ways. Especially worthy of note is Bert N. Zelman of Prentice-Hall's Project Planning Department, who contributed much "above and beyond the call of duty" in editing the manuscript and coordinating the multiple tasks of development and production of the book, and whose remarkable intellectual energy and broad scholarship greatly strengthened the final product. John J. Dunleavy, the designer, created the dynamic format of this book. Norma Karlin devoted her energy and many talents to its preparation for the press. Edward E. Lugenbeel, Neale E. Sweet, and David R. Esner of Prentice-Hall offered invaluable advice and encouragement along the way. It was a pleasure, once again, to have the benefit of Frances L. Orkin's imaginative photo research. Mary H. Fitzgerald rendered substantial aid in all stages of the book's production.

Gratitude is due to Professor James R. Averill, who worked diligently with the early versions of the manuscript and whose knowledge and judgment I hold in high regard. Mention should also be made of Mrs. Kazuko Nishita, who typed every draft of the manuscript, and whose efficiency, cheerfulness, and dependability amid many other responsibilities of her own were a great joy. The list of others who have generously contributed their knowledge and judgment includes Edward S. Katkin, Marcel L. Goldschmid, Allen Parducci, R. O. Pihl, Neil A. Carrier, Robert E. Garrison, Robert Bornstein, Rose Frank, Edward O'day, Gail Silverman, Janet Stein, Jerry Higgins, Frank B. McMahon, Charles Morris, and Edward Poindexter. Many of these persons provided extremely detailed and thoughtful critiques of tremendous value. They cannot, of course, be held responsible in any way for the book's defects, since my own judgment ex-

clusively determined the final contents. I express my gratitude to them and can only hope that they are reasonably
pleased with the outcome of their efforts.

Last and most deserving of credit is the person who day
in and day out over all the years remained encouraging, optimistic, accepting, and patient, protecting both my work commitment and my good cheer as she has always during the
writing of several other books and throughout our wonderful
28-year relationship—my wife, Bunny.   *R.S.L.*

List of Notes

What can the shadow-like generations of man attain
But build up a dazzling mockery of delight that under their touch dissolves again?
Oedipus seemed blessed, but there is no man blessed amongst men.

Oedipus overcame the woman-breasted Fate;
He seemed like a strong tower against Death and first among the fortunate;
He sat upon the ancient throne of Thebes, and all men called him great.

But, looking for a marriage-bed, he found the bed of his birth,
Tilled the field his father had tilled, cast seed into the same abounding earth;
Entered through the door that had sent him wailing forth.

Begetter and begot as one! How could that be hid?
What darkness cover up that marriage-bed? Time watches, he is eagle-eyed,
And all the works of man are known and every soul is tried.

Would you had never come to Thebes, nor to this house,
Nor riddled with the woman-breasted Fate, beaten off Death and succoured us,
That I had never raised this song, heartbroken Oedipus!

—From Sophocles' "King Oedipus," translated by W. B. Yeats (1953).

An ancient Greek legend tells of a monster known as the Sphinx, part woman, part lion, who afflicted the city of Thebes. Crouched on a rock, she stopped all passing travelers and asked them a riddle: "What animal is that which in the morning goes on four feet, at noon on two, and in the evening upon three?" When the passerby could not answer correctly he was killed and devoured. No one could solve the puzzle except one Oedipus. When posed the riddle by the Sphinx, Oedipus replied, "Man, who in childhood creeps on hands and knees, in manhood walks erect, and in old age hobbles with the aid of a staff." At this, the Sphinx was so mortified that she threw herself from the rock and perished. Oedipus thus became the savior of Thebes and was made king, much to his future sorrow. (We shall pursue his further adventures in Chapter 12.) This book concerns a greater "riddle," that of man's inner nature. To find this answer we must explore his mental life, learn how and why he thinks, feels, and acts as he does in response to the dynamic world in which he must engage in a struggle for existence.

One does not have to try to convince people of the excitement inherent in the effort to understand themselves better. Man is a curious animal. Not only does he find joy in increasing his knowledge, but his quest into the depths of his own psyche is powered by the desire to improve his lot in life. Students jam into psychology courses hoping to solve the riddle, wanting to learn what they think psychology has to teach them about their lives and their pressing personal problems. Although students' expectations about what psychology will do for them are often unrealistic in that there are few quick and easy answers to the problems of living in a complex and difficult world, psychology is, indeed, a rich and fascinating field, touching every facet of our lives. And there is no denying that it has already done much to improve our understanding of human behavior and helped to throw light on the many irrational, even self-destructive activities of man.

In most introductory psychology texts, students are presented a host of unrelated topics that professional psychologists consider representative of the discipline, skimmingly presented, and without much effort to show how these topics relate to the major concerns of mankind. During the lifetimes of many of us the automobile and airplane have emerged as the world's principal means of transportation. Radio and television have made instant communication possible around the globe. Nuclear power and bombs, rocket propulsion and space flight, high-speed computers and automation—all have put enormous power into man's hands for good or ill. In this century, we have seen the elimination or control of many diseases. Despite two highly destructive world wars and many lesser ones, numerous revolutions, massacres, and genocides, the human population is increasing at a dizzying rate. Today we are confronted with growing problems of air, water, and soil pollution and impending shortages of vital raw materials. In many parts of the globe large-scale hunger threatens. As pressures mount, there has been a significant increase in use and abuse of drugs and a rise in crime and social disorder. In the light of these major world upheavals, can psychology be presented meaningfully if it ignores such critical issues? Clearly, the problems that men and women must face in the world around them are an essential part of their psychology.

Instead of starting with the topics important to academic psychologists, the book you are about to read is unusual in that it approaches the puzzle of man's labyrinthine psyche through classical human problems that are as vital, poignant, and unresolved today as they were at the dawn of history. The focus will be on how psychology can contribute to their solution, rather than on the study of psychological methods per se. Yet it turns out that a surprising amount of basic psychology can be learned in this way.

I have tried here to tell a coherent story, to examine a number of interrelated problems in some depth, and to link them through certain central themes. Four key problem areas have been selected: (1) Since man was originally forged in the course of evolution by the pressures of biological survival and today people in technologically advanced societies are confronted with brand new environmental dangers to both survival and the quality of life, we begin in Part I by examining the *environments of man*, both physical and social, and consider their impact on him. (2) This book was written during the final phases of the prolonged and horrendous war in Southeast Asia and in a time of extraordinary violence throughout the world. The problem of war and violence is foremost in everyone's mind today. And so Part II concerns the *psychology of aggression*. (3) Mankind is also rent by divisiveness and continuing exclusion of racial, religious, and ethnic minorities. Society is faced today with growing intergroup hostility. In the light of its ubiquitousness and importance in our lives, we examine *prejudice* in Part III. (4) Many individuals fail to adapt successfully to the stresses of the modern world, and some totally withdraw from reality. In Part IV we are concerned with personal *adaptation*—and its opposite, human *alienation*. Our study of these per-

sistent human dilemmas will bring into bold relief the biosocial nature of man. Looking closely at them as we shall do may help us better to understand ourselves. And only with increased insight into our own motivations can we function effectively as concerned human beings in the society and world of which we are part.

Certain ways of thinking about the nature of man are adopted by anyone who writes a psychology text, and it will be worthwhile here briefly to acquaint the reader with the way I, as the author, think about these matters. There are a number of controversial issues that no one can avoid in presenting the subject matter, and it is best to face them squarely right at the start.

THE NATURE OF MAN

Man is a biological organism, made of many cells forming tissues and organs. He is subject to the same basic biological laws as all other forms of animal life. At the same time he is a social animal, creating a complex society and living within the social patterns he has created; indeed, he is heavily dependent on interpersonal relationships and is shaped psychologically by them from birth. Thus, if we are to understand ourselves we must take note of both the biological and social forces constantly at work in controlling our behavior and mental activity. Every psychological event is a joint product of these two interacting forces.

Our biological makeup influences the social order that we create around us. In order to survive in what can be a hostile physical environment, man must find a space in which he can feel secure. Everywhere men have learned how to use available materials to construct shelters that shut out rain or snow, keep in or keep out heat, and permit entry of sufficient light. Social institutions must somehow fulfill this biological requirement for shelter. Similarly, each society must have arrangements for mating and child rearing, since the species cannot survive unless it produces offspring and protects them to maturity. Probably for these reasons the family evolved as the basic social unit. The social structure must likewise include arrangements to provide for food, say, by organizing its people so that there is a practical division of labor, whether it be by food gathering or hunting or agriculture.

Conversely, our social patterns modify the way biological processes operate. For example, societies generally arrange time-related patterns of eating and sleeping. Sometimes the sleeping cycle follows the rhythm of the sun as it rises and sets, although in more complex societies some people play roles that keep them awake at night and asleep during the day. In most industrial societies people eat three times a day at prescribed intervals. As a result of these time-related social patterns, we acquire regular biological rhythms that determine our gastric secretions, our feelings of hunger and fatigue, and our hormonal activity. Today, when we travel by jet airplane across many time zones into a cultural setting where the eating and sleeping patterns are quite different, we will be made uncomfortable by disruption of our established biological cycle. Some time is required before this "jet lag" wears off and new rhythms are established under the altered social patterns. Similarly, although all people eat, the types of food are markedly different, ranging from raw fish to beef, goat to whale blubber, frogs' legs to grasshoppers, strictly vegetable foods to meat, and the methods of eating also vary considerably. In one culture a person may recline on chairs, in another in hammocks; he may sit on his haunches or on the ground: each of these patterns have an effect on posture and hence on the pattern of bone calcification and musculature. There is, in short, constant interplay between biological factors that influence our social patterns and social factors that influence our biological activities.

As will be seen in Parts II and III, even our feelings of animosity toward others are, in part, a product of the way we are constructed biologically, a result of the functioning of our particular type of brain and the secretions of our glands, and this pattern of behavior can be traced to our early ancestors. Yet human reactions involving hostility also depend on certain social conditions that provoke them. It is impossible to develop an adequate understanding of this or any other way of reacting to other people by focusing solely on man's biological characteristics. When we try to resolve the riddle that is man we must look to these two sets of forces, the biological and the social, since both are central in everything he does and experiences. Henceforth in this text, when biological and social factors are considered separately, it is merely for convenience of exposition and not because either approach alone can adequately explain most psychological phenomena or offers a better vantage point for doing so.

Man is also *interdependent with his environment* and cannot be understood apart from it. Indeed, the environment does make many demands on us, providing innumerable challenges to which we must respond successfully in order to survive. Behavior does not take place in a vacuum but is always occurring in an environmental context. We cannot predict human actions without reference to that context.

Nevertheless, man is not merely a passive responder to environmental stimuli that happen to come his way, nor does he become active only when aroused by such stimuli. We cannot apprehend all external events around us since there are too many—so we must be selective. It is true that some stimuli are inherently very forceful, making us look, listen, or respond. For example, a sudden loud noise will gain our attention and may be difficult to disregard even if we try. On the other hand, as a result of our biological makeup and experience, our reactions to the environment depend on the importance of the stimulus to our welfare, and we reject some inputs as irrelevant, vigilantly attend to others as potentially harmful or rewarding, and actively seek out others if they are not present. We appraise environmental events in accordance with their relative significance, searching actively for those things which will produce what we consider to be desirable ends and avoiding that which might injure or destroy us. Man is unique in the animal world in the complexity of his thought, in his commitment to and dependence on symbols, in his wide-ranging use of tools and weapons, and in the extent to which he can free himself from the tyranny of his tissues and glands and direct his life flexibly and with fore-sight. Perhaps most important from the psycho-logical point of view, man is aware of himself as moving through time and measures its pass-ing; he recognizes that he has a past, present, and future; he knows that he was born and that he must die.

WHAT IS PSYCHOLOGY?

One of the remarkable qualities of man is that he not only acts but is an observer of his own actions and is conscious of himself as a being. Perhaps the most obtrusive feature of subjective experience is our awareness of thoughts, images, feelings, moods, wishes, and intentions. Indeed, psychology began with a preoccupation with man's inner life and the nature of consciousness. There are, however, certain serious difficulties inherent in the study of subjective experience.

Although all of us are aware of our own inner experience, consciousness is a private affair, making it difficult to study with dependa-bility or objectivity. It is difficult to know what is going on in other persons' minds unless they tell us about it, and there are many reasons why we cannot fully trust what they report. People may be *unwilling* to tell us things that put them in a bad light socially, or they may desire to give certain positive impressions and therefore distort their account. They may also be *unable* (as dis-tinguished from unwilling) to tell us what is in their minds. For one thing, to report accurately and completely about such matters they must use words, and even in the richest and most versatile of human languages, many aspects of our experience are *not adequately labeled.* Thus, in some languages there are many words for things that are an important part of the everyday ex-perience of the people but cannot be translated into other languages in which such words are not required. For example, the Hanunoo tribes-men of the Philippines have words distin-guishing 92 different varieties of rice (Conklin, 1954); the Nuer people of Africa have thousands of words having to do with cattle, an important

part of their subsistence (Evans-Prichard, 1940); and the Eskimo differentiates among many vari-eties of snow. The members of these cultures can thus communicate about many nuances of their environment and experience that others cannot even conceive of, just as our own language is particularly expressive of those things which are of great importance to us but which may be missing from other tongues (Whorf, 1960). Moreover, in our own language words describ-ing various emotional states are quite limited and vague, making it difficult for us to commu-nicate such states accurately to others.

Impact of Freud's theory

One of the events that helped turn psy-chology away from the study of conscious expe-rience and made psychologists distrustful of the importance of such study was the emergence of psychoanalytic theory around the turn of the century. At that time Sigmund Freud, then a practicing neurologist in Vienna, began to pub-lish the ideas that were destined to have such tremendous impact on all the social sciences, particularly in the fields of personality, clinical, and social psychology. In his early therapeutic work, Freud sometimes made use of hypnosis, and he was struck by the fact that a large part of human mental activity is unconscious. As his psychoanalytic techniques advanced, Freud be-came sure that much of human behavior is gov-erned by such unconscious processes, by motives and emotions that are unknown even to the actor himself, much less to the casual observer. Freud suggested that we are frequently capable of *deceiving ourselves* about the bases of our ac-tions. It followed logically that the study of consciousness alone would not have very much efficacy in helping to explain a person's actions, since he could know little about the most sig-nificant portion of his mental life.

On the other hand, the actions of people are clearly of great importance to the psycholo-gist. He must pay close attention to the ways in which people behave. After all, their actions express the nature of their mental life. Thus, a primary focus of the science of psychology has come to be placed on the way people act, their treatment of others, as an expression of their inner nature.

Partly as a result of the methodological difficulties of studying consciousness and partly because there was some doubt about its importance in accounting for human affairs, the mainstream of psychology in the 1920s and 1930s turned away from the study of man's subjective, inner mental life and toward that which could be more reliably observed, namely his behavior. Behavior came to include not only motor actions and verbal reports but also observable physiological changes in response to the environment, such as the electrical activity of the brain, secretions of glands, and changes in the activity of the body (like heart rate or respiration). A new definition of psychology appeared, namely, that it was the *science of behavior*, and the strictest adherents of this approach came to be called *behaviorists.* Psychology began to model itself after experimental physics in an effort to take its place among the natural sciences. It tended at first to rule out the study of inner mental life (or the "mind") as being beyond the realm of scientific study because it could not be observed directly. Although the doctrine of behaviorism had the positive consequence of pushing psychology away from armchair speculation about mental life that was unsupported by behavioral evidence, it also had a stultifying influence on the field, leaving out all reference to the inner mental activity that governs our behavior and functions every moment of our existence, even when we sleep.

Neobehaviorism

In recent years strict behaviorism has tended to give way to a broader view often referred to as *neobehaviorism.* Although this view still acknowledges that only overt behavior is subject to direct observation, it also recognizes the key role that internal mental activity plays as mediator between environmental inputs (usually called *stimuli*) and our reactions (or *responses*) to them. Such internal mental activity (for example, motives, thoughts, and feelings) influences and modifies how we act and react. Neobehaviorism holds that the primary task of

theoretical psychology is to investigate the nature of this mental activity and how it is connected with environmental input and consequent behavior.

While the strict behaviorist understood behavior in terms of connections between stimuli and responses (S–R), both readily observable events, the neobehaviorist understands behavior in terms of internal psychological events; these are aroused by stimuli and govern the behavioral response (S–O–R, with the "O" standing for these internal events). The task of understanding behavior from this point of view can be likened to the situation one faces in attempting to understand what is happening in an experimental animal, who cannot of course speak to us to explain why he acts as he does. By observing how he acts in any given environmental context, we can make inferences about what is happening internally, for example, that he is hungry, enraged, or fearful. By his actions he communicates to us about his inner psychological processes. If our understanding is sound, we will make the correct prediction about how the animal will behave. Thus, a lion tamer usually knows (as do that animal's potential prey in the wild) when it is safe to approach the lion and when it is unsafe, from a "reading" of his psychological state. If his perception is unsound, the lion tamer is likely to find out in a hurry.

In the case of man, it is as though one were looking at a sealed electrical box whose inner workings (electrical circuits) we cannot directly observe but whose nature we can infer by noting what goes in and how this gets converted into the pattern of electrical energy coming out. (In the psychological case, the input consists of environmental stimuli and the output is behavior.)

The neobehaviorist's solution to the riddle of the mind (as a sealed box whose working must be inferred) is quite in keeping with the Freudian suggestion that most important mental activity is unconscious and hence not reportable by the person. The solution is to take what the person says about his mental life as a source of information, but with a grain of salt, recognizing that the "real" mental activity is often covered up through a process of censorship or defense (say, because its acknowledgment would be unbearably painful). In Freudian psychology, the hidden mental activities are detected by inferences on the part of the observer, if he can decipher the code. He watches for inconsistencies in what is said or between what is said and done; he also notes the way ideas slip through the censorship screen in symbolic form in dreams, in "Freudian slips" of the tongue, or in various symptoms of psychological disturbance (*neurosis*). Much may be learned, of course, through a patient's "free association" in psychoanalysis. But more about this later. The point is that we can attempt to infer what is going on inside by watching the person's behavior in particular environmental contexts. We try to formulate rules of what is going on, cast typically in terms of concepts such as motives, thoughts, feelings, and defense mechanisms; these are then linked to directly observable environmental stimuli and behavioral responses.

There are two main facets to modern psychology: The one concentrates on *behavior* and the environmental context in which it occurs; this is readily observable and constitutes the bulk of what many modern psychologists are doing at present. The other involves something that we all intuitively recognize as a major part of our lives, namely, *consciousness* (or subjective experience), which is known directly only to each person privately, although an observer can try to guess at it from what is said and done in given environmental settings. Currently, there is much renewed and growing interest among psychologists in the nature of subjective experience, stimulated partly by recognition of the striking changes in consciousness accompanying use of certain drugs and the heightened states achieved through meditation, yoga, zen, and other such means of introspection.

It is therefore sensible to define psychology as the *science of behavior and mental activity.* This definition includes inferred mental activity as well as behavior, and allows everyone (except those who reject the legitimacy of any theory about the mind) to have a piece of the psychological pie. However, there remain some very significant dissenting voices. Perhaps the most distinguished is B. F. Skinner (1938, 1961, 1971), who argues that theories about mental activities

have never been of much value in psychology and that in understanding behavior it is most important to show the relationships between the way animals react and the contingencies in their environment, that is, the rewards and punishments that follow from actions. It is mainly these environmental contingencies that shape how we behave, and Skinner believes that references to inner events such as motives, thoughts, and feelings obscure rather than clarify the laws of behavior, or at best are useless in predicting behavior. We shall encounter Skinner's ideas again in Chapter 4, when we consider the way people are influenced by their social milieu. Moreover, his views should not be treated lightly: a vital and influential new school of psychology dealing with the principles of behavior modification and therapy has sprung up in recent years, based largely on Skinnerian methods of behavioral analysis (Chapter 11).

Psychology as a science

Having used the word *science* in the definition of psychology, it is fitting to examine the question of whether or not psychology is a science at all. Most psychologists would answer affirmatively, although those wishing to emulate the more exact natural sciences might express some doubts because of the high degree of imprecision in most psychological data and theory. I would say it is a science, not because it is anywhere near as precise as physics, for example, but because it represents *a body of reliable knowledge* and *seeks by rational and observational means to expand that knowledge.* Thus, psychologists attempt not only to speculate about mental events and the rules by which they operate, but also to evaluate such speculations by checking them against the observable facts of behavior and trying to make sure the facts are dependable. Psychologists are generally committed to search for knowledge by *use of a wide array of observational and experimental methods, which can be repeated by more than one observer, permitting verification of the results.* This is the method of science. However, as James Deese (1972) has observed, psychology may at times be considered more like an *art* than a science in that some of its techniques are based on intuitive experience that is not systematically codified or always readily verifiable by means of observation. Thus, skilled therapists are able to pose questions so effectively that a patient is likely to reveal essential things about himself, while poorly trained or ineffectual clinicians sometimes ask the same things in such a way as to mobilize denials or defense mechanisms. Therefore, there is art in the practice of psychotherapy and in the assessment of personality. Great perspicacity is required for accurate observations about the behavior of people in natural or laboratory situations. Art and science are thoroughly mixed in much of professional and research psychology, just as they are in the practice of medicine.

Psychology and the betterment of human life

There are many values in science. For some social scientists it is enough to try to describe, as an artist or gifted writer might, *how* people manage their lives without necessarily attempting to determine the *causes* of their behavior or to predict their future actions. Yet, to the extent that we want to use psychological knowledge to improve the quality of life, we must (in the cause-and-effect tradition of the natural sciences) be able in some degree to *predict* human reactions on the basis of our understanding of mental activity and the conditions that influence it. If we can predict behavior, then to some degree we can *control* psychological events.

The earliest way in which man understood himself and the world was based on magic and demonology. An illness or injury was attributed to the action of an evil spirit driven to punish a transgression against the supernatural or to the action of a sorcerer hired to wreak revenge for an insult or injury. Such magical thinking is still dominant in primitive societies today and is more common within our own society than is often realized or acknowledged. This is illustrated by widespread interest in so-called occult matters (like attempts to communicate with the dead or the great fascination with black magic, voodoo, and witchcraft) and in the recent resurgence of belief in the ancient pseudoscience of astrology as a means of predicting the future. Although the interest of many people in astrology is merely playful, not a few appear to take seriously the claim that astrological charts and readings can foretell their fate by reference to the movements of planets and stars. What is remarkable and instructive about this is that belief in magic and even sorcery should gain such ready acceptance at a time when the general level of public education is higher than it has ever been in the history of civilization.

It was a major step forward for mankind when the people of ancient Greece began to substitute rational thought and observation for belief in magic and demons to explain events. The notion that there were natural causes for every event later spread to many parts of the vast Roman Empire. During this Greco-Roman era, science flourished in certain academies of learning and great strides in knowledge took place. With the collapse of Rome, this rationalistic tradition was partially buried during the Middle Ages (the so-called Dark Ages), but it began to revive again with the European Renaissance, leading during the last five centuries to a vast expansion of knowledge and technology that has changed the shape of the world.

An important factor in this expansion of knowledge was the inclination to analyze natural events in terms of cause and effect. Modern psychology, like all science, follows this naturalistic tradition. Usually these causal conditions act in complex chains or networks, and most of the cause-and-effect relationships in psychology involve mutual action and reaction: *A* says something to *B*; *B* responds; in turn, that response influences both *A* and *B* in their further interaction.

The importance of thinking in terms of cause and effect in the effort to improve man's life can be illustrated most clearly perhaps in medicine. When we know the conditions causing an illness, we can sometimes prevent or cure it by changing these conditions. We can remove diseased organs that threaten the patient's life, administer germ-killing antibiotics to his body, strengthen his bodily defenses against invading viruses by vaccination. We can try to prevent the spread of such illness by quarantining the affected individuals. In the psychological domain, we can attempt to encourage the development of successful adaptation by influencing the conditions of life under which people develop, substituting those factors which produce favorable outcomes or prevent unfavorable ones.

As was said earlier, scientific theories must be buttressed by supportive evidence. Unsupported convictions or good intentions about helping people or improving society are not enough. It would of course be desirable to have completely reliable data about the conditions shaping behavior and mental activity before we set about altering them. But man is not a laboratory animal, and rats and monkeys do not always provide adequate substitutes in psychological research. Many psychologists who want to act to improve the human condition doubt that we can wait until all the data are in. They feel that the problems are pressing and that we must make attempts to aid troubled individuals by altering the conditions of their lives. Moreover, they feel that such changes will also create a kind of laboratory for the study of human affairs in which the effects of such intervention may be observed. Often we cannot anticipate the effects of changes we produce, however, and these effects may be quite the opposite from what was intended. Do we await full knowledge so that we can be confident of the outcomes of our intervention, or press ahead though we know very little? This dilemma is one of the most excruciatingly difficult and controversial in modern social science.

The history of psycho-quackery offers a striking example of what can happen when half-baked, unproved notions about the causes of mental illness are applied to people. In the early 1920s, Henry Cotton (1922), a physician, offered the theory that mental disorders were caused by nerve poisons arising from hidden foci of infection within the body. These infections, which existed unknown to the patient, might be lodged in the teeth, tonsils, appendix, and other locations, and a logical treatment would be systematically to remove all the tissues where the poisons might be generated. Large numbers of patients were so treated. Cotton claimed great success for the treatment, and its use spread. It took a careful experiment by two other physi-

cians (Kopeloff and Cheney, 1922) to dispel this false theory and the treatment that accompanied it. They compared a group of 58 mental patients treated in this way with a comparable group of 62 people receiving no such treatment and found that those treated showed no more benefit from removal of teeth, tonsils, or whatever than did the untreated ones. A core tenet of science, let us remember, is that our hunches or theoretical speculations about the way things work must be checked in carefully reported research *that can be repeated by others.*

Unfortunately for future investigation of human problems, recent years have seen the growth of considerable distrust in the capability of science and its technology to aid mankind. Many college students have developed a disinterest in and disillusionment with rational approaches to problems, an antiintellectualism arising at a time when serious research on such problems was never more needed. One can sympathize with the feeling of this post-Hiroshima generation that science and technology has let us down as the solution to our troubles. The capability of science to create a better life in other than material ways has no doubt been oversold, and the discovery of this is a source of disappointment and disillusionment to some. Current critics of science point out that it has provided us with terrible engines of destruction (the hydrogen bomb, napalm, B-52 bombers, ballistic missiles) rather than added security and well-being. Technological expansion has also helped degrade our environment to the point of crisis. This has led to a growing sentiment that equates *all* scientific endeavors, psychology included, with antihumanism.

It is the point of view of this book, however, that humanity can best be served in the long run by increasing knowledge about the workings of the human mind and the conditions that affect it. Only in this way can we distinguish between half-baked notions of human betterment through miraculous cure-alls and sound ideas about how life can be improved. Among many scientists concerned about such matters, including psychologists, there has been a growing and important debate about whether they should become involved in public policy-making. (One example is in the area of the mass media and the issue of whether or not television programming contributes to crime and violence; see Chapter 7.) This kind of debate will undoubtedly increase in frequency and intensity in the years to come as more social scientists are called upon to help in reconstructing social policy.

The uniqueness of psychology

Throughout this book, psychology is presented as one of many interrelated disciplines, each attempting to contribute to man's self-understanding. Psychology is obviously not unique in its interest in problems of the physical and social environment, aggression, prejudice, or even mental disorder and health, although it has an especially important role to play in each of these. Rather, what makes it unique is the particular way it approaches these problems. The nature of *psychological analysis* is fundamentally different from, say, biological analysis or economic analysis. Let us take the study of aggression as an example.

From the *biological* standpoint, the seeds of aggression are transmitted to an animal by its hereditary endowment. This genetic background creates the nervous system and the set of hormones that jointly control behavior and influence aggression. The origins of all this are to be found in the evolutionary process. The biologist's task is to discover the particular cellular mechanisms involved in aggression and to identify the stimuli that trigger them, producing aggressive behavior in different animal species—including, of course, man.

The *social sciences*, in contrast, focus on aggressions of people living within a common social system, in other words, organized and behaving interdependently. The scientific task is to determine the conditions of social organization influential in aggression. For example, the *economist's* interests center on the economic conditions that encourage aggression and warfare, the extent to which economic competition among groups and nations favor aggression, the organization of skills and resources brought together in war, and the economic costs and benefits of fighting. Thus, some economists argue that World War II extricated the United States from

a severe economic depression by providing jobs through industrial and military expansion, and this represents one kind of economic analysis of war. *Sociologists* focus their attention on various social institutions as possible determinants or inhibitors of aggression, for example, the social rules by which people settle quarrels, or the power relations existing within and between societies. *Anthropologists* might be interested in comparing the patterns of aggression and war in different cultures, as influenced by their values and belief systems, whether they are nomadic or farming cultures, and so on. And *political scientists* concern themselves with the manner in which any social unit, say, a nation, comes to the political decision to go to war. The boundaries between the various social sciences are often difficult to draw sharply. The common denominator of all is that an aggregation of people is the unit of study, that is, a group or social system of some kind.

How does *psychology* differ from these disciplines, and what makes it unique? Psychology is both a social and biological science. In the biological sciences, the basic unit of study and analysis is the single cell, parts of cells, tissue systems, or the individual animal as part of a species. In the social sciences, the unit is the group, the social system. In psychology, the unit is the *single individual as a system of mental and behavioral processes*—his motives, thoughts, and feelings. Of course, psychologists also study social groups, but when they do their interest is mainly centered on how one person affects another or how the group influences the individual. It is this focus on the individual's internal motivations and responses, his mental and emotional state, that marks psychological analysis. (We shall see in Part II how psychology borrows insights from both the biological and social sciences in developing its analysis of human aggression.)

WILL READING THIS (OR ANY) BOOK PRODUCE INNER WELL-BEING?

As was noted earlier, a high percentage of students take courses in psychology in the understandable but mistaken belief that they will learn how to master their personal problems. A smaller percentage have genuine intellectual curiosity about the field. It is possible to gain some insight into oneself and one's life pattern from such courses and from general reading. Much can be learned about people in general, especially other people. However, such knowledge almost certainly cannot provide solutions to one's own deep-seated problems. Commenting on recent student unrest and widespread alienation from society, Bruno Bettelheim (1969, pp. 9, 11, 16, 35) makes this point in the following provocative passage:

It is true that those who come to the university and who are already deeply dissatisfied with themselves and society, tend to study psychology, political science, philosophy, sociology. Such students even choose psychology in the hope that to study it will add to self-knowledge (which it can) and will solve their psychological problems (which it cannot). Feeling lost in themselves, they also feel lost with others and come to think that by studying society they will feel more at home in the world, and hence with themselves. But when the study of these and related subjects fails to solve their inner difficulties, or the various problems they have in relating to others, they come to hate the university whose teaching disappoints them. They are convinced that the teaching is "irrelevant"—as indeed it is when it comes to solving deep-seated emotional problems of long standing, because it was never designed to that end.

Commonsense should tell the reader that the study of psychology offers no royal road to happiness. If it did have that effect, then professional workers in the field (like clinical psychologists, psychiatrists, social workers, and psych professors) would all be paragons of mental health. However, as a group, professional psychologists are no more healthy than any other part of the population. (Indeed, some humorists have unkindly suggested that they may be even less so.)

Psychological principles are broad generalizations, and although people share much in common they are also unique in their personal characteristics and individual circumstances. This is even true of "identical" twins. No two people are exactly alike. Their personal re-

sources, needs, and problems will also differ, and a useful principle for one person might be inadequate and even counterproductive for someone else. Because we need a limited number of general principles to reduce the total variation to more manageable proportions, anything we can say about how people ought to live or manage their affairs is likely to be overgeneral when applied to the individual. For this reason, psychotherapy must be tailored to each person, since each case is unique, although it must also operate within general principles about psychodynamics.

Furthermore, since most of us lack insight into our own behavior and mental life and the factors influencing them, the image we have of ourselves is likely to be highly distorted (as we shall see in Chapters 10 and 11). One may learn about how others deceive themselves but fail to recognize that such defenses are operating in oneself as well. It is possible to see clearly what another person must do to master his problems, but such objectivity is difficult or impossible in one's own case.

Lastly, psychological knowledge cannot provide anyone with a set of values on which to predicate his life. It is not a system of ethics. Most readers will by now have discovered that there are many divergent ethical values from which to choose, those of parents, teachers, friends, great religious leaders, philosophers, writers—and most of them are contradictory!! As will be seen in Chapter 12, psychology cannot tell us whether to emphasize self-discipline and restraint in the interest of future goals or to live with abandon and unconcern, whether to reject sensory pleasure or to cultivate it. It can perhaps help us to realize the likely consequences of commitment to one or another set of values.

In the coming pages, the complex and often paradoxical nature of man is set forth as a mystery to be solved, and psychology as one of many disciplines dedicated to solving it. The motivation and background for this dedication is partly the joy of knowing and partly the need to find answers to the enigmatic problems that have always beset the human race. These conundrums have no easy solution. In fact, the wisest readers may have anticipated that, unlike

Oedipus, we cannot yet solve the riddle, though we try to lay the groundwork for ultimate solution. Throughout this book we confront many questions about how the environment, both physical and social, has formed us, and why it is so difficult to alter it without endangering ourselves; why, in spite of the destructiveness and misery of war, men continue to destroy each other; why they hate and fear men of clans, creeds, and castes other than their own; why there are so many cases of personal breakdown, so many retreats into alienation and despair; and what, on the other hand, constitutes adaptive success and inner well-being. In trying to find answers to these and other questions, we come to understand ourselves a little better, and perhaps discover how much must still be learned. It will help the reader to recognize before he begins that psychology is a frontier science, advancing slowly toward a knowledge of man, but only on the outer edge of firm understanding.

Those who want nothing but absolute answers now and cannot be comfortable with uncertainty and disagreement at the frontier will not find psychology their cup of tea. But some who read this book may one day help to advance our psychological understanding of human problems; others will perhaps apply knowledge they have gained herein without even knowing where it came from; and many, I hope, will experience a sense of challenge and excitement, and the expansion of their intellectual horizons. Bon voyage!

23,5

At no other time in the history of psychological thought
has it been more obvious that man cannot be adequately
understood without reference to the settings in which he
lives. In Chapters 1 through 5 we shall pay close attention to those settings, starting with what surrounds man,
though being concerned as well with how he reacts to
these surroundings. We need to know the rules of our
interdependency with the environment, how we are
shaped by it and how it in turn is modified—indeed,
transformed—by us.

In the Prologue a number of problems were raised
that will be themes of this book. Some of them, such
as overpopulation and pollution, are features of the

Man is always reaching out beyond the world he sees and hears.
In every age . . . he has tried to express, even amid the confusions
of his thought and the crudities of his language, something of
that other world he only feels and does not touch or see—the
world of thoughts and ideals. Yet . . . there must necessarily
remain much that transcends the thought and language of man.
It is with the sense of this limitation that he has fashioned
symbols. He has looked at Nature and seen in its bountiful sky,
in its life-giving sun, and in its majestic storms, the embodiment,
the symbol of his aspirations. He has gone further—he has
created his own myths of the gods. (Benedict, 1959, p. 113).

physical environment; others, produced by rapid social change, represent problems of the social environment. Part I concerns both kinds of environment—man's physical setting and his social milieu.

We can easily accept the obvious fact that our surroundings have the power to affect us greatly, but we need to understand how and why this is so. Has the struggle for survival affected man's interaction with the world around him just as it has shaped all biological species during the long period of evolution from simple cells to highly complex organisms? And, similarly, how does the social environment influence our actions and reactions, shaping each of our personalities as we develop from birth to old age? We must find answers to these questions before we can hope to formulate effective solutions to the enormous problems challenging the human species today.

The five chapters in Part I each deal with different psychological facets of the relationship between man and his environments. The treatment is divided roughly into

2

3

4

*For baboons, as for many herbivores, association with other species
        on the range often provides mutual protection. . . . The ungulates
have a keen sense of smell, and baboons have keen eyesight.
        Baboons are visually alert, constantly looking in all directions as
they feed. If they see predators, they utter warning barks that
        alert not only the other baboons but also any other animals that
may be in the vicinity. Similarly, a warning bark by a bushbuck
        or an impala will put a baboon troop to flight. . . . (from Wash-
burn and DeVore, 1961).*

The newborn infant is the center of social attraction. The most
dominant adult males sit by the mother and walk close beside
her. When the troop is resting, adult females and juveniles come
to the mother, groom her and attempt to groom the infant. . . .
(from Washburn and DeVore, 1961).

8

7

For baboons, as for many herbivores, association with other species
on the range often provides mutual protection. . . . The ungulates
have a keen sense of smell, and baboons have keen eyesight.
Baboons are visually alert, constantly looking in all directions as
they feed. If they see predators, they utter warning barks that
alert not only the other baboons but also any other animals that
may be in the vicinity. Similarly, a warning bark by a bushbuck
or an impala will put a baboon troop to flight. . . . (from Wash-
burn and DeVore, 1961).

*The newborn infant is the center of social attraction. The most
dominant adult males sit by the mother and walk close beside
her. When the troop is resting, adult females and juveniles come
to the mother, groom her and attempt to groom the infant. . . .
(from Washburn and DeVore, 1961).*

8

7

9   10

two sections, one dealing with the impact of the physical
environment (Chapters 1, 2, and 3), the other with the
impact of the social environment (Chapters 4 and 5).
The problem-centered chapters (Chapter 3 on overpopulation and Chapter 5 on social change) are both
preceded by discussions attempting to provide a basic
understanding of the general principles of such impact.

   Chapter 1 adopts the psychobiological perspective,
that is, man is viewed as a biological species, the primary
orientation being survival and adaptation in a given
physical environment. (Henceforth, when referring to the
physical environment we shall drop the adjective and
call it simply the *environment.*) In many ways we can learn
about human adaptation by studying the psychobiology
of other animals, especially man's nearest relatives, the
primates. (Some of the photos accompanying these introductory comments provide an illuminating glimpse
of animal behavior in a natural African habitat somewhat like that in which the earliest traces of man have
been found; see Chapter 1.)

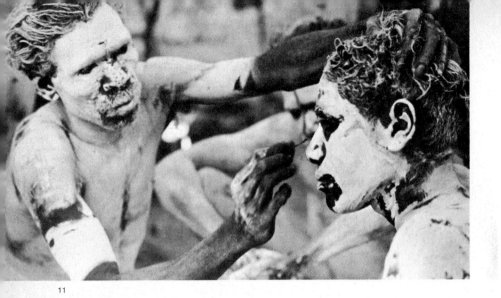

11

What then is this secret life of the Aborigines? It is the life
       apart—a life of ritual and mythology, of sacred rites and objects.
It is the life in which man really finds his place in society and
       in nature, and in which he is brought in touch with the invisible
things of the world of the past, present and future. . . . (from
       Elkin, 1964, p. 170).

12

13

14

. . . the Ammassalik [Eskimos] depend largely upon seals and
other blubbery sea mammals for their food, clothing, light, and
heat and . . . though the coastal waters are rich in these animals,
it is impossible for them to accumulate great stores of food. . . .
Therefore, when hunting is good, they eat plentifully; when
continued bad weather makes hunting impossible they have suf-
ficient stores of meat and blubber to last them several weeks; but
if conditions are unfavorable for any protracted period then
starvation faces them. . . . (from Mirsky, 1961, p. 55).

15

Among the Ammassalik, children are greatly desired. Both male
and female children are welcome since the one means future
hunters and the other means hunters' partners. No sickly child,
or one without a mother, is allowed to live, and in times of
stress it is understood that children must be sacrificed before
their parents, because even if they were kept alive . . . they
would be unable to cope with the environment and quickly succumb.
They are an investment that is not allowed to become a lia-
bility. . . . (from Mirsky, 1961, p. 75).

16

17

18

To help us understand fully man's response to the world around him, however, the psychobiological perspective is incomplete. As will be seen in Chapter 2, man is a social animal whose behavior is closely tied to symbolic mental activity. Thus, in addition to strictly biological considerations, his style of life also reflects his culture. He builds a shelter not only in an effort to accommodate to inclement weather conditions but also as an expression of socially learned ideas of "the good life." By examining how he builds his house we may gain an understanding of how he believes people ought to live together. Other expressions of his culture—his tools, his weapons, his art, his social organization—also enlighten us as to his view of the world. In short, we adopt the *psychosocial perspective*.

The reader will encounter in Chapter 3 one of the major environmental problems of our times—*human overpopulation*. The psychological impact of current accelerating population growth is analyzed, along with the psychological issues that must be faced in attempting to cope with it.

In Chapter 4, we turn to the effect of social environment on the individual, considering in some detail the nature of its psychological impact. How does the social environment into which we are born affect us as we move into and out of different social groups? How do our social groups influence our actions and reactions and help to shape our personality development?

19

20

21

Many societies display some differentiation in house form based
on [social] stratification. . . . In parts of Africa the compound
may be larger and have more retainers, wives, or cattle; the
house may be more decorated, as in Southeast Asia. . . . The
skulls or scalps of enemies may be displayed as symbols, or the
wealth and prestige of the owner may be expressed through size
and number of retainers or elaboration of carved columns, as
among the Kwakiutl. . . . (from Rapoport, 1969, p. 11).

23

24

25

I saw the Japanese moving in masses, responding to forces unknown to me, and in their faces I could see only one expression: a bewildered longing. . . . (from Paul, 1962, p. 3).

We move in Chapter 5 to the human problems posed by *rapid social change,* a prominent feature of the world we live in today. We examine the "generation gap," which is a product of rapid social change, and the struggle by the individual to preserve his identity in the face of social pressures toward uniformity. We also consider various attempts made throughout history to imagine an ideal world (*utopia*), together with some recent attempts to portray the frightening world (*dystopia*) toward which man is headed if he does not change his present course.

Illustrations: Background photo, pp. 14, 15—Tokyo rush hour crowd (Jacqueline Paul). 1. East African bush, Tanzania (Jeanne White from National Audubon Society). 2. Neutral relationship of two herbivore species, Amboseli reserve, Kenya. 3, 4. Baboon troop marching and feeding. 5. Baboons fleeing hungry lioness. 6. Baboons and other species (2–6 S. L. Washburn and Irven De Vore). 7. Baboon with young (A. W. Ambler from National Audubon Society). 8. Gibbon foot (Gordon S. Smith from National Audubon Society). 9. Grooming (S. L. Washburn and Irven De Vore). 10. Female baboon carrying young (Mark Boulton from National Audubon Society). 11. Aborigines preparing for initiation rites, Australia. 12. Bark painting, Arnhem Land, Australia. 13. Aborigine mother and child. 14. Eskimos cutting up young whale, Alaska (11–14 courtesy of The American Museum of Natural History). 15. Eskimo fishermen, Northwest Territory (National Film Board of Canada). 16. Eskimo folk art (Canadian Eskimo Arts Council). 17, 18. Stills from Robert Flaherty's classic documentary film *Nanook of the North* (from the Estate of Frances H. Flaherty; Museum of Modern Art/Film Stills Archive). 19. Pueblo, Taos, New Mexico. 20. Junks and sampans, Hong Kong (United Nations). 21. Papuan communal house, New Guinea (19, 21 courtesy of The American Museum of Natural History). 22. Downtown Manhattan (B. N. Zelman). 23. Pedestrian traffic, Tokyo (Jacqueline Paul). 24. Packed subway train (Hiroshi Hosono, Foreign Correspondents' Club, Tokyo). 25. Japanese bar scene (Jacqueline Paul).

Any attempt to understand man or any other creature psychologically without paying close attention to his physical environment would be futile. It would be like trying to understand the motion of a fish without knowledge of the properties of water or the flight of a bird without knowledge of air as a medium and of the principles of aerodynamics. In this chapter we shall examine how the environment originally made man into the creature he is and how it now influences his life style and psychological makeup. We must begin by putting ourselves in the larger context of the natural world and its evolutionary history.

MAN AS PART OF NATURE

Human behavior is the result of continuing "negotiation" between man and the environment. The environment imposes adaptive requirements on man: it serves as the source of everything material that he requires for life; it also imposes constraints on what he can do. In using environmental resources in order to live and flourish, man also alters the world in which he lives. He therefore not only is shaped by his encounter with the environment but also frequently shapes that environment.

Ecology is that branch of biological science concerned with the interrelationship of living organisms and their environment. Odum (1963) tells us that the word comes from the Greek root *oikos* meaning "house," and so ecology is literally the study of houses or, in its generally accepted sense, the study of environments (the natural "homes" or settings in which organisms live). More broadly, ecology deals with the interaction between organisms and their environment, especially as it affects their survival.

The ecosystem

The *ecosystem*, a community of organisms living within one habitat, is the basic unit of ecological study. Each component of an ecosystem vitally affects every other, and all the organisms within it are interdependent. There are three types of living things in every ecosystem: (1) *green plants,* which use light energy to manufacture food from simple inorganic substances; (2) *animals,* which consume and utilize (as a source of energy) food synthesized by green plants; (3) *bacteria* and *fungi,* which decompose or break down the complex compounds of dead organic matter, absorb some of the products of decomposition, and release substances which the plants and animals can use. There is also a fourth but nonliving component, namely, the basic elements of the environment, such as oxygen, hydrogen, carbon, nitrogen, iron, and sulfur, which frequently occur in compounds like water (H_2O) and carbon dioxide (CO_2). These are some of the inorganic substances on which all biochemical activity depends and from which primitive life forms must have sprung, perhaps around 3 billion years ago.

Plants are vital to animal life because they are the main source of oxygen; in turn animals use the oxygen and return it to the atmosphere in the form of carbon dioxide. The carbon dioxide ultimately is taken up by the plants and used in photosynthesis to produce carbohydrates, thus also providing food for animal life. In effect, the plants depend on the animals to release the needed carbon dioxide for photosynthesis, and the animals depend on the plants to provide the basis of their energy through food and oxygen. The bacteria and fungi also assist in getting the waste from animal life back into the chemical forms that both plants and animals can use. There is thus a continuous chemical cycle occurring in any ecosystem. Substances are consumed and changed and then recycled to their original form.

The biologically active world contains many types of ecosystems—seas, estuaries, and seashores; streams and rivers; lakes and ponds; freshwater marshes; deserts, tundras, grasslands, and forests. Together these ecosystems all form one vast, highly complex system, usually referred to as the *biosphere,* which includes all organisms inhabiting the soil, air, and water of this planet. The biosphere comprises only a small percentage of the mass of the earth and its atmosphere.

A sense of wonderment at the multiple varieties of natural life can be experienced when one reads some of the excellent accounts of the teeming and interdependent life found in an ordinary pond (Amos, 1970). There are many forms of aquatic plants and animals that coexist in such a pond, and

Figure 1.1 Inhabitants of a pond: (a) whirligig beetle; (b) bladderwort; (c) water strider; (d) damselfly nymph. (William H. Amos)

the numerous ways they manage to survive through individual adaptations to the same watery environment are fascinating. The whirligig beetle is one example (Figure 1.1a). When it dives to the bottom of the pond, a bubble is formed beneath its wings and at the tip of its abdomen; during the period of submersion this bubble acts as an air tank and a gill to absorb oxygen from the water and to pass carbon dioxide back into the water. In this way the insect can stay submerged for several hours. Nitrogen, a principal component of the air bubble, slowly escapes into the water and eventually the air sac collapses, at which point the insect must rise again to the surface for a new supply of air.

A thing . . . never returns to nothing, but all things after disruption go back into the first bodies of matter . . . then goodly crops spring up and boughs are green with leaves upon the trees, trees themselves grow and are laden with fruit; by them in turn our race and the race of wild beasts are fed, by them we see glad towns teem with children and the leafy forests ring on all sides with the song of new birds; through them cattle wearied with their load of fat lay their bodies down about the glad pastures and the white milky stream pours from the distended udders; through them a new brood with weakly limbs frisks and gambols over the soft grass, rapt in their young hearts with the pure new milk. None of the things therefore which seem to be lost is utterly lost, since nature replenishes one thing out of another and does not suffer any thing to be begotten, before she has been recruited by the death of some other. . . . [Lucretius, 96–55 B.C.; 1952 ed.]

Another example is the bladderwort (Figure 1.1b). At rest, the bladders seem to be flattened sacs, but when any small creature ruffles the hairs guarding the opening the bladders expand instantly and the prey is sucked into them and to its death. The marvelous and fragile water strider is able to use the surface tension of the water literally to walk or run across the surface on six long legs (Figure 1.1c). The damselfly nymph in search of food presses up from below against the surface, bending it as if it were an elastic but solid roof (Figure 1.1d). All these are special adaptations, produced by millions of years of evolution, that enable each viable organism to thrive in its own particular way in the pond setting. Man also is a specialized form of life, adapted of course to a land rather than an aquatic environment.

Because of the interdependence of living things, any change in one component of an ecosystem tends to influence all other components. An ecosystem is a delicately balanced mechanism, as indeed is the biosphere as a whole. Ill-considered actions by man, one of its residents, can disturb that balance. Substances may be used up faster than they can be replaced; toxic waste materials may build up, poisoning the water, land, or air. Such wastes (pollutants) will damage the health of all organisms, including man, that share the same environmental space.

The ecological niche

All this may seem very remote from the study of man, or from psychology, but in important ways it is the very essence of such study. An essential concept to consider here is that of the *ecological niche,* which refers to the role that any type of organism (*species*) plays within its habitat.

The characteristics of all living species, including man, must be suited to the specific environment in which they live if they are to survive. A famous example of this was given by Charles Darwin (1859), who demonstrated among other things that each of the many species of orchid has an individualized flower structure making it attractive to only one particular species of insect. In visiting that orchid and coming into contact with the special parts of the flower, the insect transports pollen which fertilizes the orchid. If the specific insect involved in this process were to disappear from the environment, that particular species of orchid could not propagate and would itself become extinct. Thus, this orchid is a highly specialized species in the ecological sense. Other species of flower are ecological generalists, that is, capable of being fertilized by many means or of surviving in many ways and under varied conditions. Man is a superb generalist, since there

(a)

are many ways and many settings in which he is able to survive as a species.

The ecological niche may be likened to the particular shelf in the library on which a book is filed or, as Odum (1963) expresses it, to the role or occupation that the organism has within the ecosystem: the habitat is the "address"; the niche is the "profession." Man, like all other species, has created a particular niche for himself in the living world. The way he acts and how he experiences things are related to the role he plays, and that role is the result of a long evolutionary process.

THE ENVIRONMENT AND MAN'S LIFE STYLE

We can make use of this powerful concept of the ecological niche to help explain the varied patterns of human life in the many parts of the globe where man exists today. By expanding the idea a bit, we can begin to understand the diverse ways in which humanity has developed in different environmental settings.

How the environment affects us

Our habitat shapes our way of life in several fundamental, survival-related ways. First, it imposes certain adaptive *demands,* meaning that one must live in certain ways as prescribed by environmental conditions. We saw this quite clearly in the brief survey of life in the freshwater pond, a habitat requiring quite different ways of getting along than in the ocean, in a forest, or in a desert. In the case of man, some people roast in steamy jungles or nearly waterless deserts (Figure 1.2); or, like the Eskimo, they live in severe cold where little grows; or they are terrorized by floods, earthquakes,

Mutual shading
minumum surface area
maximum mass

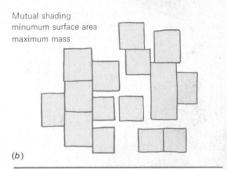

(b)

(c)

(d)

Maximum cross ventilation

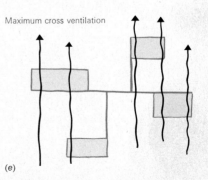

(e)

Figure 1.2 Housing patterns in different climates: (a) Yokut settlement showing brushwood shade; San Joaquin Valley, California. (b) Housing elements crowded together, typical of a hot, arid climate. This design delays entry of heat in daytime but retains it at night. Materials with high heat capacity are used, such as adobe, mud, or stone, which absorb heat during the day and reradiate it at night when it is cold. This compact geometry, providing maximum space with minimum exposure of surface area, is found in such diverse places as the southwestern United States, southern Tunisia, and the Loire Valley in southwest France. (c) Housing characteristic of such places as Singapore, Malaysia, Indonesia, the Amazon Valley, Colombia, and Haiti. (d) Seminole house, Florida. (e) Long, narrow geometry and wide spacing are typical of a hot, humid climate. Houses are designed to produce maximum shade and ventilation while holding minimum heat. (Adapted from Rapoport, 1969)

hurricanes, tornadoes; or they are threatened by virulent infection-bearing or parasitic organisms against which they must develop some natural resistance. The peoples that live in warm, humid climates must spend considerable time and energy in preserving their food against spoilage, especially if such food is scarce; this task is not nearly so important in cold climates, where food is easily preserved. Or, as another example, the sleeping arrangements of the primitive family are much influenced by climate; in cold climates, husbands and wives sleep together in the same bed in winter more than they do in mild climates (Whiting, 1964), a fact of obviously great psychological importance. Here, then, are cases where variations in style of life and in the psychological events connected with them can be understood by reference to the adaptive demands the environment imposes. The patterning of environmental demands has a great deal to do with how human populations live, what is most important to them, how they spend their time, and how they develop their skills, customs, values, and beliefs. These are clearly psychological matters of much significance.

The environment also imposes certain *constraints* on how and where people live. For example, prior to the era of modern technology, mountain ranges and seas confined peoples to certain geographical regions, and certain settings such as the hottest portions of the desert and the coldest places at the earth's poles were so forbidding that no one could live there. Moreover, at various times in history, mountain ranges, great rivers, and oceans served as major barriers against human migration and conquest. Less than half a century ago it was still widely assumed that the United States was secure against invasion from Europe because of the two oceans that protected its eastern and western flanks. That was when a strong navy could be regarded as security against attack, before the advent of atomic bombs, guided missiles, and supersonic air travel. All these radical transformations have occurred within one lifetime, and it is hard to believe that some 250,000 miles of vacuum separating the earth from the moon can no longer prevent man's presence on that satellite.

The environment provides *resources* on which survival is predicated, for example, the availability of food and various materials that can be fashioned into clothing, housing, tools, and weapons. It should be no surprise, therefore, that the ways people accomplish the major tasks of survival are linked to the physical conditions under which they live.

Most of the early attempts to link the physical environment to man's behavior emphasized gross features of the natural world such as climate and geography. Historical interest in the psychological effects of climate is reflected in

Note 1.1

Analysis of environmental effects depends on our ability to observe and measure the precise degree to which human and animal behavior is affected. Whether these environmental conditions are still in their natural state, like the Amazonian rain forest or the Australian outback, or are products of civilization, like towns or large urban centers observation and measurement are key tasks in the growing field of environmental psychology (see Craik, 1970a, 1970b; Proshansky *et al.*, 1970), as in all branches of psychological research.

One cannot, however, depend on casual impressions, which are often incorrect. Consider, for example, the situation in which we want to describe the complex interaction among members of a social group. How might one describe what is going on at a large cocktail party? Many behavioral events are happening simultaneously—competitive or aggressive interchanges, flirtations, expressions of boredom and interest, evidence of dominant and subordinate social relationships, and so on. Depending on our interests, we must concentrate on particular types of events and find some way of describing and measuring them.

We might be interested in studying the amount of aggression manifested at the cocktail party and comparing it with that found, say, at a pot party. This comparison would not be easy. For one thing, different sorts of people would probably be involved at each party. Furthermore, since people behave differently if they know they are being watched, we would have to station "secret" observers (perhaps as participants in the party), who know what to look for and can discreetly jot down all instances of aggressive behavior, noting how often they occur, among whom, with what provocation, in what setting, and so on. Of course, some forms of aggressive communication are nonverbal, and our observers would have to be alert for nuances of gesture and facial expression. Such subtleties compound the problem.

In all scientific research, before we attempt to generalize on our observations we must make sure that they are reliable. In the above case we would have to check on the judgment and accuracy of our observers by posting several of them at each party and assessing the agreements and disagree-

St. Thomas Aquinas's interesting but not very sound advice to a thirteenth-century ruler about how to select a site for a city (from Aquinas, 1938 ed., Book II, Chap. 1, p. 110):

A temperate climate is most conducive to fitness for war by which human society is kept in security. For as Begetius tells us, all people that live near the sun and are dried up by the excessive heat have keener intellects, it is true, but they have less blood, and consequently have no constancy of self-reliance in hand-to-hand fighting, for knowing that they have but little blood, they have a greater fear of wounds. On the other hand, northern tribes, far removed from the burning rays of the sun, are more dull-witted, indeed, but, because they have an ample flow of blood, they are ever ready for war. Those who dwell in temperate climes have, on the other hand, an abundance of blood and thus make light of wounds or death and, on the other hand, do not lack prudence, which puts the proper restraint on them in camp and helps them in using strategy in the field.

Well into this century there were dozens of such theories about the relationship between the environment and human behavior, most of them vague, contradictory, and poorly documented, so that it was difficult to tell the valid ones from those which were clearly wrong (Klausner, 1971). One of the perennial favorites was the effort to connect climate with delinquency and crime. For example, it was reported (Dexter, 1904) that deportment in the New York public schools, the number of murders in Denver, and the number of males arrested for drunkenness in New York City were all related to the varying meteorological conditions occurring during the decade of the 1890s. This was explained by a physiological theory that was all wrong, namely, that low temperature, absence of wind, and atmospheric dryness result in rapid metabolism, while high temperature, high barometric pressure, and high humidity lower the metabolic rate. It was further assumed that high metabolism will result in a more active individual than low metabolism, other things being equal, and thus, the conditions producing it are likely to create hyperactivity, delinquency, and crime.

One trouble with this superficially plausible analysis is that our bodies are capable of adjusting to a wide variety of climatic conditions and changes and of maintaining a physiological equilibrium (or steady metabolic state) regardless of climate. In effect, metabolism is not substantially affected by climatic variation. Moreover, had the investigator looked further into the facts he would have discovered that there is no difference in the metabolic rates of murderers, drunks, and delinquents, on the one hand, and of other groups whose social behavior is impeccable (see Note 1.1).

ments in their findings. In this way we could also screen out the effect of personal bias.

Sometimes special conditions over which we have no control may influence our results. In this instance the character of the host would probably be an important factor, as would the nature of the place in which the parties were held, how crowded the rooms were, the temperature, ventilation, even the time of day. If one were setting up both parties for purposes of this study, one would probably hold them in the same place, with the same host, at the same time of day, and so on. But even then, for the study to be valid the background of guests at each event would have to be determined, as well as their age, education level, and other such details. Environmental psychologists, who try to study people under real-life conditions, rarely can control all the circumstances to this extent.

In studies with animals, not only is the task of observing, recording, and interpreting data under diverse conditions both difficult and demanding, but a major problem is the psychological effect on the animals produced by the observer himself. Animals, just like the guests at our party, will usually act in ways other than usual when they know they are being observed.

Jane van Lawick-Goodall ran into this and other problems in her studies of wild chimpanzees in Tanzania, Africa. In order to observe these primates, who were at first very shy and fearful of human contact, she had to gain their confidence, which she finally did after a long and discouraging period during which they would not let her near them. Later, in order to observe them frequently at close range, she created a feeding station, which became the Gombe Stream Research Center. Bananas, which chimpanzees love, were placed in feeding boxes, and the chimps at first came in small groups to feed.

However, presence of the feeding station greatly increased tension and aggressiveness among the male chimpanzees of the area, since it increased their natural competitiveness and furthermore put them into conflict with local baboons, who also rushed in to get a share. Moreover, because of the presence of a steady supply of bananas, chimps began to remain near to the station and were not ranging as widely throughout the area in search of food as they previously had. Van Lawick-Goodall (1971, p. 149) and her photographer-husband left the station in the care of assistants for a while and later returned to find the following conditions: "Hugo and I . . . were shocked by the change we saw in the chimps' behavior. Not only was there a great deal more fighting than ever before, but many of the chimps were hanging around camp for hours and hours every day. . . ." Procedures created by the researchers to facilitate observation of natural behavior had greatly changed that behavior. Great effort, patience, and ingenuity had to be applied to eliminate, or at least minimize, these distortions produced by the observers' presence and actions. Steel boxes that could be opened by hidden observers at infrequent and irregular feeding times helped to restore the chimps' normal ranging patterns.

Thus, regardless of the kinds of behavior in which we are interested, both its accurate assessment in nature and determination of how it is affected by various environmental conditions require precise techniques of observation and measurement, ways of evaluating the accuracy of these observations and the validity of our interpretations, and care that the very act of making observations does not distort the natural behavior. Wherever possible, provision should be made for other researchers to repeat the observations as a check on the results.

Most observers are willing to acknowledge the possibility that weather has some connection with social disorder and delinquency. One need only think, for example, of the common expectation that urban riots are likely to occur during the "long, hot summer." But if this is true, it is for quite a different reason than originally proposed. It could hardly be the heat itself which causes the trouble, since the same pattern has been observed in San Francisco, Oakland, and Berkeley, California, which are rarely hot enough to bother anyone. A better possibility is that under warm, dry conditions there is much more social intercourse. People stream into the streets, socializing, and doing more of everything (Figure 1.3), including the criminal activities of assaulting, robbing, vandalizing property, and rioting. In short, higher degrees of social interaction probably increase the possibilities of antisocial as well as socially acceptable behavior.

Another doubtful physiological theory (Woodruff, 1905) attempted to explain how variations in human skin color came about. This physical characteristic quite obviously has great impact on people's lives, socially and psychologically, and I shall discuss this impact further in Part III. In any case, an effort was made to show that skin pigmentation (say, black versus white) is geographically distributed over the earth's surface on the basis of the adaptive need to screen out the damaging ultraviolet rays of the sun in the tropics. It was assumed that white men could not survive where the sun was strong since they lacked such pigmentation, whereas blacks could thrive in such geographical localities. This idea correctly recognizes the connection between skin pigmentation and ultraviolet radiation, but the proposed physiological mechanism is questionable. For example, Caucasians live very successfully in Iran under extremely strong sunlight, partly by laying down pigmentation as protection against the sun's rays, a process we all know as tanning.

The history of the disease rickets in the Northern Hemisphere (Loomis, 1970) seems to provide a more reasonable causal link between geography and skin color. It was known in the late 1800s that northern European infants (in London, for instance) suffered from rickets as a result of the relative absence of sunlight. The area of northern Europe lies at a latitude similar to lands that are largely uninhabited because of cold climate, for example, the Aleutian Islands, Labrador, and northern Siberia, but northern Europe is made habitable by the warming Gulf Stream. Nevertheless, the weak sun that hangs low in the sky in winter in these areas fails to stimulate the body to produce calciferol, a substance crucial in bone formation, leading to the disease called rickets. Thus, it was noted around 1909 that German children who were born in the fall and died in the spring usually had rickets, while those

who were born in the spring and died in the fall (and who experienced more sunlight) were free of that disease (Figure 1.4).

Moreover, in 1889 it was found that areas in England having heavy industrial smog showed a much higher incidence of rickets because the ultraviolet rays were even further weakened there than in areas without smog (Figure 1.5). Ultimately, it was discovered that rickets could be cured by dietary supplements containing calciferol, such as fish-liver oils, which are high in vitamin D. These substances make up for the calciferol production that is normally stimulated by the sun, just as they do in fish living below the surface of the water and receiving little or no ultraviolet radiation. It is worth noting that in the Arctic, where there is little sunlight for several months of the year, the Eskimos' diet is very rich in fish-liver oils. Starting in 1917, when cod-liver oil was first administered to black children in New York City in whom rickets was severe and widespread, the rickets was cured and further recurrences prevented.

There is indeed, as was earlier supposed, a connection between geography and the distribution of skin color throughout the world, although this relationship has grown weaker in modern times with the effects of slave traffic and migrations of blacks to the industrialized North. Before such migrations there was a strong tendency for light-skinned peoples to be living in areas far removed from the equator and for dark-

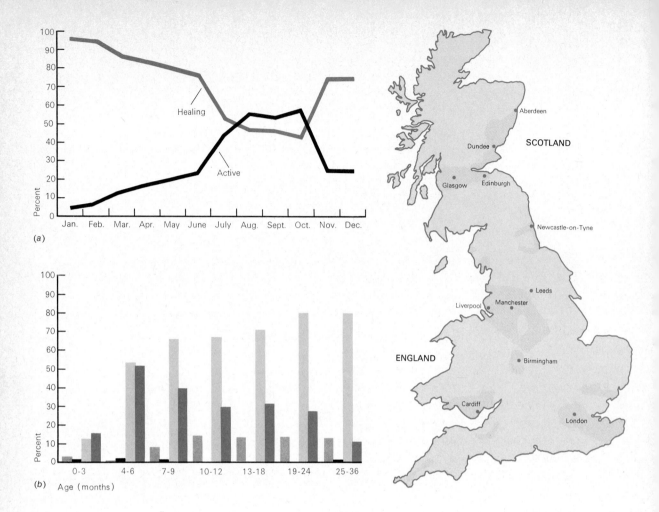

Figure 1.4 Left. (a) Seasonal variation in frequency of rickets as revealed in 386 postmortem examinations of children conducted by G. Schmorl in 1909. Children either had an active case at time of death or a "healing" case. Severity of the disease increased in the fall and decreased in the spring. (b) Effect of latitude on the incidence of rickets in children of various ages in Puerto Rico (color) and New Haven (gray), as surveyed in 1933: light bars, clinical diagnosis; dark bars, X-ray diagnosis. The difference would seem to be due to variations in sunlight at the two latitudes. (Adapted from Loomis, 1970)

Figure 1.5 Right. High incidence of rickets in industrial areas of Britain in 1889. Since diets in these industrial areas (darker color) were in general better than in poorer surrounding areas, the disease was not of dietary origin. The cause was smog that obscured sunlight. (Adapted from Loomis, 1970; see facing page)

skinned peoples to be distributed more heavily in tropical regions (Figure 1.6). In northern Europe, far from the equator and weakly lit by the sun, particularly in winter, men needed as much ultraviolet radiation as they could get to survive. Therefore, in those regions people were biologically favored who had unpigmented skin, allowing more ultraviolet radiation to stimulate the body's production of calciferol. Black-skinned peoples could get ample radiation in equatorial areas, where the sun was always strong, but not in the far North in winter. This adaptational problem was obviated, however, by the discovery of vitamin D, which substituted for the sun's action, so that today skin pigmentation is no longer clearly linked to geography.

Such an analysis helps us understand why in the past black skins predominated in one part of the world while white skins tended to be concentrated in another. It is a very clear example of the biological link between the environment, on the one hand, and human life patterns, on the other. But it also illustrates the complexity of the relationship, and the role of cultural factors as well. We shall consider cultural factors in man's response to his environment (which sometimes even transcend biological factors) in Chapter 2.

The story of skin color takes us into early biological development of the animal species called man. We need to take a broad look at the way he came to be what he is in order to have a sound grasp of his mental life. To gain the necessary perspective, we must consider human evolution.

THE EVOLUTION OF MAN

The notion that the complex organisms of the world evolved from simpler forms of life did not begin with Darwin (1859), with whom we associate the concept today, but can be found even among the writings of ancient Greeks, though it was understood quite differently then. The philosopher Anaximander (610–545 B.C.) maintained that animal life began in the sun-heated mud, which he believed once covered the earth, and that man in particular came from a fishlike form. Empedocles (495–435 B.C.) suggested that animal life began as undifferentiated living masses of tissue which became fashioned accidentally into limbs and other parts. Some of these combinations resulted in nonviable monsters; others,

Figure 1.6 Distribution of skin color around the world before 1700 A.D. (Figures 1.4, 1.5, and 1.6 adapted from W. F. Loomis, Rickets. Scientific American, 1970, 233(6), 77–91. © 1970 by Scientific American, Inc. All rights reserved.)

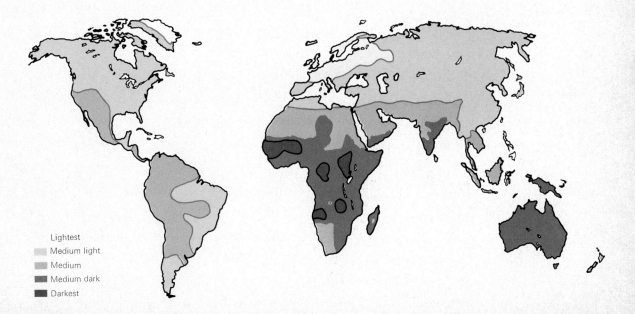

Lightest
Medium light
Medium
Medium dark
Darkest

whose parts were complementary and whose characteristics were well-adapted to environmental demands, were able to survive and flourish.

But much later, in the Middle Ages, this idea of evolution was held to be contrary to accepted religious dogma and hence heretical; among most medieval scholars, the ideas of Aquinas sufficed.

How evolution works

Darwin's great contribution was to propose an acceptable mechanism, *natural selection,* and to provide substantial evidence for evolutionary processes. And although Darwinism has been bitterly fought and often misunderstood even up to the present time,* it has become the dominant mode of thinking in the scientific world about the origin and development of the numerous and diverse species within the biosphere.

The essential idea underlying Darwinian evolution is that species survive or perish depending on their capacity to adapt, in effect, to establish an ecological niche for themselves so that they can survive and produce more organisms than are lost through starvation, disease, predation, or other hostile environmental forces. Any biological characteristic that does not favor survival, at least up to the point of procreation, will be eliminated, that is, will fail to establish itself in the population. Thus, in Darwinian theory, the fundamental mechanism of evolution is natural selection, the tendency for unfit biological species (and traits) to be eliminated in favor of those encouraging species survival.

The test of survival is not the fate of a single specimen, which is biologically unimportant, but whether a larger number of specimens in a population will survive rather than die off. For the most part, however, factors favoring species survival will also favor individual survival. This is certainly true in the higher mammals, which reproduce only a few offspring. A high percentage of these must be capable of surviving individually so that they live long enough to breed and multiply. Others, such as plants, insects, frogs, turtles, and fish, must produce huge quantities of offspring because most of them die before reproducing.

Feedback from the environment is a crucial aspect of natural selection. For example, species that live in geographic areas of limited oxygen (near the tops of high mountains) must develop special physiological mechanisms for living under such conditions, and as a result of the process of natural selection

[Charles Darwin] *began the observations which led to his theory of evolution at the age of 22, when he was a naturalist on H.M.S. Beagle, a ship which the British navy sent on a five year cruise around the world. . . .*

After passing through the Straits of Magellan the Beagle sailed northward along the Pacific coast of South America, and spent five weeks at the Galápagos Islands, 600 miles west of the coast of Ecuador. Here Darwin became aware of the fact that the principal animals were different from those of the South American coast. . . . The giant tortoises for which the islands are named were the commonest animals of the interior of the islands. Not only do these belong to a completely different group from any inhabiting the American mainland, but in addition each separate island of the Galápagos archipelago has its own particular race of tortoise. . . . In the book which he wrote about his journey [Voyage of the Beagle, 1837] *Darwin comments . . .:*

"Why, on these small points of land, which within a late geological period must have been covered by the ocean, which are formed of basaltic lava, and therefore differ in geological character from the American continent, and are placed under a different climate,—why were their aboriginal inhabitants, associated, I may add, in different proportions both in kind and number from those on the continent, and therefore acting on each other in a different manner—why were they created on American types of organization?" [From Stebbins, 1966, pp. 5–7; see also Porter and Brower, 1970, Vol. 1, pp. 100–113]

---

*Note, for example, that religious fundamentalists still struggle (and have all but succeeded) in California to have the biblical story of creation presented in the public schools side by side with the biological theory of evolution in science courses.

in which the unfit are eliminated, the successful species ultimately show biological characteristics different from those living at sea level, where the oxygen supply is rich. In short, environmental features determine the adaptive or survival value of all biological traits and which species survive or become extinct. It takes a proper match between the environment and the biological characteristics of the organism to create a viable species.

Feedback is also a fundamental principle of ontogenetic development (that is, the development of the individual organism) as well as phylogenetic development (the evolution of species). Through feedback from the environment, one learns its invariant properties, for example, by touching or picking up things, squeezing them, fleeing them, attacking them, and discovering how they respond. Thus, feedback is an essential principle of biological survival.

In the social interaction of animals, feedback is also an essential element. A mother who displays maternal behavior toward her baby is encouraged to continue, to desist, or to change how she acts by the reactions of the baby, who may cry, bite her nipples, stop crying, coo, or reach toward her. Social interaction is thus always a matter of mutual stimulation and feedback: one animal stimulates another in some way, the other responds, and this response is then perceived by the initiator of the interaction in what is sometimes called a *feedback loop*. It discovers the consequences of its actions and continuously maintains or changes its actions accordingly. Higher animals, especially man, have a remarkable capacity to perceive and interpret the environmental response, to anticipate it, and to accommodate to it in order to survive and flourish. These are psychological activities that will be considered in detail later.

A brief chronology of human evolution

It is estimated that the earth was formed about 5 billion years ago, its crust emerging as a habitable place about half a billion years later. Simple compounds of hydrogen, oxygen, carbon, and nitrogen began to be formed in these early stages and ultimately combined to become the first forms of life, namely, protists or single-celled organisms, around 3 billion years ago. This was followed by a succession of evolutionary developments leading much later to the sequential appearance of marine plants and animals, land plants, insects, amphibians, reptiles (including the dinosaurs), birds, and mammals. Man emerged from a group of mammals known as the primates (lemurs, monkeys, and apes). Recent archeological discoveries in East Africa place early forms of ape-man from 1.75 to 2.6 million years ago. Life has been evolving from the earliest life

forms for about 3 billion years, a time scale which is difficult
for any of us to grasp. Modern man represents a very recent
arrival in this long evolutionary process (Figure 1.7).

Our ideas about the succession of organisms over this
time period are fragmentary and inferential at best, although
the efforts of geologists, archeologists, and physical anthropologists to obtain evidence about this makes a fascinating story
in itself, which cannot be adequately portrayed in a brief
account. Much of the information comes from fossils (preserved remains or impressions of living creatures) found at
different layers of the earth's crust. The time period which
these layers represent is gauged from the depth of the layer
and from radiochemical dating methods.

Many species of early man have been differentiated by
scientists, and we cannot be concerned here with the complex
details or with the debates about which skeleton fragment
should be considered man and which should be regarded as
ape. The dividing line is clearly arbitrary. However, the rough
outlines of this evolution will help the reader keep the nature
of early man and the world he inhabited in perspective and
help us to understand what we are and how we got this way.

Roughly some 40 to 70 million years ago, mammals with
large and complex brains had already evolved into many
different forms in the rain forests of Central Asia and Africa;
of these forms the most advanced was the primate order,
consisting of many separate species of lemurs and monkeys.
They lived mainly in trees but some also obtained food on
the ground. Their "occupation" of aerial trapeze artist was
made possible by an intricate brain, long arms, legs, and tail
capable of grasping the limbs of trees, a high degree of sensorimotor coordination, the capability of visually discerning depth
or distance, acute hearing, and some limited ability to communicate and grasp meaning from sights and sounds. Monkeys
had also developed a family life and a sexually based division
of labor, qualities that facilitated the survival tasks of defense
against predators, the care and feeding of the young who
remained relatively helpless for quite a time, and effective
competition with other mammals in food gathering.

*Figure 1.7 (a) Evolutionary history of the primates. The dashed lines show
the most probable evolutionary relationships. Width of the colored areas indicates
the approximate abundance of each group. (Adapted from McAlester, 1968) (b)
The loris, a prosimian from Ceylon, related to the lemurs of Madagascar and
the tarsiers of Indonesia and the Philippines. Probably evolved from tree-dwelling
insectivores like the tree shrew, all prosimians have certain monkeylike characteristics, notably the grasping hand. (Courtesy New York Zoological Society) (c)
Mandrill baboon, with young, from West Africa. The wide-set eyes permit
stereoscopic vision, as in man. (d) Olive baboon from tropical Africa. (c, d: Arthur
W. Ambler from National Audubon Society)*

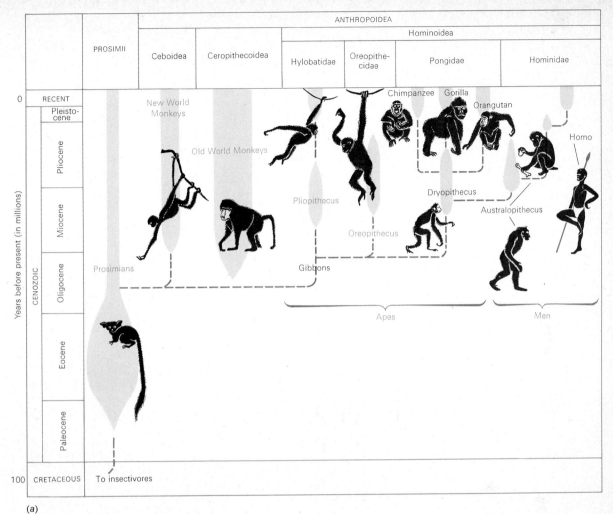

			ANTHROPOIDEA					
	PROSIMII	Ceboidea	Ceropithecoidea	Hominoidea				
				Hylobatidae	Oreopithe-cidae	Pongidae	Hominidae

RECENT

Pleisto-cene

Pliocene

Miocene

Oligocene

Eocene

Paleocene

CRETACEOUS   To insectivores

Years before present (in millions)

CENOZOIC

0

100

New World Monkeys

Old World Monkeys

Prosimians

Pliopithecus

Oreopithecus

Gibbons

Chimpanzee   Gorilla

Orangutan

Dryopithecus

Australopithecus

Homo

Apes

Men

(a)

(b)   (c)   (d)

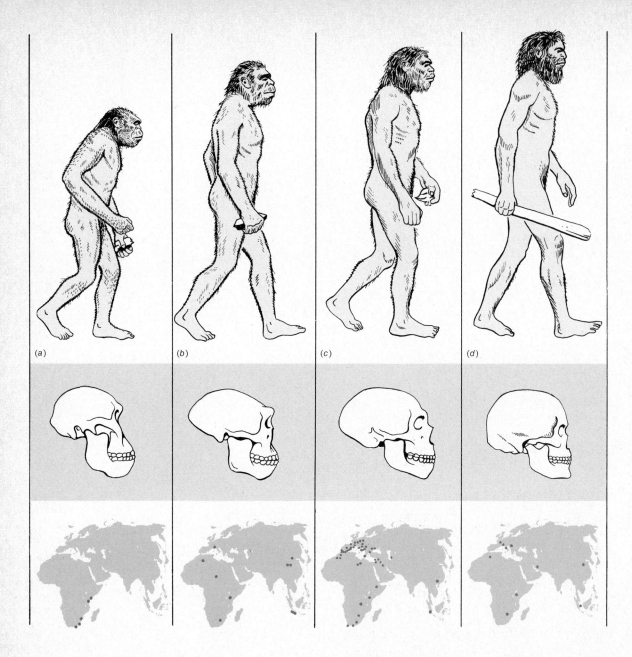

Figure 1.8 (*a*) Australopithecus africanus.
(*b*) Homo erectus. (*c*) *Neanderthal man.* (*d*)
Modern form of Homo sapiens.

For reasons not altogether clear but which probably involved changes in the environment such as those which made the dinosaur extinct, some of these monkey species began to live on the ground instead of in trees, forming a new evolutionary line, the *anthropoid apes*. This is thought to have happened about 20 or 30 million years ago. Through natural selection, those traits permitting apes to exist on the open plains survived. Such survival must have been facilitated by superior capacity to learn and to anticipate future events and plan for them (which required a larger brain), to be readily and appropriately aroused to fear and aggression when threatened or attacked, or when animal food was being hunted, to shape tools, to hold a weapon while running or walking, and to be able to communicate and cooperate socially when hunting, warding off predators, or rearing the young. These anthropoid apes split off from the tree-dwelling monkeys and established an evolutionary branch leading ultimately, though not directly, to man.

Hominoids ("ape-men") appear   The line leading to man later split off from the anthropoid apes, roughly 5 million years ago. The apes developed into one line of several species (among them the gibbon, orangutan, chimpanzee, and gorilla), as noted in Figure 1.7, which provides a rough chronology of these major evolutionary events. Man evolved from the other line in a complex series of steps the details of which are quite obscure. No one can say precisely which of the early manlike (hominoid) species should be called man. Because the changes were gradual and took millions of years, this is a matter of judgment from fragmentary evidence. The earliest beginnings of man, however, are usually assumed to have occurred after the separation between the apes and the hominids (our first human kin: family Hominidae), this difference becoming quite clearly defined more than 2.5 million years ago, according to recent archeological findings.

In the evolution of man, the most important ape-man, called *Australopithecus,* inhabited Africa about 2 to 3 million years ago. There were at least two versions of these transitional primates. The distinction is important because the earlier and larger subspecies of ape-man did not make it, so to speak, and became extinct. He had powerful molar teeth and jaws, capable of grinding vegetation, and small incisors and canine teeth so that he could not shear flesh as well as carnivorous animals can. According to Louis S. B. Leakey, who with his wife discovered the earliest known human bone fragments in Tanzania in 1959, he was largely vegetarian and his brain was very small, little larger than that of present-day chimpanzees. We can presume that he was quite limited in his ability to abstract or plan. Evidently, when food became scarce as a result of climatic changes, he could no longer compete effectively with other primates (Figure 1.8) and died out.

Hominids (the family of man) emerge   The smaller and better adapted ape-man of this new vintage apparently evolved in a somewhat different direction; deemphasizing the vegetarian diet in which hominoids originally had to compete with anthropoid apes, he turned to meat eating. This direction permitted reduction in size of the huge muscles over the temples

Figure 1.9 (a) Richard Leakey with skull found near Lake Rudolph, East Africa, evidence that an upright form of the genus Homo *coexisted with* Australopithecus *more than 2.5 million years ago. (b) Gradual evolution of man's brain has hitherto been represented as a progression from the skull of* Australopithecus *to that of* Homo sapiens. *Richard Leakey's recent discovery (see inset) challenges this smooth progression. (Photograph by Bob Campbell, © National Geographic Society)*

(a)

(b)

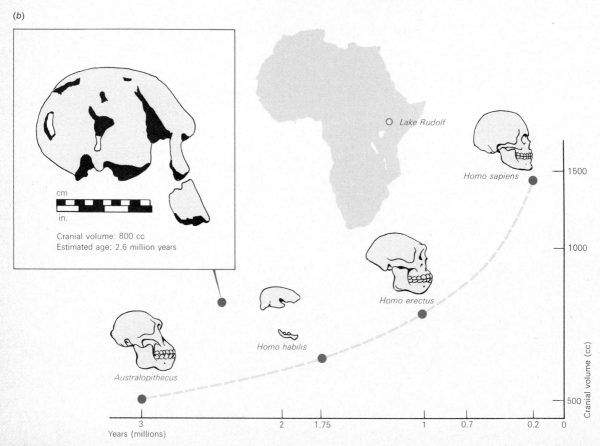

Cranial volume: 800 cc
Estimated age: 2.6 million years

Lake Rudolf

Homo sapiens

Homo erectus

Homo habilis

Australopithecus

Cranial volume (cc)

1500

1000

500

3   2   1.75   1   0.7   0.2   0

Years (millions)

used in grinding vegetation. In earlier ape-man, these muscles had originally closed right over the braincase. In later hominid species, the brain was enlarged greatly, increasing the potential for thinking and planning and for the development of manual dexterity that made use of brute force less important in adaptation. A larger brain and dexterous hands facilitated development and use of simple weapons and tools, and also allowed protoman to cooperate with his fellows in competing with scavengers (hyenas, jackals, vultures) for meat killed by the big cats. Ultimately our hominid ancestor became a successful hunter in his own right.

In late 1972, an exciting new fossil discovery was announced by Richard Leakey (Louis Leakey's son) and his wife Maeve that pushes the origins of genus *Homo* back almost a million years and alters somewhat our present understanding of the puzzle of man's beginnings. The newly discovered skull fragments found near Lake Rudolf in Kenya, Africa, reveal a man, living about 2.6 million years ago, who was a contemporary of *Australopithecus.* Prior to this new discovery the earliest known man, called *Homo habilis* by Louis Leakey, had been dated as living 1.75 million years ago. The reconstructed skull suggests a man more advanced even than *Homo habilis,* though different from our own species. The problem posed by this newly found skull is illustrated in Figure 1.9, which shows both its early placement in the evolution of man and its considerable cranial volume, about as large as the next species in the progression, *Homo erectus,* who lived about 1 million years ago. You can see that the new find is displaced from the theoretical curve in Figure 1.9b showing the progression in cranial volume from *Australopithecus* to *Homo sapiens.**

Homo erectus ("the man who stood erect") appeared approximately 500,000 years ago, and there followed a succession of many different forms such as Java man, Peking man, and Heidelberg man, whose lineal relationships to modern man are not clearly understood. *Homo erectus*'s brain was considerably larger than any previous hominid species. He was also capable of devising many different kinds of tools for hunting and obtaining shelter wherever he lived in the world, and he evidently could make use of fire, thus warming his cave or campsite, and probably cooking his meat. In one archeological site at which *Homo erectus* lived, a three-stone bola was found, an ingenious instrument twirled above the head and thrown at the feet of fleeing animals in order to bring them to the ground (Figure 1.10). Although it is also used today in modern

Figure 1.10 Killing birds with bolas.

---

*See W. Sullivan, Skull pushes back man's origin. *The New York Times,* November 10, 1972, pp. 1 and 16. Such new challenges in the attempt to trace accurately the details of man's origins are of course highly important but must not sidetrack us from our main purpose, which is to gain a general overview of human evolution and relate it to modern man's psychology.

(a)

(b)

Figure 1.11 Man the tool maker: (a) Camayura woman of the Amazon rain forest straining tapioca root in a large pottery bowl. (b) Young Camayura man shooting whistling arrow. (Courtesy of The American Museum of Natural History)

Argentina, this *Homo erectus* bola has been dated as approximately 500,000 years old, along with stone axes and the crushed bones of large animals that he evidently hunted. When this early man eventually evolved into our own modern species, the new version appeared first as Neanderthal man about 100,000 years ago.

Neanderthal man lived in Europe and Asia from 100,000 to 40,000 years ago. He could engage in the most important adaptive human functions. He used flint-pointed spears and hand axes, rudimentary fur clothing, and fire to withstand the weather. From his skeletons, tools, and the remains of game, we know him to have been good at hunting, stalking the huge mammoth and cave bear and using their tusks, pelt, and meat. He also fished and gathered fruit. But even more striking is the suggestion from archeological evidence that he did many of these things in organized groups, showing a fairly complex social organization, with stable family groups and the use of quasi-religious rituals in the burial of his dead. For example, numerous burial sites have been uncovered suggesting that considerable ceremony was employed in such burial, the corpse being interred with artifacts. In one such site in the Shanidar Cave in Iraq, traces of grains of pollen and other flower parts in the burial place have been detected by microscopic analysis, suggesting that the Neanderthal man whose bones these were and who lived 60,000 years ago had been laid to rest on a litter of flowers. All this implies that even early man had many of the rudimentary intellectual, social, and emotional properties to be elaborated so greatly later in modern men. In any event, Neanderthal man was later suddenly replaced by Cro-Magnon man around 35,000 to 40,000 years ago, a type with bones structurally much like our own. Our own type is thought to have arisen somewhat later (Figure 1.11), though he differs from Cro-Magnon man skeletally only in minor ways.

Scientists are not sure why *Homo erectus* became extinct and the new species, called *Homo sapiens* (that is, somewhat presumptuously, "man the wise"), emerged. One speculative possibility is that *Homo erectus* was too aggressive and lacked sufficient potential for social cooperation. A better possibility is that the evolutionary arrival on the scene of a newer, more able species of man led to the demise of the earlier form. One highly probable explanation is extermination as a result of major environmental catastrophes, such as pestilence, drought, or famine, and the ravages of the Ice Age known to have occurred about a million years ago, which must have grossly changed the world's climate.

Whatever the answer turns out to be about the demise of earlier species of man and the emergence of modern man, there is widespread agreement that the basic cause must have had something to do with environmental demands that could not be adequately met, creating natural selection pressures favoring only the more adaptive and ingenious advanced hominids, who ultimately survived, multiplied, and spread all over the face of the earth. Brain development must have been a crucial step.

The human brain

Although no one doubts today that the brain is the central organ of mental activity, this was far from obvious in the distant past. Even the remarkable men of classical Greece were not really very sure about it. For example, Plato (427–347 B.C.) was correct in placing the intellect in the head, but for the wrong reasons, namely, that the head was round and was the nearest part of the body to the heavens. On the other hand, Aristotle (384–322 B.C.), paying attention to careful anatomical observations, decided that the heart was the "seat of the soul," the brain merely providing the cooling system for the blood. In any event, little real advance was made in understanding the brain until the sixteenth or seventeenth century, when excellent anatomical maps of the brain became available, and serious efforts were made to identify the special functions of its different parts and of the nervous system in general (Figure 1.12).

Evolution of the brain   Man's brain is, of course, the main key to his special characteristics among the animals, as well as to those characteristics he shares with the primates from which he evolved. If we compare his brain with those of other animals, some insight can be obtained not only about its gradual evolution but also about how man's psychological characteristics came into being. Consider, for example, the matter of size. Although brain size and adaptive intelligence are by no means perfectly related, with each new species in the progression from the great apes to *Homo sapiens* we find a steady enlargement of the brain (as illustrated in Table 1.1).

Not only did brain size increase as evolution proceeded, but so did the relative size of various important control centers. What happened seems to be that in simple animals certain very rudimentary neurological structures evolved first which regulated vital physiological and behavioral activities. In early vertebrates, these structures were protuberances located at the upper end of the spinal cord and functioned in association with the eyes, mouth, and other vital organs. As animals became more complex, additional brain centers appeared, and dealing as they did with elementary and universal functions, they were not dropped as new structures were elaborated but are still found in the brains of every animal species, including our own. All animals must seek and digest food, breathe,

Figure 1.12   Early anatomists dissected the brain seeking clues about its function. This woodcut is from the famous De humani corporis fabrica *of Andreas Vesalius (1514–1564). (Library, New York Academy of Medicine)*

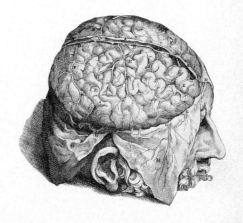

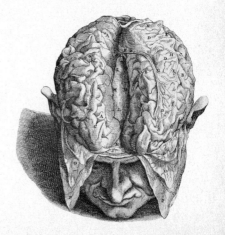

Table 1.1

Approximate cranial capacities of some apes, fossil ape-man, and modern man[a]

Primate	Capacity (cubic centimeters)
Chimpanzee	400
Orangutan	416
Gorilla	543
Australopithecus africanus (australopithecine)	600
Paranthropus robustus (australopithecine)	650
Homo erectus	775–1,000
Steinheim man	1,117
Rhodesian man	1,305
Neanderthal man	1,300–1,425
Cro-Magnon man	1,200–1,500
Recent man	1,200–1,500

[a] After M. F. Ashley Montagu (1965); M. Day (1965); and others.

maintain their internal temperature and chemical equilibrium, sleep, perceive their environments with reasonable accuracy, be alert to danger and capable of mobilizing to cope with it, and reproduce their kind. Such tasks must be managed by every animal species regardless of how primitive or advanced it is in an evolutionary sense.

On the other hand, two things seem to happen as one goes from the simpler to the more complex animals: (1) As one goes up the evolutionary scale, behavior becomes more variable. (2) The dependence of behavior on tightly wired-in neurological controls grows weaker, with more and more of the vital patterns of behavior (like fighting, fleeing, or mating) being modified and shaped by experience, or even inhibited. Along with this, there are many things higher mammals can and must do that simpler, less advanced animals cannot. For example, man has a tremendous capacity to learn from experience, to remember the past and anticipate the future, to manipulate abstract concepts, to think and reason, and to communicate by means of a complex language (Table 1.2). This means that special brain centers are found in man that do not exist in his earliest animal ancestors or that were previously developed in only a very rudimentary way. In examining and comparing the brains of different animal species, as we move up the scale of evolution we find little or no progressive elaboration in parts of the brain serving universal vital activities, such as alertness, emotional arousal, and regulation of the internal equilibrium. But those centers of the brain involved in what are often called "higher mental processes" show great changes in relative size. In man they are predominant.

If the reader examines Figure 1.13 he will observe changes in the anatomy of the brain from frog to man. The drawings show side views, and one must realize that the brain is symmetrical around a central stem or tube (the original spinal cord), so that there are actually two identical cerebral hemispheres, two olfactory lobes (for the sense of smell), and so on. Notice in this figure that there are major differences among the brains of these animals, and yet the similarities are also substantial. Careful anatomical examination leaves no doubt that all these brains are built on the same basic plan. In every case the earliest neurological part, the spinal cord, has enlarged into a bulbular brainstem, with a cerebellum (which stabilizes intricate body movements) and optic lobes (serving vision) on the top side, two olfactory lobes (serving smell) at the forward end, and two cerebral hemispheres (centers of those "higher mental processes") originating at the fore part but extending back of, and sometimes over, parts of the basic brainstem. In the human brain shown here the olfactory lobes are not visible and are comparatively little developed, while the cerebral hemispheres (together called the *cerebrum*) have developed into the most prominent portion of the brain, covering much of the rest of it.

The sizes of the brain structures correspond roughly to the importance of their behavioral manifestations in the life of the animal. For example, look in Figure 1.13 at the cerebellum of the pigeon and compare it with that of the lizard. In

Figure 1.13 Progression in the anatomy of the brain from lower to higher animals.

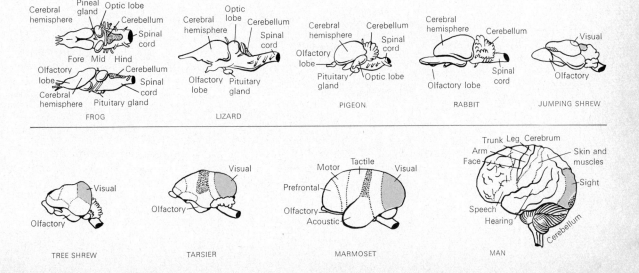

the pigeon it is relatively large and complex, while in the lizard it is small and simple, which squares with the observation that the highly coordinated bodily movements of the bird in flight require a correspondingly complex neurological control apparatus, while the limited locomotion of the lizard can be adequately served by a rudimentary organ. By the same token, the olfactory lobes of man are exceedingly small in relation to other portions of the brain, a fact which relates to his minimal use of smell, compared, say, with the jumping shrew whose life is so dominated by the sense of smell that some have very long and mobile noses (the "elephant" shrews; see Wooldridge, 1963).

The cerebral hemispheres gain in importance as we approach the human end of the evolutionary scale. In the frog, the cerebrum is only a small swelling, hardly larger than the other protuberances of the brainstem. However, its comparative size and complexity progressively grows as we proceed from frog to man. In monkeys, apes, and man, the cerebral hemispheres have grown so large that they appear as a covering that surrounds and hides most of the other regions (Figure

Table 1.2

Comparison of life-style characteristics of primates and men[a,b]

ECOLOGY			ECONOMIC SYSTEM	
Group size, density, and range	Home base	Population structure	Food habits	Economic dependence
Groups of 50–60 common but vary widely. One individual per 5–10 square miles. Range 200–600 square miles. Territorial rights; defend boundaries against strangers.	Occupy improved sites for variable times where sick are cared for and stores kept.	Tribal organization of local, exogamous groups.	Omnivorous. Food sharing. Men specialize in hunting, women and children in gathering.	Infants are dependent on adults for many years. Maturity of male delayed biologically and culturally. Hunting, storage and sharing of food.
10–200 in group. 10 individuals per square mile. Range 3–6 square miles; no territorial defense.	None: sick and injured must keep up with troop.	Small, inbreeding groups.	Almost entirely vegetarian. No food sharing, no division of labor.	Infant economically independent after weaning. Full maturity biologically delayed. No hunting, storage or sharing of food.

[a] Baboons and men are contrasted in this chart, which indicates that although primates often seem remarkably "human," there are fundamental differences in behavior. Baboon characteristics, which may be taken as representative of ape and monkey behavior in general, are based on laboratory and field studies; human characteristics are what is known of preagricultural *Homo sapiens*. The chart suggests that there was a considerable gap between primate behavior and the behavior of the most primitive men known.

[b] From S. L. Washburn and I. DeVore, The social life of baboons. *Scientific American*, 1961, **204**(6), 62–71. © 1961 by Scientific American, Inc. All rights reserved.

1.14). At the same time, those primitive centers of the brain-stem which control the activities keeping us alive and viable in a changing environment, and which we share with all other animals, have remained substantially unchanged from species to species, even among the highly complex and intelligent primate order to which we belong.

Models of how the brain works Man has attempted to understand the brain as the main organ of adaptation and mental life in many different ways, creating models that were usually based on analogies to the way other things in the physical world were thought to work (Magoun, 1963). Plato divided the soul of man into three subdivisions: the vegetative soul, serving appetite and nourishment and located in the belly and pelvis; the vital soul, concerned with body heat and located in the chest; and the rational soul, in the head. A hydraulic model was created by the Roman physician Galen (130–201 A.D.) based on the workings of the system of reservoirs and aqueducts of the Roman world. The French philosopher René Descartes (1596–1650) used an optical model, with hu-

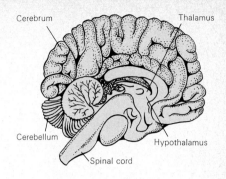

Figure 1.14 Vertical section of the brain showing the outer rind of the cerebrum (cerebral cortex, site of the higher mental processes) and some more primitive portions.

SOCIAL SYSTEM					COMMUNICATION
Organization	Social control	Sexual behavior	Mother-child relationship	Play	Use of symbols
Bands are dependent on, and affiliated with, one another in a semiopen system. Subgroups based on kinship.	Based on custom.	Female continuously receptive. Family based on prolonged male-female relationship and incest taboos.	Prolonged: infant helpless and entirely dependent on adults.	Interpersonal but also considerable use of inanimate objects.	Linguistic community. Language crucial in the evolution of religion, art, technology, and the cooperation of many individuals.
Troop self-sufficient, closed to outsiders. Temporary subgroups are formed based on age and individual preferences.	Based on physical dominance.	Female estrus. Multiple mates. No prolonged male-female relationship.	Intense but brief; infant well developed and in partial control.	Mainly interpersonal and exploratory.	Species-specific, largely gestural and concerned with immediate situations.

man impulses beamed like light rays outward from the pineal body ("the locus of the soul") to other portions of the brain. Phrenologists of the nineteenth century thought that various human activities were located in specific portions of the brain's surface; prominent bumps in the skull suggested extensive development of such activity in that person. These bumps could, therefore, be read to determine personality traits.

The most recent physiological model of the brain is linked to modern engineering and computer concepts, making use of the central idea of *feedback* discussed earlier. The brain is like any automatic mechanical or electrical control device (sometimes called a "servomechanism"), in which an action shuts off and on, or is modified, when it reaches a preset level. A good example is the ordinary home thermostat or temperature regulator. When, according to the thermometer, the temperature of the room has fallen below a designated point, which the homeowner can set to his own satisfaction, a gear closes the electrical circuit and hence turns on the heater. Similarly, when the room temperature rises above the designated point, the gearing system opens or disconnects the electrical circuit, turning off the heater. In this way, the room temperature can be automatically controlled; changes in temperature are systematically made to feed back to the heat-producing mechanism, the furnace. This is analogous to processes physiologists believe take place within the brain.

Consider the following simple example. When we walk from the daylight into a dimly lit room, the pupils of our eyes automatically enlarge or dilate, increasing the supply of light to the retina of the eye. Similarly, if the light becomes stronger, the pupils automatically contract, thus preventing damage to the sensitive nerve endings of the retina. The retinal cells picking up the light send electrical impulses to a brain center, which in turn provides electrical instructions to the muscles to either dilate or contract the pupil of the eye, just as the home thermometer turns a gear that opens or closes an electrical circuit, turning the heater on or off. There are many such feedback control loops operating within the brain—keeping our blood temperature constant at about 98.6 degrees, maintaining the sugar and oxygen level of the brain cells, and so on. Such feedback systems also operate in more complex behavioral contexts. One of the most remarkable is the one which controls coordination between the hand and the eye. The hand reaches out to touch or pick up something, and the eye gauges the distance, continually monitoring it so that we do not overreach or underreach. In effect, what we see feeds back to the control of our hand movements, and we are so experienced and skilled at this that it all occurs rather automatically, without our even being conscious of the process (Note 1.2).

Note 1.2

How do physiological psychologists find out about the various portions of the brain that govern our actions? The brain contains many different centers of neural activity, and each of these appear to play a distinct role in regulating our behavior.

Historically, this idea of a distinct *localization of brain function* has not always been taken seriously, and there has been an oscillation between such a view and the opposing idea that the brain acts as a total mass. (In the latter view, any portion is able to take over control of any psychological activity, and when brain tissues are destroyed what becomes important is how much tissue is affected rather than the specific cells involved.) The idea of localization of function began to be taken quite seriously in the early nineteenth century. At that time sophisticated efforts were first made to determine the kinds of behavior regulated by given portions of the brain. In recent years the idea of highly localized functions for specific brain centers has taken a strong hold on our thinking because of advances in technology enabling us to obtain a more precise idea of the actual anatomy of the brain.

One of the main approaches to the problem has involved careful surgical removal of certain brain tissues (so that the animal survives the operation), with subsequent observation of changes in the animal's adaptive behavior. Animals such as cats, rats, and monkeys are used for these experiments because it would be unthinkable to perform them on human subjects. Sometimes, however, during brain surgery (for removal of a tumor, say), the neurosurgeon must determine how much tissue can be removed safely. While the patient is under local anesthetic and the brain exposed, a weak electrical current may be safely introduced at specific locations and the patient asked about its psychological effects. This technique, an important part of the medical procedure, has also yielded much information about the role of various brain tissues in psychological activity (Penfield and Rasmussen, 1950). Moreover, many people have suffered brain injury as a result of accidents, and physiological psychologists and neurologists have been able to study some of the changes that result, say, in visual perception, in speech, or in abstract thought. Such patients can be

This physiological model serves well to explain the brain's control or "servomechanism" function; it leaves many questions unanswered as to that more fascinating side of man's mental activity—his creative thought!

Environmental change

As the above account indicates, man has become what he is through a long process of adaptation to his environment. No environment is static, however, and our present world is quite different from the one in which our early hominid ancestors first arose more than a million years ago (Bowlby, 1969). Man's habitat has evolved in some ways faster than he has himself. And if things keep changing at the present rate, his environment may alter even more radically in the near future.

We can also speak of man-made things as adapted to a given environment, just as we speak of biological organisms being adapted, and the problem of environmental change can be illustrated by using the automobile as an analogy. A small car might be said to be well-adapted to the streets of London. This means that it performs certain functions suitable to those streets, such as being able to move readily throughout the city by virtue of its size, speed, acceleration, braking, and turning radius. The car is well-designed (well-adapted) to London streets, but it might be poorly adapted to the American superhighway, to Alpine roads, for use in the Arctic, or in the desert. Moreover, changes in the London street scene might also make the car obsolete, just as the original "Tin Lizzie" (Ford Model-T) became obsolete. In the same way human traits are still presumably undergoing natural selection on the basis of their relevance to the modern world, and what is now biologically adaptive may be quite different from what was adaptive in past eras.

This has two important implications for our study of the effects of the environment on man. First, many of man's traits may be no longer well-adapted to the present environment, since they were evolved through adaptive struggles of the past when conditions were different. Second, many of the rapid changes in the environment today may ultimately lead to the evolution of new human traits.

About the first point that some human traits are no longer well-suited to the way we live today, an often-stated example is the emotion of anger. There was a time when men were heavily occupied in coping with predators and competing with dangerous carnivorous animals and other men for food. To do this effectively required a set of aggression-oriented attributes that permitted mobilization of added strength and energy (for fighting or fleeing) in emergency situations. Under

Note 1.2 (cont.)

tested carefully in the clinic or laboratory and the information about losses in previously intact skills may then be correlated with X-ray and other clinical evidence of the amount and type of tissue damage.

One of the most important technological advances in the study of how the brain works has been the use of an electric current applied to a very restricted portion of the brain, even to a single cell, while its behavioral effects are studied. This can be accomplished by means of a microelectrode, a tiny conductor so small as to be invisible to the naked eye, that is implanted with the use of a microscope into a specified portion of brain tissue. Delgado (1969) has shown that when one portion of a bull's brain is stimulated electrically the bull is regularly observed to charge at someone who has attracted his attention, while when another portion is stimulated the bull's attack instantly ceases. In this way Delgado is attempting to determine which brain centers are involved in aggression and in its inhibition.

Many methodological problems arise in such studies that should make the investigator somewhat cautious about his conclusions. For example, it makes a great deal of difference whether after surgery the animals are tested in the laboratory cage or observed in their natural environment. In some instances, opposite conclusions may be drawn depending on whether the animal is caged or free-roaming. Also, it is sometimes difficult to tell just how much (and exactly which portion) of the brain tissue has been destroyed surgically or electrically stimulated: destroying one portion may lead to destruction of other, interconnected portions; and even a weak electrical current will spread over a larger area. The brain is a complex organ, with all parts interconnected and highly interdependent, so that it is hard to affect one portion without affecting others. It is thus difficult to pinpoint the exact locus responsible for each observed behavioral change.

In spite of these technical problems, much has been learned about the brain from such neurosurgical methods. But we still have a very long way to go before we understand just how the brain functions as master organ of our adaptive behavior and mental life and the role of each portion within it.

In the early Pleistocene, perhaps three million years ago, crocodiles floated in the shallow lake at Olduvai where Australopithecus *left his remains, and that lake has died and come again and died many times over in the long rhythms of rain and drought that characterized the Ice Age. In Africa, where these oscillations were less violent than on other continents, many great animals still survive, but tool-users such as* Homo erectus *and his contemporaries, who were large creatures themselves, once hunted mastodons, gorilla-sized baboons, wild sabre-tusked pigs the size of hippopotamuses, and wild sheep as large as buffalo . . . on these plains. . . .* [From Matthiessen, 1972, p. 86]

such conditions, bodily changes that make possible such rapid mobilization are adaptively useful, that is, they aid in survival. In moments of danger or stress the substance *adrenaline* is secreted: thereupon sugar is released from the liver, heart rate accelerates, blood pressure increases, and more blood becomes available to the muscles and brain at the expense of the digestive tract (where it is not needed during the emergency). Certain emotional states, like rage, also play a part in reactions to threat. The present environment of man less often seems to require such drastic physiological adjustments, since the dangers modern man faces tend to be increasingly symbolic and the stresses are more intrapersonal than physical. Yet our biological makeup, compounded in the evolutionary crucible of past environmental pressures, still calls forth the physiological adjustments required by primitive man even though they now have much less utility for survival. Biological evolution is a very slow process compared with cultural evolution, and it will probably take a long time for us to lose many of our primitive attributes. Man's brief cultural history of 5,000 years is but a moment in the span of his evolutionary history of some 2.5 million years, or 3 billion years if we trace back our evolution to the one-celled protists.

One of the best-known theories of the cause of psychosomatic or stress disorders is predicated on the above analysis. In many social contexts, the physiological changes connected with anger and other crisis emotions often take place even though they are not needed. When there is no way to dissipate these impulses in major physical efforts such as headlong flight from danger or violent physical activity, tension builds up. Such emotion-charged feelings continue to smolder in day-to-day social relationships, producing psychosomatic symptoms in certain physiologically vulnerable persons. These stress disorders, as they are often called, are therefore products of evolutionary adaptations to an environment that no longer exists. (Violent sports like boxing, bullfighting, or football may help relieve the pressure of such emotions in participants—and, vicariously, in spectators; see Chapter 7.)

As to the second implication, that present-day characteristics of the environment may ultimately stimulate the evolution of new biological traits, it is not inconceivable that future generations of man may develop biological adaptations even to such noxious conditions as high levels of noise, air pollution, radiation, and an increasingly sedentary way of life, to name a few of the problems of the modern industrial world that early man did not have to face. Since evolution is still occurring, it is not unreasonable to assume that through selection new characteristics having no special value in the past will gradually emerge and be passed on to subsequent generations. In turn, it is quite possible that certain traits, well-established in past times, will drop out in the future or become

vestigial, like our appendix. There thus remains the intriguing prospect of the gradual creation of a new kind of man, although none of us will be around to greet him.

As a result of biological evolution, our bodies have developed the capacity to make many changes in response to new and unusual environmental demands. Such changes may be temporary or permanent. Examples include physiological adaptations to high altitudes, severe cold, excessive heat, or an unusual diet (Lasker, 1969).

Readers may have had the experience of being out of breath and fatigued when ascending a mountain like Pikes Peak or Mt. Evans in Colorado, both above 14,000 feet. At such elevations the air is very thin, containing much less oxygen than is present at sea level, and the muscle tissues become starved for oxygen. Within a few days in such a setting, the number of red blood cells (which carry oxygen from the lungs to the body's tissues) rises sharply to accommodate the lack, adding substantially to the oxygen supply available to the tissues, and we again feel and function comfortably. When we descend to sea level, the red cell count returns to normal. Our body has made a temporary physiological adaptation to high altitude.

But what of people who must live under high-altitude conditions all of their lives? Do such populations show permanent physiological changes? The answer seems to be affirmative, though it is not yet certain whether such physiological changes are maintained genetically as a result of natural selection pressures (and passed on to offspring) or merely acquired by everyone born at these high altitudes. There are now more than 10 million people living in the high-altitude portions (8,000 to 17,500 feet) of the Peruvian Andes Mountains, once the site of the Inca Empire, a major pre-Columbian civilization of the Western Hemisphere. One might think, therefore, that this would be an ideal human environment; but in actuality men who come up to these mountains from sea level find them to be extremely uncomfortable and difficult areas in which to live. Lowlanders suffer on these peaks from long-term or even permanent reduction of work capacity, and they undergo a number of acute physiological changes, including the rise in red blood cell concentration mentioned earlier.

Two populations of Peruvians of this region, a group of Nuñoa Indians living at high altitudes and another group living on the valley floor, have been compared (Baker, 1969). It was found that the maximum oxygen consumption of the highland Nuñoa males, hence their capacity to engage in sustained work, was great despite the reduced atmospheric pressure (and low oxygen content of the air). In contrast, when male lowlanders were brought to high altitudes, they showed significant reductions in maximum oxygen consumption and gave evidence of much discomfort. More recent evidence has

In the second half of the twentieth century, the advance of science along hundreds of fronts was changing the nature of the questions being asked concerning life, evolution, and man. While the archaeologists and paleontologists were widening their search for the record of man's origins and development, psychologists were beginning to unravel the nature of higher cognition and intelligence; molecular biologists were seeking clues to basic processes in genetics, life processes, and thought; astronomers had begun to theorize on the possibility of other planets around other suns in other universes containing other forms of evolved intelligent life. The United States and the Soviet Union had arrived at advanced plans for lunar and planetary exploration. . . . [From Marshack, 1972, p. 73]

confirmed that when Nuñoa highlanders are brought down to sea level, they too suffer considerable physiological distress, suggesting that they have more or less permanently adapted to the high altitudes and must now adapt to sea-level conditions if they wish to remain there.

In this chapter, the term adaptation has been used in the Darwinian sense, namely, that biological systems capable of living within a given environment survive (and adapt) through natural selection. This definition includes both the physiological *and* behavioral capacity to meet survival requirements within a given environment. Thus, we adapt to cold and thin air not only as a result of automatic physiological processes, such as are illustrated above with the Nuñoa Indians, but also by making clothing and burning fuel or by supplying oxygen where it normally is not present, as in high-altitude jet planes. It is in this latter sense, incidentally, that psychological questions come most clearly into focus, since mental activities such as perceiving, learning, and thinking are critical to survival in higher mammals. In short, our intelligence enables us to learn how to adapt to many hazards and changes in the world around us.

Man is capable of many kinds of adaptation to changed environmental conditions. Some of the adaptational responses are physiological, aroused temporarily or acquired over the lifetime of the individual; some are behavioral (such as building a fire, using clothing, or fashioning a tool); some are genetic, involving the evolution of new biological structures that favor species survival; and some, perhaps, are only potential, growing out of man's inventiveness and imagination, not yet required but available when needed. One cannot properly consider the future of man in the face of environmental change without taking into account these diverse possibilities.

The man-made environment

All of the above concerns the natural environment. However, much of our environment today is man-made, creating new hazards to life and limb, new ways of shortening life. These new hazards are the ironic result of technological "advances" since World War II that have produced sources of death and disability previously nonexistent, rare, or unimportant (Ford, 1970).

These new sources of death and disability are too numerous and widely recognized to require more than a passing mention to illustrate the point. They include huge numbers of deaths and disabilities due to traffic accidents, disease (such as emphysema) due to air pollution, poisoning due to lead, asbestos (used in auto brake linings), and mercury, and the misuse of drugs whose safety had not been proven (like thalidomide). Each of these instances has its own tragic record. In

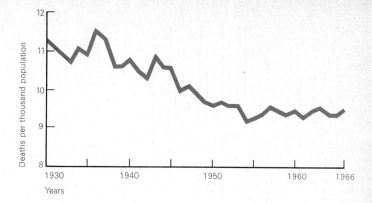

Figure 1.15 Death rates in the United States from 1930 to 1966. (Courtesy U.S. Public Health Service)

New York City the Health Department has estimated that as many as 25,000 slum children may be suffering from lead poisoning as a result of ingestion of leaded paint chipping off the walls of old buildings. No one is certain how widespread lead poisoning is throughout the United States, but it has been estimated that as many as 225,000 children are affected (Oberle, 1969). Recently, in a large Colorado town, dangerous radioactive waste filings were found infiltrated into sand used for concrete in construction of many new buildings. These are only a few of the health hazards created by modern technology.

Everyone realizes that there has been a general uptrend in life expectancy during the past few decades. In the sixteenth and seventeenth centuries in the city of York, England, only about 10 percent of the population lived to the age of 40; in the following century the percentage was even smaller (Cowgill, 1970). The aristocracy of England did considerably better, but they were relatively few in number. Moreover, this remarkably low figure for life spans some 100 to 300 years ago was not unique to such cities as York but applied widely throughout mankind, and in many areas of the world it was a good deal worse. Life expectancy in North America today is 70+ years, due in large measure to the reduction of deaths at birth and during infancy. However, improvement in the life span seems to be leveling off, and it is difficult to tell what the future holds (Figure 1.15).

CONCLUDING COMMENT

To this point, our concern has been with how man, as part of nature and as a product of biological evolution, came to be what he is. The central principle of this human evolution is biological survival—the process of natural selection through which characteristics that serve a species well in its struggle to establish an ecological niche are retained and passed on. This concept helps us understand the evolution of man's remarkable brain and with it the extraordinary human versatility in adapting to diverse and changing environmental circumstances. Our brain has enabled us to cope effectively with environmental demands, to overcome the ever-present challenges of the world around us. A new problem is whether, in continuing to exploit the resources of that world at an ever-expanding rate, man will also continue to change the natural environment in ways that lead ultimately to its wanton and irreversible destruction. (We shall consider this challenge again in Chapter 3, which deals with the increasing environmental problem caused by overpopulation.) What we are, both physically and psychologically, is a result of the world in which we live, a world whose well-being is essential to our own continued survival.

The principle of biological survival, while helping us toward an understanding of our psychological makeup and how it evolved, is nevertheless insufficient to explain everything. The culture in which we live also shapes our relationship with the environment in ways that are independent of strictly survival values and sometimes even in ways that contradict such values. Moreover, our psychological makeup itself influences how we apprehend and respond to the physical environment. We turn to such questions in Chapter 2.

ANNOTATED LIST OF SUGGESTED READINGS

Ecology

Odum, E. P. *Ecology.* New York: Holt, Rinehart & Winston, 1963 (paper). A brief, readable basic text.

Lorenz, K. Z. *King Solomon's ring.* New York: Thomas Y. Crowell, 1953 (paper). Delightful, nontechnical discussion of all kinds of animals and the ways they live, which exudes the sense of wonder and warm enjoyment of animal life keenly felt by the author, a prominent ethologist.

Evolution and adaptation

Dubos, R. *Man adapting.* New Haven: Yale University Press, 1965. Examination of the biological and social implications of modern environmental problems in a fairly nontechnical but expert fashion.

Wooldridge, D. E. *The machinery of the brain.* New York: McGraw-Hill, 1963 (paper). A very clear and readable account of the characteristics of the brain and nervous system, and how physiological psychologists think it works in such spheres as emotion and consciousness, speech, and learning and memory. Requires little prior knowledge of physiology or neural anatomy.

2,3,5

Although the environment shapes us, this influence is by no means direct and simple because, as was noted at the end of Chapter 1, the principle of sheer survival is not sufficient to account for all the variations in the way we live. Biological factors are important, but "man does not live by bread alone." Furthermore, there are many ways of surviving, or even thriving, even under comparable environmental circumstances. To better understand how man relates to his environment and tries to master the problems it poses for him, we need to turn to the psychological and social (or cultural) influences that determine how he apprehends and deals with that environment. An environmental condition is not a constraint or resource until it is perceived and conceived as such, and this recognition depends on cultural forces and internal psychological events. But how does an individual gain an understanding of his environment?

KNOWING THE ENVIRONMENT

The psychology of perception is largely the study of how our sense organs (for example, our eyes, ears, or smell and taste receptors) pick up information about the environment and how this information is interpreted. Were we not to look very closely at the process, we might get the idea that our senses merely record external reality as a camera records patterns of light and shadow on film. Yet, just as a photo needs to be composed by the photographer, who chooses where to point the lens of his camera and adjusts its focus, so perception involves a focusing and registering of the sense organs. And just as the patterns of light and dark and the hues developed on film need to be interpreted to make sense, so the impressions impinging on our sense organs and projected to our brain need

88 126 212
57   89 173
─── ─── ───
31   37   39
37
28
39
───
107

to be put together and analyzed in a meaningful way. Thus, to be accurate, the analogy between perception and a camera must include not only the recording of information (by light-sensitive paper or by the eye's retina), but it must also include the more involved mental processes of decision making about where to aim the sensory equipment and recognition of what the registered pattern means. This theme has been addressed by Kurt Koffka (1935, pp. 27–28) in the following anecdote:

On a winter evening amidst a driving snowstorm a man on horse-back arrived at an inn, happy to have reached a shelter after hours of riding over the wind-swept plain on which the blanket of snow had covered all paths and landmarks. The landlord who came to the door viewed the stranger with surprise and asked him whence he came. The man pointed in the direction straight away from the inn, whereupon the landlord, in tone of awe and wonder, said: "Do you know that you have ridden across the Lake of Constance?" At which the rider dropped stone dead at his feet.

What Koffka called the *geographical environment* (or per-haps we might use the term "objective environment") is the Lake of Constance covered with ice. In contrast, the traveler's perception (or should we say fantasy?) of the lake as a snow-swept plain is called the *behavioral environment* (or "subjective environment"). The important point here is that the man's behavior is understandable only by reference to this subjec-tively perceived environment. Presumably, if Koffka's traveler had known he was riding on ice-covered water, he would have taken another route or, at the very least, acted quite differ-ently, riding as if he were moving over glass or delicate eggs and experiencing much apprehension. The shock of discovery that his life has really been in jeopardy every minute of that ride kills him. The effects of the environment depend on the apprehension of it by the observer, on how he perceives it and interprets its significance. There are numerous illustrations of this in literature (see the margin and Figure 2.1).

The critical problem of perception is to apprehend what the environment is like "accurately" (Gibson, 1966). The nervous system has an extraordinary ability to extract specific information from the environment. Most approaches to per-ception have emphasized this "veridical" (*true*) aspect. It is a key adaptive feature of complex organisms, aiding them to survive and to establish ecological niches for themselves.

Do not be misled, however, about what this means. The notion of veridical perception, that is, perception that accu-rately reflects or mirrors the environment, has only limited validity. There is no way for man to know what the environ-ment is really like outside of what he mentally constructs of this environment by his sense organs and perceptual activity. Perception is "true" only in the sense that the knowledge

[Natasha] could only grasp what awaited her when, walking over the red cloth, she went into the vestibule, took off her cloak, and walked . . . up the lighted staircase. . . . [There] was a mist before her eyes; she could see nothing clearly, her pulse beat a hundred times a minute, and the blood throbbed at her heart. . . . The looking-glasses on the staircases reflected ladies in white, blue, and pink dresses, with diamonds and pearls on their bare arms and necks.

Natasha looked into the looking-glasses and could not distinguish herself from the rest. All was mingled into one brilliant pro-cession. At the entrance into the first room, the regular hum of voices, footsteps, greet-ings deafened Natasha; the light and bril-liance dazzled her still more. . . . [The] host-ess's eyes rested . . . on the slender figure of Natasha. She looked at her, and smiled at her a smile that was something more than the smile of welcome she had for all. Looking at her, the hostess was reminded perhaps of her golden days of girlhood, gone never to return, of her own first ball. . . . [From Leo Tolstoy, *War and peace* (transl. by Constance Garnett), p. 425. New York: Modern Library, 1931]

Figure 2.1 A girl's first formal dance seems an immense, glittering, elegant affair, even as recalled by her years later as a mature woman; the same crowded ballroom, perceived by someone older, more jaded, and less impressionable, may seem not nearly so magnificent. We have here two subjective interpretations of the same objective environment. (Scene from the Soviet film War and Peace, directed by Sergei Bondarchuk; TASS from SOVFOTO)

obtained serves us well in our interactions with the environment. Sensing heat enables us safely to avoid being burned; perceiving a crevasse enables us to avoid falling to our death. But our perceptual systems respond to only a limited percentage of the total available information. We do not perceive ultraviolet, infrared, cosmic, or X rays. Nor can we see bacteria without the aid of a microscope. Their existence is known by virtue of man's remarkable capacity for conceptualization and thought and because he can manufacture instruments (sensors) capable of supplementing his limited perceptual capability. There are countless examples of this in animal life. For example, a dog does not perceive colors; to it, the environment must look totally black and white. On the other hand, most dogs can detect odors and high-pitched sounds that man cannot. Yet our ability to reason keeps us from foolishly maintaining that the chemical substances or sound wavelengths that we cannot detect with our sense organs do not exist.

In short, our perception of the external world is a schematic affair, based on what has been required for species survival during evolutionary history, rather than a direct mirroring of all that actually exists. Our perceptual experience is so compelling, subjectively, that it is difficult to divest ourselves of the literal view that perception is the discovery of

When the moon disappears, people say that the moon has gone; and when it reappears, they say that the moon has come. But, in fact, the moon never goes nor comes. . . . The moon appears everywhere, over a crowded city, a sleepy village, a mountain, a river; it is seen in the depths of a pond, in a jug of water, in a drop of dew on a leaf. If a man walks hundreds of miles the moon goes with him. The moon does not change, but to people it seems to change. Buddha is like the moon . . . [he seems to appear and disappear] but in his Essence he changes not. [The teaching of Buddha, 11th ed. Tokyo: Bukkyo Dendo Kyokai, 1970, p. 27] how the environment truly is and to adopt a relativistic view that we detect some of the qualities of objects and events but probably cannot know all of reality.

The nature-nurture issue

Throughout the history of psychological thought there has been much research and debate aimed at pinning down those features in human behavior which are innate (inborn) and those which are learned through experience, and in no sphere of human activity has this issue been more actively fought over than in studies of perception. The nature-nurture controversy, as it has often been called, was not a constructive one when cast in either/or terms, that is, when it was asserted that a mental event was a product solely of heredity *or* learning. In every sphere of human activity, both are completely intertwined and contribute jointly to the end result. So it is with perception. Our perception of the environment is partly determined at birth by the structure of our sense organs and brain (nature) and partly the result of learning about things (nurture). Efforts to disentangle them to permit study of their influence in perceptual development are instructive.

What would a person see, for example, if he had been blind since childhood and then suddenly was able to use his eyes for the first time as an adult? Just such a hypothetical question was posed in the seventeenth century in a letter to British philosopher John Locke from his friend William Molyneux (author of *Dioptrica nova,* 1692):

Suppose a man *born* blind, and now adult, taught by his *touch* to distinguish between a cube and a sphere of the same metal, and nighly [almost] of the same bigness, so as to tell, when he felt one and the other, which is the cube, which the sphere. Suppose that the cube and the sphere were placed on a table, and the blind man be made to see . . . [could he] now distinguish and tell which is the globe, which the cube?

Locke thought he could not.

Some light is thrown on this hypothetical question by research on patients who have had cataracts surgically removed, enabling them to see for the first time as adults (Senden, 1960). At the moment of removal of bandages, the patient tends to be confused by a bewildering array of visual inputs. He appears, however, capable of distinguishing figure from background as do normal subjects, to be able to focus on figures, to scan them, and to follow their movements with his eyes. Such processes thus seem to be innate, although one cannot be altogether sure because adults have the advantage of having formed concepts that may aid greatly in figure-ground perception. On the other hand, such a patient cannot visually identify familiar objects that he has previously only touched, and if he learns to identify them visually in one situation he still may be unable to identify them in another, say, when the illumination is changed.

All this suggests that some basic perceptual activities may well be present at birth, whereas others develop gradually with experience. However, both human clinical studies of restored vision and animal experiments on visual deprivation at birth are not conclusive about the innate visual ability of the infant, since it is possible that the observed effects were influenced by deterioration of the visual apparatus during the period of blindness or visual deprivation. The most direct attack on the problem must be done with studies of newborn children, difficult as it is to estimate what a newborn babe perceives.

There have been many attempts to do the latter, but here we shall consider only one of the most interesting. It deals with the capacity to perceive height or distance. The world is so constructed that were we unable to distinguish distance we might well fall over cliffs or down crevasses (or down flights of steps, off roofs, out of windows). Most parents exercise considerable caution to protect their infant from falling out of its crib or down the stairs, believing presumably that the child has not yet learned to appreciate heights. However, studies show that small children may well have a very early perceptual appreciation of height or depth, even though they may lack the ability sufficiently to control their motor behavior so as to keep from falling.

One of the best and most ingenious experiments shedding light on this problem has been reported by Gibson and Walk (1960), who studied infants ranging from 6 to 14 months of age. In this study each child is placed on the edge of what is called a "visual cliff." This is created by a heavy glass pane on which the child can crawl, half of which rests on a solid base and half of which spans a drop of several feet. The glass on the solid side is covered with a checkered pattern, and this pattern continues down the shelf and deep "precipice" below the surface glass, enhancing the sense of depth. The effect of this arrangement is to have a bridge of glass on which the child can sit or crawl over a crevasse of several feet on one side and an apparently solid surface on the other. If the child is placed on the board in the middle of the pane of glass, on the solid side he sees a checkered floorlike area on which he can safely sit or crawl. If he turns to the side in which the checkered portion drops below the transparent surface layer of glass, and if he can perceive distance or height, then he will see a precipice. If he cannot discriminate height, one side will look the same to him as the other, and he should not hesitate to crawl out onto the ledge. This "visual cliff" arrangement is illustrated in Figure 2.2.

Figure 2.2   *The visual cliff: even infants perceive the danger of the chasm below the supporting glass bridge and typically move off it to the safer "solid" side. (From Gibson and Walk, 1960; photo by William Vandivert)*

When a child is placed on a board in the middle of the apparatus and its mother calls it, first from one side and then from the other, in nearly all cases, even at 6 months of age, he will crawl readily off the board and onto the shallow, solid side but refuse to crawl over the "precipice" side. An infant will frequently peer through the glass on the deep side but then back away. Even patting the glass on the deep side with his hands does not reassure him of its solidity. Since babies cannot be tested who are not old enough to crawl, these results do not prove that perception of depth or height is present at birth. It is clear, however, that depth perception has been established by the time the infant begins to crawl.

With other animals, the evidence shows that at least as soon as the animal is capable of locomotion, it perceives height or depth. Chickens less than 24 hours old would never step off the deep side. Goats and lambs placed on the apparatus as soon as they could stand (no more than a day old in some cases) always chose the solid side and would not move onto the deep side. Although learning is heavily involved in perceptual activities, it is quite evident that *this* perceptual capacity is present in all animals very early and probably has more to do with inborn neural properties than with experience.

Perceptual and cognitive development

At birth the physiological structure of our eyes and the nerves serving visual perception is fairly well established, and what happens when light falls on a newborn baby's eyes is not much different than it is in an adult. However, the baby does not discern this visual pattern as does the adult. At first he can hardly center his attention on anything, and he may use only one eye at birth. In a few weeks he will look with both eyes, and by the end of two months he will accurately focus on an object dangled in front of him and soon follow it with his eyes. In short, it takes some time before an infant can see objects as distinguished from their backgrounds, an ability essential to an adequate perception of the environment. At the start of life, little can be made of the complex patterns of sensory stimulation to which the nervous system is exposed, but with some experience things soon begin to get organized. Vernon (1962, p. 17) has described this feature of perceptual development as follows:

Perhaps one might call it more properly a random set of lights, noises, touches, tastes, and so on, without any connection or any known cause. However, it seems probable that within the first two months of his life the infant begins to realize that certain of these events recur regularly, and in particular that some of them frequently occur together, at the same time and in the same place or direction.

The warm touch of the nipple and the breast, the taste of the milk, the relief of his empty stomach, are pleasantly associated together at frequent and regular intervals. Indeed, it has been shown that first of all the touch of the breast, and later the movements of handling and nursing his body, become signals to the infant by means of which he anticipates feeding, though not with any clear consciousness of this.

The baby is beginning to recognize repetitive patterns in his environment, and these add significance to sensory inputs. In effect, *learning* is taking place, a psychological process we shall consider in more detail in Chapter 4 in connection with the impact of the social environment. But with learning comes the real beginning of perception as well, in the sense of apprehending and understanding the environment. It does not happen at once, but in a succession of stages, as the noted Swiss developmental psychologist Jean Piaget (1952, 1957) has pointed out. In the subsequent discussion of the main lines of perceptual and cognitive (thought) development, the main emphasis is placed on Piaget's ideas, although the work of others is also drawn upon at various points.

Piaget's main contributions are twofold: (1) a careful theoretical analysis of the development of perception and thought in children as they mature; (2) the creation of ingeniously designed tasks that help make evident the child's internal cognitive activities. The ways these tasks are performed help reveal the nature of the infant's thought processes even before it is capable of talking.

Piaget adopted a biological, evolutionary view of the growth of human intelligence, emphasizing feedback, the mechanism discussed in Chapter 1. The child comes to know his environment through his adaptive commerce with it. By acting on the environment and being acted on by it we achieve our perceptual and conceptual grasp of the world (Figure 2.3). This grasp is expressed psychologically in the form of internal representations of the world (*schemas*) that orient us and permit further acquisition of knowledge. Development of schemas proceeds in a stepwise fashion, new schemas always resting on a base of old knowledge.

Accommodation and assimilation   Psychologically, adaptation takes two basic forms: *accommodation* and *assimilation*. Accommodation is adjustment of schemas and behavior to the realities of the environment. Thus, as one reaches for an object, the distance the hand is made to travel represents an accommodation to the physical distance between the person and that object. And as one grasps the object, the spatial pattern of the fingers is an accommodation to its size and shape, adjusted through feedback from hand to eye and also employing the

If you grasp Piaget's biological perspective of intelligence, you will never be able to say what a young teacher said to me about her first graders: "But they can't think." These youngsters may not be able to speak properly or to read or to write; they may be poor in remembering or learning things by rote. But there is one thing they do, and must do, because they are children. This one thing is thinking. Six-year-old children develop. They are becoming more intelligent right under the nose of the teacher. This could not happen if they could not think. That they develop poorly in spite of schooling, instead of being helped by it, is the tragedy to which we address ourselves. This is the immediate reason that motivates me to urge all teachers to become familiar with Piaget's theory of knowledge. . . .

One problem that fascinated him . . . can be formulated in this way. If intelligent knowing is not a copy of reality, and if it does not derive primarily from the environment, how does it happen that it so perfectly fits the environment? Why is it that theoretical abstractions such as numbers and deductive reasoning have such fruitful applications in the real world?

To this Piaget suggests a biological answer, which puts him in opposition to current scientific and philosophical opinions. He denies that the general instruments of knowing, the forms of human intelligence, are discovered or learned from the environment. He denies with equal vigor that these forms are innately given or belong to a supranatural realm. He holds that human intelligence derives from the functioning of its inner structures according to a process of equilibration by way of formal abstractions. But the functioning of these structures does not take place in a vacuum. It occurs within a concrete person who lives in a specific physical and social environment, from which he learns specific things and toward which he has personal attitudes and motivation. The functioning of the structures manifests in behavior (and eventually to subjective awareness) the "objective" regulations that are internal to the functioning of all things in nature. Human intelligence is, therefore, directly related to regulations that can be observed at various levels of natural functioning. [From Furth, 1970, pp. 78–80]

sense of touch and kinesthesis (information about the movement and position of one's muscles). The object sets the requirements for the action, and these must all be taken into account in grasping the object. Similarly, and more importantly, as schemas develop they too represent accommodations to the nature of things, events, and relationships in the environment.

Assimilation is a manipulation of the external environment by the person so that it is made to conform to his requirements (goals, needs, existing conceptions). Instead of changing himself (as in accommodation), he adapts the environment to his needs. For example, wanting to make a noise, the child may seize any object at hand—a toy telephone, a spoon, a porcelain bowl—and bang with it. What determines the use of the object is not so much its normal use or value but the need simply to have an object for banging. Or, to take another example, when some of our primitive ancestors sat around a campfire built for cooking or for warmth, one of them might have carried away a burning piece of wood and used it as a torch, thus creatively assimilating an object originally intended for one purpose (giving heat) to another (providing light).

Effective transactions with the environment usually require both accommodation and assimilation. We grow not only by making our schemas fit the environmental circumstances and changing these schemas when necessary, but also by making the external circumstances fit our existing schemas, that is by assimilating events to internal representations of the world we have already forged out of past experience. We must be capable of changing ourselves and our environment to

Figure 2.3   Through commerce with the environment the child learns about things. (a, b) The long, thin object does not fit through crib bars crosswise and this child must discover some other way to make it fit. (c, d) The solution, that the object will fit lengthwise, is found by chance. (e–g) This solution is later applied to a new object. (George Zimbel; Monkmeyer Press Photo Service)

(e)   (f)   (g)

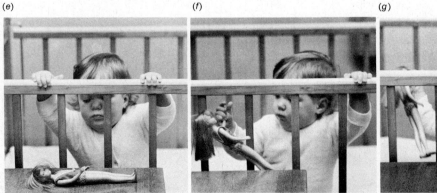

establish an effective and working equilibrium between them.

In Piaget's analysis (1952) of the progression of cognitive activity from birth to maturity, two main stages are outlined. These may be referred to as the sensorimotor stage and the conceptual or symbolic stage.

The sensorimotor stage   The sensorimotor stage lasts for roughly 2 years. Right after birth the infant makes a slow transition from purely reflexive activity, like automatically sucking, swallowing, or moving in response to stimuli, to the emergence of a limited cognitive structure. For about 6 weeks the infant sleeps most of the time, but when he is awake he is engaged in active interaction with the environment. At this time, the infant has difficulty differentiating between himself and other persons or things, as well as among the many different objects with which he comes in contact. In effect, he has not formed any concept of things outside of himself. For example, he acts as though anything with which his mouth comes in contact is suckable. Later he will come to know that some things can be sucked and others cannot or that some things taste pleasant and others do not.

During this initial stage of cognitive development, the elements of three essential later forms of thought are being established. One is the capacity to distinguish objects as such and, even more complex, to acquire a sense of *himself as separate* from other people and things. Within the first 2 years, he comes to distinguish himself from outside objects, but he is still "egocentric" and cannot place himself in the position of other people so as to recognize that they have a different point of view from himself. For example, if he is asked to point to the right hand of a person facing him, he will point to the side on which his own right hand is placed, failing to recognize that the other person is facing the other way. A second new element is a sense of the connection between things that are related in space and time; in effect, he learns the principle of *physical causality:* "If I throw this ball up, it will fall down." A third is the sense of *having an effect* on the environment that helps to establish a desire for competence and mastery of his surroundings (White, 1967): "I can make this thing move," or "If I bang it I can make a noise." Without such a sense of personal effectiveness, there can be little sustained progress toward achievement of goals in life.

Relatively early in the sensorimotor stage, at about 5 months of age, if a ball is placed beneath a blanket or behind an object the infant acts as if the ball no longer exists; however, by 8 months he will lift the blanket and try to find the ball, showing by this that he knows it has merely been hidden and that it still exists as an object even though it is out of sight. Thus, by this time he has made remarkable progress in con-

(a)

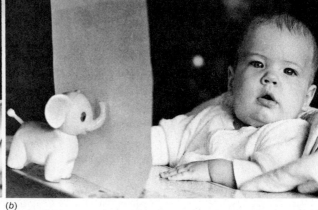

(b)

(c)

Figure 2.4 In the first few months of life the infant reacts only to objects' immediate sensory presence. (a, b) Out of sight, out of mind. By its eighth month, however, the child can conceive of the continued existence of hidden objects and will try to find them. (c–f) Out of sight, but still there. Peekaboo! (George Zimbel; Monkmeyer Press Photo Service)

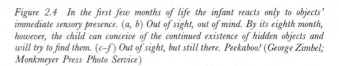

(d)

(e)

(f)

ceiving of objects more abstractly as rather stable features of the environment, even when he cannot see them (see Figure 2.4). The child has also begun to understand the causal efficacy of his own actions and to take pleasure from shaking rattles and from creating other such interesting events by his actions. By the end of this stage, he is already experimenting with objects, dropping them, say, to observe what happens. Moreover, some of this cognitive activity is now becoming *representational*, that is, it is taking place internally through images or symbols, as thoughts rather than perceptions of things.

Consider how valuable it is for a baby to learn that the same object is a constant thing, though it disappears momentarily or looks different in various positions. Before about 9 months of age, if his bottle is presented with the nipple turned away he will not try to grasp it, since it looks so unusual to him in this position that he fails to recognize it as his bottle. As he plays with objects, for example, turning his toys over in his hands, he discovers in time that each object has a constant shape even when it is seen in different aspects. Not only does he learn such "shape constancy," but he also learns how the object looks in its different aspects. But by the end of the first year of life, he shows clearly by his actions that he now recognizes things regardless of how they appear superficially in terms of the play of light on the retina of the eye. Similarly, he discovers about size and distance, and how the superficial appearance of things change as they get nearer or farther away. Things actually project smaller images on the retina at a distance than when they are close, so the child must learn to compensate for this in interpreting their size or distance; he learns that the object is not smaller but only farther away (Vernon, 1962).

66

As language develops, the child's ability to classify objects and events and to manipulate them symbolically is enlarged greatly. This ability to classify and name things would at first seem irrelevant to development of perception. Actually, it is of the utmost importance. In order to identify the important things in his environment, the child has to abstract their essential qualities so that they can be recognized in various circumstances. The number of new and unfamiliar objects he can identify continues to increase, however, and ultimately may threaten his sense of mastery. But the child learns to abstract, classify, and store away enough of the essential qualities of objects he knows to be able to handle new ones as they arise. Now, when he sees a new object, he need not compare it with every object he has previously seen but can quickly classify it into the appropriate category. He thus gains some idea of what it is and how to respond to it. The use of *words* as tags for classes of things is a great aid in remembering them. Where there is some potential danger, he now can make a rapid guess as to the situation. If feedback as the situation develops shows him that his assessment is incorrect, he can revise that judgment. In any event, operation of his sense organs combines with his growing knowledge of the world about him, his increasing ability to conceptualize or schematize the nature of things, and his preliminary use of language as an aid in such thought processes to produce the mental activity characteristic of *Homo sapiens*.

Symbolic thought From about 2 to 7 years of age, symbolic representations and their manipulation are crystallizing rapidly, and the transition is being made from mainly sensorimotor acts to covert mental acts. The latter tend to replace actions somewhat, or at least they allow the child to think before acting, to "look before he leaps." He is beginning to think in terms of classes or concepts, to see relationships, to manipulate language and even concepts like numbers. However, this is still being performed in a fashion Piaget calls "intuitive," meaning that the child's interactions with things are still quite egocentric, and above all, still tied to immediate concrete experiences rather than to abstract mental transformations of them. A good example of this is illustrated in Figure 2.5. Two containers are presented to the child—one short and wide, the other long and thin. Water is first poured into the short, wide container, and then an amount that the child can see is equal to the first is poured into the tall, thin container. Now the child is asked which container contains more liquid. You and I know that the volume of the liquid has not changed after being poured, but the child of 6 or 7 years usually says that the tall, thin container has a greater amount of water since its level is higher. The child is still

When an infant of 16 to 18 months looks for an object under a small towel under which one has previously placed a hat, not seeing the object when he removes the towel, the infant will immediately conclude that the object is under the hat. He infers this from the fact that the object was put under the towel and he does not see it when the towel is removed. . . . Thus, between the middle of the first year and of the second year there develops the elementary form of conservation which is the scheme of the permanent object. . . .

Therefore, before the operations formulated by language, there is a kind of logic of action coordination. This logic is characterized by order relations and by the hierarchical linking of the part to the whole. On the other hand, on the plane of more mature representation and thinking one can distinguish a figurative aspect tied to the representation of states and operations involving actions and their interiorization. A genetic relationship can then be postulated between these operations and the above-mentioned logic of action coordination. For example, the operation of adding two numbers [say, $2 + 3 = 5$] derives from the action of uniting objects; if one must call this uniting symbolic, this is insofar as the terms 2, 3, 5, + and = are signs and not things; but the addition that is applied to these signs is as real a uniting in the strict sense as an addition applied to objects. [From Piaget, 1969, p. 125]

(a)   (b)   (c)   (d)

Figure 2.5 The child of 6 or 7 is still tied to intuitive thinking rather than to abstract mental processes. (a) Two equal quantities of water. (b) One is poured into a taller and thinner container. (c) Now, which contains more water? (d) This one. (Felix Cooper)

Figure 2.6 Learning to control the rate of oscillation of a pendulum by means of experimentation. From 11 to 15, youngsters become adept at the logical processes required for abstract mathematics and complex reasoning. (Felix Cooper)

responding to the concrete perceptual impression. He cannot yet grasp the principle of "conservation," which is (in this instance) that the amount of water does not change merely because it is put into a container of different shape.

Between the ages of 7 and 11, the child becomes increasingly capable of employing complicated logical operations, at the same time becoming comfortable with the use of numbers. From 11 to 15 years of age he takes the last steps toward pure abstract thought and conceptualization (and can now tackle mathematical subjects like algebra and geometry). A demonstration with a pendulum apparatus is a good test of ability to reason (Figure 2.6). The girl here is given a number of objects, such as a glass bottle, dust pan, metal cup, pencil, pliers, and hammer, each of which is tied to a string hanging from the ceiling. The task is to determine whether she can control the rate of oscillation of the pendulum and, if possible, to make explicit her reasoning. In attempting to control the rate of oscillation, the child can vary the length of the string, the weight of the object fastened to it, how far the oscillation is made to extend, and the force of the push given.

In such a task it is possible to determine the child's conception of physical events by examining the logic of his analysis of the problem. Symbolic thought in this situation involves systematically separating the various factors that account for the rate of movement of the pendulum; in this way, thinking is accomplished in terms of abstract principles. The person has reached the highest stage of cognitive development if he can think and reason symbolically. In Piaget's view, the development of thought always moves in the direction of becoming increasingly independent of the concrete physical objects of the environment, growing more and more representational and abstract.

There are important practical implications of these changes in perception and thought for how society might handle its problems. It has been found, for example, that before the age of 13 adolescents usually cannot imagine the social consequences of political actions and typically think in terms of stereotyped, "black and white" opposites: "All police are good." "All police are evil." They are not yet able to analyze social problems with subtlety and realism. Before age

15, it is difficult for them even to think of the community as a whole, nor can they grasp the idea that the community has legitimate claims upon the citizen. (With increasing age and cognitive development, philosophical principles begin to play a part in their political judgments (Adelson and O'Neil, 1966).) Thus, as Piaget had suggested, from 11 to 18 years of age there is a progression from concrete, egocentric forms of thinking to more abstract, idealized ways of looking at things, and this operates in community affairs, in political thought, and in social life as well as in our own personal activities.

Moreover, people certainly do not all reach the same level of symbolic thought as they approach adulthood, so the kinds of solutions to social problems they will accept are also likely to vary. Whenever, as a society, we try to deal with social ills, certain ways of thinking are likely to cause disagreement, not because of ideological issues but simply because the level of symbolic thought required for comprehension of the subject's complexities may be beyond the grasp of many citizens. That is why the skilled propagandist or political huckster is often more effective in gaining mass response through simplistic arguments than the intellectual orator who "talks over the people's heads."

What all this means, of course, is that we cannot consider perception to be a mere reflection or recording of what is "out there." The entire process is closely linked to learning and thinking. Sensory processes, the detection and integration of physical inputs from the environment through our eyes, ears, nose, taste buds, kinesthetic and touch receptors, are certainly heavily dependent on certain built-in physiological processes, but perception goes beyond this. It involves interpretation of these physical inputs, the effective sorting and use of information received.

Such interpretation is subject to many sources of confusion and idiosyncracy. The information may be marginal or inadequate, as when illumination is poor, when events happen so quickly that they can be barely assimilated, or when contradictory data about objects and events is received. Under these conditions, internal factors loom large in determining what the person perceives and how he evaluates the data. Let us consider some examples of this.

Sources of perceptual confusion

We look at the jumble of black and white splotches on the pages of this book, organizing them instantly into letters and words or as a drawing or photo. We see a person or a chair (as figure) in a room (ground). In effect, some things in the stimulus pattern have integrity as objects and stand out against a background of other things.

A pendulum was constructed in the form of an object hanging from a string, and [then] the subject was shown how to vary the length of the string, how to change the weight of the suspended object, how to release the pendulum from various heights, and how to push it with different degrees of force. The subject was required to solve what is essentially a problem in physics: to discover which of the four factors, that is, length, weight, height, or force, alone or in combination with others, affects the pendulum's frequency of oscillation (how fast it swings). The correct solution, of course, is that the major causative factor is the length of the string: the shorter the string, the faster the oscillation. To solve the problem, the subject was allowed to experiment with the pendulum in any way he pleased. He could, for instance, make the pendulum heavy or light and see what happened. The examiner played a limited and non-directive role. He recorded the subject's experiments and verbal statements, and he intervened in the course of events to question the subject on a few points that were not clear. In addition, the examiner also asked the subject to prove his assertions when he did not voluntarily do so. To summarize, the subject assumed the role of a scientist seeking an answer by empirical means to a classical problem in physics, and the examiner recorded his behavior. . . .

. . . the adolescent [subject] begins in the realm of the hypothetical and imagines all of the possible determinants of the results. To test his hypotheses, he devises experiments which are well-ordered and designed to isolate the critical factors by systematically holding all factors but one constant. He observes the results correctly, and from them proceeds to draw conclusions. [From Ginsburg and Opper, 1969, pp. 182–183]

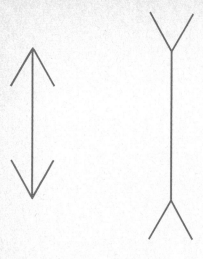

Figure 2.7 The Müller-Lyer illusion. Which vertical line is longer?

The external context The nature of perception is greatly altered, of course, if the figure itself is changed; however, the same figure can even be judged differently in the *context* of different backgrounds. This principle has produced a great many fascinating perceptual illusions well-known to psychologists interested in perception and to artists attempting to create interesting images through the manipulation of light and shadow and color on canvas. A classic example is the visual illusion discovered in 1889 by Franz Müller-Lyer, a German psychologist. It is illustrated in Figure 2.7.

Notice that the vertical line on the right seems longer than the one on the left. If you have never seen this illusion before, you may have to measure the lines with a ruler before convincing yourself that the lines are equal in length. There have been fascinating theories about the reason for this effect, one of the most recent being that the context fools us into imagining the vertical lines as part of a three-dimensional object. Thus, the vertical line at the right seems to be an edge projecting toward us, and the one on the left is an edge projecting away from us. To see this, look at the figure on the right and imagine, for example, a sawhorse, with the vertical line being the top board, and the top and bottom dashes the triangular legs standing on the ground; then look at the figure on the left and try to see the sawhorse turned upside down, with the triangular legs facing up in the air, and the top board of the horse now lying on the ground. The key mechanism in this illusion may be that things look bigger when they are close to us and smaller when farther away. It is possible that the Müller-Lyer illusion fools us into thinking the right vertical line is longer than the one on the left because the added context makes us see it as closer to us in space.

There are many such famous illusions in which an added context makes things look different. Another example is illustrated in Figure 2.8. It shows an illusion in which two actually straight and parallel horizontal lines appear markedly bowed in opposite directions as a result of the added context of criss-crossing lines. There is no need to review here the many different varieties of visual illusions. It is sufficient merely to recog-

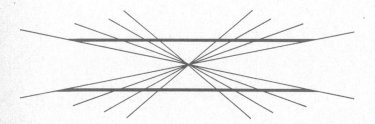

Figure 2.8 The Hering illusion. Try putting a ruler next to the horizontal lines and see what happens.

Figure 2.9 *Apparatus used in studies of space orientation. Both the subject in his chair (foreground) and the luminous rod can be tilted at will by the examiner. (From Witkin et al., 1954)*

nize that the context or background of any stimulus figure strongly influences what is perceived and may even produce subjective distortions from the objective stimulus event.

The evidence from one perceptual system is often *contradicted* by that obtained from another, and this too can be seen as an effect of the context on perception. For example, if a person is seated in a chair in a dark room and before him is placed a luminous rod, he has no trouble telling whether that rod is vertical or even slightly tilted away from the vertical position (Figure 2.9). If he is asked to correct the tilt, he can do so with high accuracy. However, suppose that the chair itself is now tilted too, say in the opposite direction. Two sources of information are now conflicting: Because the person is no longer in bodily alignment with the vertical line of sight from the rod, even a perfectly vertical rod may look tilted, and if the rod is actually tilted in relation to the walls of the room, it is a more difficult task to right it. The *kinesthetic* information (from the person's muscles), helping him orient himself to the pull of gravity, tells him one thing; the *visual* information about what is up and what is down tells him another.

Precisely this kind of perceptual situation has been studied extensively by Witkin and his colleagues (1954). They found that young children of both sexes are more responsive to visual cues (they tended to ignore the bodily cues when judging verticality of the rod); however, as they matured they shifted to a greater emphasis on the bodily tilt, stabilizing in this regard at about 13 years of age. For reasons that are not altogether clear, however, starting at about 15 years of age,

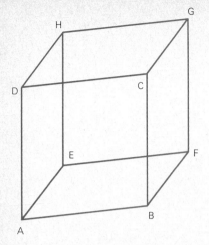

Figure 2.10 The Necker cube. Is the nearest surface ABCD or EFGH? Keep looking at the drawing for a while. What happens?

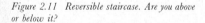

Figure 2.11 Reversible staircase. Are you above or below it?

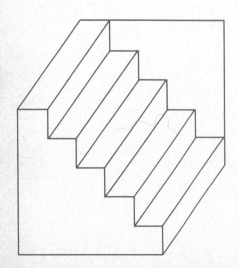

women reverse the pattern and show a sharp rise in responsiveness to visual cues while men increase in visual responsiveness only slightly. In this way, by adulthood, men and women differ in the way the contradiction of visual and bodily cues is resolved perceptually; women remain more responsive to the visual cues of verticality, while men are guided by their own body position.

Ambiguous information   There are also perceptual situations in which the environmental evidence may be assessed in two ways, neither of which is compelling enough to gain ascendancy. This happens with a type of figure drawing that "reverses," that is, is alternately perceived—first one way, then another. One such *reversible figure* was devised in 1832 by L. A. Necker, a Swiss naturalist, and since then it has been referred to as the Necker cube (Figure 2.10).

Our first perception is of a transparent box in which the *ABCD* area is the outer surface. But if we continue to look at the figure for a time, the original image seems to be erased, or rather it shifts; a new one has replaced it in which the *ABCD* area now becomes the inner surface of a transparent box, tilted in a different direction from the first construction. As long as one keeps looking at the drawing, the two distinctly different perceptions keep switching back and forth effortlessly.

Another example of a reversible figure is the drawing in Figure 2.11, in which the image changes back and forth between a staircase going up from left to right and an overhanging cornice, seen as though the viewer is underneath the staircase.

What seems to happen in the Necker cube and the reversible staircase is that each contains no clue as to which of the two images of the object is correct. The problem arises because these are three-dimensional objects represented on a two-dimensional surface, whereas in the natural context of three-dimensional space we usually know the right answer unless the cues are too weak, say, because of poor lighting, or fog, or some other impediment. This illustrates the point that perception is not a passive registering of sensory inputs but is an active process of interpreting the environment on the basis of past experience.

Psychological set   Whenever the information to be obtained about the environment is limited, ambiguous, or contradictory, idiosyncratic forces within the individual increase in importance in determining what is perceived and how it is interpreted. The person's beliefs, expectations, attitudes, motivations, and emotional concerns, factors always in some degree shaping behavior and subjective experience, are then brought more sharply into play, since the environmental con-

REPRODUCED FIGURES	WORD LIST 1	STIMULUS FIGURES	WORD LIST 2	REPRODUCED FIGURES
	Curtains in a window		Diamond in a rectangle	
	Bottle		Stirrup	
	Crescent moon		Letter "C"	
	Beehive		Hat	
	Eyeglasses		Dumbbells	
	Seven		Four	
	Ship's wheel		Sun	
	Hourglass		Table	
	Kidney bean		Canoe	
	Pine tree		Trowel	
	Gun		Broom	
	Two		Eight	

Figure 2.12   Subjects were asked to redraw the stimulus figures with either of the two word lists as "memory aids": about one-quarter of the subjects' pictures had major distortions, and 73 percent of these figures were distorted in the expected direction. See text, p. 74. (From Carmichael et al., 1932)

straints are now less clear and compelling as to how the event should be perceived, interpreted, and remembered. This principle can be seen most clearly in research on the role of psychological "set" in perceptual activity (see Note 2.1).

Set is a general term referring to a variety of cognitive, motivational, and emotional factors operating both before or during perceptual activity, which serve to orient us as to how an environmental happening should be viewed. Usually we do not see something "out of the blue" but are programmed, as it were, to perceive things in certain ways. These factors tend to guide the way in which we organize the event perceptually. Some sets arise out of the immediate situation; others are long-standing properties that operate whenever we are in a relevant situation.

In a classic study of the role of set in perception, people were presented with a series of stimulus objects and asked to reproduce what they had seen after these objects were removed from sight (Carmichael *et al.*, 1932). Prior to seeing the stimulus, subjects were told different things about what to expect. Typical results are shown in Figure 2.12 (p. 73). When subjects were given to believe that the stimulus to be seen would be a pair of glasses, many perceived glasses and reproduced the stimulus as indicated by the drawing on the left. If, on the

---

Note 2.1

In any study of perception, at least two general sets of causal influences must be taken into account: (1) physical input or display from the environment; and (2) personal characteristics of the subject. The more that the environmental display is ambiguous, the larger will personality factors loom in importance.

In analyzing psychological events, we often tend to oversimplify human reactions, to see them as the result of a single influence: a person grows angry because of an insult; he drops out of school because of a permissive upbringing; he likes a girl because she reminds him of his mother; and so on. All such statements are oversimplifications of what is, in reality, a complicated matrix of factors that have shaped a given pattern of behavior. Many causal influences are operating in any psychological happening. Everything we think, do, and feel is the product of numerous factors, both in the environment and within ourselves. This idea

is expressed by the term *multiple causation.*

When we perform experimental research on problems of perception, our study generally is designed to focus on a single or at most a few causal factors. We must remember that in nature many such factors are operating simultaneously in any psychological event.

Furthermore, various factors influencing the reaction are likely to interact, with modification of their psychological effects. One such interaction takes the following form: When the environmental inputs are strong and unambiguous, we will all perceive them in more or less the same way; however, as ambiguity is increased, persons of type A will see things differently than persons of type B. In effect, personal traits will increasingly influence what the individual sees, interacting always with the particular constraints imposed by the environmental display. The outcome will be some compromise between the environmental display and the person-

ality, each of which has some influence.

In psychological research we must therefore allow for many interacting variables. In Figure 2.9 we saw an example of contradiction between visual and kinesthetic (muscular) sources of information, an interaction among external variables. Situations in which the person wants to do two different things at the same time illustrate interactions between factors within the personality. Perhaps the most important types of interaction, however, are those in which an environmental factor interacts with a personality factor, as when people are struggling to cope with emotionally threatening experiences imposed on them from the social milieu.

Consider the following example (Lazarus and associates, 1951): A series of sentences, some emotionally threatening and some neutral, were put on a tape recorder against a background of noise which obscured them somewhat, making them difficult to hear without effort. Listeners usually could make

other hand, they were told they would see something that looked like a dumbbell, many drew reproductions like the one on the right. In effect, the stimulus object was assimilated to the concept formed by their expectations, leading to changes in detail in their memory of it as reflected in their drawings. Although the experiment is a very old one, it illustrates particularly well the overriding importance of set when the input is relatively ambiguous. The twofold result was produced in this case by making the subjects draw the stimulus object from memory, since if it had been in front of them while the drawings were made the cues from the stimulus objects would have been too compelling to distort.

Another, more recent example, and one more strictly concerned with perceptual activity rather than reproduction from memory, arises from a well-known demonstration of figure-ground instability. In Figure 2.13, as with the Necker cube (Figure 2.10), the viewer's perception of a picture shifts back and forth readily. We see a drawing of a woman. Some of us first see an attractive young woman, while others see an "old hag." After gazing at the picture for a while, it should shift from one to the other. To see the old hag, concentrate on the white projection in the middle left of the picture: you will soon perceive it as a large, somewhat hooked nose, upon

Figure 2.13 Is this a young woman or an old hag?

out only about 50 percent of the material. Then two groups of neurotic patients were selected, varying in symptoms and in their characteristic mode of coping with emotionally disturbing experiences. One group was composed of hysterical neurotics; the other, obsessive compulsives (see Chapter 10). The former are said to cope by repressing or avoiding threatening emotional material, whereas the latter handle such material by vigilance, that is, by being extremely alert to anything that might be threatening and then dampening its sting by detachment (much the way a physician or nurse keeps from being distressed at the sight of blood by being intellectually detached from it).

The tape recording of emotionally threatening and neutral sentences was played, and both types of patients wrote down what they heard. Those sentences which were easy to hear were accurately recorded by all patients, regardless of whether they were hysterics or obsessive compulsives. However,

the case was different for sentences that were difficult to hear. Since such sentences were somewhat ambiguous, personality factors played a greater role in determining what the subjects heard. Hysterics turned out to be more accurate in transcribing the neutral sentences than those which were emotionally threatening, in keeping with their tendency to handle threat by avoidance. On the other hand, obsessive-compulsive patients were more accurate in their transcriptions of the emotionally threatening sentences than the neutral ones, in keeping with their extravigilant and intellectualized way of responding to threat.

Here we see an *interaction* between two sets of causal factors in human perception, the environmental input (stimulus) and the personality. The perceptual outcome is not the result of either factor alone. When the sentences were clear and unambiguous, no differences showed up between the two groups of subjects. But when the sentences

were difficult to hear, each group tended to hear different types of sentence content better. Stimulus ambiguity increased one group's perception of threatening ideas but decreased the other's.

Personality and clinical psychologists make use of this principle in personality assessment by means of projective tests. Ambiguous perceptual material, such as ink-blots, incomplete sentences, or photos and drawings of people in unclear situations, are presented to be interpreted or completed by the person being assessed. Since the environmental inputs can mean different things to different people, personality factors will tend to shape how they handle the task. One individual may perceive a stimulus photo as portraying a domineering mother and her son, while another treats it as representing a kindly teacher and her pupil. The clinician uses such differences to make inferences about the kinds of persons he is examining. More will be said about this in Chapter 11.

(a)

(b)

Figure 2.14   (a) The young woman. (b) The hag.

which you will immediately see the horizontal line as a mouth below it, and the chin jutting out below that. To see the attractive young woman, try to view the hag's nose as a cheek and chin, with the old hag's mouth a choker necklace bisecting the young woman's neck. The eye of the old hag is the ear of the young woman.

Now if this picture, normally reversible in its figure-ground organization, is presented after subjects are first primed or "set" to see either the old hag or the young woman, the odds are that on the first showing the picture will be perceived in accord with that set. The set can be induced either by verbal preparation or by showing the subject a version of the picture that makes the cues for one or the other organization more compelling. For example, if we are shown Figure 2.14(a), the odds are good that we will then perceive the ambiguous drawing as the young woman; on the other hand, if we are shown Figure 2.14 (b) first, we are likely to perceive the ambiguous figure as the old hag. To demonstrate this effect, you might try it out with some friends to see how much influence such a set can have in shaping their perception of the ambiguous drawing.

One of the most interesting examples of the role of set or expectation in perceptual activity was reported many years ago in an experiment by Bruner and Postman (1949), who created a number of incongruous stimuli by mixing the suits and colors of a deck of cards and then tested the ease of recognition of these cards when they were flashed rapidly before the subjects. As a result of our experience with playing cards, we know that clubs and spades are black while diamonds and hearts are red. It could be said that those of us having experience with playing cards expect (are set or programmed) to see such conventional suit-color combinations. Not surprisingly, Bruner and Postman found that it was much harder for subjects to recognize clubs and spades when colored red or diamonds and hearts when colored black than with the normally colored cards.

Some of the typical errors made by subjects when presented these incongruously designed cards are interesting. One type of error was to assimilate either the suit to the color or the color to the suit; that is, a red spade might mistakenly be called a heart or diamond, or a black diamond might be reported incorrectly as a spade or club. Even more significant psychologically, however, and amusing too, were the instances in which a compromise perceptual reaction occurred, for example, when a red spade or a black heart was reported as brown, purple, rusty black, or black with red edges. In other words, faced with environmental objects that were incongruous (because they violated long-standing expectations), subjects grossly misperceived or distorted in their perceptions the actual physical structures (or *colors*) to which they were exposed. Similar distortions in perception have been shown to occur when a donkey and a leaf were presented bathed in light composed of red and green wavelengths (Duncker, 1939). The fact that a donkey should look grey and a leaf should look green led subjects to match the perceived color of the object to a comparison color that was greener or greyer (less green), depending on whether the object was the donkey or leaf.

Clearly, people normally do very well with the information they obtain about their environment. Otherwise, man could not have become a successful species biologically. The confusions and idiosyncrasies just noted are the result of the fact that, in the welter of continuing and ever-changing environmental inputs, we are forced to be selective. Moreover, many of our judgments must be made in the absence of clear and compelling information. In almost every area of social policy, for example, there are divergent interests among different social groups and major differences in how the same set of facts are interpreted. This corresponds, in some respects, to the ambiguous or confusing perceptual situations discussed above. When the inputs from the environment are clear-cut, one finds relatively little variation in the perceptual or judgmental outcome; but when the inputs are contradictory, confusing, or marginal in informational content, their interpretation depends more heavily on personal and cultural factors. (We shall see how this principle is used in personality assessment in Chapter 11.) Some of the potent cultural forces influencing human reactions to the physical environment are examined in the next section.

CULTURAL RESPONSE TO THE ENVIRONMENT

The fact that values other than those pertaining to survival are important in his life makes man different from all other creatures, in spite of the fact that he is part of the biological world. Man lives uniquely by symbols and ideologies. These are aspects of his culture. His abstract mental capacities permit him to have a sense of individual and social identity and to think of himself in terms of the past, present, and future.* An elaborate system of language permits communication with others of his species and enables him to relate interpersonally in ways characteristic of no other animal. He creates highly involved cultures consisting in part of ideologies about life and how it is to be lived, and he passes these down

---

*Jane van Lawick–Goodall (1971) thinks that chimpanzees too may have a sense of self, but if so it is a very rudimentary one compared with that of man.

It has been a summer of drought and despair. . . . The corn is stunted in the fields. Old Chief Tawakwaptiwa died in April, and a successor is not yet appointed. An undercurrent of strife and evil runs through all the villages. . . . The Snake-Antelope ceremony is the last hope, and it always brings rain. So, above as below, the sky reflects this battle between good and evil. . . .

They file into the plaza—two rows of twelve men each, . . . the Antelopes ash-gray and white, the Snakes reddish-brown and black. . . . Silently they encircle the plaza four times—a strange silence accentuated by the slight rattle of gourds and seashells. As each passes in front of the kisi [the shelter housing live snakes] he bends forward and with his right foot stomps powerfully upon the pochta, the sounding board. . . . In the thick, somber silence the dull resonant stamp sounds like a faint rumble from underground, echoed a moment later, like thunder from the distant storm clouds.

This is the supreme moment of mystery in the Snake Dance, the . . . climax of the whole Snake-Antelope ceremony. Never elsewhere does one hear such a sound, so deep and powerful it is. It assures those below that those above are dutifully carrying on the ceremony. It awakens the vibratory centers deep within the earth. . . . [From Book of the Hopi (transcribed by F. Waters), pp. 278–279. New York: Ballantine Books, 1963]

[For nearly all North American Indians] the value of ecstatic experience [Dionysian "vision"] in religion is a cornerstone of the whole religious structure. It may be induced by intoxicants and drugs; it may be self-induced—which may include such means as fasting and torture—or it may be achieved in dance. . . .

The absence of this vision complex in the Southwest [Pueblos] is one of the most striking cases of cultural resistance or cultural reinterpretation that we know. . . . No more than the Pueblos have allowed ecstasy as induced by alcohol or drugs, or under the guise of vision, have they admitted it as induced by the dance. Perhaps no people in North America spend more time in dance than the Southwest Pueblos. But its use . . . for the inducement of supernormal experience is alien to them. . . . [The] Hopi at the climax of their dances in the kivas dance upon the altar destroying the ground painting. Here there is no ecstasy; it is raw material used to build up one of the common Pueblo dance patterns. [From Ruth Benedict, 1930]

to subsequent generations through education and imitation. Thus, men acquire social values and personal goals that mobilize and sustain their activities. Ideological values may even transcend survival values at certain times, when men will risk their lives to preserve them. Cultural values greatly affect how the people of a society apprehend and relate to their physical environment.

The existence of water in the environment, for example, is a fact of great biological importance. But physically water is merely a chemical compound of hydrogen and oxygen that has no social relevance except in terms of how it is used within a culture. Water can provide a medium for swimming, fishing, or baptizing, as well as being a vital substance for drinking, washing, or cooking. Although it is a physical object of great importance, it can thus also serve as a social symbol for certain human activities that are culturally determined. Water can of course be drunk without the act having any social relevance, but a swimming pool, a fishing rod, or a baptismal font has meaning as a social object or symbol only within a culture that uses it. Thus, since baptism is practiced only by certain religious groups (cultures or subcultures), an Australian aborigine who knows nothing of Christian rites will not conceive of water as a baptismal agent. It is the culture in which man lives that gives the water social meanings beyond the strictly biological one.

Apollonian versus Dionysian life styles

Ideally, to illustrate the effect of cultural factors on outlook we should compare divergent patterns of cognition under similar environmental conditions. But this is not easy, since no two environments are exactly alike. However, if we make some minor compromises, we can indeed find interesting examples of different cultural reactions to the environment that at the same time cannot be readily explained by differences in the physical conditions of life. One such example is Ruth Benedict's (1934) classic comparison of the Pueblo Indians of the American Southwest and other Indian cultures (like the Apache) thriving under fairly comparable semidesert conditions in the western plains, the Mojave Desert, and the arid parts of northern Mexico.

No one knows what made the Pueblo Indians first settle in cliff dwellings and valley cities in Arizona and New Mexico over a thousand years ago in a nearly waterless valley. Although the land seems forbidding, this culture flourished before the Spanish *conquistadores* came looking for cities of gold in this part of the world. By that time the Pueblos had already abandoned their cities in the high cliffs and in the valleys and settled along the Rio Grande in villages they still occupy. Their

(a)

(b)

(c)

culture, unlike that of most other Indian communities, did not disintegrate with the coming of the white man but is still preserved in the Acoma, Zuñi, and Hopi tribes of the southwestern United States.

Drawing upon anthropological sources and the writings of others (for instance, Morris, 1942), Benedict described the Pueblos as an *Apollonian* culture, whose life styles were in marked contrast to the *Dionysian* patterns of other Indian groups. These terms refer to two distinct world views. (Dionysus was the Greek god of wine, object of a religious cult, who represented sensuous, frenzied, orgiastic, and irrational values. Apollo was the Greek god of manly beauty, art, poetry, and wisdom, celebrated for being temperate and rational.)

The Dionysian, as the German philosopher Friedrich Nietzsche portrayed him, struggles for meaning in life by attempting to break down the usual limits of existence, to reach the infinite, to escape from the boundaries imposed by his senses, and to thrust himself fully into another order of experience. He values frenzy. He sees himself, as did Faust, as a force forever combating obstacles. Conflict is the essence of existence.

The Apollonian, in contrast, distrusts such values, and in their place emphasizes order, balance, and moderation. For him the ideal world is harmonious. He strives to avoid disruptive psychological states, outlaw extremes from his experience, and find a middle road. Even in dancing, as Nietzsche put it, the Apollonian "remains what he is, and retains his civic name."

No people is entirely one thing or another, or lives strictly in accordance with a single life theme. The concepts of Apollonian and Dionysian life styles are gross abstractions that mainly attempt to capture the flavor of important and contradictory world views. Nevertheless, to a considerable extent the Pueblos would seem to be largely Apollonian in outlook and institution, while the other North American Indian cultures appear to be passionately Dionysian (Figure 2.15).

(d)

Figure 2.15 Apollonian (a, b) and Dionysian (c, d) rituals among American Indians. (a) Sober Snake ceremony of the Hopi tribe (Pueblos) of Arizona, painted by Fred Kabotie, Hopi artist. (b) The Pueblo rain seeker; photo by Rodman Wanamaker. (c) Frenzied Bison dance of the Mandans, a Sioux tribe of North Dakota, drawn from life by Charles Bodmer in the 1830s. (d) Blackfoot Indian engaged in the Torture dance in quest of vision; rare photo taken by R. N. Wilson in Alberta, Canada, in 1892. See comments by Ruth Benedict in margin of p. 78 and in text. (a–d: Courtesy of The American Museum of Natural History)

The first world was Tokpela [Endless Space].

But first, they say, there was only the Creator, Taiowa. All else was endless space. There was no beginning and no end, no time, no shape, no life. Just an immeasurable void that had its beginning and end, time, shape, and life in the mind of Taiowa the Creator.

Then he, the infinite, conceived the finite. First he created Sótuknang to make it manifest, saying to him, "I have created you, the first power and instrument as a person, to carry out my plan for life in endless space. I am your Uncle. You are my Nephew. Go now and lay out these universes in proper order so they may work harmoniously with one another according to my plan."

Sótuknang did as he was commanded. From endless space he gathered that which was to be manifest as solid substance, molded it into forms, and arranged them into nine universal kingdoms: one for Taiowa the Creator, one for himself, and seven universes for the life to come. Finishing this, Sótuknang went to Taiowa and asked, "Is this according to your plan?"

"It is very good," said Taiowa. . . . [From *Book of the Hopi* (transcribed by Frank Waters), p. 3. New York: Ballantine Books, 1963]

One of the Pueblo tribes, the Zuñi, was described by Benedict (1934, p. 54) as "a ceremonious people . . . who value sobriety and inoffensiveness above all other virtues." Their rituals are memorized so as to be letter-perfect, for each detail has magical value in dealing with the gods. They are highly traditional. Their prayers are not the outpouring of the human heart, but rather in a mild and ceremonious fashion they ask for rain, for an orderly life, pleasant days, a refuge against violence, and to be blessed with happy women.

Dancing is a major feature of ceremonial life, as it is with the other Plains Indians. Pueblo dancing is not of the frenzied type, bent toward ecstatic experience, but restrained, disciplined, and highly traditional. The Pueblo dancers feel thoroughly identified with the forces of nature, which they hope will resonate to their purposes. On the other hand, in the Navajo fire dance the dancers race around a blazing fire, each grasping a burning strand and striking the dancer ahead. They wildly circle closer and closer to the leaping flames. Bourke (1892, p. 585) writes as follows about Apache dancing:

These three dancers (medicine men) were naked to the waist, and wore beautiful kilts of fringed buckskin bound on with sashes, and moccasins reaching to the knees. In this guise they jumped into the center of the great circle of spectators and singers and began running about the fire shrieking and muttering, encouraged by the shouts and the singing, and by the drumming and incantation of the chorus which now swelled forth at full lung power.

As the volume of music swelled and the cries of the on-lookers became fiercer, the dancers were encouraged to the enthusiasm of frenzy. They darted about the circle, going through the motions of looking for an enemy, all the while muttering, mumbling, and singing, jumping, swaying, whirling like the dancing Dervishes of Arabia.

Generally, the Pueblos regard alcohol with repugnance, rejecting and distrusting any experiences that transport the person out of ordinary bounds and forfeit his sobriety. Nor do they understand self-torture, which is so common among other Plains Indians. Even death is treated in as controlled and moderate a fashion as possible, though Pueblos experience sorrow and acknowledge the loss.

In contrast, in a Yuman tribe cremation after the death of an individual (the body and all his personal property are burned), the scene is frenzied and wild. The mourners wail and cry as the flames of the funeral pyre rise, tearing their hair and scratching their faces. The women rip off their dresses and throw them into the fire.

The Apollonian Pueblos do not see the gods as having it in for them, as evil forces to be placated. It is foreign to them to see the universe as a place of conflict between good and evil (as the Judeo-Christian religions have taught). They view the world as a harmonious whole. Nor do they view the seasons or man's life as a race between life and death. Both life and death are always present, and death is not a denial of life. They have a sense of oneness with the universe. The heroism, violence, ecstasy, and struggle against obstacles of the Dionysian tribes has no place in the Apollonian cosmic view.

This contrast between the Dionysian and Apollonian life style among different Indian groups dramatically illustrates how highly diverse ideologies and life styles can emerge under comparable environmental conditions. It is a strong testimonial to the capacity of culture to shape man's way of thinking about nature and his response to it.

The feeling of control over things

Recently in the social sciences great interest has developed in another aspect of man's outlook toward his environment, namely, the extent to which he feels he has power over external events. Cultural anthropologists have found numerous variations in this regard among people of different cultures. Psychologists have shown that even within the same culture people vary considerably in this respect and that such outlooks are related to how well the individual is coping with problems of living. Let us first consider the cultural examples.

Gillin (1967) has compared two cultures living within the same city of Central America (San Carlos, Guatemala), namely, the Ladinos (Spanish-speaking people of mixed or pure Spanish descent) and an Indian population.

The Indian group views its environment passively, idealizing a peaceful adjustment to it. Their world is believed to be controlled by unseen powers, and man is conceived as being able to do nothing to change the rules or affect his destiny. He is therefore wise to bring himself into conformity with the scheme of things, opposition being useless against God's will. The Ladinos, in contrast, are an aggressive people, seeking to control and dominate the universe and believing it amenable to human manipulation. For the Ladino, even God favors the strong and powerful.

The same contrast can be found among groups living in our own urban centers, some of whom (like the San Carlos Indians) feel helpless or powerless to do anything about their lives, while others conceive that they can, to some extent, control their destiny (like the Ladinos). For example, feelings of utter powerlessness have been noted in the urban industrial slums of the West (for instance, in San Juan, Puerto Rico, and in Mexico City) by writers such as Oscar Lewis (1966). He refers to the way of life of such groups as the "culture of poverty." As a result of continuously negative experiences with life, poverty-stricken people often (though not always) develop

Many years ago when our grandparents foresaw what our future would be like, they spoke their prophecies among themselves and passed them on to the children before them.

"Cities will progress and then decay to the ways of the lowest beings. Drinkers of dark liquids will come upon the land, speaking nonsense and filth. Then the end shall be nearer.

"Population will increase until the land can hold no more. The tribes of men will mix. The dark liquids they drink will cause the people to fight among themselves. Families will break up: father against children and the children against one another.

"Maybe when the people have outdone themselves, then maybe, the stars will fall upon the land, or drops of hot water will rain upon the earth. Or the land will turn under. Or our father, the sun, will not rise to start the day. Then our possessions will turn into beasts and devour us whole.

"If not, there will be an odor from gases, which will fill the air we breathe, and the end for us shall come.

"But the people themselves will bring upon themselves what they receive. . . . [Time] alone will tell what the future holds for us." [From *The Zunis: self-portrayals* (trans. by Alvina Quam), p. 3. Albuquerque, N.M.: Univ. of New Mexico Press, 1972]

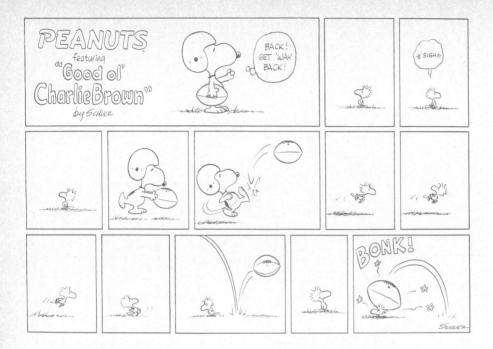

Figure 2.16 It would seem that for poor Wood-stock, the locus of control is decidedly external. (Drawing by Charles Schulz; © 1970 United Feature Syndicate, Inc.)

the outlook that there is nothing they can do to change their circumstances—they are so poor that they cannot even gain a toehold to climb out of their lowly condition, and even if an opportunity appears they cannot recognize it or do anything about it. They are oriented toward the present rather than the future and seem unable to defer immediate gratification and plan for the future in order to advance occupationally and economically.

Psychologist Julian Rotter (1966) speaks of a similar contrast in outlook between those in our society who *internalize* responsibility and power, that is, assume that they have the means to influence events, and those who *externalize* them, in other words, assume that any outcome is a product of external forces over which they have little or no control. Given the same circumstances of reward and punishment, desires, opportunities, and handicaps, "externalizers" are likely to do little to master or change the conditions of their lives, while "internalizers" generally exert considerable effort to improve things and blame themselves when they go wrong (Figure 2.16). Internalizers seek professional help for their problems, since they believe that their own defects prevent them from having satisfactory lives; externalizers tend to reject psychotherapy, since they blame uncontrollable external events for their plight (say, poverty or governmental indifference).

Recently a study of tornado deaths in various parts of the United States has produced striking evidence that culturally based outlooks like the above affect physical vulnerability by influencing what the individual will do when faced with an environmental disaster (Sims and Baumann, 1972). Injuries and deaths from tornadoes in Alabama, for example, are disproportionately high, compared with Illinois, another tornado area, and this difference cannot be explained by reference to physical factors such as frequency and severity of storms, population density, or adequacy of housing. In Illinois the predominant method of keeping informed about the impending crisis was by means of the mass media, such as radio or television, while Alabamians reported vaguely watching the sky or looking at the clouds. Illinoisians were five times as likely as Alabamians to take concrete action, such as seeking shelter, taking precautions, or alerting others. Consistent with this difference in coping behaviors are the general outlooks of the people of the two subcultures concerning the forces that control life events. The Illinoisians were more autonomous, more prone to see themselves as responsible for managing their own lives, and more confident of their effectiveness than the Alabamians, who tend to see themselves as governed by external forces outside their control such as fate, luck, and (particularly) God. Here we see not only the impact of culture on how people perceive the world, but we also have an opportunity to observe how this outlook leads to divergent actions with unequal effects on the chances of survival against an environmental danger.

All this is indicative of the potency of culturally based orientations to life in influencing the way a people (as well as a person) deals with the environment. Along the same lines, it has often been suggested that technologically oriented industrial development first occurred in western Europe partly because of its ideology of mastery and control over the environment rather than of resignation to or a sense of oneness with it. One recent writer (White, 1967) has put forth the fascinating thesis that there is a religious origin to our traditional Western ethic of taming or attacking nature. He notes that the pagan belief in many gods was ultimately replaced by another outlook, that of the single deity in Hebrew and Christian theology. In primitive societies living under a pagan pantheon, every natural thing was presided over by a spirit. The whole of nature was sacred. This restrained man from wantonly destroying living things, since such destruction might enrage the spirit in charge, and therefore to cut down a tree or kill an animal safely required that the spirit first be placated. Pueblo Indians beg forgiveness when they fell a tree or kill a jack rabbit. Mayans pray when they cut down trees to clear land. Pygmies think that they have to restore the balance of nature when they upset it. It is rather typical of primitive man and to a lesser extent of peasant peoples that there is no sharp dividing line between man and nature, an outlook in keeping with the ecological viewpoint discussed in Chapter 1 (see the margin).

White suggests that by substituting the one God of Christianity for the many gods of paganism, the exploitation of nature without fear and guilt was made possible. First of all, man could elevate himself above the animal world in his own eyes (for example, only he was said to have a soul), and he could come to believe that nature had no reason to exist except for his benefit. This is one interpretation of the Old Testament story of the sacrifice of the lamb by Abraham to spare his son, Isaac. The sacrifice equals man's elevation over the animal world or, more broadly, the preservation of man at the expense of nature. There have also been dissenters from this theme, however, one of whom was St. Francis of Assisi, who proclaimed the spiritual equality of everything in nature and demonstrated this ideology by preaching to animals. Still, the dominant ideology of the modern Western world was that all nature, like the Garden of Eden, was placed on earth for man's special benefit. In White's view, this ideology helped push the West toward development of technology for control of the physical environment. If this view is correct, the causal link between Western ideology and its remarkable industrial development of the past four hundred years would provide a fascinating instance of the impact of culture on man's relations to his environment.

Cultural versus survival values

Cultural factors sometimes even act antithetically to biological needs. To preserve cultural values and the social forms of life as we know them, societies often take courses of action that, in spite of rationalizations to the contrary, may impair the survival prospects of people living within them. There is a long list of common examples: Although wars are sometimes said to be fought to protect and defend a people, they are often unnecessary, unwise, and even self-destructive, and this implies that ideological values (nationalism, fanatic patriotism) have gotten in the way of survival. The viability of our world and security of people everywhere are no doubt threatened by a wasteful and futile international arms race. There is little doubt too that we are endangering our health by unbridled industrial and commercial expansion destructive of the environment. This expansion is undertaken to fulfill economic goals (increased "gross national product") at the expense of other features of life. And for ideological reasons we continue to maintain archaic laws against widespread social offenses such as prostitution and adult homosexuality (non-victim crimes), thus diverting law enforcement resources from really violent crimes that endanger the lives of our citizens.

The man and son . . . [take] the store of piñon nuts gathered by a pack rat for winter eating—replacing the "take" with an equal amount of grain. [From The Zunis: Self-portrayals, p. vii. Albuquerque, N.M.: Univ. of New Mexico Press, 1972]

By failing to invest in real psychological rehabilitation of people in prison, we commit increasing numbers of men and women to lives of desperation and crime in which they become predators upon the rest of society. Punitive ideologies that blame economically marginal groups such as slum dwellers, the aged, and the educationally deprived for their plight may well alienate large numbers of people, increase the likelihood of crime, and endanger the security of the rest of society. As a final example, recently the governor of California vetoed a bill which would have eliminated the requirement that public school children obtain parental consent before learning about venereal disease. Insofar as this makes it more difficult to teach the causes of such disease to schoolchildren, at a time of rampaging incidence of venereal disease that is reaching epidemic proportions, such action to preserve the traditional attitude toward sex probably increases the dangers to the physical well-being of our youth. It is always a matter of judgment, of course, as to whether a given course of action will threaten or enhance public security and well-being, but the argument that physical survival can be endangered by ideologically based decisions is unassailable.

Sometimes ethical values must take precedence over survival values, however. Survival as a biological principle is ethically neutral—the biologically fittest survive, while those lacking adaptability perish. If we blindly applied this principle of natural selection to the problem of air pollution, there is little doubt that the biological laws of survival would take over. Were we not to clean up the air (it would be cheaper not to), then numerous people would grow sick and many would die; the problem of overpopulation would be alleviated. Those with weaker lungs would succumb to respiratory diseases (this is evidently already happening in the case of emphysema), and others with tougher lungs would survive. Eventually, after many generations, evolutionary changes in man's lungs probably would produce a new breed for whom pollution might no longer pose a significant problem. But in the process, we would be callously casting aside all humanitarian values that make life worthwhile. "Our best interests" are often divided between values of sheer physical survival (for the individual, for the group, or for the nation) and maintenance of important cultural or ethical standards. Such standards are uniquely important to man, who lives by symbols that are both endearing and provoking. Our cultural values guide us in seeking long-range improvements in the human condition. Culture itself has evolved, via the transmission and preservation of useful ideas (in literature, history, science, philosophy, art), from generation to generation.

Although I have been saying here that cultural factors are important in the way man handles his life and the physical

(a)

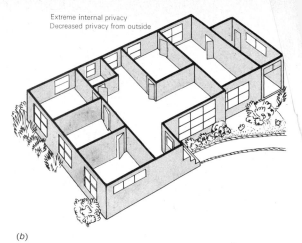

Extreme internal privacy
Decreased privacy from outside

(b)

(c)

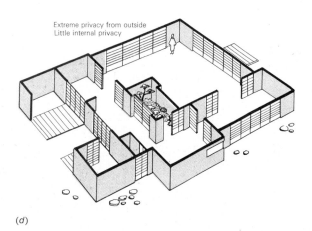

Extreme privacy from outside
Little internal privacy

(d)

Figure 2.17 Privacy realms: effect of cultural factors upon house design. (a,b) The American house has many windows and is subdivided into several rooms. There is maximum internal privacy and less privacy from the outside. (c,d) The Japanese house turns a blank façade of high fences, walls, or closed screens to the outside world; but inside there is little concern about privacy and people can hear each other through the paper screens, which may often be left open for ventilation so that the whole house can be seen through. Thus there is maximum privacy from the outside and little internal privacy. (a: Felix Cooper; c: Hiroshi Hosono, Foreign Correspondents' Club, Tokyo)

world in which he lives, I seem to be hedging on whether they are more important or less important than survival factors. The question is not very meaningful in the abstract, since sometimes cultural factors will transcend biological ones and at other times be dwarfed by them. Biologists and cultural anthropologists generally weigh these factors as one would expect them to from their respective vantage points. For example, in a fascinating book on the kinds of houses built in different parts of the world, Amos Rapoport (1969) considers culture as the primary force in house design, and climate and geography as merely secondary modifiers. The physical setting provides mainly the possibilities, but the choice of style and materials reflects cultural taboos, customs, and tradition.

Rapoport shows how cultures differ in their definition of basic needs, family structure, position of women, attitude toward privacy (Figure 2.17), and forms of social intercourse, and how such differences lead to differently designed dwellings. For example, the levels of lighting desired are quite different from culture to culture, even between England and the United States, in spite of the fact that one would expect the visual requirements to be similar. Although resting is a basic need, the people of some cultures rest by squatting (in parts of Asia), others stand on one foot (Australian aborigines and some Africans), and still others sit. Moreover, the manner in which sleeping is accomplished may vary: people may sleep in a bed or on a mat on the floor; they may also differ in the quantity of sleeping space which they require.

It might be well to conclude this discussion by quoting a passage from Rapoport (1969, p. 47):

> Given a certain climate, the availability of certain materials, and the constraints and capabilities of a given level of technology, what finally decides the form of a dwelling, and moulds the spaces and their relationships, is the vision that people have of the ideal life. The environment sought reflects many socio-cultural forces, including religious beliefs, family and clan structure, social organization, way of gaining a livelihood, and social relations between individuals. This is why solutions are much more varied than biological needs, technical devices, and climatic conditions, and also why one aspect may be more dominant in one culture than it is in others. Buildings and settlements are the visible expression of the relative importance attached to different aspects of life and varying ways of perceiving reality. The house, the village, and the town expresses the fact that societies share certain generally accepted goals and life values. The forms of primitive and vernacular buildings are less the result of individual desires than of the aims and desires of the unified group for an ideal environment. They therefore have symbolic values, since symbols serve a culture by making concrete its ideas and feelings. At the same time, house forms, more than other artifacts, are influenced and modified by climatic forces, choice of site, and availability and choice of materials and construction techniques.

In a Western-style building, a window, no matter how large, is not generally considered to be an entrance or an exit, but the mobile partitions [shoji] of a Japanese house serve as both windows and doors.

It is their mobility, of course, which enables these sliding partitions to play their role in the merging of indoor and outdoor space. Unlike solid walls, or even walls supplied with an abundance of doors and windows, they form no permanent boundary between outdoors and indoors, whether physical or psychological. When they are closed, it is only for the sake of convenience, and they may be readily opened to enlarge the living space and permit free and intimate contact with nature. . . .

The shoji have an essential role in creating the atmosphere of a room. . . . When they are closed on a cool day, they serve as a kind of screen on which the silhouettes of trees and other outdoor objects may appear. When the two central panels of the customary set of four shoji are opened, the garden is viewed in the manner of a framed picture. In the heat of summer all four panels may be lifted out and a bamboo blind hung in their place, so that the room seems to become a part of the outdoor space, while the breeze is allowed to sweep freely into the house. In winter, if the house is furnished with snow-viewing shoji, the lower panels of glass may be exposed by raising the paper panels that cover them, and the outdoor scene can be viewed without discomfort from the cold. . . . [From Itoh and Futagawa, 1969, p. 159]

CONCLUDING COMMENT

We can see that no simple, universal human outlook toward the physical world is born of the requirements of biological survival. Although our perception is in remarkable accord with the information provided by the environment, partly as a result of the inherent physical properties of our sense organs and partly as a result of our experience with the environment from the earliest days of our lives, personal and cultural influences also play a central role in the ways we apprehend the world and deal with it, especially under conditions in which the informational output of the environment is ambiguous.

This is important because these very differences in outlook affect how we act toward the environment and determine the solutions we select for the problems it presents. To cope with such problems, not only must we think about them in terms of our biological survival, but we must also take into account the powerful psychosocial forces influencing our response to the environment. In fact, personal and cultural values are often pitted against biological survival values. Moreover, as we saw in connection with the divergent styles of thinking about tornadoes, various individuals and social groups are likely to have divergent perceptions and interpretations of given environmental problems, and in consequence will cope with them differently as well. These insights about the way psychological and social factors control our interaction with the environment will stand us in good stead as we consider the problem of overpopulation in Chapter 3.

ANNOTATED LIST OF SUGGESTED READINGS

Perception

Vernon, M. D. *The psychology of perception.* Middlesex, England: Penguin Books, 1962 (paper). A very thorough, systematic, and clear presentation of perception psychology, somewhat dry but well worth reading.

Froman, R. *Science, art, and visual illusions.* New York: Simon and Schuster, 1970 (paper). One of the most interesting brief accounts of visual illusions and their bases, explaining how great Western art has made use of illusions.

Phillips, J. L., Jr. *The origins of intellect: Piaget's theory.* San Francisco: Freeman, 1969. Ginsburg, H., and Opper, S. *Piaget's theory of intellectual development: An introduction.* Englewood Cliffs, N.J.: Prentice-Hall, 1969. Two brief accounts of Piaget's stages of cognitive development, presented for students of educational psychology.

The environment and social science

Klausner, S. Z. *On man in his environment.* San Francisco: Jossey-Bass, 1971. Advanced analysis of man's response to the environment from the point of view of sociological theory, and a consideration of the implications of such theory for social planning and social policy.

Klausner, S. Z. (ed.) Society and its physical environment. *Annals of American Academy of Political and Social Science,* 1970, **389,** 1–115. Collection of professional articles on the threats imposed by present environmental problems, and on the social science issues in dealing with these.

Rapoport, A. *House form and culture.* Englewood Cliffs, N.J.: Prentice-Hall, 1969 (paper). A very interesting and readable account of how culture and physical conditions determine the designs of dwellings all over the world. Illustrates very well some of the ideas presented in this chapter.

Environmental psychology

Craik, K. H. Environmental psychology. In *New directions in psychology* (K. H. Craik, B. Kleinmuntz, R. L. Rosnow, R. Rosenthal, J. A. Cheyne, and R. H. Walters, eds.), Vol. 4, pp. 1–122. New York: Holt, Rinehart & Winston, 1970. Wide-ranging chapter reviewing the major problems of the emerging discipline of environmental psychology.

Proshansky, H. M., Ittelson, W. H., and Rivlin, L. G. (eds.) *Environmental psychology: Man in his physical setting.* New York: Basic Books, 1971. A varied collection of articles dealing with theories of environmental influence and research on environmental planning.

Nowadays, as in past eras, the environment imposes urgent biological, social, and psychological demands on man. We still face many of the same old natural disasters—hurricanes, earthquakes, tornadoes, fires, tidal waves, floods, and droughts—that man has always had to face, although modern technology provides increasing control over some of them. On the other hand, thanks to modern technology our world is becoming more and more polluted with noxious chemicals. Large numbers of people lack adequate housing and food, live insecurely in cities rife with crime, in harsh urban environ-ments often totally unrelieved by natural beauty. We are harrassed by noise, hazardous travel to work or play, and a host of other ills deriving from modern existence. However, here I shall discuss in some depth the problem of overpopula-tion because it encompasses many other difficulties of modern life which are created or compounded by the population explosion. Overpopulation also has profound psychological consequences, and perhaps more than any other environ-mental problem its solution will depend on a knowledge of psychological principles.

GROWTH OF THE WORLD'S POPULATION

Not long ago I tried to attend a symposium on popula-tion on the Berkeley campus, held in the largest lecture hall available there. I arrived 45 minutes ahead of schedule and to my chagrin found a line of waiting people that stretched far out of sight around several adjacent buildings. The hall was totally full long before I reached it, and there were also hundreds of people behind me who could not get in. Several of us afterwards mused at the irony of not being able to attend a lecture on overpopulation because there were too many

*Figure 3.1 Lucy's view of the world. (Drawing by Charles Schulz; © 1967
United Feature Syndicate, Inc.)*

people who wanted to hear it. Since then the experience has symbolized for me two interconnected facts: first, the sudden great interest in the population problem; secondly, the increasing numbers of people in the same urban community competing for the limited supply of space and other resources. One sees this in many contexts, especially in urban centers, at a popular play, movie, or restaurant on Saturday night, in the parking lots and spaces on and off campus and in the business and theater districts, on the commuter highways, on vacation roads during any summer weekend, and so on. All of this crowding takes place in a country that has relatively low population density (people per square mile) compared, for example, with a country like India, which has an extraordinarily high population density.

The Population Reference Bureau reports that an average of 3.9 babies were born in the world every second in 1969, that is, 190,000 each day, 1.3 million each week, and 72 million each year (Figure 3.1). Forty years ago, the rate was only about 20 million a year. It has been estimated that the American population will reach 300 to 350 million by the year 2000. If you think the towns and cities have gotten crowded in recent times, imagine what they will be like in 25 years with about one-third more people.

On the other hand, the situation may be changing rapidly in the United States. For example, revised projections are being offered by some demographers (population specialists) on the basis of a sharp dip in the American birth rate that became evident in the 1970 census. It may well be that our actual population in the year 2000 will be closer to 250 million, and it is not inconceivable that population growth here might ultimately even slow to a trickle as a result of reduced average family size. Demographers are still not able to forecast such changes in human reproductive behavior, since these depend on a complex of psychological, sociological, and economic factors. They can project ongoing trends into the future as long as these remain fairly stable. Accounting for the recent change in the United States picture are such factors as chang-ing attitudes of Americans toward having children, especially on the part of women, growing concern with overpopulation and environmental deterioration, more liberal birth control and abortion laws, and new methods of contraception, partic-ularly the pill. But it is sobering to realize that the United States population problem is still small compared with that of most developing nations of Asia, Africa, and South America.

Some notion of the rate of expansion of the human race can be gained from Figure 3.2, which shows the population believed to have existed during the Paleolithic period ("Old Stone Age"), its growth up to the present, and its estimated growth by the year 2000 A.D. You will observe that there were roughly 5.32 million people on earth 10,000 years ago in the year 8030 B.C. It had taken almost a million years to get to that number from a population size of only about 125,000 in Early Paleolithic times. By about 1800 A.D., the figure had reached 906 million. It was 2.4 billion in 1950, it now exceeds 3.5 billion, and it is predicted to be 7.5 billion in 2000 A.D., a population explosion indeed! The world's population has been growing at a geometric rate; this is often expressed in terms of "doubling times," that is, the number of years it will take for the existing population to double. Paul Ehrlich (1968) gives the following approximate sequence of doubling times over the history of mankind: 1,000,000 years; 1,000 years; 200 years; 80 years; and 37 years in 1960. Thus, the rate at which the world's population doubles is rapidly increasing and, by the same token, the doubling time is rapidly decreasing. If things continue at the present rate, it will take only about 37 years for the population of the world to go from approximately 3 billion to 6 billion. That should happen before the end of this century, as is shown in Figure 3.2.

Two parents produce many more than two additional people when they have two children, and this is often difficult to understand. Just as dollars added as interest in a bank account will themselves earn more interest if they remain in the account, so the people who are added to the population themselves produce more offspring; they too increase their numbers at compound interest, as it were. The original couple is likely to be still alive when their grandchildren are born, and in turn these grandchildren may produce offspring during the lifetime of the original pair (see also Table 3.1 on page 99). Instead of merely replacing themselves, the couple has multiplied itself severalfold. Thus, the drop in doubling times is surprisingly rapid as the population grows. And it is also the reason why the United States population could continue to grow to 250 million by the year 2000 (and 350 million a hundred years hence), even should the average family size be held down to only two children.

YEARS AGO	CULTURAL STAGE	AREA POPULATED	ASSUMED DENSITY PER SQUARE KILOMETER OF LAND	TOTAL POPULATION (MILLIONS)
1,000,000	Early Paleolithic		0.00425	0.125
300,000	Middle Paleolithic		0.012	1.0
25,000	Late Paleolithic		0.04	3.34
10,000	Mesolithic		0.04	5.32
6,000	Village farming Early urban		1.0 0.04	86.5
2,000	Village farming and urban		1.0	133
325	Farming and industrial		3.7	545
175	Farming and industrial		4.9	728
75	Farming and industrial		6.2	906
25	Farming and industrial		11.0	1,610
10	Farming and industrial		16.4	2,400
AD 2000	Farming and industrial		54.8	7,500

The rate of population growth is obtained by simply subtracting the death rate from the birth rate. The birth rate consists of the number of births each year per thousand people; the death rate is the number of deaths each year per thousand people. If we subtract the latter from the former we have the approximate rate of increase, ignoring of course immigration or emigration. Thus, if the birth rate is 30 per thousand and the death rate 10 per thousand, the population growth will be about 20 per thousand, which expressed as a percent or rate per hundred is 2, very nearly the United States figure. If the birth rate and the death rate are close to each other, the rate of increase will be negligible or zero; if the birth rate and the death rate are discrepant, there will be either population growth or decline.

Another important fact of population growth is that "developing countries" such as India, China, Kenya, Nigeria, Turkey, Indonesia, the Philippines, Brazil, Costa Rica, and El Salvador have far higher rates of growth than "developed countries" such as the United States, Austria, Denmark, Norway, the United Kingdom, Poland, Russia, Italy, Spain, and Japan. You can see this principle clearly in Figure 3.3, in which

Figure 3.3   Projected population of developed and undeveloped nations from 1830 to 2000 A.D. *(From United Nations Association, 1969)*

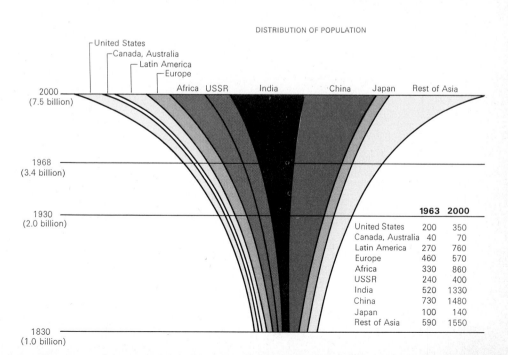

DISTRIBUTION OF POPULATION

	1963	2000
United States	200	350
Canada, Australia	40	70
Latin America	270	760
Europe	460	570
Africa	330	860
USSR	240	400
India	520	1330
China	730	1480
Japan	100	140
Rest of Asia	590	1550

the cone reflecting United States population and its growth is not very wide compared with that of India, China, the rest of Asia, Africa, and South America.*

Moreover, if we think of the population sizes of countries in relation to the wealth and natural resources of the world, then some interesting facts emerge. Some countries, such as the United States, have much wealth and relatively small populations, while others, such as India, are teeming with people but have little wealth per capita. The former countries have a small average family size, whereas large families are the rule in the latter. Therefore, if one redraws the map of the world imaginatively as one demographer has done so that the sizes of the continental land masses reflect the ratio of population to wealth instead of their actual geographical size, the world map develops some fascinating distortions. This is shown in Figure 3.4.

If the level of industrialization in China could be increased to the point that each Chinese family possessed an automobile and other amenities of industrial society, the effect on China and the entire world would be catastrophic.

This observation immediately raises the point, of course, that the [United States] should be considered overdeveloped by virtue of having attained a level of per capita consumption far in excess of that to which the bulk of humanity can realistically aspire. Some very basic figures shed light on the development dilemma. There are currently at least 750 million people in mainland China. By contrast, the population of the United States is slightly over 200 million. Since there are more than 3.5 Chinese for every American, it would require some 3.5 times the present United States resources consumption to sustain China at current American levels. . . .

An "Americanized" China would consume nearly eight billion metric tons of coal equivalent in energy each year, more than the present total world consumption. To the extent that energy consumption is a reasonable index of environmental impact, these numbers mean that raising Chinese energy consumption to the American level would amount to doubling the environmental impact of [man]. . . . [Denis Pirages and Paul Ehrlich, Stanford University]

PROBLEMS CAUSED BY OVERPOPULATION

The population explosion is creating many new biological, sociological, and psychological problems for mankind. Among these are (1) increased pollution; (2) excessive demands on the food supply; (3) depletion of the world's natural resources; (4) damage to the quality of life.

Pollution

There is a close, though by no means perfect, correlation between population and pollution. This is a main theme of Paul Ehrlich's well-known book entitled *The Population Bomb* (1968) and in fact is one of the reasons discussions of overpopulation and pollution are so often linked. Added numbers of people means more sewage pumped into rivers, bays, and marine areas, more garbage and refuse to be disposed of, more factories producing the goods that people need or want and pumping wastes into air and water, more electricity whose production results in smoke or heated effluents, and more toxic pesticides to protect the increasing amount of food required, all adding to pollution.

It is not necessary to dwell at length on our modern problems of environmental protection; these are amply detailed in today's mass media. Alarm about the problem was

*The difference in projected world population between Figure 3.2 and Figure 3.3 merely reflects variation in demographers' estimates due to the large number of variables affecting population growth. These are approximations based on how the variables are taken into account, rather than precise estimates.

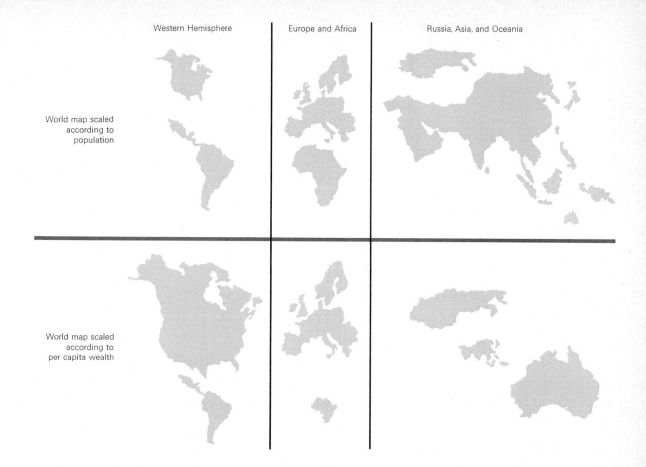

Western Hemisphere | Europe and Africa | Russia, Asia, and Oceania

World map scaled according to population

World map scaled according to per capita wealth

sounded early by such writers as Rachel Carson (1962), and many others continue nowadays to push for corrective societal action. Any of us who live in cities are likely to have experienced choking and eye-smarting smog (Figure 3.5). There are many industrial air polluters, but pollution is likely to be worst in and around large cities. Here are the heaviest concentrations of people and automobiles. Los Angeles typifies the problem. A 60-mile circle drawn around the city of Los Angeles encompasses 10 million Californians, who live on less than 5 percent of the land of the state and account for more than 50 percent of its population, jobs, income, cars, and telephones. Twenty-five years ago, most of the electricity for this area was generated by hydroelectric plants producing no air pollution. By 1970, 90 percent of Los Angeles' electric power was being generated by steam plants burning natural gas or fuel oil, some of it high-sulfur oil that produces a smoke extremely destructive to houses, boats, cars, vegetation, and lungs. At the current rates of demand for electricity, by 1980 Los Angeles County

Figure 3.4 A new view of the world, scaled according to population and per capita wealth for the year 1969. The figures are as follows: Africa, 344 million people, $140; Asia, 1,990 million people, $184; Latin America, 276 million people, $385; Soviet Union, 241 million people, $890; Europe, 456 million people, $1,230; Oceania, 19 million people, $1,857; North America, 225 million people, $3,399. (Map concept and data from the Population Reference Bureau, as presented in the San Francisco Examiner, *Dec. 21, 1969, Sec. B, p. 2)*

(a)

(b)

(c)

Figure 3.5   Los Angeles (a) and New York (b) enveloped in smog. (c) City and state officials standing atop a mountain of garbage, one day's accumulation, at a landfill in Staten Island, New York. (d) Italian worker in the industrial area of Marghera, near Venice. Air pollution in the area has become so acute that 205 local factories have been ordered to supply their 50,000 workers with gas masks. (a, b, d: Wide World Photos; c: The New York Times)

(d)

will be generating roughly two and a half times the electrical energy being used today—and of course more and more smog.

An expert on preventive medicine, Amasa B. Ford (1970), has recently used the expression "ecological casualties" to refer to victims of medical damage from air pollution and has provided some useful statistics documenting the alarming health hazards from it. She observes that during the past decade the relationship of chronic bronchitis and emphysema to air pollution has become increasingly evident. In the United States and the Netherlands since 1950, for example, death rates from these disorders have more than doubled. Sudden increases in respiratory illness and death became evident during the severe smog in London in 1952, when 4,000 more than the usual number of deaths were recorded for a 5-week period. Hospital admission rates and the average length of stay for persons suffering from respiratory and circulatory disorders have been shown to be correlated substantially with changes in the atmospheric concentration of pollutants such as carbon monoxide, sulfur dioxide, and oxides of nitrogen. The task of identifying the role played by various air pollutants in respiratory and circulatory diseases is made difficult by virtue of the fact that these diseases are also caused and aggravated by other factors, such as smoking, age, and climate. Nevertheless, ". . . the fact remains that 18,763 more deaths were attributed to these two causes [bronchitis and emphysema] in the United States in 1966 than 10 years earlier—an increase of almost two and a half times, and observed at all ages above 35. If only one half of these increased deaths were attributable to air pollution, this would still amount to nearly 1000 additional deaths a year. . . . The price of a polluted atmosphere in terms of illness and reduced functional capacity may be greater than its cost in years lost through premature deaths" (quoted from Ford, 1970, p. 258).

The important thing to bear in mind is that pollution is, in large measure, a product of the population explosion: too many people are pouring their wastes or effluents, whether produced by their natural bodily processes or by industrial processes, into the ecosystem. And, as was noted in Chapter 1, this means simply that the natural recycling process that restores these waste substances to forms usable by living organisms is being overwhelmed and that the wastes accumulate. This could happen regardless of industry, but the latter has multiplied the power of mankind to pollute, so that even a comparatively small number of people in a given space can be too many for healthy and aesthetically pleasing living.

Excessive demands on the food supply

None can say with any precision how much food will be needed for the population projected by demographers for future years, nor the maximum amounts of food our present or future technology is capable of producing. There seems to be little question, however, that much of the present world population is seriously underfed, and even in the United States there is a disturbingly high incidence of semistarvation and malnutrition. Moreover, if the present rate of population growth continues unabated, sooner or later there will be insufficient food supplies for all the world's people. (It must be acknowledged that projections as to the capacity of this planet to feed its population are debated by the experts, with Ehrlich being among the more pessimistic, although he has much competent company, probably the majority of specialists.)

Actually the spectre of food shortage connected with expanding population is not a new idea. The first man to argue persuasively that the rate of population growth exceeded the capacity of the world to produce food was Thomas Robert Malthus (1766–1834). In an optimistic era when the dominant viewpoint was that the world was entering a period of increasing and unlimited progress, Malthus (1798; reprinted 1964) argued that great natural principles would limit this progress. He formulated the principle that ". . . population, when unchecked, increases in a geometrical ratio, and subsistence . . . in an arithmetical ratio." If so, it would be inevitable that the food supply must become inadequate—that is, it is only a matter of time, assuming population growth remains unchecked, or the capacity to produce and distribute food cannot be correspondingly raised. Malthus was thus the first major Cassandra of population growth.

(a)

(b)

Figure 3.6 Irish potato famine of 1846 to 1851.
(a) Distribution of clothes to ragged children. (b)
Funeral of one of the many victims of starvation.
(a: Culver Pictures, Inc.; b: Illustrated
London News, *Jan. 30, 1847)*

As in Malthus's day, there are those today who array themselves on the other side of the issue, pointing to major increases in food production in the recent past and in the projected future as a result of advanced agricultural methods, for example, extensive use of pesticides, new and more productive strains of grain, and more widespread use of fertilizers and irrigation. (Note, by the way, that pesticides are also sources of pollution and are destroying large numbers of birds and other animals and insects.) The annual report of the United Nations Food and Agriculture Organization (FAO) for 1969 implies that fears of a "Malthusian catastrophe" have been rendered groundless by the recent growth and dissemination of agricultural technology all over the world. The report argues that the undeveloped nations of the world increased their agricultural production by 5 percent in 1967 and 2 percent in 1968, and the growth trend continues. FAO Director-General A. H. Boerma even warned that by 1969 "excess supplies, not only of cereals but also of butter and dry skim milk, reached proportions that led to serious problems in the commodity markets, and . . . a further expansion of stocks seemed to be in the offing."

On the other hand, a rather disturbing essay by Bruce Wallace (1972) in a recent book on social biology suggests that complacency of the sort illustrated in the previous paragraph could be very dangerous. Wallace recounts the tragic yet fascinating story of the potato famine in Ireland during the years from 1846 to 1851, in which a million persons in that small country perished, and more than 1.5 million others emigrated, mainly to the United States. The famine set in motion a period of economic decline in Ireland that has lasted nearly until today, causing severe and disruptive changes in family life. Even in the previous century, Ireland had food problems. In 1729 Jonathan Swift published his famous satiric essay entitled *A Modest Proposal,* suggesting tongue in cheek that the problem could be solved by eating young children, a solution that would not only reduce the population size but also help feed Ireland's starving millions. Swift wrote, "I have been assured by a very knowing American of my acquaintance in London, that a young healthy child well nursed is at a year old a most delicious, nourishing and wholesome food, whether stewed, roasted, baked, or boiled, and I make no doubt that it will equally serve in a fricassee, or a ragout" (Figure 3.6).

Prior to the famine and between 1779 and 1841, the Irish population had increased from a relatively stable 3 million persons to about 8 or 9 million, due in large part to the potato crop which provided a far greater yield per acre than the grain the English and Scottish peoples used for their staple food. Since a family could easily grow a year's supply of potatoes on a small piece of land, and needed little else to start married life, family holdings were divided again and again many times

Table 3.1

Comparison of population (*A*) producing four children per couple by age 20 with population (*B*) with four children per couple by age 30[a]

Years from beginning	Relative sizes of populations		Ratio
	A	*B*	*A/B*
0	1.0	1.0	1.0
10	1.4	1.3	1.1
20	2.0	1.6	1.2
30	2.8	2.0	1.4
40	4.0	2.5	1.6
50	5.7	3.2	1.8
60	8.0	4.0	2.0
70	11.3	5.0	2.3
80	16.0	6.4	2.5
90	22.6	8.0	2.8
100	32.0	10.1	3.2
110	45.3	12.7	3.6
120	64.0	16.0	4.0

[a] From Wallace (1972, p. 77).

over to accommodate young couples 16 to 18 years of age. Marrying early, they had children at regular one- or two-year intervals and so produced ever-increasing numbers of children and grandchildren. The effect of this social pattern on population growth may be seen in Table 3.1. Two populations are compared: population *A* produces an average of four children per couple by the age of twenty; population *B* produces four children per couple by age thirty. Both populations will double in size each generation, but over a period of many years they will produce markedly different numbers of persons because the generations in population *A* will occur much more rapidly since they start 10 years earlier than in the case of *B*. Within 60 years population *A* will become twice as large as population *B*; in 120 years, *A* will be four times as large as *B*. Anyway, such an expansion took place in Ireland and led to disaster.

In 1845 the situation collapsed as a result of a fungus blight that struck the Irish potato. The entire Irish crop of potatoes was decimated, and there were no food reserves to be tapped. Moreover, food could not be imported because of the British Corn Laws, which, in order to protect the income of British farmers, made it illegal to import grain into the British Isles. In Ireland, thousands starved to death. Others were forced to emigrate. A downward economic spiral was set in motion. As a result of this disaster, marriage patterns were altered permanently. In Ireland today, men do not generally marry until their fathers retire, nor are they apparently willing to accept wives younger than themselves, so marriages are late and reproduction much curtailed.

Wallace sees the Irish situation of 1845 as a warning to ourselves, and believes we may have also laid the foundation for a similar disaster. For example, the United States no longer has much food to spare. Surpluses are required to support the expanding populations of other nations. In late 1972 the Soviet Union purchased nearly the whole American surplus of cereal grains as a result of severe shortages caused by failure of substantial portions of the Russian crop. China and India are also large-scale importers of cereals. As a result of mechanization and advanced technology, fewer persons in the West are now engaged in agriculture, with less than one person in 20 needed to farm in order to feed the other 19. Moreover, American farms are increasingly large and devoted to raising single crops, which also encourages the spread of disease and insect pests, and heroic procedures (such as use of massive doses of pesticides) are required to resist them. What appears to be efficiency is not really efficient at all, in that it is expensive in critical resources such as fuel energy to extract and distribute the food calories we eat. Wallace likens our present arrangement to that of a shipwrecked man who is adrift at sea and must rely on fish to survive. If it takes him 175 to 200 calories to catch a fish which supplies 100 calories of energy, then he is using up too much energy for what he is getting and he is slowly starving to death. In gasoline for distribution of food alone, we are spending more energy to supply people with food than that food is worth. From this point of view, our agricultural activities are only superficially efficient; they are costing too much. Not only have we created a shaky food supply edifice making us vulnerable to a catastrophe analogous to the Irish potato famine, but future generations must pay the excessive costs of our overutilization of vital resources. Like the Irish before the famine, we are operating on the hazardous presumption that we will always have food for our skyrocketing population. Wallace writes (1972, p. 82):

No matter how the situation is rationalized, our food-getting procedures are at best only temporarily successful. The reckoning may not hit the present middle-aged generation: it will in all likelihood hit our grandchildren. There may be an euphoria that envelops a skin diver who returns from an underwater hunt with a one- or two-pound fish on his spear; in the long run, however, he cannot live on euphoria. The highly touted agricultural system of the United States is at the moment euphoric; the euphoria will vanish when the true cost of food for feeding hundreds of millions or billions of persons becomes apparent.

Depletion of the world's resources

Another problem caused by population growth is an increased demand on the world's dwindling natural resources. Industrially developed countries require many substances to maintain their economies. These include the world's limited stores of fuel oil, without which no modern industrial society can run efficiently; unpolluted fresh water for drinking, recreation, and industrial usage; metals and minerals, many of which are in relatively scarce supply; wood for housing construction and paper products; animal wool and hides for clothing and shoes. The supply of these natural substances is not inexhaustible. Production of synthetic substitutes, when possible, is costly in terms of the energy required.

Wealthy nations and wealthy families use up more of the resources of the world than do the poor. The consumption figures for the United States are astonishing. Every year we use well over half of the raw materials consumed by the world, yet we constitute only one-fifteenth of the world's population. Moreover, this discrepancy between ourselves and the rest of the world grows greater each year. Looked at from the point of view of the individual, it has been estimated that in his 70-year life span each American baby will consume directly or indirectly 26 million gallons of water, 21 thousand gallons of gasoline, 10 thousand pounds of meat, 28 thousand pounds of milk and cream, $5,000 to $8,000 in school building materials, $6,300 worth of clothing, and $7,000 worth of furniture (based on the 1966 value of the dollar). Ehrlich (1968, p. 149) sums it up: "It's not a baby, it's a Superconsumer!" This accelerated rate of use has now reached proportions that alarm ecologists all over the world.

Clearly, as the number of people increases, so will the size of the problem. If all the highly populated nations of the world manage to create technological societies comparable in industrial output to those of North America and Western Europe, and their populations continue to grow at the present rate, almost certainly there will be the "ecocatastrophe" of which Ehrlich warns. Perhaps even the life-preserving substances of the biosphere will be destroyed, even the very air we breathe. This is a possibility that cannot be ignored.

Damage to the quality of life

The presence of excessive numbers of people is, as we have just seen, a physical danger to the survival of those now living and surely to unborn generations; it also threatens to make life more unpleasant in the psychological sense, particularly for those who presently enjoy high standards in the qual-

The trees of Niu Shan [Mountain] were once beautiful, but as it was situated near the borders of a large State, they were hewn down with axes and hatchets. How could the forests retain their beauty? Still, through the ceaseless activity [of vegetal forces] day and night, and the fertilizing influences of the rain and the dew, [the mountain was again] not without buds and sprouts . . . ; but then came cattle and goats to browse upon them. To these things is owing [its present] bare and stripped appearance, and people seeing it suppose that it was never finely wooded. But is this the nature of the mountain? [So also] of what properly belongs to man—shall it be said that the mind [of man] was without benevolence and righteousness? The way in which a man loses his proper goodness of mind is like the way in which the mountain is denuded of trees by axes and hatchets. Hewn down day after day, how can [the mind] retain its beauty? [Mencius (Meng Tzu, 372–289 B.C.) The Works of Mencius (trans. by J. Legge). Hongkong: Hongkong Univ. Press, 1960]

ity of their lives. We must now make a fundamental distinction between two terms: (1) *overpopulation* refers to excessive numbers of people in the world at large; (2) *high population density* indicates excessive amounts of people per square mile, city block, individual home or room. The United States, for example, has high population density mainly in its great urban centers, but there are vast areas in which very few people live because there are limited ways of making a living there. Moreover, a city may have a relatively low population density in its affluent neighborhoods, but density per dwelling may be very high indeed in its poorest slum districts. Some nations, like Sweden, Australia, and Canada, are still sparsely populated, but even there people tend to pack into major urban centers such as Stockholm, Sydney, or Montreal.

Population density is a physical variable, that is, it refers to how many people occupy a given unit of space, but it is not a psychological variable: people living under conditions of high population density may or may not feel *crowded*, depending on their expectations, their cultural experience, and their personal needs. As we learned earlier, people often perceive and appraise similar conditions quite differently. Therefore, it is not always easy to predict their psychological reactions without reference to personal and cultural factors shaping how they think and feel. *Crowding* is thus a judgmental matter and a psychological variable, whereas high population density concerns the actual spatial configuration within which people live (Stokols, 1972). This is a very important distinction, one which many research workers in the field of urban environments and population problems have often failed to make. It becomes critically important when we are trying to assess the psychological and social consequences of population growth and its effect on the quality of life. For example, a person may feel crowded among strangers but quite secure and comfortable in the same space with an equal number of friends.

Effects of high population density Do high population densities produce important negative psychological effects? If so, at what level does overpopulation become psychologically destructive? As might be anticipated from Chapter 2, this is not easily answered. The factors making people happy or unhappy, effective or ineffective, are quite variable. For example, although the American poor have more television sets and other goods, on the average, than the poor of under-developed countries, they often seem to be more alienated from society, a result perhaps of the discrepancy between the American ideal (or expectation) and American reality. Moreover, well-to-do people often like to "rough it," to go camping or hiking, living for a while under a measure of hardship without many of the products of modern technology to which they are normally accustomed.

Some people living under conditions of very high density may display high morale and even enthusiasm for their way of life. They would not trade the advantages of a teeming metropolis for the greater spaciousness of more rural settings. One of the problems of evaluating the effects of high density is that often other negative conditions are likely to be correlated with it, for example, crime, filth and disease, lack of privacy, or traffic congestion. Since these negative conditions are not necessary correlates of high density (some very affluent people live in high-density high-rise buildings under extremely pleasant and spacious personal circumstances), it is difficult to tell whether those people living in great urban centers like New York City who are troubled or unhappy feel this way merely because of high population density or because of other factors. We must therefore be careful about assuming that high population density as such is always perceived as crowding or that it automatically creates psychological discomfort, without specifying in more detail whether and under what conditions this happens, and why (see Galle *et al.,* 1972).

How might high population density harm people? There seem to be at least two main lines of reasoning: one, that it increases the competition for available space and resources, putting people under severe stress; the other, that high density leads to anonymity or impersonality, thus weakening vital social bonds and leaving the individual more alienated.

Evidence of *increased stress* is largely derived from animal rather than human studies. The physiological and behavioral effects of severe population density in animals are substantial (Christian and Davis, 1964), and one researcher (Calhoun, 1962; see Figure 3.7a) has coined the term "behavioral sink" to refer to gross distortions of behavior that have been observed, including disruption of courting, nest building, and sexual activity, and increased social disorganization. There is an increased incidence of aggressive assaults on other animals in the colony (Klepinger, 1965; Thiessen, 1966). The following account comes from a newspaper interview with John Calhoun by Tom Huth of the Washington Post Service (*San Francisco Chronicle,* May 9, 1971):

Dr. John Calhoun's laboratory mice are dying. They are doomed, he says, to extinction.

Physically they are healthy—to him they are even beautiful. But most of them are withdrawn, uncomplaining, uninvolved, without aggression. And they are without sex, so they are dying.

They are dying of overpopulation. And, Dr. Calhoun says, there are lessons for man in his grim little mousery.

Calhoun works as a research psychologist fot the National Institute

(a)

(b)

Figure 3.7   (a) *John A. Calhoun stands in his "mouse universe," designed for study of overpopulation and crowding.* (b) *Thousands of West Germans sunbathing at a beach on the Baltic coast.* (a: National Institute of Mental Health; b: D.P.A./Pictorial Parade)

Anyone who reflects these days on the relationship of man and earth must eventually
find himself operating at two levels of awareness.

He worries about his house and his car, his
income and his possessions in the usual way.
He gets angry at politicians when the power
fails and his air-conditioner stops. He hopes
his union will get that wage increase, or the
company whose stock he owns will sell more
of its new gadgets.

But all the time he knows that the premises
of that life are false, that before long it must
give way. For even a little serious thought
will have made him aware that all the "progress" and "growth" of modern economic life
are based on the plundering of a finite environment. And the thin crust of earth and air
and water that sustains us is near its
limits. . . .

The Ecologist, a British magazine, published
the "Blueprint for Survival." First it set out
the reasons for urgency. For example, resources are running out under the pressures
of exponential growth: Ecological demand
will multiply by a factor of 32 over the next
66 years at present growth rates. Can anyone imagine the earth meeting such a requirement? Even if we stop population
growth completely in developed countries in
thirty years, and the rest of the world in
seventy, world population will stabilize at
more than four times present numbers. One
may argue over this figure or that, but it is
impossible to resist the conclusion that a
crisis is coming.

The Blueprint proposed an integrated program to meet the crisis. It rested on a call
for abandonment of some basic human
ideas: the instinct for fertility, the worship of
economic growth, the tendency of our culture to become more industrialized, urbanized, centralized.

Those are demands for the most immense
changes in human attitudes. [Anthony Lewis,
Life and politics. The New York Times,
Jan. 17, 1973]

of Mental Health. In the beginning, he put eight white mice, four pairs, into an $8\frac{1}{2}$-by-$8\frac{1}{2}$ foot galvanized steel universe on the upper floor of a corrugated iron building at the National Institute of Health's animal farm in Montgomery County, Md.

The mice had warmth, food, no disease, no predators. In a little more than two years there were 2200 of them. But by that time they were not mice, Calhoun says. They were something else, non-mice, their social organizations destroyed and their behaviors deformed by overcrowding.

Now 600 of them have expired and the other 1600 will too, Calhoun says. There has not been a mouse born in more than a year; the youngest is 40 years old in terms of the human life span. The females are passing menopause. Soon time will run out: the process will be irreversible; life will be death. . . .

The eight original animals quickly multiplied to 150, which he says was the ideal number for the setting because it provided each mouse with the right amount of interaction to maintain gratification and stability. In nature, the population would remain steady at about 150.

"Organisms fabricate products and also dispose of them," he explains. "So in nature the capacity to fabricate—fertilization—is geared to disposal factors—disease, predators, migration. We've eliminated them all."

The population of the colony quickly jumped to four times the optimum, or about 600. The adults already had formed 14 distinct social groups, which they apparently considered the comfortable number. When the young ones reached maturity and tried to join groups, they were rejected, except for a few who managed to replace some of their aging brethren.

Most of the young mice, about 400 of them, withdrew in a huddled mass in the middle of the cage. "They were treated as sticks and stones," Calhoun says. "Once rejected they were outside the system. They were extremely violent, they would attack and slash and turn on a neighbor and bite," attempting to reduce social contacts.

Aside from such impressive evidence with a few species of animals under *very severe* conditions of population density, we still know too little about the feeling of being crowded and its effects on people, aside from some more or less common-sensical speculation. Many questions might be asked. For example, aside from its unpleasantness, does jamming people for brief periods into subway cars (as in Tokyo, Japan, where professional pushers with white gloves literally pack the cars during rush hours) have a significant impact on their long-term psychological state? Tokyoites seem to be extremely stoic about this discomfort and indignity. To what extent is such crowding tolerable, and under what conditions? Are there cultures under which high density and lack of privacy are not regarded negatively because it is expected, as in Hong Kong or Tokyo?* In an American slum tenement, is it the crowding or other features (loss of dignity, grinding poverty, hopeless-

*Reexamine the photos on pages 23 and 24 in this light.

ness) that are particularly damaging to human sensibilities and morale? What expectations and attitudes are capable, on the one hand, of increasing the sensitivity of people to crowding or, on the other, of insulating them against it? More research needs to be carried out around these central questions pertaining to the psychological impact of high population density on individuals.

There has been recent speculative interest in the problem of human *alienation* under high density conditions—but precious little usable research. The argument runs something like this: when large numbers of people live in close proximity, there is an increase in anonymity and loss of social identity. The city dweller is in a state of continual isolation amid crowds of people as he strolls the streets, when he shops in large supermarkets, as he sits in the bus or subway. This frees him from social obligations but also makes him feel isolated, lonely, and alienated. He would presumably be swamped psychologically if he tried to concern himself with the private concerns of so many other people. As Stanley Milgram (1972, p. 1) puts it, "Nothing is more characteristic of urban life than the fact that we often gain extreme familiarity with the faces of a number of persons yet never interact with them. . . . I have stood at a commuter station for several years, often in the company of people whom I have never gotten to know (familiar strangers). The faces and the people are treated as part of the environment, equivalent to the scenery, rather than persons with whom one talks, exchanges greetings." In the midst of a crowd, one is a nameless stranger, free to go beyond the usual social restraints (Figure 3.7b). In contrast, in the small, intimate community (which is rapidly disappearing all over the industrialized world), the individual knows and is known to nearly everyone else. This gives him a social identity and encourages a degree of social responsibility. In such circumstances he is less likely to act antisocially without endangering his place in that community and his own sense of self.

But is it really true that populations of large metropolises manifest a higher rate of antisocial behavior than those of smaller, more intimate communities? We tend to think so, but we cannot answer this question with certainty because the casual observations we have are difficult to interpret. The problems of answering this question can be highlighted by an interesting but totally inconclusive study (Zimbardo, 1969) comparing a large city (New York) with a much smaller one (Palo Alto, California). We can learn something by reviewing this study, even though it does not provide a completely dependable answer.

A deserted automobile was left for 64 hours near the Bronx campus of New York University, with its license plates removed and the hood open. Another car, treated in the same

Note 3.1

The study of Latané and Darley (1969, 1970) described on pp. 106–109 illustrates one of the major research strategies used in psychology, namely, *laboratory experimentation.* This should be distinguished from *naturalistic observation,* which is another major approach to obtaining psychological knowledge. We can get a clearer understanding of why Latané and Darley did what they did if we ask first how they might have studied the problem of bystander apathy by naturalistic observation and consider the difficulties this would have posed.

Actually, their first approach to the problem was a naturalistic one, since before doing an experiment they carefully studied the reports of interviews with spectators to get some idea of what had actually happened and how the bystanders had felt and acted. This initial inspection led them tentatively to reject the notion that the bystanders failed to intervene because they were apathetic, and it suggested the hypothesis that presence of others inhibits intervention by diffusing responsibility and providing reassurance to each bystander about his inaction. However at this stage the hypothesis was only an unproven hunch that needed to be tested further. One obvious way to do this would be to examine many similar incidents involving a victim and bystanders and to determine whether the bystanders intervened or failed to do so in each case. This would be naturalistic observation and comparison of real-life events. If Latané and Darley's hypothesis is correct, then bystander intervention should occur more often when there is a lone observer than when there are several observers.

However, one trouble with approaching the problem by means of naturalistic observation is that similar events do not occur very often. Many months or years may pass before such an incident recurs. A second difficulty is that the investigators obviously cannot be present when the event is occurring and must depend on the accuracy of spectators' memories and their willingness to report honestly. In so emotionally charged a situation, investigators often have difficulty getting accurate accounts from people feeling guilty or ashamed of their behavior.

Perhaps the most important difficulty in using naturalistic observation here is that

manner, was also left for the same period of time near the Stanford University campus in Palo Alto. Within the first 24 hours, the car left in New York had been stripped of all movable parts, and after 3 days it was a useless hunk of trash. Most of the vandalism occurred during daylight hours (observers had been stationed nearby to check the action). The Palo Alto car was untouched.

In interpreting this finding, one difficulty is that just the mere fact of large population alone (in New York) would increase the statistical chances of vandalism, theft, or any antisocial act. For example, New York contains about twice as many drug addicts (a major source of crime) as any other major American city, certainly a much higher number than a community like Palo Alto; New York also has a larger number of juvenile delinquents and vandals. Thus it is not possible to say with certainty what it was about New York or Palo Alto that accounted for the difference—the size, density, and anonymity of the urban atmosphere, the percentage of criminals, or other factors peculiar to these communities. There is also the question of how typical New York City is of major metropolitan communities. Only were we to leave cars similarly in a number of other large cities and small towns could we begin to separate out the specific factors that lead to such antisocial behavior patterns. Notions about the role of population density in affecting the behavior, attitudes, and morale of people have yet to be tested systematically in well-designed research.

The phenomenon of "bystander apathy" The urban center is often the scene of another phenomenon that has gained considerable attention of late, the failure of people to help when another person is in trouble. This so-called bystander apathy has been attributed to moral callousness and dehumanization often assumed to be characteristic of situations of high population density. The best known example is the case of Kitty Genovese, who in New York City on a March night in 1964 was attacked as she came home from work. Thirty-eight of her neighbors saw her plight from their windows, but no one came to her assistance or even called the police, even though her assailant took over half an hour to murder her. This type of situation was the stimulus for an interesting series of studies by Bib Latané and John Darley (1969, 1970), who tried to assess some of the social forces at work in such an incident.

Latané and Darley suggest that although witnesses to an emergency often do nothing to help the victim, the terms apathy, indifference, and unconcern do not accurately describe their reactions. In the Kitty Genovese case, for example, the witnesses continued to stare out of their windows, fascinated perhaps, possibly distressed too, although they did not act to help her. Inhibiting helpful action by spectators were a host of psychological factors—fear of being harmed themselves, difficulty in recognizing what must be done because of the unusual nature of the event and its suddenness, and (perhaps among the most important) the assumption that someone else would surely act. The authors make the interesting suggestion that, contrary to popular judgment, helpful interventions are less likely when there is a group of onlookers than when the witness is alone (see Note 3.1 *after* reading text, pp. 107–109).

Latané and Darley (1969) performed a number of experiments, each of which support the thesis that bystanders in groups are less likely to intervene than if they are alone. One example will suffice to show how they approached the problem, an experiment they refer to as "A lady in distress."

The subjects, undergraduate students at Columbia University, waited in a room thinking they were to participate in a market research study. In one condition, they waited with a friend; in another, with a stranger; and in a third, they waited alone. They had all been led into the testing room by a young woman who was unknown to them. While waiting, they heard the young woman, who had now gone into an adjacent room, climb onto a chair, fall, and evidently hurt herself. Via a tape recorder they heard a loud crash and a scream as the chair apparently collapsed. The woman moaned, "Oh, my God, my foot . . . I . . . can't move . . . it. Oh . . . my ankle. I . . . can't get this . . . thing . . . off me." She cried and moaned for about another minute, with the cries becoming more subdued and controlled, and finally muttered something about getting outside, knocked over the chair as she pulled herself up, thumped to the door, and closed it behind her as she left. The entire tape-recorded incident took two minutes.

Seventy percent of the students hearing the accident alone in the closed waiting room offered to help the victim before she left the other room, whereas only 10 percent of those waiting with someone else whom they did not know did so. If the other person in the waiting room was a friend, at least one person intervened in 70 percent of the pairs. This is actually considerably less than the 70 percent of those waiting alone because in the former condition there are twice the number of people available to act. When those who did not intervene were interviewed about their behavior, most said they had decided that the problem of the victim was not too serious, some thought someone else would or could help, and three said they did not want to embarrass the victim. Nearly all maintained that had there been a "real" emergency, they would have been among the first to help. Perhaps people are less afraid also of possible embarrassment in acting in front of a friend (who is not likely to misinterpret such behavior), or they may be more worried about the embarrassment of not

each such incident will differ from every other case in the number and type of bystanders, the kind of victim (woman or man, friend or stranger), and the nature of the victim's plight. Furthermore, the problem for the bystander could vary in many diverse ways: the risks of intervention might be greater in one incident than in another; or in one situation the bystander might be able to keep his role private while in another it might be public. Each of these conditions could have an important bearing on the likelihood of intervention. Every natural situation is a highly complex event, and it is difficult to isolate for analysis any single factor as affecting the behavioral outcome. Since the situation of interest to Latané and Darley varied according to whether the bystander was alone or with someone else (stranger or friend), it was necessary to find some way of separating out this variable and assessing its influence. For such a problem the laboratory experiment is often a good solution.

The general strategy of the experiment is to make some psychological event occur in the laboratory, to manipulate certain conditions (the *independent variables*) that could affect the behavioral outcome (the *dependent variables*), and to observe and measure that outcome very carefully. This laboratory event is an attempt to simulate certain of the basic elements of the real-life setting under controlled conditions that the experimenter wishes to isolate for study. It is thus a mockup of real life, but since no two psychological events can ever be exactly alike, what happens in the laboratory is merely analogous to the real-life event rather than identical to it. On the basis of the experimental findings that bystander company suppresses intervention in behalf of the victim, one might suppose that in a real-life incident with only one bystander rather than the large number that watched the Genovese murder the result might have been different because responsibility for doing something would not have been so diffused. There are, of course, many variables other than the one of interest to the experimenter. But in any given experiment, the researcher is attempting to isolate one or two such elements in order to examine their influence on the behavior in question.

The research of Latané and Darley illustrates what has been said above. They set up a laboratory model of the Genovese case and performed a series of experiments based on that model, one of which has been described in the text proper. In other experiments, different kinds of situations were created (such as an epileptic having an attack, or danger to the bystanders themselves) in order to determine the generality of the hypothesis of bystander intervention. No other elements that might have had an influence were allowed to vary from experimental setting to setting, although such variables would be part of the total context of real-life events of this type. In effect, these other variables were *controlled*. This allowed the experimenters to draw conclusions about just one or two variables, namely, the significance of whether the bystander was alone or in the company of others and whether the others were friends or strangers.

Although the strategy of the experiment offers many advantages, there are also many problems in its use in psychological research. For example, the experimenter must make the laboratory event a realistic model if he wants to apply his findings to life, a model that other investigators can duplicate so as to determine whether the findings are dependable. In actuality, the subject in such experiments knows he is in a laboratory, yet he must react naturally for the experiment to be valid. The subject must believe, for instance, that the cries of the experimenters' confederates are not fake but suggest rather that they are in real distress. If the acting is wooden or the situation improbable, then the laboratory model is worthless. Furthermore, there must be nothing in the behavior or words of the experimenter to bias the outcome, and this is not so easy to guarantee. When these and other requirements are not met, any conclusions drawn by the experimenter on the basis of the observations are likely to be false, since they would only apply to the artificial scene in the laboratory and not to the real-life setting.

We shall see many other examples of experimental research used by psychologists. In each case the experimenter has tried to create a laboratory model of some real-life event or process to see how it is affected by certain conditions that he can manipulate. The experimental approach is a very powerful tool for obtaining psychological knowledge, for analyzing complex events into their essential elements and relationships, and for testing whether they occur under given conditions. But in many spheres of psychological inquiry experimental methods have severe limitations, and naturalistic observation is more suitable.

It is virtually impossible to study intense emotions in the laboratory, or the ways people cope with severe danger, threat, or loss, without engaging in practices that might be quite damaging to individuals and hence go beyond appropriate ethical constraints. We can, of course, create mild emotional situations in the laboratory, but these are merely pale shadows of the sometimes intense emotions that people experience in their daily lives. Thus, whatever laboratory experi-

acting in a friend's presence. Latané and Darley (1969, p. 260), write analytically as follows:

The presence of other people can also alter the rewards and costs facing an individual bystander, perhaps most importantly, the presence of other people can alter the cost of not acting. If only one bystander is present in an emergency, he carries all of the responsibility of dealing with it.

Put differently, we might note that in the Genovese case the bystanders could not watch each other closely, and each alone might have assumed that someone else was calling the police. A lone bystander, however, cannot so easily avoid the responsibility and must take all the blame for not acting.

The other experiments involved quite different emergency situations, staged however as in the instance just described. It was found that in general people were less likely to take socially responsible action if other people were present than when alone. It did not matter whether the situation involved general danger, a victim of an accident, or a criminal against whom the group could readily unite.

The authors believe that there are two main reasons for the inaction by a group of onlookers: (1) the apparent lack of concern on the part of the others watching could lead each individual to interpret the situation as less serious than he might otherwise think; and (2) the presence of others diffuses the responsibility for dealing with the situation. Thus, although there may be "safety in numbers" in the sense that a person is less likely to be a victim if he stays in a crowd, the old adage is not true in instances where one needs help from others when in trouble.

About the issue of whether the crowded city creates apathy and alienation, Latané and Darley are highly skeptical. They believe the person watching may not act, but he is by no means indifferent. Having once determined some of the psychological reasons underlying the failure of bystanders to help, they find it necessary to reject the concept of bystander apathy or callousness as explanations. Concluding their findings, Latané and Darley (1969, p. 404) state:

Although the results of these studies may shake our faith in "safety in numbers," they may also help us begin to understand the frightening incidents in which crowds have heard but not answered a call for help. They suggest that the immediate social environment is more important in determining a person's reaction to an emergency than such vague cultural or personality concepts as "apathy" and "alienation due to urbanization." They also help explain why failure to intervene seems more common in large cities than in rural areas. When an emergency arises in a large city, a crowd is likely to gather; the members of the crowd are likely to be strangers; and it is likely that none of them will know the victim. These are exactly the conditions that, in our experiments, led to the fewest attempts to help. [See Note 3.1, pp. 106–109, for further thoughts on these studies.]

These studies do not directly tell us, of course, about population density and its effects, since they do not compare the behavior, say, of urban and rural subjects or settings, or high and low density conditions, although they do have a connection with the density problem because bystander behavior was compared under group and individual conditions. There is also evidence that such behavior varies considerably from city to city (Paris, Athens, and Boston; see Feldman, 1968), but the details of such variation are not well established. However, we can begin to see the fascinating specific possibilities in the general question of how the quality of life is affected by high population density.

DYNAMICS OF POPULATION GROWTH

Are problems of overpopulation or high population density unique to the human species, or are they features of the animal world in general? The answer is complicated. No other contemporary species has had man's astronomical and continuing growth in population, although this has been true only in comparatively recent times; before the development of agriculture and technology the human population was fairly stable. But animal populations do have overpopulation and high density problems, and many once well-established species have become extinct under changing environmental conditions (as was pointed out in Chapter 1). Indeed, Charles Darwin first came across the idea of the struggle for survival on reading Malthus's essay (1798) on geometric population growth and limited food supply. Today, biological scientists believe that much insight may be gained about human population problems from a knowledge of how population is regulated in nature, and we shall give some attention to this here.

The population of most plant and animal species is regulated by a combination of biological and social forces influencing survival and reproduction. Populations are not self-limiting; they tend to grow at geometric rates unless or until this growth is checked by outside forces such as food limitations of the ecosystem. In some cases, animals may literally eat themselves out of food and shelter, as the lemmings (small, mouselike rodents) apparently do; when this crisis occurs, lemmings launch into an apparently suicidal migration down to the sea, where they drown themselves!! Ethologists believe that this mass suicide is really a headlong and unsuc-

ments tell us about human emotions must be based on weak levels of emotional arousal, and our generalizations must, if possible, correct for the error. Perhaps the rules of emotion are different for mild emotional states than for intense ones; and if our knowledge is based solely on the former (created in the laboratory), then our interpretation will be incorrect. Such a limitation does not apply in animal research, but then there is considerable hazard in applying animal data to man. Nor does it apply to the many psychological problem areas that are socially or emotionally quite neutral, as when we want to discover experimentally how some physical or social variable affects perception, thought, or memory. For large areas of psychology, the laboratory experiment is a prime tool. But the reader should keep in mind both the advantages and the limitations of laboratory experimentation as a source of psychological knowledge.

In looking at Nature, it is most necessary . . . never to forget that every single organic being [is] . . . striving to the utmost to increase in numbers; that each lives by a struggle at some period of its life; that heavy destruction inevitably falls either on the young or old, during each generation or at recurrent intervals. Lighten any check, mitigate the destruction ever so little, and the number of the species will almost instantaneously increase to any amount. . . . [From Darwin, 1859]

(a)

(b)

Figure 3.8 (a) Some of the thousands of young people who attended a free rock concert in Central Park, New York City. (b) Still photo from the film Gimme Shelter, which presented a live Rolling Stones concert in California that drew tens of thousands from all over the United States. The concert was marked by sporadic outbursts of violence and at least one homicide that could be attributed to the overcrowded conditions. (a: The New York Times; b: Courtesy of Cinema 5 Ltd.; The Museum of Modern Art/Film Stills Archive)

cessful search for another habitat that can accommodate the excess population; a few lemmings succeed in finding new abodes and perpetuate the species, but vast numbers are drowned in the headlong rush. How human beings would behave under similar circumstances can only be conjectured (Figure 3.8).

In general, however, most animal population levels are quite stable, fluctuating around a fairly steady norm (Wynne-Edwards, 1965). Their population size and density level off before the available space is completely saturated. Such regulation depends on a number of processes, including competition for food and space, the action of predators who kill and eat them, and the toll of parasites or disease. There is, moreover, a kind of feedback control from the conditions of the environment (see Chapter 1). If the population density within the habitat gets too great for all the animals to feed and breed, competition forces the less favored individuals to starve, restricts them from breeding, or exposes them to predators.

Many animal species, such as the great apes, develop *social hierarchies* of authority, or "pecking orders." The expression *pecking order* comes from the social pattern of feeding in fowl in which the dominant bird takes charge and pecks at the food until he is satisfied, upon which the next subordinate in line takes over, then the next, and so on. In very many species the strongest and most aggressive animals establish a *territory* wherein they have best access to the available food supply. In the mating season, dominant males will seek to control as many females as they can, leaving subordinate animals "out in the cold" (Figure 3.9). Dominant animals satisfy themselves first in all things, threatening and chasing off subordinate competitors. When established, the hierarchy is usually quite stable, especially in times of relative plenty. Under conditions of crowding and scarcity, however, and in the mating season, this stability is weakened, and competition and conflict increase.

In any case, when population density increases and the food supply grows scarce, the very subordinate individuals, who are isolated on the fringes of the colony away from the best sources of food, begin to die of starvation and fall prey to roving predators who are likely to attack a lone animal more readily than one in the center of the colony. In addition, the increase in competition or stress leads to secretion of certain hormones of the adrenal glands. This has the biological effect of reducing breeding and survival rates. Such hormones induce more miscarriages in females and in addition weaken the animals' resistance to disease (Christian and Davis, 1964). These biological and social mechanisms result in an increase in the death rate and a reduction of the birth rate, hence they serve to lower the population density until the available food again rises above that needed to feed the colony. When this happens the same forces (lowered death rates and increased birth rates) that allowed the upsurge in the population density in the first place are again set in motion. Thus, an *equilibrium* in population sizes and densities is continuously maintained, with minor fluctuations around the norm limited by environmental conditions (mainly food supply, predators, and disease). Maintenance of this equilibrium (*homeostasis*) prevents most animal species from overexploiting their habitats and thus using up the vegetation and other vital natural resources.

Wynne-Edwards (1965) thinks that although these homeostatic regulatory mechanisms operated in very early man, they are no longer effective in the case of modern man. In early Paleolithic times there was little change in population size for a long period because man was a food gatherer and hunter. When shortages prevailed, human population growth was inhibited by infanticide, abortion, abstention from intercourse, cannibalism, tribal warfare, human sacrifice, and of course by starvation and disease, as in lower animals. The big change in man's situation occurred with the shift from hunting and food gathering to agriculture, which made it possible to produce more and more food as needed by the growing population. Another significant change has been produced in recent times by the advances in medicine that have sharply lowered the death rate. Wynne-Edwards (1965, p. 1548) agrees with Ehrlich and other ecologists in their concern with the growing population crisis. He writes, "It becomes obvious at last that we are getting very near the global carrying capacity of our habitat, and that we ought swiftly to impose some new, effective, homeostatic regimen before we overwhelm it . . ."

There is a great temptation to draw parallels between biosocial mechanisms observed in overcrowded colonies of animals and human behavior on a planet whose "carrying capacity" is soon to be reached. When Ehrlich (1968) suggests that war, famine, and pestilence will operate to regulate human population if it goes beyond some as yet undefined level (an extension of Malthusian views), he is saying that primordial catastrophic forces analogous to those in lower

Figure 3.9 Male sage grouse engaged in plumage displays on their strutting ground as part of the competition to establish sexual hierarchy; the dominant male becomes "master cock," attracting and mating with most of the hens. (Hugh M. Halliday from National Audubon Society)

animals will take over in man if his population growth is not regulated by sociopolitical means, either voluntarily by people everywhere or involuntarily by governmental edict. Man is capable of regulating his actions through cultural and sociopolitical means. These play as great a part in human population dynamics today as do biological factors. The problem of reducing population growth is obviously one of getting human couples to prevent or terminate pregnancies beyond a certain number.

PSYCHOLOGICAL ISSUES OF POPULATION GROWTH

Cultures vary in the attitudes they inculcate in their people toward having children and population control. The usual forms of control include sexual abstinence, abortion, and direct birth-control techniques. Based in part on observations of primitive tribes such as the Yanomamös, who live in the Venezuelan interior and have had little contact with modern man, it has been speculated that the slowness of increase in the total human population up to 10,000 years ago was probably in large measure due to the practice of spacing children through intercourse taboos, long periods of breast feeding, abortion, and infanticide, leading to an effective live birth rate of one child every 4 to 5 years (Neel, 1970). It is also notable that the population of Europe, which nearly doubled in the years between 1750 and 1850, was probably kept from even greater growth by the widespread practices of celibacy and infanticide (Langer, 1972). Usual methods included dosing the baby with gin or opiates, starvation, strangulation, or smothering, and, perhaps the most common of all, abandonment (Figure 3.10). It is also of great interest that the introduction of legal abortion in Japan after 1947 markedly lowered the number of births from 2.6 million in 1947 to 1.6 million in 1960 (Lerner, 1968).

In a recent review and analysis of the problems of population control (Fawcett, 1970), three public attitudes toward regulation of births were distinguished: (1) those urging greater efforts to influence people voluntarily to limit childbearing; (2) those proposing either positive or negative inducements, such as taxation credits or charges; and (3) those advocating compulsion, for example, mandatory sterilization of individuals with large families. One can readily see that many ethical as well as practical issues are involved in each of the above approaches, and each has its advocates and critics. However, in the final analysis, barring the third rather extreme solution, all public policies must be relevant to the ultimate decision-making power that each couple has over its actions. What each

Figure 3.10 William Hogarth's "Gin Lane," a view of eighteenth-century London. Casual infanticide seems to have been the order of the day: in the foreground a baby is falling to his death while his mother sits in a drunken stupor; in the mid-background another child has somehow become impaled on a spit; and at the far right an infant is being soothed with a glass of gin. (The Metropolitan Museum of Art, Harris Brisbane Dick Fund, 1932)

couple does depends on how it views the matter. The crucial decisions must be made in homes and medical offices where contraception, abortion, and sterilization are accomplished. We are dealing here with fundamental psychological questions related to deeply ingrained human motives, ways of thinking and believing, and emotional patterns. The attitudes of people resulting from these psychological processes must be reckoned with in order to formulate effective social policy. In the brief discussion that follows we shall consider the motives for having or not having children, attitudes toward the control of population growth, and other emotional factors that get in the way of rational social policies.

Motives for having or not having children

Obviously, the sexual drive underlies human conception. This drive probably has little or nothing to do with wanting children, but it is undoubtedly one of the major reasons people do have them. In nature it is mainly the sexual drive that

Figure 3.11 Cartoon by Leo Garel. (Reproduced by special permission of PLAYBOY *Magazine; copyright* © *1967 by Playboy)*

"No, we're not especially crazy about kids. They're sort of a by-product."

results in procreation, and in all probability only man recognizes the connection between sexual intercourse and childbirth. Children are conceived with or without actual planning on the part of parents, and the *desire* to limit family size may not be effectuated unless there is careful planning (Figure 3.11). Rainwater (1960, p. 53) writes about this in ironic fashion, as follows:

When the event to be planned is as significant as parenthood, the dynamics of choice are likely to become even more muddled, particularly since what one is planning is not really parenthood at all, but nonparenthood. One who exercises the choice to do nothing at all, to plan only in the negative sense, is quite likely to become a parent.

Leaving out the desire for sexual intercourse, the biological motive for having children usually derives from presumed *maternal instincts* or *drives* that in lower animals are obviously biologically predetermined but have a much greater component of learning in *Homo sapiens.* Important too may be the feminine desire to experience childbirth (even if there is no interest in rearing the child), to breastfeed a baby, to cuddle an infant next to the skin; members of both sexes may enjoy taking care of a child or playing with it. (Animal pets, as everyone recognizes, are often substitutes for children.) Evidence that such desires are somehow part of a woman's or man's basic biological equipment is very meager, although it seems likely that some such inclinations may be inborn.

The above issue is actually a very important one for many modern women who want to change their social role from one of mother and homemaker to that of an active professional career. Should there be a strong biological urge toward motherhood, then the choice not to have children might produce long-range psychological deprivation. The counter-argument of women's liberationists is that even if it could be demonstrated that most women "need" to have children in a strictly biological sense, apart from their socialization in a culture that trains them from childhood for this role (Bem, 1970, pp. 89–99), there would still probably be great individual differences in the strength of this need, and it is highly likely that many women could live rich and satisfying lives without having children. The question is currently being hotly debated by biological and social scientists.

There are, of course, many other motives for having children, other than simple biological urges. There is much social pressure on the young couple to have a baby, partly from the cultural norm which makes the family the basic unit of life (and views having children as good and right) and partly from the couple's parents, who are frequently anxious to have grandchildren. Grandchildren provide an extension of the maternal and paternal role that has been interrupted by the maturation of their own children, and many mothers and fathers look forward again to taking care of their son's or daughter's baby at a time when they are experiencing the "empty nest" syndrome of the middle-aged.

Figure 3.12 The modern small family: "A girl for you and a boy for me." (Mimi Forsyth; Monkmeyer Press Photo Service)

In many cultures, having children has been viewed as an economic advantage, especially in the case of the boy, who in preindustrial societies could work the land, hunt, and fish, or in other ways contribute to the family's economic welfare. Childbearing often serves to strengthen the woman's or man's ego: the woman may wish to validate her femininity; the man to demonstrate his virility. Sometimes a couple with marital problems seeks children in order to hold the marriage together in the belief that they will get along better once they have a child. Similarly, a couple with one child often decides to have a second on the assumption that an only child is harmed in some way. Couples with only boys or girls frequently want another baby so that both sexes will be represented, sometimes trying again and again without success (Figure 3.12). An important reason for large families is the constraint against contraception because it is a religious duty to procreate.

These motives for wanting children have been listed by Pohlman (1969), who has written one of the few psychologically oriented analyses of the motives for having children. In the context of population control, such lists of motives for having children suffer from several serious limitations in helping us understand the data on human fertility. For one thing,

Note 3.2

This discussion of the motives for having or not having children points to a very important general question about the concept of motive in psychology. What sort of an idea is this? How can Pohlman (1969), for example, one of the investigators of the motivation for having or not having children, speak knowledgeably about such motives? Above all, how can we determine what individuals really want?

The concept of motive is an intellectual tool used by psychologists to make sense out of the way a person or animal acts. They are theoretical "constructs," to use an expression commonly used by psychologists, just as are genes in biology or electrons in physics. Genes cannot be seen directly, but are presumed to exist as carriers of heredity from parents to children. (Biochemists have found that they are complex molecules, *deoxyribonucleic acid,* or DNA.) The electron is a basic particle hypothesized by physicists to explain matter and energy. The behavior of these particles cannot be known directly but is inferred from their causes and effects. Motives, too, are inferred from their effects, and sometimes from the conditions that bring them about.

Psychologists frequently use two related terms—drive and motive. *Drive* refers to a vague state of tension or restlessness in the organism which through experience (learning) becomes linked to behavior capable of reducing that tension (see Chapter 6). A good example is hunger. The tension is produced by not eating for a time, and the person or animal must learn to find food and eat it in order to reduce the tension. *Motive* has more of a psychological connotation, that is, it implies an urge to perform a specific behavior, and therefore that a psychological connection has been made between the drive tension and the behavior that terminates it. Some drives and motives result from the biological construction of the organism (innate drives), and others are acquired largely through experience, as in the case of the motive to have children. Any motive is known to us through only two sources—presence of the conditions that bring it about, and thoughts, behavior, or feelings that result from its presence.

Our everyday language uses comparable though perhaps less systematically differen-

wanting a child (or some children) is not the same thing as wanting a *given number* of children, say, two versus five. Relatively little attention has been given to the latter question. Furthermore, a mere list of motives for having children is insufficient to help us understand the psychodynamics of procreation. It does not tell us, for example, how the various reasons for having children are put together within a particular person or couple making the decision, including the most and least important motives on the person's list of priorities or the weighing of the various motives to have or not to have children. Moreover, couples may not be very conscious of many of their motives. They may not acknowledge or even be aware of the extent to which their wish to have a baby is the result of social pressure, and this pressure may not be in accord with their main psychological interests or needs as individuals or as a couple. The decision-making process is thus difficult to assess.

The social scientist who has given most attention to the psychological meaning for the individual and the conjugal couple of sex, marriage, contraception, and having children is Lee Rainwater (1960, 1965), whom I quoted earlier. Most other psychologically oriented studies to date have centered on the characteristics of individuals, and they have failed to reveal much relationship between such characteristics and patterns of fertility of couples. Rainwater's studies, in contrast, focus more on the couple as a unit than on the individual. Rainwater's method was to interview many couples representing various social classes and religious affiliations. His findings suggest that couples who prefer small families are likely to be husband-dominated or jointly organized conjugal relationships, have interest in activities outside the home, and include a wife who is uneasy about or negative toward homemaking. Large families seem to be sought on the other hand by couples whose values are oriented toward children and the home, for whom sexual relations are especially important, and who identify failure to want children as an instance of selfishness (see Note 3.2).

The attitudinal norm observed in Rainwater's interviews is not comforting for those who are concerned about overpopulation. It is that *couples should not have more children than they can support, but they should have as many children as can economically be managed.* Hence, to have a smaller number is an expression of selfishness or neuroticism, and to have more than can be supported is to display poor judgment or lack of discipline. In short, the value expressed is that "the good person in a good world has a large family."

The large family has, of course, been traditional throughout history. Most of our grandparents grew up in such a family, and there is no denying the psychological security of being part of an extended, close-knit kinship group, with many brothers and sisters, uncles, aunts, and cousins to whom one can relate (Figure 3.13).

Although not as common today, the large family still has many strong adherents. A family living in a middle-class section of a major American city was recently interviewed. The parents are 53 and 43 years of age and have 18 children, ranging in age from 22 years to 5 months. As the mother describes it, "The kids arrived one at a time. It is not as though we had all 18 at once. We never planned 18. We just let it happen." The couple presented a picture of well-being. The wife reported that she always feels good while pregnant and that their sex life is the same as it was 23 years ago, when they got married. The husband, who holds three jobs, indicated that economically things were not always easy. But the older children help out with part-time work after school, and others help in household chores. The children are also active in community life. Both parents are very proud of their family.

Rainwater (1960, pp. 81–82, 86) has examined in a highly sophisticated way the meaning of sex, marriage, and having children for each couple he has interviewed:

Two aspects of being a parent are important in connection with family planning: the meaning of the biological fact of becoming a parent, and the meaning and function of children in the lives of their parents. The first has to do with very deeply felt conceptions of oneself as a man or a woman, the second with the ramified ways in which the psychosocial identity of father or mother is defined in action.

To impregnate and to become pregnant signify to the individual a kind of categorical maturity as adult human beings; the natural consequence of sexual intercourse fixes more permanently and obviously than can the private experience of love-making the status of adulthood, of being grown up. . . .

Once children have arrived, they take on different meanings; they come to be individuals to whom one must relate and whose independent existence must be taken into account in the way the husband and wife live. The relatively simple meanings which *having* children represent become much more complex as the children become psychosocial realities as well as biological events.

Efforts everywhere in the world to get people to reduce the size of their families are confronted not only by the problem of ignorance about contraception but also by widespread absence in individuals and families of planning for the future. Equally important as psychocultural facts are very strong personal motives, ethical values, and religious traditions concerning child raising and family life. Obviously, we need to know more about how children are valued by different groups within our own society and in other societies. It is one thing to help get people who already want fewer children to succeed

tiated terms. We speak of people having needs, wants, wishes, desires, and aims or goals. These are variants of the general idea of motivation, each with its own special implication. For example, the word *need* implies something necessary or vitally important; we not only want something, we need it. Some of these needs are the result of our biological makeup, and in others certain activities and goals have become enormously important to us through learning. The word *wish* also means something that we desire, though it is not necessarily attainable. When we wish ("I wish I were a rich man"), we are fantasizing about what the desired state would be like. And in our daily lives, we often make educated guesses or inferences about a person's inner motivational state from what we observe in his behavior.

Let us again take the comparatively simple instance of hunger. We look for evidence of causal antecedents such as food deprivation (time since the last meal) and of resultant actions (seeking food and eating), actions that subside once the drive has been satisfied. We can estimate the intensity of the drive from the intensity of the behavioral effort and its persistence. In the human case, we can also examine the extent to which the individual is preoccupied by thoughts and emotions (or fantasies) involving food. For example, in studies of human semistarvation during World War II, male volunteers who were restricted to a very limited intake of food for several months reported thinking almost continuously about eating, and instead of putting pinups of scantily clad women on their walls, they put over their beds color photos of succulent foods cut out of magazines.

How might we study the more complicated case of motives related to having children? Of significance here are social pressures urging men and women to validate their role in life by having children. Until recently, such pressures were quite widespread and strong. Today, however, more people are beginning to challenge this notion, and there is less uniformity in this regard.

Most often the motives for having or not having children can be inferred from what the person says (as in Rainwater's studies), though as we know such statements cannot always be accepted at face value. We can also gauge the nature and strength of various motives for or against having children by observing certain patterns of behavior from which the wishes of the person and his or her fears can be inferred. We might note that a particular woman spends much time with her neighbors' or friends' children, playing with them and cuddling them. A childless couple may go to a physician to determine why they have not conceived and take steps to correct the problem. Or the couple may speak about their childlessness with distress or with evidence of disappointment. The strength of the motive for having children can be guessed at from the frequency and intensity of such behavior. On the other hand, there might be clear evidence of desire for children, yet simultaneous evidence of fear about pregnancy, delivery, or child rearing on the part of the woman, in which case we can infer the existence of a strong conflict of motives. And if one assumes that many motivational factors are beneath the surface of awareness, fantasies about children can be detected from projective tests (see Chapter 11), which sometimes reveal what the person cannot tell directly to anyone, perhaps even to himself.

in this wish, but it is another matter to try to influence people whose personal needs, values, and ideologies favor large families or lead them to reject any interference or alternative outlooks. These are complex psychological and cultural issues about which there is much yet for social scientists to learn.

Attitudes toward control of population growth

Surveys reveal that the average couple in the United States today desires between two and four children. A recent study (Van Tienhoven and associates, 1971) put the average preference at 2.9 children, but there is also a considerable range above and below. For example, as many as 65 percent of couples wanted three or more children, well above the level needed to maintain the present population size, and a fair proportion wanted less. Marked differences between lower- and middle-class groups used to be found in family size preferences, but these seem to be narrowing today, perhaps as a result of the mass media that express and disseminate largely middle-class standards to the whole population, thus leveling class differences. Recent studies (Westoff and Bumpass, 1973) have also shown that American Roman Catholics have drastically shifted to the use of birth control practices officially disapproved by their church. By 1970, two-thirds of Catholic women in the United States were using contraceptives, and for women under 30 this figure reached three-quarters. This was so even for those otherwise actively religious, for example, those receiving Communion at least once a month.

However, striking ethnic differences in family size preferences have recently been emerging, with some minority groups (especially blacks and chicanos) feeling keenly that they need large families to increase their social force in the white-dominated society. Many members of these ethnic minorities (especially males) have expressed dismay and anger at the widespread tendency of intellectuals to embrace the need for population control; they may perhaps be replacing Catholics as the staunchest defenders of the right to have large families. These minority groups often see efforts to control population growth as directed primarily against them, and they see in the population growth issue mainly an effort to hold them down by limiting their numbers.

Speaking before the organization of Planned Parenthood–World Population, Andrew Billingsley, Vice President for Academic Affairs at Howard, a black university, has characterized population control programs as "overt racism with overtones of genocide." He stated that whites have decided that the black population is getting out of control and must be curbed, although blacks constitute only 15 percent of the

Figure 3.13 The traditional large family. (Courtesy of Dr. David Miller)

people of the United States. Instead, he argued, "the greatest population pressure lies with the white middle class, which is the most destructive of national resources, environment, space, money, power, and control. If population control programs are to be imposed, begin with the class that has more than its fair share of everything." It is ironic that the population crisis is now also caught up in the web of racial and ethnic stereotypes, accompanied by mutual hatred and distrust.

These ethnic complications have drawn the following forceful comment by Paul Ehrlich: "It is hardly surprising that, upon seeing the ODC's [overdeveloped countries] grab vastly more than their share of the world's wealth, people of the UDC's [underdeveloped countries] are suspicious when the ODC's talk of population control. They are suspicious for the same reasons that our own suppressed minorities are suspicious when they hear affluent whites talk of population control. The message they get is 'there are too many of you nonwhites and we don't want to share what we've got with you; therefore we want to reduce your numbers.'" Ehrlich's answer is that everyone will enjoy a higher quality of life if population growth is controlled and that simple arithmetic shows that no one's problems will be solved without population control, including the problems of the "have-nots" of the world. He

Today . . . the great peril to mankind does not stem from the actions of any one regime, party, group or class. Rather it is the family of man itself which poses that threat, exposed as its own worst enemy and at the same time, alas, as the worst enemy of the rest of creation. If there is to be hope of saving mankind, mankind must first be convinced of this. [Claude Lévi-Strauss, quoted in *The New York Times*, Jan. 21, 1972, p. 47]

uses the analogy of the earth as a spaceship, rather than as a place of unlimited bounty, and suggests that we must learn to live as though we had limited resources and space, a point that applies to everyone, rich and poor, black and white. We can see in this explosive issue how psychological and cultural factors play a crucial role in efforts to control worldwide population growth.

These differences in the attitudes of ethnic groups toward family size and population control have been further documented by Buckout (1972). A mixed ethnic group of 267 unmarried undergraduate students were surveyed, including 80.9 percent white, 9.1 percent black, 5.3 percent Spanish surname (chicano), 3.0 percent Oriental, and 1.5 percent Native American (Indian). The mean age was 22 years, and there were an equal number of males and females. In addition, 26.6 percent were Catholic, 34.6 percent Protestant, 3.0 percent Jewish, 5.2 percent had other religious ties, and 28.8 percent reported no religious preference. In all these characteristics, as well as in income and educational level, the sample studied was quite representative of the overall population of California where the study was made. Each subject was interviewed by a person from his own ethnic group and asked questions about personal desires about future family planning, attitudes toward sterilization, abortion and birth control, and toward various social policies about population control.

It was found that the ideal family size for this sample was 2.6, males reporting 2.4 and females 2.7. However, there were marked ethnic differences. Blacks in the sample desired 4.1 children, and chicanos 4.0. These latter groups were strongly antagonistic to coercive population controls, especially mandatory sterilization, and they were less favorable than whites even to voluntary limitations of family size. Sterilization of males was seen by many blacks as likely to reduce masculinity, or to increase effeminacy (an entirely incorrect belief also shared by many whites, which is likely to be an important psychological factor in the individual response to many birth-control measures). A large portion of those asked indicated that they approve of the "pill" for contraception, however the numbers favoring the pill are lower for blacks and chicanos than whites.

Buckout concludes that birth control should not be forced upon minority groups who feel threatened by such a prospect, since it would only further widen the gulf already existing between them and the white community and would probably be counterproductive. These variant beliefs and attitudes of members of ethnic minorities must somehow be taken into account in any sociopolitical program aimed at lowering population growth rates by changing behavior patterns.

Why do so many people refuse to play their part in solving the population problem? One of the psychological obstacles to reasonable action is ignorance. If people have no idea as to the nature of a problem or what to do about it, then even a highly threatening situation cannot provoke them to take therapeutic action. Another obstacle has to do with the sense of powerlessness many people feel over their fate; such a feeling of powerlessness encourages a fatalistic outlook and passivity or inaction (see Chapter 2). The action needed is sometimes awkward or painful, or must be sustained for a long time. Moreover, in a situation where the person is threatened by some future harm and feels he cannot do much about it, or that any corrective action is coupled with other major psychological costs, he is capable of selectively attending to the evidence and convincing himself that there is indeed nothing to worry about. Then the warnings seem to fall on "deaf ears," and we get an impression of great inertia in spite of serious danger.

People are remarkably capable of protecting themselves against threatening thoughts and information, including those related to dangers in the environment with which they do not know how to cope or which seem somewhat remote or vague, or when the solution is itself threatening to other important goals and values. These forms of coping make it possible for the person to minimize the seriousness of the danger and to feel reasonably comfortable while he proceeds to do what he has always done. The following paragraphs depict some of the standard ways people defend themselves psychologically.

"Après nous le déluge" This famous French quotation is attributed to Madame de Pompadour, mistress of King Louis XV of France, whose reign preceded that of Louis XVI and the French Revolution that wiped out this monarchy. It means, "After us, the flood," or, in a sense, "Who cares what happens after we're gone?" There are three varieties of this way of thinking. In one, the person acknowledges readily that he is contributing to the miseries of those who follow him, and he takes the honest though self-centered position that the problem is not his lookout. In the second version the individual refuses to acknowledge to others that he does not care in the least about what happens to the next guy, though he can admit it to himself; he fears only the social disapproval or punishment to which he would be subjected were he to admit to others his selfishness and social indifference. Outwardly such

a person might support social efforts to slow the rate of population growth, but privately he does whatever is convenient for himself. In the third version, the individual does not even acknowledge to himself his indifference to the issues, and he would feel keen guilt if he were made to recognize it. He will go to some lengths to maintain this self-deception, but with often unaccountable lapses. Although he can never accept the similarity of his own attitude to that of King Louis XV's favorite, nevertheless he does not trouble himself too much about the overpopulation problem until it presses in upon him.

"I won't listen" (selective inattention)   Unlike the Pompadour type, this person is admittedly quite threatened and disturbed over what is said to be happening to the world, but he seems unable to deal with such threats—they only add to an already intolerable burden he has to bear—and the only way he can obtain relief is to *avoid* attending to any messages that bring it to mind. He may make certain not to read anything in the newspapers or magazines alluding to the subject or to turn off television programs discussing it. "Keep it light" is the motto. "We have enough to cope with without constantly being reminded of this business." Naturally, there will be occasions when the subject cannot be avoided, in which case this person experiences bursts of anxiety or depression, but such spells are generally dealt with by avoidance of the painful subject whenever possible (Figure 3.14).

"It's not true (or, it's not that bad); and even if it's true, what I am doing is justified"   A personally very useful way of responding to evidence that something is wrong in the world in which we live is to *deny* it. If the source of the threatening input is discredited, then we can go on our merry way without a moment's care. There is no cause for alarm. Or even if one acknowledges that a problem exists, it is clearly not serious; besides, the United Nations (or God) will somehow manage to take care of it.

This device is a favorite of smokers who are confronted by massive evidence that smoking is a hazard. Such persons may acknowledge that there is some risk to others yet deny vigorously that there is any serious probability that themselves will succumb to lung cancer or cardiovascular disease. To further "rationalize" this denial, they will point to the much higher probability of being killed in an automobile accident; or they will argue that it is more hazardous to quit smoking because then they will become overweight.

Similar rationalizations may be found in defensive thinking about population pressures. For example, it may be pointed out that it has not really been proved *conclusively* that we cannot feed the world's growing population indefinitely.

Figure 3.14   One world view from "The Lumpits." (Drawing by Mal Hancock; © Washington Star Syndicate, Inc.)

("Perhaps something will turn up. After all, no one has a crystal ball.") Or a person may see the problem only in terms of others ("those poor people of India"), rather than himself. Some people react to the vigorous warnings expressed by ecologists and demographers by deciding that such people are "alarmists," or "agitators," or "left-wing intellectuals" who are attacking the American way of life and certainly ought not to be believed. Thus instead of being concerned with the threat of overpopulation, they turn their attack upon those who warn about it. ("It's all a Communist plot to weaken our economy.") Finally, there is the view that no individual can do anything about such a vast problem all alone; the solution requires a mighty global cooperative effort, which is just not feasible right now. (This is similar to the assertion that one's vote in an election is lost among millions, so why really bother about going to the polls?)

We can thus see that such defensive *denial* of danger is often coupled with various *rationalizations,* in which supportive reasons are given for lack of concern. Such denial and rationalization may be shared by large numbers of people facing the same problem.

"I won't get involved" One of the most common defenses against an impending threat is that of *detachment* or disengagement. If we see the victims of a disaster as less than human, then we need not be disturbed by what has happened to them. Once we decide to look at an unpleasant reality from a strictly intellectual viewpoint, we can analyze its components, getting distance from it, and the poignancy of the human condition it bespeaks need not trouble us. By using the defense of detachment or intellectualization we are thus able to read about or view with equanimity the most severe devastation of our environment and to maintain a posture of cool disengagement from the problem. In the past, psychologists have tended to overlook the extraordinary capacity of man to protect himself in this way because such forms of self-defense have previously been treated as manifestations of psychopathology.

The foregoing discussion hardly exhausts the range of psychological defenses people use in coping with threat. It is clear that any attempt to solve the highly charged problem of overpopulation must take us into the arena of the emotional and irrational. We shall have occasion again to consider defense mechanisms in other parts of this book, for example, in connection with psychological health and pathology (Chapter 10). We will see that although such defense mechanisms help people to feel better temporarily and to avoid incapacitating emotion, they are also obstacles to accurate perception of the threat and hence to effective remedial action when such action is possible (Figure 3.15).

Figure 3.15 A clash of attitudes. (Drawing by Mal Hancock; © *Washington Star Syndicate, Inc.)*

The young generation . . . the articulate young rebels around the world . . . are at home in this time. Satellites are familiar in their skies. They have never known a time when war did not threaten annihilation. Those who use computers do not anthropomorphize them; they know that they are programmed by human beings. When they are given the facts, they can understand immediately that continual pollution of air and water and soil will soon make the planet uninhabitable and that it will be impossible to feed an infinitely expanding world population. They can see that control of conception is feasible and necessary. As members of one species in an underdeveloped world community, they recognize the invidious distinctions based on race and caste are anachronisms. They insist on the vital necessity of some form of world order.

They live in a world in which events are presented in their complex immediacy; they are no longer bound by the simplified linear sequences dictated by the printed word. In their eyes the killing of an enemy is not qualitatively different from the murder of a neighbor. They cannot reconcile our efforts to save our own children . . . with our readiness to destroy the children of others with napalm. . . . Old distinctions between . . . ''my'' group and ''theirs''—the outsiders, the alien—have lost their meaning. They know that the people of one nation alone cannot save their own children; each holds the responsibility for the others' children. [M. Mead, *Culture and commitment*. Garden City, N.Y.: National History Press (Doubleday), 1970]

We are dealing here also with a very general problem of conflict between immediate interests of the individual and long-range interests of the community, a problem that exists whenever people must share a common property, such as a park, a street, a forest, a river, or any resource. The "common good," especially extended into the distant future, is an abstraction, but one's "personal good" is immediate and pressing. To the former we react by thinking, "Why should I bother? What good will it do me?" For the community to act in conservation of important environmental values, most people must first recognize that their own long-range interests are involved, and this is sometimes difficult to see or believe. We are asked to sacrifice our own immediate and very evident interests for uncertain ones in the future and for people whom we neither know nor especially care about. In such a context one wants to know at the very least that most other people are also making comparable sacrifices. Moreover, many people have difficulty accepting present sacrifices (say, to save money, or to become educated) for their own future gain. Why then should it be surprising that they are even less willing to make sacrifices for the abstract and vague welfare of large numbers of strangers, in the distant future, after they are gone? Such altruism is a highly fragile and infrequent human value compared with the motives of immediate self-interest. It is no wonder then that the social task of coping with overpopulation and pollution is so difficult and that the desirability of having minimal population growth can be widely accepted without being necessarily acted upon.

A key theoretical and practical issue imbedded in the above point is of the greatest importance. It concerns the complex relationship between attitudes and values, on the one hand, and behavior or action, on the other (see Chapter 9). Social psychologists have often tried to understand human behavior by reference to the attitudes that presumably underlie it. We are said to express hostility behaviorally (in words or by physical attack) on the basis of feelings of anger; we avoid people or places presumably on the basis of fear or other negative feelings and attitudes; we behave listlessly on the supposed basis of feelings of depression or hopelessness about a situation; or we seek others' company and behave positively toward them because we like them and enjoy being with them.

Quite commonly, however, perhaps more than psychologists have been willing to acknowledge, attitudes and behavior are poorly correlated. We may hold one attitude but wish to convey the impression of a different one, perhaps because we judge that our real feelings would be condemned. Moreover, we express an attitude in our overt behavior only when we believe that we can effect the outcome we desire; should we see no such hope, then there would be little point in acting.

Thus, many of us may feel that population growth must be curtailed somehow and yet be unwilling to accept those concrete social policies which would restrict our individual freedom to do as we choose.

CONCLUDING COMMENT

In treating the problem of overpopulation as a growing crisis of the environment, some of the major ecological principles discussed in Chapters 1 and 2 have been highlighted. We can, for example, try to understand the population crisis from the point of view of biological survival (as in Chapter 1), centering our analysis around the available food supply, changing birth and death rates, and the things that happen when competition for necessary space and resources grows intense under high population density. The pessimism of many writers about the problem is predicated on the conviction, based on analogies to biological processes in the animal world, that in the absence of sociopolitical solutions the proliferating human population will ultimately be reduced through apocalyptic catastrophes of famine, pestilence, and massive warfare.

More attractive sociopolitical solutions, such as the voluntary or compulsory reduction of family size to a point approximating "zero population growth," though obvious and logical, face a host of contrary personal and cultural values that illustrate one of the central themes of Chapter 2, namely, that survival values alone cannot explain man's approach to his environment. When, for example, some minority groups support the idea that they must reproduce extensively to overcome oppression by the majority, or when individual families choose for ideological or religious reasons to have four, five, six, or ten and more children, then psychological and cultural forces are operating in opposition to long-term biological survival of the species.

What will happen in the future about the environmental problem of overpopulation rests on our ability to evaluate and change people's attitudes and actions with respect to family planning. Most people today regard very negatively the forcible control of procreation by government. Yet if we continue indefinitely to serve our own individual or group desires as we have in the past, it is likely that the world will be inundated with people beyond the point where rational solutions are still possible. But can the widespread restraint required to avoid this eventuality be accomplished, and by what means? No one knows the answer, and the critical nature of the problem recommends, certainly, that intensive study be made of motives for child rearing and family planning in various parts

If man wants an extended future, . . . if he wants to avoid the pattern of boom and collapse, he will have to give up the philosophy of growth. Is that socially conceivable? The more one thinks about what is asked, the more staggering are the implications. [Anthony Lewis, To grow and to die: II. *The New York Times,* Jan. 31, 1973]

of the world. Psychology must certainly be at the forefront of this study. Over and above such research, however, it is now imperative that the peoples of the world develop a sense of urgency about the problem, a feeling that cannot be acquired until the devastating effects of overpopulation on the quality of life are truly grasped and feared.

ANNOTATED LIST OF SUGGESTED READINGS

Overpopulation and the environment

Ehrlich, P. R. *The population bomb.* New York: Ballantine Books, 1968. A very readable, if alarming, account of the population crisis and its consequences for humanity.

Hardin, G. (ed.) *Population, evolution, and birth control.* San Francisco: Freeman, 1964, 1969. An interesting collection of pieces dealing with the population problem, the dynamics of population, demographic issues, evolution, and birth control.

Wallace, B. *Essays in social biology,* Vol. 1: "People—their needs, environment, ecology." Englewood Cliffs, N.J.: Prentice-Hall, 1972. A series of fascinating essays and readings in social biology, applying the methods of scientific analysis to environmental problems of our times. Requires no previous knowledge of biology.

Overpopulation and psychology

Fawcett, J. T. *Psychology and population.* New York: The Population Council, 1970. A brief but comprehensive and highly respected examination of various psychological issues that have an important bearing on social and political programs attempting to put limits on population growth.

Pohlman, E. H. *Psychology of birth planning.* Cambridge, Mass.: Schenkman, 1969. Analysis of psychological questions involved in the sociopolitical management of population, including the motivations for wanting and not wanting children.

Just as one is born into a physical environment, so every person also enters a social environment that has a major impact on how he thinks, feels, acts, and reacts throughout his life. Our task in this chapter is to try to understand how this social environment affects us psychologically.

THE SOCIAL SETTING

We live in the midst of a complex web of human relationships, ranging from intimate family life to larger social entities (like the religious denomination, ethnic group, or nation to which we belong). Most of us are only barely aware of how elaborate is our daily social behavior (Goffman, 1971). We obey complex rules of pedestrian traffic on busy streets, follow the usually accepted ways of behaving in a crowded elevator or subway, reveal delicate nuances of meaning in our everyday conversation and in our richly expressive body gestures, and behave suitably at weddings, funerals, meals, in a college class, with someone of the same sex and someone of the opposite sex, and so on. Much of this complex tuning of our behavior to social rules occurs more or less automatically without our even being aware of it, yet it embodies an intricate pattern of social interaction. For each social context we must learn a host of rules that guide us in how we are to think, act, and feel. These rules establish the social realities of the setting into which we are born and through which we move daily. These social realities were here long before each of us arrived on the scene and will still exist after we are gone. We react to them as though they were stable fixtures of the external world, just as we react to the physical environment.

However, society and its culture are human products, growing out of traditional ways of thinking, feeling, and doing

Only at [the] point [when social institutions are passed down to the next generation] does it become possible to speak of a social world at all, in the sense of a comprehensive and given reality confronting the individual in a manner analogous to the reality of the natural (physical) world. . . . To take the most important item of socialization, language appears to the child as inherent in the nature of things, and he cannot grasp the notion of its conventionality. A thing is what it is called, and it could not be called anything else. All institutions appear in the same way, as given, unalterable and self-evident. . . . [The] institutional world transmitted by most parents already has the character of historical and objective reality. The process of transmission simply strengthens the parents' sense of reality, if only because, to put it crudely, if one says, "This is how these things are done," often enough one believes it oneself. . . . [From Berger and Luckmann, 1966, pp. 56, 57]

things. These ways began long ago as matters of convenience or necessity, but once established they tended to persist, becoming habitual social patterns handed down from one generation to the next (Berger and Luckman, 1966). As habitual patterns are transmitted from generation to generation they become fixed social institutions, unchangeable rules of conduct. Their original existence as merely convenient ways of doing things then becomes less obvious, less easy to perceive. For a child, they are *the* social world into which he is born and over which he has only limited control, the social conventions to be obeyed. Subsequent generations must learn about this social order as they must learn about the natural environment. Since we grow up within a social milieu, each of us is to some extent a product of it. During our entire lifetime our modes of thought, feeling, and acting are shaped by it, especially in the formative years.

People living within the same social setting do not always perceive social reality in the same way, just as their perceptions of physical reality may also differ. To some extent, each individual's social reality is his own private, subjective world that is never completely shared with others. We have our own projects, meanings, and consciousness, our own thoughts, feelings, wishes, and acts. What each of us knows is not exactly like what anyone else knows, and therefore the way social reality is constructed in our minds differs from person to person. The sociologist and anthropologist, as well as the psychologist, must take this fact into account. Sociologists recognize variations among members of different groups each with their own cultural backgrounds and experience. Thus, social reality to an Asian peasant is not exactly the same as social reality to an American serviceman stationed in Asia. Even within the same society, social circumstances are likely to differentiate the way in which subgroups conceive of the social world. An American black living in an urban ghetto conceives of the social environment of his country quite differently from an affluent white American living in a small, all-white suburban township. Even the same religion is experienced very differently by sharecroppers, factory workers, merchants, millionaires, and intellectuals. As a result, the social scientist's task of describing social reality *objectively* is very difficult. Indeed, in a sense there are many truths, not one.

Still, in spite of these group and individual variations, there is considerable overlap among the ways different groups and individuals conceive the world. We recognize that we live with others in a common social world and that there is a degree of correspondence between our meanings and theirs. That is why we can speak of a social environment, just as previously we could speak of a physical environment, and why we can sensibly ask about how people respond to its influence. And so in our analysis of this social influence, we must continue to utilize the concept of adaptation with which we were pre-occupied in Chapters 1 and 2.

We can be affected by the social environment either in an *immediate,* contemporaneous fashion, or *developmentally* over a lifetime of social interaction. The former concerns our immediate, here-and-now actions and the reactions of other people to them, while the latter pertains to our past interactions with people as they have influenced our personality development. The remainder of this chapter is organized around these two modes of social influence.

PRESSURE FROM THE IMMEDIATE SOCIAL SITUATION

Since the 1930s, there has been great interest in the effects of social groups on individuals. Such interest has been heightened by intense scholarly debate about the allegedly increasing tendency toward conformity and uniformity in the modern world. A number of creative social scientists have also developed ingenious methods for studying the problem of social influence experimentally.

Experimental examples

An excellent starting point for our discussion is an unusual phenomenon investigated by Muzafer Sherif (1935) called the *autokinetic effect* ("autokinesis" means self-regulated movement). This is the tendency of a stationary light to seem to move when there are no external reference points by which an observer can fix its position. This effect once posed a real problem for bomber pilots flying in formation, since at night they often used the lights of the plane ahead to set their course; because the lights seemed to move in an erratic, confusing fashion (in the dark sky there were no reference points), the pilots sometimes became disoriented and flew off course. The problem was ultimately solved by using lights that blinked on and off.

Sherif made use of this subjective phenomenon to study the influence of other people upon the way we see things. He put subjects into a totally dark room with a single point of light, told them that the light was moving, and that their task was to estimate how far and in which direction it moved. When working alone, a subject developed his own stable autokinetic movement pattern. For example, one person would see the light as exhibiting little movement (say, 1 or 2 inches) to the left, whereas in another case it would seem to move many

The reality of everyday life further presents itself to me as an intersubjective world, a world that I share with others. This intersubjectivity sharply differentiates everyday life from other realities of which I am conscious. I am alone in the world of my dreams, but I know that the world of everyday life is as real to others as it is to myself. Indeed, I cannot exist in everyday life without continually interacting and communicating with others. I know that my natural attitude to this world corresponds to the natural attitude of others, that they also comprehend the objectifications by which this world is ordered, that they also organize this world around the "here and now" of their being in it and have projects for working in it. [From Berger and Luckmann, 1966, pp. 22–23]

feet to the right. This pattern of movement became a given subject's individual norm or standard, which he tended to follow consistently from trial to trial.

Now, however, when another subject was introduced into the room and asked to describe the light's movement, his presence and perceptual report greatly influenced the first subject's pattern. Sherif cleverly used confederates for this. Without the knowledge of the subject, the confederate was instructed to make his estimates consistently larger or smaller, and in a different direction, than that of the subject. Over several trials this gradually led to a change in the subject's estimates in the direction of those of the confederate. Though the experimenter emphasized that the subject should give his own opinions, a new norm became established as a result of the social pressure of conflicting estimates. This new norm was a compromise between the subject's original one and that of the confederate. Moreover, the new standard persisted even when the subject was again allowed to work alone, suggesting that the change was not merely slavish conformity to the confederate's report but was actually a more fundamental change in the way the light now seemed to move. The Sherif experiments with the autokinetic effect were dramatic early demonstrations of the powerful effect others can have on one's individual judgments.

From the point of view of our present understanding, it was perhaps not very surprising that the autokinetic phenomenon used by Sherif proved so vulnerable to social influence. In the absence of external anchor points to help define the location of the point of light, the judgmental task used by Sherif must be considered ambiguous* and highly susceptible to social suggestion and influence. There were, in effect, no right or wrong answers, since any movement of the light at all was a self-generated illusion. It could be argued, perhaps, that the effects would have been very different if the judgmental task was unambiguous and clear. Under such conditions one might expect that the social pressure would fail to alter what the person saw and hence reported. Some years later, this possibility was followed up by Solomon Asch (1952a, 1956), using such an unambiguous perceptual task in a series of innovative experiments that had a major impact on subsequent research on group processes.

Asch set up a situation in which subjects had to say which of three comparison lines was most similar in length to a standard line (as in Figure 4.1). Naturally, the differences in length could have been made very small and difficult to detect, which would have increased the ambiguity of the task. Asch, however, chose to make the task easy and the answer

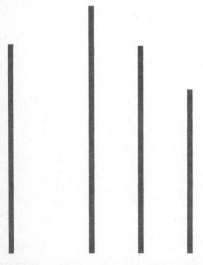

Figure 4.1 A typical stimulus in the Asch study (1952a). Subjects were shown all four lines simultaneously and asked which one of the comparison lines, A, B, or C, was most similar in length to line X. When confederates unanimously reported the incorrect answer (say, C), subjects conformed by giving the same wrong answer about 35 percent of the time.

X   A   B   C

*See Chapter 2.

Table 4.1

Distribution of errors when subjects performed Asch's task alone and under group pressure[a]

Number of errors	Frequency of errors when subject was exposed to group pressure	Frequency of errors when each subject worked alone
0	13	35
1	4	1
2	5	1
3	6	—
4	3	—
5	4	—
6	1	—
7	2	—
8	5	—
9	3	—
10	3	—
11	1	—
12	0	—

[a] From Asch (1952a, p. 5).

unequivocal, as is illustrated by the fact that when it was performed alone, subjects made virtually no errors. The procedure for evaluating the effects of group influence was to set up a series of trials in which subjects made a number of comparisons in the presence of others. Each of the other supposed subjects was a confederate of the experimenter, programmed to behave in a particular way without the real subject knowing anything about their collaboration (Table 4.1).

For each new subject a new group of from three to eight people was created. In a group of eight, seven were confederates of the experimenter who gave judgments as previously planned. The group was arranged so that the real subject always gave his judgment last. Imagine yourself in a room with seven other "peers," each giving his judgment as you await your turn. For the first two trials everything goes well, the confederates each announcing the answer which seems correct to you. Then suddenly on the third trial and thereafter, each of the confederates reports an answer different from what your senses tell you is correct; for example, in the problem in Figure 4.1, they announce their answer is *A*! This is the situation Asch's subjects faced. In contrast with the errorless performance of the subjects when working alone, in the group situation of social pressure, subjects made errors in the direction of the group judgment more than one-third of the time (Table 4.1). Some subjects yielded or conformed (accommodated) on every trial, others never conformed, while still others did so only from time to time (see Note 4.1).

Subsequent studies, many of them by other researchers, have pinned down some of the conditions under which the incidence of yielding is made greater or less. These are summarized below. For example, yielding to group pressure occurs regardless of whether the task is ambiguous, as in statements of opinion, or unambiguous, as in statements of fact. It will occur even when the answers given by the group are clearly ridiculous, for example, that men are 8 to 9 inches taller than women or that male babies have a life expectancy of 25 years. It also occurs even when the subject cannot see the others in the group, as long as he believes they are present and he discovers their answer. As might be expected, degree of conformity is reduced, though by no means eliminated, if the voting situation is made anonymous and the subject thinks he is overhearing the other judgments through an error of the experimenter.

The size of the majority against the subject is an important factor in affecting degree of conformity. Yielding is not as great, though it is still substantial, when the majority con-

Note 4.1

What would Asch (1952a, 1956) have been able to say about social pressure had he studied subjects only in the group setting? It would then have been impossible for him to conclude with any confidence that the presence and actions of the confederates were responsible for the subjects' judgmental errors. This is because he could have had no way of knowing how many errors subjects would have made in the absence of social pressure. Asch could, of course, have looked at the pattern of errors and noted that they corresponded to the answers given by the confederates, but this would not have been definitive since there were only two possible choices besides the correct one, and certain errors might have been more likely than others with or without social pressure.

The methodological principle being stated here is of the utmost importance in

any kind of research. We usually speak of it as the *principle of control.* It is necessary to have a comparison or "control" condition against which to compare the experimental effects in which we are interested. Other examples of this can be seen in studies described in earlier chapters. For example, in research on the functions of brain tissues (see Note 1.1) in which certain tissues are removed, it is necessary to compare the behavior of animals so treated with that of animals untreated by surgery. A similar point was implied in the discussion (in the Prologue) of the claim by Henry Cotton that surgical removal of foci of infection in the body cured mental patients. It was not until a controlled experiment was performed, comparing the patients so treated with a group not treated, that it became clear that the removal of tonsils, adenoids, or appendixes has no psychotherapeutic value.

Sometimes ordinary control or comparison groups are inadequate to test for the effects observed because they fail to control for some other factors that might be operating along with the experimental manipulation. For example, the surgical removal of foci of infection could theoretically have helped some patients (though it seems not to have in this study), but not for the reason given. Patients so treated can sometimes be influenced by the attention given to them, or by their own belief that surgery will help. In such a case, any improvement that might be observed in the treated group could have nothing to do with actual removal of tissue.

This phenomenon is sometimes referred to as the "Hawthorne effect," alluding to a famous industrial study at the Hawthorne works of the Western Electric Co. in Chicago (Roethlisberger and Dixon, 1940). The researchers at the Hawthorne plant began with

sists of only two others. Increasing the majority beyond two results in a large jump in the incidence of yielding, but above three or four there seems to be only a slight additional increase. The largest majority ever studied has never gone beyond 16. There is thus no research to tell us whether resisting a thousand people is more difficult than resisting three or four, although it is plausible that additional increments beyond a certain number of people would make little or no difference.

Furthermore, the more confidence a subject has in the group (for example, if it is regarded as highly expert or is composed of high-status persons), the greater is the pressure toward conformity. In the same vein, if there has been a history of disagreement from the start (say, if even on the first trial the confederates choose an incorrect answer), pressure to conform is less, possibly because such a history erodes confidence in the group. And if the subject finds himself with an ally later on, that is, another member of the group emerges who starts to give the same answer that a nonconforming subject would have given, yielding is reduced sharply. Cohesive groups—those with a strong *esprit de corps* or with whom the subject feels closely identified—produce more conformity pressure than groups without such cohesiveness. Women yield more than men, perhaps because of the traditional feminine role most women have internalized in our society, although no one to my knowledge has yet tried the conformity experiment with

the notion that better lighting in the plant would increase worker efficiency. The plant lighting was varied for an experimental group but not for a control group, and indeed, as the lighting was made brighter, worker output went up. However, it also improved to the same degree in a control group not so treated. The experimental group continued to improve in performance even when the lighting was later gradually reduced to as little as ordinary moonlight, demonstrating that it was not the lighting but something else which accounted for the changed performance. What had happened was that this evidence of interest on the part of management in working conditions had improved employee morale, and the effect of higher morale accounted for increased output in the experimental and control groups alike.

In the same way, treating patients with drugs (and other new procedures) will often result in apparent improvement in the patient's mental state, not because of the chemical effect of the drugs per se, but because of the belief on the part of the patient that he will be helped. Because such belief can be communicated by the physician, the research design must control for this or make possible assessment of such effects. One method to accomplish this in drug research is to use *placebos* (sugar pills that look and taste no different than the drugs). If the patients taking the placebo improve as much as those taking the actual drug, then it cannot be the drug which produced the effect but merely the administration of it, especially when the experimenters and the patients have positive expectations. Researchers also use the so-called double-blind technique, in which neither the immediate experimenters nor the subjects know who is getting the real drug

and who is getting the placebo. In this way the researchers' knowledge cannot subtly affect their behavior toward the patients.

The principle of control states that if the researcher wishes to ensure that it is the condition of the study (his experimental manipulation) which influences the subjects and not some other factor, he must utilize comparison conditions that allow him to rule out all other factors. In the Asch studies (1952a, 1956) of the effects of group pressure, subjects made judgments under such pressure and without it (the control condition). The results in Table 4.1 show clearly that when alone subjects made very few errors compared with subjects influenced by the group, leaving no doubt that the errors were indeed the result of social pressure. Research designed to show particular effects must have such controls; otherwise no confident conclusion can be drawn.

militant advocates of women's liberation. Conformity is also greater in early adolescence (age 13 to 14) than later on (18 to 21). Finally, certain personality variables, which seem to have to do with high self-esteem, self-confidence, and intelligence, dispose the person to remain more independent from social pressure, and hence they reduce yielding (see Freedman *et al.*, 1970, for a more detailed review).

Studies in the field

If we extend the question of immediate social influence to the more general realm of psychological outlook, or ways of thinking and feeling, we should also find that the social group is a powerful source of influence. Field research on the political attitudes of young people, both before going to college and as a result of the college experience, provides some very important insights into how this works. For example, national surveys of high school seniors (for instance, see Jennings and Niemi, 1968) reveal that when both parents are agreed about their political preferences, the young people favored the same political party in 76 percent of the cases, with only about 10

Figure 4.2   The Bennington effect. (Drawing by Saxon; © *1963 The New Yorker Magazine, Inc.)*

"They sent her to Bennington to lose her Southern accent, and then she turned her back on everything."

percent actually reporting the opposite preference. The percentage of agreement with parents appears to be higher at a younger age and decreases somewhat as the child grows older. It has been observed, for example, that almost 80 percent of grade school children agree with the party preference of their fathers (Hess and Torney, 1967), while only 50 to 60 percent of those in college do (Goldsen *et al.,* 1960). As a further illustration of the role of one's social group in the formation of outlooks or attitudes, 90 percent of marriage partners voted for the same political party.

As the child grows older, the social groups to which he is regularly exposed may change considerably. For example, if he lives at college instead of in his parental home, the social pressures of the home are gradually weakened and the new social atmosphere at college gains in importance. Even in high school today peer influences seem to be gaining in importance for the young person in contrast with parental influences, a social change which is a source of much family conflict and distress (see discussion of the "generation gap" in Chapter 5). Some classic research observations about such peer influences at school were obtained at Bennington College by Theodore Newcomb (1943), and the results seem just as relevant today as they were roughly 30 years ago, although the students and atmosphere at Bennington have greatly changed since that time (Figure 4.2).

Bennington College in Vermont was (and is) a small and exclusive college for women. It contained for its time a very liberal faculty, strongly "New Dealish" in political orientation. In those days, however, most of the students came from quite affluent and conservative upper- and middle-class homes. For example, in 1936, over two-thirds of the parents were affiliated with the Republican party. As one might anticipate 62 percent of the freshman students favored Alfred Landon, the Republican candidate, over Franklin D. Roosevelt, the Democratic candidate. However, the students became increasingly liberal politically during their four years of attendance at Bennington. This is illustrated by the fact that in that same presidential year, 1936, 43 percent of the sophomores and only 15 percent of the juniors and seniors favored the Republican candidate. They had responded to the social atmosphere in which they lived by making a deliberate choice away from their parents and toward the new community, as is illustrated by the following interview statement (Newcomb, 1943, p. 134):

All my life I've resented the protection of governesses and parents. At college I got away from that, or rather, I guess I should say, I changed it to wanting the intellectual approval of teachers and more advanced students. Then I found that you can't be reactionary and be intellectually respectable.

And another student reported (Newcomb, 1943, p. 131):

> Becoming radical meant thinking for myself and, figuratively, thumbing my nose at my family. It also meant intellectual identification with the faculty and students that I most wanted to be like.

Newcomb and colleagues (1967) did an interesting follow-up study roughly 25 years later on the students originally interviewed and also examined the campus for any changes in the institution itself. As to the original student women, those who had changed in the liberal direction during their college years had retained the college-induced liberal attitude. For example, 60 percent of the women who had graduated from Bennington in the late 1930s supported the Democratic candidate (John F. Kennedy) in the election of 1960. In contrast, comparable middle-aged women of the same social class, that is, college-educated, Protestant, living in the Northeast, and in the upper 1 percent of the population socioeconomically, preferred Kennedy in less than 30 percent of the cases. Similarly, in the 1964 election, 90 percent of the Bennington graduates preferred Lyndon Johnson to Barry Goldwater, while only about two-thirds of comparable women who had not gone to Bennington preferred Johnson. Interviews revealed that the former also showed a slight "conservative drift," a finding which is consistent with many other studies showing that a shift toward a conservative outlook tends to take place at

Note 4.2

In Note 3.1, dealing with Latané and Darley's research on "bystander apathy," it was pointed out that one of the major advantages of the laboratory experiment is that it allows more precise manipulation of conditions thought to have a causal influence on behavior and subjective experience, permitting the controlled isolation of that condition so that its effects alone can be properly assessed. Usually in nature, many causal influences are operating simultaneously and it is difficult reliably to determine which are important and how they work.

However, the laboratory experiment also has certain limitations and disadvantages compared with naturalistic or field research. What are some of the limitations of laboratory experimentation as a source of depend-

able knowledge? One of the most important ones is that it is difficult in the laboratory to discover the ordinary behavior of people or animals when left to their own resources in their natural setting. We have learned little from laboratory research about, say, love, humor, sadness, disappointment, frustration, cooperation, or altruism, to mention a few qualities of great importance in the lives of men and women. Though we can perhaps isolate and study some of these human qualities, we cannot tell under laboratory conditions just how common and important they are in our everyday lives. Nor do we learn how people manage their major problems of living without observations in the field.

Another difficulty is that sometimes the findings of the laboratory are discrepant from

related findings in nature. It has been reported that baboons in zoos and primate laboratories evolve patterns of dominance and submission (see Chapter 6) on the basis of physical intimidation and brute power, but observations of baboons in their natural habitat suggest that leaders and followers emerge mainly through such attributes as superior cunning, sexual expertise, and attractiveness, and that physical intimidation and brute power seem to be less important (Washburn, 1963). Many controlled laboratory experiments on pain and pain-relieving drugs produce findings that do not square with their effects in clinical situations such as surgery or military and accidental injury: compounds that relieve pain in the former setting often fail to do so in the ward of a

around the age of 30. However, to a striking degree the attitudinal changes initiated at Bennington were found to be stable, and (according to Newcomb *et al.*, 1967) after graduation they were reinforced by the selection of husbands and new friends with a liberal political stamp (see Note 4.2).

Of interest also were changes found in Bennington itself over the elapsed quarter of a century. In the 1930s, a majority of the parents, and the students on their arrival at the institution, had been conservative. However, during the ensuing years the college had developed the reputation of being extremely liberal, so that by the 1960s conservative families were no longer sending their children there as freely. Newcomb's follow-up studies show that in the early 1960s a majority of the parents of Bennington women were now affiliated with the Democratic party. This means that today the liberal college atmosphere at Bennington would act mainly to reinforce the liberal outlook now predominant among the students rather than to change it from conservative to liberal.

This finding that a college environment had been a major force in shifting students' outlooks from conservative to liberal has enormous political and social implications, and these have not been lost on conservative thinkers. For one thing, the data reinforce apprehensions of many conservative parents about the political atmosphere of the campuses to which they send their children. *National Review* (1965), a conservative magazine edited by William F. Buckley, Jr., reported a smaller-scale survey of twelve diverse United States campuses

---

hospital (Beecher, 1956, 1959, 1960). It has also been shown that animals can be conditioned to behave in certain ways in training, but after a time these artificially learned behavior patterns tend to drift toward patterns that are closer to the animals' natural, innate tendencies. For example, chickens that have been taught to dance will, in the natural setting, drift toward persistent scratching behavior, a prominent feature of their natural response pattern in their native habitat; or the pig who has been trained to pick up a coin and carry it gradually begins to drop it and "root" it with his snout along the way, thus showing how strong is the natural habit of the animal (Breland and Breland, 1966). One experimenter (Epstein, 1962, pp. 269–270) put it this way:

The experimental method is necessarily an artificial one. Herein lies both its strength and weakness. Because of its artificiality, experimentation is able to establish causal relationships under highly controlled conditions, which makes it eminently suitable for testing theory. However, where an attempt is made to understand events in the natural world, which all theory must eventually do if it is to be more than an intellectual exercise, it is necessary to bridge the gap between the natural event and the experimental situation. Because an event can be produced in the laboratory does not mean that the event is so produced in the natural world. Because a child can be shown to learn by trial and error in the laboratory does not mean that this is the way he learns in everyday life. . . .

Since 1930, American psychology has favored the laboratory experiment as the method of choice for investigation of problems, and indeed this method has much going for it, notably its capacity to permit careful and precise measurements and to isolate conditions for study of their effects, uncontaminated by the multiple other conditions usually operating in nature. Some problems are best tackled in this way, while others are best studied in the natural setting. Both approaches are indispensable, and one without the other is likely to produce distorted notions about what we are and how we work, psychologically (Willems and Raush, 1969).

in 1963, producing interesting findings parallel to that of Newcomb and his colleagues. The magazine concluded that "The influence of the liberal arts faculty, then, is apparently a paramount factor in determining the political complexion of these college students whose views were flexible when matriculated" (*National Review,* 1963, p. 281). Responding to this, social psychologist Daryl Bem (1970, pp. 85–86) observes sardonically:

> If you are a reader of the *National Review,* you will know that there was little joy in the editorial room when these data came in. But editor William F. Buckley, Jr. never loses his cool. The *National Review* would never say out loud that "the diabolical influence of the leftist liberal arts faculty, then, is the paramount factor in seducing the malleable minds of our finest youth." But they must have been thinking it.

Social pressure is surely a factor of the utmost importance on the world scene, both at the national and international level. For example, using the term *groupthink* for the tendency of individuals to conform to the group, Janis (1972)

Figure 4.3   High-level groupthink: President Johnson chairs a meeting aboard Air Force One during the escalation phase of the Vietnam War. (Y. R. Okamoto photo; Lyndon Baines Johnson Library)

has analyzed several recent and tragic adventures of the American government (the Bay of Pigs invasion of Cuba and the Indochina War) to illustrate how groupthink contributed to those mistakes in committees composed of presidential advisers that were charged with the task of setting policy. All participants in groupthink believe unquestioningly in the inherent morality of their in-group, and this leads them often to ignore the ethical and moral consequences of their decisions. For example, one very influential former adviser, historian Arthur Schlesinger, Jr., had doubts about the morality of the Bay of Pigs adventure. He presented his strong objections in a memo to the President and the Secretary of State, but suppressed them when he attended the group meetings of the Kennedy advisers. Thus, group pressure tends to prevent expression of views that are out of step with the prevailing sentiment, increasing the likelihood that the group will act without consideration of all of the factors that should be examined in any decision. Similar processes were also at work in the decision making that led to large-scale commitment of American troops in Vietnam under President Lyndon B. Johnson (Figure 4.3).

The above observations have provided important evidence on social influence and the conditions under which it operates. The immediate group (parents and peers) is clearly a very powerful influence on how the person thinks, feels, and acts. However, we must still explain this influence and attempt to outline the psychological mechanisms involved.

The ways social influence works

Careful interviews by Asch (1952b) of his subjects after the experience of group pressure (illustrated earlier in Figure 4.1 and Table 4.1) suggest some fertile hypotheses about mechanisms of social influence. Each subject who yielded to group pressure was confronted with his performance afterwards and asked for an explanation. Some subjects readily admitted they believed that the other participants had been wrong but described great conflict and distress at being deviant. To avoid this dilemma, they evidently consciously chose to go along with the group. Another group of subjects also reported experiencing distress but reconciled the difficulty in their minds by assuming that they had somehow misunderstood the task. In effect, they went along with the group, thinking that they themselves had been in error. On rare occasions a subject would express surprise and confusion when told of his mistakes, reported not remembering any problem, and denied being influenced by the group.

Three distinct processes of adapting to (coping with) group pressure are suggested by these interview responses: (1) The group is a powerful agent, capable of disciplining the individual; hence he feels safer when he avoids exposing him-

On March 11, about a week after my return from Latin America, I was summoned to a meeting with the President in the Cabinet Room. An intimidating group sat around the table—the Secretary of State, the Secretary of Defense, the director of the Central Intelligence Agency, three Joint Chiefs resplendent in uniforms and decorations, the Assistant Secretary of State for Inter-American Affairs, the chairman of the Latin American Task Force and appropriate assistants and bottle-washers. I shrank into a chair at the far end of the table and listened in silence. . . .

[Matters] were still very much in flux. No final decision had yet been taken on whether the invasion should go forward at all and, if so, whether Trinidad should be the landing point. It fell to Allen Dulles [Director of Central Intelligence] and Richard M. Bissell, Jr. [Deputy Director for Operations], as the originators of the project to make the main arguments for action. . . .

Bissell was a man of high character and remarkable intellectual gifts. His mind was swift and penetrating, and he had an unsurpassed talent for lucid analysis and fluent exposition. He had committed himself for the past year to the Cuban project. . . . Yet he recognized the strength of his commitment and, with characteristic honesty, warned us to discount his bias. Nonetheless, we all listened transfixed—in this meeting and other meetings which followed—fascinated by the workings of this superbly clear, organized and articulate intelligence, while Bissell, pointer in hand, would explain how the invasion would work. . . .

The determination to keep the scheme alive sprang in part, I believe, from the embarrassments of calling it off. As Dulles said at the March 11 meeting, "Don't forget that we have a disposal problem. If we have to take these men out of Guatemala, we will have to transfer them to the United States, and we can't have them wandering around the country telling everyone what they have been doing." What could one do with "this asset" if not send it on to Cuba?

The contingency had thus become a reality: having created the Brigade as an option, the CIA now presented its use against Cuba as a necessity. Nor did Dulles's arguments lack force. Confronted by them, Kennedy tentatively agreed that the simplest thing, after all, might be to let the Cubans go where they yearned to go—to Cuba. . . . [From A. M. Schlesinger, Jr. *A thousand days: John F. Kennedy in the White House,* pp. 240–242. Boston: Houghton Mifflin, 1965]

self as deviant. (2) People need confirmation from others of their judgments about the world. They therefore look to others in evaluating the adequacy of their own understanding and change their approach when they seem to be out of step. (3) People require approval and acceptance from others, sometimes so strongly that they tend to conform automatically without seeming to realize that they are doing so. Let us look at each of these a bit more closely.

Power of the group   It is by no means unrealistic to be distressed or uneasy about deviating from the norms of a group of which one is a member, since groups have the power to discipline members, and indeed they normally do so. The manner in which groups exercise their power over deviant individuals was well demonstrated in a classic and ingenious experiment by Stanley Schachter (1951). Schachter created a number of "natural" groups by advertising for college students who wanted to engage in discussions of current social issues. When each group first met they were asked by the organizer to discuss and make recommendations about a juvenile case that was currently pending in court. A delinquent was to be sentenced shortly for a crime, and the group was asked to determine whether it would recommend clemency or strong discipline to the presiding judge. The case was presented in such a way as to favor clemency. Following in the experimental tradition of Sherif and Asch, Schachter employed accomplices to create certain patterns of conformity and deviancy in the group. Three accomplices were assigned to each group, and they played three social roles: a *conformer* who always adopted at the outset the dominant position taken by the group; a *deviate,* who invariably took a position opposite from that of the group; and a *recanter,* that is, one who began with a deviant position but later revoked it, seeming to be won over to the dominant viewpoint, in which position he then firmly remained.

Schachter found that these three types of persons were treated quite differently. In general, groups punished the deviate for his heresy and treated the conformer and the recanter alike (after the latter came over to the group position). At the beginning of the discussions, for example, the group directed intensive conversation toward the deviate and the recanter, probably in an effort to convert them. However, as time passed without their being able to change the deviate's position, members of the group stopped talking to him. As part of the experiment, each group was later told there were too many members for effective future discussions, and each member was asked to evaluate every other member to determine democratically who might be eliminated from membership. The groups usually tended to rate the deviate as less acceptable than the other two confederates, thus making his expulsion a likely punishment for his failure to conform. Moreover, when committees were organized to carry on the administrative business of the group, such as determining the topic for discussion, announcing meeting times and places, and the like, the deviate was not often elected to important committees where power might reside, though he was frequently selected for unimportant (powerless) committees where labor was required (see Figure 4.4). Studies such as this point up the power of the group over the individual, and its tendency to reject the individual who persists in maintaining attitudes that run counter to the group norm. There is little doubt that this tendency of groups is one of the major mechanisms of immediate social influence.

From Schachter's research much has been learned about the price of being a deviate. Less attention has been given to what may be a more important aspect of the problem, namely, the adaptive struggle each person faces in such a situation and the ways he attempts to cope with it. Clearly, yielding to group pressure is one way of coping. One can simply cease to be deviant. Field observation and personality studies of yielding and independence show that people will often go to great lengths to conceal their deviancy (Freedman and Doob, 1968). Thus, attempts are made to hide their identity by some atheists, Jews, communists, light-skinned Negroes, homosexuals

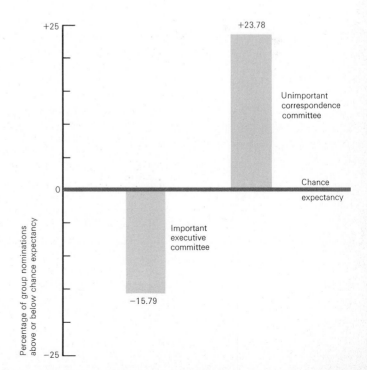

Figure 4.4 Assignment of "deviates" to important and unimportant committees, shown as percentage of nominations above or below chance expectancy. (Adapted from Schachter, 1951)

and other sexual deviates, ex-criminals, even geniuses, in short, anyone who is likely to be maltreated for being what he is.

In a penetrating analysis, Goffman (1963, p. 74) describes such tactics of concealment (or "passing") in detail, commenting, "Because of the great rewards in being considered normal, almost all persons who are in a position to pass will do so on some occasion by intent." During the Depression of the 1930s, when jobs were scarce, some Jews increased their chances of being hired by wearing a crucifix around their necks; today, some atheists may attend church and even move their lips along with the congregation while prayers are being said; some communists sign loyalty oaths; and so on. It is true that of late there have been many interesting changes in the social climate. Many homosexuals, traditionally given to concealment, are now publicly identifying themselves to an unusual degree, or (as some offended and hostile heterosexuals put it) openly "flaunting" their sexual deviancy. Nonconformity on many fronts—women's lib, long-haired youth, hippies, yippies, black activists, gay activists—has been in vogue. But the severe punitive power of society toward deviancy remains intact, and there are signs that the period of "permissiveness" may be coming to an end (Figure 4.5).

We shall return to the conflict between social norms and personal values later.

Figure 4.5   An uninhibited gay couple stepping out. (Susan Ylvisaker; Jeroboam)

Need for confirmation from others   Other people constitute important sources of information on which we often depend. They may know things that are of value to us: how to swim or ride a bike; how to fix a plumbing leak or TV set; how to buy a car without getting a "lemon." In the wild also, many animals depend on each other for warnings of danger. Man is similar to such animals in this regard. There is the familiar practical joke in which one person stands on a busy streetcorner looking up at the sky, upon which all the passersby also stop to look up and find out what is happening. Only a rare passerby will not do so. We all have the human need to gain the support of others in our judgments, and we tend to rely on their judgments as well. This behavior is part of the general human tendency to cluster in times of danger (Figure 4.6).

By the same token, if an individual suddenly discovers that his answers to a series of problems are different from those of others, he is likely to wonder about his own judgment. He may think that perhaps he has misunderstood the situation. Throughout our lives, and especially in childhood, we need confirmation from others about our own judgment and skills. We learn about our own competencies, in large measure, from the way others regard them—in school, in sports, in work, in social relations, and so on. Our appraisals of ourselves are very

of thinking, feeling, and acting of that society, since the former (the culture) can only be known by reference to the patterns that are shared by most or many members of a society. Nevertheless, we can think of a cultural pattern as the existing social environment into which the members of a given society are born, and we can understand the modal (typical) personality of individuals living within it as the product of *socialization*, that is, the effect of growing up in and adapting to that culture. And we can then ask how individuals come to reflect the culture into which they are born. To consider social influence in personality development, we must therefore look to studies by social anthropologists on the lives of people living in divergent cultures.

Marked differences are especially obvious when the outlook of our own society is compared with those of primitive societies. Those who have read Margaret Mead's (1935) account of the sex roles of males and females in the Tchambuli tribe in New Guinea must think immediately of current trends in Western society. Men and women of the Tchambuli culture appear to have reversed the traditional sex roles, women being considered naturally aggressive and domineering, while men are thought of as sensitive and artistic. Sex roles are strongly culturally determined.

It is not necessary to look to the disappearing primitive societies to find marked culturally based differences in outlook and patterns of living. One need only live for a time in the many-faceted subcontinent of India or in the cultural mosaic of Southeast Asia to sense the tremendous variations in outlook existing among the peoples of the world. The reader should also recall the comparison by Ruth Benedict (1934) of the Apollonian Pueblo Indians and the many Dionysian tribes of North America (see Chapter 2). This comparison is just as relevant here as it was there.

Even in Japan, where there has been a rapid shift in recent years away from distinctively Japanese cultural traditions to a way of life far more similar to that of the Western world, there remain strong underlying cultural patterns of thought and action that sharply distinguish Japanese society from our own. This has been nicely illustrated by anthropologist William Caudill (1959) in a comparison of Japanese and American attitudes toward alcohol and its use. Although both Japanese (especially men) and Americans drink a great deal, there is little alcoholism in Japan as this might be defined in the United States. A whiskey advertisement in a popular magazine in Japan points up the Japanese attitude. It shows a pleasant old gentleman smilingly anticipating the pleasure of drinking the six bottles of whiskey he has been saving up, while his gray-haired wife is kneeling on the floor and counting her money. The advertisement caption says, "To each his own

the researcher's interpretative stance, and the researcher has the obligation to show that his interpretation is justified by evidence. Of course, the findings must be objective, and if they are dependable, then other experimenters can later repeat them. But different interpretations of the data must also be considered.

One usually finds an intimate tie between psychological theory and what we observe in human behavior. An investigator cannot look at everything. He must make interpretive choices about what is significant, what to look for, and what the behavior he observes means. It is important to bear in mind that psychological studies do not occur in a vacuum, but reflect our theories of human behavior and subjective experience.

The Japanese consider our American total abstinence pledges as one of the strange vagaries of the Occident. So too they regard our local agitations to vote our home area dry. Drinking sake is a pleasure no man in his right mind would deny himself. But alcohol belongs among the minor relaxations and no man in his right mind, either, would become obsessed by it. According to their way of thinking one does not fear to "become" a drunkard any more than one fears to "become" a homosexual, and it is true that the compulsive drunkard is not a social problem in Japan. Alcohol is a pleasant relaxation and one's family and even the public does not consider a man repulsive when he is under the influence of liquor. He is not likely to be violent and certainly nobody thinks he is going to beat up his children. A crying jag is quite common and relaxation of the strict rules of Japanese posture and gestures is universal. . . .

Conventional Japanese strictly separate drinking from eating. As soon as a man tastes rice at a village party where sake is served it means that he has stopped drinking. He has stepped over into another "circle" and he keeps them separate. At home he may have sake after his meal but he does not eat and drink at the same time. He gives himself up in turn to one or the other enjoyment. [From Benedict, 1946, p. 189]

Serenely [the Japanese mother] expected everyone to do as she approved; there was no scolding nor arguing, but her expectation, soft as silk floss and quite as strong, held her little family to the paths that seemed right to her. [Quoted by Benedict, 1946, from E. I. Sugimoto, *A daughter of the samurai*, p. 20. New York: Doubleday, 1926]

One of the reasons why this "expectation, soft as silk floss and quite as strong," can be so effective is that training is so explicit for every art and skill. It is the habit that is taught, not just the rules. Whether it is proper use of chopsticks in childhood or proper ways of entering a room, or is the tea ceremony or massage later in life, the movements are performed over and over literally under the hands of grownups till they are automatic. [From Benedict, 1946, p. 281]

happiness," reflecting one typical family pattern in which the wife manages the money and gives her husband an allowance with which to do his drinking. When he comes home drunk, the wife is likely to greet him, help him off with his shoes and clothing, prepare a snack for him, and assist him to bed without a complaint. Nor is this drinking pattern traditionally subject to much social criticism, although this may be changing somewhat. It is highly unusual for a Japanese man to drink during the working day. Rather, he waits for evening, or vacation, or some other suitable occasion, and he does not anticipate rejection or criticism from others because of his drinking, since he does not allow it to interfere with the discharge of responsibilities (Figure 4.7). In contrast, there is considerable guilt connected with heavy drinking in the United States, and such drinking not infrequently produces a deterioration in the person's work and social relations, and sometimes leads to the unhappy spectacle of the "skid row" alcoholic.

One of the most interesting research comparisons of psychological differences among people growing up in two different cultures has been made with Irish- and Italian-Americans (Singer and Opler, 1956). What makes this comparison particularly interesting is that the contrast is found within our familiar Western world. Singer and Opler observed the behavior patterns and mental symptoms of Irish-American and Italian-American schizophrenics, all suffering from serious mental disturbances, and linked these to differences in outlook between the two ethnic groups.

Sixty male schizophrenic patients in a mental hospital in New York City were carefully examined by means of observation, case history data, and personality tests. The patients were all Catholic, ranging in age from 18 to 45, comparable in education and socioeconomic status, hospitalized at about the same time, and all being between first- and third-generation Americans. Half were Irish-American and half Italian-American. The only important way in which the two groups differed was in their Irish or Italian ethnic background.

The choice of these two ethnic groups was predicated on known differences in family structure and values. The researchers wanted to determine the extent to which such ethnic differences, even following emigration from their original cultures, would be reflected in observable patterns of disturbed behavior. The Irish mother usually plays a dominant and controlling role in the family. Furthermore, in the Irish family, sexual activity is subordinated to procreation, celibacy is encouraged, courtship lacks intensity and is drawn out, and marriage is typically delayed for a long time. (The reader may recall from Chapter 3 that this social pattern of delayed marriage was brought into existence during the Irish potato famine

(a)

(b)

*Figure 4.7 "To each his own happiness":
Japanese family patterns. (a) Husbands making
a big night of it, out on the town. (b) The wife's
domain—the home. (Jacqueline Paul)*

in the mid-nineteenth century, dramatically altering a very
different previous pattern of early marriage that had resulted
in an astronomically rapid growth in population.) In the modern Irish, sexual feelings are commonly thought of as sinful
and are thus a source of considerable guilt. The Italian pattern,
in contrast, involves a dominant father. Sexuality is not only
acceptable but is cultivated as a sign of healthy maleness, as
any woman who has visited Italy and had her bottom pinched
can attest. Thus the Irish cultural pattern tends to be one of
inhibition, delay of gratification, and maternal domination,
while the Italian pattern encourages the expressive acting out
of feelings and a male-dominated family life. It would not be
surprising, therefore, to find patients of Irish and Italian descent showing quite different psychodynamics.

"As the twig is bent,
the tree's inclined."

Figure 4.8 Environmental molding of personality. (Drawing by O. Soglow; © 1937, 1965 The New Yorker Magazine, Inc.)

Singer and Opler's data revealed, indeed, that the Irish patient was far more inhibited than the Italian, was more beset by fear and guilt, and felt considerable hostility to female family members, although largely he inhibited these feelings. He was also frequently alcoholic (in 19 of the 30 patients), a symptom which was very rare in the Italians (found in only one of the 30 patients). The Italian patient, on the other hand, was far more emotionally expressive and overtly hostile, although he did not attack female family figures but usually aimed his hostility at the male parent.

These findings, like many others dealing with cultural and subcultural variations, highlight the point that an individual's way of thinking and living, and even his way of being mentally ill, is linked to the culture or subculture from which he has sprung. The social environment is somehow incorporated into our personalities, becoming an integral part of our being, and influencing our modes of thought, feeling, and action in countless ways throughout our lives. This process has been called *socialization,* and we must consider how such a process might work (Figure 4.8).

Ways society shapes our personality

Four main mechanisms of lifelong social influence will now be considered: (1) reward and punishment; (2) imitation and identification; (3) performance of role behaviors; and (4) the search for meaning and identity. All four mechanisms are undoubtedly operative in the development of personal outlooks and life styles, supplementing or contradicting each other, depending on the particular case. Debates about which is more important or dominant in one or another context need not concern us in our examination of each.

Reward and punishment One of the oldest traditions in the psychology of learning is that behavior and psychological reactions are acquired because of their consequences for the person or animal, that is, as a result of positive or negative effects. This principle of *reward and punishment* is parallel with the evolutionary concept of natural selection, which stresses *feedback* from the environment as the major determinant of whether or not a biological trait will survive and flourish. You will recall from Chapter 1 that a biological trait enhancing the species' chances of survival is perpetuated, while one which is nonadaptive is lost because with it the species fails to reproduce faster than it succumbs to environmental hazards.

When we consider behavior in the individual organism, we find that in the course of development actions leading to harm (and often pain) will tend to be rooted out, while those leading to adaptive outcomes (and satisfaction) will be acquired and repeated. The actions of each organism produce environmental consequences which in turn affect the actor, either positively or negatively. Through such environmental feedback, patterns of behavior are learned or unlearned. The principle of reward and punishment says simply that *we tend to learn that which results in rewards and fail to learn, or unlearn, that which results in punishment.* This enormously useful psychological principle is sometimes referred to as the *law of effect.*

A few decades ago, an exciting discovery appeared to link the mechanism of reward and punishment to stimulation of certain regions of the brain. James Olds had been investigating brain functions in the rat with microelectrodes (electrodes so tiny that they can introduce electrical stimulation to a very small brain tissue area), when he accidentally discovered that mild current delivered to an area near the *hypothalamus,* an important region of the midbrain (see Figure 1.14), led the rat to return repeatedly to the spot in the cage where it had received the stimulation. Later research showed that rats would learn to perform an act (like pressing a bar constructed in the cage) just to produce this electrical stimulation. It was as if the stimulation was pleasurable and the animal wanted it. In fact, it was evidently so rewarding, animals would press the bar at phenomenal rates, averaging over 2,000 times an hour for as long as 15 to 20 hours until they dropped from exhaustion (Olds and Olds, 1965). This phenomenon has since also been demonstrated with cats and monkeys. So rewarding is the stimulation that even very hungry animals, on a starvation diet for up to 10 days, will accept a more painful shock to obtain it than they will to obtain food. However, if the electrodes are implanted in the wrong area of the brain, such animals will stop responding and avoid the bar area, indicating that electrical stimulation of other, adjacent areas is unpleasant or punishing. Moreover, strong or prolonged stimulation to the same area that is rewarding is aversive, the animal avoiding it if possible. One of the intriguing possibilities in all this is that a brain center has been discovered that controls what is rewarding or pleasant; however, physiological psychologists are not agreed on this, and other hypotheses have been proposed. For example, it may be that stimulation of this particular hypothalamic area suppresses the sensation of hunger, thereby replacing the animal's normal feeding behavior. Perhaps further study of this phenomenon will provide an understanding of how the brain acts in the context of reward and punishment.

When a child engages in behavior that is rewarded by its parents, or when it expresses attitudes that lead to positive outcomes, such behavior patterns or attitudes are likely to be stamped in, that is, learned as habitual responses. Thus, when a boy shows interest in what the culture defines as masculine

[Another] . . . *control system involves behavior feedback influences, mainly in the form of reinforcing consequences. An organism that responded foresightedly on the basis of informative environmental cues but remained unaffected by the results of its actions would be too obtuse to survive for long. In fact, behavior is extensively controlled by its consequences. Responses that cause unrewarding or punishing effects tend to be discarded, whereas those that produce rewarding outcomes are retained and strengthened. Human behavior therefore cannot be fully understood without examining the regulatory influence of reinforcement. . . .*

In the minds of most people, reinforcement is usually equated with tangible rewards and punishments. Actually, human behavior is largely sustained and modified by symbolic reinforcers . . . in the form of verbal approval, reprimands, attention, affection, and rejection. . . . [From Bandura, 1973, p. 47]

As children grow older, more explicit sex-role training is introduced. Boys are encouraged to take more of an interest in mathematics and science. Boys, not girls, are given chemistry sets and microscopes for Christmas. Moreover, all children quickly learn that mommy is proud to be a moron when it comes to mathematics and science, whereas daddy knows all about those things. When a young boy returns from school all excited over a biology class, he is almost certain to be encouraged to think of becoming a physician. A girl with a similar enthusiasm is told that she might want to consider nurse's training later so she can have an interesting job to fall back on in case—God forbid—she ever needs to support herself! A very different kind of encouragement. And a girl who doggedly persists in her enthusiasm for science is likely to find her parents as horrified by the prospect of a permanent love affair with physics as they would be by the prospect of an interracial marriage. [From Bem, 1970, p. 91]

things (engaging in sports; playing with building toys, electric trains, or toy guns; acting aggressively), his parents are likely to react with pleasure and approval, thereby encouraging him in this direction. On the other hand, if he exhibits interest in what are considered feminine things (playing with dolls; playing house), his parents are likely to show disapproval and may even punish or shame him, removing the toys. On the other hand, girls are often subtly encouraged to adopt a pattern of behavior and a set of attitudes that the culture views as suitably feminine. In this way, masculine and feminine attitudes are supported by parents and other adults with whom the child comes in contact. Over the long period of childhood and adolescence these attitudes become an important part of the developing personality, generally giving a boy masculine characteristics and a girl feminine ones.

Advocates of woman's liberation recognize this when they criticize the pattern of sexual identification encouraged in our society. They argue that there is no inherent biological reason why boys should grow up career-oriented and girls should especially want to engage in homemaking and child rearing. The only reason for this pattern, they say, is its systematic inculcation by parents and the rest of society. Although this assertion may be overstated and overlooks possible biological roots of many masculine and feminine behavior patterns, it does warrant serious consideration. As we saw earlier, Margaret Mead's (1935) studies of the Tchambuli indicate that other male-female roles are indeed possible.

There can be no challenge to the point that continual reward and punishment applied to children and adolescents is an extremely powerful though not infallible social force, producing stereotyped social roles of men and women in most societies, including our own. Similarly, when a person is rewarded for what he does or thinks by getting the things he wants (such as money, candy, good grades, praise), it increases the tendency for him to behave in this way. Conversely, punishment for undesired behavior, such as driving too fast, making noise in the library, using disapproved language, stealing, or fighting, is likely to inhibit or "stamp out" such behavior in the future. In military training, young men must unlearn some of what they have learned as children, and new attitudes suitable for combat are "stamped in" through military discipline. In short, our behavior, attitudes, and habits are determined by whether or not they produce positive or negative feedback within a given environment. Such learning is often called *conditioning.*

The discovery of conditioning has had a major impact on our modern theory of learning. What is now known as *classical conditioning* has its origins in some famous experiments performed by the Russian physiologist Ivan P. Pavlov

(1849–1936). Pavlov placed a dog in a harness to study the nervous reflexes involved in salivation and digestion; he noticed that the flow of saliva was influenced not only by food placed in the dog's mouth but merely by the sight of food. Pavlov realized that some purely psychological process was taking place. The saliva flow, which is the inborn physiological response to the presence of food in the mouth, had become "conditioned," as Pavlov put it, to the sight of the food. Such a conditioned response depended on the pairing of several essential elements: (1) there had to be an "unconditioned stimulus" (food), which naturally, that is, without learning, produces the salivation (the unconditioned response); (2) these must be paired with a conditioned stimulus (the sight of the food or some other stimulus normally not capable of producing the reaction—say, a light, a tone, or a noise), so that through experience or repeated pairings it eventually comes to elicit the response (the salivation). In effect, the salivation now occurs to the light, for example, because the light has become a signal to the animal of the coming of food (Figure 4.9). The salivation which was originally an unconditioned response to food now becomes a conditioned (learned) response to the signal that food is coming. Or, put differently, appearance of the food is the "reinforcement" for the "expectation" generated by the signal.

Much research since Pavlov's experiments has been directed at discovering the rules of classical conditioning: the relations between each stimulus and response element; how a conditioned response, once acquired, is extinguished or unlearned; how one stimulus relates to another (as from one particular light or tone to another); and so on.

The *generalization* of a learned response from one stimulus to another is a very important problem that goes to the heart of the role of learning in psychological development. *Stimulus generalization* occurs when a response conditioned to a specific stimulus is triggered by other similar stimuli. Thus, if Pavlov's dog learns to salivate to a musical tone of a tuning fork, say, middle C, he will also salivate to somewhat higher or lower tones without any further experience. The more similar is the new tone to the original one, the greater the likelihood that salivation will occur and the more complete the response will be (say, in respect to the amount of salivation). This is extremely important for learning because we are rarely exposed to two situations that are exactly alike. Classical conditioning would have little significance without such generalization. Because of generalization, the response can be spread over a wide range of similar stimuli.

Consider, for example, a child who has been accidentally conditioned to react with great terror to the sight of a dog because that dog once growled or jumped all over him, fright-

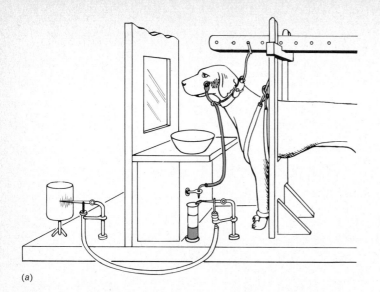

(a)

Figure 4.9 Pavlov's famous conditioning experiment. (a) Dog is strapped into a harness to minimize irrelevant movements (responses) and to help him focus on the critical stimuli. The tube attached to the salivary gland collects saliva that is secreted, the number of drops being recorded on a revolving drum. A one-way mirror allows the experimenter to observe the dog without distracting him from the food (unconditioned stimulus) or from the tone or light (conditioned stimulus). (b) Photo taken in Pavlov's laboratory of another variant of this experiment. Note tube into stomach, which permits extraction and measurement of stomach juices secreted in response to the conditioned stimulus. (Sovfoto)

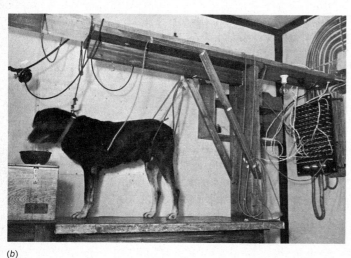

(b)

ening him badly. Such fear produces marked changes in heart rate, blood pressure, and a host of other bodily changes. Next time the child sees a dog like the original one, he again experiences great fear and all the accompanying physiological effects. Because of stimulus generalization it need not be the same dog; any dog, or any furry animal, may now evoke the conditioned response. The child has acquired a reaction much like a phobia through stimulus generalization.

By the same token, a conditioned response may be eliminated by arranging things so that the stimulus occurs without the conditioned response, using the contrary process of *extinc-*

tion. On a limited basis, this process has been used in the treatment of some incapacitating phobias acquired via classical conditioning. Many years ago, Mary Cover Jones (1924) treated a three-year-old child whose fear of a white rat had generalized to other furry animals and objects, such as rabbits, fur coats, and feathers. The problem was to confront the child with such an animal under conditions in which the conditioned fear response did not occur, a difficult task indeed. Jones first presented the child with food he liked under conditions of high security and with other children present, bringing in a much-feared rabbit only at a great distance. During many subsequent trials, the animal was very gradually brought closer so as to avoid triggering the conditioned fear response until eventually the child became used to the animal's presence and the fear was extinguished. Such procedures are the basis of certain modern methods of "behavior therapy" in which undesirable emotional symptoms are extinguished by counter-conditioning procedures. There is reason to think, however, that such procedures work only in fairly uncomplicated cases; much doubt remains about such treatment for severe phobias and other emotional disturbances in which the symptoms are thought to derive not from simple conditioning but from deep, unconscious conflicts or psychoneurotic disturbances. More will be said about this in Chapter 11.

The discovery of classical Pavlovian conditioning was a momentous one because it suggested a way to study learning in all animals, including man. For a while it was thought that such conditioning was the basic mechanism on which all learning was built, even including the most complex forms of learning in higher animals. Now, however, psychologists recognize that classical conditioning is only one form of learning, albeit an important one. Several other varieties of learning have since been discovered and explored.

Another important learning pattern has been called *operant conditioning* (or *Skinnerian conditioning,* after psychologist B. F. Skinner, who has devoted many years to investigating this phenomenon). When you teach a dog to obey commands such as "Stay" and "Come" or to do tricks such as rolling over or fetching, you are using operant conditioning. Unlike classical conditioning, in which there is a natural, biological basis for the response (food triggers salivation; an emotional stimulus produces hormone secretion by a gland), in training a dog to come on command you have to first get the animal to make the response before you can get him to do it under command or signal, since there is no ordinary stimulus to which it is attached biologically. The response is something he can do naturally, and you want it to be elicited by your command, but it must come first before he can be "taught" to do it at the proper moment. Skinner (1971) calls reactions such as

It is now clear that we must take into account what the environment does to an organism not only before but after it responds. Behavior is shaped and maintained by its consequences. Once this fact is recognized, we can formulate the interaction between organism and environment in a much more comprehensive way. [From Skinner, 1971, p. 18]

Figure 4.10   B. F. Skinner, leading investigator of operant conditioning. (Courtesy of B. F. Skinner)

Figure 4.11   Another way to look at conditioning. (Drawing by Birkett, Punch Magazine; © *1971 Toronto Sun Syndicate, Inc.)*

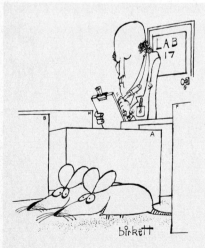

"I'm getting him conditioned beautifully—every time I run through the maze, he throws me a bit of cheese."

salivation or blinking of the eye *respondent behavior;* they are responses to specific stimuli and seem to be under the control of such stimuli. The term *operant behavior* is used to refer to actions that seem to be spontaneous and perhaps internally provoked rather than being a response to a specific external stimulus, as in the case of salivating to food (Figure 4.10).

A Skinnerian experiment on operant conditioning consists of putting an animal, such as a rat or pigeon, in a box in which there is a movable bar; when pressed down, this bar releases a pellet of food (the reward). As the rat moves about, he accidentally presses the bar and the food falls into the tray. The rat eats the food, and so the bar-pressing act is rewarded. If the bar pressing continues to lead to food, the rate of bar pressing increases and is "reinforced." On the other hand, if food no longer appears, the bar-pressing response is "extinguished" (Figure 4.11).

In operant conditioning, just as in classical conditioning, it is possible to explore systematically the conditions under which changes in animal behavior take place in response to changes in the environment. For example, one can determine systematically the frequency of reward that works best to produce learning of the desired response. Research has shown that skipping the reward on occasional trials is useful because the emerging habit is more resistant to extinction, meaning that it remains in force longer in spite of later cessation of the reward. Or, one can also determine systematically the rewards that work best in the learning of a habitual response. Such knowledge is important not only for what it tells us about animal behavior and capabilities, but because patterns of learning such as the above also have their counterparts in human life, giving rise to practical questions such as, "How consistently or in what pattern should one reward a child for something he does, and what kinds of rewards work best for a five-year-old child, a ten-year-old, or an adult?"

One of the most interesting features of the operant-conditioning pattern of learning is its capacity to permit the "shaping" of behavior, that is, if the animal is capable of making the desired response, it can be systematically modified in any direction by subtly manipulating the reward. For example, a pigeon can be made to hold its head high as it walks by rewarding every occasion when it raises its head slightly above average and not rewarding the "wrong" response. Pigeons have also been taught by Skinner to play a limited version of ping-pong through operant-conditioning principles. Animal trainers use essentially the same procedures, and the marvelous repertoires one sees in circus animals, and also those of trained whales, porpoises, and seals seen at marine exhibits, illustrate the power of operant-conditioning principles in systematically training and *shaping* the behavior of animals.

Such principles have also proven very useful with man, since he also responds to his environment through feedback. Studies of human conditioning have great relevance to problems of education and in treatment of mental patients and children with learning defects. One recent book (Mehrabian, 1970) attempts to spell out the practical procedures for experimental conditioning in man and discusses implications of its use. There is also a growing school of psychotherapy, referred to as behavior modification or behavior therapy, in which principles of conditioning (both classical and operant) are used in the treatment of phobias, sexual impotence and frigidity, and other adaptive problems (Figure 4.12). One thriving school of psychopathology tends to explain abnormal or deviant patterns of behavior in terms of faulty conditioning or disturbed patterns of reward and punishment from the social environment (see Ullmann and Krasner, 1969). More will be said about this too in Chapter 11.

There is much debate about the exact mechanisms by which the pairing of stimuli and responses or rewards and punishments leads to systematic changes in adaptive behavior. For some theorists, such acquired behavior changes are best explained by reference to complex cognitive events within the individual. The contrast between the simple, conditioning view of learning and a cognitive approach might be symbolized by the distinction between learning by rote memory and drill versus learning by understanding principles and perceiving relationships. Thus, for example, Edward C. Tolman (1948) thought of learning, even in relatively simple animals like the rat and certainly in man, as involving a kind of *cognitive map* or representation of a situation. Learning takes place through

The trouble is that when we punish a person for behaving badly, we leave it up to him to discover how to behave well, and he can then get credit for behaving well. But if he behaves well for reasons we have just examined, it is the environment that must get the credit. At issue is an attribute of autonomous man. Men are to behave well only because they are good. Under a "perfect" system no one needs goodness. [From Skinner, 1971, pp. 66–67]

Figure 4.12   Behavior control in action. (Drawing by Tandberg; © 1971 United Feature Syndicate, Inc.)

signs, that is, a learned expectation that one stimulus (such as a correct turn in a maze or a dead end) will be followed by another. In many cases, instead of learning a fixed sequence of stimulus and response elements, we learn a complex cognitive scheme (or "map") of the situation, as when a child learns to walk from his home to school he recognizes the many "signs" along the way. From this standpoint the way people *interpret* (or *misinterpret*) the contingencies of their lives becomes especially important. If they believe fallaciously that some action will lead to reward, and never catch on to their misapprehension, then that action will probably continue to be performed rather than eliminated. *Actual* reward and punishment may often be less important in controlling human behavior than *expectations* about them.

Skinner himself regards as unscientific and misleading any speculation about inner mental events such as cognitive representations, associations, and the like. What must be discovered, says Skinner, are the environmental rules or contingencies experienced by the person or animal in the course of his life, and these guide how he acts and reacts. Thus, these two patterns of learning, classical and instrumental conditioning, merely provide some of the data about how our behavior

Note 4.4

Again and again in psychology we come across the term *theory,* and while we are considering theoretical debates about the nature of learning, a few words are in order about what this term means. One of the major tasks of any scientific effort is to bring order and meaning to the multitudes of observations about the world. Psychology is no exception. Psychological theories represent a systematic intellectual effort to make sense out of multiple observations.

A theory is a kind of cognitive map of some portion of the world: in psychological terms, it may be an analysis of people and what makes them tick. A theory deals largely with unobservables, with processes, rather than with things that can be measured directly. It is speculative or interpretive rather than observational (empirical or factual). The word "model" sometimes is used instead, pointing up the fact that theories commonly attempt to explain a phenomenon by analogy to some other well-known mechanism of the physical world, as when we say that the brain

works somewhat like the feedback mechanism of a thermostat (see Chapter 1).

Some psychological theories are extremely ambitious in attempting to encompass much or everything that is known about human behavior, just as Newtonian physics and later Einsteinian physics are attempts to account for all of the known physical world. Alternatively, theories may be limited to a narrow segment of human behavior and experience, say, how the person responds to threats, how social motives arise and shape actions, or why a psychotic patient has hallucinations. Large-scale theories are made up of many components, each of which are tied together by certain assumptions and principles about the world.

Competing psychological systems make somewhat different theoretical assumptions about man and how he is influenced, and they construct differing analytic models of the processes involved in thought, feeling, and action. Such theories often differ in fundamental outlook. Psychologists often

hold divergent philosophies of science and have different outlooks about what theories are supposed to do. Some may believe that the primary aim of a theory is to make possible the practical prediction and control of human behavior, testing only how well they succeed at this; others may see theory as a means of bettering our knowledge, regardless of whether it has instant practical uses.

Theory is constructed partly by means of *inductive* reasoning, that is, by moving from the particular observation to a general concept or principle. First we observe something and then consider what it could mean in a more general sense. Theories are evaluated or tested mainly by *deductive* reasoning, that is, by going from the general principle to the particular case. We reason as follows: "Given this or that theoretical principle or process, certain things should follow," and then we look to see whether or not the expected relationships (hypotheses) are indeed found. Thus, theory and empirical observation are closely intertwined and the

is shaped by the environment through reward and punishment; but how these data are interpreted varies greatly among the psychological theories of learning. Although they have been merely touched upon here, these are by no means trivial debates, and many psychologists concerned with psychological development and learning have devoted their lives to testing out the extent to which the various theoretical approaches are fruitful in helping us understand human and animal behavior patterns (see Note 4.4).

There are of course innumerable cases, to be found in the daily newspapers, in which no amount of punishment seems to have been capable of "stamping out" undesirable behavior, for reasons which are not entirely clear. Despite punishment and threat of punishment, aggressive, antisocial behavior of delinquent youngsters and criminal adults has obviously not been reduced. Very often the parent who severely and consistently punishes his child for aggressive, antisocial acts succeeds only in fixing (even encouraging) such acts rather than eliminating them. In such an instance, one might reason that punishment has been ineffectively applied, or perhaps that its effective use is difficult to accomplish in real-life, nonlaboratory situations. Parents of delinquents and criminals

activities of observing nature and trying to make general sense of it are continuous in psychology, as in all scientific disciplines. Since theories are provisional ways of trying to understand the observed phenomena of the world, physical or psychological, they are constantly being revised or dropped in favor of other models as new facts emerge.

Psychologists generally consider the best theories to be those which can *encompass the largest range of facts* about the psychological world within a self-consistent analytic system. All theories in use help us to do this more or less, so that other criteria of good theory are also relevant. One of these is that the theory be *vulnerable to disproof;* that is, one should be able to conceive of observations that would make the theory untenable. Many of our theories are stated so loosely that it is difficult to imagine how they might be disproved, but they may have temporary utility in guiding the direction of our thought and observation until restated or refined later on. Another criterion of good

theory, considered by many to be the most important one for a developing science, is its *fruitfulness.* Does it, in effect, lead to new observations that improve our understanding? Many theories that have ultimately been discarded in favor of newer ones have been very fruitful in this sense, though inadequate in other ways. Other theories seem not to generate any research and new findings. Finally, other things being equal (for example, two theories may be equally effective in accounting for observations), good theories are also *elegantly simple* in that they depend on a minimum of assumptions and propositions about the phenomena under consideration. Such a theory is powerful in that a few basic propositions enable us to make sense out of manifold observations. Psychology, which is a recent science and is a long way from such elegance and precision, has long envied physics in that its basic theoretical propositions about the physical world have great power.

The technical concerns and debates in

the philosophy of science as applied to psychology are a good deal more complex than have been indicated here, but the reader should not be overwhelmed by this thought. When all is said and done, the most important thing to remember now is that all theoretical attempts in psychology are highly fluid and tentative, often dealing with different psychological arenas rather than being directly competitive in trying to account for all the known facts. Throughout this text casual reference will often be made to theory, to tentative principles or rules, to guesses and hypotheses about empirical relationships, and to inferences from and interpretations of observations. This is all part of psychology's effort to make sense out of whatever facts are in evidence in various areas of human behavior and experience. For the interested reader who wants to go deeper into the philosophy of science, especially as it applies to the social sciences, one of the best sources is a book by Abraham Kaplan (1964).

are very likely to have been punitive, physically cruel, and rejecting in their treatment of the child, as William and Joan McCord (1956, 1958) have pointed out in their studies of delinquency. There is also the aberrant phenomenon of *masochism*, in which sexual arousal is dependent on, or at least facilitated by, physical or psychological punishment; instead of such punishment extinguishing sexual feelings and gratification it actually strengthens them. The masochist therefore will seek rather than avoid punishment. Clearly the line between pain and pleasure is somewhat blurred in such cases.

Persistence of aggressive disobedience in spite of frequent and severe punishment (as well as masochistic longing for punishment in many wrongdoers) renders corporal punishment an often ineffective means of reducing antisocial acts. Better ways must be found to change such behavior. We need information about the conditions under which punishment does or does not work to control antisocial activity. Any given type of punishment is probably only one factor in a complex mixture of pain and pleasure. Perhaps while the child is being physically hurt, he is also being simultaneously rewarded by having emotionally aroused the parent. In some cases punishment may be the only form of psychological contact between the parent and the child; in others, its negative effects may be mitigated and its significance altered because the child welcomes it as a sign of parental interest, which though painful, is often preferable to indifference. The fact that in delinquents punishment has often been associated with parental rejection may facilitate the delinquent child's retaliatory rejection of the parent and strengthen his building resolve to go his own way or to beat the parent at his own game. In this connection, Sheldon and Eleanor Glueck (1950) long ago suggested that the delinquents they had studied were unimpressed with punishment because they had had so much experience with it from rejecting parents. Punishment means much more when it comes from someone who you believe loves you and who you respect than when it comes from someone who appears to reject or hate you and does not have your best interests at heart.

In sum, we are beginning to recognize that the effects of punishment depend on a host of other factors, such as how consistently it is administered, whether it is used jointly with reward, the attitude with which it is given, the values of the person and his peers (for example, whether he thinks he is right or wrong or how his peers feel about his "infraction"), and whether the child believes he can control by his own actions whether he will receive punishment, reward, or neither. Moreover, the reader will recall from Chapter 2 that those who feel powerless to influence by their actions whether they are rewarded or punished are likely not to be very much affected (see Rotter, 1966). In any event, some learning psychologists have either rejected punishment as an educational device or have reservations about its general effectiveness. A major debate about its values and limitations has been going on in psychology and education for some time. It is clearly an important problem with major practical consequences for child rearing, education, and the judicial and penal system.

Imitation and identification   Another reason why punishment often fails is that a different, sometimes contradictory learning process is also at work simultaneously, namely *imitation* and *identification*. What happens is that when children observe their parents punishing them for their aggressiveness, the parents are also providing a model that the children imitate and identify with (Figure 4.13). Social psychologist Roger Brown (1965, pp. 394–395) puts it this way:

> Parents who beat their children for aggression intend to "stamp out" the aggression. The fact that the treatment does not work as intended suggests that the . . . theory is wrong. A beating may be regarded as an instance of the behavior it is supposed to stamp out. If children are more disposed to learn by imitation or example than by "stamping out" they ought to learn from a beating to beat. This seems to be roughly what happens.

The statement that we develop attitudes by imitating models is incomplete, however, since this still does not give us rules about the kinds of people who come to be models for children and about the traits selected or rejected for imitation. Every parent recognizes that his child has acquired some of his attitudes, values, and behavior patterns, but obviously not all. Some have evidently come from the child's mother and others from his father. Other adults within and outside the family may also have served as models. Why has he modeled himself after some and not others? Why has he picked up some traits and not others from the people he has used as models? The answers to these important questions are still very fragmentary.

There are at least three likely bases for the selection of a model. One is the *similarity between the child and the parent.* Freud assumed that the boy develops masculine attitudes and behavior patterns because he recognizes his sexual similarity to the father; both have a penis and are males. Conversely, the girl takes on the attitudes of the mother, whom she resembles sexually. The die is thus cast for sexual and social identification and development. This is reinforced, of course, by other actions of the parents. By reference to sexual similarity, Freud attempted to explain not only the formation of general attitudes and personality patterns but sexual roles as well.

Another possible factor in modeling is the parent's *power to control* the good things of life (Bandura and Walters, 1963).

"This will teach you not to hit people."

Figure 4.13   Or, don't do what I do, do what I say! (Drawing by Stanley Stamaty; © 1951 The Saturday Review Associates, Inc. Used with permission.)

There are several reasons why modeling influences play a paramount role in learning in everyday life. When mistakes are costly or dangerous, skillful performances can be established without needless errors by providing competent models who demonstrate how the required activities should be performed. If learning proceeded solely through direct experience, most people would never survive their formative years because mistakes often result in fatal consequences. Some complex behaviors, of course, can be produced only through the influence of models. If children had no opportunity to hear speech, for example, it would be virtually impossible to teach them the linguistic skills that constitute a language. Where certain forms of behavior can be conveyed only by social cues, modeling is an indispensable aspect of learning. Even in instances in which it is possible to establish new skills through other means, the process of acquisition can be considerably shortened by providing appropriate models. [From Bandura, 1973, p. 68]

[If] man's sense of guilt goes back to the murder of the father, that was undoubtedly an instance of "remorse," and yet are we to suppose that there were no conscience and feelings of guilt before the act on that occasion? If so, where did the remorse come from then? This instance must explain to us the riddle of the sense of guilt and so make an end of our difficulties. And it will do so, as I believe. This remorse was the result of the very earliest primal ambivalence of feelings towards the father: the sons hated him, but they loved him too; after their hate against him had been satisfied by their aggressive acts, their love came to expression in their remorse about the deed, set up the super-ego [conscience] by identification with the father, gave it the father's power to punish as he would have done the aggression they had performed, and created the restrictions which should prevent a repetition of the deed. And since impulses to aggressions against the father were repeated in the next generations, the feelings of guilt, too, persisted, and were further reinforced every time an aggression was suppressed anew and made over to the super-ego. At this point, it seems to me, we can at last clearly perceive the part played by love in the origin of conscience and the fatal inevitableness of the sense of guilt. It is not really a decisive matter whether one has killed one's father or abstained from the deed; one must feel guilty in either case, for guilt is the expression of the conflict of ambivalence. . . .
[From Freud, 1968, p. 66]

Other things being equal, the child should imitate the parent who is most capable of creating desirable outcomes and to want to be like him or her so that he too will achieve this power to master the environment. This principle also implies the sort of traits selected as desirable; those which appear in the child's mind to give the parent maximum control over life's desirables should be more attractive than those which are either irrelevant or thwart effective living.

The third basis of modeling is the need of the relatively powerless child to neutralize the threat imposed by the powerful parent or parent-substitute. This process has been called "identification with the aggressor" by Freud, who has written extensively about it (1961). *Identification with the aggressor* grows out of the Oedipus complex, that is, the idea of a family triangle of love and hate in which the boy competes with the father for the mother and the girl is in competition with the mother for the father. How this triangle originates is not important here. It was presumed by Freud to be a universal feature of human development. The fact of its existence poses a crucial problem for the child, and its resolution represents an essential step in normal psychological development. The boy is no match for the father, who is obviously big and powerful and whose potential retaliation for the boy's competitive aggression is fantasized to take the form of castration, —the cutting off of his genitals, hence loss of his masculinity. The girl has a similar problem in competing with the mother, whom she sees as having lost her penis as a consequence of the same struggle when she was a child. During the period before puberty, the child usually resolves this problem by the process of identifying with the aggressor, that is, by repressing the offending and dangerous sexual urges toward the opposite-sexed parent and the competitive hostility toward the like-sexed parent, and in this way saves himself (or herself) from the danger since the parent-competitor no longer has any reason to threaten harm. In this process of defensive identification, the child begins to take on the attitudes, values, and behavior patterns of the same-sexed parent, identifying defensively with that parent (see also Chapter 12).

Before we leave the process of imitation, something should be said about whether such conforming actions are merely external and superficial or whether the individual takes the model's attitudes and behaviors on as integral parts of his own personality. Social psychologist Herbert Kelman (1961) has suggested that in socialization there can be a wide range of involvement, from *compliance* (the superficial adoption of an outlook or attitude merely for display) to *internalization* (the identification spoken of by Freud and involving relatively permanent, fundamental, and unconscious acquisitions to the personality).

The most limited degree of conformity, that of compliance, comprises our most superficial response to social pressures: we do or say what is expected of us only because we think it will impress others and make them respond positively to us. We might laugh at someone's jokes (say, those of the boss or teacher) even if they do not seem funny, and in doing so hope to ingratiate ourselves with that person (Figure 4.14). Somehow one usually recognizes this as a "dishonest" act, yet it is embedded so firmly in the fabric of our social life that it takes place in the main with little conflict or distress and perhaps even without much awareness.

At the other end of the continuum is complete internalization or identification. In such instances, the models presented by the parent or others result in imitation that is not just "skin deep." Rather, the internalized attitudes become part of our own value system, thereafter functioning automatically and perhaps also unconsciously. Our most important outlooks and attitudes are probably internalized quite early in life; although they may be overlaid by later adult modes of thinking and feeling, deeply internalized attitudes are especially resistant to change, even when they are rejected on the surface. In Freudian thought the emotional contents of the "primitive unconscious" governs many of our adult patterns of behavior without our awareness of its influence.

The above distinction has also been expressed differently, namely, as two levels of personality, the surface and the underlying or deep level. Compliance is acting in accord with social

Figure 4.14   The amiable employer-employee relationship—a million laughs! (Drawing by J. J. Dunleavy)

"Now that I've complimented you on your work, and you've laughed at my little jokes, let's return to this matter of your salary."

[The] social learning theory of sex role development tends to emphasize different employment of rewards and punishments contingent upon the child's sex. The processes considered in social learning theory are based on this manipulation of punishments and rewards, which produces sex-appropriate behavior within the context of social agents (family, friends, or peers), with subsequent generalization of this learning in response to others. The adoption of sex-appropriate behavior is reflected in the increased frequency with which such behaviors occur in the repertoire of the boy or girl. Following this initial learning, a new and more powerful method of acquiring sex role occurs through imitation learning, which is simply the observation of an appropriate model's behavior resulting in the acquisition of additional and complex behavior patterns. Apparently, imitation learning does not require the child to perform the learned behaviors immediately or to receive reinforcement of the new behavior patterns. Finally, the most complicated sex-appropriate patterns of behavior are gained by the developing child without evident reinforcement by other agents, which has led social learning theorists to posit the mechanism of identification, termed identificatory learning, which implies that the child develops a drive or motive to be like a model, typically the parent of the same sex. This particular explanatory concept is usually employed to account for the acquisition of complex, integrated patterns of sex role behavior which were not preceded by any specific training. . . . [From Rosenberg and Sutton-Smith, 1972, pp. 54–55]

Figure 4.15 Establishing his role: the little shaver. (Robert Smith; Black Star)

pressures merely on the surface; underneath, either unknown to the observer or even to the actor himself, contrary outlooks and attitudes are also present and influential in the person's life. Asch's (1956) subjects who gave an answer they knew to be wrong were displaying compliance, while those subjects who were genuinely surprised at their "mistakes" and did not sense that they were responding to social pressure appear to have automatically internalized the views of the group and thus minimized, perhaps by repression, any conflict between themselves and others. By accommodation, their own identity and that of the external social world was made harmonious.

One of the major tasks each person must face is in some obscure fashion to be able to synthesize the often contradictory forces of individuation and socialization, remaining a separate and independent entity while not being alienated from the social world in which he lives (Rank, 1952; Fromm, 1955). This individual problem has several important implications for moral development. One person may behave in accordance with certain firm standards of morality because he feels these standards deeply. Another, appearing to act equally morally on the surface, may do so not out of conviction but because it is the way current societal norms or authorities tell him to act. For him, morality is largely a matter of conformity to rules of the moment, and if these rules change, his standards of conduct will change too.

This question also affects education. We speak here of "formal" education (that is, teaching in school or by parental injunction) versus "informal" education (when the child models his behavior after the parent's conduct). Many primitive societies do not have formal schools, although parents systematically train their children to perform the skilled tasks required for the adaptive functioning of the individual and the society. In complex advanced societies, technology and societal values are inculcated in youth through systems of formal schooling, so that standards of culture are maintained from generation to generation.

When children are educated in school or through other formal efforts specifying what they must believe and how they are to act and feel, what is typically assimilated by the child is how he "ought" to behave. However, this behavior is rarely internalized. Real internalization is more likely to occur from informal modeling of adult figures (Figure 4.15), and this can be contradictory to what is learned formally, though it need not be. For example, we are likely to learn what our parents, ministers, or teachers would like us to believe about God, democracy, proper social conduct, morality, and such. But we are also likely to acquire through imitation or modeling the patterns we see in our elders. Formal education often produces superficial social behavior, outlooks, and attitudes, in short, compliance, but whether we take on these traits by internalization may well depend on the conduct of the adults whom we model. The child may be taught not to lie both at school and by parental injunction, but at the same time he may observe his parents lying to him or to friends and relatives. Under these circumstances, and if he has a positive relationship with his parents, the child may learn "correct" ways of behaving, which he can display appropriately as needed, but he may also internalize his parents' ways of thinking, feeling, and acting, which are quite contrary to what he has learned formally. One of the major problems of growing up is coming to accept such discrepancies between the way our heroes behave and the patterns of conduct they urge on us—"Do as I say, not as I do."

The playing of social roles Although conventional wisdom suggests that outlooks and attitudes cause actions, there is abundant evidence that the opposite is also true, namely, that behavior causes outlooks and attitudes, although in such matters it is usually very difficult to unravel causes and effects. One example is the observation (Lieberman, 1956) that the attitudes of a group of factory workers changed sharply when they were either promoted to the role of foreman or elected to the position of union steward. As common sense suggests, those who were made union stewards become more prounion, while those who became foremen shifted their attitudes in favor of management. These cognitive-affective changes took place shortly after the new role was undertaken. Later, however, when economic conditions forced some of the foremen to go back to the rank-and-file status, their attitudes reverted back too. In short, changes in behavior or, more strictly, in the behavioral roles people play, also seem to result in changes in attitudes (Bem, 1970).

Quite a few research studies have dealt with this phenomenon. An example is a field experiment at Yale by Arthur Cohen (Brehm and Cohen, 1962). The event precipitating the research was a student "riot" in which the New Haven police had intervened, leading to accusations of police brutality, and highly emotional and bitter feelings on the part of most of the student body. Cohen selected students at random and asked them to write a strong essay entitled "Why the New Haven Police Actions Were Justified," thus arguing in favor of the police. Some of the students were offered ten dollars to write the essay, some five dollars, others one dollar, and still others fifty cents. Having written the essay, each student was also asked to indicate his actual opinion of the police actions, and the opinion of a comparison group that had not written the essay was also obtained in the same way. This procedure was employed to discover whether the behavior of writing the essay in favor of the police action would result in a more favorable attitude toward the police, and whether the amount of money used to induce the student to write the essay made any difference.

Cohen found that there was no difference in attitude between the students who were paid either five or ten dollars for writing the essay and those in the comparison group who never wrote the essay; both groups still considered the police very unjustified. However, students who had been paid one dollar became significantly more favorable to the police actions following the writing of their essays, and those paid only fifty cents were made even more favorable by the essay-writing task. In short, the less they were paid, the more they changed in the positive direction.

Most explanations of this type of finding have emphasized the need to justify the prior actions that have been taken, in this case the essay. If you have been paid handsomely (ten or five dollars), there is no problem for you to resolve since you can easily attribute your stance to the money you have received rather than to an initially favorable attitude. If, on the other hand, you have been paid very little, then to go on record in favor of the police must somehow be justified in some other way, since otherwise it seems to reflect on your actual feelings in the matter or makes you appear rather foolish. By admitting a moderately favorable attitude, you justify rationally your willingness to write a favorable essay. Many decisions, taken for other reasons at the outset, are afterwards justified by a shift in expressed attitude to make such decisions comprehensible. However, the extent to which the attitude really changes or merely reflects a superficial saving of face is not clear. Another possibility is that in marshalling arguments in favor of the police action, new thoughts about the event had been entertained, allowing perhaps a real shift in attitude.

In any event, psychologists have become keenly aware that one way to change attitudes may be to have people play social roles to which they are unaccustomed. Whatever explanation is offered, observations such as the above provide examples of the shaping of attitudes by actions. Such a possibility is very important from a practical standpoint, since many efforts to change attitudes of prejudice, for example, hinge on laws designed to force behavioral compliance (for example, to end segregation by busing children to desegregated schools). The effect of these laws on attitudes depends on the possibility that people will change how they feel if they can only be made to change their behavior. To what extent and under what conditions "stateways can make folkways" or, more accurately, laws that are obeyed can make attitudes, is still an open issue requiring considerable further study.

The search for meaning and identity   The chief limitation of the three mechanisms described above is that they imply a passive human animal, shaped by external rewards and punishment, by the observed actions, thoughts, and feelings of parents and other adult models, or by actions forced by imposed social conditions. One gets the image of the child picking up the outlooks of parents and of the larger society as a sponge soaks up fluid, with little or no selectivity or judgment.

However, no child ever comes out exactly like a parent; quite the contrary, although there is much that he picks up from his family and the larger culture, each child grows up into a distinctive adult with qualities of his own and with new attitudes, values, and behavior patterns not found in the parents and other adult models. There are two parents rather than one, and countless others on whom the modeling is based. Rewards and punishments vary too, even within the same family. So the child is exposed not to one consistent pattern of influence but many and often contradictory patterns from which he must pick and choose a course of his own. Thus, a better metaphor for the process of socialization than a sponge soaking up influence would be that of a selective filter. Each of us is an evaluating, searching being. Our experiences are constantly being filtered through a perceptual and cognitive sieve in accordance with our own requirements and unique judgments. We are not simply "conditioned," if by this is meant that we respond exclusively to a neat calculus of pain and pleasure. We can break our so-called conditioning; indeed we can and do look beyond the immediate rewards and punishments and our limited models of childhood, and in the process of growth establish new outlooks. Thus, in addition to the more or less passive conditioning processes, each person's outlook and life style are created through an active searching for meaning in life and, to the limits of his intellectual powers, an effort to construct a workable and consistent scheme by which he can understand himself and the world in which he lives (see, for example, Frankl, 1963).

We know very little about how this works, but one of the favored principles is that people always seek to maintain *consistency*. The theme of self-consistency has had a long history and tradition in psychological thought, and it has taken several different forms. One is expressed in the psychology of conflict and its resolution. We are said to face conflict throughout our lives. Some conflicts arise between the needs of the individual and the demands of the environment, as in the case of sexual impulses that are disapproved of by society. Other conflicts are intrapsychic, that is, they operate within the person, as when a person feels strong hostility toward others but has internalized moral standards treating such hostility as reprehensible. Freud built his theory of the mind largely out

The role of power in American life is a curious one. The privilege of controlling the actions or of affecting the income and property of other persons is something that no one of us can profess to seek or admit to possessing. No American ever runs for office because of an avowed desire to govern. He seeks to serve—and then only in response to the insistent pressure of friends or of that anonymous, but oddly vocal, fauna which inhabit the grass roots. We no longer have public officials, only public servants. The same scrupulous avoidance of the terminology of power characterizes American business. The head of the company is no longer the boss—the term survives only as an amiable form of address—but the leader of the team. . . . [Despite] this convention, which outlaws ostensible pursuit of power and which leads to a constant search for euphemisms to disguise its possession, there is no indication that, as a people, we are averse to power. [From J. K. Galbraith, American capitalism, p. 25. Boston: Houghton Mifflin, 1956]

of the ways people experience and deal with conflicts (between biological impulses, which he called the *id,* and external realities as perceived by the person, the *ego;* and between either of these and the social conscience—the *superego*). He viewed psychopathology as the inadequate resolution of such conflict.

The essential feature of conflict between two impulses is that resolution of the struggle by gratifying one impulse requires frustration of the other one. A harmonious or consistent psychological structure is not possible unless the basic conflicts of living are resolved, since they imply that the individual will be torn continuously between contradictory or incompatible impulses and attitudes. Sometimes the emphasis in the consistency principle is placed on the ways an individual learns to resolve conflict (Miller, 1944; Lewin, 1935), sometimes on the pathological consequences (Freud, 1936, 1961), and sometimes on the way the person seeks consistency, or avoids it, in attitude and behavior (Festinger, 1957).

In social psychology, the consistency principle has been a major influence for many years and is perhaps best illustrated by the concept of *cognitive dissonance.* Leon Festinger (1957) maintained that if the cognitive elements of an attitude, that is, any knowledge, opinion, or belief about the environment, oneself, or one's behavior, are *inconsistent* or contradictory, this will motivate one to attempt to eliminate the inconsistency by some cognitive change. An example might be an American Jew who has been steadily opposed to American participation in the Indochina War and who in consequence experienced cognitive dissonance (conflict) after the Six-day War between the Arabs and Israelis in 1967. His position about how the United States should respond to Israeli needs for military support seemed to contradict his antiwar position that the United States should not interfere in the fate of other nations such as Vietnam. This inconsistency involves distress or tension that might be resolved by changing his stance on Vietnam (for example, by becoming a "hawk") or by rejecting the idea of United States responsibility for Israel. Many people in this bind have actually resolved it by doing just this, while others have solved the problem by further differentiating their position on war, arguing that not all wars are bad, only some.

The essential idea put forth here is a simple one, namely, that as individuals struggle to fashion their views of themselves and the world in which they live they seek to create a self-consistent, harmonious system of outlooks and attitudes as a platform on which to build their lives. Wherever possible, outlooks and attitudes will be constructed that do not contradict one another in their basic cognitive elements or premises. When an individual fails in this, as to some extent he must, he experiences tension or distress, which motivates use of any of a variety of psychological devices that permit him to cope with the conflict and resolve it.

Although the idea of a motive to preserve cognitive consistency has been a most popular approach to the study of attitudes in the laboratory, questions have been raised about the extent to which the principle can be generalized to naturally occurring events in real life. It has been suggested, for example, that in the normal course of events people neither look for or notice such inconsistencies and often appear to tolerate them without being particularly troubled (see Freedman, 1968). With this in mind, Irwin Silverman (1971) has studied the way people handle naturally occurring cognitive inconsistencies. The personal crisis undergone by Senator Edward M. ("Ted") Kennedy, an important public figure, seemed to be an ideal situation in which to examine this. Kennedy's career and public support were endangered by a July 1969 episode that took place on an island off Cape Cod, Massachusetts, leading to the death of a girl with whom he was driving late at night after a party. His car plunged off a bridge on a country road and into an estuary, a dangerous body of rushing water. Kennedy managed to save himself, but the girl drowned.

The Senator pleaded guilty to leaving the scene of an accident and was given a two-month suspended sentence. Newspapers and magazines had a field day. Much of the public (well over a third) felt that Kennedy had "failed to tell the real truth" in the matter, as was revealed by a Harris poll in August 1969. Many questions seemed to be left unanswered. Chief among these was the reason for Kennedy's long delay in reporting the accident, during which he had evidently returned to his hotel and then to the scene of the party on Chappaquiddick Island before making his report.

Silverman constructed a questionnaire to assess the extent of attitude change toward Kennedy as a function of these events. The questionnaire was administered during the third week following the accident to a sample of 35 faculty members, 57 graduate students, 8 undergraduates, and 2 laboratory technicians at the University of Florida at Gainesville. All but 11 of the subjects were male, about half being in the early twenties, but with some subjects ranging in age up to the early sixties. This sample of people is hardly representative of the population at large, but it is nevertheless instructive to see how this group reacted to this tragic event.

The results of Silverman's survey are too extensive and complex to review here. However, certain of his findings bear particularly on the capacity of people to tolerate cognitive inconsistency. Silverman found, for example, that those respondents who reported not having changed their favorable attitude toward Kennedy after the incident showed a greater degree of tolerance for inconsistency than would be expected from the principle of cognitive consistency. For example, of 49 subjects maintaining highly positive attitudes toward Kennedy even after the accident, 29 percent reported believing that his court sentence had been too lenient; 61 percent believed that a private citizen would have been treated more severely; 65 percent admitted the possibility, if not the probability, that the drowned girl's life might have been saved if Kennedy had not delayed reporting the accident; 20 percent admitted the possibility that Kennedy was aware of the added risk to her life when he did delay; and 64 percent thought that his delay was probably or definitely based, at least partly, on concern for his reputation. Yet in spite of these very damaging beliefs, these subjects persisted in their highly positive view of Kennedy, both as a person and as a potential candidate for President (see Note 4.5).

In addition, of this group of 49 subjects who stated not having changed their positive opinion of Kennedy, only 37 percent excused him for the delay in reporting the accident, as evidenced by their failure to mention the supportive reasons

Note 4.5

Silverman's research (1971) on the effects of the Chappaquiddick incident on attitudes toward Senator Edward Kennedy raises the important question of the *representativeness* of the subject samples used in that study and in psychological research in general. We are usually not interested only in the particular people studied in such research, but seek to generalize from those people to large groups or to people in general, how they think, feel, and act, and the factors that influence this.

Silverman was trying to say something about the American public at large, or perhaps about people of any country, and the generalizations about cognitive inconsistency reflect this very broad concern. However, a glance at the characteristics of the people he questioned makes evident that they are not a representative or large sample of Americans. His subjects were predominantly males working or studying in a university setting located in a particular part of Florida. In consequence, we cannot be sure that what he found applies to all or most people, though it certainly could.

Public opinion surveys of attitudes toward social or political issues, or toward products in the marketplace, face exactly the same problem. When a poll is made of public attitudes toward, say, a national candidate for political office, the accuracy of the poll is ultimately tested in the election itself. Such polls are frequently accurate even though based on a comparatively small number of people. This is accomplished by well-established techniques of obtaining so-called stratified or *representative samples*. If the pollster wishes to predict the election results, his survey should be limited to those who are eligible to vote. Representativeness is accomplished by arranging to have the exact proportion of individuals of different types that is found in the voting population at large. Thus, a representative sample will include the same proportion of whites, blacks, chicanos, Orientals, wealthy, poor, Protestants, Catholics, Jews, people in the North, South, East, and West, from cities or rural areas, and so on, as is found in the voting public at large. Any group that affects voting behavior must be taken into account; otherwise the estimate will be off the mark.

The same principle applies more or less to research on psychological processes, though it is seldom taken as seriously in practice. For example, much psychological research is done with college sophomores who are most accessible to study, and doubts have sometimes been expressed about whether what is learned with students is applicable to the population as a whole. The problem is not so acute in some types of research, especially that which is oriented toward processes thought to be universal in mankind, though we cannot assume that they are universal without comparable studies with many kinds of people. In the absence of evidence that a generalization applies universally, we must always also have some reservations about this. As our knowledge advances, we are able to refine our generalizations more and more, and to state the exact conditions under which they apply. Such detail is as important in the advancement of our understanding as are the broad generalizations themselves. And if we are interested in the application of psychological knowledge, such precision is absolutely necessary. For example, in psychotherapy (see Chapter 11), knowledge that a particular approach works with some kinds of people and not with others obviously is of the utmost importance.

cited by Kennedy himself, namely, shock, exhaustion, disorientation, and the effects of brain concussion; 39 percent also stated in place of these excuses that the real reason was his fear of political and/or personal repercussions; 10 percent thought that he was too intoxicated at the time of the accident to present himself to the police; and 24 percent believed that he spent the time during the delay trying to find a way to conceal his role in the event. Surely, these latter two beliefs, that he was drunk and that he was trying to conceal his part in the affair, would seem to raise serious questions as to his fitness to head one's government. Yet 51 percent of those who remained faithfully supportive of Kennedy listed at least one of the three above reasons for Kennedy's delay in reporting the accident, namely, fear of the repercussions, intoxication, and attempting to cover up.

Silverman gives several possible explanations of this tolerance of apparent cognitive inconsistency. One explanation suggests an almost defiant or defensive loyalty to the man in a context of devoted past support of him and his family. It is as if, says Silverman, one learned that a beloved friend had committed some terrible sin, and confronted with this one responds, "I know what he did and I deplore it, but I still love him as much." Another explanation argues that the attitudes and beliefs of people in this situation were actually consistent if viewed in a larger framework, that of Kennedy's potential for public service. That is, those who remained positive toward Kennedy wished to interpret the delay in reporting the incident as not being morally reprehensible but as a necessary and pragmatic act designed to protect his political and personal future. In this connection it is interesting that attitudes toward him as a person seemed to be less susceptible of change, at least in many respondents, than those related to his being a political figure. For many subjects, the delaying actions might have reflected bad judgment in a crisis (raising questions about him as a national leader), but they did not necessarily impugn his moral character. Thus, there may well be a double standard of values for the ordinary man and for the important public personage.

It thus appears quite possible that there are limitations to the idea that cognitive inconsistency is always a major source of tension, discomfort, or stress and that it necessarily creates a powerful motive to reconcile the conflict. As Rosenberg (1963, p. 11) pungently stated the reservation:

The most obvious unresolved problem . . . [confronting the models of cognitive consistency] . . . is that the arousal of inconsistency which all of them assume to be motivating is often nothing of the sort. . . . I can like Adlai Stevenson a lot, name fifteen different virtues that he possesses and, while continuing to maintain strong positive regard for him, I can note that everyday he looks more unesthetically paunchy, that he has sometimes argued disingenuously in the Security Council and that he may well be more than a bit indecisive.

In any case, the principle of cognitive consistency, and the issues raised above, are of concern in psychological development because each new addition to the emerging personality of the developing child confronts thoughts, feelings, and actions that have already been established and with which it is either consistent or inconsistent. As the personality system becomes more and more complex, it should also become increasingly resistive to contradictory additions, since these would threaten the psychological edifice that has already been constructed. Another way of saying this is to note that people become less flexible as they mature, perhaps because there is a complete personality system to protect and it is better established when we are mature than when we are children. Note, however, that as this process of solidification of a personality structure proceeds, less and less are we talking about the *formation* of ways of thinking, feeling, and acting, and more and more are we considering the possibilities of personality *change* as new experiences challenge or threaten the existing structure.

CONCLUDING COMMENT

In this chapter we considered the problem of pressure to conform exerted by the social group on the individual, and we weighed the things that make an individual responsive to such pressure. None of us is immune to social influence although we like to think of ourselves as independent in thought and action, and indeed some of us are more so than others.

From the standpoint of the individual, social pressures constitute problems to be solved. We must cope with these all our lives, and sometimes the struggle involves enormously high personal stakes, hence is frought with emotional possibilities. Since social pressures engender conflicts and threats, they also play an important role in emotional disorders, helping to create symptoms of stress and disturbances of interpersonal relations. Consider, for example, the person caught in a real-life version of the Asch experiment on conformity. If we place ourselves in his shoes, we can appreciate his distress, and vividly sense the struggle of someone who in trying to relate to the world in which he lives finds himself momentarily isolated and confused. Just how people struggle with such problems will be examined in detail in Part IV.

Beyond these pressures of the immediate social situation, social influences shape the developing personality of the individual throughout his life from the moment of birth on. They do so through four fundamental mechanisms: reward and punishment; imitation and identification; playing of social roles; and the search for meaning and identity. These mechanisms are not mutually exclusive nor can we say just yet which ones, if any, are most important, or how they combine as they surely do in any individual case to create a complex personality. Yet it is by psychological processes of development such as these that different cultures and subcultures influence the patterns of thinking, feeling, and acting of their members, and it is only by understanding how this works that we can hope to alter the psychological makeup of persons, or of peoples, for the better.

The possibility of affecting personality development through our knowledge of such mechanisms is a two-edged sword. Clinicians, for example, have the positive goal of trying to help people to develop without crippling psychological ailments or self-destructive hangups. As parents we would like to have the knowledge to do so with our children. As social planners we would like to create social conditions that will benefit as many people as possible. To be able to do so, however, implies (somewhat frighteningly) that a powerful, knowledgeable person or agency might also be able to use conditioning methods in a Machiavellian fashion to assert a self-seeking mastery over society. Such a possibility has led to vigorous debate among biological and social scientists about the values and dangers of social conditioning. For some, the solution to man's problems lies in influencing his socialization by controlling his environment (for example, see Skinner, 1971), a prospect alarming to many thoughtful people. For others, the solution must be sought in use of effective mind-altering drugs (Clark, 1971) to eliminate destructive aggressive tendencies. And still others see the ultimate utopia in terms of the capacity to influence the human brain through electrical and chemical stimulation (Delgado, 1969) or in the manipulation of human genes (Davis, 1970). No one, of course, phrases this interest in influencing human psychological development in Machiavellian terms, but rather these proposals are always expressed as aimed at helping or improving the human condition.

Two simple and fundamental points must urgently be made about all this ferment. First, in spite of highly emotionalized characterizations of the potential for controlling and manipulating human psychological development, there appears to be little present evidence that we will have the knowledge or power actually to do so in the foreseeable future. Second, and far more important, man is an enormously complex creature, and though subject to influence, he is also more

Just as we have previously noted national differences in concepts of time and space, there are vast differences in ways of gesturing despite the fact that most individuals would consider such gestures to be natural. If an American were asked to point to himself, he would most likely point to his chest. In response to the same question, a Japanese would point to his nose. [From DeVos and Hippler, 1969, p. 325]

resistant to such influence than is usually acknowledged (see also Chapter 9). In spite of the most concerted efforts of parents, children continue to grow up as independent individuals, often very different from what their parents intend, and sometimes even from what they themselves intend. It is a denigration of the human psyche to see people simply as products of reward and punishment, or of the social roles they play, or of the process of imitation of parental models. We are, to be sure, all of these things. But we are also more, as I have tried to suggest in this chapter. On the basis of our present understanding, it would seem more profitable to work toward a real understanding of the mechanisms underlying personality formation than to brood about some future electronically controlled, computerized dictatorship. It will not be at all easy to convert human beings into mindless robots. We shall return to this problem in Chapter 5, which deals with social change and its psychological consequences.

ANNOTATED LIST OF SUGGESTED READINGS

Pressures of the immediate social situation

Bem, D. *Beliefs, attitudes and human affairs.* Belmont, Calif.: Brooks/Cole, 1970 (paper). Interesting discussion of the cognitive, affective, behavioral, and social foundations of beliefs and attitudes, and their significance in human affairs.

Freedman, J. L., Carlsmith, J. M., and Sears, D. O. *Social psychology.* Englewood Cliffs, N.J.: Prentice-Hall, 1970 (especially Chapters 7, 10, and 11). A basic and readable text in social psychology with excellent summaries of research on conformity, the consistency principle, and social pressure.

Lewin, K. *Resolving social conflicts: Selected papers on group dynamics*

(Gertrude W. Lewin, ed.) New York: Harper & Row, 1948. A collection of essays by one of the past giants of group dynamics.

Mehrabian, A. *Tactics of social influence.* Englewood Cliffs, N.J.: Prentice-Hall, 1970 (paper). Readable and authoritative discussion of the shaping of human behavior through the principle of environmental reinforcement.

Skinner, B. F. *Beyond freedom and dignity.* New York: Knopf, 1971. Examination of the technology of shaping behavior by the author of *Walden Two.* Skinner believes that the use of punishment has blocked development of more effective cultural practices and that the environment must be changed if man's traditional goals of freedom and dignity are to be at-

tained; very unpopular with "humanistic" psychologists.

Social influence in personality development

Brown, R. *Social psychology.* New York: The Free Press, 1965 (especially Chapters 8, 9, and 10). An excellent and distinctive textbook of social psychology with particular strengths in showing how psychological development and personality are forged out of social living; also discusses contemporaneous social influence effectively.

Lazarus, R. S. *Personality.* Englewood Cliffs, N.J.: Prentice-Hall, 1971 (paper). Brief textbook which, among other things, examines social forces as developmental determinants of personality.

We have just examined the ways in which society influences our thoughts, feelings, and actions and considered how social pressure tends to shape our personalities. This analysis proceeded from the assumption that the social world in which we live is a relatively stable system and hence is likely to be passed on from one generation to the next. Such an assumption, although reasonable, tends to deemphasize social change and its implications for human behavior and personality development. Just as man's physical environment constantly is changing, so his social environment is also in a state of flux. In this chapter we shall consider the psychological effects of social change.

In the development of mankind there have been two kinds of evolution, biological and sociocultural. Biological evolution was dealt with in Chapter 1. We noted there that early versions of *Homo sapiens* were not very different biologically from man today. Clearly, biological evolution is a very slow process. Most geneticists believe that man is continuing to evolve slowly, but no marked changes in his biological makeup have occurred in the past 30,000 years (Dobzhansky, 1962). With improved diet men have become taller, and their average life span has increased, but these changes are largely the result of cultural, not genetic, factors.

The rate of change in human culture and social structure over the past 5,000 years has been very rapid. Aldous Huxley (1965, p. 32) expresses this contrast between biological and sociocultural evolution very well:

Anatomically and physiologically, man has changed very little during the last twenty or thirty thousand years. The nature of genetic capacities of today's bright child are essentially the same as those of a child born into a family of Upper Paleolithic cave-dwellers. But whereas the contemporary bright baby may grow up to become almost anything—a Presbyterian engineer, for example, a piano-playing Marxist, a professor of biochemistry who is a mystical agnostic and likes to paint in watercolours—the [Paleolithic] baby could not possibly have grown into anything except a hunter or food-gatherer, using the crudest of stone tools and thinking about his narrow world of trees and swamps in terms of some hazy system of magic. Ancient and modern, the two babies are indistinguishable. Each of them contains all the potentialities of the particular breed of human being to which he or she happens to belong. But the adults into whom the babies will grow are profoundly dissimilar; and they are dissimilar because in one of them very few, and in the other a good many, of the baby's inborn potentialities have been actualized.

By far the most vigorous, though somewhat repetitious, documentation of social change has been made in the popular book *Future Shock* by Alvin Toffler (1970). Toffler's theme is that the social world is not only very different today from that of the past but that the rate of change is accelerating rapidly, seriously undermining the stability of our world. Today's education, argues Toffler, must prepare people for living and getting along with rapid change. Social change has been particularly spectacular during the past 300 years or so. Toffler suggests, provocatively, that "Almost as much has happened since I was born as happened before," and he elaborates this electrifying thought as follows (Toffler, 1970, p. 15):

This startling statement can be illustrated in a number of ways. It has been observed, for example, that if the last 50,000 years of man's existence were divided into lifetimes of approximately sixty-two years each, there have been about 800 such lifetimes. Of these 800, fully 650 were spent in caves.

Only during the last seventy lifetimes has it been possible to communicate effectively from one lifetime to another—as writing made it possible to do. Only during the last six lifetimes did masses of men ever see a printed word. Only during the last four has it been possible to measure time with any precision. Only in the last two has anyone anywhere used an electric motor. And the overwhelming majority of the material goods we use in daily life today have been developed within the present, the 800th lifetime.

Much of Toffler's book is in the form of illustrations of this accelerated rate of cultural change about which we are all intuitively aware. One example will suffice to point up what he is saying. In 6000 B.C., the fastest mode of long-distance transportation was the camel, which averaged about 8 miles per hour (mph). This maximum speed went up to about 20 mph about 4,400 years later in 1600 B.C. with the invention of the chariot. Nearly 3,500 years later, the first mail coach operating in England in 1784 averaged only 10 mph. The steam locomotive introduced in 1825 could go only 13 mph, and the sailing ships of the time could muster only half that speed. By the 1880s, with advances in the steam engine, railway locomotives could attain 100 mph. From here on the pace

The course of the flight up and down was exceedingly erratic, partly due to the irregularity of the air, and partly to [my] lack of experience in handling this machine. The control of the front rudder was difficult on account of its being balanced too near the center. This gave a tendency to turn itself when started, so that it turned too far on one side and then too far on the other. As a result, the machine would rise suddenly to about ten feet, and then as suddenly dart for the ground. A sudden dart when a little over 120 feet from the point at which it rose into the air, ended the flight.

As the velocity of the wind was over 35 feet per second and the speed of the machine over the ground against the wind ten feet per second, the speed of the machine relative to the air was over 45 feet per second, and the length of the flight was equivalent to a flight of 540 feet made in calm air.

This flight lasted only 12 seconds, but it was nevertheless the first in the history of the world in which a machine carrying a man had raised itself by its own power into the air in full flight, had sailed forward without the reduction of speed, and had finally landed at a point as high as that from which it started. [Orville Wright]

(a)

(b)

(c)

(d)

Figure 5.1 Acceleration of air transport in this century. (a) Wilbur Wright soaring aloft on one of many experimental glider flights at Kitty Hawk, North Carolina, on October 10, 1902; the aircraft had a wing span of 32 feet and supported a pilot in winds of medium velocity. (b) The next year, December 17, 1903, Orville Wright made the first successful takeoff, under power, of a heavier-than-air craft, with brother Wilbur running alongside one wing tip. This flight lasted 12 seconds; the longest flight that day, by Wilbur, was for 59 seconds and went 852 feet. (c) The twin-engine Douglas DC-3, standard airliner of the late 1930s, could carry a maximum of 31 people, including a crew of three, at top speed of 235 miles per hour; fully loaded its range was 340 miles. (d) The supersonic Concorde, an Anglo-French cooperative venture, has four turbojet engines, cruises at 1,400 miles per hour, and can carry up to 128 passengers 4,000 miles in some 3.5 hours. (a,b: Library of Congress; c: courtesy of the National Air and Space Museum, Smithsonian Institution; d: British Aircraft Corporation (USA) Inc.)

of technological development boggles the mind. In only 58 years after the 100-mph locomotive, the fastest speed quadrupled to 400 mph with the propellor-driven airplane of 1938. Less than twenty years later this speed limit was doubled with the advent of jet airliners (Figure 5.1). By the 1960s, rocket airplanes were approaching speeds of 4,000 mph, and space capsules were circling the globe at 18,000 mph and traversing the quarter of a million miles from the earth to the moon in three days! The same accelerated progress can be found in virtually all of man's technological capabilities.

These changes in speed of transportation are important in human terms in that they have brought the world's peoples close together (for example, it now takes as little as 9 hours

(a)

(b)

Figure 5.2 Few things of importance now happen in the world without our being there via instantaneous electronic communication. (a) Hooded Arab gunman negotiates with West German police from balcony of Israeli residence at Olympic Village, Munich, September 5, 1972, while a worldwide TV audience watches. Israeli athletes were held hostage inside as police and cameramen surrounded the building. (b) The tragic ending: wreck of helicopter that transported the Arabs and their hostages to the airport, where a shootout and grenade explosion resulted in the death of all the athletes. Two days later the TV cameras were trained again on the continuing "live" Olympic spectacle. (a: Wide World Photos; b: United Press International Photo)

to get from San Francisco to Tokyo by ordinary passenger jet, and the new supersonic Concordes will be much faster). Communications satellites now make it possible for hundreds of millions of people around the world to sit in their living rooms and simultaneously watch "live" events, some of great moment and emotional impact. Thus, probably more than a billion people were onlookers while the tragic events unfolded that culminated in the massacre of Israeli athletes by terrorists during the Olympic games in Munich, Germany, in the late summer of 1972. Instantaneously transmitted pictures gave glimpses of the terrorists and the German police, showed the helicopters whirling away from Olympic Village to the airport, and finally let us see German officials announcing the tragic ending. A play-by-play visualization of what transpired during the day-long siege was presented to a worldwide TV audience (Figure 5.2).

With such instant communications it is now virtually impossible for anyone to remain isolated within his own narrow social sphere. Increasingly the whole world is becoming a single social entity, like the small community of yesteryear. The cliché "Isn't it a small world!" is now a reality, and with this new reality comes the breakdown of many of the geographical and cultural barriers that used to keep many tribes and nations isolated from one another.

As we saw earlier (in Chapter 4), our social milieu greatly influences our developing personalities. Thus, any rapid change in this social environment has profound psychological implications. Such change imposes tremendous adaptational demands upon the individual, who must constantly cope with new problems. Those who as children were socialized to one set of conditions, as adults must learn to live in a new world with social patterns and values very different from the ones that have been internalized as stable features of their personalities. In our own times, the traditional culture that has been passed down from earlier generations, the culture of our parents and grandparents, is rapidly changing before our eyes. Under such conditions certain strains in the social fabric are inevitable. It is now common to speak of a *generation gap*. Examination of this phenomenon, so familiar to us all, may throw some light on the special problems of psychological development that seem to characterize our frenzied times.

THE GENERATION GAP

Anthropologist Margaret Mead (1970) has studied the interaction between generations and has described three cultural patterns. In one type, at least three generations are living together at the same time—grandparents, parents, and their children. As the child grows up he is likely to take for granted and accept the culture unquestioningly as it is passed down by his forebears. This type arises from a stable social pattern, and it produces a traditional culture with high stability and only slow change. This is the way things once were in Europe and the United States before the speedup of change that Toffler (1970) writes about.

In the second type, it is not the elders who provide the models for the growing child's attitudes and behavior, but rather the child's present generation of peers or contemporaries. Mead thinks that this is now the pattern of present-day Western society, brought about by the rapid changes forced upon it by technological advances and by their social consequences, for example, the isolation of the nuclear family in which only two generations live together, the parents and the children. The sense of continuity with older generations is lost, and the stable base for all cultural values grows shaky. Under such conditions, says Mead (1970, p. 38), a generation gap develops: "In the United States, as one son after another, in one home after another, disagreed with his father and left home to go West or to some other part of the country, the circumstance that these battles were recurrent in most households came to have the appearance of the natural order of relations between fathers and sons." Such generational conflict ultimately required the open and conscious forsaking of traditional patterns maintained by the parents and grandparents and the seeking of new models.

The third type, Mead argues, is a new cultural form that is now slowly emerging in face of the unknown and uncertain nature of the future world. Today's young generation approaches life as explorers rather than retainers and communicators of the past. They seek new ways rather than old ones because new approaches are desperately needed to provide solutions to problems that are unique to our times. Never before, says Mead, has there been such a complete break between one generation and the next. Because cultural evolution is now so rapid, the changes demanding new solutions take place within a single lifetime, and the younger generation can no longer look to the past for answers (see Note 5.1).

Components of the generation gap

A generation gap is manifest when the experiences, attitudes, values, and ways of life of one generation differ sharply from those of the next. Such a gap can be either "real" or a product of age; that is, parents, as a rule, will think differently from their children simply because people of 40 years of age, say, are psychologically different from people of 20.

Note 5.1

What Margaret Mead (1970) has to say about social change, family life, and the generation gap is, of course, speculative theoretical analysis, though it is not without supportive observations. We must realize that any such observations entail a correlation (parallel relationship) between changing social values and changing patterns of family life, and she has interpreted this correlation in terms of cause and effect. She concludes that the altered structure of family life in recent times, with parents and children living apart from grandparents rather than in the three-generation home, has significance as a cause of the generation gap in life styles and values.

However, correlation does not necessarily mean causation. It is possible that the generational changes are correlated with generational isolation because they are both the product of other social changes, such as increased mobility, greater financial security, effects of industrialization and automation on work attitudes, or loss of intimate social ties that were once part of life in small, tight-knit communities. All these might well produce significant changes in human values and behavior. Moreover, the causal relationship could even go the other way round, with changes in generational attitudes driving parents and children apart.

Any correlation has four possible interpretations: If factor *A* is correlated with *B*, (1) it may mean that *A* causes *B*; or (2) it may mean that *B* causes *A*, or even that both are interdependent, each helping to produce the other through feedback (for example, if one person expresses hostility to another, that person may in turn respond with hostility, which will then trigger even more hostility from the first person, and so on); (3) *A* and *B* might be related because of some third, as yet undetermined factor; (4) their relationship might occur purely by chance. By searching through statistical records, we might perhaps discover that, say, the number of trees cut down in Canada over several years is correlated with the number of people killed in the Vietnam War in those years, most probably a totally meaningless chance relationship. Statisticians are continually turning up such coincidences.

This is always the problem with correlational analyses and is one of the arguments in favor of experimentation, in which some factor is manipulated to determine whether it has certain effects on some other factor. Thus, in medical research, one can establish that a microbe is the causal agent of a disease if one can show that when a person (or animal) is exposed to it, he (or it) contracts the disease. Experiments can often be conducted that demonstrate such causal relationships, as in the case of Walter Reed's studies of yellow fever during the building of the Panama Canal. Reed exposed some subjects to the mosquito carrying yellow-fever virus and prevented such exposure in others, and demonstrated in this way that the mosquito was the carrier of the disease agent. In study of most human psychological ills, analogous experimentation cannot be undertaken for obvious practical as well as ethical reasons.

How might we seek to test Margaret Mead's ideas? One possibility would be to compare families in which parents, children, and grandparents have remained together within the same household with families in which the nuclear family (parents and children) was isolated. If Mead's analysis is correct, there should be greater generational differences in the latter than in the former. (To my knowledge, such a study has never been done.) We would have to weigh other factors of importance that might be responsible for any obtained differences. For example, the intact three-generational families might live in communities (say, in farming areas) where there is less mobility and where generational differences are slight even in small nuclear families.

Often, especially in social and personality research, we have to settle for correlational studies in the field and must cautiously draw our conclusions, knowing that they cannot readily be proved by experimentation. This is one of the reasons why there is likely to be so much disagreement and controversy in the social sciences, even when the data themselves are not in question. In every field or clinical study, multiple factors are operating that could have an influence on the outcome. Thus, selection of any one causal factor is very difficult. Similar reservations were implied in Note 2.1, in which we noted the multiple causation of behavior and the complex interactions among the many factors shaping how we think, feel, and act.

Some of what has been called a generation gap is merely the natural result of age differential, and as such it should disappear as the young grow older. However, the "real" aspect of the generation gap refers to changes in social conditions under which children live today as compared with those of their parents when they were children. Most of the time, both of these ideas are mixed together—the age differential and the altered way of life in a different social era. Regardless of its causes, a generation gap usually gives rise to generational conflict, mutual arguments and unhappiness over divergent ways of life.

It is really quite difficult to document whether "real" generational differences today are greater than in the past because we have no adequate measure of social change (as economists have quantitative indices of economic change). Moreover, there has always been generational conflict. We find it in the Bible, in classical Greek drama, and as a theme of Shakespeare's *Henry IV* and *King Lear*. Such conflict is described in many social science treatises of the recent past on adolescence, with its intense turbulence and rebellion. Today, the impression is that generational conflict is unusually strong, and as a result of its treatment in the mass media we are all very conscious of it.

In generational conflict, the older generation is usually unhappy with the younger, and vice-versa, and a rather gusty rhetoric develops about what each thinks is wrong with the other. This is exemplified by the well-publicized statements of certain youths that no one over 30 can be trusted. And there has been ample counterattack, as in the case of the man who, when asked how the present generation differed from those of the past, replied in the public press, "I think this generation stinks!" (a remark that also reveals the anger and frustration so widespread in our society these days—see Figure 5.3). Similar anger at rebellious youth is also illustrated by the off-year election campaign of 1970, with vigorous condemnation by high officials of permissiveness in American society and on the nation's college campuses, an episode in which the administration attempted to capitalize politically on the deepening polarities, fears, and hostilities in the electorate.

Although it is not by any means universal, there is a widespread feeling on the part of middle-class parents that their children have had it too easy, that they are not appreciative of the struggles their parents experienced roughly 20 years earlier, and there is much dismay on the part of the older generation at what they see as a breakdown of values in their children. In turn, considerable hostility and condemnation is expressed by the young of their parents' outlook and way of life. All this gives rise to the impression that there is indeed a growing void between one generation and the next.

New moralities

There do seem to be new values and concepts of morality among many of the young, although these values also have counterparts in ancient philosophical movements (say, among the ancient Greeks) and throughout history. Psychologist Robert T. Hogan (1969) sees moral opinion in the United States as being presently divided into two camps—proponents of "traditional moral values"; and those adhering to what he calls "the new moralities." Included in the latter category are "situation ethics" (Fletcher, 1966), which takes the position that there are no universal standards of morality; that things are right or wrong in accordance with the situation. (There is one absolute standard, "love," which when well served is always good and right in every situation.)

A vignette from the film *The Rainmaker* provides an illustration of situation ethics. The rainmaker makes love to a lonely girl in a barn, ostensibly with the intention of providing her with a sense of womanliness and to give her hope that she can have marriage and a family. Ultimately the girl's brother, morally outraged, threatens to shoot the rainmaker, but the wise father of the girl takes away his pistol saying, "Noah, you're so full of what's right, you can't see what's good." In situation ethics, the father is seen as a moral hero, and the rainmaker's "loving" but traditionally immoral act is applauded. The value expressed here is that we should not hesitate to break a law that is in all conscience unjust (in effect, unloving). We can all recognize other versions of this dictum, such as statements at the Nuremberg trials of Nazis in 1945 arguing that men should be bound by a higher law than mere obedience to their superiors, and the principle was affirmed

Figure 5.3 Young antiwar protesters arrested and corralled behind hurricane fencing in Washington, D.C., May Day, 1971. (Charles Harbutt; Magnum)

in these trials that the evil orders should have been disobeyed. The same principle is expressed in the limited privilege legally given to our own soldiers in the code of military justice to disobey a military command if it violates higher principles; and it is also evident in many instances of civil disobedience.

The philosophical and emotional issues touched here are excruciatingly difficult to resolve, and they have been examined by thoughtful men throughout history. Acceptance of the "new morality" also reflects, in part, a rejection of traditional, established values and institutions, whatever they are. Sometimes they also express a loss of confidence in the power of reason and of traditional intellectual standards to govern our lives. In their place is put human passion, said to be more trustworthy than reason and restraint, which are seen as warping and distorting the "true" nature of man through hypocrisy and by rigid rules that seek order but not justice. What is not dealt with effectively in the "new moralities" is the perennial problem of self-deception, that is, the tendency of people to justify almost anything they do and to distort their own self-seeking motives. Nevertheless, the positive intent is to challenge rigidly conventional systems of morality, which have often failed dismally to provide justice, humanity, and love, and to counter these with better principles that are more in tune with human needs and feelings.

The emergence of the "new morality" is but one evidence of the generation gap, of the rejection of tradition, and of the search for alternative values on which a meaningful life in today's world might be sustained. The success or failure of this effort is less relevant to our present thesis than the fact of its existence and of the communication problems it must pose today between parents and their children. Such ideological generational conflicts are certainly far more important than the more superficial issues of hair and clothing style or other minor areas of contention between the generations (Figure 5.4).

Worldwide nature of the problem

Generational conflict is hardly unique to the United States but is happening to some degree all over the world. All technologically oriented societies are confronted by the same problems and share the same worldwide system of instant communications. This may be seen even in those countries whose cultural traditions have been quite different from ours. An excellent example is Japan, a country with extremely strong and unified traditions lasting for centuries (Figure 5.5). Japan's headlong movement into the technological-industrial era, especially since World War II, has resulted in changes that make the older generation feel abandoned by their children.

(a)

(b)

(c)

At one time older men and women in Japan had important family responsibility and authority, and this pattern of the veneration of the old extended into social, business, professional, and political life, even when such a system of seniority succeeded also in stifling the young. Increasingly now, however, older people in Japan are feeling useless, empty, lonely, and ignored by their children. Precisely this pattern of change has also characterized the nations of Western Europe and the United States, only it began earlier there. For example, in Japan about 80 percent of people over 65 years of age still live with their families; in England, 42 percent; and in the United States, only 28 percent. Nevertheless, the complaint is increasingly heard in Japan that the daughter-in-law, for example, works and wants the husband's mother (once a proud

Figure 5.4 Then and now: (a) 1944—Some of the 25,000 bobby-soxers, all Frank Sinatra fans, waiting in line to see their idol at the Paramount Theater, New York City. At left, two girls hold up their hero's photo. (b) 1965—At Buckingham Palace, London, a few of the thousands of young girls awaiting their beloved Beatles, who were to be presented to the Queen. (c) 1970—Rock music festival in Powder Ridge, Connecticut, called off because of a court injunction, produced this impromptu scene, as youngsters staged a nonmusical festival of their own. (a,c: United Press International Photo; b: Central Press/Pictorial Parade)

(a)

(b)

Figure 5.5 *The disappearing cultural past: old and new in Japan. (a) A family, part of a big crowd at Meiji Shrine, Tokyo, during the New Years holidays. Clothes are traditional, except for one modern touch—the fur wraps. (b) Formally attired women studying the traditional tea ceremony at a special school. (c) Crowd in downtown Tokyo, all in modern garb. (d) Young motorcyclists, revved up and raring to go. (a,b: Hiroshi Hosono, Foreign Correspondents' Club, Tokyo; c,d: Jacqueline Paul)*

(c)

(d)

matriarch in the home) only for a babysitter. In a country where age traditionally required respect and bestowed authority, this social change is highly disturbing to the roughly 7.5 million people over 65 who no longer feel a sense of dignity in their old age as a result of the disappearance of the older traditions.

Social change does of course require that each generation grow up in a world slightly or markedly different from the one from which it sprang, and thus, as Mead says, parents cannot know intimately many of the experiences of their children, any more than children can know a large proportion of the experiences of their parents, except insofar as these can be imagined through empathy and the existence of some common core of shared experience. Were there no social change, there would be no "real" generation gap (although there might well be generational conflict, because older people see things differently than young ones). The faster or more marked is the social change and the turmoil it brings, the more marked should be the gap between generations.

How wide is the generation gap?

There are reasons to be wary about the allegation that the fundamentals of life have changed as much as is claimed and that the generation gap applies to all segments of the population, young and old. One could argue, in fact, that there is a continual *need for social change,* since outside of that perfect world which has never existed except in myths, every social system has numerous defects making for perennial injustice and creating large gaps between social ideals and social reality. Therefore, certain groups will be having a bad time while others are fighting to preserve the status quo. Certain kinds of social change are desirable and even necessary, and to those for whom things are particularly bad (like disparaged minorities, the poor, the handicapped) the absence of progress is a tremendous provocation to unrest. Perhaps there has been insufficient change in the fundamental ways we get along in society rather than too much.

Social change, for example, has not kept up with the vast new body of knowledge available to those who are exposed to the mass media of the world in this electronic age. To many young people, society still seems stuck in the old ways. They feel that little effort has been made to eliminate structural poverty, or near-Victorian hypocrisy about sex and sex roles, or racism, war, and excess materialism. Youth often sees society as static, bogged down by inertia, rather than changing or moving ahead.

Is there really so much more change taking place within our society than has occurred in other periods of history?

Could there be more social change today than was experienced in the nineteenth and early twentieth centuries by immigrant families during the massive migrations from Europe and Asia to the United States? What could be more uprooting to a family and engender more change in its way of life than to leave the "old country" and settle in a new one, with its new values, ways of thinking, customs, and language. In such great migrations, throughout the history of man, the social change was not gradual but almost instantaneous. This was rapid social change indeed, and clearly brought with it much conflict and distress, both for the older generation and for the new.

In the face of the emotionally charged atmosphere within which the generation gap is usually discussed, it is pleasant to find a humorous portrayal of it by satirical columnist Arthur Hoppe (*San Francisco Chronicle*, November 9, 1970). In his usual *reductio ad absurdum* style, Hoppe writes:

Once upon a time there was a young man named Horatio Alger who lived in a country suffering under a Great Depression.

Times were terrible. Horatio couldn't find a job. He had to share a run-down flat with ten other unemployed bums. They wore odd, cast-off clothes. They had no soap, no razor blades, no privacy and not much hope.

And all they had to eat were beans, bagels and boiled rutabagas—day after day.

"But I shall persevere!" said Horatio grimly. "I shall persevere so that my son will have a better life. He will have a decent home, decent clothes, decent food and a decent job. He shall never have to live like this."

And Horatio persevered.

He found a job lifting bags and toting bales for 20 cents an hour, 12 hours a day. He suffered. He persevered.

He formed a union. He called a strike. The police clubbed him on the head. The Establishment scorned him as 'an anarchist' and a 'troublemaker.' He suffered. But he persevered.

"I must do my part to reform society and make this a better world," he said. And he did.

Thanks in part to his efforts, times changed. Minimum wages, old age pensions, unemployment insurance and the eight-hour day came into being. Prosperity gradually returned.

At last Horatio's suffering and perseverance were rewarded. Like most of his generation he now had a decent home, decent clothes, decent food, a decent job, two cars in the garage and chicken every Sunday.

And he had a son, Horatio Junior.

"It was all worth it," said Horatio proudly and happily as he watched the lad grow up, "to know that he will never have to undergo what I underwent."

Junior, as sons inevitably will, grew up. "What, Dad," he asked one day, "should I make the goal of my life?"

"Why, son," replied Horatio with some surprise, "the goal of life, of course, is to get a decent job so that you can have a decent home, decent clothes, decent food, two cars in the garage and chicken every Sunday."

"But I've already got all that," said Junior. And a week later he dropped out.

Junior joined a commune and lived in a run-down flat with ten other unemployed bums. They wore odd, cast-off clothes. They had no soap, razor blades or privacy and, in conformity with their Zoroastrian religion, they ate nothing but beans, bagels and boiled rutabagas—day after day.

The police clubbed them on the head. The Establishment scorned them as 'anarchists' and 'troublemakers.' But Junior persevered.

"I must do my part," he said, "to reform society and make this a better world."

"But why, son?" cried Horatio, wringing his hands. "Why?"

"The trouble with you, Dad," said his son sadly, "is that you don't understand the finer things in life."

MORAL: Cheer up. Our grandchildren will be just like us.

Hoppe, of course, is saying here that the more things change, the more they are the same. He, like many others, does not accept the notion that the present generation gap is much wider than it always has been.

Much of what is said about the generation gap applies to only a limited percentage of the youthful population. The impression that there is such a gap, and that it is large, stems from the many visible instances of youthful rebellion and counterculture activities, as well as the very vocal and often rigid response of many of their elders. But the evidence is also persuasive that a considerable majority of young people are not very different from their parents in outlook, expectation, and aspiration.

Some evidence for this assertion comes from a Gallup poll late in the presidential campaign of 1972 showing that as of late August that year, little more than two months before the election, Nixon was leading McGovern in the under-30 voter group by 61 to 36 percent. This may only mean that the liberal Democrat simply had not impressed the young voter as a potential President, rather than that they supported "the establishment," but such figures are hardly consistent with the claim of predominant disaffection among today's youth.

More systematic data are available from a comparison of the conceptions of the good life of American college students in 1950 and 1970 (Morris and Small, 1971). The sample is unfortunately limited, including mainly students in philosophy courses in a wide variety of colleges all over the United States; it is thus heavily biased toward the humanities and social sciences, and against those in the professions and natural sciences, who (both students and professors) are known to be more conservative. The comparison was based on the same

Innovations, whether they are technological or social, require, the creative efforts of an inventor. Who are these persons? What makes them create new things? Are they different from others? . . . They are believed to have characteristics which, although not socially deviant, suggest that such persons do not readily accept the typical social routines that provide the stability most people need. They are not content with the status quo. Unlike the antisocial psychopath, however, they do not turn their wrath upon society but rather attempt to change it by the invention of something new. . . . Since the innovator does not conform to all social norms directly nor accept all of the values of his social group, he can be defined as an individual who has not been completely "socialized" by his society. His discontent with current practices serves as the basic motivation for the invention of something new, whether it is a physical object, such as a car, or a new form of social organization, like a new school. This same discontent probably pervades the basic personality of revolutionaries, leaders of social movements, and others concerned with changing their society. Thus it appears that the inventor is a person who is basically dissatisfied with contemporary living and who is concerned about the future. [From Fairweather, 1972, p. 7]

measure, a "Ways to Live" scale consisting of 13 possible conceptions of the good life in which the respondent must indicate how much he or she personally would like to live each of the alternatives. For example, Way 5 is to "act and enjoy life through group participation," Way 7 is to "integrate action, enjoyment, and contemplation," Way 10 is to "control the self stoically," and Way 12 is to "chance adventuresome deeds." In addition to this, students in the 1970 study (but not in 1950) were asked, "Do you feel that our society is satisfactory for the development and expression of your own particular abilities and wishes?"—and to explain why or why not.

The most striking finding was that the 1970 American college student did not differ greatly from the 1950 student in his ideals for living. The researchers express some surprise at this, though they suggest interpretively that even the 1950 students, like the 1970 ones, did not conform to the traditional stereotypes of American youth; in effect, the main personal ideals about life appearing in the 1970 group had already been present in 1950 and are thus not new. The only really striking change in values occurred in response to Way 1: "preserve the best that man has attained." Between 1950 and 1970 there was a marked drop in the acceptance of this outlook. Way 1 expresses conservatism in its most positive sense, and nationwide in 1950 college students thought of this positively; in 1970 they gave it a somewhat more negative rating. Thus, in 1970 students were less tradition oriented than in 1950. Here is an explanation of Way 1 as it was described to the subjects:

In this design for living the individual actively participates in the social life of his community, not to change it primarily, but to understand, appreciate, and preserve the best that man has attained. Excessive desires should be avoided and moderation sought. One wants the good things of life but in an orderly way. Life is to have clarity, balance, refinement, control. Vulgarity, great enthusiasm, irrational behavior, impatience, indulgence are to be avoided. Friendship is to be esteemed but not easy intimacy with many people. Life is to have discipline, intelligibility, good manners, predictability. Social changes are to be made slowly and carefully so that what has been achieved in human culture is not lost. The individual should be active physically and socially, but not in a hectic or radical way. Restraint and intelligence should give order to an active life.

Although the question was not asked in 1950, almost half the students in the 1970 sample did not believe that present-day American society is favorable for realizing the life they would like to live. (Notice, by the way, that this finding could be put in the opposite fashion having a somewhat different feeling tone, namely, that less than half the students felt that they could not realize the life they would like to live in present-day America.) In terms of the point being developed here, a very substantial proportion of today's college youth can be said to have values about the good life that are not so very different from those of youth two decades ago, that is, the previous generation. For them the generation gap is nonexistent, or at least not evident in the expressed positive values of living revealed in this study.

Thus, what Mead and others are talking about could well be a comparatively small segment of youth rather than youth in general. She could be right in another sense, that this small force could be today's cadre for tomorrow's groundswell. However, in purely statistical terms it is an exaggeration to say that this is how youth of today, collectively, looks at things. Such a claim highlights the dangers inherent in *generalizing* about whole populations of people from unrepresentative samples that are obtrusive and hence capture our attention.

Without some generalizations about people and social settings, there would, of course, be nothing worth saying. The science of man would be reduced to describing concretely every individual and his specific social setting, and we would be unable to categorize or abstract those things which groups or populations may have in common. Thus, although one must acknowledge that every person is different from every other person, there are also properties that people share, and one of the tasks of social science is to identify these common properties. Every generalization is, therefore, an attempt to find a principle for simplifying an overwhelmingly complex and detailed panorama of variation; at the same time, each such generalization is a potential source of error in the sense that in making it we must overlook the differences between people in favor of the similarities.

Nevertheless, we have the obligation to ask how accurate and useful a generalization is, and to pin down where it fits and where it does not. The problem gets particularly acute when the generalization is so sweeping that it presents a severely distorted image of what exists. Nowhere is there a better example of the danger of this than in the emotional, value-laden hyperbole applied in discussions of a nation's or group's modal personality. One has the impression that there is both truth and severe distortion in this concept, depending on how the point is made. The emphasis turns on which of the facts an analyst pays attention to and how the facts are interpreted. In an excellent discussion of the problem, Grossack and Gardner (1970, p. 115) put the matter as follows:

. . . one may note the same fact, say anonymity in the city, and call it atomism or individualism, depending on one's perspective and what one wants to prove. As with statistics, the game of national character has many rules and is designed to trap the unwary and

I admit we should follow some basic rules but first you should look at who is making the rules. Sometimes I walk down a deserted beach listening to the waves and birds and I hear them forever calling and forever crying and sometimes we feel that way but everyone goes on with his own little routines, afraid to stop and listen for fear of cracking the nutshell.—The answer is out there somewhere. We need to search for it. [Shannon Dickson, a 15-year-old Texas boy, quoted in Mead (1970)]

the incautious. Those European analysts who look at America through Teutonic or Gallic or Leninist lenses are likely to interpret a social event like a race riot quite differently from social scientists raised in the Middle West who are ministers' sons. One analyst may infer that violence is becoming rampant in America, another that the proletariat is asserting itself, another that Negroes no longer fear police brutality, another that blacks resent police brutality, a fifth that the Negroes' lot is improving, a sixth that it is desperate. And, in a curious sense, they may all be right, for their analyses may apply to different segments of the rioters, or may be applicable at different times.

Most discussions of the current social scene, understandably oriented to abstracting, generalizing, simplifying so that the facts can be made manageable, also tend to overgeneralize about gross and complex populations such as youth, students, the older generation, silent Americans, hardhats, blacks, other ethnic minorities, as though whatever is said about them represents dominant trends within these populations and, what is worse, accurately characterizes each of its individual members too. Data are usually absent or not cited. Such unscientific and stereotypical thinking stems from a combination of strong ideological commitment to certain concepts and the absence of detailed facts. This is perhaps the most dangerous trend in the great bulk of discussions of social change and generational conflict. We must be more precise about various groups in a society, and social scientists have become increasingly wary about speaking in overgeneral terms.

Figure 5.6   The campus scene—two examples. (a) Life amid the ivy, Cornell University. (b) At Berkeley, maximum variety: hip, straight, and far out. (a: Cornell University photograph by Sol Goldberg; b: Jim Cron; Monkmeyer Press Photo Service)

(a)

(b)

Moreover, recognition of this often comes as a bitter disappointment to young people who sense a likemindedness about current social problems in their own campus population only to discover belatedly that their campus is not a perfect microcosm of the whole country or world (Figure 5.6). As John Hersey (1970, p. 12) in his last book, *Letter to the Alumni,* has artfully stated it:

It is not only inaccurate, it is positively harmful to lump the various student types, the revolutionaries, the activists, the meliorists, the individualists, the constitutionalists, the conservatives, the reactionaries, the anti-socials, the apathetics, the hippies and yippies, joiners and doers, druggies and drunks, jocks and cocks, Women's Libs and feminine flirts, gay boys and "sexist" men, grinds and goof-offs and flick buffs, and guitar pluckers and motherfuckers and gentle souls and thoughtful loners, and givers and takers and breakers and makers—*all* under the heading of a unitary concept "student." Or arrogant troublemaker. Or for that matter, "beautiful youth." I myself will repeatedly fall victim to the generalizing fallacy in this letter, as for concision I even lump individuals into types, or talk about "what students want," or rudely address you as if alumni were all alike. There are many variants of bull shit, and many views of reality. It is not easy to distinguish between them, even in oneself. But how easy it *seems* when we look at a group toward whom we feel hostile!

Cycles of child rearing

For social change to have an impact on the growing child, it must be reflected in the way parents or parent-substitutes rear their children. Parental influence is obviously of great importance to the young child, though later on influences outside the home grow in importance. Social changes in child-rearing patterns are not new, and the many viewpoints about how one should treat children have shifted back and forth frequently over the past century between two extremes, namely, a discipline-oriented pattern and a permissive pattern. It might be well to examine this in the context of our discussion of social change and the generation gap.

This oscillation in child-rearing viewpoints has been described in detail by Celia B. Stendler (1950) covering a 60-year period. Unfortunately, comparable study has not been done between 1950 and the present. She observed that from 1890 to 1900 the tender-minded view prevailed. The growing child was seen as a delicate flower that needed cultivation with love and gentleness. An editor of a magazine of the day devoted to child rearing wrote, "Love, petting and indulgence will not hurt a child if at the same time he is taught to be unselfish and obedient. Love is the mighty solvent." And another editor outlined a plan for dealing with a boy who was labeled lazy, careless, and good-for-nothing. He wrote in exhortation, "I thought I would try to win him with love alone, and never strike him. . . . Mothers who have trouble with their children, bring them up the Christian way . . . with a loving and tender heart, and you will surely succeed. . . ." (Stendler, 1950, p. 122). From this perspective, the child must be led not driven, persuaded not commanded (Figure 5.7). Consistency and firmness should be tempered with understanding and justice. Corporal punishment is undesirable.

However, from 1910 to 1930, the predominant mood of child rearing had shifted to the tough-minded outlook. If a child refused to obey a parental command, the parent was to demand complete obedience lest it be "doomed to depravity" or spoiled. The demand for obedience was a contest of wills that the child must be made to lose; all this was to be done much as one tames or "breaks in" a horse. A child had to be raised on a rigid schedule, with times fixed for when it was to eat and even for its other body functions. For example, a bowel movement had to be experienced every day, and strong purgatives such as castor oil were used if the child's intestines did not operate according to the required household rhythm. If a baby cried or was hungry before the scheduled feeding time, it had to wait until that feeding time arrived. Mothers were exhorted in child-rearing magazines that only such tight discipline would produce a sound adult. No deviation from the set pattern was to be countenanced. As everyone knows, this pattern shifted during the 1930s toward a more liberal, tender-minded, child-centered outlook, emphasizing spontaneity, individuality, and creativity.

"Now son, isn't this better than hanging around your pad smoking grass."

Figure 5.7   The generation gap. (Drawing by J. J. Dunleavy)

The oscillation between these positions in the history of child rearing is a fascinating story of ambivalence, with one outlook tending to dominate in a given era only to lose out to the other outlook later. Unfortunately, it seems extremely difficult for society to adopt a reasonable balanced position, although individual families may buck the general trend. Typically we go from one extreme to the other in spite of evidence that both positions have some useful things to offer but that neither is adequate. For example, Diana Baumrind and A. E. Black (1967) at the Institute of Human Development of the University of California at Berkeley studied three groups of youngsters and their parents for 8 years (see also Baumrind, 1971); they found that those parents who were most warm and permissive brought up children who lacked self-reliance and self-control. Moreover, children of authoritarian parents were discontented, withdrawn, and distrustful. In contrast to both these extremes, however, the middle group of children, whose parents were controlling and demanding yet also warm, rational, and receptive to the child, turned out to be the most self-reliant, self-controlled, inclined to explore and try out things, and content with themselves and their relationships with others. Such data suggest that either extreme of authoritarianism or permissiveness results in harmful consequences. Perhaps we should avoid the periodic emotional swings between tough- and tender-mindedness. What seems to happen in such swings is that the ills of society tend to be blamed simplistically on whatever pattern of education and child rearing has existed during the immediate past (cast usually in extreme, stereotypical fashion), and so that pattern is abandoned for the equally extreme and stereotypical alternative that other generations of parents had tried but found wanting. In short, we flip-flop from one outlook to the other, although neither is capable of resolving our social ills and each creates its own special problems.

Furthermore, it was discovered in the 1940s (Davis and Havighurst, 1946) that there were sharp social-class differences in attitudes toward child rearing. Middle-class parents were found to be much stricter than lower-class parents, particularly in such things as the age of toilet training and weaning, with middle-class parents beginning such disciplinary pressures earlier than lower-class parents. This difference was assumed to be a stable distinction between the social classes until it was reported by Sears and associates (1957) that this difference had all but disappeared. In fact, the middle-class mothers they studied in Boston were actually slightly more permissive toward their children than lower-class mothers. What had happened to eliminate or reverse the earlier class differences?

Urie Bronfenbrenner (1958) has suggested a two-stage process. First, literate middle-class mothers and fathers of the

1930s had been reading magazines on child rearing advocating permissiveness and relaxed attitudes. With the advent of mass communications, in turn, lower-class parents had begun to imitate the pattern displayed by middle-class parents; although the latter group had already begun to leave that position, the former had not yet caught up with the change. Thus, when middle-class parents dropped the strict disciplinary values with their children, the class differences tended to *disappear* and to some degree even reverse themselves slightly as lower-class families now were emphasizing self-reliance and independence. Bronfenbrenner cited a study by Martha Wolfenstein (1953) in support of his contention that middle-class patterns had changed. She had analyzed the contents of a magazine on child rearing called *Infant Care* published by the United States Children's Bureau between the years 1929 and 1938. The shift in attitudes was much in evidence there, as Bronfenbrenner had claimed.

But what had produced the shift in the attitude toward child rearing among the experts writing in such magazines? The answer is obscure. It is possible, for example, that instead of parents being influenced by the professionals as Bronfenbrenner assumed, there was a major change in values in the educated segments of the society at large, and the experts merely were part of this movement rather than its cause. At the turn of the century and in the 1920s, many of our social mores were changing, evidenced, for example, by a sharp rise in the divorce rate and an increase in sexual freedom. The traditional Protestant ethic of self-control and self-denial was also losing force among a large segment of the United States population. What caused such major cultural change is not clear, but it evidently did occur and is reflected in a reversal of the way a large proportion of American families viewed the rearing of their children. In the future, the increased impact of mass media such as films and television make unlikely any further tendencies toward class differentiation in child-rearing attitudes.

In this brief history we see a prime illustration of how changing social patterns have affected psychological development through their impact on child-rearing practices. At one time parents pressed for discipline and self-control in their children, both in word and act, and their children expressed these values in the way they conducted their own lives. The generation that grew up in the depression years of the 1930s had certain attitudes toward work and study, toward borrowing and spending, toward success and failure and how these are achieved. These attitudes were probably never completely lost in these adults. But changes in child-rearing attitudes in the 1940s and 1950s have infiltrated the ways in which they, in turn, reared their own children. And the children of this period (who are now raising babies of their own) have acquired modes of thinking and feeling quite different from those of their parents and in accord with the newer, permissive patterns. We ask why our children are different from us, but we bring them up differently, so they ought to be different. It is possible that further changes will occur, and perhaps we shall have an eventual return to a more discipline-centered pattern, as the pendulum swings once again.

UNIFORMITY VERSUS PLURALISM

The problems of social change, and the social pressures on the individual discussed in Chapter 4, raise another interesting question: Has our society been moving toward increasing uniformity and away from *pluralism* (that is, a society with a wide variety of life styles and ways of thinking, feeling, and acting) over the course of recent decades? No doubt every social system must be capable of getting its members to do what is needed for it to survive and flourish. This means a degree of conformity or, if you like, accommodation to the demands and constraints of that system. But for each individual, membership in society must not be at the cost of losing his own psychological identity. Each of us needs some sense of unity with the social world in which we find ourselves and some sense of our own uniqueness as well. When developmental influences are multiple rather than unitary, the outcome is likely to be somewhere in between the extremes of a uniform and a pluralistic pattern (Figure 5.8).

The nature of American society has been the subject of much thought and debate by social analysts for nearly 150 years. Modern critics who have attempted to evaluate American life have posed the question as follows: Is the United States a "mass society," characterized by excessive uniformity and overattention to the immediate social fashions and proprieties?

Social change and the American character

In the 1950s, one of the most influential and controversial studies of mass society was made by David Riesman (1950) in a book entitled, *The Lonely Crowd: A Study of the Changing American Character* (for a nineteenth-century view, see Alexis de Tocqueville's *Democracy in America,* first published in 1835, reprinted in 1954). The debate that was ushered in by Riesman's analysis is germane to our present concern with social change. On the basis of examination of the contents of the mass media and other observations of the American scene, Riesman argued that the predominant pattern of life in the

Figure 5.8 New rules for old. (Drawing by J. J. Dunleavy)

"Listen, Bert, on this campus we don't dig those conformist clothes."

United States had been shifting from two older types that he called "tradition directed" and "inner directed" to a new type referred to as "other directed." *Tradition directed* meant that people tended to act as their forefathers had, with patterns of behavior and values dictated largely by clans, castes, professions, guilds, and the like, social groupings that had endured for centuries and whose values were modified only very slightly through succeeding generations. Persons living in accordance with this style would continue to conform or accommodate to these traditional values. During the nineteenth century, however, the dominant American character structure had become *inner directed*. Exemplars of this pattern were believers in the "Protestant ethic," a value system in which one worked and saved, sacrificing present pleasures for future success. According to the Calvinist tradition, such people are members of the "elect," that is, persons marked for salvation. Inner-directed persons were organized or directed from within in the sense that their values had been implanted by their elders early in life, and their behavior was guided toward whatever means they believed would help them achieve these internalized goals. The heroes of this style of life were the rugged individualists, people like the protagonists of Horatio Alger's novels, which carried such provocative titles as *Strive and Succeed, Success Against Odds, Sink or Swim,* and *Survive or Perish* (Figure 5.9).

The new, emerging character type of modern America of the post–World War I era, was the *other-directed* person. He was shallower, freer with his money, friendlier, less certain of himself and his values, and more in need of approval from others. His life was neither guided by traditional values or by a set of inner standards acquired from his parents but by an externally derived, shifting set of contemporaneous social norms communicated by those around him. In short, he was without roots, a conformist to the crowd, vulnerable to its approval and disapproval and subject to the loneliness that comes from the absence of internal strength. This transition had come about, suggested Riesman, because of technological advances in industry, transportation, and communications leading to greater interdependence among people. No longer could even the most individualistic member of society manage his affairs without the skills and labor of others. However, although men grew increasingly interdependent, they also became more estranged from each other with the atrophy of family ties and frequent challenges to old faiths and traditions. The absence of such firm anchors creates *the lonely crowd*, a society of anxious people, jammed together in crowded urban centers yet isolated psychologically from one another.

Riesman's analysis set in motion a sharp debate. Some questioned whether his characterology was an accurate description of Americans—those on the political left argued, for

Figure 5.9   One of the most popular themes of your grandparents' day. Has the "counterculture" changed things much? (Private collection)

example, that American businessmen were still inner-directed egotists. Others doubted whether most people could be typed into such pure and stereotyped categories. These criticisms were particularly telling because of the informal, casual methods of observation employed by Riesman. Yet in his enunciation of "ideal" types, Riesman was trying to bring into sharp relief the most salient traits of people living in our society rather than proposing that most people neatly fitted such abstractions. His work succeeded in stimulating much renewed interest in the American social scene.

A short time later, another widely read and influential sociological analysis, one quite compatible with that of Riesman, was offered by William H. Whyte, Jr. (1956). It was given the somewhat mocking title, *The Organization Man.* Whyte studied a community in a small suburb of Chicago called Park Forest. He lived there as a "participant observer," circulated questionnaires, conducted interviews, attended community meetings, and read what was printed within the relatively new suburb in order to get a picture of its life style and values. Whyte was particularly interested in what he perceived to be the changing pattern of American capitalism and the consequences of this pattern for the people working within corporations as rising young executives. The earlier business ethic in the United States had been highly individualistic and cut-throat, with ingenuity, resourcefulness, and even deviousness rewarded if it succeeded in successful capitalistic expansion. This ethic had given business a bad name, and with the advent of unionism and of increasing federal regulation, there was great pressure to change the earlier image. This was attempted through advertising, better treatment of employees, and the hiring and promoting of a very different type of man than had been previously sought, one who could "fit in" with the corporate structure, be loyal to it, avoid rocking the boat, and present a good appearance in public. The new dictum was described by Whyte (1956, p. 43) as follows:

Be loyal to the company, and the company will be loyal to you. After all, if you do a good job for the organization, it is only good sense for the organization to be good to you, because that will be best for everybody. There are a bunch of real people around here. Tell them what you think and they will respect you for it. . . . A man who gets ulcers shouldn't be in business anyway.

This new type of "organization man" came to live in Park Forest. He was ambitious but not too much so—since that might disturb things in the well-functioning organization. He was taught or believed that creative ideas came from the group rather than from the individual. He was rootless in the sense of having little concern with older family ties or with geographical areas to which one might feel he belonged. He never dwelt on where he had been and always assumed he would ultimately leave (he must be transferred to move up) and move to another community in a different part of the country. The community in which he lived contained no given standards, traditions, or sense of values, and there was much pressure for participation in its communal life. It was largely classless; nearly everyone was accepted regardless of previous income or life history. There was much opportunity for friendship, but the deviate was punished by exclusion. Whyte (1956, p. 401) describes the dilemma of the organization man in terms quite compatible with those of Riesman before him:

. . . the increasing benevolence of human relations, the more democratic atmosphere, has in one way made the individual's path more difficult. He is intimidated by normalcy. He too has become more adept at concealing hostilities and ambitions, more skillfully normal, but he knows he is different and he is not sure about the other. In his own peculiarities, he can feel isolated, a fraud who is not what he seems.

He is in an organization but not of it. He cannot fully be himself, since he must submerge himself and conform to the group in order to function successfully within the system. He needs the approval of the group to survive and flourish.

Surface uniformity and underlying diversity

Thus far the sociological analyses and observational studies cited here have emphasized conformity to external social norms as the lot of the average man of our contemporary society. Such a bleak view of the modern American has become very fashionable. It merged with the tendency, illustrated by a popular piece by Jane Jacobs (1961), to attack the homogeneous American middle-class suburb (Figure 5.10). This was a logical extension of Riesman's and Whyte's work, because Americans have tended to cluster since World War II in suburban settlements ringing the central city, communities celebrated in Malvina Reynolds' well-known song "Little Boxes" for their homogeneous "ticky tacky" houses, cars, dress, and manners. At the same time, critics have cried nostalgically for the return of heterogeneous communities where people of different classes and interests can mix freely, although one is forced to wonder whether these have ever really existed. All along there have been dissenters who have questioned the accuracy of this description of the American scene by Riesman and Whyte. These dissenters affirm instead that what has been emphasized are surface manifestations and that the more fundamental character of the population is far from stereotyped and conformist. Two recent exponents of this position, Daniel Bell and Herbert Gans, imply that diversity and individualism

Little boxes

Little boxes on the hillside,
Little boxes made of ticky tacky
Little boxes on the hillside,
Little boxes all the same.
There's a green one & a pink one
   & a blue one & a yellow one,
And they're all made out of ticky tacky,
   and they all look just the same.
And the boys go in-to business
   and they marry and raise a family in
Boxes made of ticky tacky
   and they all look just the same.

And the people in the houses
   all went to the university
Where they were put in boxes
   and they came out all the same
And there's doctors, and there's lawyers
   and there's business executives
And they're all made out of ticky tacky
   and they all look just the same.

And they all play on the golf course
   and drink their martini dry
And they all have pretty children
   and the children go to school
And the children go to summer camp
   and then to the university
Where they all are put in boxes
   and they come out all the same.

Little boxes on the hillside.
Little boxes made of ticky tacky
Little boxes on the hillside,
Little boxes all the same.

"Stedman, what's this I hear about your wife having another baby?"

is as strong now as it has ever been if only one looks more closely at things and interprets with less bias.

Bell (1962) questions even the logic of the concept of "mass society," the assumption that because people are thrown together socially and live or work in similar settings, they are necessarily alike in thought and feeling. You will recall in this connection Kelman's distinction in Chapter 4 between superficial compliance with social pressures and internalization of them. Bell (1962, p. 27) pursues a similar line in the following passage:

Individuals are not *tabulae rasae* [blank tablets or slates on which things are written]. They bring varying social conceptions to the same experience and go away with dissimilar responses. They may be silent, separate, detached, and anonymous while watching the movie, but afterwards they talk about it with friends and exchange opinions and judgments. They are once again members of particular social groups. Would one say that several hundred thousand or a thousand individuals home alone at night, but all reading the same book, constitute "mass"?

Bell feels that critics of the so-called mass society have been fooled by appearances. They observe people doing similar things, living in the same sort of houses, driving similar cars, and conclude erroneously that they think alike, that they are alike in character. Such a view, says Bell, is really a veiled attack on the masses as "mindless" by the alienated intellectual with a different set of values from the rest of society. Our egalitarian-oriented society holds the desirable value of making possible widespread material betterment, greater opportunity for the exercise of talent, and appreciation of culture and

197

education by the largest proportion of people possible. Such aspirations should not be equated, however, with conformity or the loss of individuality. Such a set of ideals increases the prospects of privacy, free choice of friends and occupations, the chance of gaining status on the basis of achievement rather than birth or assignment by the state, and a plurality of standards and norms. Indeed, suggests Bell, the facts about our society suggest anything but the elimination of individuality; quite the contrary, there is a plethora of variation.

Consider, for example, that during the late 1960s and early 1970s there has been great social unrest, marked conflict between groups, and the absence of a unified national purpose. On the one hand, one may be critical of such lack of unity, but it hardly suggests uniformity of viewpoint. There are organizations to the far right, the new left, beatniks, hippies, yippies, acid heads, conservatives, liberals, black power advocates, Presbyterians, Jews, Catholics, Baptists. There are dozens of different ethnic groups, which as we have recently discovered, never fully lost their original identity in the "melting pot." Bell's critique is particularly telling with respect to the extreme protagonists of the idea that we have developed into a "mass society" of robots, thinking, feeling, and wanting the same things and living in precisely the same style. But it also illustrates that in this area of sociological analysis, the same facts, because they are quite incomplete, are easily interpreted in diverse ways, depending on different ideological premises upheld by the social analysts.

Herbert Gans (1967) has studied the community of Levittown, a planned setting of inexpensive housing located in New Jersey. The community was comprised largely of young, working, or lower-middle-class people, somewhat more heterogeneous than Whyte's Park Forest, not as well-to-do, but also suburban.

One matter of great interest to Gans was how the various subpopulations within Levittown fitted themselves together. Gans rejects as invalid the popular image of suburbia in which people must conform or be rejected. He describes Levittown as a community where each group maintains its own identity, has its own values, attitudes, goals, politics, and interests yet remains on reasonably good terms with the other groups. Each group is only marginally affected by the presence of the others, their different life styles, values, and goals. They are concerned with compatibility; but propinquity does not make for friendship, nor does it lead to an abandonment of individual ways of thinking. Compatibility is achieved by civility and making surface concessions rather than by fundamental conformism. The groups do confront each other hastily from time to time when community policy must be developed, for example, in the instance of controversy about the operation of the school

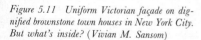

Figure 5.11   Uniform Victorian façade on dignified brownstone town houses in New York City. But what's inside? (Vivian M. Sansom)

system, a problem that frequently presents one of the trouble spots in such communities. Generally such confrontations do not get out of hand and there is give and take. There is, acknowledges Gans, a high degree of conformity in Levittown, but it takes the form of sharing of useful ideas and superficial concession to the communal setting rather than slavish copying of others to avoid differences. The population has not become outgoing, mindless conformers but remains a collection of individuals and subgroups retaining the social aspirations with which they came to the community. Gans (1967, pp. 165–167) gives the following interesting defense of suburban life:

> There is no question that Levittown is quite homogeneous in age and income as compared to established cities and small towns, but such comparisons are in many ways irrelevant. People do not live in the political units we call cities or small towns; often their social life takes place in areas even smaller than a census tract. Many such areas in the city are about as homogeneous in class as Levittown, and slum and high income areas, whether urban or suburban, are even more so. Small towns are notoriously rigid in their separation of rich and poor, and only appear to be more heterogeneous because individual neighborhoods are so small. All these considerations effectively question the belief that before the advent of modern suburbs Americans of all classes lived together. . . . Critics of the suburbs also inveigh against physical homogeneity and mass-produced housing. Like much of the rest of the critique, this charge is a thinly veiled attack on the culture of working-class and lower-class people, implying that mass-produced housing leads to mass-produced lives. The critics seem to forget that the town houses of the upper class in the nineteenth century were also physically homogeneous; that everyone, poor and rich alike, drove mass-produced homogeneous cars without damage to their personalities; and that today, only the rich can afford custom-built housing. [See Figure 5.11.]

Clash of ideologies

Balanced against this highly gracious pattern of relating to neighbors and avoiding conflict among the diverse ways of thinking to be found on the American scene, as in most other social systems, are the frequent explosions that take place when people allow their intense commitments to an ideological position to spill over into bitter quarrels. We fight wars over ideologies, wax eloquent about them, love and hate as a result of them, and devote stupendous energies to their defense, especially when they are tied up with our individual and collective identities (Note 5.2). The following newspaper story* is merely one of countless daily examples within our society.

The setting was an address by women's liberation militant Ti-Grace Atkinson, in an auditorium of Catholic Univer-

*Reported in the *San Francisco Chronicle,* March 12, 1971, p. 3.

Note 5.2

In reading the accompanying text discussion one must not gain the impression that only the layman is caught up in such struggles over ideology and that scientific research is free from the intrusion of emotional factors. Though they value objectivity and indeed require that research observations be capable of verification, scientists are people, subject to the same ideological biases as anyone else, which is why scrupulous research methods are of vital importance in evaluating conclusions. Lord Bertrand Russell, the noted British philosopher, put it somewhat sardonically this way:

> One may say broadly that all animals that have been carefully observed have behaved so as to confirm the philosophy in which the observer believed before his observation began. Nay, more, they have all displayed the national characteristics of the observer. Animals studied by Americans rush about frantically with an incredible display of bustle and pep, and at last achieve the desired result by chance. Animals observed by Germans sit still and think, and at last evolve solutions out of their own inner consciousness.

The problem is, of course, greatest in those scientific fields wherein what is studied has great impact on people's lives. Nowhere has this been more evident than in research on the highly charged issue of the respective roles of heredity and environment (nature versus nurture; see Chapter 2) in the determination of human intelligence and adaptation. This is because political ideology is tangled up in this issue, some believing that people adapt unsuccessfully because they are biologically or morally lacking (conservative ideology), and others that adaptive trouble and poor achievement arise from defects in the social environment (liberal-radical ideology).

One of the most fascinating attempts to tackle this problem is a study of eminent scholars who had expressed their political ideologies in their writings and also published research on the heredity-environment issue (Pastore, 1949). Twenty-four scientists were studied whose research on the nature-nurture issue took place from 1900 to 1940. The list included biologists, psychologists, anthropologists, and sociologists, and included such notables as Francis Galton,

William McDougall, Edward L. Thorndike, Henry H. Goddard, Lewis M. Terman, James McK. Cattell, and John B. Watson among the psychologists; William Bateson, J. B. S. Haldane, and Hermann J. Muller among the geneticists; and other leaders in their fields, like Karl Pearson, statistician, and Franz Boaz, anthropologist. These names may mean little or nothing to most readers, but to professional workers in these fields, the list is a "Who's Who" of distinguished men.

On the basis of their published statements about socioeconomic matters, 12 of the scholars were classed as liberal or radical, and 12 as conservatives, and the social ideologies they expressed were examined in relation to their stand on the nature-nurture issue. It was found that 11 of the 12 liberal-radicals took an environmentalist (nurture) stand in their research, while 11 of the 12 conservatives were hereditarians (nature). Later studies have tended to confirm this link between ideology and the way scientists tackle problems that have emotional relevance in human affairs (Tompkins, 1965).

This does not mean that scientific research is necessarily or automatically biased by ideology or that such bias cannot be controlled or corrected for, but only that it is always a danger and that we must be constantly on guard against it. The dangers are greatest not only where the issue being studied involves ideological polarities, but also where comparatively little is known about a problem or methodology for tackling it is still weak. Thus, the status of behavior genetics as a field was quite primitive at the time that the 24 scholars were actively working, and they easily fell into traps (such as overgeneralizing from a narrow context) that the modern behavior geneticist should be better able to avoid. Yet the alert reader will also recognize that emotional traps still lie in wait for the unsuspecting scientist, as is evident in the heated debates today about the racial inheritance of intelligence, with scientists still taking sides on either the hereditarian or environmentalist position.

Indeed the prevalence of bias is the most forceful argument against accepting casual impression as opposed to careful observation and measurement in psychological research, since such impression is more easily influenced by ideological biases; one must seek the highest precision and control possible in the design of research (see Note 4.1). The traditional scientific requirement that observations made by one researcher be replicated (duplicated) by others helps prevent inadvertent and unrecognized bias that can distort our study of phenomena.

sity in Washington, D.C. She was discussing the virginity of the Virgin Mary and is reported to have said that Mary, and women in general, had been badly used by the Catholic Church in the doctrine of the virgin birth of Christ. This doctrine, she said, emphasized and institutionalized the enslavement of women, forcing many of them into a kind of prostitution as wives. The altercation began when Kathryn Buckley Bozell, who edits the conservative Catholic magazine *Triumph,* was apparently so offended by Ms. Atkinson's attack on traditional church ideology that she attempted physically to strike the militant leader as she delivered her address.

Afterwards, Mrs. Bozell reportedly rushed outside the auditorium, knelt on the sidewalk, said a rosary, and shouted, "To hell with Catholic University." She also is reported to have said that Ms. Atkinson "can attack the Catholic viewpoint all she wants to, but I couldn't let her insult the Virgin Mary." Ms. Atkinson later countered with the observation that Mrs. Bozell was "a prostitute for her husband as well as the Catholic Church." Catholic University had attempted to bar Ms. Atkinson from speaking, but the student groups that invited her obtained a court order affirming that she was constitutionally entitled to make her address.

Episodes of this kind, in which there is an emotional and sometimes violent confrontation between ideologies, are common. The many state laws in the United States (all now abolished) banning the teaching of Darwin's theory of evolution is a classic example, and continuing efforts along these lines by fundamentalist religious groups, even up to the present in many parts of the country, illustrate the persistence of this perception of Darwinian theory as a serious threat to church values and ideology. Other examples include passionate anti-communism, patriotism, and Marxism. The point is that ideologies and the symbols representing them are not merely detached, intellectual conceptions of the world but may be clung to with intense passion. Perhaps because it is so important to people to try to find meaning and a coherent frame of reference for viewing life, death, and the world in which they live, any threat to or attack on the central ideology is likely to elicit strong emotional reactions, ranging from anxiety to intense anger or even depression. It is generally in the interest of people in the same community to keep such emotional explosions from breaking out, of course, and neighbors of diverse convictions usually manage to coexist in comparative tranquillity, creating at least the appearance of homogeneous ways of thinking, feeling, and acting. In recent times there have been occasional violent exceptions, however (Figure 5.12).

The concern with conformity and the spectre of a mass society, which was widespread and fashionable in the fifties,

Figure 5.12 Clash of ideologies: police barricades separate crowds as hostility escalates in Canarsie, middle-class section of Brooklyn, during 1972 struggle over busing of children into neighborhood schools. (Charles Zanlunghi)

seems now to be giving way to a new and opposite alarm, that our society is fractionating and moving toward anarchy and that this might ultimately lead to government repression. As the distinguished British scholar Lord Kenneth Clark has expressed it in a newspaper interview in 1972, "Without any doubt the great fear of our time is that anarchy beyond a certain point will produce a reaction. It always does. It did in Rome. Military or fascist or communist, call it what you will, an authoritarian reaction. The question is how far people can live without some kind of framework without lapsing into anarchy. . . . In your country (the United States) the law is no longer held in the same respect, is it? Religion has no effect. A lot of people were taught at home. What parents said was wrong was the basis of morality. No young person is going to swallow that now." Clark is referring to the loss of shared belief in our society (the very opposite of the older concerns of Riesman and Whyte). Although he supports dissent and challenge to our institutions, he is troubled by what he believes to be the completeness of the revolt against *all* institutions, *all* rules. Although the revolt is understandable, indeed, as he

201

says, "You couldn't do much worse than the old institutions and rules did in the last 40 years," the attack on all institutions also has very serious consequences for civilization, leaving nothing to hang onto, with the conceivable result that there will be an opposite reaction yielding the interposition of an authoritarian regime.

Clark's impressions are supported by evidence that in the United States trust in government is at a low ebb. Data obtained in a recent survey from the University of Michigan has suggested that in the 6-year period between 1964 and 1970 cynicism or lack of trust has risen among whites from 20 to 39 percent, and even more so among blacks. This includes, incidentally, cynics both of the political left and of the right, and the distrust cuts across political party lines.* Thus, the central problem of American society today is probably not a trend toward increasing uniformity; rather, it may be the inability of society to find a unified direction that will permit it to get down to the difficult business of solving the many nagging social problems that still plague it. Clearly our social world is changing, and with this change new problems are arising for all of us collectively and for each of us individually.

*Since this was written, public disclosures emerging from the Watergate scandal have rocked America and confidence in government has diminished far below what it was when the above survey was made (see Note 9.9).

Note 5.3

A word might be added here about the study of literature in general to reveal the nature of society (present and past) and the ways people thought, felt, and acted in various periods of history. We cannot enter past civilizations as the social anthropologist can do with primitive cultures still extant. Therefore, to reconstruct man in his previous societies requires materials from them that have been preserved and that can be analyzed.

Imagine yourself, for example, as an explorer from another world who has landed on earth in the vicinity of the United States but can only remain for an hour or two. Suppose too that you have had no previous source of information about this culture, but you have the ability to learn language rapidly. What would you pick up on this visit to learn about the people living on this part of the globe? One obvious source would be books, newspapers, magazines, comic books, and even advertising brochures and posters. By studying these, much could be learned about the people, how they think, feel, and behave.

In a book devoted to the sociological use of literature and popular culture in studies of social and psychological history, Lowenthal (1961, p. xii) puts it as follows:

Popular commodities serve primarily as indicators of the socio-psychological characteristics of the multitude. By studying the organization, content, and linguistic symbols of the mass media, we learn about the typical forms of behavior, attitudes, commonly held beliefs, prejudices, and aspirations of large numbers of people. At least since the separation of literature into the two distinct fields of art and commodity in the course of the eighteenth century, the popular literary products can make no claim to insight and truth. Yet, since they have become a powerful force in the life of modern man, their symbols cannot be overestimated as diagnostic tools for studying man in contemporary society.

Lowenthal gives many examples of this use

of literature and the popular media to study peoples in times past, two of which are noted below. The dramatist Pierre Corneille, a major spokesman for the French absolute monarchy, lived and wrote during the first three quarters of the seventeenth century. As a child of his times, Corneille viewed man as unable by his very nature to impose order on himself and his affairs without the direction of a powerful state authority. In contrast, Henrik Ibsen, the nineteenth-century Norwegian dramatist, living and writing at a time in which the middle-class values were predominant, portrayed his characters as highly competitive in all their public and private affairs. At the place and time of these writers, both sets of character traits were thought to be innate, though the contrast between those periods makes it clear that the character traits diversely painted by Corneille and Ibsen must have had social origins.

One of the most extensive anthropological studies of a society and its people was done by Ruth Benedict (1946) without the

ATTEMPTS TO IMAGINE THE FUTURE: DREAM OR NIGHTMARE?

If we accept the principle that social change is necessary, or at least inevitable, then we can also entertain the possibility of influencing such change for the better. We can at least try to imagine what sort of ideal world might be possible. Throughout history there has been frequent dissatisfaction with the existing social order and a reaching toward better intellectual and moral systems. Many utopian literary works have been written, some of which (such as Plato's *Republic*) were conceived as long ago as classical Greek times, and some of which are of the most recent vintage [B. F. Skinner's (1961) *Walden Two,* Herbert Marcuse's (1961) *Eros and Civilization,* or Charles Reich's (1970) *The Greening of America*]. These works reveal much about the perceived failures of various social orders, as well as the fundamental assumptions about the nature of man held by their authors. Study of early utopian writings can help us assess the reactions of people to the times in which they lived, as well as their fantasies and dreams of the future (see Note 5.3).

investigator ever having been to that country. During World War II there was great governmental concern in the United States about what to expect of the Japanese people after military victory had been achieved. There was also concern about the problem of how to achieve victory with a minimum of casualties. It was not clear whether the Japanese would surrender when it became clear that they could no longer succeed militarily or whether it would be necessary to engage in a bloody fight for every square inch of their country. The long history of self-imposed isolation from the rest of the world and Japan's difficult ideographic written language had resulted in an absence of dependable knowledge in the United States about Japanese culture.

As a cultural anthropologist, Ruth Benedict agreed to undertake a study of the culture and the people. Obviously she could not visit Japan during the war, and therefore she could only rely on indirect methods to learn about it. These methods consisted of exten- sive interviews with expatriate Japanese living in this country, and an extensive examination was made of Japanese literature for clues about the people's social structure, codes of conduct, values, and modes of thinking, feeling, and acting. One result of this effort was Benedict's famous book *The Chrysanthemum and the Sword.* Another was increased sophistication on the part of the American government about the Japanese nation and how to manage the postwar occupation in 1945. (See marginal quotations from this remarkable work, presented in Chapter 4, page 146.)

There is an obvious limitation to the use of mass media and literary works (like the utopian novels discussed in the text) to make inferences about the social structure of the times and the psychological status of people living in them. Fiction often portrays only selective types of people rather than a broad spectrum of the population. And only a small proportion of any given population might be literate (or able to read such works), a diffi- culty not so serious in modern times in the case of mass media such as movies and television. But the general problem is the uncertain *representativeness* of the themes observed in literature for the populations living in particular places and times (see Note 4.5, page 168).

Nevertheless, the other available information about past societies and people is subject to similar limitations and is not more reliable. Historical accounts are often quite limited and traditionally do not address themselves sufficiently to the psychological characteristics of a people or to their daily activities and customs. Histories are also often rather biased and selective. But the greatest literary works of past eras do, indeed, describe behavior patterns consistent with what else is known from other sources about life in those times. Much that is psychologically relevant can be gleaned from careful study of these works about how man at different times in the world's history has understood himself and his society.

The word utopia was coined by Sir Thomas More (1516). It was derived from the Greek root "topia," that is, an existing and ongoing place. Utopia literally means no place that really exists, and utopian writings have tackled the philosophical task of trying to imagine a better (or, in some cases, worse) social order than presently exists. As Edwin Warner puts it in a *Time* Magazine article of January 18, 1971 (p. 19):

Utopia is not meant to be lived in. At its best, it is a model for the exemplary life, not a guide to reality. As he brought his majestic *Republic* to a close, Plato acknowledged that he had written it to build a better city within the heart of man. We live in a world that is part reality, part dream; the tension between the two is the source of our creativity. . . .

The idealized society in utopian literature is also sometimes called *eutopia,* the place of the good life. Many writers have written anti-utopias, or *dystopias.* Examples of the latter are Aldous Huxley's (1932) *Brave New World,* George Orwell's (1949) *1984,* and Anthony Burgess's (1962) *A Clockwork Orange.* The visions in these books are nightmares of a world gone crazy rather than fantasies of the good life.

Frank Manuel (1965) has analyzed utopian thought, and divides it into three major categories. Here I shall refer to these as (1) benign utopias; (2) programs for the good life; and (3) individually centered utopias. These correspond roughly to some of the historical changes in outlook toward society that have occurred from ancient to modern times.

Benign utopias

In early utopias up to the nineteenth century, including Plato's *Republic,* the good life is conceived as depending on a wise social order and power is vested in a benign, though authoritarian, state. It was assumed that all conflict, dissension, and hostility generates an unhappy social climate; by establishing a firm and stable social order such conflicts were to be eliminated. Laws and institutions would be devised to maximize the loving tendencies in man's nature. This would result in a life of continuous pleasure, subject only to the natural ills of disease and old age, and even these might be greatly reduced. In some of these Greco-Christian utopias, the main force creating dissension is the uncontrolled longing for property, and with the development of a communal social order it was presumed that equality, peace, and a contempt for riches would be achieved.

In this mode of utopian thought, the state is all-powerful, and as in the case of Plato's *Republic,* governed by an elite of wise men. Emphasis is placed on a stable social order, with

The object of this part is to bridge, as rapidly and vigorously as possible, the transition from the year 1970 to the year 2036. An age of enormous mechanical and industrial energy has to be suggested by a few moments of picture and music. The music should begin with a monstrous clangor and come down to a smoother and smoother rhythm as efficiency prevails over stress. The shots dissolve rapidly on to one another, and are bridged with enigmatic and eccentric mechanical movements. The small figures of men move among the monstrosities of mechanism, more and more dwarfed by their accumulating intensity.

An explosive blast fills the screen. The smoke clears, and the work of the engineers of this new age looms upon us. First, there is a great clearance of old material and a preparation for new structures. Gigantic cranes swing across the screen. Old ruined steel frameworks are torn down. Shots are given of the clearing up of old buildings and ruins.

Then come shots suggesting experiment, design, and the making of new materials. A huge power station and machine details are shown. Digging machines are seen making a gigantic excavation. Conveyer belts carry away the debris. Stress is laid on the work of excavation because the Everytown of the

change minimized, and institutions arranged so that change would neither be needed nor sought. Utopia is usually created in these tales by an enlightened despot who maintains the system in a strict but just fashion. The maximum good is represented as tranquillity, and only moderation is regarded as pleasurable (Manuel refers to them as "utopias of calm felicity").

This utopian conception is derived from certain psychological assumptions about the nature of man—that to be happy he needed only sensate comfort, food, clothing, sexual gratification, and protection against foreign enemies. An educational system would smoothly transmit the calm felicity from one generation to the next. As Manuel (1965, p. 300) puts it, "There were general needs for religious adoration, a bit of good clean fun in the evening, amiable conversation, the respect due to one's age and sexual status, but there were no powerful drives and no stormy passions to upset the equilibrium. . . . The mood of the system is sameness, the tonus one of Stoic calm, without excitement." Thus, by implication, boredom is not generally conceived to be a problem by these writers. The main focus is placed on the elimination of crisis, conflict, strong emotion, uncertainty, and instability—the pure Apollonian world! Still, only a particularly placid kind of man could find total self-fulfillment in such an environment, surely not the hero, entrepreneur, saint, or ascetic.

Programs for the good life

The tone of utopian thought changed drastically around the time of the French Revolution, when calm felicity was no longer seen as the ideal state of mankind. New definitions of man's nature were developing that cast doubt on the tradition in Greek and Christian thought of the superiority of man's rational processes over his passions. Important in this new era was the spreading industrial revolution, bringing growing awareness of the poverty and misery of urban industrial workers, a new historical consciousness emphasizing change and progress, increased emphasis on the need for equality (which had been absent in the previous authoritarian utopias), and the emergence of a romantic cult of self-expression and individuality. Thus the new utopias became dynamic and open-ended rather than static and closed (Figure 5.13).

The onrushing technological revolution in Western society threatened the individual with loss of identity and anonymity, so the new utopian order would attempt to preserve what was being endangered. The new assumption was that once man's needs for love and creative self-expression were satisfied, there would be little need to acquire power over

year 2036 will be dug into the hills. It will not be a skyscraper city.

A chemical factory, with a dark liquid bubbling in giant retorts, works swiftly and smoothly. Masked workers go to and fro. The liquid is poured out into a molding machine that is making walls for new buildings.

The metal scaffolding of the new town is being made and great slabs of wall from the molding machine are placed in position. The lines of the new subterranean city of Everytown begin to appear, bold and colossal. . . .

FINALE

An observatory at a high point above Everytown. A telescopic mirror of the night sky showing the cylinder as a very small speck against a starry background. Cabal and Passworthy stand before this mirror.

Cabal: "There! There they go! That faint gleam of light."
Pause.
Passworthy: "I feel—what we have done is—monstrous."
Cabal: "What they have done is magnificent."
Passworthy: "Will they return?"
Cabal: "Yes. And go again. And again—until the landing can be made and the moon is conquered. This is only a beginning."
Passworthy: "And if they don't return—my son, and your daughter? What of that, Cabal."
Cabal (with a catch in his voice but resolute): "Then presently—others will go."
Passworthy: "My God! Is there never to be an age of happiness? Is there never to be rest?"
Cabal: "Rest enough for the individual man. Too much of it and too soon, and we call it death. But for MAN no rest and no ending. He must go on—conquest beyond conquest. This little planet and its winds and ways, and all the laws of mind and matter that restrain him. Then the planets about him, and at last out across immensity to the stars. And when he has conquered all the deeps of space and all the mysteries of time—still he will be beginning."
Passworthy: "But we are such little creatures. Poor humanity. So fragile—so weak."
Cabal: "Little animals, eh?"
Passworthy: "Little animals."
Cabal: "If we are no more than animals—we must snatch at our little scraps of happiness and live and suffer and pass, mattering no more—than all the other animals do—or have done." (He points out at the stars). "It is that—or this? All the universe—or nothing. . . . Which shall it be, Passworthy?"
[From the filmscript of *Things to Come* by H. G. Wells, 1935. Reprinted by permission of the Estate of H. G. Wells.]

Figure 5.13   H. G. Wells's vision of the underground city of the future, as projected in this still from the motion picture Things to Come, *produced in 1936 by Alexander Korda. Although this scene is set in the year 2036, it does not look particularly futuristic to our eyes today. Science fiction, it seems, can hardly keep ahead of the rush of events. (Photo from National Film Archive, London)*

others. Human energies could be turned from exploitation of man by man to exploitation of nature. Outlets were to be created to divert murderous passions into more innocent channels. The critical thing was to provide for each man's needs. For Karl Marx this meant putting an end to working-class poverty. For others, the Marxist dictum "each according to his needs" was enlarged to include the actualization of the individual in psychological terms as well. Power was to be restored to the people, because society did not need to be ruled and policed but rather *administered* by wise leaders, including scientists and technical experts. Still, the state was of the essence because it was only through its power, through technological exploitation of nature and the concerted efforts of its

people, that the means of subsistence and the wealth needed
for the good life for all could be achieved. Thus, nineteenth-
century utopians, including Americans such as Edward Bellamy (1888; reprinted 1967) in his novel *Looking Backward:
2000–1887,* did not reject the concept of a strong central government within which people went about their socially useful
tasks. Bellamy wrote of an ideal society in the year 2000, a
Golden Age with "substitution of scientific methods of an
organized and unified industrial system for the wasteful struggle of the present competitive plan." According to orthodox
Marxists, only at some later stage, presumably after a complete
reorganization and reeducation of all elements of society, could
the state be allowed to "wither away."

Individually centered utopias

With few exceptions (for example, Skinner's *Walden Two*),
the modern crop of utopians treat the political state as anathema. The social order is viewed as the source of repression
of the potential good in man. These utopians seek to free the
individual from the twin yokes of psychological repression (as
exemplified by the Viennese society of Freud's youth, in late-
Victorian times) and of political suppression of human freedom and decency (as exemplified by the modern all-powerful
totalitarian state). The recent utopian emphasis is thus clearly
both psychological and political.

Consider Stanley Kubrick's 1972 film *A Clockwork Orange,*
based on the Burgess novel, one of the dystopias noted earlier,
for what it shows about people's fears in our complex world
of technological power (Figure 5.14). The film can be regarded as one man's vision of what is in store in the near-
future—roving gangs stealing, raping, terrorizing, and killing,
with a police equally vicious, and a society geared to the
absolute control of all human impulses that are not useful
to it. Perhaps most frightening is the coldness and mechanical
dehumanization of people when they engage in their destructive acts, and of the government when it deals with the
individual. The "hero," Alex, is part of this world of terrorism
and sadism, a killer who is sent to prison for 14 years,
after he has murdered a woman for fun.

Submitting to an experiment in conditioning (designed
to relieve prison congestion, because more room is needed for
political prisoners), he is turned into a conforming moral robot
who becomes physically ill in the face of sex or violence. He
has been made into a mechanical robot, a "clockwork orange,"
without the possibility even of moral choice. However, after
he has been rendered harmless and is released, he then falls
prey to his former victims.

The film, unfortunately I think, vindicates Alex's ugliness

[All of us] are victims in mind, body, or soul, in one way or another, of the present barbarous industrial and social arrangements, and . . . we are all equally interested, if not for ourselves, yet for our children, in breaking the meshes which entangle us, and struggling upward to a higher, nobler, happier plane of existence. [Edward Bellamy]

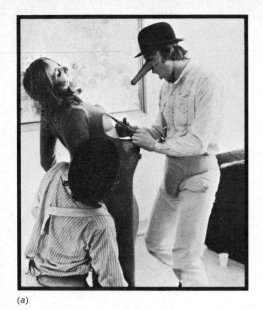

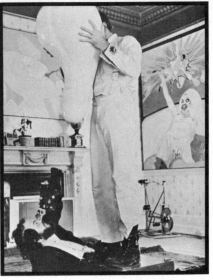

(a)

(b)

Figure 5.14 Dystopia: a nightmare vision of the future, as portrayed in Stanley Kubrick's A Clockwork Orange: (a) Alex and his gang break into a house and rape a woman after binding and gagging her husband. (b) The murder scene, with Kubrick and his camera in place of the victim. (c) The newly reconditioned, nonviolent Alex is assaulted by his former victims. (From the motion picture A CLOCKWORK ORANGE; © 1972 Warner Bros. Inc.; photos from the Museum of Modern Art/Film Stills Archive)

(c)

by making his impulse-ridden, sadistic life seem no worse, perhaps even more attractive, than the garbage-strewn, cold, soulless world around him. As critic Pauline Kael puts it, the "straight" people seem to be more twisted than Alex, since he suffers, while they are inhuman and incapable of suffering. Like Aldous Huxley's *Brave New World* of drugged, conforming humanity, and George Orwell's *1984* with its "big brother," endless warfare, and total government control, *Clockwork Orange* pushes the theme of conditioned man as the hapless victim of a superregulating, dehumanizing state apparatus.

It is this same theme that evokes the frequently negative reaction to B. F. Skinner's (1961) vision of a good society controlled by conditioning, although in criticizing his stance it is often forgotten that there could be no functioning society of any sort without some degree of conformity or socialization. Skinner has pointed out, for example, that our traditional concepts of individual freedom and dignity get in the way of progress, because they have allowed people to do as they please, and when left to their own devices, people do what comes naturally, such as aggressing, polluting, reproducing, and over-populating the world. Therefore, it is essential that we begin to control human behavior through conditioning, and to re-design the social system to make people behave better so that the culture can be strengthened and perpetuated. Such social controls would systematically provide rewards and punishments (see Chapter 4), mainly rewards, in order to help people do what is necessary to promote a peaceful and altruistically oriented world, free of the main social evils of our times and of the past. It is not surprising, of course, that the utopian image Skinner sets forth is often seen as a nightmare not unlike Orwell's *1984*, dominated in all probability by an elite cadre, maybe of behavioral scientists (or someone using behavioral scientists). Yet what Skinner has to say is certainly worth reading and thinking about since mass conditioning, for good or ill, already surrounds us to a considerable extent in the form of high-pressure advertising, politicised education, and official propaganda campaigns of all kinds.

The dilemma, of course, is how to preserve the most valuable qualities of humanity in this time of increasingly centralized authority. The most serious spectre before most creators of utopias and dystopias is the dehumanization of man through exaggerated social conditioning, and modern utopian heroes tend to be those who refuse to succumb and who remain deviant.

Modern would-be utopians have faced a difficult psychological dilemma, posed by Sigmund Freud's psychoanalytic writings and to some extent by a common misinterpretation of Darwinian evolution. Darwin's concepts of adaptation created for some the image of man, like a wild beast, fighting tooth and claw for survival. This image is predicated on the assumption that the biological nature of man required that he compete for social survival, just as "survival of the fittest" marked the evolutionary adaptive principle in lower animals (see Chapter 1). Actually, Darwinism does not state that the animal who can fight best survives but only that a species whose biological structures are best fitted for *whatever* kind of environment it may live in will survive. There may be no direct competition at all in the sense of one organism surviving at the expense of others, although such competition often occurs. However, the widely held but incorrect extension of Darwin's

"The real power, the power we have to fight for night and day, is not power over things, but over men." He paused, and for a moment assumed again his air of a schoolmaster questioning a promising pupil: "How does one man assert his power over another, Winston?"

Winston thought. "By making him suffer," he said.

"Exactly. By making him suffer. Obedience is not enough. Unless he is suffering, how can you be sure that he is obeying your will and not his own? Power is in inflicting pain and humiliation. Power is in tearing human minds to pieces and putting them together again in new shapes of your own choosing. Do you begin to see, then, what kind of world we are creating? It is the exact opposite of the stupid hedonistic Utopias that the old reformers imagined. A world of fear and treachery and torment, a world of trampling and being trampled upon, a world which will grow not less but more merciless as it refines itself. Progress in our world will be progress toward more pain. The old civilizations claimed that they were founded on love or justice. Ours is founded upon hatred. In our world there will be no emotions except fear, rage, triumph, and self-abasement. Everything else we shall destroy—everything. . . . [From George Orwell, 1984, pp. 269–270. New York: Harcourt Brace Jovanovich, 1949]

ideas to society, sometimes referred to as "social Darwinism," posed a dilemma for utopian writers who adopted it. How could biological man be accommodated within a social order that also permitted the good life for all, with humaneness, cooperativeness, and peacefulness?

Freudian theory also posed a dilemma for utopians because the essence of what Freud was saying is that man is not the rational animal he once thought himself to be. Quite the contrary, below the surface of his rationality lay the really important, powerful, unconscious determinants of his behavior and feelings, the biologically based sexual and aggressive drives. Freud (not Darwin) quite explicitly argued that man was instinctively an aggressive animal, that violence of man against man seemed to be inevitable, and that the only hope was to redirect ("sublimate" was his actual term) this aggressive drive toward socially useful and constructive activities; however, it could never be completely bottled up. A strong social order was essential for man's well-being, since otherwise his brutish nature would take over and be terribly destructive. Social repression of man's instinctual urges could not entirely hold down these drives without also creating neurotically warped personalities representing the breaking out of these

Figure 5.15   Another dystopian projection of the near future, where all books are forbidden and government-controlled television reigns supreme. Here we see firemen busy hunting down and destroying illegal reading matter, a scene reminiscent of the Nazi book-burning rampages of the 1930s. (From the film FAHRENHEIT 451, *directed by François Truffaut, based on the Ray Bradbury story. Courtesy of Universal Pictures; photos from the Museum of Modern Art/Film Stills Archive)*

(a)

(b)

repressed urges. From such a standpoint, what kind of utopia could be envisaged for man? Only a completely rational and loving man could make such an ideal possible, and Freud had shown that man was not like that.

The utopian works of the past several decades have, by and large, taken one of two alternative routes to the solution of this dilemma of man's assumed brutish nature. In the first, a world is imagined in which the imperious forces of man's animal body are left behind in favor of the *spiritualization* of mankind. This kind of utopia is not built on the gratification of the senses but on the strengthening of the spirit so that the body can be transcended and hence made less important. Then brotherhood and communion can be achieved. This solution is reminiscent of the Christ ideal and is not at all alien to the precepts of Buddhism. Religious experience becomes the highest good. One may find some aspects of this approach in the later writings of psychologist Abraham Maslow (1968), who increasingly emphasized "peak experiences" as one of the hallmarks of his view of the healthy personality. We shall return to these ideas in Chapter 12.

The other route turns on exactly the opposite premise and involves a redefinition of Freud's assumptions about the necessity of repressing man's instinctual urges lest they destroy him. The argument states that it is precisely the fact of social repression of man's sexuality that leads him into frustration, misery, and aggression toward his fellow man. The solution is therefore the *enhancement and fuller expression of the senses,* with all human activity sexualized. With the fullest gratification of the human body and an emphasis on man's loving poten-tial, an end to the more destructive aspects of man's social life can be visualized because frustration is thereby banished. Instead of placing man under some controlling state or politi-cal dominion, as was the style of most preceding versions of utopia, the new utopians move toward anarchy on the as-sumption that man needs to be freed from external constraints to regain individual identity and the essential humanness that he has lost. Widely read examples of this latter approach are the works of Norman O. Brown (1959), Herbert Marcuse (1961), and Charles A. Reich (1970). Although there are im-portant differences in each of these visions of utopia, they share this common theme of the dehumanization of man by a re-pressive, competitive, bureaucratic, elitist, and class-structured society. Some recent science fiction films, such as Jean-Luc Godard's *Alphaville* (1965), François Truffaut's *Fahrenheit 451* (1966), and Stanley Kubrick's *2001: A Space Odyssey* (1968), also deal with this theme (Figure 5.15).

One can see in even this brief examination of utopian writing that in every era man has expressed his discontent with

Though I attain Buddhahood, I will not be satisfied until people all over the world are influenced by my spirit of loving compassion that will purify their minds and heal their bodies and lift them above the things of the world. [The teaching of Buddha, 11th ed., p. 96. Tokyo: Bukkyo Dendo Kyokai, 1970]

And [Jesus] said to his disciples, "Therefore I tell you, do not be anxious about your life, what you shall eat, nor about your body, what you shall put on. For life is more than food, and the body more than clothing. Consider the ravens: they neither sow nor reap, they have neither storehouse nor barn, and yet God feeds them. Of how much more value are you than the birds! And which of you by being anxious can add a cubit to his stature? If then you are not able to do as small a thing as that, why are you anxious about the rest? Consider the lilies, how they grow; they nei-ther toil nor spin; yet I tell you, even Solomon in all his glory was not arrayed like one of these. . . ." [The Gospel according to St. Luke, 12:22]

the existing social environment and dreamt of a better life. This cursory review has had to overlook many important variations and nuances in the multitude of utopian works that have been published since Plato's times. My purpose here has been to point up the changing concepts and values of man about himself and his social environment as revealed by utopian writings.

[One can subscribe to the view] that the life of man in society, while it is incidentally a biological fact, has characteristics which are not reducible to biology and must be explained in the distinctive terms of cultural analysis: that the physical well-being of men is a result of their social organization and not vice-versa; that social improvement is a product of advances in technology and social organization, and not of breeding or selective elimination; that judgments as to the value of competition between men or enterprises or nations must be based upon social and not allegedly biological consequences; and finally, that there is nothing in nature or a naturalistic philosophy of life which makes impossible the acceptance of moral sanctions which can be employed for the common good. . . . [From Hofstadter, 1944]

CONCLUDING COMMENT

The focus of this chapter has been on social change and the implications of such change for social behavior and personality development. Social change creates what has been called the generation gap, transitions in patterns of child rearing, and differences in the orientation of new generations toward their lives. There is also justifiable debate about the extent and nature of the social changes we are undergoing. There have been numerous conflicting studies of the changing American character, and debates about whether or not we are a mass culture. As long as there has been written history people have expressed dissatisfaction with the existing social order and have tried to imagine a better world in which to live. Utopian novels or essays tell us a great deal about how people in different eras saw their societies and hoped to change them. Comparable analyses can be found today, although the notions of what is wrong with the social system and how it should be refashioned have changed greatly over past eras.

Can we have an effect on the changing social world, helping to shape it in directions that will improve the lives of people in our own society and throughout the world? It is difficult to say. Perhaps so. We hope that we can, since clearly there is need for change, although there is little agreement over the kinds of change that are needed and possible to eliminate the thorniest problems of the human race. To speak sensibly about change and its implications requires that we understand better how people are governed by the physical and social environment in which they live. Hence what we have learned in Part I serves as a good background for our examination in coming chapters of some other major ills that beset mankind and threaten its very self-destruction. Our understanding of these problems must transcend ideological dogma and be predicated as much as possible on reliable knowledge before we can venture to solve what has always seemed insoluble. We now turn (in Parts II and III) to two of the major quandaries that have confronted humanity since the dawn of time—man's aggression and man's prejudice.

ANNOTATED LIST OF SUGGESTED READINGS

The nature of our society

Grossack, M., and Gardner, H. *Man and men: Social psychology as social science.* Scranton, Pa.: International Textbook Co., 1970 (paper). A pleasant and interesting brief text about our society from the point of view of social psychology; written for beginning students.

Utopian writing

Daedalus: Journal of the American Academy of Arts and Sciences, Spring, 1965, Vol. 94. This whole issue of the journal is given over to a series of excellent (though somewhat advanced) discussions of utopias, their history and significance.

Cultural change and the generation gap

Mead, Margaret. *Culture and commitment: A study of the generation gap.* Garden City, N.Y.: Natural History Press/Doubleday, 1970. A brief book attempting to explain today's generation gap in terms of changes in relationships between grandparents, parents, and children brought about by technology-induced mobility; takes the position that culture as handed down from the past is disappearing in the face of totally new demands on present and future generations.

Toffler, A. *Future shock.* New York: Random House, 1970. Extensive documentation of many of the facets of social and technological changes that man has undergone during his history, with some interesting speculation on the impact of these changes on our way of thinking and reacting.

To judge from remains of predators found at his sites, early man
was an increasingly effective creature, who drove such unaggres-
sive daylight hunters as the cheetah and the wild dog from their
kills. In the dark, he was at a disadvantage and took shelter,
leaving the hunt to leopard, lion, and hyena, but in the day,
confronted with his sticks and stones, strange upright stance,
and the shrieks, scowls, and manic jumps of primate threat dis-
play, these more dignified creatures probably gave way. [From
Matthiessen, 1972, p. 106]

No characteristic of man has been more important or more continuously a problem throughout history than his aggressiveness. In its multiple forms, aggression is held responsible for man's considerable mastery of his environment, for his achievements in building and maintaining strong social systems, and for his awesome destructiveness toward other men and what they have built. No one can construct a psychology of human behavior without taking aggression into account. Today the study of man's aggressive nature becomes especially urgent, not merely because our own society is living through a period of considerable turmoil and violence but because the engines of destruction that man has built and that are now at the disposal of leaders of hostile nations are frightful in their power. It has never been more important to try to understand this Janus-faced tendency of man—one side evidently capable of

2   3

4

5

6

bringing him to the heights of personal, social, and cultural achievement; the other side capable of destroying all civilization and life on this planet.

The term *aggression* is used in many different senses, covering a wide range of human behavior. One of its common meanings is conveyed by the word "assertiveness," or even "aggressiveness," which is best defined as competitive striving as distinguished from passivity or indifference. Thus, when a football player plays a hard and driving game, we say he is aggressive; or when a child rebels against authority, struggles for independence, or strives to gain *power* or *mastery* over his environment, he too is being aggressive. We say he is *attacking* problems, *getting his teeth into* them, or *overcoming* difficulties. Although such assertiveness and aggression may be fashioned out of similar human tendencies, they are not the same thing, if we mean by aggression what most psychologists do, namely, the *effort to harm or threaten* another person.

One difficulty produced by the failure to distinguish in our language between assertiveness, on the one hand, and anger, hatred, or hostility, on the other, is that we might think of all aggression as "bad," although the assertive traits just noted have been extremely valuable to man in his striving to control the circumstances of his life, to defend himself against innumerable dangers, and to establish his dominant position among all organisms of this world. Assertiveness does not automatically imply destructive behavior or the urge to harm others, and we should be careful to distinguish these separate but probably related meanings. Thus, if one speaks of aggression as "the dark side of man," certain forms of destructive actions or impulses are meant. In a sense, then, aggression may be a cloud "with a silver lining" whose dark side we must learn to control. In this text, when the term aggression is used from now on it will mean the effort to harm and destroy, or the threat to overcome by force, rather than the quality of competitive assertiveness.

When psychologists use the term aggression in the sense of violent combativeness, they also tend to exclude what biological scientists often refer to as *predatory aggres-*

[The] evolution of social fighting has proceeded independently in
different species, with the result that . . . it serves a variety of
social functions. The most general of these . . . is the availabil-
ity of social space, but agonistic behavior may also regulate the
availability of mates, as in deer and sage grouse; the division
of food, in dogs and wolves but not in mice; and the availability
of breeding territories in many species of birds. [From Scott,
1970, p. 570]

9

10

After the prey animal has been maneuvered within reach begins the central event in the predatory sequence: capture. . . . The first stage . . . consists of a final lunge and grab when the distance between the predator and the prey has been reduced to a yard or less. If the chase has been a cooperative venture, more than one chimpanzee may catch the prey. . . . The killing is normally brief. If the prey is in the grasp of a single chimpanzee, the chimpanzee may bite the back of the prey's neck or twist its neck in both hands. Alternatively, the chimpanzee may stand upright, grasping the prey by its legs, and strike its head and body against the ground or a tree trunk. If the prey is caught by more than one chimpanzee, it may be torn apart as each captor tugs on a different limb: in this way killing and dividing are accomplished simultaneously. [From Teleki, 1973, p. 37]

11

sion (or *predation*), that is, the carnivorous behavior occuring widely throughout the animal kingdom in which one animal hunts and kills another for food. As we shall see in Chapter 6, such predatory activity occurs for very different reasons and with other motivations than aggressive forms of destructive behavior. There are thus good grounds for excluding predation from the psychological treatment of aggression, although some anthropologists think of predatory aggressiveness as the evolutionary basis of all other kinds. In any case, aggression as a human social problem could have little to do with such food-getting activities of predators, in which emotions such as hate play no part, although both forms of behavior tend to be lumped together in common speech.

12

Violence is not always a negative phenomenon, except to the absolute pacifist. Whether or not violence is "bad" is a matter of one's point of view and the circumstances. Throughout history, struggle against evil oppression has required violence. Few people would disapprove, say, a violent revolt by the inmates of Nazi concentration camps in World War II against their brutal SS guards. Remember too that societies, good ones as well as bad, maintain order by the implicit threat of punitive violence and by carrying out this threat when laws have been disobeyed. The existence of law enforcement (police, courts, jails) always implies that transgressors will be prevented from illegal acts either by physical restraint or by the prospect of punishment, which in many parts of the world still includes the death penalty. It is sometimes difficult, as we all know, to evaluate dispassionately just how much force and police power is required to maintain public order—or when such violent enforcement becomes excessive.

What is the relation between aggression and violence? Clearly some forms of aggression are nonviolent and relatively subtle, as when one person attacks another verbally, criticizing him "for his own good" or perhaps even in highly disguised, underhanded fashion. Violent aggression, on the other hand, may range from mild confrontation and threat to a clash causing severe injury or death. Physical restraint is a form of violence, although it may do little physical harm; it may of course

13

14

Mankind has for many thousands of years conducted experiments
in the eating of human flesh, and has not found it wanting.
Especially it has proved to foster the feeling of solidarity within
the group and of antipathy toward the alien, providing an in-
comparable means of gratifying with deep emotion the hatred of
one's enemy. Cannibalism was proved to be extraordinarily well
qualified to provide the excitement of the ultimate aggression. . . .

[The] Indians of Vancouver Island found a heightened excitation,
disciplined in endless ritual and taboo, in a ceremonial show of
cannibalism. Secret societies of the men were all important . . . ;
the whole winter was given over to their rites . . . ; membership
was limited to first sons of noble birth. When it was time for
such an one to become a member of the society, he retired to the
forests . . . and it was said that the spirits had taken him. Here
an almost mummified corpse was prepared and smoked, and at
the appointed time, in the midst of great excitement, the noble
youth returned to the village with the Spirit of the Cannibal
upon him. A member of the society carried the corpse before him,
while with violent rhythms and trembling of his tense body, he
rendered in dance his seeking for human flesh. He was held by
his neck ring that he might not attack the people, and he uttered
a terrible reiterated cannibal cry. But when he had bitten the
corpse, the ecstasy left him, and he was "tamed." [From Benedict,
1959, pp. 44–46]

be highly offensive or psychologically damaging to the person. Thus, there is an intimate relation between aggression and violence, but not an identity.

Some of the most interesting examples of human aggression are expressed as ridicule so thoroughly disguised that the victim does not even recognize it as such. An excellent example of disguised attack are, of all things, the jingles of Mother Goose! Consider the familiar lines shown at the right. These seem like harmless nursery rhymes to us now but in reality were devastating criticisms of personages of the British royal family and relate to political events of the seventeenth century.

In this verse, known to most of us from childhood, is craftily interwoven the bitter story of James Stuart (1688–1766), pretender to the throne of England. James Stuart, illegitimate son of James II, soon after he was born was smuggled into the bed of Mary d'Este, the royal mistress. It was then claimed that he was the King's lawful heir. Although this claim was rejected and the deception revealed, the resultant uproar contributed to the downfall of the King himself. James II was deposed the same year, 1688, and had to flee into exile. The baby on the tree top refers to the royal child. The cradle rocking in the wind is an allusion to the winds of adversity that blew against the illegitimate royal baby and ultimately sent crashing down not only the baby's claim to the throne but the very throne itself. The verse is thus a veiled and pungent criticism of King James, disguised because of the danger of too open and direct

Hush-a-bye, Baby, on the tree top,
When the wind blows, the cradle will rock;
When the tree shakes, the cradle will fall,
Down will come Baby, and cradle, and all.

15

an attack on powerful authority. This illustration points up the reason for extending our concern with aggression to its most subtle as well as its more obvious forms.

Although aggression of man against man and conflicts leading to war between nations have always produced great human suffering, today the threat of utter annihilation hangs over the whole earth like the sword of Damocles. The potential devastation of war has been growing by leaps and bounds over the last several hundred years. In the 126 years between 1820 and 1945, it has been estimated that 59 million people were killed in murderous attacks and deadly conflicts of all kinds. These figures ignore the enormous additional cost of warfare—in disease, economic depletion, destruction of property, and dislocation (which the United States alone of the major participants of World War II escaped), as well as innumerable permanent injuries inflicted on both civilian and military personnel. The high incidence of civilian deaths and injuries in modern war is attributable to changes in both the technology and rules of warfare. Less than 5 percent of the population was involved in the European wars of the seventeenth and eighteenth centuries, whereas nearly the entire adult population was engaged in World War II, not merely at the fighting front but in producing the services at home necessary for war. Thus, warfare limited to military combatants has changed to "total war"; such struggles are no longer won when the enemy army is defeated but only when the whole enemy society has been rendered unable to

16

17

18

While violence breeds violence, it can also act as a vaccine. This dual truth of experience has often been proved. To-day, the very fact that the world has suffered so badly from the plague of war twice within a generation may increase the counter-active effects. Besides war-weariness, there are other important psychological factors that may help to create conditions favourable to a renewed period of limitation. The multiplication of machinery has sterilized the romance of war, by diminishing the value of human qualities. Courage and skill are of little avail against a superiority of machinery. The bomber has extended the dehumanizing effect of artillery; the flying bomb, the rocket bomb, and the atomic bomb have carried it further in turn. Such weapons make nonsense of the soldierly idea that success in war is a proof of a people's virility and virtue. They have reduced men to the status of rabbits in a laboratory experiment. That unromantic truth may have a better chance of being generally recognized in the aftermath of the Second World War. [From Liddell Hart, 1947, pp. 116–117]

continue the fighting, often by devastating aerial attack.

Primitive man fought in hand-to-hand combat using clubs and spears; only in recent historical times has he acquired guns and explosives that enable him to kill a few score at a time; and the past half century has given birth to continuously more massive engines of destruction (culminating in hydrogen bomb warheads transported by electronically guided rockets) that can kill vast populations in a single moment. The first, most

primitive atomic weapons killed more than 250,000 people at Hiroshima and Nagasaki on August 6 and 9, 1945, and left large numbers terribly injured. The cities were leveled. One now hears projections of hundreds of millions killed and injured in a first strike by the Soviet Union or the United States, and these figures ignore the multiplication of casualties that surely would result from retaliatory actions. There is every possibility that such an atomic war would destroy all life on earth.

Although it is unlikely that The Bomb is the only cause of our present preoccupation with violence, it has most likely led to an increasing concern with the implications of death and dying, a subject that was taboo

In Hiroshima at 8:09 A.M. on August 6, 1945, at a height of
    600 meters . . . above the center of the city, an atomic bomb
composed of uranium-235 exploded. It was the time to prepare
    breakfast, so that not only the heat from the atomic bomb but
also fires from charcoal braziers contributed much to the conflag-
    ration. Approximately 6000 youngsters and older students . . .
were in the streets, engaged in voluntary tasks of clearing the
    ground [forming fire lanes, a precaution against expected in-
cendiary bombing], and many adults were on their way to work.
    . . . The atomic bomb exploded over the heart of the city, and
almost two-thirds of the 90,000 buildings within 25 square
    kilometers were destroyed. [Approximately 260,000 people were
killed, and 163,000 were injured by burns and exposure to radia-
    tion.] The fires that followed immediately after the explosion be-
came a major conflagration and spread in all directions, covering
    a circular area of 11 square kilometers. Most of the fires were
extinguished by evening. At the instant of the explosion, the
    sky was filled with a bluish-white flash, and this was followed
by a sound like that of thunder. The sun was obscured, and the
    sky was hidden by yellow, white, and brown smoke for about
20 minutes. About 60 minutes after the explosion rain began
    to fall, which lasted until evening at the hypocenter. . . . The
rainwater appeared blackish for the first two hours and then
    gradually changed to ordinary transparent rain. . . . [From
Watanabe, 1965, pp. 486–487]

in decades past. Destructive violence holds the center of our attention, and we search for understanding and remedies. In recent years Americans have seen a President (John F. Kennedy), a Senator and presidential candidate (Robert F. Kennedy), and a distinguished winner of the Nobel Peace Prize (Martin Luther King) assassinated. Students on several college campuses have been killed by police or National Guardsmen, and in turn policemen are being gunned down in ever-increasing numbers, escalating the violence markedly. In the United States the rate of violent crimes, including murder, forcible rape, robbery, and aggravated assault, has increased dramatically during the past decade. And the increasing worldwide incidence of terrorism, assassination, kidnapping, skyjacking, and numerous other acts of violence have forced the problem to every nation's attention. Man the killer continues to play the dominant role on the world scene.

We shall consider in the next two chapters whether there is any direct connection between aggression in man and aggression in lower animals. Is man's aggressive behavior similar to that of lower animals, and in what ways? What are the biological forces in animals that account for their patterns of aggression and violence? Are such forces present in man, and how do they work?

Another class of questions concerns the extent to which patterns of aggression are learned. How and under what conditions does such learning occur? Under what social conditions will each form of aggression manifest itself? What are the personality characteristics of aggressive and nonaggressive individuals?

In man, of course, there is a complex interaction between biological forces and social forces. Different patterns of aggression are acquired under various conditions of life. How can biological dispositions to aggression and violence in man be modified or redirected by social forces? What other properties of man can be brought into play in the control of aggression? Are aggressive forces at work in the individual also operative in the group or nation, or must other factors be weighed as well? Can we explain societal forms of aggression in the same terms as we explain individual forms?

23

24

*The fateful question [for] the human species seems to me to be
whether and to what extent the cultural process developed in it
will succeed in mastering the derangements of communal life
caused by . . . aggression and self-destruction. In this connection,
perhaps the phase through which we are at this moment passing
deserves special interest. Men have brought their powers of sub-
duing the forces of nature to such a pitch that by using them
they could very easily exterminate each other to the last man.
They know this—hence arises a great part of their current unrest, their dejection, their mood of apprehension. [From Freud,
1968 ed., p. 80]*

25

26

One of the most untenable features of the present
literature on aggression is the tendency by many writers
to take an either/or position on the role of biological
and social factors. Although protagonists of these two
views often seem to claim a corner on the truth, each
alone is only partly correct. Ultimately the answers will
depend on the fusing of both sets of insights into a common theory, based on the interplay of factors. We shall
explore the most provocative and useful ideas of each
group in the next two chapters, with some occasional
rather tentative efforts to show their interaction.

Illustrations: Background photo, pp. 214, 215—Intertribal warfare among the Dani highlanders of New Guinea (photo from *Dead Birds,* 1963, filmed by Robert Gardner and Karl Heider; Contemporary/McGraw-Hill Films). 1. Gu, god of iron and war, sculpture from Dahomey, Africa (Musée de l'Homme, Paris; photo: Eliot Elisofon). 2. Lion pride with zebra kill (Mark Boulton from National Audubon Society). 3. Threat display of angry baboon (photo courtesy of Thomas McKern). 4. Male sage grouse in mating display. 5. Male gazelles fighting. 6. Combat dance of male rattlesnakes. 7. Gannets nesting, Bonaventure Island, Quebec. 8. Fighting gannets (4 Harry Engels; 5,7 Leonard Lee Rue III; 6 William B. Allen; 8 Allan D. Cruikshank: all from National Audubon Society). 9. Chimpanzee eating young baboon that it has hunted and killed. 10. Chimp using its teeth to break into skull; although chimps often participate in meat-sharing clusters, the brain is a prized portion, not to be shared. 11. Young chimp requesting by hand gesture some of the food that its mother is chewing (9–11 Photos taken at Gombe National Park, Tanzania, by Geza Teleki). 12. King Kong (photo courtesy of Mark A. Binn). 13. Masked dancers at Kwakiutl Cannibal ceremony, Pacific Northwest Coast. 14. Kachina dolls representing ancestral spirits of the Pueblo Indians. 15. Kikuyu tribal conclave, Kenya (13–15 Courtesy of The American Museum of Natural History). 16. Machine gunners in World War I (U.S. Signal Corps photo). 17–19 The Western Front, 1916 (Imperial War Museum, London). 20. American military cemetery in Belgium. 21. Magdeburg, Germany, April 1945 (20,21 U.S. Army photos). 22 Hiroshima (U.S. Air Force photo). 23. B-52 bomber. 24. Atomic bomb victims, August 6, 1945. 25. Bikini atoll. (23–25 Wide World Photos). 26. Hanoi, December 1972 (A.F.P./Pictorial Parade).

The topic of aggression falls within the fields of motivation and emotion. The concept of *motivation* refers to drives, wishes, intentions, and goals. These terms concern events taking place within the person or animal, brought about partly by internal physiological conditions (as in hunger) and partly by the stimulating conditions of the environment (such as the sight of food, or signals of the presence of food) that generate motivated behavior (like searching for food, eating). Under such conditions we say that the person or animal is hungry, or has the drive to eat. In the case of aggression, one speaks of the drive or intention to attack someone and the aggressive actions that accompany it. We shall examine here the biosocial mechanisms underlying such motivated aggressive behavior.

The language of *emotion* also refers to certain inner events that are brought about by certain kinds of commerce between the person or animal and his environment. Thus, when danger is perceived, we become frightened, a state that consists of the recognition of danger, the feelings (or *affects* as they are usually called) connected with this recognition and which we call fear, a stirred-up bodily state, and perhaps actions normally associated with this state, such as fleeing or freezing (when alarmed, many animals will suddenly become motionless for a few moments). The cognitions, affects, and behaviors associated with the various emotions are usually distinctive enough to be referred to by different names, such as fear, grief, depression, guilt, joy, relief, or love. In the case of aggression we speak of the emotion of anger or rage and the actions involved in attacking someone; frequently such attacks are triggered by threats (real or imagined) that the attacker perceives as coming from another individual.

The differences between a motive and an emotion need not concern us greatly here. These concepts provide somewhat

Figure 6.1 Lulu, with her infant daughter Patty Cake, born at the Central Park Zoo, New York City. Baby gorillas, like other primates, are quite helpless at birth and would not survive if their mothers were disinterested in caring for them. (The New York Times)

different perspectives about similar or closely related psychological events, the psychology of motivation emphasizing the direction and coordination of human effort, that is, its goal-directedness, and the psychology of emotion emphasizing states of excitement, subjective affects, bodily disturbances, and emergency actions. Anyway, aggression (and anger) can be regarded as both a motive and an emotion. The scientific task in each case is the same, namely, to specify the nature and rules of this commerce with the environment, including the properties of the person or animal, and of the environment too, that bring about an aggressive response or a state of anger rather than some other type of reaction.

Since motives and emotions are certainly part of man's biological heritage, we must also examine them in other animals to determine similarities and differences. This will help us to locate their evolutionary origins and to identify the special biological properties of man that leads him to react to certain internal and external conditions in certain ways. The kind of interaction with the environment that leads to aggression may be found universally in the animal kingdom, so it is reasonable to think that human patterns of aggression derive in some measure from our biological inheritance.

In order to survive, animals must engage in certain vital activities: *feeding; mating; parental behavior* (to insure the survival of the offspring until they can fend for themselves; see Figure 6.1); *avoidance of or escape from danger; exploration* of the environment so as to develop competence; and *aggression,* a type of behavior that performs a number of key functions in survival, as we shall see. Animal species that can do all these things effectively have a far better chance of perpetuating themselves, hence evolutionary selection pressures favor development of these traits (see Chapter 1). Each member of a given species is so constructed that it has internal drives to do those things which must be done for its survival. Such innate, inherited drives have been grouped historically under the broad category of "instinct."

THE DOCTRINE OF INSTINCT

Around the turn of the century, the concept of *instinct* was widely employed by psychologists to explain the behavior of organisms, including man. One of the most influential writers of the time, William McDougall (1918, p. 30), defined instinct as "an inherited or innate psycho-physical disposition which determines its possessor to perceive, or pay attention to, objects of a certain class, to experience an emotional excitement or a particular quality upon perceiving such an object, and to act in regard to it in a particular manner, or at least, to experience an impulse to such an action." (Note that emphasis here should be placed on the words *inherited or innate.*)

One of the problems was to catalog the instincts in man, that is, to list the basic instincts that could account for all human behavior, and McDougall's list started off modestly enough with the following items: flight, repulsion, curiosity, pugnacity, self-abasement, self-assertion, parental, reproductive, hunger, gregariousness, acquisitiveness, and constructiveness. However, there was a disturbing tendency for the list to grow as new writers suggested more and more examples of instinctual behavior not covered by the basic list, and it became clear that the concept as it was being used was not helping at all to explain things; it had become merely a label for a given type of behavior, masquerading as an explanation. Thus, if one asked why people fight, the circular answer was, "That is the way man is; he has the instinct to fight." And so on with gregariousness, play, sports, gambling, or eating apples in one's own orchard. Any kind of behavior one wanted to explain was attributed to the mysterious force of instinct, and in turn the instinct was defined by the behavior it was designed to explain in the first place.

To make the concept of instinct scientifically useful, however, required evidence of the nature of the specific instinctual mechanism and the conditions under which it operated. Otherwise the reasoning would lead nowhere. Such evidence was not forthcoming at that time; it was not until more recent times that ethologists began systematically studying animal behavior more closely. Thus, early versions of the concept of instinct were largely ways of concealing our ignorance of the human mind by pointing vaguely to man's inborn nature. As a result, the concept was severely attacked and went into eclipse for many years, especially in psychology, although it was never completely abandoned. The idea of instinct is undergoing some resurgence of late as a result of a growing tradition of competent ethological and psychobiological research of the sort that was lacking in Darwin's day and during the first several decades of the twentieth century. However, as we shall see shortly, new versions of the concept are taking forms very different from earlier ones.

There are actually two main variants of the instinct doctrine: (1) Adaptive functions such as maternal behavior, attachment, and aggression are *innate drives* or needs operating within the animal. (2) Certain kinds of behavior are *innate responses* that are triggered by some suitable external stimulus. Each of these variants has been used in attempts to explain aggression in terms of instinct.

Aggression as an innate drive

If aggression is an innate drive, it would follow that we "have to" engage in aggressive acts or else suffer from mounting tension or discomfort; we are literally "driven" to this by our biological makeup. To grasp this fully requires also that we understand the principle of *tension reduction.*

In the philosophy of hedonism, man seeks only pleasure and the avoidance of pain. The principle of tension-reduction likewise states that all behavior (in man as well as in other animals) can be understood as an effort to reduce tension or pain. This was one of the ways psychology tried to link adaptive behavior to biology, and it fit well within the Darwinian tradition because biological survival obviously depended, in part, on the maintenance of the proper internal state; for example, we cannot live without food or water and an appropriate body temperature. A delicately poised, balanced state of the tissues has to be maintained, even though this balance is constantly being disturbed by changes in the environment or by demands made upon the system. *Homeostasis* is the process by which a balance is maintained in the inner economy of the body (Cannon, 1939).

To a considerable extent this internal homeostatic equilibrium is maintained by automatic processes regulated by hormones and the nervous system and acting somewhat like a home thermostat when it turns on the furnace as the temperature falls below the "set" point and turns it off again when the temperature rises above that point (see Chapter 1). Nevertheless, these automatic, internal forms of regulation are not the whole story. To survive, an animal must ward off external attack, seek food and water, find or build shelter, and so on, thereby engaging in vigorous interaction with the environment. This is where the psychological principle of tension reduction comes in. Through it, all behavior is understood as an effort to preserve an equilibrium, both within the body and in its relations with the environment. Though some maintenance actions are innate (like defecation and urination), in many instances we must learn through experience what is necessary to minimize or eliminate tissue deficits, for example, to reduce thirst by drinking certain liquids (water, milk) and not others (sea water, urine). In any event, from the tension-reduction point of view a satiated animal is a quiescent animal; an animal with a tissue deficit is a tense or restless one, in a state leading ultimately to action that may reduce tension and thus facilitate survival.

Notice that the idea of tension reduction invites an emphasis on simple inborn bodily needs or drives shared by all mammals, such as hunger, thirst, or sex. An early version of the idea that man inherited a biological tendency to aggression from his animal ancestors was that aggression was such an inborn or innate drive. Man "had to" engage in aggressive behavior just as he "had to" eat, or else suffer pain or tension.

Freud's views   Sigmund Freud was one of the major spokesman for this innate drive concept of aggression. In his early theorizing about human instincts or drives he had ignored aggression, not even writing about it until he was 59 years old in 1915 (during World War I), roughly 20 years after he began evolving his psychoanalytic theory (Figure 6.2). When he finally did become interested in aggression, at first he adopted a way of thinking quite similar to that of many psychologists today, namely, that aggression was a reaction to the frustration of other innate drives. But by 1920 he was treating aggression as a separate innate drive as powerful as sex. One of the things that evidently influenced him greatly was the ubiquitousness of human savagery and war, which he regarded as evidence of the "dark" or animal side of human nature. In 1930, with the world in economic and political turmoil but with the outbreak of World War II still 10 years off, Freud expressed a pessimistic outlook on the difficulty of restraining human savagery, as is illustrated by the following rather bitter passage from *Civilization and Its Discontents* (reprinted in 1957, pp. 85–86):

> The bit of truth behind all this—one so eagerly denied—is that men are not gentle, friendly creatures wishing for love, who simply defend themselves if they are attacked, but that a powerful measure of desire for aggression has to be reckoned as part of their instinctual endowment. The result is that their neighbor is to them not only a possible helper or sexual object, but also a temptation to them to gratify their aggressiveness on him, to exploit his capacity for work without recompense, to use him sexually without his consent, to seize his possessions, to humiliate him, to cause him pain, to torture and to kill him. *Homo homini lupus**; who has the courage to dispute it in the face of all the evidence in his own life and in history? This aggressive cruelty usually lies in wait for some provocation, or else it steps into the service of some other purpose, the aim of which might as well have been achieved by milder measures. In circumstances that favour it, when these forces in the mind which ordinarily inhibit it cease to operate, it also manifests itself spontaneously and reveals men as savage beasts to whom the thought of sparing their own kind is alien. Anyone who calls to mind the atrocities of the early migrations, of the invasions by the Huns or by the so-called Mongols under Jenghiz Khan and Tamurlane, of the sack of Jerusalem by the pious Crusaders, even indeed the horrors of the last world-war, will have to bow his head humbly before the truth of this view of man.

*Man is a wolf to man.

(a)

(b)

(c)

Figure 6.2   (a) Sigmund Freud and his sons Ernst (left) and Martin in 1916. With both sons in uniforms of the Austro-Hungarian Army, Freud was very conscious of the World War and its horrors. (b) Australian troops pass through devastated Chateau Wood near Ypres, in Flanders, Belgium, in October 1917. (c) Horses struggle through knee-deep mud during Battle of the Somme, November 1916; the ground has been churned up by continuous heavy artillery bombardment. (a: By courtesy of Mrs. E. Lucie Freud; b, c: Imperial War Museum, London)

Freud used the term *death instinct* (or *Thanatos,* after the Greek god of death) to refer to the innate, self-destructive drive in man from which aggression toward his fellow man is derived. *Thanatos* is opposed to *Eros,* the instinct toward life (named for the Greek god of love). Freud saw the urge to self-destruction as analogous to the physical principle of the dissolution of matter. This self-destructive urge is deflected for a time during life, and in this brief period *Eros* prevails and the energy of the death instinct is turned outward against others. Sometimes, however, the life instinct fails, as in suicide, or when a person unconsciously seeks to destroy himself through alcoholism or drug abuse, or by exposing himself needlessly to dangers (as in high-risk activities such as skydiving, auto racing, or tightrope walking; Figure 6.3). When the innate self-destructive energies are turned outward, man acts violently to preserve his own life and to destroy others.

Implications of the innate drive theme   Certain conclusions about the control of human aggression flow from the foregoing drive concept, and these should be examined briefly. In the instinctivist view, not only is aggression inevitable in human affairs, but it must be regarded as a desirable feature of man's psychic apparatus, since his intense aggressiveness is the means by which he has protected himself against his enemies and survived in the competitive struggle with larger, more powerful beasts. And, to carry this argument up to the present, only if modern man is permitted to express or discharge this inherited aggressive drive can he be considered psychologically healthy. But the drive or instinct, if one adopts such a view, must be controlled somehow, since in its primitive form it results in great social harm.

Figure 6.3   Stuntman Stephen Ladd entering a flaming tunnel of straw bales during a performance at a trade show in Epping, England, in November 1972. Seconds after this picture was taken, the motorcycle lost power and its 25-year-old driver was burned to death. (Wide World Photos)

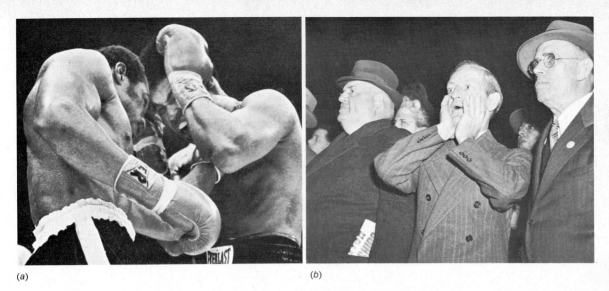

(a)

(b)

Figure 6.4 Modern gladiatorial combat. (a) His jaw broken by a punch thrown earlier in the bout, Muhammed Ali grimaces in pain as Ken Norton connects with a left to the chin. The San Diego match went the full 12 rounds, and Ali—virtually unrecognizable at the end—lost on a split decision. (b) At another fight, in New York City, in September 1941, excited fans look on as heavyweight champion Joe Louis knocks out challenger Lou Nova. (Wide World Photos)

Innate drives can be inhibited and yet at the same time expressed in alternative, socially desirable ways. Such rechanneling or "sublimation," as this is called, depends on proper child-rearing practices and the evolution of suitable social structures. The right kind of inhibition is one that permits substitute outlets for the energy, enabling discharge of the drive but turning it into socially constructive or at least harmless enterprises, such as competitive games and sports, "fighting" against natural obstacles, "attacking" social injustice, or "striving" to achieve (see Figure 6.4). Freud believed, in fact, that the works of man and the entire social structure could be explained as a sublimation of sexual and aggressive energies. But the trick is to provide adequate channeling. The severe restrictions and the failure to provide adequate releases can lead to neurotic and psychotic psychic disturbances; too weak restrictions (excessive permissiveness) can lead to defects of character, such as *overly aggressive* or violent personalities.

One can see, therefore, that treating aggression as an innate drive also implies that the positive or desirable aspects of aggression, such as all kinds of striving, are strictly sublimations of the more fundamental urge to harm. This is one of the implications of Freudian theory that troubles many thoughtful psychologists who see in this view a negative message about man, namely, that it is only by taming his "bad

233

animal instincts" that man can become good, altruistic, and humanitarian. In passing I might note that personality theorists after Freud (for example, Fromm, 1955; Maslow, 1968) have argued for an opposing point of view that is now being called "humanistic psychology" (for example, Maddi and Costa, 1972). One of its tenets is that man's positive and distinctly human qualities are also a natural part of his biology, rather than a derivative of socialization, and that these qualities are too often suppressed by a destructive social environment. (We will consider this idea further in Chapter 12.)

Problems with instinctivism Not only was there little evidence from the realm of biology to support the idea of a death instinct (except the obvious fact that all organisms die), but the idea of a physical system "running down" is a rather poor analogy to self-destructive urges. It is sensible to say that man, like all systems, ultimately runs down, but this is hardly tantamount to his having a death instinct, or a *death wish,* as Freud often referred to its psychological expression. Such an analogy illogically personifies the dissolution of tissues, making it a "desire" for death, or for the tranquillity of nothingness or Nirvana. This illogical feature, and the difficulty of obtaining any evidence with which to evaluate such a concept, led to widespread rejection of the death instinct by professionals, even many of those sympathetic to psychoanalysis in general (see Fenichel, 1945).

What is rejected in the Freudian view is not the implication that aggression in man has biological origins, but the idea of *innate drive,* that is, that energy from this self-destructive drive automatically builds up in the person unless there is some opportunity for its release in aggressive actions, just as pressure builds up in a steam boiler unless released through valves or by explosion. This energy or drive model of motivation and emotion is sometimes referred to as the "boiler analogy." There is thus postulated a *need* to express aggression, which if not gratified will result in mounting discomfort and other disturbances. It is the basis of the common idea that the "discharge" of anger is essential because it "lets off steam" just like an overloaded boiler.

Actually, the boiler analogy gets its strongest support from comparison with another biological urge that Freud thought was closely linked to aggression, namely sex. Abstinence from sex appears to make people more responsive to sexual stimulation. "Wet dreams" in men are a particularly good example of the build-up and discharge of the sex urge. Sex does seem to work as the drive-concept indicates, by a gradual increase in the drive tension through hormonal activity, leading ultimately to discharge. It is thus sensible to think of sex as an innate "urge" whose expression relieves,

(a)   (b)   (c)

discharges, or releases "pressure" or tension. For example, in his research with the stickleback fish, Tinbergen (1951), another protagonist of the drive concept, showed that as sexual abstinence was prolonged, males became increasingly indiscriminate in their sexual approaches to females. Normally, such male fish will make sexual advances only to suitable models of the female presented by the experimenter (and of course to real females); but under increased sexual tension from hormone build-up, they made advances to very inadequate models considerably distorted from the "real thing." The only awkwardness in this concept as applied to sex is that people also find the stimulation or build-up phase of sexual excitement pleasureable rather than painful, up to a point.

However, there is serious doubt that the innate drive concept can be soundly applied to aggression. There is no suitable evidence making it reasonable to say, for example, that an animal or person has a built-in drive to attack or fight and that when the energy of this drive is blocked from discharge it mounts, creates drive tension, and must therefore be discharged somehow. Research in man has also revealed that the "discharge" of aggression is as likely to increase the chances of further attack as to decrease it (the release is not necessarily "cathartic"), a result out of keeping with the concept of aggression as a kind of drive or energy needing to be released.

Although the innate drive concept as applied to aggression may not be altogether sound, it still has enough adherents to require that it be represented seriously in any treatment of aggression, and many of us who see the arguments against it still feel some nagging doubt, especially in the light of the obvious gratification and even joy that people can feel at others' suffering, even when this joy is suffused with guilt (Figure 6.5). As Freud (1959) put it in a letter to Albert Einstein in 1932 entitled *Why War?*, ". . . there is no use in trying to get rid of men's aggressive inclinations. We are told that in certain happy regions of the earth, where nature

Figure 6.5 Public savagery. (a,b) President Jean-Bédel Bokassa at the prison in Bangui, Central African Republic, in July 1972, when he ordered his soldiers to beat men imprisoned for theft with clubs. "Thieves must all die," he declared. "There will be no more theft in the Central African Republic." Of the 46 men beaten, at least three died. Their corpses were put on public display with the battered survivors, many of whom appeared near death. (Photographs by Hughes Vassal and Henri Bureau; Gamma) (c) In Dacca, East Pakistan (now Bangladesh), in December 1971, Bengali militiamen stab their bayonets into victims executed for collaboration with the West Pakistani Army during the civil war. (This photo was part of a series for which photographers Horst Faas and Michel Laurent of the Associated Press won a Pulitzer Prize; Wide World Photos)

provides in abundance everything that man requires, there are races whose life is passed in tranquillity and who know neither compulsion nor aggressiveness. I can scarcely believe it and I should be glad to hear more of these fortunate beings . . ." At about the same time as Freud's letter, Ruth Benedict (1934) was pointing out that Eskimos and Mission Indians could not conceive of organized battles of tribe against tribe; others have noted that warfare was absent among the Andaman Islanders, the Arunta, the Western Shoshoni, the Yahgan, and other cultures. However, in deference to Freud's view, in such societies there is no absence of aggression, although the forms of violence might be different, occurring for example as homicides and interfamily feuds rather than tribal warfare. The question still remains, therefore: Why is man so aggressive so uniformly all over the world, if there is no simple biological drive to be so? We shall see later (and in Chapter 7) that a frequent answer tends to be that if man is uniformly aggressive it is because the external conditions of his life continually generate aggression. Anyway, it seems best to say that the issue of an innate aggressive drive still remains in doubt, at least in the minds of many. Were Freud even partly right, it would greatly affect how we are to deal with the problem.

There are some simple primitive tribes which have punitive sanctions for all killing, and these tribes have no idea what war is. Just after the First World War, I was living with the Serrano Indians of Southern California, who had this uncivilized peculiarity. The reverberations of the great struggle had reached them only faintly, but they were bewildered. This expedition overseas, they had thought at first, was like a dangerous journey down into the country of the Gulf of California, and they could understand that a man might lose his life on such a trip. The enemy, too, venturing into such country, might be decimated. But American soldiers apparently killed men, and these Indians speculated that then they would not be returning to their own country after the war. Would not punishment be in store for them? My explanations fell on uncomprehending ears, for they had no double standard which would serve to set apart the Battle of the Marne from a drunken brawl in which men knifed each other in the back after a bottle of firewater.

A primitive tribe in order to judge as these Serrano Indians judged must live in very special conditions. Either they must have a little island all to themselves, or they must have good natural boundaries, or they must live in regions and own possessions which more restless people have not coveted. Most primitive tribes are not so isolated as this or not so poor, and to them the double standard in homicide is upheld by their everyday experience. [From Benedict, 1959, p. 371]

Aggression as an innate response

This approach to aggression, and many other of the phenomena that fall within the traditional concept of instinct, predominates today and is nicely expressed by John Scott (1958, pp. 63–64):

The important fact is that the chain of causation [of aggression] in every case eventually traces back to the outside. There is no physiological evidence of any spontaneous stimulation for fighting arising within the body. This means that there is no need for fighting, either aggressive or defensive, apart from what happens in the external environment. We may conclude that a person who is fortunate enough to exist in an environment which is without stimulation to fight will not suffer physiological or nervous damage because he never fights. This is a quite different situation from the physiology of eating, where the internal processes of metabolism lead to definite physiological changes which eventually produce hunger and stimulation to eat, without any change in the external environment.

We can also conclude that there is no such thing as a simple "instinct for fighting," in the sense of an internal driving force which has to be satisfied. There is, however, an internal physiological mechanism which has only to be stimulated to produce fighting. . . .

How the response is aroused   The vital interplay between internal biological factors and external, environmental stimulation in shaping what many have called instinctual behavior can be illustrated by the work of ornithologist Daniel S. Lehrman (1964) on the reproductive cycle in the ring dove. The cycle appears similar to most other instinctual behaviors in that a predictable, stereotyped pattern is displayed that, on closer inspection and research, turns out to be quite modifiable and dependent on the nature and timing of the environmental and hormonal stimulation. Although it does not deal with aggression, we can apply it to aggression nonetheless.

The seemingly stereotyped pattern looks like this: When a male and female ring dove with no previous breeding experience are placed together in a cage with a glass bowl and some nesting material, courtship occurs; the male struts about, bows, and coos at the female. After some hours, they select the glass bowl (or any other concave place), crouch in it, and give distinctive coos. The male gathers materials for the nest, and the female constructs the nest while standing in the bowl. After a week or so of this nest building, during which copulation has also occurred, the female seems to become strongly attached to the nest as evidenced by the fact that she resists being dislodged from it. She is about to lay her eggs. Seven to eleven days after the onset of courtship, she produces the first egg, usually around five o'clock in the afternoon. She sits on the egg, then lays another one, usually about nine the next morning. During that day, the male usually takes a turn sitting and thereafter the two birds sit alternately, with the male typically sitting about 6 hours during the middle of the day and the female the rest of the time. In about 14 days the eggs hatch, and the parents feed the young a liquid secreted from the lining of their crops (a pouch in their gullet). When the young are about 10 or 12 days old, they leave the nest but continue to beg for and receive food from the parents until they are about 2 weeks of age, at which time the parents become increasingly unwilling to feed them, and the young are forced to learn to peck for grain on the floor. This terminates the reproductive cycle. When the young are about 25 days old, the male again starts the courting behavior, and the entire cycle lasting 6 or 7 weeks begins again as before. This behavior seems much like the homing in pigeons or the migration of fish and birds in its apparent universality and biologically stereotyped details, and it illustrates the kind of seemingly built-in patterns that led early investigators to postulate instincts. However, Lehrman's work helps identify the actual internal and external influences bringing each aspect of the pattern about (Figure 6.6).

The *hormonal influences* are illustrated by the fact that when the female dove is first placed in the cage, her oviduct weighs about 800 milligrams (mg), but when she lays her eggs after having proceeded through courtship and nest building, it weighs about 4,000 mg. Similarly, gradual changes occur

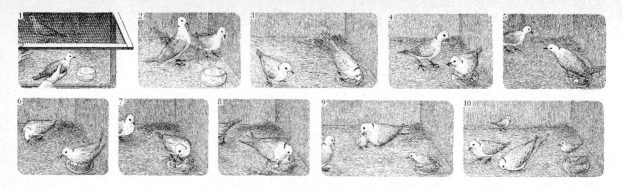

Figure 6.6 Pattern of reproductive behavior in ring doves. There is an interplay of internal and external factors, in step-by-step progression, from the initial courting and nest-building behavior through the final care and feeding of the young. See text for details of the cycle. (From "The Reproductive Behavior of Ring Doves" by Daniel S. Lehrman. © 1964 by Scientific American, Inc. All rights reserved)

in the birds' crops that are necessary to prepare them for feeding the young and in the male's testes preparing him to copulate.

Lehrman's research has shown that this pattern of behavior, though having a large hormonal component, is also highly dependent on *environmental events* or stimuli to trigger the secretion of these hormones, which in turn help initiate the appropriate actions. He has shown, for example, that if the birds are placed in a cage in which there are nesting materials and two eggs already laid, the birds do not sit on them but act as if the eggs were not there. Instead of sitting they proceed in sequence to court, build their own nest, lay their own eggs, and only then to sit on them. The lone female lays no eggs; she needs the sight of the male. A lone male has no interest in nesting materials, eggs, or young; he must be stimulated by the female.

Thus, the behavior pattern is by no means entirely determined from within but depends also on the timing of environmental events that set in motion the internal (hormonal) ones controlling (in ways that are still not clear) the behavior necessary for nest building, copulation, egg laying, and feeding of young. In short, as McDougall had argued, instinct is merely the *disposition to respond* in some given fashion to some suitable *external stimulus,* although Lehrman finds the term instinct misleading and hence undesirable. For the reproductive behavior cycle of the species to take place, exactly the right combination of stimuli and mutual actions is required, each occurring at the proper moment. This revised conception of biological factors in adaptive behavior (which are no longer seen as strictly internally controlled sequences of action) represents a major step forward from earlier ideas of rigid instinct and allows for the elaborate interplay of both biological and social forces in the control of adaptive behavior (Figure 6.7).

Applied to aggression, the implications should be clear. Even in lower animals aggressive behavior is not explained by reference to an oversimplified instinct principle, that is, by the unfolding of a purely internal, genetically controlled set of actions. Although there are undoubtedly physiological (neurological and hormonal) mechanisms involved in aggression, they represent only part of the explanation, since aggression depends also on environmental stimulation and regulation.

In the quotation from Scott (1958) cited earlier, the argument is made that there is no spontaneous stimulation for fighting arising within the body (as in an innate drive), but that aggression requires some kind of stimulation from the outside. In psychobiological terms, whatever it is that man inherited from his animal ancestors which makes him aggressive must be an innate disposition to react with aggression when activated by an appropriate external stimulus. If the appropriate *releasing stimulus* for aggression is presented to a member of a given animal species, including man, then that animal should attack; if such a stimulus does not materialize, then the animal should not attack, nor will he suffer any ill-effect or build-up of tension in consequence.

Releasing stimuli The general idea that certain external stimuli release innate emotional and motivational patterns has become a strong modern tradition in psychobiological studies of both fear and aggression in animals. In the case of *fear*, it has been observed that rats, dogs, and even human children

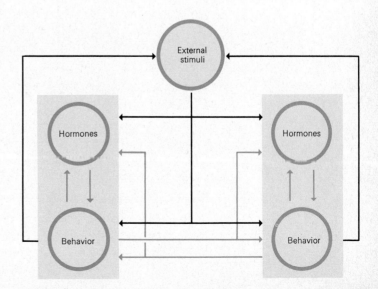

Figure 6.7 Schematic representation of the complex way in which hormones regulate the cycle of reproductive behavior in ring doves and are in turn affected by external stimulation. (From "The Reproductive Behavior of Ring Doves" by Daniel S. Lehrman. © 1964 by Scientific American, Inc. All rights reserved)

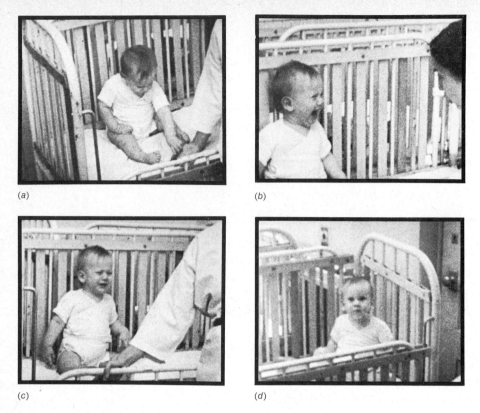

(a)

(b)

(c)

(d)

Figure 6.8   Fear of strangers in a young child. Film sequence shows infant (a) playing calmly, then (b) frightened by a strange face, (c) still anxious, and finally (d) calm again. (Reproduced from the film Anxiety *by Rene A. Spitz, M.D.; courtesy of the New York University Film Library)*

Figure 6.9   Fear and threat responses in Rhesus monkeys. (a) Threat response of a mother in "defense" of her infant. (b) Young monkey in a strange environment responds to a fear stimulus by attachment to a surrogate mother. (c) "Crying" response of an infant monkey deprived of its surrogate mother in a strange environment. (d) Fear response of young monkey to the hostile advances of an adult. (e) Threat response of an adult male. (Wisconsin Primate Laboratory)

(a)

(b)

(c)

can usually be made fearful by a painful stimulus, by sudden loud noises, by loss of support, or by strange surroundings. A dog is usually frightened by seeing a balloon being blown up, by seeing his master in unusual clothing, or in the presence of a strange person. Primates (monkeys and apes) become fearful in the presence of many things, including a carrot of unusual shape, a biscuit with a worm in it, or a doll. Nearly all chimpanzees are terrified by the sight of a life-size clay model of a chimpanzee head without the body, often screaming at it and running away from it (see Donald Hebb, 1946). Infant chimpanzees, like human infants, are frightened of strangers, and the age at which this occurs in chimpanzees is about 4 months. Such fears in children appear to be widespread, if not universal, at around 6 to 8 months of age. At that time of life, if a child is confronted with a strange adult, he will usually exhibit marked fears, a reaction that tends to disappear as he matures further (Figures 6.8 and 6.9).

Hebb has proposed that the property all fear-inducing objects have in common is strangeness; the child or animal must have matured to the extent that it can distinguish the familiar from the unfamiliar. In this connection, it is also tempting to speculate on the widespread nature of certain unreasonable fears in humans, for example, of spiders and snakes, in spite of the fact that few people have ever had a physically painful or harmful experience with them. Likewise, there could be an innate tendency in people to fear occult phenomena, such as dead bodies rising up from their graves (Figure 6.10). Such fear is part of the thrill of seeing those horror movies during which the spine tingles at the critical moments. At such a film many a young child will hide his head, clutch at a parent, or begin to cry. There may be nothing particularly surprising in the long history of demonology in human affairs, and Hebb would probably have little difficulty assimilating occult fears to the idea of fear of the unfamiliar or strange. A complicating feature of this is the possi-

Figure 6.10 Nosferatu, a bloodthirsty predecessor of the famous vampire Count Dracula, gazes at us longingly in this still photo from the 1922 horror-film classic from Germany, directed by F. W. Murnau. (The Museum of Modern Art/Film Stills Archive)

(d)

(e)

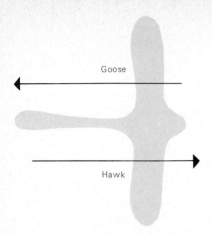

Figure 6.11　This silhouette resembles a hawk when moved to the right, and its moving shadow triggers escape responses in young turkeys. When the same silhouette is moved to the left, however, it casts a gooselike shadow and does not trigger the escape mechanism. (After Tinbergen, 1951)

Figure 6.12　The male stickleback will ignore the top model but will attack any of the lower ones, all having the right coloration. (After Tinbergen, 1951)

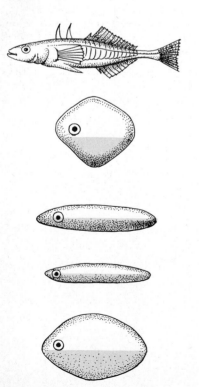

bility that many things for which there is widespread fear might also have unconscious, symbolic significance in the Freudian sense. Thus, a snake may symbolize a threatening male genital organ, which in many cultures is surrounded by severe social taboos. A snake is also scary, of course, simply because it may be poisonous: man and his early tree-dwelling primate ancestors have always been threatened by snakes, who move as easily in trees as upon the ground.

In other animals, similar fear responses are common. For example, in fowl, the short, fat-necked silhouette of a hawk (a major predator of such birds) is capable of producing fear even when it is seen for the first time, whereas a long, narrow-necked silhouette (resembling a goose, which is of course non-predatory) will produce no alarm. When the hawk silhouette is moved backward (see Figure 6.11), it becomes a goose silhouette and no longer triggers the fear response in fowl.

In the case of *aggression,* similar innate triggering mechanisms have been demonstrated in many animals, including numerous fish, insect, and fowl species. Such releasing mechanisms are apparently species specific, that is, the stimuli capable of producing aggression are peculiar to each species. Tinbergen's (1951) work with the stickleback fish offers a good example. Aggression behavior in the male stickleback can be released merely by the sight of the red underbelly of another male of the same species invading his "territory." Such a specific stimulus would have no significance whatever for any other species of animal. The male stickleback seems to be built with the innate tendency to react with aggression to that particular visual-stimulus pattern (Figure 6.12), and the aggressive response can be triggered even by a stickleback "model" that is very unlike the real fish in appearance as long as the underbelly is painted red. A more exact model lacking this specific red coloration will fail to trigger the aggressive response (see Note 6.1, p. 244).

Aggression directed toward members of the same species usually includes threat gestures or displays of various kinds, in which one animal challenges another in a dominance struggle. Such threats signal to the other animal the intent to attack; likewise, when the animal is submissive or is experiencing the emotion of fear and is likely to withdraw, its body and face present a characteristically different conformation. It is obviously of importance for animals to be able to recognize accurately such varying expressive patterns so that their own behavioral response can conform accurately to actions of other members of their species. And such recognition does indeed occur, as a result of both innate and learning processes. In Figure 6.13 we see drawings of a wolf's face and head in various conformations signifying imminent withdrawal or attack. Expressive patterns may thus serve as stimuli eliciting

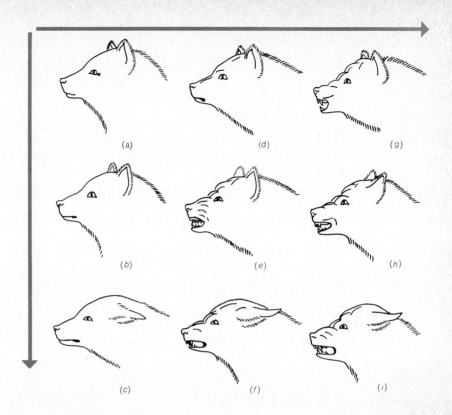

(a) (d) (g)

(b) (e) (h)

(c) (f) (i)

Figure 6.13 Facial expressions of the wolf that signify various intensities of flight or threat intentions: (a–c) readiness to flee; (a–g) increasing aggression; (e,f,h,i) various combinations (superpositions) of facial expression, revealing ambiguity of intention. (After Lorenz, 1953)

aggression or withdrawal in other animals, although reactions to such stimuli in higher animal species such as anthropoid apes are likely to be far less automatic and much more influenced by past experience and learning than in Tinbergen's fish or fowl.

Are there specific releasers for aggression in man? As was pointed out in Chapter 1, built-in patterns of response to specific stimuli are less evident as we advance from lower to higher animals, but they are not entirely ruled out, as we saw in the case of the child's fear of strangers noted earlier (Figure 6.8). If so, then there may be standard environmental conditions that tend to arouse aggression in higher animals, including man. Conditions producing *pain* or *frustration* have been suggested as stimuli for aggression in higher animals, although aggression is not the only response to such conditions.

Frustration and aggression   The idea that frustration antecedes aggression received its strongest and most influential support in a famous monograph by Dollard and associates (1939). This distinguished group of psychologists defined frustration in very general terms as "an interference with the occurrence of an instigated goal-response at its proper time

243

in the behavior sequence," and the response of aggression as any "sequence of behavior, the goal-response to which is the injury of the person toward whom it is directed." Emphasis was placed by Dollard *et al.* on the external stimulus event that brings about the interruption or frustration and not on the emotional reaction (say, anger) produced by it.

There has been considerable debate about the major premises set forth by Dollard *et al.* in their monograph linking aggression to frustration. Most of the argument has been over the definition of frustration, particularly over whether any kind of interruption of a goal response arouses aggression, or only certain kinds. Some writers have suggested that a distinction must be drawn between frustrations involving ordinary deprivations (like absence of food or water) and those involving threats to the person's identity or self-esteem (see, for example, Maslow, 1941, 1943; Rosenzweig, 1944; Pastore, 1952; and Sargent, 1948). These theorists proposed that in

---

Note 6.1

Tinbergen's research (1951) on the innate releasing mechanisms of the stickleback fish highlights the difference between circular attempts to explain behavior by reference to some mysterious force within the organism and research that succeeds in pinning down specific causal conditions within or without the organism. *Circular reasoning* has been mentioned earlier in this chapter in connection with the doctrine of instinct. When a hypothetical mechanism has not been grounded in observable conditions, the proposed scheme is merely a theoretical pointer rather than an adequate explanation, although it can sometimes turn attention in the right direction and lead in that way to real knowledge.

Tinbergen watched the male stickleback go into his routine of attack on another male of the same species who entered his territory, and in the tradition of the instinct concept Tinbergen assumed that the male must be programmed to fight other male sticklebacks, but what was the nature of this programming? One answer might be found in the stickleback's nervous and hormonal systems, but Tinbergen was a naturalist rather than a physiologist, and he was not led to study the fish's anatomy and physiology for a clue. However, he could perhaps discover just what the fish was programmed to re-

spond to in the environment. He reasoned that the response might either have something to do with the particular shape or conformation of the other male stickleback or it might have to do with the bright red underbelly only found in the mature male. By a series of clever experiments using models, Tinbergen was able to show conclusively that the attacks had nothing to do with the body shape of the other fish but were triggered only by the red coloring on the fish's abdomen (as shown in Figure 6.12). In this way, Tinbergen was able to take speculation about instinctual pressures out of the realm of circular reasoning, which merely points to some mysterious internal force, and move toward knowledge of the exact way in which the patterned response of intraspecies attack is initiated in the stickleback.

Earlier in this chapter some other examples of circular reasoning were mentioned. One instance is the suggestion by Freud that people who expose themselves continuously to dangers (like professional soldiers, bullfighters, or sky divers) may be unconsciously seeking death in such ways. A similar process has been suggested as the explanation of why young terrorists (be they Arab refugees, Japanese students, black militants, or whatever) risk their own survival in violent activities involving a high probability of self-

destruction. The problem with such explanations is that no way has been found to test the proposed mechanism underlying this "death wish." We cannot predict the exact conditions under which this supposed unconscious mechanism will or will not function, nor do we know the early influences that lead to such self-destructive behavior. Without such information, the reasoning is unsupported, and most thoughtful analysts are reluctant to choose it over other more obvious explanations for soldiering, bullfighting, or black militancy. Circularity of reasoning also plagues the notion, mentioned earlier, that the work of artists or surgeons, say, represents sublimation (rechanneling) of sexual or aggressive urges.

In Note 3.2, which dealt with motivation, it was shown that circular reasoning may be avoided by establishment of rules regarding inference of motives within the individual. To support our motivation concepts (which were characterized as intellectual tools to help explain behavior), we must do the same sort of thing that Tinbergen has done: we must identify the causal conditions of a given drive or motive and ultimately relate these conditions to the specific kind of behavior from which the inference about inner mechanisms has been made.

man aggression is a response only to the latter, that is, to threats to the person's identity or some central or essential aspect of his being. As Karl Menninger (1942) has noted, although on the surface having one's toe stepped on appears trivial, anger is often produced because the incident is interpreted by the victim as an attack on his ego. From this standpoint, if the injury is produced inadvertently, anger is less likely than if injury is intentional, because in the latter instance the victim feels belittled or demeaned. When there is actually no intent to injure but some doubt remains, an apology often solves the problem of bruised feelings. More will be said about this question of intent in Chapter 7.

Another criticism of the treatment of frustration and aggression by Dollard *et al.* (1939) was that it did not seem to encompass some known eliciters of aggression in higher animals, including man (Durbin and Bowlby, 1939; and Seward, 1945). Durbin and Bowlby have suggested that fights between children and among apes break out for three reasons: (1) over disputes concerning possession of external objects; (2) because of resentment at the intrusion of a stranger into the group; and (3) because of frustrations as defined by Dollard *et al.* The first two reasons do not seem easily assimilable into the usual definition of frustration, unless one treats possession of objects and being among familiar animals as "goal-responses" that are being interfered with. More likely, frustration is just one of the causes of aggression.

In any event, the original frustration-aggression concept was important because it turned psychological attention toward the nature of the *transaction* taking place *between the organism and its environment* that might account for aggression or its absence. Psychologists began to focus their attention upon observable *external events* that might have causal significance for aggression. However, the frustration hypothesis tried to encompass too much within the general concept of frustration and failed to make several important distinctions. No account was paid to the way in which an individual interprets the significance of the stimulus. There was also no distinction between an injury that had already occurred and one merely anticipated or threatened. Current formulations (for example, see Berkowitz, 1962a, 1962b) have greatly enlarged the original concept and filled in many of the earlier gaps, based on a large body of experimental data on the situational determinants of aggression.

The hunt for a universal releaser of aggression in animals and man was the product of relatively simplistic thinking often found in the early stages of research. Only with increased comprehension of the subject do we begin to recognize the complications and qualifications that must necessarily be placed on an overgeneral hypothesis. Such increasing sophis-

(a)

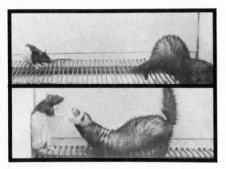

(b)

Figure 6.14 Animals become highly aggressive when given a painful electric shock; under the stimulus of pain, they will attack and try to destroy almost anything in the vicinity, including animals that are usually feared and avoided, or even inanimate objects. (a) Raccoon attacks and bites stuffed toy immediately after shock. (b) Ferret attacks hooded rat on being shocked. (Dr. Nathan H. Azrin)

tication is well illustrated by the work of Nathan Azrin (1967) on the environmental basis of aggression in animals.

There had been earlier observations (Miller, 1948) that when an electric shock was delivered to a lone rat's feet it would attempt to escape or would "freeze" into immobility, but when a group of rats in the same cage were shocked in this way they immediately began attacking one another. Similar observations were made by Azrin and his colleagues. It was learned that aggressive behavior could be elicited in many (but not all) types of animals by a painful stimulus, the number of attacks increasing with increases in the intensity, duration, and frequency of the pain (shock) stimulation (Figure 6.14). Moreover, it was not a predatory reaction, because hunger did not have an appreciable effect on the number of attacks. Biting was a prominent part of the aggressive reaction, and it appeared to Azrin that the aim of the attack was not merely to ward off or defend but to injure or destroy. He also found that a pain-induced attack would be directed not only at another animal in the cage, even an animal whose retaliation could kill the attacker, but at any object that was attackable, such as a stuffed toy model of an animal or a tennis ball hanging from a string. (People also often strike at things when angry—as when a person strikes the ground in a rage with his golf club or tennis racquet after missing a series of shots; infant temper tantrums are an extreme form of this phenomenon.)

Later Azrin shifted from the stimulus of physical pain to other stimuli such as the withdrawal of an expected reward, and here too "psychological pain," as Azrin referred to the frustration, led to attack reactions. Further research demonstrated that painful stimuli such as electric shocks produced attack behavior only when the animals could not avoid them. Thus, it would appear that avoidance behavior is also a common reaction to pain, and that attack and fear responses are perhaps linked. However, aggression might well be learned as the *fundamental response* (regardless of the possibility of avoidance responses) if "counteraggression" were always effective in eliminating the pain. Azrin thinks that pain or frustration arouses a state in animals such that it is rewarding for them to injure or destroy. This is probably true in the wild, where the source of pain is usually another animal.

Interplay of biological and learning processes Early attempts to tighten the loose concept of instinct created an artificial dichotomy between inborn patterns and learning. A pattern of behavior was said to be instinctual only if it occurred throughout the species, involved a complex series of actions, and was clearly not attributable to learning. According to this definition, behavior patterns could be regarded as instinctual only in lower organisms on the evolutionary scale, such as insects, fish, reptiles, and birds, and most human behavior patterns were ruled out because they contained a large component of learning.

As was pointed out in Chapter 1, emotions and learning take on particular importance in the higher species for whom the behavior patterns necessary for survival are not automatic, with no prearranged guarantee that they will take place when needed. Instead, these necessary behavior patterns are heavily subject to modification through learning. The emotional reaction in situations of potential or actual danger, such as separation of mother and infant or predatory attack, helps ensure that decisive adaptive behavior will take place to protect the individual frequently enough to preserve the species. Weak efforts are likely to be insufficient in situations of real danger; hence the arousal of emotion takes up the slack of the absence of automatic, built-in mechanisms in higher mammals and makes more likely the mobilization of a major adaptive effort. In short, emotions may be said to act as facilitators or multipliers of adaptive impulses. As a result of their operation, no animal is likely to "sleep through" the presence of a signal of real danger or to respond too weakly—one cannot relax while massively aroused—because once a situation critical to survival is recognized, the whole organism is launched into mobilization for coping with it.

Nevertheless, even higher animals still retain some of the biological pressures and controls that are useful in guaranteeing behavior adaptive for the species. We might connect such biological dispositions to social patterns of behavior in man by briefly outlining three themes concerning the development of motives in general: (1) by considering ways in which innate biological forces affect the development of social patterns of behaviors; (2) by recognizing distinctions between various kinds of social behavior, some of which may be closer to biological origins and others more embedded in cultural patterns; and (3) by acknowledging that more than one process may be taking place at the same time and even having a similar effect.

1. One of the ways biological factors might influence the acquisition of social motives is to make it easier for an individual to learn some types of behavior than to learn others. For example, aggression might be inhibited or controlled under some circumstances yet become the dominant reaction when man feels threatened. The inhibitions, therefore, might be very fragile, while the tendency to aggressive behavior might be strong. Indeed we do speak of uncontrollable rages, of being blindly angry, of going berserk, and so on. Conditions

might still be created in which aggression would be made less likely, but it would remain very difficult to control in the face of the strong evolutionary forces supporting it. Thus, to say that as we learn aggressive behavior we can also learn to inhibit it, that we can learn to feel sympathy as well as hostility toward other men, does not imply rejection of the idea that innate biological factors support aggression under given circumstances and that these are strong enough to override the learned forces of inhibition.

Perhaps the fate of Mahatma Gandhi's philosophy of nonviolence as it has evolved in modern-day India is an illustration of the fragility of such religious and ethical inhibitions in the face of stronger pressures favoring the response of aggression, especially when the inhibition is out of keeping with social conditions. In Gandhi's time, during their struggle for independence, the Indians under Britain were unarmed and militarily weak except for their vast masses, which made noncooperation and nonviolent protest highly effective and direct violence a poor tactic under the prevailing circumstances. Today, however, the state of India, governed by Gandhi's disciples, has become more powerful than her neighbor, Moslem Pakistan, and hence she can take the wraps off earlier Hindu ethical inhibitions (favoring nonviolent resistance) and revert to the more prepotent response, direct attack, when her leaders feel that Indian territory (in Kashmir) or interests (in Bengal) are being infringed upon.

2. Social behavior patterns may differ markedly in their dependence on biological and social factors; therefore, lumping them all together may obscure rather than clarify the manner in which biological and cultural forces interact. There are many social behavior patterns in man that have parallels in other animals and are clearly essential to survival, for example, maternal behavior, attachment, sex, and aggression. These kinds of behavior are obviously socially motivated (as opposed to simple physiological drives such as hunger and thirst), since they are nearly always interpersonal in character. But it is difficult to deny that in mammalian species they depend heavily on inborn (hereditary) mechanisms that are products of evolutionary adaptation.

On the other hand, other socially motivated patterns, such as striving for achievement, commitment to studies or to work, seeking social status, or desire for approval, would appear to have less direct and less evident biological bases and greater dependence on what is learned from a particular cultural pattern. For example, anthropological data suggest that achievement motivation varies greatly in importance and form of expression from one culture to another or at different periods of human history (see McClelland, 1961). In understanding such motives, it might be more fruitful, therefore, to examine the manner in which cultural values are transmitted to the individual and assimilated by him in socialization than to search for neurohormonal determinants and for parallels among more primitive animal species.

In any event, assuming a person who is strongly disposed biologically to be physically active and pugnacious and who grows up under cultural conditions that push him to strive for dominance over his compeers, the two forces, biological and cultural, may well combine to produce an individual who is more aggressive than average. Again we can see that cultural learning and biological disposition need not be at odds as explanations of the resultant motivational pattern (see the quotation in the margin).

3. There is no reason why several acquisition processes may not take place simultaneously in the development of many social motivations. For example, a child may develop a strong achievement motivation partly as a result of high physical energy and restlessness, partly because his lower-middle-class parents drum it into his head that he must advance economically and socially, and partly because he is punished for starting fights with other youngsters. In one learning process the mother systematically rewards her child for striving to achieve until ultimately he internalizes this value as his own. The other learning process involves substitute behavior, as aggressive reactions aroused by suitable stimuli are blocked by social pressure and redirected into socially acceptable forms of aggression (such as competitiveness and striving for achievement). The mix of biological and social factors may be quite varied, resulting in a wide range of different outcomes.

The above arguments are, of course, built on certain broad assumptions, but they point to one way in which innate, biological forces might interact with multiple cultural learning processes in the development of social motives. The important points to recognize are (1) that any tendency to create a sharp dichotomy between biological and learning theories of the origin of social motives is misleading and unconstructive (see Beach, 1955); and (2) that even divergent hypotheses about the social acquisition process itself need not be mutually contradictory but may well apply in different degrees and under different conditions of development.

The main trouble with the entire foregoing discussion is that aggression has been treated as a single kind of response regardless of the species in which it occurs or the physical and social conditions under which it takes place. Such a simplistic view is not warranted. Distinctions were made in the introduction to Part II between human assertiveness and aggression,

Besides marriage the Kwakiutl [of the Pacific Northwest Coast] recognize murder as an equally valid method of adding to one's privilege and rank. A man claims as his own all the names and special privileges of his victim. Some of the most valued of these are the winter ceremonial dances. If a man met the owner of a dance and killed him, he could assume the right to give the dance himself. A commoner would hardly avail himself of this method of rising in status unless he had enough property to validate his assumption of the dance prerogatives. In the past, a number of wars were conducted primarily to increase the number of tribal names, crests, and dances. [From Goldman, 1961, p. 180]

the latter involving anger, hostility, or the intent to injure, and in the complex patterns of aggression displayed by other animal species. We must also differentiate between *predation* (when one animal stalks and kills another for food) and *combattiveness* in self-defense, in defense of young, and in intraspecies aggression. Predation, a *food-getting* activity, is often not classified as a form of aggression, which may be seen as a *social* activity evolving from various *defensive* behavior patterns. Aggressive behavior toward members of the same species occurs in struggles for hierarchic dominance, in sexual rivalry, or to protect territory.

In the case of man, it may be important also to distinguish between an impersonal aggression or attack without anger (as in prizefighting or other aggressive sports, in business competition, or when bombs are dropped under orders against an enemy one never sees) and aggression accompanied by feelings of hostility or extreme rage (see Chapter 7). Furthermore, some types of human aggression go all the way to total destruction of the enemy, while other forms of antagonism are strictly verbal and stop short of doing bodily harm. Sometimes the aggression is physical and violent, whereas at other times it is subtle and perhaps not even perceived by the victim. Recognition of such distinctions is of vital importance if we are looking for the stimulus conditions (releasers) of aggression, since one form of aggression may be provoked by quite different external circumstances than another (Moyer, 1967); it has also been shown that in each of the different forms of animal aggression (say, sexually competitive or territorial) the physiological processes taking place in the animal also differ (Rothballer, 1967). In short, the general term *aggression* is much too broad and loose, and the existence of various subvarieties clearly implies somewhat different psychobiological principles. Ultimately we may find that different explanations for the various forms of "aggression" will be required, with a distinct term for each form (see Note 6.2).

EVOLUTION OF HUMAN AGGRESSION

When we speak of the psychobiology of human aggression, we start with the assumption that man has received the physiological equipment (for example, nerves and hormones) underlying his patterns of aggression from animals preceding him on earth. As we saw in Chapter 1, we do indeed share much of our biological structure with our animal forebears. Although some of our innate behavioral responses to environmental stimuli are also part of this inheritance, new patterns have certainly emerged in man that cannot be found previ-

Note 6.2

This problem of how finely to slice the behavioral pie is a very common one and bears some comment here. Notice that in the text proper the question has been raised about how broad our definition of aggression ought to be. Should it include predatory aggression as well as defensive aggression, territorial aggression within a species, behavioral aggression with and without anger, anger without behavioral aggression, and so on, or are these quite distinct phenomena, unrelated to each other? Another way to view this is to ask what all these various forms of aggression have in common and how they diverge. Lumping all within the same broad category of "aggressive behavior" is done because we presume that they all share some important property or properties in common, as to causal conditions, pattern of response, or internal mechanism.

We often first make progress in science by noticing similarities among various phenomena and by drawing them all together within the same concept. This seems useful as a first step in understanding each phenomenon. Thus, many very different behavior patterns are classified within the concept of stress, or of motivation, emotion, defense mechanism, or whatever. Soon, however, we begin to recognize that we may have encompassed too much under one category, or perhaps we learn that while all these subvarieties have something in common, they also display important differences. This is a more advanced stage of knowledge: by differentiating among these subvarieties, we are led to discover new causes, effects, and mechanisms that help increase our accuracy in predicting events of interest to us. Thus, in the case of the broad concept of stress, we begin to recognize that the phenomena of psychological stress differ from those of physiological stress, and although these overlap somewhat in some of their effects (they may both produce comparable organic changes in the body), they also obey different causal rules. For instance, the bodily effects of psychological stress are much influenced by the way a person construes a situation, while physiological stress will always lead to about the same bodily effects regardless of how the situation is interpreted. In the same way, the differentiation of several forms of aggression will help us achieve a precise understanding of their causation.

ously in the biological world. But when we consider human psychology vis-á-vis animal psychology, this is still much too general a statement. We must determine what is new and what is inherited and how each element enters into our lives. In the present case we must ask which of the many patterns of aggression that animals display have contributed to particular kinds of human aggression.

Two very general types of aggression found in animal life have been emphasized in psychobiological speculation about the origins of human aggression, namely, "interspecies aggression" and "intraspecies aggression." Both were probably highly important in the evolution of human aggression, although there is considerable debate as to how these forms might have contributed, and relatively little solid data about the details of the evolutionary process.

Interspecies aggression

The term *interspecies aggression* refers simply to aggression between animals of different species, as when a lion attacks a zebra, or a baboon defends his troop by fighting when threatened by one of the predatory cats. Most interspecies aggression takes the form of predation or defense against predatory attack. Predation, that is, attacking and eating other animals for food, is one of the most general of zoological patterns; it can be found in the simplest single-celled organisms and all the way up to the largest and most complex. Pericles (498–429 B.C.) noticed this too: "'Master, I marvel how the fishes live in the sea.' 'Why, as men do on land: The great ones eat up the little ones.'"

The popular image of animals either fighting or fleeing each other, however, is exaggerated. Animals of many species often share the same habitat, usually being rather indifferent to each other and going their separate ways. When not engaged in the hunt, even carnivores seem to be peaceful and attract little attention. More accurate information about animals in their natural settings is available today than it was to those early writers about aggression. For example, Freud had striking misapprehensions about how animals got along. He seems to have helped further the stereotype current during his time of the animal world as living "tooth and claw," engaged in an endless and savage struggle for survival. In recent years, efforts have been made by ethologists and zoologists to correct this erroneous impression. In the popular "true-to-life" motion picture *Born Free,* we have an attempt to show African lions as gentle and loyal if treated decently, like "man's best friend," the dog.

Most monkeys and apes survive quite well on a diet of fruit and vegetables and they are usually regarded as vegetar-

By the same token, we bring order to human personality studies by grouping people into general types or classes, based on the many variables by which individuals differ. But we always know that each person is a unique blend of traits, and the grouping of many people together within one category does some violence to this psychological principle. Even though many people may share one or two traits in common, they also always differ in other important ways. The test of how broadly we should slice the pie is how useful any given system of classification is in helping us understand and predict whatever is of immediate interest. As was noted in the Prologue, when we are dealing with a single individual, say, someone in psychological difficulty, we have to zero in on his or her particular problems and recognize the ways in which they are different from those of every other person with whom we may have worked; of course, our more general concepts should help guide our approach to these problems, but it is the individual nuances that count in psychotherapy. We are always operating with some form of classification, frequently with very large slices (often too large), and always seeking to add finer detail but to bring the details into the larger context. In short, we advance first by generalizing and then by seeing finer distinctions.

ians, although some also do a certain amount of meat eating. There have been many field observations of baboons hunting and eating monkeys; and chimpanzees are also known to kill and eat monkeys, young baboons, bush pigs, and bush bucks (Teleki, 1973). Like man, chimpanzees are *omnivorous*, meaning they eat everything. Moreover, primates are endangered by predators such as leopards and cheetahs. Therefore, inter-species aggressive tendencies in primates would yield the double adaptive advantage of increasing the range of food supplies and of providing a basis for self-protection against predators. By and large, primates are rather aggressive animals, so there is no reason to be surprised at man's aggressive tendencies. For some scientists, the key element in this aggressiveness is man's emergence as a highly successful predator. For them this is the critical link in the evolutionary chain to aggression in man (see also Washburn and Hamburg, 1968; Southwick, 1972).

In Chapter 1 it was suggested that the early hominid species made an important transition from a primarily vegetarian diet, which was the main staple of the anthropoid apes, to a carnivorous (meat-eating) diet. Although carnivorous activity was already present in the anthropoid apes, it flowered according to Leakey (1967) in the transition from ape to man. Leakey argues also that man was offensive in odor to the lion and other jungle cats and therefore did not need the great physical strength and long canine teeth and claws of other primates to avoid being eaten. But he did have to make the important transition from vegetable food to meat, and this was managed essentially through the use of sharp cutting tools to scavenge for flesh and ultimately to kill his own prey. The natural aggressiveness that was already present in primates must have stood protoman in good stead in his transition to hunter, and it surely helped him enormously in competing for meat with anthropoid apes and other predators. With a larger brain and greater manual dexterity, he could develop weapons enabling him to attack animals from a distance. And once man used weapons to attack and kill other primates, as has been shown by archeological evidence, Leakey believes that only a short further step was required for this aggressive pattern to be extended to other men. As man advanced in sophistication, he also advanced in his power to kill, from sticks to weapons that could be thrown or hurled, to bows and arrows, guns, guided missiles, and eventually nuclear warheads attached to rockets that can kill anywhere on the globe.

Many anthropologists in addition to Leakey (for example, Washburn, 1959; Freeman, 1964) believe that man's aggression against other men is, in part, an extension of his having become a carnivore. Leakey viewed early man as becoming a major aggressor only as a result of his need and ability to kill for food in competition with other species and later in competition with members of his own species. So competitive predation is seen as a cornerstone in the evolution of aggression in man.

This evolutionary scenario runs as follows: (1) The transition from vegetarian to meat eater probably at first involved scavenging for meat scraps in competition with vultures, jackals, and hyenas. Early man, roaming in the plains of East Africa, where the earliest skeletons of hominids were found by the Leakeys, was probably not disdainful of a bit of leftover carrion when food was scarce. Indeed, it has been reported in Africa that men have eaten meat of animals (elephants) dead more than eight days when survival was at stake. Men learned to catch insects and fish, and trap small reptiles, birds, and mammals for food. (2) Later in human evolutionary development man became a highly efficient predator, hunting in groups, eventually with weapons that could overcome his inability to run down game or to overpower it physically. Such hunting parties made use of various strategies—joining forces to beat the bush, surrounding prey, and hunting up-wind (something that lions and other cats have evidently not learned to do). (3) Some writers have also proposed a man-hunting and cannibalistic stage in which prisoners of tribal war were sacrificed and eaten. Evidence of cannibalism has frequently been noted by paleontologists and archeologists who have studied Stone Age remains (fossils and artifacts) in many parts of the world (see Marshack, 1972), including Europe, Asia, the Americas, Africa, Australia, and Oceania. Today there are a few protein-poor societies in which it still occurs, such as among the headhunting tribes of New Guinea and Borneo; even among modern men there are accounts of cannibalism on rafts, in prison camps, after natural disasters, and in famines under desperate survival conditions. A recent case has been reported among survivors of a downed Uruguayan airliner who were stranded in the high Andes for 69 days (Figure 6.15).

Figure 6.15 Two bodies lie in the snow beside the fuselage of a Uruguayan Air Force plane that crashed in the Chilean Andes and was not found for 69 days. Of the 45 persons aboard, members of a Uruguayan soccer team and their supporters, only 16 survived. Some of the survivors acknowledged that during their two-month ordeal they ate parts of the victims' bodies to stay alive. (Wide World Photos)

The Maoris of New Zealand, before the [can-
nibal] feast, took from their enemies the ex-
quisitely tattooed heads which were their
incomparable pride, and setting them on
posts about them, taunted them after this
fashion:

"You thought to flee, ha? But my power over-
took you.
You were cooked; you were made food for
my mouth.
Where is your father? He is cooked.
Where is your brother? He is eaten.
Where is your wife? There she sits, a wife for
me!"
[From Benedict, 1959, p. 47]

Freud says of the brothers: "Cannibal savages as they were, it goes without saying
that they devoured their victim as well as
killing him." He takes this cannibalistic act
for granted as the consequence of the first.
From the viewpoint of those cannibal savages themselves . . . the priority of aims
belongs obviously to the eating: the killing
was, so to speak, the necessary act pre-
paratory to devouring the victim. . . .
Cannibals devouring a body with relish present a picture of "nature red in tooth and
claw." Father-murder is an atrocious crime.
The eating of the killed father is for persons
of our civilization so unimaginable that the
act is outside the range of our imagination.
We can still imagine, although even that is
difficult, that a young son in rage kills his father, and we sometimes read of such cases
in our newspapers, but eating of the killed
father is not believable and is unheard of in
every sense of the word. Killing of fathers
is outdated, but eating them is decidedly
obsolete. Yet the killing as well as the eating
of parents is well proved by the testimony
of missionaries and anthropologists who
lived with cannibal tribes of today. It is, however, remarkable that even with those savage people dead relatives are often killed
and eaten by a neighboring tribe, which is
asked to dispose of the old ones. [From Reik,
1957, p. 171]

Freud, in his concept of introjection (identification), proposed that the developing child orally incorporates (in fantasy) a loved object as part of the process by which the child takes on, in effect, *eats,* the attributes of the parent (Freud, 1933). This relates to sacred blood rites known to occur in numerous primitive cultures, such as the Australian Aborigines. And this view has been developed by Theodore Reik (1957) in his book *Myth and Guilt,* in which he links the story of the Garden of Eden to primitive man's killing and eating of the father, an act symbolized by Adam and Eve's eating of the forbidden fruit from the Tree of Knowledge. Whether this is merely fanciful or a useful speculation, it is not totally implausible that a change in species feeding patterns (from vegetarian to omnivorous scavenger to carnivorous predator) taking place as recently in evolutionary history as 2 million years ago would leave very strong traces in the psychobiology of that species. Or, put differently, man might still display strong residuals of this evolutionary history, thereby justifying Washburn's (1959) statement that, "It is easy to teach people to kill, and it is hard to develop customs which avoid killing." This would be so because killing for food is a deeply ingrained force in the human psyche, and education for killing would jibe with man's acquired predatory disposition (Figure 6.16).

One of the major troubles with this line of reasoning is that although men might have acquired some of their aggressive patterns by becoming meat eaters and successful predators, and although this diet might even have altered their biology and through this their psyches, this theoretical sequence is grossly oversimplified against the multiple other happenings of major importance in the physiological and social development of modern man. For example, the human brain has enlarged from roughly 600 cubic centimeters 1.75 million years ago to perhaps 1,500 cubic centimeters at present (see Table 1.1), so lots of other things were happening along with the proposed transition to predation. Consider also the multiple biological, social, political, historical, economic, and cultural factors in the progression from scavenger to predator to tribal warrior (man-killer, sometimes man-eater, later man-enslaver) to agriculturalist-feuder to citizen-soldier to "specialist" (aviator, missile expert, nuclear physicist, general, espionage agent, assassin, guerrilla, riot policeman, terrorist). There is clearly no simple parallel between the animal predatory instinct and human aggression as it manifests itself today. Whatever man's origins, he has come a long way since then. The problem is that the psychobiological explanation alone somewhat obscures many complex social aspects of man's aggression. But more of this later (Chapter 7).

Another problem with this line of reasoning about predation and human aggression is that it probably under-

Figure 6.16 Slaughter of a pig for a tribal feast in the New Hebrides Islands of the South Pacific. (© Kal Muller/Woodfin Camp)

states the aggressiveness of protoman before the transition to predator in the light of evidence of intraspecies aggressiveness in other mostly vegetarian or omnivorous primates, for example, the chimpanzee, baboon, gorilla, and—the most aggressive of them all—the gibbon, whom we have not considered here. One could, for example, just as easily argue that man became a meat eater, a predator, because he was already a pretty aggressive animal, and that this aggressiveness made it possible and even likely for him to attack and kill other species for food. When competition for food became a problem, the existence of aggressive tendencies would have been quite handy in the service of attacking other species. Although there is apparently no way to resolve this speculative conflict as yet, I believe a better case can be made for the view that development of predatory behavior was more the consequence of man's already existent aggressive nature than the cause. In all likelihood, both types of tendencies went hand in hand, one facilitating the other in the evolution of mankind, but social or intraspecies elements have been much emphasized in recent writings.

Intraspecies aggression

The most vigorous and popularized speculations about the biological evolution of aggression in man come from writers intrigued by patterns of *intraspecies* aggression (aggression toward members of the same species) in the animal world and the ease with which human parallels or analogies can be drawn. When we think of aggression as a social problem, we do not usually have in mind the hunting or killing of animals for food but rather man's destructiveness toward his *own species*, as in war, murder, child beating, and the like. Two fascinating themes may be found in the writings of those who see human patterns of aggression as having their biological roots in animal intraspecies aggression. The first stems from the observation of certain parallels in animal intraspecies aggression and man's social behavior, namely, the presence of dominance hierarchies, territoriality, and sexual competition in both. (These were touched on briefly in Chapter 3 in the discussion of population dynamics.) The second has to do with biological controls that ordinarily keep social aggression in animals from getting out of hand but which seem to have broken down in the case of man.

Dominance hierarchies   The tendency is found widely among animal species to form dominance hierarchies in which the most aggressive and impressive member of a group (usually male) tends to control most of the activities of the other animals, being the first to feed, choosing the most favorable place at a water hole, mating with the females he chooses, in short, being on top of the heap. Although such hierarchies may be simple or highly complex, all the animals in a group arrange themselves roughly in accordance with their places in the social order. Thus, in any social interchange between two animals, one is usually dominant, the other submissive, and the latter generally defers to the former.

The manner in which the dominance hierarchy or social order was initially established is of interest. Calhoun (1948, 1950) studied a rat colony under as natural conditions as possible for two years, the animals being restricted only by a fence around the large living area. Rats close to the food supply established themselves in holes and were avoided by outlying rats who never got as much food as those in favored positions (this is an example of "territoriality," to be discussed shortly). As a result, the latter were in poorer physical condition and had a low reproductive rate. This social arrangement was established not by violent fighting but by what Calhoun called "psychological drubbing." An older rat would seize a young rat who wandered into an area occupied by the adult,

As long as the male wrasse, a family of fish inhabiting Australia's Great Barrier Reef, stays alive, he dominates his harem of three to six females, keeping each in her place in the well-ordered hierarchy below him. But when he dies, an extraordinary transformation takes place in the top-ranked female. Within a matter of days she undergoes behavioral and physiological changes that turn her into a full-fledged male, dominating the remainder of the harem.

Apparently, an Australian zoologist who studied the fish reported in . . . Science, dominance of the male is required to suppress a natural tendency to change sex. When a female suddenly finds herself not dominated, she takes on the male's aggressive behavioral patterns within hours. . . .

shaking it, and chasing it away without biting or inflicting harm. In this way a well-organized society was formed, with the young or less vigorous rats learning to avoid the dominant, established rats. Destructive fighting was controlled unless alien rats entered the picture, the population size was experimentally allowed to become too large, or the food supply and living conditions deteriorated markedly.

We saw earlier that a somewhat different type of social order exists among baboons (Washburn and DeVore, 1961), with dominant males controlling females and juveniles. Many species of birds and mammals have their own means of establishing dominance hierarchies. A fascinating example in fish was recently reported by D. R. Robertson, an Australian zoologist studying tropical fish at the Great Barrier Reef (see the margin, pp. 256–257).

Territoriality Another important property of intraspecies aggression is the strong tendency in most animal species to acquire and possess *territories* (often the ground closest to the food supply) and to hold them against competitors. Territorial behavior is found in lower animals on the evolutionary scale, such as fish and fowl, as well as in the highest animals such as primates. The strongest or most aggressive and impressive males take over the most desirable territory and the weakest or most submissive are dispossessed. The territory is the animal's base for purposes of feeding, breeding, and rearing of the young.

One can see this very readily in mating behavior—in the migratory seal, to take one example. In mating season (spring) the males begin to arrive from southern waters at the same Arctic site they visit every year. Each male stakes out a part of the beach, attacking any other male who encroaches, and waiting for the arrival of the females. When the females arrive, the biggest and strongest bulls (sometimes colorfully called "beachmasters") appropriate as many females as each can handle, establishing a harem that is defended within the territory against would-be competitors throughout the mating period. Ultimately in the fall, when the cubs are mature enough, the colony departs again for southern waters, only to return the following year to live through the same territorial mating pattern.

Sexual competition A relatively stable and peaceful animal colony can be aroused and even disrupted socially in its dominance and territorial patterns as a result of seasonal mating activity (when the females go into heat, or *estrus*). Sherwood L. Washburn (personal communication) and others (Wilson and Boelkins, 1970) have observed that the frequency of aggressive behavior and deaths in male monkeys is highest dur-

The study by Dr. D. R. Robertson of the University of Queensland in Brisbane, Australia, was confined to the species of wrasse known as Labroides dimidiatus, a brightly colored tropical fish varying in size from three to six inches. . . .

Dr. Robertson said his findings were based on observations of wrasse harems in the wild. In all, he and his colleagues saw 26 sex reversals take place, five naturally occurring and 21 experimentally induced by removing the male.

In four other cases, there were two equally ranked females next in line after the male. His removal caused each to transform into a male. The new males then split the harem and went their separate ways.

"Approximately one and a half to two hours after male death," Dr. Robertson wrote, "maleness appears in the form of the special male aggressive display that the new 'male' starts performing to the females of its group.

"The switchover to male courtship and spawning behavior takes somewhat longer but can be partly accomplished within one day and completed within two to four days." Within that period of time the female's ovaries gradually change their characteristics. Small bits of tissue capable of producing sperm emerge from dormancy within the ovaries and develop, transforming the ovary into a testis.

"Probably all females are capable of changing sex and most (possibly all) have testicular elements within perfectly functional ovaries," Dr. Robertson wrote of the wrasse. "The tendency of any female to change may be actively suppressed by more dominant individuals in the hierarchy."

Dr. Robertson said that the typical harem exhibited a linear dominance pattern, with the male dominating the top female and she, in turn, dominating the second highest female and so on to the youngest fish at the bottom of the order. . . .

The internal mechanism of the transformation is poorly understood but it is believed to be under the control of hormones produced in response to environmental conditions including, presumably, the stress of being dominated. [From Boyce Rensberger. The New York Times, Sept. 19, 1972, p. 26]

ing the reproductive season. One researcher (Carpenter, 1942, 1964) was able to reduce the level of aggression in a colony of rhesus monkeys by allowing no more than one male for every five females; in a later study, the ratio was changed to one male for every twenty females, with a consequent further reduction in aggression.

Evidently several factors account for this effect, particularly the glandular changes accompanying estrus and the competition aroused over mating. The role of glandular activity has been demonstrated by injecting male sex hormones into castrated male chimpanzees. Such hormonal activity would occur naturally in the mating season through the special stimulation provided by the females in heat. In one study (Clark and Birch, 1945, 1946), two male chimpanzees who had been castrated were given hormonal injections while they interacted in a cage. Before the injections they had been put in a competitive situation by placing just one peanut between them in the cage, over and over again. As is typical of many animal species, a dominance-submissive relationship or pecking order had been established, the same male usually taking the peanut first until he was satisfied. When injections of the male sex hormone were given only to the subordinate chimp, he overturned the dominance relationship and established himself as the dominant chimp. In this and other species, injections of the male sex hormone increased aggressiveness (or perhaps reduced fear), with the implication that aggression is at least partly controlled by biochemical substances. It also suggests that the widespread tendency of males to be more aggressive than females might have some hormonal basis, as might the increased aggressiveness of females when defending their newborn young.

In man it has been shown that the amount of testosterone (a male sex hormone) normally produced by the body and coursing in the blood differs among human males, and this

Note 6.3

In the research of Persky *et al.* (1971), degree of hostility and level of the sex hormone testosterone were said to be correlated + 0.66. Since such parallel relationships or correlations have been mentioned many times in this book, by now the reader probably has developed an intuitive sense of what is meant when we say that two variables are correlated or linked. However, we must consider more closely just what is meant by the term "a correlation of + 0.66"—without getting so technical that those without much mathematical background will be unnecessarily put off. The basic outlines of the concept are really quite simple and straightforward.

A correlation involves interdependence between two sets of mathematical variables (values); when arrayed against each other, they will rise and fall together in corresponding fashion. A simple example is height and weight. We know intuitively that these two measures are highly correlated: someone who is tall is likely to weigh more than someone who is short. Similarly, there is usually high correlation between a person's grades in high school and those in college. A *correlation coefficient* states mathematically how closely the two sets of measures are related, which is expressed as a numerical value between 0.00 and 1.00. A correlation of 0.00 means there is no statistical relationship or link between the measures, and 1.00 means that the relationship is perfect (we never find such a perfect

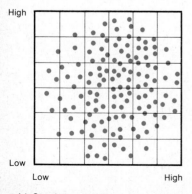

(*a*) Correlation = 0.00

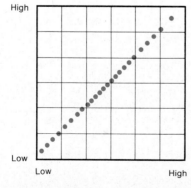

(*b*) Correlation = + 1.00

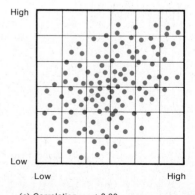

(*c*) Correlation = + 0.30

amount is strongly related to measures of hostility and aggression derived from questionnaires (Persky *et al.*, 1971). The male sex hormone level was higher in young men (averaging 22 years of age) who indicated in their answers that they often felt hostile and acted aggressively than it was in those who did not, although this did not hold for older males (averaging 45 years of age). Such a finding is consistent with the idea that hostile and aggressive tendencies are encouraged or intensified by such hormones, although a cause and effect relationship is not proved. It is possible, for example, that hostility and aggressiveness in men generate such hormones, rather than the other way around, although the latter interpretation is thought to be most reasonable by physiological psychologists and endocrinologists. Another problem is that there were no direct measures of hostility and aggressiveness in this study, and we cannot be absolutely sure that what the male subjects reported about themselves is an accurate reflection of their actual behavioral reactions in social situations. Nevertheless, findings such as these suggest that the relationship between sex hormone level and aggression found in animals may also apply to man, though probably to a lesser extent (Note 6.3).

Adaptive advantages of intraspecies aggression What might be the utility of intraspecies aggression that has permitted it to be retained and passed along through the millions of years of animal evolution? On the surface, it would seem that intense competition and physical conflict among members of one species would impair rather than enhance that species' chances of survival. Clearly there must be important compensatory factors that make such behavior worthwhile.

In the case of *dominance,* once established a hierarchy actually provides a high degree of stability and order among the animals living within the same area as a colony or troop. By means of such "pecking orders" conflict and competition

relationship in psychological research). A correlation can be *positive*—as one measure goes up so does the other; or it can be *negative*—as one measure goes up, the other goes down. Height and weight are positively related. Age past 40 and the ability of a person to read fine print are negatively correlated. A positive relationship is shown by putting a plus sign (+) before the correlation coefficient, and a negative relationship is shown by a minus (−) sign.

So far so good. Now what about different degrees of correlation between 0.00 and 1.00. The graphs below (called scattergrams) show six simulated correlations, some positive, some negative, for two sets of variables. One is displayed on the vertical axis and the other is placed on the horizontal axis, each pair of measures forming a single data point on the graph: that is, Subject 1 gets a particular score on one test and another score on a second test; subject 2 also has two scores; and so on. For each subject, the score on the first test is placed on the vertical axis, and the score on the second is placed on the horizontal axis; both combined into one data point represent how far up and how far across they go on the two axes. You will notice that in the case of perfect correlation (Graphs *b* and *d*), the data points form a straight line: if one variable is low, then the other will be low; if one variable is high, then the other is high too. Graph *b* shows a positive relationship, while Graph *d* shows a negative one.

Notice that in a zero correlation (Graph *a*) the scores on one measure are only randomly related to those of the other, and one gets a picture of chaos rather than of orderly arrangement. We cannot estimate from one measure where the other paired measure is likely to fall. There is no statistical relationship. Graphs *c, e,* and *f,* on the other

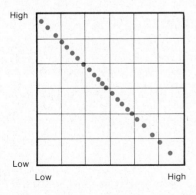

(d) Correlation = −1.00

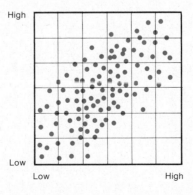

(e) Correlation = +0.60

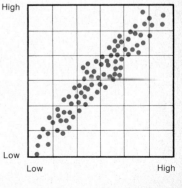

(f) Correlation = +0.90

hand, show intermediate degrees of relationship. As we move from a correlation of +0.30 (Graph *c*) to one of +0.60 (Graph *e*), we see that the data points begin to converge increasingly on a line going from lower left to upper right. By the time we reach Graph *f*, the relationship is quite strong, though not perfect, and there is considerable likelihood that a low score on one measure will indicate a low score on the other.

One practical value of a correlation is that we can increase the accuracy of our guess about a variable, say, a person's college grades, if we know the other variable, say, his high-school grades. If the correlation is very high, knowing an individual's high-school grades will allow us to predict with fair accuracy what he will do in college. If the correlation is low, our guess will be much more chancy.

Now to return to Persky *et al.* (1971) and the relationship between hostility and testosterone production. This particular correlation was +0.66, a moderate relationship more or less like the one shown in Graph *e*. Persky *et al.* have also provided a scattergram of this relationship (Graph *g*), and we can see that as degree of hostility on the horizontal axis increases, the subjects' testosterone production rate (in milligrams per day) also increases. The line (called a *regression line*) in Graph *g* indicates the average of all the data points, and the points falling above it represent too much testosterone production for the level of hostility, while the points falling below the line represent cases in which testosterone production was too low for the hostility scores. In a perfect correlation, all points would have fallen on that line. The higher the correlation the less scattered are the scores from the regression line.

There are actually many ways of determining and expressing a relationship be-

are resolved, and once established a dominance hierarchy means that each animal, by and large, "knows his place," and submissive animals normally do not go beyond the point of prudence in challenging the dominant ones. Of course, such hierarchies are established through much struggle and experimentation, one animal challenging another in many an aggressive contest. The patterns are always changing and gray areas do indeed exist—as when young male baboons are maturing and establishing their place in the hierarchy, or when old males are losing their powers to intimidate younger ones (or when they are injured or become sick). Thus, a young male baboon engages in much rough-and-tumble play with his fellow males in the process of discovering his metal, but he has a long way to go before he attains the dominance status of a full-grown male in the upper rungs of the hierarchy or even in relation to "adolescents" and adult females who are still bigger and stronger than he is (Washburn and DeVore, 1961). In the course of his development, he will gradually move up through the ranks; he will pass the adult females and ultimately compete with full-grown males, probably dominating some and being dominated by others. As a dominant male he will defend the females and their young against outside threats. In times of food scarcity, overpopulation, invasion by another baboon troop, or predation by another species, in short, under all sorts of critical conditions of life, stable dominance patterns may become disrupted and severe conflict will likely ensue.

Calhoun (1948, 1950) set up controlled conditions under which a rat colony was permitted to establish a stable dominance pattern after the usual initial period of instability and competition. He then introduced a second colony of rats into the same habitat, thereby severely upsetting the ecological balance. The result was great loss of life among both colonies, especially the invading one, as a result of intense and destructive aggression that totally disrupted both colonies' social order and stability. The reader may recall the discussion of Calhoun's research in Chapter 3 (Figure 3.7a) from the perspective of overpopulation.

Washburn and Hamburg (1968) have also described a group of macaque monkeys who had lived in captivity without serious fighting for two years under the dominance of a single male. On removal of the dominant male, the social order at first continued as before for two weeks. However, then the animal that had been number two in the hierarchy attempted to assert his power, upon which competition and serious fighting broke out all over. Two infants were killed and several adults received severe bites, something that in the normal course of events would not have happened. Under favorable environmental conditions, especially in the wild, well-estab-

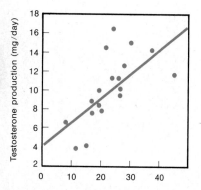

(*g*) Sum hostility scores

lished dominance patterns prevent fighting and provide the animal colony with a stable social order.

One of the most widely respected proposals about the adaptive function of *territorial* conflict is that it prevents overcrowding that would make the environment uninhabitable (Eibl-Eibesfeldt, 1967). Ecologists, who are concerned with the balance of nature, have stressed this point, and have expressed fears that the absence of human population control will result in the environment becoming increasingly uninhabitable through overexploitation. Territoriality protects the environment by producing wider spacing of animals (a reduction of population density), and keeps the population size from eroding supplies of food and other needed resources (see Chapter 3). Conservationists do the same thing when they permit hunting in certain seasons to thin out the excess population of deer, migratory fowl, and other wildlife; sometimes natural regulation is insufficient to maintain the well-being of the animal colonies (especially when man has eliminated too many of the natural predators, such as wolves, foxes, tigers, and hawks—all endangered species).

Do animals often kill?   Whatever the layman's impressions might be, animals of the same species do not typically injure each other seriously in their fighting over territory or in dominance or mating contests, although they sometimes do. Often the "fight" is a ritualized display in which one animal threatens the other, with the less dominant or less impressive individual backing down and leaving the field to the other before there has been any actual physical clash. The exceptions occur under conditions in which the well-established dominance hierarchy has broken down, as in overcrowding or confinement, when a colony is invaded by an alien group, leading to excessive competition, combat, and death, or under other stress conditions that are not yet well understood. It has been suggested that our predominant experience with animals in the abnormal situation of captivity has led us to overestimate the extent to which animals injure or kill members of their own species in the wild. This point has been made by many scientists (Lorenz, 1964; Mathews, 1964; Scott, 1958; Eibl-Eibesfeldt, 1967) who have closely observed the behavior of animals in their natural settings.

Observations by Eibl-Eibesfeldt (1967), for example, suggest that lethal injuries do not usually result from intraspecies fighting because, along with their ability to inflict damage on each other, many animals seem to have developed special inhibitory mechanisms, or they have modified their ways of fighting with their own species in order to avoid inflicting actual damage. For example, poisonous snakes do not bite each other (this would be deadly and soon lead to their

tween two variables, and the correlation coefficient described here is merely one, albeit one of the most accurate and useful in psychological research. Most research in psychology is designed to test whether a relationship exists between two or more variables, and if these variables are suitably scaled, the degree of such relationship can be determined. There will be many more occasions in this book in which correlations are referred to, and it will be useful to keep in mind the basic outlines of what has been presented here.

extinction) but wrestle with each other in accordance with fixed rules. In one species of poisonous snake, *Crotalus ruber*, male rivals raise the forward third of their bodies from the ground and strike at each other with their heads, not opening their mouths when doing so. Eventually, one of them becomes exhausted and gives up, or is forced to the ground and pressed there by a loop of the other's body.

Marine iguanas, large numbers of which occupy the rocky coasts of the Galápagos Islands, provide another illustration of intraspecies aggression without lethal results. During breeding, the males occupy shore territories where they live with several females. When a rival male comes near, the holder of the territory makes a threatening display, opening his mouth, nodding his head, walking up and down stiff-leggedly in front of his rival, and showing his lateral side with his top crest erected (see Figure 6.17). If the rival takes up the challenge and answers with the same threat display, fighting takes place. The iguanas rush at each other but only feign biting; their struggle takes the form of a lowering of heads and bumping together harmlessly. The hornlike scales covering the top of their heads interlock, and each tries to push the other away. Sometimes they pause in this, show a frontal threat display, nodding with the mouth open. The fight ends when one animal is pushed off the rock or surrenders by lying flat on his belly. The winner then immediately stops fighting and assumes a posture of threat display, waiting for the rival to leave. The whole fight has been a highly ritualized event, like a tournament, in which the stronger animal wins without hurting the loser. In intraspecies aggression in most animals, damage that would be disadvantageous to the species is avoided by the presence of behavior on the part of the loser which serves to inhibit further attack. Such ritualized patterns, differing

Figure 6.17 Galápagos marine iguanas in combat. (a) A head-to-head confrontation. (b) The fight is over: iguana on left assumes submissive posture, while his victor assumes dominant posture. (Dr. I. Eibl-Eibesfeldt)

(a)

(b)

only in specific details, occur in a large number of fishes, reptiles, birds, and mammals.

Aggression in the apes The picture of intraspecies aggression in primate species such as baboons, gorillas, and chimpanzees is of particular interest because of their evolutionary proximity to man (Washburn and Hamburg, 1968; Southwick, 1972). More observations in the natural setting have been made of baboons (for example, see Washburn and DeVore, 1961) than of any other anthropoid ape, perhaps because they live mainly in the open rather than in forest areas. Baboon society is organized around very strict dominance hierarchies. Full-grown males, much bigger, stronger, and more aggressive than females, are at the top of the hierarchy, and there is usually one large male who has first access to sexually receptive females, engages in more aggression, leads the troop in counterattacks against predators, protects subordinate members of the troop, and most often is treated in a submissive manner by the others (Figure 6.18).

Intraspecies aggression in baboons usually consists of ritualized threats, chasing, and brief fights that usually stop short of serious injury. After the exchange of a few nips or bites the loser assumes a submissive attitude, running away, lying on the ground, displaying what is called a "fear grin," and the like. By this behavior the loser inhibits the victor from further aggression. This type of conflict occurs at a high rate with constant expression and reassertion of dominance-submissive relationships taking place. A threat involves opening the mouth wide to show the teeth (as in a kind of yawn), pacing about tensely, raising the eyebrows, barking, grunting,

Figure 6.18 Marching order of a baboon troop. The dominant males accompany the females with infants in the center of the troop. Other males and females precede and follow the central group. A group of juveniles is seen in the lower part of the figure. Two females in heat, or estrous (swelling shown by colored markings), are each accompanied by a male. (From Primate behavior: Field studies of monkeys and apes, *edited by Irven DeVore (1965). Reprinted by permission of Holt, Rinehart and Winston, Inc.)*

roaring, teeth grinding, ear flattening, raising the hair on and about the head, shaking rocks and branches, all directed at the challenger. If the offending animal withdraws, that is usually all there is to it. Often, when a dominant animal threatens a submissive one, the latter will take it out on the animal below him in the hierarchy (behaviorists refer to this phenomenon as *displacement*), and so on down the line, thus further reinforcing the existing dominance hierarchy. But if the threat escalates into a fight, the animals charge, hit, push and rub each other on the ground, and bite either with minor nips using the incisors, or sometimes use the canine teeth to produce more serious wounds.

In contrast with the popular stereotype of the gorilla as a ferocious beast, in his natural habitat he is the most mild and relaxed of all the anthropoid apes (see Schaller, 1964). Gorillas appear to be totally vegetarian, living in rather cohesive groups numbering from about five to thirty animals, foraging for food and moving about in a leisurely manner. Generally they feel secure against predators (except man). Like the baboon, gorilla groups also tend to live under the dominance of a single large male. However, there is much less conflict among the gorillas than among the baboons, with placidity and tolerance appearing to be the usual norm. The assertion of dominance is likely to be accomplished by a brief stare, a single tap with the hand, and sometimes an incipient charge. Rarely is there any biting or wrestling. Usually the submissive animal moves away when given any of the above signals. The ritualized chest beating we associate with the gorilla is often performed only by full-grown males in response to man, other groups of gorillas, or the threat display of another animal. These rather placid patterns of aggressive behavior apply only in situations where there is ample food and lack of danger, and gorillas, like other species, show a breakdown of the stable social pattern under conditions of environmentally produced stress.

Chimpanzee social organization, in contrast with that of baboons and gorillas, is rather loose. These are evidently the brightest of the nonhuman primates, and they have even been shown to make use of simple tools. There is a shifting array of small groups that may merge together temporarily into larger bands, then break up, and reform. There is no tightly knit primary group which always remains together. The dominance by a strong male, so important in baboon and gorilla society, seems less important among the chimpanzees than the individual affectionate ties between mother and children and among others in the colony. Feeding often occurs in "sharing clusters," with no strict hierarchy established in the sharing of food (van Lawick–Goodall, 1972; Teleki, 1973).

One day when Mike [the new top-ranking male chimpanzee] was sitting in camp, a series of distinctive, rather melodious pant-hoots with characteristic quavers at the close announced the return of Goliath [the former champ], who for two weeks had been somewhere down in the southern part of the reserve. Mike responded immediately, hooting in turn and charging across the clearing. Then he climbed a tree and sat staring over the valley, every hair on end.

A few minutes later Goliath appeared, and as he reached the outskirts of the camp clearing he commenced one of his spectacular displays. He must have seen Mike, because he headed straight for him, dragging a huge branch. He leaped into a tree near Mike's and was motionless. For a moment Mike stared toward him and then he too began to display, swaying the branches of his tree, swinging to the ground, hurling a few rocks, and, finally, leaping up into Goliath's tree and swaying the branches there. When he stopped, Goliath immediately reciprocated, swinging about in the tree and rocking the branches. Presently, as one of his wild leaps took him quite close to Mike, Mike also displayed, and for a few unbelievable moments both of the splendid male chimpanzees were swaying branches

There is considerable interspecies aggression in chimpanzees, who unlike gorillas seem to engage in some predation, eating insects and bird eggs, hunting and killing young baboons, monkeys, bush pigs, and other small mammals and insects (see Introduction to Part II). There is also considerable intraspecies fighting, but this rarely leads to killing. Establishment of the dominance pattern, however, is similar to that of other primate species, built largely around threat displays such as glaring, waving of arms, running toward the adversary, ground slapping, branch shaking, and loud vocalization. The animal that is threatened or attacked usually runs off, sometimes screaming loudly, or he makes appeasement gestures, such as displaying a "fear" grin or touching the dominant animal on the arm, lip, or scrotum. The displacement seen in the baboon seems to be even more common in the chimpanzee (Figure 6.19).

Parallels with human aggression   The temptation is very great to see analogies between animal patterns of hierarchical, territorial, or sexual competition and patterns of human conflict; such parallels have been enthusiastically seized upon by many writers (for example, Ardrey, 1966; Lorenz, 1966). Man does indeed live in dominance hierarchies (or "pecking orders") involving social class and status, and social scientists tell us that they are found in virtually all human societies. Throughout history territoriality has played a key role in relations between adjacent tribes, nations, or empires. In our own times, both territoriality and struggles for dominance are

within a few feet of each other until I thought the whole tree must crash to the ground. An instant later both chimps were on the ground displaying in the undergrowth. Eventually they both stopped and sat staring at each other. It was Goliath who moved next, standing upright as he rocked a sapling; when he paused Mike charged past him, hurling a rock and drumming with his feet on the trunk of a tree.

This went on for nearly half an hour: first one male and then the other displayed, and each performance seemed to be more vigorous, more spectacular than the one preceding it. Yet during all that time, apart from occasionally hitting one another with the ends of the branches they swayed, neither chimpanzee actually attacked the other. Unexpectedly, after an extra long pause, it looked as if Goliath's nerve had broken. He rushed up to Mike, crouched beside him with loud, nervous pant-grunts, and began to groom him with feverish intensity. For a few moments Mike ignored Goliath completely. Suddenly he turned and with a vigor almost matching Goliath's, began to groom his vanquished rival. There they sat, grooming each other without pause for over an hour. [From van Lawick–Goodall, 1971, pp. 125–126]

Figure 6.19   Savannah chimpanzee beating a stuffed leopard with a stick. The test was performed with chimps captured in the wild at nearly adult age; consequently they must have known leopards as predators prior to capture. (© A. Kortlandt; all rights reserved)

still present in the form of intense individual and corporate competition for wealth and power. Under capitalism, a high value is placed on private ownership, and to the most successful competitor go the greatest rewards, the biggest status symbols. As in the animal world, one has little difficulty in identifying those at the top of the hierarchy. Traditional hierarchical societies, be they oligarchies, monarchies, or autocracies, frequently depend on family inheritance more than on actual competition to establish social rank. Dynamic societies that permit competition to change the hierarchical structure are said to have high *social mobility*—individuals can move up through their own efforts or down as a result of incompetence or misfortune. In the eighteenth and nineteenth centuries and early decades of this century, American society was highly mobile, with many great fortunes won and lost.

The ideology of socialism emphasizes egalitarian rather than hierarchical principles, and the various Marxist governments in existence today are all committed either to temper the effects of open competitiveness or to abolish it totally by limiting the extent to which acquisition of wealth is permitted. If such egalitarianism could be shown to operate smoothly, some doubt might be cast on the potency of man's assumed innate competitive tendencies. But most societies are mixtures of outlooks and politicoeconomic arrangements, and seldom is the reality much like the stated ideals. All one hears (from inside) about the communist countries of the world makes it clear that elitism and hierarchical social structure obtain there as well as in capitalist societies, although perhaps with different status symbols (though not very different: a key requirement for top Soviet officials is apparently a large, luxurious *dacha* in the country). George Orwell (1954) said it very clearly in *Animal Farm,* his satiric tale of an animal revolution on a farm in which the oppressive humans are dispatched and the beasts take over under the leadership of the pigs. Orwell's sardonic conclusion is that very soon after the revolution the slogan "All animals are equal" changed to "All animals are equal, but some animals [the pigs] are more equal than others."

American society would appear to be ambivalent about its ideals and practices. In our stated outlook (the Declaration of Independence and the Constitution), we seem to reject the principle of dominance or status—in an egalitarian democracy "all men are created equal," and any idea of royalty or status achieved by birth is denied—but in practice we have a strong class system. Moreover, at the same time as we espouse the idea of equality and humanitarianism, we also clearly embrace the principle of "free enterprise," competitive striving in which there must be winners and losers. Our love of competition is often held responsible in large measure for our great economic power, although actual economic competition in many areas (such as communications and transport) is sharply curtailed by law, and our industrial pattern has many features of the monopoly or cartel.

Man seems also to be highly *territorial*. Not only is a high value placed on private ownership and wealth, but psychologically we identify with our property (a piece of land, a house, an automobile), which often becomes an extension of our egos, and we defend our possessions and our egos vigorously. A man will often regard the size of his desk, or whether he can have a rug for his office or a key to the executive washroom, as more important than the amount of his salary. There is no doubt that man engages in a great many activities that appear roughly analogous to struggles for dominance and territory in other animals. Thus, the major thrust of the concept of the origins of social aggression in man is that his competitive and territorial tendencies derive from innate universal biological forces.

Many scientists, particularly social scientists, are rather wary of this unrestrained use of parallels between animal intraspecies aggression and the human variety in attempts to understand and explain the latter. One danger in doing so is that we already know from animal studies that the patterns of dominance and territoriality are highly variable, differing from species to species, and differing in the same species under various environmental conditions. It is only by specifying the conditions under which such aggression will or will not occur that we can understand it and predict it. More hard evidence is required identifying the type of environmental conditions (social, cultural, economic) under which human aggression frequently occurs (see Chapter 7), and the internal neural and hormonal mechanisms regulating it.

How, for example, would animal aggression look if animal species other than man had and could use the sophisticated technology of man? A silly question perhaps, but as we shall see shortly the technology of weapons is an important factor in human aggression, making it unique. Because man is a tool-, weapon-, and fire-utilizing animal, possessed of massive power for destruction, human aggression cannot be adequately understood or controlled merely by reference to its parallels with animal aggression. We must discover the exact way it works in particular human contexts (Ashley Montagu, 1968).

Causes of war   There is great debate among anthropologists about the causes of war. Vayda (1968) has argued that territorial conflict has as much to do with the food supply in man as in other animals, and that when a group's per capita food supply begins to decline within a given territory intragroup tensions increase; when they reach a certain peak, re-

Aggressive behavior is most frequent, diverse, and extensive when a sample population of animals of the same species has no organization or is in the process of becoming organized into grouping structures, or when groups are threatened by others of the same species, or when there are unresolved drive tensions within organized groups, as during the early phases of the breeding season. The animals of the Santiago Island rhesus colony fought persistently during the early stages of the colony's organization. Many individuals, especially infants and early juveniles, were killed. Some were driven into the sea. . . . Peripheral males surrounded the colony, there was a high incidence of driving attacks, and the whole colony was in a state of great tension. [From Carpenter, 1968, p. 54]

[In New Guinea] (1) a diminishing per capita food supply and increasing intragroup competition for resources generate intense domestic frustrations and other in-group tensions; (2) when these tensions reach a certain level, release is sought in warfare with an enemy group; (3) a result of the warfare is reduction of the pressure of people upon the land, either because of heavy battle mortality or because of the victorious group's taking its defeated and dispersed enemy's territory; (4) the reduced pressure on the land means that . . . domestic frustrations are arrested and other in-group tensions can be kept within tolerable limits. . . .
[From Vayda, 1968, p. 88]

lease is then found in warfare against a neighboring group, decreasing population pressure or increasing the available territory, and making the in-group tensions more manageable once again. Such a hypothesis draws on the psychobiological notion of territoriality as seen in animals, and it evidently fits the warfare patterns Vayda has observed among tribes in New Guinea. However, it does not do so well for tribal societies (the Yanomamö) that Chagnon (1968a, 1968b) has studied in the Venezuelan interior. The Yanomamö practice slash-and-burn farming and there is sufficient jungle land for all, although the tribal units are kept very small to prevent population pressures on the available resources. This is managed through infanticide and by division of the tribe when its population exceeds about 80. Warfare between tribes is very frequent, but not over land so much as over women, who are the principle commodity of exchange and the means for the formation of essential kinship alliances. The rules, in effect, are quite different in the two societies studied by Vayda and Chagnon, though each is easily mobilized for war making. Thus, reference to territorial mechanisms in animals as the explanation for warfare between tribes is too simple to explain the pattern of armed conflict in these two cultures.

What does seem to emerge here is that in both cases *conflict arises over possession of resources whose ownership confers increased power upon the holder*—land in New Guinea, women in Venezuela. Similar power struggles on a far grander scale occur today on the world stage, often over highly symbolic issues of "national prestige." Modern "civilized" conflict leading to warfare also has its rituals of dominance and submission, conducted by statesmen, generals, and diplomats. Elaborate parlays often precede and follow armed clashes.

Only when we have advanced to this stage of detail can we evaluate the implications of intraspecies aggression as a biological disposition in man. Is biological pressure toward territoriality and dominance strong enough to control human behavior regardless of all inhibitions arrayed against it? Just how is such pressure manifested in our brain and glands? If such pressure is weak, then there is no reason why it may not be resisted, redirected by learning, or transformed by a different set of social controls than we now employ. When one of the popularizers of the view of man's aggression as an extension of animal territoriality, Robert Ardrey (1966), uses the title *The Territorial Imperative*, he is suggesting, in effect, that such biological pressure cannot be resisted, although there is absolutely no evidence about the actual nature of this pressure, much less its strength and the way it might work. Thus, if we are not careful, uncritical acceptance of this sort of doctrine will take us back to the circular and unfruitful instinct position from which we started before the turn of the century. We can be fascinated by such analogies, and even come to believe that using them to set the direction of future research may be very fruitful, but we must also guard against overemphasizing the human-animal parallels at the expense of not seeing the differences and believing we understand something when we do not.

How similar is human and animal aggression? Waelder (1960, p. 147), a psychoanalyst of the innate-drive persuasion writes:

. . . when terrible things, cruelties hardly conceivable, occur in men, many speak thoughtlessly of "brutality," of bestialism, or a return to animal levels. . . . As if there were animals which inflict on their own kind what man can do to man. Just at this point the zoologist has to draw a clear line: these evil, horrible things are no animal survival that happened to be carried along in the imperceptible transition from animal to man; this evil belongs entirely on this side of the dividing line, it is purely human. . . .

And Anthony Storr (1968), also a Freudian, puts the same point thusly:

In our brief review of aggression in other species, we concluded that even animals which prey upon one another do not rejoice in cruelty for its own sake. . . . Yet men, with hatred in their hearts, take pleasure in prolonging the agonies of helpless victims, and show extreme ingenuity in devising tortures which cause the maximum pain and the minimum risk of a quick ending. The relation of predator to prey (or dominant to subordinate) cannot be called sadistic without robbing the adjective of its meaning; for the enjoyment of another's pain is, so far as one can tell, peculiar to human beings.

The human enjoyment of death for its own sake, as seen in the ritualistic spectacle of the bullfight (Figure 6.20) or in hunting for "sport," is certainly unmatched elsewhere in the animal kingdom.

The dilemma is that human social aggression has surely gone far beyond the mainly ritualized aggression found in animals. Man maims and kills his own kind at a prodigious rate unmatched by any other species on earth. Intraspecies aggression in other animals is rarely fatal, except under rare conditions. Scientists adopting the psychobiological perspective have acknowledged the above dilemma, although it is most likely to be emphasized by those who dispute the comparability between aggression in man and other animals. Those more favorable to the search for animal bases for man's aggression have tried to resolve the dilemma by assuming that in the course of his evolutionary and social development man has *lost some of the controls* that protect lower animals against unbridled and destructive aggression. Konrad Lorenz (1964, 1966) is probably the foremost exponent of this position.

The Dugum Dani, who live in the New Guinea highlands, exemplify a warrior society. . . . In the Dani culture men from villages separated by agricultural gardens regularly engage in intertribal warfare that is one of the most valued activities in Dani life. The Dani do not fight for land, food resources, or conquest of opponents; rather, fighting serves social and spiritual purposes.

Dani warfare, which is highly stylized, is performed in designated battlefields adjacent to the villages. Sentries maintain continuous surveillance from high watchtowers to safeguard against enemy ambushes. Men are armed wherever they go so they can be readily summoned to combat surprise raids. Indeed, much of Dani life is organized around warfare, including such activities as extended guard duty, fashioning weapons, cutting grass to prevent ambushes, and performing magical practices to secure defense systems. Formal battles are initiated by shouting a challenge across the no man's land. After ritualistic confrontations between advance bands of warriors, the combatants, armed with spears and bows and arrows, engage in repeated brief clashes of deadly fighting throughout the day.

Though the origin of the institutionalized warfare remains unknown, fighting is instigated and perpetuated largely by feared consequences of unavenged spirits. . . . [From Bandura, 1973, p. 108; see also R. Gardner and K. G. Heider, Gardens of war: Life and death in the New Guinea Stone Age. New York: Random House, 1969]

Figure 6.20 A young bullfighter basks in approving applause after successfully dispatching his bull in the arena in Arles, France. (Photo by Lucien Clergue, 1968 Photography Annual; from United Press International)

Lorenz's main argument is that although man shares with lower animals the same propensity for aggressive behavior, through evolution he has lost the specific controls that protect these animals from unbridled aggression. Remember that as we go from lower to higher animals on the evolutionary scale, we also move toward greater variability and flexibility of behavior; there is more freedom from strict biological controls, in this case controls that restrain the killing of members of one's own species. Most animals can retreat easily before the fatal damage has been done. The winner seems to exhibit no need to pursue the retiring loser—the fact of his submission settles the matter. The case changes, however, when the fighting animals are kept together in a cage where escape is impossible. Lorenz notes, for example, that if two rival pigeons are kept together in a cage, one will strip the other of all its exposed feathers and ultimately kill it. Although the pigeon would not normally be regarded as a vicious animal (its beak, for example, is not a particularly dangerous weapon), such species can be more murderous than the wolf when the opportunity for escape is eliminated. Man, says Lorenz, shows an aggressive process analogous to that of caged animals. Because of weapons that kill fast, the victim does not have the opportunity to withdraw or redress the injury, thus preventing the victor from inhibiting his attack. In short, man's weapons are so effective that the killing is done before the murderous aggression can be inhibited by escape or submission.

Furthermore, *ritualized aggression* is found mainly in animals capable of establishing strong bonds or affective ties, as in stable mating, maternal behavior, and other forms of inter-animal relationships. This, says Lorenz (1964, p. 48),

will certainly *not* be news to the student of human nature, to the psychiatrist and the psychoanalyst. The wisdom of the old proverbs as well as that of Sigmund Freud has known for a very long time indeed how closely human aggressiveness and human love are bound together.

No organism is known, claims Lorenz, that shows the tendency to form strong bonds or attachments and is at the same time devoid of aggression; however, highly gregarious creatures such as many fish and birds who live peacefully in flocks do not display bonds but live without individual ties.

Lorenz's theme is supported by many ethologists. Eibl-Eibesfeldt (1967) has added a further thought—that man actually does have some special mechanisms that could help prevent the killing of a conspecific, although these are not strong enough or rapidly enough aroused to control the new and deadly weapons that have become part of our environment. Introspection tells us, says Eibl-Eibesfeldt, that mentally healthy people can feel pity and that such a reaction is elicited by submissive acts on the part of persons, just as the submissive postures of some animals induce inhibition of further assault. A person may fall to his knees to show vulnerability, or raise his hands to show he is weaponless and friendly, and he may cry or plead. Indeed, such actions tend usually to inhibit further aggression, but a gun can kill so fast that the opponent often has no opportunity before his demise to appeal for pity or surrender (Figure 6.21). Man is, of course, the only animal who kills in a disciplined way under *orders* or is subject to the incitements of war propaganda (see Chapter 7).

Social control of aggression   Man must discover new means to modify his aggression. He must develop social and psychological modes of preventing violence. Who could argue with such a reasonable point! But how? One possibility might be to ban weapons, although this, of course, is easier said than done. It is probable that such a ban, if successful, would at least cut down the incidence of homicide.

Historian Arthur Schlesinger, Jr. (1968) has noted, for example, that states with adequate gun laws (New Jersey, New York, Massachusetts, and Rhode Island) have much lower rates of murder than states with no or weak gun laws (Texas, Mississippi, Louisiana, and Nevada). In countries with strong gun laws, rates of homicide are also low compared with the American rate, which is about 3.5 murders per 100,000 population. In Great Britain, where police generally do not carry guns, the rate is 0.05, and in Japan it is 0.04 per 100,000 people. In Canada, where police *do* carry guns as in the United States, the rate is 0.52 per 100,000, ten times the British rate but only one-seventh the American rate. Why the difference? The evidence is suggestive rather than conclusive because other cultural factors in these countries could be contributing to the differences (Note 6.4). But gun laws illustrate a form of social control designed to serve as a substitute for the instinctual controls that Lorenz says are absent in highly evolved man. Social psychologists often make the same proposal, though for quite different reasons than those cited by Lorenz.

With respect to this problem of social controls, ethologists such as Lorenz also argue that the encouragement of ritual aggression in man, as in competitive sports, that is, combat which stops short of injury or killing, would help matters by reducing the destructiveness now associated with territoriality and dominance struggles. Thus, on this point Lorenz is allied with Freud, but for different reasons. As Freud saw it, it was important for man to have an outlet for pent-up innate aggressive drives. For Lorenz, the point is that by ritualizing aggression, that is, hemming it in with all sorts of rules and

Figure 6.21 Child accompanies his father to street execution of Pakistani collaborators in Dacca, Bangladesh, in December 1971. Civil strife of this kind frequently produces the most extreme examples of fractricidal violence, with lust for revenge leading to excesses of cruelty and mass slaughter of prisoners. (Popperfoto; Pictorial Parade)

codes, a man could win in a symbolic territorial argument and yet maintain his dominance without killing. For Lorenz it is the winning that is important, no matter how it is accomplished. But for Freud it was the discharge of aggression in killing or producing suffering in another that was important. Lorenz points to the more gentlemanly arts of combat practiced by knights in tournaments during feudal times, as well as other highly socialized and ritualized contests. He is not very specific, however, about how to get men to accept the ritual winning or losing, in short, about how man could be stopped from "playing for keeps."

For the social scientist, this problem is one of socialization and of developing and keeping a set of appropriate cultural values. Within our society at present, we attempt to control individual violence by instilling children with cultural values against killing (albeit weak ones), as well as by a system of laws and law enforcement. We know, however, how inadequate these means have proved, especially with respect to the most alienated people of a society. Thus, the crucial question of how to achieve the desired social conditions is left unanswered by extrapolations from concepts such as innate territoriality and dominance striving.

The idea that aggression can be ritualized as a social institution, thus decreasing its more destructive consequences, may be found in the writings of a number of cultural anthropologists. Its role has been reviewed and analyzed by Norbeck (1963), who cites many examples among various African cultures. One example is the *inowala* ceremony of the Swazi people, in which the king, members of the royal family, and all subjects of the kingdom participate. Aggression against the king is expressed through a ritual drama portraying the many dangers the king must face in his job, especially the hatred and hostility of rivals in the royal clan. It also expresses the sympathy of the people for their king and their loyalty to him. The songs of the ritual, sung by the people, repeatedly stress hatred in the third person (he, they) or the second person (you), as in the phrase, "You hate the king," and a portion of song that states: "King, alas for your fate, King, they reject thee, King, they hate thee." Such hostility, presumably felt by the people, is said to be expressed in the safer and more acceptable ritual form, thus controlling the impulses of rebellion and solidifying the people behind the ruler. One way of looking at such expressions, from the drive point of view, is that it is a form of catharsis (self-purification or purgation) that banishes the threat of disunity imposed by conflicts and allows formalized group expression rather than dangerous individual expression. Actually, Norbeck has expressed doubt that this cathartic interpretation of the function of such rituals is sound, arguing that although such rituals are no doubt socially im-

Note 6.4

In comparing the gun laws of different states with their homicide rates, Schlesinger (1968) is suggesting a correlation between the two, although he has not ordered these variables numerically in such a way as to obtain a correlation coefficient (described in Note 6.3). Aside from the statistical aspects, this is another instance in which a causal inference is being derived from a correlation. Schlesinger is assuming that the strength of the gun laws, and hence the accessibility of guns, influences whether there will be many or few homicides in a community. Perhaps so. But we should be cautious here since, as was pointed out in Note 5.1, p. 177 (which the reader might wish to review), correlation does not prove causation. The causal sequence might be the other way around, or there might be some third factor, say, social stability or mores, which influences both the gun laws and the incidence of murder. To check on this we would want to consider in what ways New Jersey, New York, Massachusetts, and Rhode Island as a group of states differ from Texas, Mississippi, Louisiana, and Nevada, other than in the accessibility of guns. Or we might compare the homicide rates in other states (or countries like Australia) where guns are easily accessible. If some third factor were responsible for the other two, we would probably find some areas where guns are readily available but where murder is rare. We could then try to pinpoint this crucial missing factor.

portant, their relationship to direct aggression and violence have not been firmly established.*

The airing of grievances on very formal occasions in other African cultures, such as the Bemba (Evans-Pritchard, 1956) and in the songs of the Chopi that describe social injustices and are often critical of those in authority (Tracey, 1948), represent other examples of ritual aggression. The mocking songs of medieval kings' jesters in Europe fall into the same category. In our own culture, satiric humor and lampooning of authority figures serve this function. It is not infrequent to find employees or student groups constructing skits at annual parties in which their employers, supervisors, or professors are treated satirically, often with more than a little hostility. It used to be common for graduate students of psychology in many departments around the country to have such occasions annually. The faculty would come and be "roasted," smiling all the while they were the butt of student jokes and not-so-veiled attacks. To some teachers it was far worse than being directly attacked, however, to be totally ignored by the students. Although the interpretation that these ritual forms of aggression serve the function of minimizing the more destructive forms is controversial and not really established by empirical research, ritual aggression remains an idea widely subscribed to in the search for potential ways of controlling violence through various types of social institutions.

There are other possible explanations for the unusually deadly aggression displayed by man. One of the most reasonable is that man's mental capacities enable him to construct elaborate hostile beliefs about other men, especially when he conceives them to be his enemies (Frank, 1967). Man often comes to see his enemies as the incarnation of all evil, who must be destroyed for his own safety, or for the good of his tribe or nation, or for some higher religious or moral purpose. Unlike the chimpanzee, who quickly "makes up" after an aggressive encounter, man may conceive that the loser is leaving the field with deep and abiding hostility, only perhaps to return later to get revenge. This type of reasoning, and the ability to place oneself in another person's shoes, may be uniquely human because of man's sense of past, present, and future time. It is illustrated in numerous stories of bloody feuds, of killing and revenge and more killing to prevent retaliation: such tales are found everywhere—in American folklore, in accounts of "payback" among the New Guinea highlanders, and in the ancient Icelandic sagas (see the margin).

Thus, man's unique powers of imagination and complex

[Among the Ifugao of the Philippine Islands, the] intentional killing of a person must be avenged by the victim's kinsmen. Thus a killing always leads to a blood feud that may continue ad infinitum. . . .

The avenging of a murder has been institutionalized in headhunting. It must be understood that murder rarely occurs among families living in the same valley, and, when it does take place, public pressure is sufficiently great to prevent a blood feud from starting. But to avenge a death attributed to someone from over the mountains, from another valley, is one of the noblest deeds an Ifugao can accomplish. It gives him great prestige; it is a blessing for the whole community. . . .

Headhunting is rarely an individual undertaking. A small party of six to ten men form an expedition and proceed with as much precaution as possible to avoid danger to themselves. The victim is ambushed and speared. All then scramble for the head. When they are a safe distance from the enemy territory, the headhunting party gives a loud shriek of victory as a signal that a head has been taken. The village that has lost a head is stricken with the greatest grief. Men and women clamor for vengeance. The decapitated victim is brought back to the village and insulted and maligned to excite his soul to vengeance. It is not long before the men, stung into action by the reproaches of the women, organize a retaliatory expedition. In this way the blood feud goes on interminably. [From Goldman, 1961, pp. 168–169]

---

*Surely the tragic dramas of classic Greece, such as those of Sophocles and Aeschylus, employed the cathartic principle. In more recent times, the yearly reenactment of the Easter Passion, the betrayal, trial, and crucifixion of Christ, has a similar quality.

social codes and dogmas often overpower any empathy and forebearance he may feel towards his fellow man. In contrast, the lower animal, who inhibits his attack when his opponent submits to him, does not have the mental powers to imagine that this now submissive adversary may later return to renew the challenge. His actions are geared to the here and now and not to the future, which he cannot grasp.

These are imaginative speculations about various biological factors in man's intraspecies aggression. They have intrigued many, particularly those whose outlook resonates with notions of a competitive and acquisitive social order. By the same token, they have offended many as well, perhaps for similar reasons. Although we have no final answers concerning the evolutionary origins of man's aggression, these ideas provide possible directions for further inquiry. Their mere incompleteness is no reason to reject them summarily at this stage.

CONCLUDING COMMENT

Man's biological heritage is no doubt a factor in the patterns of aggression he displays, probably a very important one. The scientific problem, however, is to tie down how this genetic heritage operates and interacts with social forces. In this chapter, various competing theories of its mode of operation were considered, including the concept that aggression is an innate drive and the alternate one that aggression is an innate response to certain external stimuli that trigger it. Attempting to link human aggression to evolution, some writers have stressed man's emergence as a successful predator, while others have stressed intraspecies patterns such as struggles for dominance and territory. Such speculations make the assumption that there are universals in human and animal aggression, that useful parallels can be drawn between aggression in animals and aggression in man, and there has been no lack of ingenuity in suggesting such parallels.

However, it is evident that the key scientific question concerning human aggression has not yet been tackled in adequate detail, namely, "How does man's aggressive disposition as a member of the animal kingdom actually operate in the context of human social life?" In this connection, although it is valuable to seek parallels, one must also keep in mind the differences, and it is essential to determine how and to what extent the social conditions under which people live modify or transcend the biological pressures. Human patterns of aggression are sufficiently varied to suggest that they have much to do with such the prevailing social environment, as we shall see in the next chapter.

When Sigmund and Skjold got back from the east, Hallgerd told them that Thord was still at home, but that he was to ride to the Althing [Parliament] in a few days' time.

'This is your chance to get him,' she said. 'If you don't get him now, you never will.' Some people came to Hlidarend from Thorolfsfell and told Hallgerd that Thord was there. Hallgerd went to Thrain Sigfusson and the others and said, 'Thord is now at Thorolsfell. Your best plan is to kill him on his way home.'

'That's what we'll do,' said Sigmund.

They went out and got their weapons and horses, and rode away to lie in wait for him. . . .

A little later, Thord came riding towards them.

Sigmund said to him, 'Give yourself up, for now it is time for you to die.'

'Certainly not,' said Thord. 'Come and fight me in single combat.'

'Certainly not,' said Sigmund. 'We shall make full use of our advantage in numbers. It's not surprising that Skarp-Hedin is so formidable, since the saying goes that one-fourth comes from the foster-father.'

'You shall feel the full force of that,' said Thord, 'for Skarp-Hedin will avenge me.'

Then they advanced on him, but Thord defended himself so well that he shattered both their spears. Then Skjold hacked off his arm, but he fought then with his other arm for a short time until Sigmund ran him through and he fell dead to the ground. They covered him up with turf and stones.

Thrain said, 'We have done an evil deed, and the sons of Njal are not going to be pleased when they hear of it.'

They rode home and told Hallgerd, who was delighted over the killing. But Ranneveig, Gunnar's mother, said to Sigmund, 'It is said that the hand is soon sorry that it struck, and so it will be here.' [From *Njal's Saga* (trans. from the Icelandic by M. Magnusson and H. Palsson), pp. 111–112. Baltimore, Md.: Penguin, 1960]

The concept of instinct

Beach, F. A. The descent of instinct. *Psychological Review,* 1955, **62,** 401–410. A very valuable, brief discussion of the history of instinct as a concept, considering the erroneous tendency to dichotomize innate and experiential factors.

Berkowitz, L. *Aggression: A social psychological analysis,* Chap. 1, pp. 1–25. New York: McGraw-Hill, 1962. An excellent review and critique of the instinct approach to aggression.

Eibl-Eibesfeldt, I. *Ethology: The biology of behavior* (transl. by E. Klinghammer). New York: Holt, Rinehart & Winston, 1970. Surely one of the best and most complete examinations of animal behavior and instinctual patterns, probably difficult for the beginning student but rewarding.

The psychobiology of aggression

Ardrey, R. *The territorial imperative.* New York: Atheneum, 1966. A popularized, gung-ho presentation of human aggression as seen from the standpoint of its biological origins in animal territoriality.

Ashley Montagu, M. F. (ed.) *Man and aggression.* New York: Oxford Univ. Press, 1968. A series of fascinating essays attacking the psychobiological stance of Konrad Lorenz, Robert Ardrey, and others, though unhappily some of the authors seem to make the opposing error of supposing that the problem of man's aggression is strictly social.

Carthy, J. D., and Ebling, J. J. (eds.) *The natural history of aggression.* New York: Academic Press, 1964. A series of symposium articles by biological and social scientists (mainly the former) dealing with patterns of aggression in animals and various biologically oriented hypotheses about them and their implications for human warfare.

Clemente, C. D., and Lindsley, D. B. (eds.) *Brain function,* Vol. V: *Aggression and defense.* Los Angeles: Univ. of California Press, 1967. A symposium of mainly biologically oriented writers on aggression, with a special focus on brain and hormonal mechanisms.

Lorenz, K. *On aggression.* New York: Harcourt Brace Jovanovich, 1966. A short, readable, and popularized account of the parallels between human aggression and intraspecies aggression in animals, written by a highly respected ethologist.

Storr, A. *Human aggression.* New York: Atheneum, 1968. A brief, readable account of the dynamics of aggression from a more or less Freudian point of view, emphasizing the instinctual origins of aggression in man.

van Lawick-Goodall, Jane. *In the shadow of man.* New York: Dell, 1972 (paper). Superb account of life among wild chimpanzees at Gombe National Park on Lake Tanganyika, by a remarkable young woman with a keen perception of animal behavior and a strong empathy with the chimps as individuals; contains valuable descriptions of social aggression, predation, and toolmaking in these primates.

I have pointed out elsewhere that as we go up the phylogenetic ladder (or evolutionary series), behavior becomes both more variable and less dependent on innate or built-in mechanisms. Another way to say this is that when behavior is wired into the animal in a fixed fashion, the animal does not require much (if any) experience to engage in the types of behavior that promote species survival. But such automatically elicited reactions do not happen so readily in higher animals, and primates are the least fixed in their behavioral repertoire and in the environmental stimuli that elicit the response. More than any other species, the behavior of man is greatly dependent on learning, and hence he is more readily able to profit from experience. He is thus capable of flexibly adjusting his behavior and way of life to changes in environmental conditions.

Although this ability to learn and be flexible is highly adaptive, it also creates vulnerability of a sort. As Breger (1973) puts it: "If *nothing* was built-in—if the species was completely open to learning—then individuals might develop who failed to care for their young, or weren't much interested in sexual reproduction, or in fighting off predators. What is needed—and, in fact, what seems to have evolved in primates—is a system which confers value on the crucial, survival related areas while at the same time leaving the way open for a good deal of learning."

This is precisely what seems to happen in the case of human aggression. To a greater extent than any other animal man has evolved in a social context, and we cannot hope to understand his aggression or, for that matter, his great capacity for cooperation, sympathy, empathy, self-sacrifice, ability to defer immediate gratification, involvement with religious and ideological symbols as well as material things, and the tremendous strength of bonds which tie him to other persons, without paying close attention to the social setting in which he lives throughout life. The task of the present chapter is to specify how the social environment shapes the individual's aggressive patterns of behavior.

LEARNING AGGRESSION

We learn how to injure others effectively with fists, knives, guns—or words. The most sophisticated forms of attack require that we know other people's vulnerabilities and how to protect ourselves from retaliation. Thus, one of the earliest things a young draftee with no military experience is taught in the army is how to kill another man effectively. In World War II (and no doubt in other wars), considerable effort was expended in training new GIs to give up the niceties of more gentlemanly forms of combat. This was called "dirty fighting." The gallant and chivalrous rules of fisticuffs or dueling that presumably give the opponent a fair chance had to be suppressed; such decency could not be afforded in hand-to-hand combat. To survive in war men were instructed in the art of ambush and sneak attack: the enemy soldier must be killed by stealth if at all possible. Recruits also learned where to stick a bayonet or knife so that it would penetrate the skeletal armor, and other such useful skills. The popular Japanese martial arts of *karate* and *judo* have been described as "scientific dirty fighting" in that they are efficient methods of killing *without* the use of weapons. The same principles apply to learning effective means of verbal attack. Doing verbal injury to someone depends on knowing his personal sources of guilt and the ways in which he can be shamed or discredited in the eyes of others. Clearly, much learning is involved in all forms of social aggression.

We learn also to attack under certain social conditions and not under others, and to direct our attack at one kind of object (animal, person, or institution) and not at another. Until quite recently, psychologists tended to assume that certain animals (predators) automatically attacked other species (their prey or other natural enemies) on the basis of invariant instinctual patterns. The tendency of cats to kill mice and rats was generally assumed to be inborn and not subject to learning or unlearning. Therefore, it provoked much astonishment when A. Y. Kuo (1930) demonstrated that cats could easily learn to live peacefully with rats. Whatever inherent tendency cats have to attack rats can be modified quite readily by rearing them together. Kuo studied three groups of kittens. One was raised without ever seeing rats, a second group observed their mothers killing rats, and a third was reared together with rats from infancy. After four months, 43 percent

Figure 7.1 Minnie the cat and her pet rat settle down for a snooze after dinner. (London Daily Express/Pictorial Parade)

of the cats who had never seen a rat had killed at least one rat placed in its cage; 85 percent of those who had watched their mothers kill rats had done so; but none of the cats raised with rats had killed one, though they were given the same opportunities. Thus, even where the biological pressures favoring it are strong, aggression toward objects can be inhibited or modified through learning (Figure 7.1).

A great many similar studies have clearly shown that in socially aggressive animals such as the rat and mouse the tendency to fight or not fight is much influenced by learning. It has been demonstrated, for example, that success and failure (a form of reward and punishment—see Chapter 4) have a powerful influence on fighting. The animal that has been successful is much more likely to fight subsequently than one who has had many failures or than an animal with little past experience at fighting (Scott, 1958, 1962; Seward, 1946). If two mice are allowed to fight repeatedly, they form a dominance relationship such that the mouse which is beaten will always run away and never fight, and he is likely to behave this way in contacts with other mice. When it is so arranged that certain male laboratory mice have constant success in fighting, they become so ferocious that they will even attack females and young, something they ordinarily will not do. Unlike untrained mice, these "fighting mice" attack quickly, savagely, and efficiently, with little display of emotion. They have become "killers."

By the same token, mice have also been trained not to

279

fight. Since male mice ordinarily neither attack females nor fight over the possession of females as other animals do, inexperienced males were permitted to live with females for a few weeks to build up an "inhibition" against fighting with their cage mates. Then the males were taken out of their cages, held by the tail and stroked on the back, a treatment they did not like and which would ordinarily provoke aggressive behavior. When they were placed back in their cages with the original female with whom they had lived, they still did not fight. Finally a few males so trained were placed together in a pen with one or two females; significantly there was no fighting, even though placing two males alone together would ordinarily result in fighting. They had been trained not to fight. Such training has also been successfully employed with dogs. Every time a puppy playfully attacked his handlers, he was picked up and held with his feet off the ground, making him helpless. The tendency to bite ceased. Even fox terriers, usually very aggressive animals, could be trained in this way not to bite, even playfully.

For obvious reasons, there are no comparable human studies, but certain religious groups have provided what might be called "field experiments" by teaching their members from childhood to be peaceful. One such group is the Jehovah's Witnesses, a Christian sect membership in which has been recognized as the basis for conscientious-objector status in the draft and whose members suffered greatly at the hands of the Nazis, who put them into concentration camps during World War II because of their refusal to fight. Another such sect is the Quakers, whose religious training encourages an attitude of "turning the other cheek" when attacked. In addition to such religious groups within society that have strong feelings of abhorrence about overt aggression, countless individuals somehow emerge from childhood with comparable ideologically based convictions. As everyone knows, during the Vietnam War an unusually large number of young men refused to enter the armed services on such grounds, and some even left the country rather than participate in the war. Individuals can develop strong emotional values against violence even within a larger society that treats aggression in a generally positive light.

In our consideration of psychosocial aspects of aggression to follow, we shall not be concerned directly with the details or mechanisms of learning and socialization, per se. Some of these have already been touched on in Chapter 4. The reader should refer back to this earlier discussion to keep firmly in mind how aggression can be learned as an adaptive response, rechanneled into socially acceptable forms, or inhibited. Our concern here is with factors or conditions in society and within the individual that encourage aggression (Figure 7.2).

(a)

(b)

Figure 7.2 The war game. (a) Young boys play at being soldiers amid the rubble of a "no-go" area of Ulster, Northern Ireland. (b) The real thing—children clash with British troops in Belfast. In a typical pattern of hostilities, children incite the soldiers, screaming obscenities and throwing bottles and stones. The troops bide their time behind riot shields. Numerous adults stand around as onlookers. In a pervasive atmosphere of fear and hate, threat and counterthreat, is it surprising that children grow up to see violence as normal? (Photos by Mike McQueen and Colman Doyle; Camera Press London/Pictorial Parade)

A number of things interact in the arousal or inhibition of aggression in man: (1) the provocation; (2) the cultural climate; (3) psychological mechanisms in the assimilation of aggressive behavior; (4) social controls; and (5) individual personality dynamics.

Provocation

Frustration and threat have already been touched on in Chapter 6, since they are important not only in human aggression but in animal social (nonpredatory) aggression as well. If one treats aggression as an innately disposed response to specific external conditions, which is the stance adopted here, then we must examine the social factors creating frustration or threat conditions that provoke the aggressive response.

As we turn from lower animals to man, what is regarded as frustrating or threatening depends greatly on the *personal meanings* any situation conveys. For example, a young child may grow angry in response to pain, but an adult may treat such pain as something that must be tolerated or as a challenge to be overcome. Frustration of any kind may be readily accepted if compensated for by something of greater importance, such as high social esteem, wealth, power, the sympathy of others, and the like. Thus, one man's frustration is another's challenge or glory. And the same injury which is lightly passed off in one social context may be the stimulus to intense anger in another. Clearly, recognition of an *intent to injure* is crucial in the arousal of anger and aggression.

If you are kicked unintentionally while someone is struggling to pass by in a narrow theater aisle, the psychological implications of this act are quite different than when you are kicked on purpose, although the actual physical damage may be the same. The psychological state of the offender is presumed to be quite different in each of these two instances, and you will probably react differently to an injury that seems intentional than to one judged as accidental. In the former case, you will be offended and angry and may well retaliate; in the latter, you may feel some fleeting anger at the offender's carelessness but will probably tend to suppress it.

The intent to injure is judged from the behavior of the offender during and after the injury. This is clearly a psychological matter. For example, an "Oops, I'm sorry" may obviate any irritation or anger that might have been elicited. Some people are hypersensitive to injuries and likely to interpret any, no matter how trivial, as intentional insults. Usually, however, the total behavior of the offender and the context in which the offense occurs are the external social cues on which an interpretation of his intent will be based. But a judgment as to whether an injury was or was not intended is not always easy to make. A great many injurious acts are ambiguous as to intent and hence difficult to weigh objectively. Sometimes even an apology does not much soften the offense, since for one reason or another the victim feels that the offending person has not taken sufficient effort to be careful; the victim may feel too lightly treated, and this in itself may serve as an assault on his self-esteem. One cannot resist the thought, "He did that on purpose," or "By his indifference he has insulted me." Have we not all had the impulse to step on a person's feet as we passed by in the theater because we felt that the seated person was not trying hard enough to make room for us to get by? Similar violent impulses often occur on the highway (Figure 7.3). Might we call this "territoriality" in man?

Eric Berne (1964) has written an amusing but perceptive book on the fascinating "games people play" with each other. These games involve events taking place on two or three levels simultaneously—the surface level of interpersonal maneuvering in speech and action, the underlying level of intentions and feelings, and sometimes the unconscious level as well. Some of these games involve hidden forms of aggression, a

"Get off the road!!!"

Figure 7.3   A territorial struggle on the highway. (Drawing by J. J. Dunleavy)

kind of "one-upmanship" in which the underlying intent is
to get the upper hand over someone. Although such "games"
are usually not acknowledged openly, the hostility they mask
is not always hard to perceive. The "Schlemiel game" (Berne,
l964, p. 114) illustrates some of these methods of thinly disguised insult, perceived intent, and subsequent rage, and it
is fun to examine in this context.

The [term] "schlemiel" . . . [is] a popular Yiddish word allied to
the German and Dutch words for cunning. The Schlemiel's victim
. . . is colloquially called the Schlemazl. The moves in a typical game
of "Schlemiel" are as follows:

1W. White spills a highball on the hostess's evening gown.

1B. Black (the host) responds initially with rage, but he senses
(often only vaguely) that if he shows it, White wins. Black therefore
pulls himself together, and this gives him the illusion that he wins.

2W. White says: "I'm sorry."

2B. Black mutters or cries forgiveness, strengthening his illusion
that he wins.

3W. White then proceeds to inflict other damage on Black's property. He breaks things, spills things and makes messes of various
kinds. After the cigarette burn in the tablecloth, the chair leg through
the lace curtain and the gravy on the rug, White's Child [the infantile
or childish aspect of his personality] is exhilarated because he has
enjoyed himself in carrying out these procedures, for all of which
he has been forgiven, while Black has made a gratifying display of
suffering self-control. Thus, both of them profit from an unfortunate
situation, and Black is not necessarily anxious to terminate the
friendship.

As in most games, White, who makes the first move, wins either
way. If Black shows his anger, White can feel justified in returning
the resentment. If Black restrains himself, White can go on enjoying
his opportunities. The real payoff in this game, however, is not the
pleasure of destructiveness, which is merely an added bonus for
White, but the fact that he obtains forgiveness. . . .

*Figure 7.4 The schlemiel game. You supply the
dialogue. (Drawing by J. J. Dunleavy)*

Note that here when one speaks of the "intent" to harm, the
aggressor may not even be conscious of any aggressive motivation behind his behavior (Figure 7.4). There are two sets of
perceptions involved in any interpersonal event of aggression,
that of the aggressor and that of his victim, and because these
perceptions take place in two individuals, they have some
independent aspects as well as overlapping ones. This makes
the psychological nature of such an event highly complex.

Consider the following example of ethnic hostilities: A
black man accuses whites of racism because he feels put down
and otherwise injured by the system that whites identify with
and defend. Whites, in turn, may experience no awareness of
hostility or intent to injure blacks and may therefore be
mystified by the accusation. Part of the problem is that the
black is particularly sensitive to the white's behavior toward

In the second period I had my first major fight of the season. And the events leading up to it typify what ignites most hockey fights. . . .

Tardif—a strong young forward, six feet tall and 180 pounds—and I collided in a corner, which is normal enough. Still, when this happens the sticks and elbows and thick leather gloves come up instinctively. Now one of three things can happen: the players back off and forget the whole thing, which happens most of the time; the players each wait for the other to back off, finally being peaceably separated by a linesman; or the clash escalates from elbows in the ribs to gloves in the face to fisticuffs. Very simply, it's a case of action and reaction. I got a shot in the nose and decided to retaliate. War was on. . . . [From Brad Park, with Stan Fischler, *Play the man*. New York: Warner Paperback Library, 1972, p. 52]

Figure 7.5   Fun and games on the ice. (Photo by Barton Silverman)

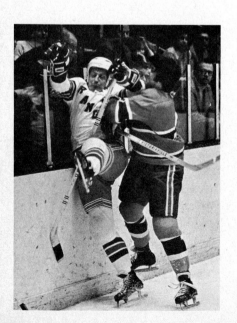

him (as most minority groups are toward members of the culturally dominant group—see Part III). He feels that whites have been tacitly accepting or supporting the system. His anger is not unlike that of the victim of the person seated in the theater who fails to move his feet to allow ready passage. It is based on an implicit (though perhaps not actually "intended") attack in the form of indifference or lack of consideration for another's plight.

One way of inferring whether there is intent to injure is to examine the social context of the aggression. An *arbitrary injury* is one which the offender was not forced into making by circumstances beyond his control; it is probably intended. A *nonarbitrary injury*, on the other hand, really could not be helped. The terms "arbitrariness" and "intent to injure" refer to two closely related psychological concepts—the former focusing more on the outward manifestations from which an inference is made about the offender's motivation, the latter focusing on the events presumably taking place in the offender's mind.

Burnstein and Worchel (1962) gave male students the task of discussing a case history of a juvenile delinquent. Various groups did this under three conditions: no frustration; arbitrary frustration; and nonarbitrary frustration. In both conditions of frustration, a confederate in the group repeatedly interrupted the group discussion, delaying it so that no conclusion could be reached within the set time limit. In the nonarbitrary version, the confederate prominently displayed a hearing aid which was apparently broken, this providing a reasonable excuse for his irritating behavior. The absence of such an excuse characterized the arbitrary-frustration condition. In the no-frustration condition, no such interruptions were encountered by the group.

Subjects in all three groups were later given the opportunity to express negative attitudes (a form of aggression) toward the confederate and other members of the group by means of the disguised task of making ratings of each person's skill in conference discussion. This could be done under three subconditions created by the experimenters: in one, the ratings were made privately; in the second, they were public; and in the third, the ratings were private and the form of the negative rating was nonpunitive (no harm could come to the person being criticized). This latter condition should create, according to Burnstein and Worchel, the least constraints against aggression, since the negative evaluation was secret and the rejected individual not harmed.

As anticipated, more negative feelings (implying anger) were expressed to the offending person (the confederate) under both conditions of frustration compared with the nonfrustrating condition. This was found to be even more so under the private, relatively nonpunitive situation than when the ratings were public and punitive. But most important for the point in question, less aggression was directed at the person who did the interrupting with the hearing aid than at the one without the hearing aid. The latter's behavior seemed unreasonable (arbitrary). (See Note 7.1.)

Burnstein and Worchel think that when the social norms against expressing aggression through criticism are reduced in strength, more latent direct aggression is released. In their experiment, the hearing aid, with its implications that the confederate's unpleasant behavior could not be helped because of his defect, led to inhibition of the *expression* of anger by the other members of the group, who would not want to attack someone unfairly when the frustrating behavior was not especially blameworthy and caused by one toward whom sympathy rather than criticism should be directed. We cannot tell for sure from the evidence presented here whether feelings of anger were reduced in the nonarbitrary-frustrating conditions or were simply not aroused. Perhaps both kinds of processes, reduced levels of anger and the inhibition of aggressive behavior, were involved. This is one of the most sticky problems in psychological research on aggression. Intent to injure and anger associated with aggression are internal states whose presence we can only guess at from behavioral evidence. Yet such internal states make a big difference in the implications imputed to our actions. Other studies (for instance, Epstein and Taylor, 1967) also strongly suggest that in man it is the *interpersonal implications* of an injurious action more than the injury itself that are important in generating feelings of ill-will toward the person who produced the injury, as well as the likelihood and strength of the retaliation.

Anger can occur without aggressive acts (as when they are inhibited), and aggression can occur without anger. Examples of the latter include the businessman who is striving to put a competitor out of business but feels no anger or hostility toward that individual, whom he may not even know personally. Prizefighters seek to injure their opponents in the ring, and hockey players shove, hook, trip, or strike opposing team members as a normal part of the competitive sport without necessarily feeling anger (Figure 7.5). In modern warfare, soldiers fire their weapons or drop their bombs, often without ever seeing the enemy they are trying to kill. Although such aggressive actions can be accompanied by anger, they need not be. An act of aggression can have many different internal psychological accompaniments, each with its own mechanism. If the observer is to distinguish between these various mental states, he must be able to tell when behavioral aggression is occurring without anger or when anger is occurring without behavioral aggression.

Note 7.1

In Burnstein and Worchel's experiment (1962), aggression was measured by evaluation of negative attitudes expressed toward the confederates. The experimenters placed the aggression on a crude measurement scale and compared the three groups of subjects in the average amount of aggression each displayed. Most psychological research requires some such quantitative evaluation of varying psychological states or reactions.

There are times when it is necessary to compare only the quality or type of a reaction, or merely whether or not it occurs. However, more sophisticated comparisons in psychological research require measurement of quantity (*quantification*) and hence the use of numbers. The simplest quantification of psychological states is by counting the frequency with which something happens. Yet even for this we need some kind of scale so that we can evaluate the frequency or strength of the response.

Suppose that we ask a subject to administer a series of electric shocks to someone as part of an experiment, and we take as an estimate of degree of aggression the voltage he selects for the administered shock. On the apparatus we have placed a scale ranging from low to high voltage, and we observe which voltage the subject selects under various conditions. Now if we want to say something about the degree of aggression as a function, say, of frustration, we can increase some of the subject's feelings of frustration by various experimental procedures. We then observe that the frustrated group administers an average shock intensity of 100 volts, while the average is only 50 volts in the nonfrustrated group. We are thus measuring degree of aggression along a quantitative scale, just as Burnstein and Worchel did with the amount of criticism directed at the confederates. We are, in effect, translating the subject's behavior into numbers which stand for the strength of his aggressive reaction to the frustrating condition.

We should be very cautious about our conclusions, however. We must be quite sure that these numbers express the internal state of the person or the intensity of his aggressive behavior, even though this assumption seems reasonable on its face. We cannot be confident that his choice of a

100-volt shock means that he is twice as hostile as someone who has administered a 50-volt shock. It is not unreasonable to assume that the former represents *more* aggression than the latter, but we cannot really say how much more. We are not, after all, measuring physical characteristics such as height and weight. A weight of 100 pounds is clearly double that of 50 pounds; that is how the scale is designed. But the subjective choice of whether to administer a shock intensity of 50 or 100 volts is another matter. We have no way of knowing whether the quantities shown on the voltage scale are equivalent in psychological terms to the degree of aggression. Actually, all we can say with any confidence is that a high score on the voltage scale seems to indicate increased degree of aggression, but we cannot gauge the amount. A jump from 20 to 30 volts on the scale might represent a greater change in psychological state than one between 50 and 60 volts, yet both differences would be scored as 10.

Thus, in assessing the study of Burnstein and Worchel (1962), we are on safer grounds if we limit ourselves to saying that one group showed more aggression than the other, rather than saying precisely *how much more*. Similarly, in most psychological work, any measurement system we use in attempting to quantify psychological states is likely to be only a rough approximation of the inner reality.

The cup of blessing that we bless, is it not the sharing of the body of Christ? And the bread that we break, is it not the partaking of the body of the Lord? [1 Corinthians 10:16]

. . . Grant us therefore, gracious Lord, so to eat the flesh of thy dear Son Jesus Christ, and to drink his blood, that our sinful bodies may be made clean by his body, and our souls washed through his most precious blood, and that we may evermore dwell in him, and he in us. Amen. [Order for Holy Communion, in The Book of Common Prayer]

This is a problem of greater significance for the study of human aggression than for that in other animals, because concern with internal events such as affects or feelings is less common among most animal behaviorists than among psychologists dealing with people. One can probably also infer emotional states in animals on the basis of expressive behavior, although some psychologists are reluctant to do so even in humans. Lorenz (1966, p. 19) suggests that anger has no part in predatory interspecies aggression, that is, when an animal is attacking prey:

From many excellent photographs it can be seen that the lion, in the dramatic moment before he springs, is in no way angry. Growling, laying [the] ears back, and other well-known expressive movements of fighting behavior are seen in predatory animals only when they are afraid of a wildly resisting prey, and even then the expressions are only suggested.

Cultural climate for aggression

As will be remembered from Chapter 4, the social setting in which we live and grow up helps to shape our thoughts, feelings, and actions. This mental climate also affects individual and group patterns of aggression. We shall here consider four facets of this: violence in myth and fantasy; violence via the mass media; cultural variations in violence; and violence as it is manifested in the world around us.

Violent fantasy   Our fantasies as expressed in ancient myths, in literature, film and drama, and in the bedtime stories we tell our children are often more gory than the most extreme and bizarre realities. These fantasies are instructive if we are interested in the cultural and psychological forces connected with human aggression and violence. Certain religious practices are also highly suggestive. For example, ritual animal slaughter as practiced in Judaism probably has some symbolic connection with primitive ritual sacrifice, perhaps even human sacrifice (see Chapter 6). Such a connection is even more obvious in Christianity: St. Paul in his letter to the Corinthians (see margin) makes a central point of the *real* presence of Christ's blood and flesh in the Eucharistic ritual. He notes that such a concept was an effective means of promoting Christianity in Greece, where the tradition of eating meat symbolic of Dionysus, the Greek god of orgiastic religion and wine, was strong among the people. (In Euripides' classic tragedy *The Bacchae*, a king who foolishly spies on Dionysian ritual "mysteries" is torn to pieces by frenzied women.) Pike (1876) has observed that in sixteenth-century England denial of Christ's *real presence* at the ritual was one of the heretical offenses for

Figure 7.6 Man's myth of the ravenous beast, as fantasized on film: King Kong, the mighty ape, running amok. (© 1933, RKO Radio; photo courtesy of Mark A. Binn)

which people were punished under church law by being burned at the stake.

Often our legends, myths, and "fairy tales" express terrifying fantasies of castration (of the god Cronus by his son Zeus), of witches eating children or being popped into ovens (*Hansel and Gretel*), of wolves eating up grandmothers (*Little Red Riding Hood*), of man-eating ogres (*Jack and the Beanstalk*), of cowboys and Indians killing each other with gusto, of King Kong the movie monster (Figure 7.6), and Godzilla arising from the sea and destroying cities and multitudes. Some of these fantasies have been interpreted from the Freudian point of view as expressing symbolically many of man's most fundamental suppressed fears and wishes (Storr, 1968). *Hansel and Gretel,* for example, may be seen as an expression of a fundamental conflict in the relationship of mothers to children; on the one hand, the child's dependency and need for protection; on the other, the child's rage and frustration over the lack of power this dependency entails. Hansel and Gretel have a mean step-mother, and the witch can be thought of as another "bad" mother; in the end both the witch and step-mother are dead, and the children live happily ever after. In *Little Red Riding Hood,* the wolf and the grandmother can also be seen as opposite facets of the same person—the frightening and destructive parent, and the kindly and concerned parent. (For a further discussion of symbolism, see Note 7.2.)

Many classic works of literature are filled with violence. Homer's *Iliad* is a long and bloody war epic. Even the Bible, from the story of Cain and Abel on, is replete with tales of violence and slaughter. It is sufficient here to recognize that an atmosphere of aggression is all around us, often expressed symbolically and in distorted form; it is part of our daily fare of fantasy and fiction, in movies and on television, and is at the core of those innocent "fairy tales" we tell our very young children. Perhaps these tales are a working out of some of mankind's primitive wishes and fears, as Freud has suggested (Abrahams and Dundes, 1969; Dundes, 1971). But they also help prepare each generation for mankind's violent ways.

Violence via the mass media   In our own times of mass production and mass consumption, even violent fantasies are manufactured wholesale. The mass media (television, movies, newspapers, "comic" books, magazines) play a large role in communicating the prevailing cultural outlook to the young.

Note 7.2

When Storr (1968) says that the mean stepmother and witch in *Hansel and Gretel* represent a bad mother, or that the wolf and the grandmother in *Little Red Riding Hood* stand for frightening and supportive parents, respectively, he is speaking about the use of symbols in human thought, fantasy, and emotion. A symbol is anything, a word, number, object, image, or design, that stands for or refers to something other than itself (see Brown, 1958). Therefore, it conveys meaning by pointing beyond itself, as with the dollar sign ($) that stands for money, and everything else that money implies, or the national flag that symbolizes a whole nation, its values, institutions, and people. Thus, symbolic thought is not limited to words alone, though words are our most important symbolic tools of thought and communication.

Most of the linguistic symbols we use have meanings that are more or less clear and conventional (widely agreed upon), and many other ordinary symbols also have agreed-upon meanings. However, for certain

individuals or groups of individuals, there are instances when symbols depart from their conventional meanings: for some people the dollar sign is a valued prize; for others it is a hated symbol of greed and moral decay. Symbolic meanings are thus not always constant.

What about the symbols interpreted by Storr (1968) and in the accompanying text, that is, the witch and stepmother, or the grandmother and wolf? Like other psychoanalytic writers before him, Storr is suggesting that these human and animal characters have widely agreed-upon (perhaps almost conventional) symbolic meanings, at least in the fairy tales in which they are embedded. These stories portray common human family situations involving powerful feelings of hate, love, and fear. As such, one function of such symbols is to disguise the negative feelings because they are threatening or uncomfortable to recognize. Most of us do not wish to acknowledge our feelings of hatred for our mothers and fathers, though they usually are

the other side of our feelings of love. Thus, the appeal of *Hansel and Gretel, Little Red Riding Hood,* and other such fairy tales is that they express many of these hidden negative feelings toward close family members (mothers, fathers, sisters, brothers, and spouses), yet do so without forcing us to face the reality of such feelings because the real persons are disguised or symbolized in the stories. Dreams too are thought to express forbidden impulses and feelings through symbols that disguise them.

Along similar lines, consider the underlying symbolism of the Shirley Temple films of the 1930s, which were enormously popular then and probably can still sometimes be seen on television today. One thing that impressed me was that in none of these films, as far as I can remember, did little Shirley have a real living mother actively present in her life. She was always "Daddy's girl." Mother had either died, or was somewhere else out of reach, a distant figure of no importance. There was rarely even a little

But when children observe violence via these media, is there significant influence on their own aggressive behavior?

In his book on aggression, Berkowitz (1962) noted that a team of investigators (Schramm *et al.,* 1961) had made a tally of the program contents of five television channels in a large urban area in the United States in 1960. During the 100 hours of their investigation about 24 percent of the programs from Monday through Friday specialized in violence, these being either Westerns or crime programs. Since the observations were made between the hours of 4 and 9 P.M., a high percentage of children were probably watching. Aside from the cartoons, which themselves usually contain a high incidence of aggressive violence under the guise of comedy, the 100 program hours included 12 murders, 16 major gunfights, and 42 other violent scenes including gunplay. These figures do not seem atypically high for aggressive content on television. For example, in 1954 other monitors had reported seeing over 6,800 aggressive incidents in a single week on the New York channels. Similar statistics have been reported in other countries. Himmelweit *et al.* (1958) reported that in Great Britain about 20 percent of the shows in 1956 contained hostility as a *dominant theme* during peak viewing hours of children (5 to 9 P.M.). Crime and violence also abound in the pages of children's comic books (Wertham, 1954, p. 229), and as

sister or brother to disturb this joyful arrangement. One might speculate about how this variation of the family triangle emphasized by Freud (see the Oedipus and Electra complexes discussed in Chapters 4 and 12) contributed to the amazing appeal of the Shirley Temple films, and to what extent this father-daughter pattern (with mother missing) was deliberately and knowledgeably planned or simply happened, proved successful, and so was followed in subsequent films. Anyway, much of their emotional appeal rested on their subtle and mostly symbolic portrayal of one of the strong and yet suppressed wishes of little girls—to be the sole object of fatherly love.

This way of thinking raises the important question, however, of the universality (as well as validity) of the meanings attributed to fairy-tale or dream symbols. Carl Jung (1960), the prominent Swiss psychiatrist, believed that many symbols were universal and stemmed from man's common animal ancestry. If so, then "wolf" as a symbol, say,

would imply to everyone a destructive and frightening agency of some kind. One can see that if we were to interpret dreams in accordance with this assumption, the existence of universal themes would make the task of interpretation much simpler. One would need only to translate the symbols in accordance with their universal meaning. Thus, in a dream, eating a meal together with someone of the opposite sex would, perhaps, mean having sexual intercourse, a long weapon might mean a penis, and a round orifice might signify a woman's vagina. If, on the other hand, symbols were idiosyncratic and their meanings depended on personal experience, it would be necessary to gain more specific information from the individual in order to interpret the symbolic dream content.

There are probably three sources of symbolic meaning in our emotional life: (1) On the basis of our similarly structured nervous systems and certain common human experiences, some symbols probably have com-

parable meaning for many or perhaps even all people. (2) The unique character of each of our life histories also contributes to the acquisition of symbols that have meanings specific to each one of us, or that might perhaps be shared by a limited class of people like ourselves. (3) The meaning of a symbol is probably also influenced by the context in which it appears. Thus, the wolf in *Little Red Riding Hood* conveys the idea of a destructive and frightening being; hence, it stands for such a being whether it is a parent or someone else. In another story, however, "wolf" might stand for all those misunderstood animals (and people) who are really very nice and lovable but who are improperly stereotyped as destructive and evil. Just such a story was presented on television not long ago as a nature study of wolves in the wild, pointing out how misunderstood wolves are, and showing them in a highly sympathetic light. (In Chapter 12 a psychoanalytic dream interpretation is given involving Freudian symbols.)

(a)

(b)

Figure 7.7 The standard ending for every Western movie—the shoot-out scene. (a) Glenn Ford and Broderick Crawford have it out in Fastest Gun Alive. *(b) At the climax of Akira Kurosawa's most famous Japanese "Western,"* Seven Samurai, *Toshiro Mifune and Takashi Shimura confront the bad guys with swords drawn, in the midst of a torrential downpour. Always among the most popular of film genres, "Westerns" are now being made in Italy and Spain. (a: Culver Pictures, Inc.; b: The Museum of Modern Art/Film Stills Archive)*

Berkowitz notes, ". . . it is practically impossible for the modern child to escape scenes of aggression and lawlessness in the mass media." As will be seen below, it is not clear what the effects of such exposure to aggression and violence are on the development of aggressive patterns of behavior—this is still a major research question—but the fact of such exposure is certainly illustrative of the aggressive interest typical of the culture in which we live (Figure 7.7).

Many experts appear to doubt that television is a major contributor to violence, believing that rather than shaping aggressive behavior the contents of the mass media reflect already established tastes, standards, and wishes of viewers. Nor is there much new in the enjoyment people have experienced in watching violence in their entertainment. As we have seen, from the earliest oral literature of man, his folk sagas and myths, to the popular fiction of our own time, his literature has always been full of violence and tragedy; even the comedies contain a great deal of thinly disguised aggression. Nevertheless, although Berkowitz (1962, p. 62) agrees that the communications media do not play the *major* role in delinquency and crime, he argues that under certain conditions they can increase the likelihood of violence in particular individuals:

To deny that TV violence and crime is a major cause of juvenile delinquency is *not* to say that aggressive scenes have no influence on a child's behavior. Only systematic quantitative research can determine what these effects might be. After reviewing such research we . . . cannot be altogether sanguine about media violence. Scenes of crime and aggression in television, movies, or books heighten the probability that some child in the audience will behave in a hostile fashion, particularly if he has aggressive dispositions.

290

But why is violence so popular in fiction and on the screen? Theoretically, two psychological functions are played by fantasy and entertainment. One involves the process of "wish fulfillment," that is, the acting out of frustrated desires in our imagination while we watch a play or movie. The second involves the learning of values and expectations about the world and the creating and strengthening of habits. When we become engrossed in dramatic entertainment, or in fact any play activity, we are discovering and trying out modes of behavior and ways of coping that may have utility in real life, either now or in the future (see Erikson, 1950). The little girl who plays with dolls is, in a sense, practicing being a mother as she talks to the "baby," and diapers, feeds, or scolds it. She has patterned this activity on her perceptions of her mother. She may not make use of this practice in the "mother role" for many years, but it will become relevant and be drawn upon when she fulfills that role as an adult.

If wish fulfillment remains strictly in fantasy, in play, daydreams, or night dreams, there is no problem. However, if such fantasies are acted out in real life, or if the child (or adult) learns from television that the violent modes of conduct he sees are acceptable so that he fails to distinguish between fantasy and reality, then serious social problems may be created. One of the things children must learn as they grow up is how to make this distinction between the make-believe world and the real world. The reader may recall as a child having awoken from a dream badly frightened and still uncertain that the experience was only a dream. Such confusion between fantasy and reality generally decreases as the child matures, and for this reason stable adults are probably less influenced by mass-media violence than are young children, especially when it is fictional rather than real aggression as in newscasts of actual events. Fortunately, most of the time the adult observer can discount what he sees as "not true," and little or no connection is drawn between events in his own life and those in the movie or play. But with children and some disturbed adults there is less certainty of this separation between fact and fantasy (Figure 7.8).

(a)

(b)

Figure 7.8 Video violence—fiction and reality. (a) Three prison inmates execute a stool pigeon with acetylene torches in Brute Force, *a film often shown on television. (b) In a videotape replayed on TV news programs around the world, a would-be assassin is seen rushing at Imelda Marcos, wife of the President of the Philippines, as she handed out awards at a beautification contest in a Manila suburb. Before the assailant was shot and killed, Mrs. Marcos was slashed on the arms as she tried to fend off his knife. (a: © 1947, Universal Pictures, Inc.; photo courtesy of Mark A. Binn; b: Wide World Photos)*

In one study of television and aggressive behavior (Eron, 1963), hundreds of third graders and their parents in a semi-rural county of New York were interviewed to determine the frequency of TV viewing in the children and to identify their favorite programs. In addition, the children's aggressiveness was assessed in school by asking each child to rate every other child in the class on many kinds of behavior, including aggressiveness. Then the TV programs preferred by each child were rated by observers for the degree of violence displayed. Table 7.1 shows that more aggressive boys watched more violent programs. This relationship did not apply to girls.

Some years later, Eron and his colleagues (1972) did a follow-up study of the same children when they were 19 years old. The most significant finding was that the preference of boys for violent programs as shown in the third grade was significantly correlated with their aggressive behavior even 10 years later as rated by both peers and by themselves. However, their later TV viewing habits (when they were 19) bore no relation to rated aggression, as they had in the third grade. Two interpretations suggest themselves. One is that what they watched in the third grade might have had some effect on degree of aggressiveness both then and later. An alternative interpretation, equally plausible, is that the more aggressive boys came to prefer more violent TV programs. Studies such as this cannot definitely prove that viewing of fictional TV violence increases aggressive behavior (review Note 5.1, p. 177).

A frequent type of research on the problem of the influence of the mass media is illustrated by the following experiment (Berkowitz and Green, 1966). The subjects were 88 male university students. They were paired, and one of the two, the *subject,* was given a problem-solving task to perform, while the other, an *accomplice* of the experimenter, was given the responsibility of administering from 1 to 10 electric shocks to the subject from another room. Later, these roles were reversed to permit study of the subject's degree of aggressive response. At the first meeting, the accomplice was introduced by name. For

Table 7.1

Mean scores for aggressiveness of third graders (boys), as rated by classmates, correlated with violence of their favorite television programs[a]

TV viewing as reported by	No violent programs	One violent program	Two violent programs	Three violent programs
Mother	14.44	14.97	18.32	28.54
Father	12.44	14.23	18.92	20.67

[a] Adapted from Eron (1963, p. 195).

half the subjects he was introduced as Kirk Anderson, and for the other half, as Bob Anderson, for reasons that will be seen shortly.

Two experimental treatments were provided: (1) the subject was handled "neutrally" by the accomplice, that is, he was given only one shock after his work on the task; or (2) he was angered by being given seven shocks. After this both subject and accomplice were shown one of two movies. Half saw a 7-minute scene from an aggression-related movie, *The Champion,* in which Kirk Douglas plays a boxer who is brutally beaten in a prize fight; the other half saw an exciting movie of a horse race that involved no aggression. Then the roles of the subject and accomplice were reversed and the subject was allowed to shock the other person after his performance of the problem-solving task.

Berkowitz and Green found that the greatest number of shocks were given by subjects who had the combined experience of being angered, had witnessed the prize fight, and whose paired accomplice had been named Kirk. In short, seeing the aggressive movie increased the aggression of those men who were already primed to attack (they were angry over being abused), and this aggression was heightened by the accomplice having a name linking him with previously viewed violence.

There are documentated cases where aggressive scenes on television or in the movies or comic books *appear* to have excited violent acts. One case (Schramm *et al.,* 1961, pp. 55–56) involved a Los Angeles housemaid who caught a 7-year old boy sprinkling ground glass into his family's food. He reported seeing this done on television and wanted to find out if it would really work. There is also the case of a murder stimulated by a movie about a deranged killer. Another incident reported in the press involved two high school youths who reenacted a switchblade fight they had seen in a TV movie about juvenile delinquents. One of the boys required emergency surgery as a result. However, such incidents are relatively infrequent; they are the exception rather than the rule, because in most cases the other factors disposing people to engage in violence are weak or absent. Only a small proportion of the audience is evidently directly aroused to aggression by what they see. Most people do not have the immediate cause for anger or the strong aggressive habits required to act violently in response to the TV violence. The media have the greatest likelihood of producing aggressive violence when the audience is already angry or when the person watching is strongly disposed to engage in aggressive acts. Undercontrolled children are more vulnerable than more discriminating and self-controlled adults.

Berkowitz (1968) also makes the interesting observation that in studies where movies on television show justifiable violence, for example, where the victim pays in kind for his own crimes, the effect is to increase aggressive behavior in the audience; however, when the violence seems excessive, audience aggression is likely to be inhibited and its reaction one of horror. Thus we have the paradox that if the film maker wants to teach the lesson that "crime does not pay," he must be very careful how he punishes the criminal, since appropriate punishment seems to encourage the expression of aggression in the audience, whereas unreasonably cruel and excessive punishment will have the opposite effect. But the line between justified aggression and unjustified aggression is unclear, and much depends on the viewer's interpretation of what he sees. There is also the danger of an increased tolerance effect, as the audience becomes inured to higher and higher levels of violence.

The effects of the mass media are, like most psychological processes, evidently more complex than often assumed, and subject to no simple generalization. Although the consensus at present seems to be that the effects of fictional violence via the mass media are limited, it is quite possible that there are long-range and insidious consequences which are difficult to detect and measure. More research must also be done on the effects on children of real-life violence seen on news programs. Addicted young TV viewers no doubt find the line between "make-believe" and "real" to be rather fuzzy. The problem is far from being settled, and we shall surely see much more speculation and work on it over the next decades.

Cultural variations in violence   Great differences also exist in the patterns of aggression and violence seen in various parts of the world, at various times in history, and even among different communities within our own country. There are cultures, for example, the Saulteaux society, a branch of the Algonkian Indians of the Labrador peninsula of North America, where open quarrels are avoided at all cost, and hostilities are dealt with either by indirect aggression (gossip behind the person's back) or by sorcery and magic (Hallowell, 1940). Such institutionalized modes of overt aggression occur in a culture in which there is no war with other tribes and in which there are no official records of murder or suicide and few open expressions of anger or quarrels ending in physical assault. This is not to say there is no hostility; quite the contrary. Although superficially there seems to be a spirit of mutual helpfulness and sharing, there is much hostility, but it remains intrapsychic or is handled indirectly. Among the Algonkians, this inhibition of aggression is a socially sanctioned ideal that seldom breaks down in actual practice. Much may be learned from such cultural patterns of aggression—how they were created, how they influence the individuals in the society, and

Women are the primary source of quarrels [among the Ammassalik Eskimos] and such quarrels are carried on between individuals in a variety of ways. They may lead to murder, to revenge by theft, or to a drum match. Quarrels may occur between a man and his wife, between two men, or between two women. In any case there is no attempt on the part of outsiders to interfere in any way. . . . Drum matches are held both summer and winter. While this is a juridical procedure and a method of settling disputes, yet it conforms to the wider social pattern of singing songs for pleasure. (In fact old drum-match songs constitute part of the rep-

what their consequences are for the society as a whole and for the personalities of its members.

Recently a Stone Age tribe, the Tasadays, has been discovered living in a remote part of Mindanao (one of the Philippine Islands), the members of which appear extraordinarily peaceful and easygoing (see MacLeish and Launois, 1972). Consisting of 27 members at this writing, the Tasadays appear to have originated elsewhere, perhaps in the Malay-Indonesia archipelago, becoming nearly isolated after settling in their inaccessible rain-forest area of the Philippines. There are few such groups still uninfluenced by the modern world, and they are of great interest because of the possibilities they offer for study of how primitive man actually lived and supported himself. Observers report no evident hostility among the members and a high degree of mutual support and cooperativeness. They are food gatherers and, like early man, do not engage in agriculture or animal husbandry. Everything is shared. They only recently learned to hunt and trap animals from an outsider, and have now acquired a taste for meat. The existence of this tribe is particularly interesting in the light of the usual speculations about patterns of aggression in early man and about the evolution of aggression in general (see Chapter 6). Surely the Tasaday tribe does not seem to fit the usual conception of man as a highly aggressive animal. Whether this is typical of early man, or whether there is any typical pattern, is of course not established from this isolated example.

As noted briefly in Chapter 6, the Eskimos have had no wars, but this is not because violence is eschewed. These people of the Far North are forced by environmental conditions to live in tiny family groupings that are extremely widely dispersed much of the time. Occasional fighting and some homicides occur among Eskimos, but no long blood feuds, possibly because of the severe environmental conditions. The fierce struggle for survival against the elements, the low population density, and the need to expend maximum energy in obtaining food—all operate against continual interpersonal violence. The Ammassalik Eskimos of Greenland have evolved instead the interesting institition of the "drum match" (Mirsky, 1961; see descriptions in the margin).

Certainly physical conditions of life, as well as cultural responses to them, are heavily involved in the evolution of particular patterns of violence among different societies. However, truly peaceful societies, where interpersonal competition exists without aggression, are quite rare in human history.

Violence in America   In every major community of the United States one reads or hears daily about assaults and murders. In 1960, the city of Philadelphia, with a population

ertory of songs sung during the long winter nights.) Both men and women may sing, but they must do so in the traditional style which governs every expression, tone, sound, and movement, and those who cannot master the style are ashamed to sing or touch the drum. A match of this kind is not settled in one encounter, but is carried on for years, the parties taking turns visiting one another. For each new meeting the parties prepare and practice new songs, in which the crimes are vastly exaggerated, or, if they can find no new material that is suitable, they may father new crimes on their opponents or reproach them for deeds which may have been merely intended but never committed. They can enumerate the faults of the opponent's family, living and dead. The opponents stand facing one another. They sing one at a time while the other party stands quietly and listens. The singer mocks the other in a number of ways, by snorting and breathing right in his face, by butting him with his forehead so that he tumbles over. The listener accepts this with the greatest composure and even laughs mockingly to show the audience his indifference. When the singer is about to butt him he shuts his eyes and advances his head to receive the blow. The match can thus go on all night, each man taking turns in beating the drum and singing but otherwise not budging from the spot. In the intervals between songs and before and after the match, the opponents do not show the slightest sign of their hostility but appear to be friendly. This is carried on before a large audience which follows every word and movement with keen enjoyment. A man has often several drum matches going on at the same time and, if during the years in which a match is going on one of the parties dies, the survivor prides himself on it and boasts of this fact to others. The same pattern that is found in these juridical drum matches is found in matches similarly carried on just for pleasure. In fact drum matches are the chief pastime of the Ammassalik. [From Mirsky, 1961, pp. 68–69]

of 2 million, had about the same number of criminal homicides as all of England, Scotland, and Wales combined, with a total population of 45 million; Philadelphia had about the same homicide rate as the United States as a whole (5.1 per 100,000 people). More than 9,000 people died in the United States that year as a result of murder and manslaughter.

Every evening, in recent years, television news programs have been filled with vivid stories from around the world of wars, riots, assassinations, and massacres. Domestic news is of violent crime, skyjacking, kidnapping, assault, murder, and rape. To the extent that this becomes a significant part of the climate of human interaction, it is no surprise that many people who are emotionally disturbed, deeply frustrated, and unbalanced will express their problems in the common social currency of anger and violent aggression, sometimes drawing on feelings of ethnic, racial, or class hatred (Figure 7.9). When killing surrounds us, some people in trouble fall into step and become killers. The cultural climate of widespread aggression

Figure 7.9   On January 8, 1973, in downtown New Orleans, six people were killed and 17 others wounded by sniper fire from the top of the Howard Johnson's Hotel. (a) A police sharpshooter in his vantage point looking down at the hotel roof. (b) After a 28-hour gun battle, a police assault team finally reached the roof to find the riddled body of one gunman, a young black. He had previously been in the navy, from which he received a less than honorable discharge, and had become very bitter about American society. Incidents such as this, in which someone goes berserk and tries to kill everyone in sight, although fortunately infrequent, seem to occur with a certain regularity, especially when firearms are obtained easily. Another such case, involving a young man who was despondent about family troubles, occurred in Natick, Massachusetts, in May 1971. He held police at bay for several hours with two rifles, two pistols, and a shotgun. (Wide World Photos)

(a)

(b)

serves as a medium of influence and suggestion, enticing any susceptible person to respond to frustration, lack of hope, alienation, or mental imbalance with violent acts. These are often rationalized as being part of the sociopolitical conflicts of our times. It does not discount the personal distress of the individual committing such acts to recognize that he is playing a part in a drama that has as its background the entire cultural milieu. The present cultural climate offers models and strong encouragement to these often tragic forms of self-expression.

Certainly not all violence, by any means, is the result of emotionally disturbed, "crazy" people going beserk. When the cultural climate is favorable to violence, perfectly ordinary people can participate in it, assimilating its values as their own. Many people grow up in what has sometimes been called "subcultures of violence" (Wolfgang and Ferracuti, 1967): in such milieus individuals are prone to solve their problems by means of aggression. In some parts of Italy and Mexico, for example, citizens frequently settle private disputes by resort to physical conflict, often leading to bloody family feuds. In the film *The Godfather* we have a fictional illustration of such a subculture. And in Central and South America, the code of *machismo* provides the tradition of males proving their manhood through violent conduct. The culture of the United States is itself extremely varied, consisting of many ethnic communities, often deriving their values from a European mother culture or evolving new values under severe conditions of oppression and poverty. Some of these are specially oriented toward violence. In such subcultures, aggressive behavior is prescribed for certain types of situations. Not all individuals necessarily adopt the violent values of this code, but many fully assimilate it and become violence-prone persons. Those who do, see the world in terms of fear and aggression and respond to it accordingly (see Toch, 1969). Many juvenile delinquents view themselves as tough, powerful, fierce, and fearless, and want to become even more so. Their prestige in their own subculture is thought of as dependent on the ability and willingness to fight. This is well illustrated in such films as *Rebel Without a Cause* and in Leonard Bernstein's music drama *West Side Story*, a tragic ghetto love story of a Romeo and Juliet caught in warfare between two ethnicly different street gangs, the Jets and the Sharks.

In their book, *The Courage of His Convictions*, Parker and Allerton (1962, p. 93) quoted an habitual criminal who describes the violent environment in which he was reared:

Violence is in a way like bad language—something that a person like me's been brought up with, something I got used to very early on as part of the daily scene of childhood, you might say. I don't at all recoil from the idea, I don't have a sort of inborn dislike of the thing, like you do. As long as I can remember I've seen violence in use all around me—my mother hitting the children; my brothers and sister all whacking our mother, or other children; the man downstairs bashing his wife and so on.

Strange as it may seem, one of the most common forms of violent assault is directed at children, frequently infants of no more than a few months of age. They are often beaten so severely that they are permanently maimed or die. Laski (1966) reports, for example, that over the course of a single year in England, the National Society for the Prevention of Cruelty to Children dealt with 114,641 cases of suspected *child beating*, of which 39,223 cases appeared in court. Such behavior is typically rationalized by the parent as an effort to discipline the child, but the severity of the punishment belies the explanation. There is evidence that a high proportion of child beaters have themselves been beaten by their own parents.

Menninger (1963, p. 217) cites the following newspaper vignette:

Erie, Pa., Sept. 15 (AP)—A young father being tried on a murder charge in the death of his 6-year-old son, told a criminal court jury that he beat the boy with a belt for refusing to tell where he had hidden a toy hammer.

"I told Jackie a father sometimes has to do things to their children they do not like," Ralph J. Hoge, 26, of Harbor Creek, Pa., said Tuesday.

Dr. James E. Wallace, pathologist at Hamot hospital, previously testified the boy died last May 30 as a result of repeated blows, "probably 100." There were at least 93 abrasions on the child's body, he said.

District Attorney Damian McLaughlin has indicated he would seek a second-degree murder verdict with a maximum penalty of ten to 20 years in prison.

"Jackie told me, 'I still love you, daddy,'" Hoge said. "Those were the last words my son said to me."

Surely in such cases, when the child survives the maltreatment, the seeds of terror and rage sown early greatly increase the likelihood of a later pathological tendency toward physical aggression. One might guess that such experiences either push the person toward the extreme of readily engaging in violence or toward an extreme fear of it.

Psychological mechanisms in assimilation of aggressive behavior

The line of reasoning that some cultures or subcultures are more violence-prone than others has been used by some to explain the systematic slaughter of 6 million Jews and other

unwanted groups by the Nazis in World War II (Figure 7.10).
Thus, historian William L. Shirer has maintained that there
was a basic flaw in the German character that explains the
readiness to obey Hitler and to follow and support him in
his evil course. This is an appealing idea for most of us, and
possibly it has some truth in it. It helps us to feel properly
horrified and maintain our feeling of personal purity and
superiority, seeing ourselves as incapable of such horrendous
acts. It also helps us to ignore the ugly events within our own
history, including frontier murders, frequent lynchings, human
slavery, treachery to the Indian, and our continuing history
of warfare. We must face the fact that we all have the potential
for violence under suitable cultural or social conditions. Kurt
Vonnegut, Jr. (1967) put it this way in *Mother Night:* "If I'd
been born in Germany I suppose I would have *been* a Nazi,
bopping Jews and gypsies and Poles around, leaving boots
sticking out of snowbanks, warming myself with my sweetly
virtuous insides." The "flaw" may well be in all of us.

What could the nature of this flaw be? Two psychological
mechanisms are of special importance here in that they both
make it easier for a person to accept violence as a solution
to his problems: one is the tendency to be obedient to authority; the other is the ability to detach oneself from the suffering
of others.

Obedience   A remarkable and disquieting piece of research
on the subject of obedience to cruel, inhuman orders was
performed by Stanley Milgram (1965a, 1965b). Initially,
Milgram had intended to begin his study in America and then
to take his research to Germany so that he could compare
Germans with Americans, but he never did so because what
he found out about Americans made it useless to continue the
study elsewhere.

Milgram's procedure involved a clever ruse. Subjects
were obtained by advertisements in a local newspaper. Milgram set up what appeared to be a learning situation in which
there was a teacher and a learner (who had been allowed to
meet briefly and then chosen for their tasks, apparently at
random). The "teacher" was in reality the experimental subject, and the "learner" was a confederate strapped into a chair
in another room and "programmed" to behave in a prescribed

(a)

(b)

(c)

Figure 7.10.   The Nazi holocaust. (a) *Charred bodies in the furnace at Buchen-
wald concentration camp, near Jena, Germany, in April 1945.* (b) *In another
camp, piled corpses of prisoners murdered in the final days of the war by retreating
German troops.* (c) *The aftermath: at the International Military Tribunal in
Nuremberg, Nazi leaders being tried for crimes against humanity and genocide.*
(U.S. Army photos)

fashion. The confederate had been chosen by Milgram to appear as an innocent-looking, mild-mannered man. The teacher asked the learner certain prescribed questions. Whenever the learner made an error, the teacher was instructed to push a button that supposedly delivered an electric shock to the learner (no shock was actually used). Following each error, the strength of the shock, as indicated on a dial, was increased. After it reached a certain level, the confederate began to protest from the next room. For example, at 75 volts, he would grunt; at 125 volts, he would give increasing evidence of distress, with statements such as "Hey, that really hurts"; at 180 volts, "I can't stand the pain, don't do that"; at 195 volts, complaints of heart trouble; and so on. If and when the teacher-subject protested, the experimenter would insist in a firm and authoritative tone that he continue. Not until the subject absolutely refused to go on with the experiment did the "learning situation" finally end. It was thus possible to determine how far subjects would proceed to follow orders and administer shock in spite of acute distress and possible danger to the other person. As voltage levels continued to rise, evidence of the learner's distress grew still stronger. He gave an agonized scream at 285 volts. At 315 volts, all sounds stopped, and there was an ominous silence from then on.

The striking finding of Milgram's initial study with American males living in New Haven, Connecticut, from 20 to 50 years of age, ordinary people such as you and I, was that 65 percent of the subjects did what they were told and kept shocking the learner *all the way up to the limit* of 450 volts, even after he had entirely stopped responding to the learning task. Milgram was able to obtain similar results even when he had the research moved to a rundown office building in Bridgeport, Connecticut, and advertised under the fictitious name "Research Associates of Bridgeport." This was done to dissociate it from Yale University, on the assumption that subjects might have been too much influenced by the reputation of so prestigious an institution. Although this did reduce obedience, 48 percent still went through the procedure all the way. They were willing to torture and perhaps even kill another person merely on the say-so of someone in authority. They did not always do this cheerfully, and many complained strenuously, but they did it. They often appeared to be distressed, like Asch's subjects described in Chapter 4. Some argued with the experimenter, questioned him, expressed doubt, sought reassurance, but nearly two-thirds of the men in New Haven and about half of the men in Bridgeport continued nonetheless to shock the "victim" as demanded by the person in authority. Perhaps some assumed that the person in charge would not let anything terrible happen, but they had no real factual basis for this faith (Note 7.3).

Note 7.3

When Milgram's experiments (1965a) were reported, they received a troubled reaction on the part of many psychologists who felt that Milgram had gone beyond proper ethics in the treatment of human subjects. These experiments had appeared at a time of growing concern about the proliferation of deception experiments in which there was the possibility of psychological harm to subjects, and Milgram's studies especially highlighted this concern. Much debate ensued about the ethics of human experimentation and the obligations of experimenters to their subjects, and this debate has continued right up to the present.

Deception had long been used in social psychological experimentation; recall, for example, the early studies of Asch described in Chapter 4. By the 1960s it was felt by many that such frequent deception not only damaged the public's confidence in psychological research but also violated the subject's right to know the treatment to which he would be exposed. The aspect of Milgram's research that was most disturbing was the potential anguish generated in the subject who continued to shock the "learner" even after he had given evidence of much distress, and the possibility that the subject's realization that he had acted reprehensibly might be damaging to him and leave a permanent scar. Such a consequence is, of course, not inherent in the use of deception, though in these particular experiments the subject's belief in the reality of the situation was critical to success of the study. Those psychologists most offended by this type of procedure began to call for a "bill of rights" for human subjects, and efforts got under way in the profession to create a code of conduct for experimenters. Governmental agencies responsible for granting of funds also began to require the monitoring of research with human subjects to assure (1) that subjects would not be harmed physically or psychologically; (2) that their privacy would not be endangered; (3) that they would not be coerced into participation; and (4) that wherever possible they would know the procedures to which they would be exposed so that they could freely and knowledgeably refuse to participate.

The issue of ethical experimentation is by no means simple. For one thing, many im-

Milgram interprets these data as evidence that under the authority of others people can abandon the sense of responsibility for their destructive acts, conceiving of themselves as the instrument of authority rather than as acting on their own. In real life this may be seen in numerous genocidal massacres that have occurred in recent wars. Large-scale killing of civilians was common in World War II. In the prolonged Indochina conflict, thousands of individual atrocities took place, apart from the slaughter of the massive bombings. There are reliable reports of prisoners dropped from helicopters, of torture and death during interrogations, of people shot in their rice paddies in "free-fire" zones where anything that moved was "officially" considered to be the enemy, of people killed for sport like game animals, sometimes shot from passing air and land vehicles, and on and on. Such cases became so common that they were no longer considered newsworthy by war correspondents, and only one, the My Lai "incident," raised much public outcry.

The point of bringing to the reader's attention the brutality of Americans in war is not to focus upon this nation as particularly evil or remarkably savage. It is not. Monstrous conduct can be found everywhere—the French are reported to have massacred 6,000 civilians at Haiphong and 12,000 civilians at Philippeville, Algeria; in Russia under Stalin huge numbers of citizens were murdered; mass atrocities were committed by the Belgians when they ruled the Congo, the Turks in Armenia after World War I, the Germans in Russia and the Japanese in East Asia during World War II, the Indonesians, the Sudanese, the Nigerians, more recently the Pakistanis and Indians, and now the Catholics and Protestants of Northern Ireland. In citing the brutality of our adversaries, we need not overlook our own and that of our friends. Rather, we must get over the idea that savagery in war is limited to other, "evil" peoples and that it is not part of our own behavior pattern. We can never hope to understand violence and aggression until we examine it without the distortions and rationalizations generally used to justify such conduct.

The important point is that neither the Nazi genocide nor the My Lai massacre was an extraordinary act of depraved men, however offensive these seem to us, but only a short step beyond the standard policy of the German war machine or of the American armed forces in Vietnam (Opton, 1971). Comparable things have happened frequently throughout the history of the world. It appears that people are quite capable of justifying killing when it is performed for country, tribe, group, or whatever seemingly legitimate authority, or for God, right, or truth, however these are defined.

We thus see that obedience to Adolph Hitler's murderous mythology did not reflect a unique character defect of the German people. It revealed only the widespread human tend-

portant questions concerning human behavior cannot be tackled experimentally without some use of deception by the experimenter, and such questions might therefore never be answered. This could be a major loss to mankind. Thus, the possibility of making discoveries important to human welfare must be balanced against the potential harm to the subjects, and this kind of judgment is not easy to make.

Furthermore, there is no actual evidence that Milgram's subjects, or those in other studies using deception or stress conditions, were indeed harmed in any way. Milgram points out that afterwards all of his subjects were debriefed and then allowed to see that the "learner" was unharmed; moreover, they were given a full picture of the study, including the fact that the "learner" was a confederate who had not actually been shocked. Milgram believes that later debriefing and discussion with a subject can usually overcome any uneasiness over having acted badly, and he states that there was no indication of any permanent trauma. People are seldom so vulnerable as to suffer permanent harm and can sometimes gain in insight through such experiences. Milgram did his best to leave his subjects with the impression that they had acted as most people do. Ironically, with some possible exceptions, laboratory experiments are usually incapable of generating much emotion in subjects, in spite of the concerns expressed by those who attack the ethics of human experimentation.

Many critics of experiments such as Milgram's remain convinced, however, that harm may be caused by such research with human subjects. Other psychologists consider the issue to be largely a "tempest in a teapot," charging that the critics are worried about imaginary injuries to subjects rather than real ones. Usually they do not deny the obligation of the researcher to be actively concerned about the rights and welfare of human subjects, but believe that regulation of experimental procedures is dangerous and mostly unwarranted. No one has done a survey of American psychologists to see where most opinions about this lie, but published letters and debates indicate that a considerable division exists among psychologists about the way the question of ethical responsibilities should be resolved. This division falls partly along ideological lines, and may also be based on what psychologists actually do. Psychological practitioners and researchers using field and clinical methods are more likely to denigrate the value and importance of laboratory experimentation, while psychologists heavily involved in human experimentation believe that the experiment is the ideal research method and are deeply concerned about the possibility of severe bureaucratic restrictions being imposed on laboratory work.

The issue of the ethics of human experimentation is difficult to resolve in the abstract, and it is even difficult to deal with dispassionately in the context of particular experiments. The Milgram experiments, more than any others in recent years, point up the dilemma precisely because they generated such strong reactions in the subjects. The reactions of readers will undoubtedly vary considerably, just as they have among professional psychologists, and it is likely that debate will continue for a long time on this issue. If you had to conduct Milgram's experiment, would you do it?

ency to be obedient to legitimized authority, though perhaps this is stronger in some societies than in others. Americans are not insulated against this tendency. They are probably as capable as any other group of rationalizing violence, of diffusing responsibility for destructive acts to others (for example, the President, or his appointees). Ironically, it is exactly this willingness to subordinate one's will to that of one's social group that makes an orderly society possible. Man's tendency to accept the authority of the group, to obey the person in power for the sake of the common good, is thus a double-edged sword. It holds us together as a family, tribe, community, or nation, but it also enables us to accept and even participate enthusiastically in destructive and often quite hideous acts of aggression toward others.

Dehumanizing one's "enemies"   The capacity of people to distance themselves psychologically from those whom they torture or destroy is a major factor in warfare and one of the most powerful forces permitting us to maim, torture, and kill others. The violent behavior noted earlier is quite common (though not universal) in combat soldiers and reflects the fact that in combat a man comes to think of the enemy as less than human (Sanford and Comstock, 1971). Consistent with such an outlook is the statement "The only good dink is a dead dink," a comment attributed to an American soldier in Vietnam (quoted in the *San Francisco Chronicle* of December 1, 1969). Similar views have been expressed about demonstrators on college campuses and reflect a similar mentality, composed of one part hatred and one part the perception of demonstrators as less than human. Consider the following comment from a 19-year-old infantryman: "I think someone ought to kill those long-haired, queer bastards back in the world. Anyone who demonstrates against the war ought to be lined up and killed, just like any gook here" (*San Francisco Examiner,* November 23, 1969). Not long after this statement, imagination became grim reality with the tragedy at Kent State University in Ohio (Figure 7.11).

Consider the perception of the police implicit in the use of the term "pig," so common these days among alienated youth and minority groups. Such stereotyping is no more justified than are racist or ethnically prejudiced expressions of hate. Only those who still see no harm in disparaging terms such as "nigger," "kike," "wop," "spic," or "chink" can have any justification for the mindless use of a term like "pig." It is likely that this stereotyped view of police officers as the evil, hostile enemy has encouraged violent attacks on them just as use of the other disparaging terms has been part of the assault on minority groups to which they were applied. These stereotypical images make it easy to see human beings as nothing but targets, objects ripe for extermination. When one group begins to regard another in this way, the subsequent step toward a decision to exterminate the "others" becomes easier, and certainly the tacit acceptance of such acts makes them more likely. And of course violence breeds more violence. Even if originally the harassed police officer lacked all prejudice, he will soon come to see all members of groups in which such hostility has been expressed as part of a continuing threat to his own safety, a sort of stereotyping in reverse. This encourages retaliative measures, justified as self-protection against a hostile enemy: "Shoot first and ask questions later." Growth of such stereotyped thinking, in which all members of a group are seen as evil and threatening, is undoubtedly a major factor in the present escalation of violence in the United States and around the world.

Portrayal of other peoples or nations as threatening and less than human is a common feature of war propaganda as well. An interesting example is the following passage from Stagner (1961, pp. 34–35):

Whittlesey (1942) reproduced a propaganda map issued by Nazi Germany early in the campaign against Czechoslovakia. It visualized that small nation as a dagger aimed at the heart of Germany, with bombers readily capable of saturating the German nation. What it ignored was the much greater extent to which Czechoslovakia was at the mercy of Germany, a fact which became apparent in 1938. One need not assume that the German author was aware of this distortion; consider the excitement in the USA today over the situation in Cuba, which is even less capable of mounting an assault on our country. Looked at from the other side, note that Americans approve strongly of the ring of air bases we have built around Russia, many of which are as close to that nation as Cuba is to ours.

Figure 7.11 Bayonets fixed, Ohio National Guardsmen move in on students at Kent State University on May 4, 1970. When the smoke cleared, four students were dead and eleven wounded. (Wide World Photos)

The perceptual distortion here arises from the fact that we perceive our nation and its purposes as good and pure, hence our bases are no threat to anyone. Russia, on the other hand, is obviously bad, cruel and untrustworthy, hence Russian bases are a great menace to world peace. Please do not interpret my remarks as implying that a Russian base in Cuba would be innocent and virtuous; what I do want to observe is that objectively similar events look quite different when viewed through nationalistic spectacles.

Along similar lines, N. Cohen (1967) has demonstrated how large numbers of ordinary people in Germany accepted the mass extermination of Jews by the Nazis on the basis of skillfully disseminated lies about the danger the Jews posed to the state. It was constantly repeated that they were part of a worldwide conspiracy, determined to undermine the state and achieve supreme power. Even the medieval fantasy of Jews as child murderers was revived. One could therefore destroy them without question. As counterpoint to this picture of Jews as evil incarnate, German "Aryans" were idealized. Thus, through widespread distortions of reality, a weak minority came to be regarded as potentially powerful and dangerous and worthy of the worst possible persecution, justified by the need to save "our fatherland." Very similar points have been made about recent American conceptions of Russians as enemies and of similar Russian views of Americans (Gladstone, 1959).

Social controls over aggression

There are a variety of institutionalized social patterns capable of inhibiting individuals from engaging in proscribed forms of aggression. Some forms of social control of aggression in animals seem to have counterparts also in man. We noted in Chapter 6 that when animals of many species become organized into social *dominance hierarchies* and *territorial systems,* the regular relationships between them consist, in large measure, of patterns of threat and avoidance: the dominant animal

Figure 7.12 Lucy illustrates the principle of deterrence. (Drawing by Charles Schulz; © 1971, United Feature Syndicate, Inc.)

threatens, and the subordinate animal submits before actual fighting breaks out. There are rough human parallels. In a stable social system, a low-status person often avoids displaying aggression, at least openly, against a high-status person in spite of provocation (see A. R. Cohen, 1955; Graham *et al.,* 1951; Kelley, 1951; and Thibault and Riecken, 1955). Presumably retaliation from a high-status individual carries with it considerable danger. Other things being equal, it is a truism that the vulnerable employee, dependent child, or powerless citizen has good reason not to attack his boss, parent, or authority figure who is capable of doing him harm (Figure 7.12).

As in animal life, when a human social system is well established and stable, there is minimal aggression; however, when there is social disorganization, aggression and violence become more frequent. Indeed, there is much sociological evidence that aggressive violence increases during periods of marked social change (Fried, 1970), and criminologists make the same point about the instability of family life in the backgrounds of many violent persons. A historical example of the increase in aggressive violence as an accompaniment of social change were the witch hunts of the Middle Ages (from around the twelfth century to as late as 1692 in Salem, Massachusetts). Psychiatric historians (Alexander and Selesnick, 1966) suggest that the burning of thousands of people as witches was, in part, a response to growing threats to Catholic church authority and to popular insecurity arising from debilitating wars, famine, and plague that wiped out about half the population of Europe (see Figure 7.13). Witch burnings had a revival as late as the seventeenth century, participated in by Protestants and Catholics alike, due to the upheaval in society produced by the Protestant revolt and the subsequent religious wars. Breakdown of the social structure (and probably the increased levels of individual frustration and threat it caused) no doubt underlies both terrible periods of widespread inhumanity.

Nevertheless, by far the most important form of social control over aggression in man are the *pressures imposed by the group on the individual* that were discussed in Chapter 4. To the extent that people feel others will disapprove of them, reject them, withhold rewards from them, or punish them, antisocial behavior, including aggression, will tend to be inhibited. In any society, however, there are usually small pockets of dissidents whose social standards are at odds with those of society at large and for whom disapproval by the majority is of no importance compared with the approval they obtain from the group with which they identify. For secret cabals of assassins and terrorists and for members of hooded societies like the Ku Klux Klan, ordinary social codes seem not to apply. Because they are influenced by like-minded individuals, the usual codes have little power over them, although they may be quite

(a)

(b)

(c)

Figure 7.13 Witch hunting in Denmark, as depicted in Carl Dreyer's powerful historical film Day of Wrath. *(a) An old woman is tortured by interrogators seeking to extract a confession of use of witchcraft. (b) She is carried to the pyre on which she is to be burned to death. (c) The web widens, as the heroine (young woman at left) is accused by her fanatical mother-in-law of resorting to sorcery to harm others. Dreyer made this film in Denmark in 1943 during the German occupation. Although the military censor permitted the film to be released, once its political implications dawned on the German authorities it was quickly suppressed. (© 1943,* PALLADIUM *of Copenhagen; courtesy The Danish Film Museum)*

sensitive to social pressures within their own group. When such dissident groups become large and powerful, as they have in Northern Ireland, society faces civil war.

Because the quieter forms of control of aggression inherent in social disapproval and withholding of rewards do not always succeed, every society makes use of forcible means of controlling offenders through a system of criminal justice. Punishment can be an effective preventive measure against destructive aggression, up to a point, but its effectiveness depends on considerations such as the nature of the punishment, its swiftness and sureness, and the extent to which it is regarded as just and even-handed. For some individuals, punishment seems to have very little coercive power (see Rotter, 1966, as discussed in Chapter 4). In times of social disorder and economic unrest, as respect for authority begins to weaken, the temptation is to mount ever-increasing punitive force against offenders, but this also conflicts with the need of every society to be cohesive and to have the bulk of its people willing voluntarily to abide by its standards. Increasingly violent law enforcement, especially when it is directed at a substantial proportion of the populace, is hardly compatible with the ideals of a free and democratic society. The problem of "law and order" has of late produced extensive national debate and conflicts about policy, but clearly such issues cannot be isolated from other politicoeconomic strains upon the social fabric.

Under conditions of major social unrest things can degenerate to such an extent that the mere presence of policemen or other law-enforcement officials may serve as the proverbial "red flag" does to a bull, that is, instead of preventing violence they may increase the chances of violent aggression. To alienated persons or groups, police or soldiers are agents and symbols of the "system" or those in power; if the system is anathema or hated, then those representing it are also likely to be hated.

Much also depends on the interpersonal interaction taking place between the law officer and the civilian. As we have seen, much aggressive behavior results from a series of actions and reactions, with one person goading another to aggression, and vice-versa. Hans Toch (1970) has shown that assaults on police officers tend to occur in a rather similar fashion in many instances, following from a series of interpersonal "games" in which both participants play their part. Each step escalates until an assault and arrest becomes virtually inevitable. In the general case, there is a first peremptory order or action on the part of the officer, followed by a contemptuous response; then perhaps the seizing of the antagonist by the officer; and finally the confrontation escalating into physical combat. Toch describes an instance of such a confrontation between a black boy who was sitting on a school yard bench late at night and an arresting police officer.

The incident proceeds as follows: The boy reported that he was on his way home and for the moment sitting on the bench when the police officer stated he wanted to talk with him. The boy replied that he had done nothing wrong. The officer then went to his car and talked on the radio. Both insisted they did not want any trouble, and the officer then began a sort of cat-and-mouse attempt to apprehend the boy, who decided to play games of his own and ran off. The boy perceived the policeman as arbitrary, and his stubbornness and resentment were mobilized. The officer responded with irritation and the determination to catch the boy, and thought he heard him utter a threat on his life. He became convinced that the boy was dangerous and maybe a "nut," and concluded that he must be stopped. He got to within 5 or 6 feet of the boy and reportedly said, "Now look, I don't want to shoot you" to shock the boy. Finally he managed to grab the boy by the arm. The boy responded with an obscenity and refused to get in the police car. Toch (1970, p. 168) describes this stage of the confrontation as follows:

The officer has [now] parlayed himself into a state of such fear that he loses control of himself, and even offers to shoot the young boy. He then attempts to physically control the dangerous monster he has mentally created, all the while continuing to exaggerate the magnitude of the opposition. This new development, of course, presents the boy with a somewhat different type of playmate from the "dumb cop" whom he had originally tackled.

There followed a physical struggle between the two, both badly frightened of each other and convinced they were engaged in a desperate fight to the death. At last the boy was subdued and placed in custody. According to Toch, this type of confrontation, and those instances which have gone tragically further, represent meetings between two violence-prone persons, each instigating the other to aggression, both "programmed" for each other, both pressing each other's aggression button (Figure 7.14). The pattern of interaction in this instance is very helpful in revealing the social dynamics of one type of aggression, in which fear, hostility, and prejudice each play their part (see Note 7.4).

Personality dynamics of aggression

The previous sections have dealt mainly with factors in the sociocultural setting that influence aggression. Such factors help create aggressive personalities through the mechanisms of social influence. Their effects are complicated and not alto-

Note 7.4

The accompanying quotation from Hans Toch (1970) and the research studies on individual personality dynamics to be described on subsequent pages should remind the reader of the principle developed in Note 2.1 about the *interaction* among two or more sets of causal conditions. Human psychological reactions are likely to be products of many kinds of interacting variables, the most important of which derive both from the individual's personality and from environmental conditions to which he is exposed.

Figure 7.14 An all too familiar stance in human relations, both domestic and international. (Drawing by Mal Hancock; © Washington Star Syndicate, Inc.)

gether understood, however, and many individuals grow up in a violent social setting without themselves developing aggressive personalities. Our concern here is with the personality dynamics that may account for such variations among people. The problem has been well stated by Hans Toch (1969, pp. 194–195):

Personality can intersect with group norms in one of several ways. For one, personal needs will dictate how well subcultural teachings are assimilated. Ultimately, it is the individual who decides whether violence is to be eagerly adopted, casually rehearsed, or totally ignored. And given the rewards of violence, weak egos are apt to best assimilate violence-prone lessons. . . . Cultural definitions can reflect all manner of personal sensitivities and can accommodate every stage of maturity in interpersonal dealings. Thus, subcultural prescriptions for violence may not specify whether insults should be sought out or reacted to, whether aggression should take physical or verbal forms, whether the individual should lead or follow in matters of aggression. Whereas the subculture of violence promotes violence, it does not prescribe the violent encounters of individual members. The nature of the person's violent acts can therefore reflect both the spirit of the times and the unique contribution of his [own] needs.

Everyone has met individuals who seem to have a low threshold for anger and who readily boil over into rage at what another person would not regard as even the slightest of provocations. One version of this pattern is the man who is normally meek or mild but who when drunk tears up the house, rages at people, and even attacks them physically. There is evidence that alcohol in sufficient quantities releases anger that is normally inhibited and increases the power-centeredness and aggressiveness in normally well-controlled people. Following such an episode, one such person might appear to feel deeply sorry or guilty for the explosion and seek to make amends, whereas in other cases he might give no evidence of remorse or concern in his later interactions with the person whom he has attacked. Some people display nearly continuous overt contempt toward everyone else or toward certain classes of people, for example, those in authority or those who do not share their own personal values. For such people, their regular stock in trade is a cool, biting sarcasm that never seems to build into strong emotional outbursts. Some people may relate to others with what appears to be compliance and cooperativeness, but their every action is designed to undermine others' authority or suggestions in a task-oriented situation. Clinicians have used the expression passive-aggressive personality to label this pattern. The patterns of aggression found among people are, in short, rich and varied. Such a pattern is often quite consistent within each individual, suggesting that it is deeply engrained in his character.

When Paddy Leonard called him he found that they were talking about feats of strength. Weathers was showing his biceps muscle to the company and boasting so much that the other two had called on Farrington to uphold the national honour. Farrington pulled up his sleeve accordingly and showed his biceps muscle to the company. The two arms were examined and compared and finally it was agreed to have a trial of strength. The table was cleared and the two men rested their elbows on it, clasping hands. When Paddy Leonard said "Go!" each was to try to bring down the other's hand on to the table. Farrington looked very serious and determined. The trial began. After about thirty seconds Weathers brought his opponent's hand slowly down on to the table. Farrington's dark wine-coloured face flushed darker still with anger and humiliation at having been defeated by such a stripling.
"You're not to put the weight of your body behind it. Play fair," he said.
"Who's not playing fair?" said the other. . . .
A very sullen-faced man stood at the corner of O'Connell Bridge waiting for the little Sandymount tram to take him home. He was full of smouldering anger and revengefulness. He felt humiliated and discontented; he did not even feel drunk; and he had only two-pence in his pocket. He cursed everything. He had done for himself in the office, pawned his watch, spent all his money; and he had not even got drunk. He began to feel thirsty again and he longed to be back again in the hot reeking public-house. He had lost his reputation as a strong man, having been defeated twice by a mere boy. His heart swelled with fury. . . .

Aggression as an expression of unconscious forces Psychodynamically oriented psychologists and psychiatrists (such as those with a Freudian outlook) tend to view much aggression as a product of unconscious forces having their origin early in life but whose symbolic, personal meanings carry over into the present. The individual is assumed to be reacting to another person "as if" that person were really someone in his childhood. Indeed, we often become angry or hostile without being readily able to explain why. The reaction seems excessive or unjustified, and it seems in such instances as if the provocation must somehow be internal rather than situational. Even if we find immediate rationalizations to explain it, the anger stems mainly from past and forgotten relationships. Nevertheless, although the "real" reason for the anger may be unremembered past hurts and threats, there is always a present situation to which we are reacting, and when it is said that we are "reliving" an event in the past, some feature of the present situation must revive or symbolize that past history, however obscure it may be.

There are a number of ways this might work. One is by the mechanism of *displacement*. Here aggression is altered in its expression, sometimes without our realizing it, by the target shifting from the object toward whom the hostility is actually felt to an alternate object. One reason for such a shift may be that the original person is too powerful to attack. Another reason is that we may have strong internalized restraints against expression of aggression, especially toward certain persons who are important to us, such as our parents or mates. For example, a woman suddenly has an upwelling of anger toward the waiter in the restaurant at which she is eating with her date, but does not know why her feelings are so strong. The anger is, in reality, felt toward her date. She cannot acknowledge this because the date is, without her realizing it, a replica of her father whom she admired and feared. In her childhood she suffered much guilt and anxiety whenever she was provoked into anger at him. The date has said something which offended her greatly. The old experience is not remembered, yet it operates to inhibit the expression of anger toward her date who represents, in reality, her father. Instead, it is displaced to the waiter, who serves as a scapegoat and who may have been just unpleasant enough to justify her hostility. In any case, she lashes out at him in an exaggerated way, much to the perplexity of everyone watching.

Some students may have read the short story by James Joyce entitled *Counterparts*, which has displacement as its main theme. A father beats up his child in place of the many adults who during the day have frustrated and demeaned him but against whom he is too powerless to dare express aggression. Such scapegoating (the tendency to blame weaker, often

He loathed returning to his home. When he went in by the side-door he found the kitchen empty and the kitchen fire nearly out. He bawled upstairs:
"Ada! Ada!"
His wife was a little sharp-faced woman who bullied her husband when he was sober and was bullied by him when he was drunk. They had five children. A little boy came running down the stairs.
"Who is that?" said the man, peering through the darkness.
"Me, pa."
"Who are you? Charlie?"
"No, pa. Tom."
"Where's your mother?"
"She's out at the chapel."
"That's right. . . . Did she think of leaving any dinner for me?"
"Yes, pa. I—"
"Light the lamp. What do you mean by having the place in darkness? Are the other children in bed?"
The man sat down heavily on one of the chairs while the little boy lit the lamp. . . .
"What's for my dinner?"
"I'm going . . . to cook it, pa," said the little boy.
The man jumped up furiously and pointed to the fire.
"On that fire! You let the fire out! By God, I'll teach you to do that again!"
He took a step to the door and seized the walking-stick which was standing behind it.
"I'll teach you to let the fire out!" he said, rolling up his sleeve in order to give his arm free play.
The little boy cried "O, pa!" and ran whimpering round the table, but the man followed him and caught him by the coat. The little boy looked about him wildly but, seeing no way of escape, fell upon his knees.
"Now, you'll let the fire out the next time!" said the man, striking at him vigorously with the stick. "Take that, you little whelp!"
The boy uttered a squeal of pain as the stick cut his thigh. He clasped his hands together in the air and his voice shook with fright.
"O, pa!" he cried. "Don't beat me, pa! And I'll . . . I'll say a Hail Mary for you. . . . I'll say a Hail Mary for you, pa, if you don't beat me. . . . I'll say a Hail Mary. . . ." [From James Joyce, Counterparts. In *Dubliners*, pp. 118–122. New York: Modern Library, 1926]

helpless persons or groups for a frustrating situation) is a form of displacement frequently found in prejudice and will be considered further in Part III. Because the evident object of an aggressive attack is sometimes not the primary one but rather a substitute for it, displacement can lead to confusion in our understanding of any aggressive act unless we can identify its hidden dynamics.

　　Animals also show a pattern that seems quite similar to displacement in man, although presumably it does not involve the symbolic and unconscious processes that Freud ascribed to human versions. Miller and Davis (see Miller, 1948) trained rats to strike one another after receiving electric shocks. If however, no other rat was in the cage, the lone rat would strike even a celluloid doll. Similar research by Azrin was cited in Chapter 6 (see Figure 6.12). In that chapter, we also saw instances of displacement in primate dominance hierarchies, in which a threatened, subordinate animal would turn on an animal lower down in the pecking order rather than fight one above him in rank.

　　Another special kind of dynamic process in aggression proposed by Freud goes by the name "sublimation." As in displacement, *sublimation* involves a transformation of the original hostile impulse into an entirely different form. However, while in displacement the transformation is in the person toward whom the aggression is directed, in sublimation the very aim of the hostile impulse itself is altered. For example, certain constructive forms of behavior such as medical surgery or butchering of animals for food are considered by psycho-

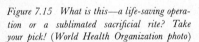

Figure 7.15　What is this—a life-saving operation or a sublimated sacrificial rite? Take your pick! (World Health Organization photo)

analytically oriented writers to be manifestations of aggressive sublimation (Figure 7.15). The choice of such occupational activities is said to be based on unconscious destructive urges (the "death instinct") that have been transformed into socially desirable activities in order to "discharge" the original urge safely or in a way more compatible with other values.

If the surgeon's cutting up of human bodies could validly be regarded as a transformed expression of instinctual aggressive urges (a highly doubtful assumption to those who are not in complete accord with the occasionally topsy-turvy concepts of psychoanalysis), then we would properly have to include such acts in our definition of aggression. Yet to do so would greatly complicate the definitional problem by dangerously enlarging the concept of aggression. We must remember that psychoanalysis deals with individual patients, and it is possible that incorrect assumptions may be drawn from limited evidence. A solution, of course, is to reject this particular hypothesis, that is, that there are innate aggressive *drives* which must be discharged by such presumed transformations. Many psychologists of late have been increasingly critical of the drive concept, whether one is speaking of an acquired drive aroused by external conditions or an innate drive in the Freudian sense. This is one of the major issues about which theoretically oriented psychologists are still in disagreement.

Traits inhibiting aggression Some personality traits appear to result in the inhibition of aggressive reactions to threatening and frustrating conditions, and attention should be paid them here. Such personality traits, including the capacity to inhibit impulsive actions and the need for approval or for warm relations with others, influence whether or not an aggression-provoking situation can trigger our anger.

Because frustration or threat and resulting anger are so common in human affairs, a major social task for each individual is the management of his own aggressive impulses. When a person regularly fails to adapt his reactions to the practical demands of life, he may come to the attention of clinicians and therapeutic efforts may be in order. Many such persons have failed to acquire internal controls or the *capacity to inhibit actions.* Such individuals boil over easily and, when angry, lash out impulsively. Impulse control is generally weak in young children but increases with maturity. Comparisons of people who actually commit suicide or engage in physical assault with those who only threaten suicide or employ verbal threats rather than physical assault suggest that physically violent people are immature developmentally; they lack self-control (see Kruger, 1954; Misch, 1954). Clinical evidence suggests that many psychopathologically aggressive, assaultive people tend to be impulsive, are unable to accept delays or frustrations, and have a low resistance to temptation. In short, they tend to act before they think.

In this regard, Livson and Mussen (1957) studied nursery-school children who were given candy with the stipulation that they could either eat it all or defer eating it until later, at which time they would be given more candy. Reports from teachers about the aggressive behavior of each child were obtained, and it was found that children who had saved the candy and refrained from eating it all at once exhibited less aggression than those who had not displayed such self-control. Such impulse control is precisely the sort of thing middle-class parents tend to encourage in their children. They are urged, for example, to accept the frustrations of studying, saving, or working now in order to earn a richer life later on.

Another personality trait associated with the inhibition of aggression is the *need to be liked or approved* by others. Such people are less likely to behave aggressively than those for whom approval is of little importance. The reader will recall the study by Breger (1963), cited in Chapter 4, in which persons who conformed readily to social pressure inhibited hostility even when it was provoked by others. Thus, those who have a strong *need for approval* might feel themselves too threatened to take the risk of attacking another person, perhaps even when such behavior is called for in self-defense.

In one fascinating study, this process was studied carefully (Conn and Crowne, 1964). First a large group of male undergraduate college students was tested to assess the strength of their need for approval. On the basis of the answers, two groups were selected for the experiment—one with a high need for approval (those scoring at the upper extreme); the other with a low need for approval.

Some of the questionnaire items used to measure need for approval appear in the margin of this page. Note that each question, when answered as indicated here (true or false) contributes to the score for approval motivation.

Next each subject was brought into the laboratory and joined with an accomplice of the experimenter, introduced as another subject. Together they were given the opportunity to win up to 5 dollars in a competitive game. At this point the experimenter was called out of the room, whereupon the accomplice proposed a way for them both to maximize their winnings and eliminate their risk. If the subject agreed, the two entered into collusion to "fix" the game. When the experimenter returned the game started. The accomplice then proceeded to violate the agreement with the result that he won most of the money at the expense of the subject. A control group was given the same treatment except without the accomplice's treachery.

At the conclusion of this assault, the subject and accom-

Item 2. I never hesitate to go out of my way to help someone in trouble. (True)

Item 4. I have never intensely disliked anyone. (True)

Item 6. I sometimes feel resentful when I don't get my way. (False)

Item 9. If I could get into a movie without paying and be sure I was not seen, I would probably do it. (False)

Item 13. No matter who I'm talking to, I'm always a good listener. (True)

Item 21. I am always courteous, even to people who are disagreeable. (True)

Item 28. There have been times when I was quite jealous of the good fortune of others. (False)

Item 30. I am sometimes irritated by people who ask favors of me. (False)

[From D. P. Crowne and D. Marlowe, *The approval motive.* New York: Wiley, 1964]

plice were escorted into another room to wait for the apparatus to be ready for the next part of the experiment. While they waited, the accomplice acted in a euphoric fashion, making bad jokes, laughing, and playing makeshift games in which he tried to involve the subject. If the subject mentioned the violation of the agreement the accomplice laughed and replied offhandedly, "Well, that's the way it goes."

During the waiting period, observations were made of each subject's behavior from behind a one-way mirror. The observers looked for expressive or verbal behavior suggesting either anger or accommodation to the euphoric mood. For example, a subject might laugh heartily, or grin, thus giving evidence that he was accommodating to the mood encouraged by the accomplice; or he might frown or look disgusted, which could be evaluated as refusal to participate. Other examples of hostility or resistance to the social pressure by the subject include verbal comments such as "Act your age," or "Why don't you sit down." From these observations ratings were made of the extent of hostility or euphoria displayed by the subjects toward the accomplice. Those who detected the false window, or who surmised the contrived nature of the situation, were eliminated from the analysis.

The experimenters found that subjects who had a high need for approval displayed significantly less hostility, joining in with the accomplice more than did the subjects low in approval need. No such difference was found in the control group. This observed pattern was graphically described by Conn and Crowne (1964, p. 177) as follows:

The two distinctive behavioral patterns displayed by the high- and low-need-for-approval groups in reaction to instigation to anger clearly suggest two modal resolutions to the problems of handling this arousal. After being treated in a dastardly manner by the experimental accomplice, approval-striving S's [subjects] endorsed by word and action the simulated jubilation of the accomplice and interacted with him as a friend and admirer. In dramatic contrast is the reaction of the low-need-for-approval S's. Following the same instigation to anger, they became sullen and resentful in facial expression and communication and refused to endorse the accomplice's "ode of joy." Instead they directed derogatory comments at him and spurned his invitations to play.

Conn and Crowne suggest that the subjects high in need for approval had unconsciously developed a social style of life which avoided hostility and assertiveness because it might lead to disapproval.

Another study (Gordon and Cohn, 1963) tackled the matter of the inhibition of aggression somewhat differently. Instead of selecting people varying in the need for approval, they tried to induce *affiliative* (friendly or sympathetic) feelings

Man is in motion toward the world and toward his like. A movement of aggression which leads to enslavement or to conquest; a movement of love, a gift of self, the ultimate stage of what by common accord is called ethical orientation. Every consciousness seems to have the capacity to demonstrate these two components, simultaneously or alternatively. The person I love will strengthen me by endorsing my assumption of my manhood, while the need to earn the admiration of the love of others will erect a value-making superstructure on my whole vision of the world. [From Fanon, 1967, p. 41]

in children to see whether such feelings would inhibit aggression. Nursery-school children were exposed to two different conditions—one in which the children were told a touching story about a lonely dog seeking playmates, and another in which a neutral story was told about a dog's search for a ball with which to play. The first story might be expected to arouse affiliative feelings or impulses in the children, because the efforts of the dog to find playmates should correspond to emotions the children probably have felt and could share. After hearing these stories, both groups of children were presented with a play situation in which one of two dolls was supposed to have frustrated the other, and they were asked questions about the alleged or fantasied frustration. It was found that the children whose affiliative feelings were aroused by the emotional story (the dog seeking playmates) expressed significantly less aggression concerning the vicarious doll frustration than those who heard the neutral story. Perhaps one means of reducing aggression is to arouse a conflicting motive or feeling. The capacity of sympathetic feelings to inhibit aggressive behavior should remind us of the suggestion by Eibl-Eibesfeldt (1967), noted in Chapter 6, that feelings of pity are one of the traits in man that act as a control against unbridled aggression in a fashion analogous to the response of dominant animals to submissive signals sent out by subordinate animals when they turn off the attack.

Anger and depression   Clinicians sometimes see anger in a troubled person as a positive or constructive intrapsychic process, to be welcomed rather than suppressed. Anger often represents an active struggling by the individual against external and internal forces that constrict him. Anyone who has lost the capacity for anger has probably also lost his verve and will to live. Such a person often suffers from severe depression, withdrawing from social interaction and from active striving and involvement of all kinds.

Depression is a mental state of helplessness and hopelessness in the face of overwhelming personal problems. The deeply depressed person seems to have given up all hope. He may wish to end his own life, though often he is unable to take such drastic action. Such feelings are also common in persons who have undergone severe personal loss, following which life seems meaningless and futile. In many cases of severe depression, the nature of the problems about which the person despairs may not even be clear to the sufferer himself, much less to his friends and family who often cannot find in his circumstances anything that would seem to justify his state of mind. Yet the clinician presumes that real causes for the feeling of hopelessness do exist at some level of the mind.

In such persons, signs of anger are a positive indication

of a return of vitality and indicate a renewed effort by the person to confront his problems. In this sense, therefore, anger and aggression are often viewed psychologically as being a healthy reaction or counterforce to depression. To remain in a state of profound depression and despair for long is to be destroyed psychologically as a functioning person. Displays of temper, even extreme outbursts of rage, however poorly directed and unrealistic they may be, are very probably essential components of the human psyche; they are necessary elements of each person's defensive arsenal in the struggle to cope with life's problems.

IS WAR INEVITABLE?

In this chapter we have been examining the conditions of social living and human personality that contribute to individual aggression. But what of collective forms of aggression (that is, by the social group acting as a mass)? There are many kinds of collective aggression: riots, lynching, capital punishment (legally sanctioned killing), and open conflict between groups, as in labor disputes, gang warfare, civil strife, and wars between nations. Of these, warfare is the most destructive since it leads to the most widespread damage, death, and injury, and it imposes today the greatest threat to organized civilization and to the preservation of the biosphere with its many forms of life. As we come to the close of the discussion of aggression, something should be said about the possibility of controlling or even limiting destructive aggression in man, particularly war.

Is war inevitable? Although many of us believe that the answer is negative, there is really no definitive answer. Throughout this chapter we have seen many of the features of human biology and society that favor the outbreak of war and other forms of destructive violence. Changing these social and biological features offers some hope for the control or elimination of war. However, since the history of mankind is one of nearly continuous warfare or destructive aggression, we must have no illusions about the chances that this perennial problem will easily give way to rational solution.

There are some severe complications. We must recognize first that there are many people who do not even regard the goal of eliminating violence as desirable; for them, as for the ancient Spartans, warfare is a valued way of life, perhaps the only one they can conceive. Perhaps even more important, not all human aggression need be regarded as negative, as was intimated earlier. The biological disposition to aggression probably facilitated man's self-defense against predators and

When we survey the present state of the world, it is difficult to see any check upon the destructiveness of warfare—if war breaks out between nations that have different systems of government, different ideologies, and are able to convert all the resources of science into instruments of destruction. Looking at the situation through present-day eyes, it seems vainly optimistic to hope that any civilized limitations can be revived. Yet an historical sense provides a foundation for hope. Since sanity could be recovered, and common sense reassert itself, after such a prolonged orgy of violence as the Thirty Years War of the seventeenth century, it is not impossible that a reaction from the disorders of the last thirty years might see a twentieth-century revival of reason sufficient to produce self-control in war, if not the abolition of war.

While violence breeds violence, it can also act as a vaccine. This dual truth of experience has often been proved. To-day, the very fact that the world has suffered so badly from the plague of war twice within a generation may increase the counteractive effects. Besides war-weariness, there are other important psychological factors that may help to create conditions favourable to a renewed period of limitation. The multiplication of machinery has sterilized the romance of war, by diminishing the value of human qualities. Courage and skill are of little avail against a superiority of machinery. The bomber has extended the dehumanizing effect of artillery; the flying bomb, the rocket bomb, and the atomic bomb have carried it further in turn. Such weapons make nonsense of the soldierly idea that success in war is a proof of a people's virility and virtue. They have reduced men to the status of rabbits in a laboratory experiment. That unromantic truth may have a better chance of being generally recognized in the aftermath of the Second World War. [From Liddell Hart, 1947, pp. 116–117]

has also contributed to his strong sense of personal identity. Without this aggressive disposition, it is quite likely that man would not have succeeded so well in competing with other species and mastering his environment, and he might still be living largely under Stone Age conditions. The dilemma here is that man's aggressive tendencies have made him both a builder of civilizations and their destroyer. As we saw earlier, any attempt to excise all human aggression would probably weaken man's constructive side as much as his destructive side. We must somehow learn to control or rechannel our aggressive behavior so that, as psychoanalyst Erich Fromm (1956) puts it, we can become truly "human."

There is another complication that is perhaps the most difficult of all. We must recognize that although they overlap in important ways, the dynamics of individual and collective aggression are not exactly similar. We cannot explain war entirely by reference to psychological events that take place in the individual. War involves a mobilization of masses of people and their subjection to a military machine that has scant concern for individual psychology, except as it affects the "war effort." When a nation mobilizes itself for war, many of its people may not agree with the decision. As Andreski (1964, p. 131) notes, "It must not be forgotten how often direct compulsion had to be used not only in recruiting soldiers but also to make them fight." The nation-state goes to war as a result of complex sociopolitical decision-making processes, often involving what are believed to be vital economic and strategic interests; that is, one or more governments decide to fight. How this happens is a problem of great human concern, but we can barely touch on it here (see Zawodny, 1966; Fried *et al.*, 1968; Wright, 1968; Pruitt and Snyder, 1969).*

Not all international conflicts lead to war. When two nations are at loggerheads, hostilities may sometimes be averted through diplomatic deals, trade agreements, non-aggression pacts, and the like. Great displays of force, as in war "games" (maneuvers), naval visits to "show the flag," and grand military parades, have often served as substitutes for actual hostilities. Sometimes military demonstrations and threats lead to a backing down of the weaker side. But such power displays usually produce intense armaments races, like those which preceded both World Wars I and II, in which maintenance of "credibility," or ability to bluff in the international poker game, is the key consideration. In our own times, the great powers are all armed to the teeth with awesome and devastating weapons, and the poker game might well transform itself into Russian roulette.

*For other studies of this problem, see the Suggested Readings at the end of this chapter. New books in this area are also emerging regularly (for instance, Bandura, 1973).

Anyone who writes about the control or elimination of war must be very diffident about doing so, since all that we have learned tells us that the problem is extremely complex and there is no simple answer. We cannot escape the nagging feeling that so far scholars have but scratched the surface of this enigmatic problem. Clearly the study of war goes beyond the single discipline of psychology, which deals with personal decision-making processes essentially from the "inside" view. Although individual and mass psychology certainly plays a part in national decisions, any attempt to understand the causes of war must extend into the domains of political science, economics, sociology, and anthropology. A multidisciplinary approach is needed (see the Suggested Readings for this chapter).

For those of us who are concerned about these massive problems of man, there often comes an overwhelming sense of our own individual helplessness. What can we do to change man or the social settings in which he lives? To change one thing is to affect many others, and we have seen how difficult it is to create conditions controlling aggression without altering many other valued features of human life as we know it. It is unfortunately much easier to see what needs to be done than to suggest how such changes ought to be brought about.

Nevertheless, let us consider the available options. There would seem to be two directions in which we can go toward creating alterations in man's condition that might help to control or eliminate war. First, based on the assumption that the aggressive response to threat (or imagined threat) is a strong biological disposition, we can attempt to alter man's psychobiology through the massive use of drugs, conditioning, and the like (see Chapter 5). It is highly doubtful, however, that such alteration is either practicable or desirable. To do so requires far more knowledge than we now have and, were it feasible, use of any such power to shape human psychobiological characteristics would impose awesome and highly dangerous responsibilities on political leaders.

The other direction seems to be more promising and is based on the premise that destructive aggression is not inevitable despite our strong biological predilections toward it. We have seen that aggression is also strongly under the control of social learning. The key to its control therefore lies within the social structure under which man lives, and its ultimate control depends on that social structure. Our problem, therefore, is to work toward social changes that maximize such control without damaging other valued human traits.

Following the ideas developed in this chapter, one might start with the *provocations* to aggression, namely, oppressive and threatening conditions that lead people to violence. Margaret Mead (1968) and others have stressed the importance of re-

In the future, the quality of a handful of scientists may weigh more heavily than any conscript mass of infantry, reducing to absurdity the quantitative value of human numbers, while nullifying both the appeal and the power of 'militarism.' Such a revolution in warfare makes its limitation more urgent, but also more practicable. The obvious road is through the establishment of a United States of the World, to which the different nations would yield their separate control of destructive forces. But the experience of history shows that progress is rarely attained in the obvious way—more often along some indirect approach. A realism that fails to see the need of a world order is more unrealistic than any idealism, yet a sense of realities shows all too clearly the unlikelihood of its early fulfilment in a common government. In advance of world federation, agreement to apply a world-wide system of qualitative disarmament could diminish the danger. In advance of this, the re-establishment of a code of conduct might, at the least, help to improve the inadequate insurance that nations can derive from pure reliance on their own armed strength. The chances would be increased if the renewal of such a code between nations was supported by a similar revival of good manners within nations. Nazism was a domestic upheaval before it became an external explosion, and it was only one expression of a world-wide symptom.

Manners are apt to be regarded as a surface polish. That is a superficial view. They arise from an inward control. A fresh realization of their importance is needed in the world to-day, and their revival might prove the salvation of civilization. . . . For only manners in the deeper sense—of mutual restraint for mutual security—can control the risk that outbursts of temper over political and social issues may lead to mutual destruction in the atomic age. [From Liddell Hart, 1947, pp. 116–117]

ducing human deprivation and frustration by halting pollution and deterioration of the biosphere and cutting the rate of global population growth to bring it into balance with the food supply and other vital resources. Such a suggestion is predicated on the importance of hunger, scarcity, and crowding. Undoubtedly there is a direct link between overpopulation and aggression. On the other hand, hostility and alienation in people is often less tied to their objective circumstances than to the gap between their expectations and reality. In any case, desperate people (and nations) have little to lose by destructive aggression, and changes that increase their sense of well-being could go a long way to reducing the aggressive provocations (Figure 7.16).

The *cultural climate* of aggression is also an important area of potential social change, and we need to work toward eliminating the aggressive models we present to our children and to make more clear the distinction between aggression in fantasy and in reality. We might begin by eliminating war toys and by toning down some of the excessive violence depicted in the mass media. It would help also to draw a sharper distinction also between anger and overt aggression. Children need not be ashamed of feeling angry at times, but must learn to express it in behavior that is not harmful to others.

Little is really known about the social systems under which peacefulness rather than aggression is the life pattern. Anthropologist Ruth Benedict had great interest in this and compared a number of different cultures varying greatly in aggressiveness. She introduced the term *synergy* to refer to the extent to which the institutions of a culture made it possible for the individual to provide simultaneously for his own advantage and that of the group. On the matter of aggression and synergy she wrote (see Maslow, 1964, p. 155):

. . . the conclusion that emerges is that societies where non-aggression is conspicuous have social orders in which the individual by the same act and at the same time serves his own advantage and that of the group. . . . Non-aggression occurs [in these societies] not because people are unselfish and put social obligations above personal desires, but when social arrangements make these two identical.

Our culture, like most of those cultures we admire, has moderately low synergy, that is, our life is predicated on competition, and we usually assume that we must sacrifice our own selfish interests if we are to contribute to the group. Competitive curve grading in school is a good example. There is only so much room for A's, and B's, so that in taking an exam if your neighbor gets a higher score you will have less chance of getting the most coveted grade. This social arrangement

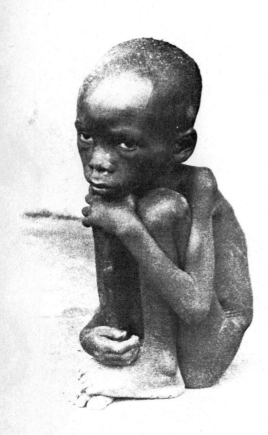

Figure 7.16 *Starving Biafran child during the Nigerian Civil War, Christmas 1969. How many other children around the world are victims of malnutrition? How many die of hunger every day? And those that survive and reach adulthood, what kind of men and women will they be? (Wide World Photos)*

makes it less likely that there will be positive feelings and mutual cooperation, since one's gain is another's loss. Whether synergistic relationships between individuals and nations can ever be achieved on a worldwide scale is not altogether clear, but the basic idea is certainly worthy of further examination (Figure 7.17).

Our own culture is quite inconsistent about its values concerning competition and aggression. Although most Americans profess Judeo-Christian ideals in which "turning the other cheek" is highly valued, this religious ethic is not really widely internalized or practiced, which shows that mere inspirational attempts to urge people toward peaceful values are insufficient to alter actual behavior; in contrast, in our most cherished national myths we admire the "manly" virtues of the fast-drawing gunfighter, the person who when called upon can "take care of himself" in a fight, the war hero who shot down twenty enemy planes, the woman in the frontier stockade who kills numerous attacking "Indian savages" alongside her husband. Writing about the American scene, Schlesinger (1968) has said that we have "a bad inheritance so far as violence is concerned. . . . We began, after all, as a people who killed red men and enslaved black men."

Figure 7.17 (a) Margaret Mead in Bali, Indonesia, being introduced to a baby, Bajoeng Gede. (b) Ruth Benedict, 1887–1948. (a: Courtesy of Dr. Margaret Mead; photo by Ken Heyman; b: photo by Blackstone–Shelburne, New York)

Our society also tends to be ambiguous in its outlook on the release or inhibition of a person's aggressive potential (Frank, 1967). On the one hand, *intra*societal aggression such as rebellion and mob violence is condemned; on the other hand, *inter*societal aggression (against an external foe) is welcomed and praised as wholesome, patriotic, and heroic. We also encourage fierce economic and scientific competition and intensely competitive, often brutal sports. Frank makes an interesting contrast between the form of aggression encouraged by capitalism and that favored by communism. Capitalism favors individual competition, communism encourages group competition. Aggression flourishes however in both.

If man has a strong, biologically based disposition toward aggression, we must find ways of undermining its *social and psychological supports.* Earlier we considered two such supportive mechanisms, namely, the tendency to be obedient to authority and the tendency to dehumanize the "enemy." Thus, for those who view war as an abomination, it is always disturbing to see national leaders whipping up violent feelings of hatred as part of a mobilization of public opinion behind policies to which they are committed. Such leaders in all likelihood reflect the ongoing outlooks and sentiments of the society at large, and perhaps it is too much to expect them to move against the natural tendencies of the populace from

Figure 7.18   Despite intense ideological differences, hostility between nations can sometimes be rechanneled into nonviolent directions. Here Chen Pso-ching of China (right) plays Dal Joon Lee, United States table tennis champion, in Los Angeles. Doug Stewart of New Zealand is umpire. (U.S. Table Tennis Association)

which they have sprung. But one major change in our cultural climate must be an increased capacity of individuals to think for themselves and to reject authority figures who pursue destructive policies. We must come to value diversity rather than conformity to a single view. Clearly this is a lot easier said than done.

The very tendency of people to subordinate themselves to the group makes it possible for them to work together toward valuable common goals. It is perhaps ironic that man, who began his evolutionary career as the quarry rather than the hunter, came to control nature through his capacity for cooperation and social coordination; this comparatively small and weak mammal, hunting in armed packs, became the most potent and feared of animals. Man's unique ability to plan and act in concert became his most powerful weapon. By capitalizing on division of labor and improved social organization, men were able to build villages, towns, cities, and civilizations. But hand in hand with these advances came improved means of destruction: stones became spears and cannons and ballistic missiles; war canoes became battleships and nuclear submarines; bands of part-time warriors became standing armies and navies; and temporary war chiefs became career generals and admirals.

The mythic forces underlying warfare have not altered much since the Stone Age, however. Intense loyalty to the clan or tribe combined with ferocity in defense of its lands and in pursuit of *mana* (see margin) are still extant as rabid patriotism, love of glory, and hatred of the foe. Yesterday's witch doctors and shamans are today's ideologists and propagandists, statesmen and liberators. But in modern war man's ability to mobilize the social group psychologically for maximum effort has turned against him and become the potential means of his own destruction. All-out nuclear warfare will have no heroic victors and no glorious victories.

Allport (1954) suggests that we must now learn to identify our social group with the *community of man* rather than with the community of the nation-state or any other subgroup (Figure 7.18). But this world outlook is not today held by many. Indeed it may only be a utopian ideal, since it overlooks the real conflicts of interest that exist in a world in which the vital resources are not shared by all. Also, people seem best able to identify strongly with limited groups such as the family or tribe.

Although as individuals we of course have little control over the social climate, the possibilities of change in social conditions remain the most intriguing and promising avenues along which we can move toward reduction of destructive aggression. We must recognize that any such changes are certain also to produce much social instability, and we have already learned that social stability inhibits aggression while

It is . . . not too difficult to trace the transition from the individualism within the [Maori] tribe to the aggressive, ruthless type outside. The individual identified himself too closely with his tribe to do other than fit his personal qualities to the cultural ideals and requirements. The "chip on the shoulder" attitude was canalized outside the group. Maori war [in New Zealand] throws this into sharp relief.

Individuals who were more than normally aggressive, that is, accomplished ruffians, might prove to be great nuisances at home; and if they went into the enemy's territory on a foraging expedition and were killed, though the tribe might be secretly relieved, it nevertheless went to war. No quarter or generosity was shown between opposing sides in time of war. "A man's mana [inner power] increased according as he could destroy the mana of the enemy, no matter how he did it." Lying, theft, cunning, deceit, treachery, cruelty, in short, anything and everything was legitimate. "Manslaying," said the Maori, "is one of man's most important activities, it is . . . the great game; better to die weapon in hand than by lingering sickness of old age." [From Mishkin, 1961, p. 453]

instability promotes it. This fact must be faced by those who are anxious for instant and massive change on a global scale in order to correct injustice.

But clearly some basic transformation in the human condition must come in the not too distant future if man is to survive; mankind cannot live perpetually under the menace of annihilating war. Although our tendencies toward cooperation, sympathy, and love are fragile and easily disrupted, especially when conditions favoring violence remain widespread, there is really no reason to look on these conditions as immutable (see Maslow, 1967, 1968; also Fromm, 1955). We saw in Chapter 5 that the social environment has been anything but permanent throughout human history. Our expanding knowledge of the way social conditions affect human interaction for good or ill may make it possible to take steps that will bring about this vital transformation.

In periods of great crisis, men have sometimes mobilized themselves for cooperative effort in the common interest. They then have demonstrated the same courageous determination in positive, constructive activities as they have shown in massive destructive efforts in times of war. If we think of man's first 2 million years as his childhood, then he is now about at the age of adolescence, of juvenile delinquency. If he gives himself time, he may yet grow up and find the collective will to transcend his violent nature.

CONCLUDING COMMENT

In this chapter we have considered aggression as a phenomenon of social learning, just as in Chapter 6 the focus was on aggression as an expression of human biology. The main emphasis in Chapter 7 was on the social and personal factors contributing to aggression or its inhibition, including the interpersonal conditions provoking it; the cultural climate; some of the psychological mechanisms (such as obedience to authority and the tendency to dehumanize one's enemies) making it possible to injure others with minimal inhibition and distress; social controls that inhibit aggression; and personality dynamics in patterns of anger and aggression.

The task of eliminating human violence, including warfare, will not be easy without some fundamental changes in social conditions on a worldwide scale. But such changes are not impossible, given man's enormous capacity for behavioral variability.

One of the most powerful divisive forces that lead to conflict in today's world is racial, ethnic, and religious prejudice. We will consider this problem in Part III.

If not in the interests of the state, do not act. If you cannot succeed, do not use troops. If you are not in danger, do not fight. A sovereign cannot raise an army because he is enraged, nor can a general fight because he is resentful. For while an angered man may again be happy, and a resentful man again be pleased, a state that has perished cannot be restored, nor can the dead be brought back to life. Therefore the enlightened ruler is prudent and the good general is warned against rash action. Thus the state is kept secure and the army preserved. [Sun Tzu (4th century B.C.), *The art of war* (trans. by S. B. Griffith). New York: Oxford Univ. Press, 1971]

Psychosocial treatments of aggression

Berkowitz, L. *Aggression: A social psychological analysis.* New York: McGraw-Hill, 1962. One of the most respected psychological treatments of aggression; a text dealing with most of the important psychological issues, from the neobehaviorist standpoint.

Megargee, E. I., and Hokanson, J. E. (eds.) *The dynamics of aggression.* New York: Harper & Row, 1970. A brief set of readings covering mainly the psychosocial side of aggression, focused on research questions.

Scott, J. P. *Aggression.* Chicago: Univ. of Chicago Press, 1958. Examination of aggression in both its psychobiological and psychosocial aspects.

Zawadny, J. K. (ed.) *Man and international relations.* Vol. I: "Conflict." San Francisco: Chandler, 1966. Extensive collection of reprinted short articles on various facets of human aggression, mainly from the psychosocial standpoint. Many of the articles are very useful, though the book is somewhat confusingly organized.

Multidisciplinary approaches to violence and war

Frank, J. D. *Sanity and survival: Psychological aspects of war and peace.* New York: Random House, 1967. A thoughtful, readable, and brief attempt to summarize what is known from a biological and social standpoint about the causes of war and the ways that might be conceived for controlling or ending it.

Graham, H. D., and Gurr, T. R. (eds.) *Violence in America: Report of the National Commission on the Causes and Prevention of Violence.* New York: Signet Books—New American Library, 1969 (paper). A collection of articles on the history of violence and crime in the United States and its patterns, including vigilante movements, class violence, racial violence, rebellion, and a discussion of overcrowding and aggression.

Fried, M., Harris, M., and Murphy, R. (eds.) *War: The anthropology of armed conflict and aggression.* New York: The Natural History Press, 1968. An edited collection of anthropological articles covering in depth such topics as effects of war, the ethology of human aggression, the nature of warfare, and its prevention.

Mead, M. (ed.) *Cooperation and competition among primitive people.* Boston: Beacon Press, 1961. A valuable survey, first published in 1937, of life among thirteen remote primitive tribes, with much useful data on many aspects of social aggression and cooperation.

Pruitt, D. G., and Snyder, R. C. (eds.) *Theory and research on the causes of war.* Englewood Cliffs, N.J.: Prentice-Hall, 1969. Excellent collection of articles mainly dealing with the sociopolitical aspects of war and the way decisions about it are made. More than any other book, this seems to be oriented toward some of the practical problems of international conflict and tension.

Rose, T. (ed.) *Violence in America.* New York: Vintage Books, 1969 (paper). Collection of articles on violence with a historical perspective and with strong political overtones.

Sanford, N., and Comstock, C. *Sanctions for evil: Sources of social destructiveness.* San Francisco: Jossey-Bass, 1971. An unusual collection of essays by psychologists, psychiatrists, and sociologists dealing with the ways society justifies cruelty and violence and the psychological processes that are part of this.

Short, J. F., Jr., and Wolfgang, M. E. (eds.) "Collective Violence." *Annals of the American Academy of Political and Social Science,* 1970, 391 pp. Collection of articles on mainly the sociopolitical aspects of collective violence such as riots and war.

Wright, Q. The study of war. In *International Encyclopedia of the Social Sciences* (D. L. Sills, ed.), pp. 453–467. New York: Macmillan, 1968. A brief but informative review of war as a human social problem.

[*The National Socialist folkish philosophy*] *believes in the necessity of an idealization of humanity. . . . But it cannot grant the
right to existence even to an ethical idea if this idea represents
a danger for the racial life of the bearers of a higher ethics; for
in a bastardized and niggerized world all the concepts of the
humanly beautiful and sublime, as well as all ideas of an idealized future of our humanity, would be lost forever. . . . [From
Hitler, 1943 ed., p. 8]*

1

Prejudice is thinking ill or well of some person or group without basis in actual fact or experience; in psychological terms, it is therefore an *attitude*. Although a prejudice can be positive as well as negative, it is especially in its negative sense that it poses a destructive social problem. The problem is a classic one in human affairs and is known to have existed as long as there have been records of human social life. For its victims, prejudice is a problem of central importance and poignancy. As will be seen in Chapter 9, one of the most destructive features of prejudice is the feeling of disparagement, of being "put down," that comes from being subject to chronically hostile attitudes. Social aggression, discussed in Chapter 7, is often linked to attitudes of prejudice, and we frequently observe how closely the two problems are interconnected.

    Discrimination is the action side of prejudice. That is to say, while prejudice refers to an attitude held by one person toward another person or group—a combination of thinking and feeling—discrimination consists of negative *acts* directed against the target of prejudice. These can range through a host of lesser acts, such as desecration of group religious or ethnic symbols, restrictions of citizenship, imposed social inequalities, and exclusion or avoidance, to the extremes of physical beatings, forced labor, lynchings, massacres, pogroms, deportations, and genocidal extermination. There are numerous more subtle forms of disparagement, which cause great psychological harm. In Chapter 9 we shall

325

All the human culture, all the results of art, science and technology that we see before us today, are almost exclusively the creative product of the Aryan. This very fact admits of the not unfounded inference that he alone was the founder of all higher humanity, therefore representing the prototype of all that we understand by the word "man." He is the Prometheus of mankind from whose shining brow the divine spark of genius has sprung at all times, forever kindling anew that fire of knowledge. . . . It was he who laid the foundations and erected the walls of every great structure in human culture. [From Hitler, 1943 ed., p. 3]

2

3

4

see that prejudiced attitudes and discriminatory behavior are overlapping but not perfectly correlated events.

In America, if you are black, Amerindian, or of Oriental, Jewish, Mexican, or Puerto Rican descent, you have no doubt experienced prejudice in some form or another. If you are a woman you have been discriminated against; likewise, if you are homosexual. Actually, there is probably no one who has not at some time been a victim of prejudice, because prejudice is a nearly universal quality of human thought. Thus, beside the major victims of prejudice, there are numerous other groups toward whom some prejudice is common in the United States: Catholics, Lutherans, Mormons, Italians, "WASPS" (white Anglo-Saxon Protestants), old people,

10

8

9

5

6

11

The Tidal Wave of Unwelcome Aliens

National States Rights Party's Most Important Program

Details How To Ship Negroes Back To Africa

12

hippies, eggheads, professors, foreigners, and so on; indeed, nearly every visible group in the society. In short, just about everyone participates to a greater or lesser extent in this process. Some instances are pernicious, of course, and these are the manifestations of group hatred that raise prejudice to the position of a major social evil.

Like all inferred psychological states, it is not easy to pin down exactly what we mean by the term attitude, and all psychologists do not agree on the same definition. Most commonly, however, attitude is defined as a *tendency to react favorably or unfavorably toward some object, idea, person, group, or situation.* Because this list of terms is such a cumbersome mouthful, hereafter I shall refer to them collectively as the *object* (or *target*) of an attitude. The word "tendency" in the definition above implies that one need not always react in the same way, but rather that there is a disposition to do so. Moreover, the reaction need not be overt, as when a person feels hostile but does not wish anyone else to know about it. Put very simply, and without some of the technical considerations of when and how they are expressed, attitudes can be thought of as likes and dislikes, and prejudice is an attitude of liking or disliking someone merely because he is a member of a particular group.

The two chapters that follow divide the problem of prejudice into its main components. Chapter 8 deals with prejudice as a social phenomenon, a part of the

13

social environment into which all of us are born. Prejudice is encouraged by the nature of social relationships, such as the existence of in-groups and out-groups, the human tendency to think about social groups in terms of stereotypes, the pressures from one's own group to react to outsiders in certain ways, the existence of competition between groups, the constant struggle of subgroups within the larger society to retain their own identity, and the often visible differences among groups based on ethnic characteristics and styles of living.

Chapter 9 focuses on the *individual* aspects of prejudice, including the reactions of the victims and the psychodynamic mechanisms involved. We shall also consider the difficulties in eliminating prejudice from human society.

We hold these truths to be self-evident, that all men are created equal; that they are endowed by their Creator with certain unalienable rights; that among these are life, liberty, and the pursuit of happiness. That, to secure these rights, governments are instituted among men, deriving their just powers from the consent of the governed. . . . [The Declaration of Independence, 1776]

16

330

Every group that is a victim of prejudice experiences and copes with this problem in somewhat distinctive ways depending on its specific circumstances, and a complete analysis would of necessity consider the history and circumstances of each such group. Thus, prejudice in the case of the Jew is a product of historical circumstances that have faced the Jew throughout a history extending roughly over two thousand years in which he was an unwelcome resident in Western countries after having been driven from his own homeland. Likewise, prejudice toward the American black cannot be adequately understood without reference to the historical event of slavery and its consequences. The problems of discrimination toward women require an understanding of the origins and patterns of male-female social roles and relationships. And in the case of other target groups, such as homosexuals, there are also special features that make each case unique.

Nevertheless, in spite of these differences, there are also common features stemming from the ways society tends to be organized and the way people think, feel, and react psychologically. Thus, it is fruitful to examine the common features and to search for principles that apply to all. Although the treatment here tends to lump all victims together, we must bear in mind the distinctiveness of each group's (and individual's) history and experience.

17

18

Although one cannot with certainty rule out the possibility of racial differences in potential for competence, the whole issue is of very little import so long as the great majority of black, Puerto Rican, and Indian children grow up in poverty with extremely limited opportunities to acquire the language and number abilities and the motivation that underlie full participation in our society. [From Hunt, 1969, p. 238]

20

21

23

22

The White Christian Nordic people of America are being threatened by a tidal wave of color, descending upon our nation from
all parts of the world. In this perilous hour of history, America
is being saturated with mongel [sic] blood from throughout Asia.
Yellow mongolians from throughout the Asian world are descending upon America in unprecedented numbers. In ever increasing
numbers the blacks from throughout the interior of Africa are
flooding the shores of America and again, our nation is being
saturated with wave after wave of colored blood. From throughout
the countries of South America and the West Indies a tidal wave
of BROWN beats relentlessly upon the American coast from
Florida to Southern California. This alien tide of yellow, brown
and black is now on the very pinnacle of swallowing up the
white nordic blood that developed and originated the great nation
we call America. . . . [From the Editorial, National Chronicle,
Feb. 8, 1973, p. 1]

24

25

26

27

There is, of course, insufficient space here to develop a case history for every major group that has been victimized by prejudice, and so the illustrations given in the next two chapters have, perforce, been limited to a few groups. The choice is partly arbitrary and partly based on the available literature. This means that certain groups are either absent from the illustrative discussions or underrepresented, not because their cases are less important or poignant, but because it was thought best to concentrate on a few groups for purposes of analysis.

We shall consider mainly the case histories of the Jew and the American black. The former has been the victim of prejudice for a very long time and anti-Semitism is regarded by many social psychologists and sociologists as the classic case of prejudice. The plight of the American black is much in the focus of attention today. Blacks represent about 11 or 12 percent of the United States population and the issue is of enormous scope for American society. The problem of sexual discrimination is now coming to the fore, and this is also considered here, though not as extensively as the problem deserves. Many other equally important target groups might have been selected for study: the Latin American (chicanos in the West and Puerto Ricans in the East); the Native American Indian; the Japanese- and Chinese-American; and numerous victims of ethnic,

28

29

30

Give me your tired, your poor,
Your huddled masses yearning to breath free,
The wretched refuse of your teeming shore,
Send these, the homeless, tempest-tossed, to me:
I lift my lamp beside the golden door.
[Emma Lazarus, The New Colossus: Inscription
for the Statue of Liberty, New York Harbor]

racial, religious, and caste prejudice in other countries.

It is my firm belief that for all these groups many of the general rules considered in Chapters 8 and 9 apply. There is, in the main, a common pattern of reaction and a common set of processes at work in all prejudice, though the emphasis will tend to shift with different conditions. The reader is invited to test out the ideas presented here on cases not discussed. How does the method of analysis being used apply in such cases, and where does it require supplementation or modification?

Illustrations: Background photo, pp. 324, 325—The Klan rides, in scene from D. W. Griffith's *Birth of a Nation,* 1915 (Museum of Modern Art/Film Stills Archive). 1. Charred victim of SS troops, Germany, 1945 (U.S. Army photo). 2. Recruitment poster: "The German student fights for Führer and nation in the ranks of the National Socialist Students League" (Library of Congress). 3. Young Nazis burning books, Berlin, 1933 (United Press International Photo). 4. Jewish couple forced to wear yellow Star of David, Berlin, 1941. 5. Anti-Semitic boycott. (4,5 Wide World Photos). 6–9. Deportation of Jews, Warsaw Ghetto, 1940–1941. 10. Lampshade made of human skin, from Buchenwald Concentration Camp, presented as an exhibit at the Nuremberg Tribunal on war crimes. (6–10 Courtesy of YIVO Institute for Jewish Research, Inc., New York). 11. In late 1945, German civilians forced to file past bodies of Jewish women starved to death by SS troops in 300-mile march across Czechoslovakia (U.S. Army photo). 12. Items from the white-supremacist press (private collection). 13. Racist graffiti near Lincoln Memorial, Washington, D.C. (Wide World Photos). 14. "Separate but equal" facilities in Southerntown, U.S.A., when segregation reigned (Charles Harbutt; Magnum). 15. Strange fruit: victims of lynching in Columbus, Mississippi, 1935 (United Press International Photo). 16. American Indians, father and son (Bruce Davidson: Magnum). 17. Guatemalan girl. 18. Young girl from Mali. 19. Filipino woman. 20. Mexican community leader. 21. Schoolboys, Upper Volta. 22. Montage: the family of man. 23. Mother and child, Mauritania. 24. Young Japanese. 25. Young Americans. 26,27. Girl and boy from Romblon Island, Philippines (17–24, 26–27. United Nations; 25. Exxon Corporation). 28. Asian refugees arriving in Britain with all their remaining possessions in their hands, after being ejected from Uganda by President Idi Amin's Africanization decree (Central Press/Pictorial Parade). 29. Hutu refugees from Burundi, Central Africa, where 150,000 of their tribe were slaughtered in an officially inspired pogrom (Wide World Photos). 30. Elderly Vietnamese (United Nations).

All of us are capable of prejudice, though some maintain and act out such attitudes to a greater degree than others. It is certainly important to explore the varying proneness of individuals to be prejudiced and the psychological forces within us that are at work in prejudice. However, we shall leave this for Chapter 9. Here we will begin with the effects of the social environment itself. Prejudice is encouraged (or discouraged) by certain social conditions, and we shall be concerned here with characteristics of society that influence prejudicial attitudes and choice of targets. We shall consider such characteristics as formation of in-groups and out-groups, unfavorable group stereotypes, peer-group pressures, group competition and conflict, social change and disruption, and the struggle between tendencies toward assimilation of minorities and tendencies toward maintenance of distinctive group identities. All of these social conditions are important in prejudice.

IN-GROUPS AND OUT-GROUPS

Man's social life, while not a direct cause of prejudice, at least sets the stage for it. From the day we are born we are members of groups. The first and most obvious such group is the family. This may be the nuclear family of father, mother, and children. Or it may be the extended family (found in cultures such as that of India today or among our recent ancestors in the West), including grandparents, uncles, aunts, and other relatives, either all living under one roof or at least in regular and frequent social contact. As our understanding of the world grows from the limited view of the very young child to the expanding concepts of the school-age child, the adolescent, and the adult, we come to recognize that we belong to other social categories: we are blacks, Jews, males, females,

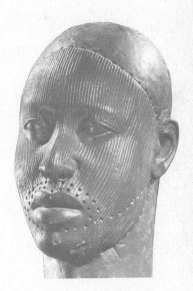

Americans, Americans of Irish descent, alumni of Berkeley or Brooklyn College, Republicans, dentists, professors, or students. We belong simultaneously to many groups, some small, others large, some positively viewed, others negatively.

What is particularly important here is the image people have of themselves. People tend to think of themselves and members of the groups they identify with as "we"; in contrast, "they" are all the others, members of groups with whom there is no identification.* For the dominant members of society, *we* refers to the elite "in-group" and *they,* to the subordinate "out-group."

Belonging to a particular group is a highly valued thing when it places one among the elite of a community. In other instances, however, feeling part of such a "we" can be mainly negative and carry some sort of social stigma. All this depends a great deal on one's own inner beliefs and value system, as well as those of the community in which he lives. Thus, being a professor may be highly valued in one portion of the community but be quite negatively viewed by other elements of society; its prestige value may also change in the course of time.

The existence of in-groups and out-groups creates the crucial background for prejudice. Loyalty to one's own group is likely to imply differential evaluation of *we*'s and *they*'s. Indeed prejudice has commonly been fostered and exploited by politicians appealing to such *we–they* sentiments as ultra-nationalism and racism, the belief that only one's own people are good or right. Differential interests among groups facilitate the cementing of in-group loyalties and intergroup conflicts. The "common enemy" is easily viewed contemptuously. Thus, the psychological advantages of strong identification with a group may be paid for by an accentuation of hostile feelings against "outsiders," negative perceptions of threat from such aliens, and a tendency to reject them or be hostile to them.

Allport (1954, p. 42) illustrates this in-group–out-group tendency as follows:

Because of their basic importance to our own survival and self-esteem we tend to develop a partisanship and ethnocentrism in respect to our in-groups. Seven-year-old children in one town were asked, "Which are better, the children in this town or in Smithfield [a neighboring town]?" Almost all replied, "The children in this town." When asked why, the children usually replied, "I don't know the kids in Smithfield." This incident puts the initial in-group and out-group situation in perspective. The familiar is *preferred*. What is alien is regarded as somehow inferior, less "good," but there is not necessarily hostility against it.

*The reader might do well to review the discussion in Chapter 4 on imitation and identification.

Does in-group loyalty automatically require feelings of antagonism toward out-groups, with attendant intergroup conflict?
Social psychologists are not in agreement on this point. Many
writers think so, believing that group cohesiveness requires a
common enemy. Others have taken the position that although
hostility toward out-groups helps strengthen in-group cohesion, it is not absolutely necessary. Anthropologists have shown
that out-groups may be viewed either as the threatening
enemy, to be defeated in order to preserve the in-group, or
as valued and appreciated trading partners, although this is
rather more rare. The problem, of course, is how to develop
an appreciation of human diversity. In our shrinking modern
world, where international economic coordination is becoming
a vital necessity, perhaps we shall come to see all of mankind
as our "trading partners" and the basis of our loyalty will be
expanded. We might then learn how to defeat the real common
enemies of man—disease, overpopulation, hunger, and poverty. Some feel that space exploration can also provide the
outward challenge that will bring humanity together, although
till now the "space race" has been largely a nationalistic competition for prestige with overtones of militarism. It is not yet
clear just how man, whose history has been a steady progression from clannishness, to nationalism, to racism and imperi-
alism, can now cultivate a larger loyalty to the worldwide
family of mankind.

UNFAVORABLE GROUP STEREOTYPES

There is a natural human tendency to classify and generalize about objects, people, and events. Our beliefs are derived
from a limited number of direct experiences or from things
we have been told by others. These limited instances can only
be systematized by us in a useful way if we are able to *generalize*
them to a larger class of events. Thus, extending from our
limited experiences and from what we have heard, we may
conceive of all life in the city as hectic, freedom as always
desirable, all Chinese as industrious, all students as radical
activists, and so on. In making such generalizations, we have
leaped from a few limited experiences to a whole class of
events, all of which we cannot possibly know about personally.
(In fact, the word prejudice itself comes from the Latin, *prae-
judicium*, a preliminary judgment before all the evidence is
heard.) As it turns out, cities are not always hectic, nor are
all Chinese industrious. When we treat all such instances as
if they were alike, we are fitting them to our preconceptions,
our *stereotypes*. It is important to recognize that the process by
which we create stereotypes is not in itself unnatural or illogi-

cal; rather it is the usual way in which elementary beliefs are organized into principles by means of which we try to order our experience and give meaning to a world that would otherwise seem chaotic. Stereotypes are thus *generalized beliefs*. But usually they are at least partially incorrect because they ignore all nuances of individual variation, and they play a central role in what we call prejudiced attitudes (Brigham, 1971).

This idea is very important. It means that in our ordinary struggle to make sense out of the world, each of us carries the seeds of prejudice because we tend to simplify and generalize, to place many diverse events and objects into a common class or category. This process is necessary to human analytic thought (it underlies scientific thinking), but it also involves varying degrees of inaccuracy. For maximum accuracy we must make precise distinctions between the individual instances of a given class and determine the extent to which qualities attributed to the class are indeed possessed by each individual case. In human terms, stereotyping becomes highly inaccurate and sometimes destructive when it is applied to all members of a large social group regardless of individual differences. Such broad characterization represents prejudice. A positive stereotype, say, that Americans are a superior people, involves essentially the same mode of thinking. We do not usually think of this positive form of prejudice as a social problem because it does not seem particularly injurious to anyone, though of course it does imply the existence of inferior people as well. Generally, though, when we speak of prejudice we mean negative stereotypes formed about groups and applied to individuals.

Figure 8.1 "To bait fish withal: if it will feed nothing else, it will feed my revenge." Actor Joseph Schildkraut as Shylock. (Museum of the City of New York)

Examples of stereotyping

Every society has certain stereotyped ways of thinking about various groups of people, fixed or exaggerated pictures (either positive or negative) of them that are widely shared by the population. These stereotypes constitute a feature of the social environment into which we are born. Examples include "All lawyers are crooked," "All Jews are shrewd," or "All blacks are lazy." Children learn these widely shared beliefs and judgments from their parents, teachers, and other adults, and they are passed down from generation to generation (see Chapter 4). Because they are often accepted as more or less axiomatic truths, they resist further analysis and are seldom subject to close scrutiny or demands for proof.

An interesting example of such a negative stereotype may be found in William Shakespeare's *Merchant of Venice* in the character of Shylock, the Jew (Figure 8.1). Although we cannot learn much from it about the actual situation of Jews in Renaissance Europe, we can learn much about the great dramatist Shakespeare. Despite his depth of poetic vision into the human condition, he could not rid himself of all the prejudices of his times. Shylock, a money lender, is portrayed as an angry, grasping, unforgiving, money-hungry man, more interested in his wealth than even in his own daughter. In contrast Antonio, a rich Italian merchant, is characterized as a lovable patrician, decent and honorable through and through, though victimized by misfortune. The evil Jewish usurer, whose forte is kicking a man when he is down, demands a pound of Antonio's flesh (his heart) as payment for an outstanding debt. Eventually, thanks to some pretty shrewd tricks by Antonio's clever lady lawyer, Shylock is stripped of his wealth, forced to convert to Christianity, and barely spared his life. The comedy ends on this happy note. Presumably Elizabethan audiences loved every minute of it. How did this prejudicial view arise?

During the Middle Ages, Jews were greatly restricted in the economic activities permitted them in most of the European countries to which they had been dispersed. At first, only a small fraction were traders, many others being artisans and craftsmen, some even farmers. However, when they lost their civil rights and the right to own land around the fifth century A.D., a high proportion of Jews were pushed into marginal economic activities. Later, they were herded into ghettos and their freedom of movement was severely curtailed (Figure 8.2). Among the major restrictions were the occupations into which they could go. Since they could neither be farmers nor own landed property and often were not allowed into artisans' guilds, they were drawn more and more into trade.

By the tenth century, Jews had become the chief merchants of Europe. In their role as international traders, they brought into contact Christians and Moslems, who were frequently in a state of hostilities with each other. With the growth of cities in the ensuing centuries mercantile business became increasingly profitable, and more and more Christians turned to commerce. Since the latter had rights of citizenship, they had great competitive advantage over the Jews, and soon outnumbered them in trade. There was increasing pressure in many towns to eliminate the Jewish merchants as rivals and to exclude them from all trading. At around this time money, which had hitherto not been an important feature of economic life, began increasingly to replace barter as the means of exchange. Although the church prohibited Christians from lending money at interest (called *usury*) canon law did not apply to Jews. Jewish merchants, who were being increasingly restricted in their regular trades, began to lend money at interest. This made them targets of attack, as we saw in the image of Shylock. But with the growth of a money economy, more and more non-Jews secretly turned to banking as a profitable livelihood, in spite of canon law. In Renaissance Italy, these bankers included members of the foremost Italian families, some with high ecclesiastical connections. Soon Christian

Salarino: *Why, I am sure, if he forfeit, thou wilt not take his flesh; what's that good for?* Shylock: *To bait fish withal: if it will feed nothing else, it will feed my revenge. He hath disgraced me, and hindered me half a million; laughed at my losses, mocked at my gains, scorned my nation, thwarted my bargains, cooled my friends, heated mine enemies; and what's his reason? I am a Jew. Hath not a Jew eyes? hath not a Jew hands, organs, dimensions, senses, affections, passions? fed with the same food, hurt with the same weapons, subject to the same diseases, healed by the same means, warmed and cooled by the same winter and summer, as a Christian is? If you prick us, do we not bleed? if you tickle us, do we not laugh? if you poison us, do we not die? and if you wrong us, shall we not revenge? If we are like you in the rest, we will resemble you in that.* [From William Shakespeare, *The Merchant of Venice*, Act III, Scene 1]

Figure 8.2 The Jewish Ghetto of Lublin, Poland, in drawing by Lionel S. Reiss. (Collection, The Jewish Museum, New York)

bankers wanted to drive Jews out of money-lending activities as well. Anti-Semitism, both official and unofficial, grew rapidly in consequence of this competition.

Actually, only a tiny percentage of Jews of this period were wealthy, and most were quite impoverished. Feudal princes in control of cities would sometimes offer protection to Jews in exchange for financial assistance. But this protection usually continued only as long as the princes needed money. Subsequent oppression of Jews was frequently severe, as we shall see later. There developed out of this matrix the distorted image of the Jew as the crafty money lender and usurer, even though banking soon became respectable and mainly the province of non-Jews. This myth has come down through history, and modern propagandistic attacks still denounce the Jews as "international bankers" controlling the financial affairs of the world. In actuality, although there are some famous Jewish bankers, notably the Rothschilds in Europe, the banking business is generally dominated by non-Jews. In the United States, executive positions in the top echelons of finance are held by Jews in a percentage substantially lower than their percentage of the population at large. But, as we shall see, the persistence of hostile stereotyping, in total disregard of the truth, is one of the hallmarks of prejudice. Simpson and Yinger (1965, p. 201) summarize the situation thus:

> Those who speak of the "Shylocks" in medieval ghettos seldom ask themselves: What were the rest of the townspeople doing? How could they have borrowed, had they not been earning enough to meet a high interest on loans? The tradition-minded peasantry may have opposed the Jewish merchant and money-lender because his activities were bad according to their standards, but the Christian townspeople attacked the Jew because his activities were good—i.e., profitable. Having found trading a profitable venture, many Christians, by the thirteenth century, had turned to banking. The church's condemnation of usury was not enforced or it was circumvented by accommodating formulas. Anti-Semitism, involving both projection (the Christian bankers were perhaps not without some guilt feelings) and economic conflict, was a natural product of this situation.

There have been many studies of social stereotypes in the United States. In one of the earliest by Katz and Braly (1933) the following traits were ascribed to Jews by college students with high agreement: Jews are shrewd, mercenary, industrious, grasping, intelligent, ambitious, and sly. Later studies (Gilbert, 1951; Karlins *et al.,* 1969) have revealed similar stereotypes, although there were some changes in recent years, the most important being the reluctance of students to express stereotypes because of the unreasonableness of being forced to make generalizations about people, particularly those whom they have hardly ever met. One student noted, "I refuse to be a part of a childish game like this. . . . I can think of no distinguishing characteristics which will apply to any group as a whole." It would appear that some students of today are more sophisticated about prejudice and more wary of falling into the trap of stereotyped thinking.

In the 1930s, stereotyped descriptions by American whites included characterization of blacks as superstitious, lazy, happy-go-lucky, ignorant, and musical (see Katz and Braly, 1933). More recently, Bettelheim and Janowitz (1950) found that the list had grown longer: it was said that blacks are sloppy and filthy; they ruin property values; they take over neighborhoods and force out whites; they are lazy and slackers at work; they have a low character (immoral and dishonest); they have lower standards of behavior; they are ignorant and have low intelligence; they are troublesome and cause disturbances; they spend all their money instead of saving it; they smell bad; they carry disease. Still more recently, Maykovich (1972) has observed changes in the stereotypes held about blacks by white adults. The main contemporary characterizations are that blacks are musical, pleasure loving, loud, lazy, happy-go-lucky, sensitive, and quick-tempered.

A questionnaire administered to 74 college men and 80 college women (Broverman *et al.,* 1972) has confirmed the impression that stereotypical pictures of the qualities of males and females in our society are also widespread. What is the content of such stereotypes? They found that women are perceived (by both men and women) as relatively less competent, less independent, less objective, and less logical than men. On the other side, men are perceived as lacking interpersonal sensitivity, warmth, and expressiveness in contrast with women. In addition, the masculine traits are typically considered more desirable than the feminine ones, and women see themselves more negatively than men do.

Developing the case that prejudicial stereotypes about women's nature and appropriate social roles have long existed, Sandra and Daryl Bem (1970) provide the following examples from the writings of St. Paul in the Bible:

> For a man . . . is the image and glory of God; but the woman is the glory of the man. For the man is not of the woman, but the woman of the man. Neither was the man created for the woman, but the woman for the man. [1 Corinthians, 11 : 7–9]

And similarly,

> Let the woman learn in silence with all subjection. But I suffer not a woman to teach, nor to usurp authority over the man, but to be in silence. For Adam was first formed, then Eve. And Adam was not deceived, but the woman, being deceived, was in the transgression. Notwithstanding, she shall be saved in childbearing, if they continue in faith and charity and holiness with sobriety. [1 Timothy, 2 : 11–15]

Incidentally, biologists are quite convinced that mammalian embryos are female in appearance at the outset and that the penis is an enlarged clitoris, with physiological maleness resulting from the activities of male sex hormones (androgens) set into action genetically through the presence of a male chromosome that establishes the sex of the offspring. Thus, it would seem that the "rib" really belonged to Eve, not Adam, in the story of creation. But more seriously, the implications of many of the biblical references to women are that woman's position is automatically defined as inferior and as a servant to man, a pattern that has tended to dominate thinking all over the world. Consider also the Jewish Orthodox morning prayer:

> Blessed art Thou, oh Lord our God, King of the Universe, that I was not born a gentile.
> Blessed art Thou, oh Lord our God, King of the Universe, that I was not born a slave.

Blessed art Thou, oh Lord our God, King of the Universe, that I was not born a woman.

And the Koran, the sacred text of Islam, states:

Men are superior to women on account of the qualities in which God has given them pre-eminence.

Women are of course not a minority out-group, since they comprise slightly over 50 percent of the world population. Nevertheless, many of the things one can say about prejudice and discrimination as they apply to minority out-groups can also be said about women. Women have been and are still exposed to certain negative stereotypes about their psychological characteristics and social roles, and the women's liberation movement is attempting to attack and change these stereotypes and the restricted social and occupational roles that are rationalized by them.

Characteristics of stereotyping

Stereotypical pictures held about minority groups are usually quite contradictory and serve mainly to justify already existing dislikes. In the case of the Jew, for example, two opposing images are commonly maintained, both of which cannot be true: all Jews are seclusive and clannish; all Jews are pushy and intrusive (Adorno *et al.,* 1950). Allport (1954, p. 195) cites the following conversation to illustrate the point:

Mr. A. I say the Jews are too much alone; they stick together, and are clannish.
Mr. B. But look; in our community there are Cohen and Morris on the Community Chest, several Jews in the Rotary Club and Chamber of Commerce. Many support our community projects. . . .
Mr. A. That's just what I was saying, they're always pushing and elbowing their way into Christian groups.

What plainly happens is that people who dislike Jews [for whatever reasons] subscribe to any and all stereotypes that would justify this dislike, whether or not the stereotypes are compatible. Whatever Jews are like, are not like, do, or don't do, the prejudice finds its rationalization in some presumed aspect of "Jewish essence."

The process taking place in such negative stereotypes is sometimes referred to as the "self-fulfilling prophecy." Simpson and Yinger (1965, p. 122) analyze it as follows in the context of white racism:

If a group of forces [associated with slavery, for example] have created an inferior status for a minority, there will appear, both as rationalization of the discrimination shown and as a result of the fact of observation of that inferior status, an attitude of prejudice

Is there a seed of the Serpent on this earth today? Are there a race of Devils living on this earth who are flesh and blood beings? We are convinced that there is a serpent race, the very offspring of Satan, living upon this earth today and working toward the total destruction of true Christianity. I am further convinced that this serpent race is a race in every sense of the definition of race, since they have, for several thousands of years upon this planet, worked for the total destruction of white Christian Civilization and are by blood descent traceable back into history for thousands of years. They do possess all of the necessary physical characteristics and traits necessary to constitute a race and must in every sense of the biological and physiological meaning of race, constitute a people which we can accurately describe as Race. Most Christians refer to the serpent race by the name Jew. [From C. Magno, Adam & Eve and Satan The seed of the serpent. In National Chronicle, February 15, 1973, p. 1]

toward the minority group. Such prejudice will block members of the "inferior" group from the life chances necessary to advancement. By limiting the opportunities of a minority group, by segregating it, by putting it at every competitive disadvantage, the prejudice helps to create the very inferiority by which it seems "justified" in the minds of the dominant group. Start out by saying that the colored man is inferior; use this as the reason for giving him poor schools, poor jobs, poor opportunities for advancement; and one soon proves himself correct by creating and enforcing that very inferiority. This, in turn, will deepen the prejudice, which again, will further restrict the opportunities of the colored person.

People like to think of themselves as rational and do not usually accept the idea that their judgments of others may be prejudicial. They can usually find ample confirmation of prejudices in the behavior of the minority group; but the negative actions of which it is accused are often the *result* of its low status rather than the cause. Nor do stereotypes require the support of any actual experience. Most studies of prejudice demonstrate that people will freely express prejudicial attitudes toward groups they have never once met.

Allport (1954, p. 7) discusses this latter feature of prejudice as the theory of the "well-deserved reputation": when a person is asked about the grounds for his negative attitude toward some group, he argues that he is not prejudiced and that anyone can see why that group of people is unpopular; *they deserve it.*

It is not easy to say how much fact is required in order to justify a judgment. A prejudiced person will almost certainly claim that he has sufficient warrant for his views. He will tell of bitter experiences he has had with refugees, Catholics, or Orientals. But, in most cases, it is evident that his facts are scanty and strained. He resorts to a selective sorting of his own few memories, mixes them up with hearsay, and overgeneralizes. No one can possibly know all refugees, Catholics, or Orientals. Hence any negative judgment of these groups as a whole is, strictly speaking, an instance of thinking ill without sufficient warrant.

Not only do stereotypes of groups vary on the basis of historical circumstances, but they have different *social uses* as well (Simpson and Yinger, 1965). For example, one group of stereotypes might be aimed at keeping down a group that is already deprived, while another is used to push down a group that has already achieved some degree of competitive power. Thus, the picture of the American black as lazy, shiftless, irresponsible, unintelligent, and unappreciative of the finer things in life is a similar picture to that drawn for the Polish worker in Germany during the late 1800s and the migrant to California from Oklahoma and Arkansas ("Okies") during the depression of the 1930s. (One should note that these migrants of the 1930s were mainly white Anglo-Saxon Protestants.) American blacks, Polish workers, and migrant farmers have in common their economically and socially depressed status. In sharp contrast are the stereotypes of Jews, Greeks, Syrians, Armenians, Japanese, and Chinese. These groups have generally managed to gain an economic toehold within the dominant society in various settings, and they have often been pictured as too ambitious, crafty, and aggressive.

One of the remarkable features of the process of stereotyping is that members of minority out-groups construct essentially the *same* prejudicial images of other minorities as do members of the majority in-group; not surprisingly, their picture of themselves usually tends to be more favorable. For example, it has been observed that Jewish and non-Jewish children showed great similarity in their rankings of various ethnic groups (Zeligs and Hendrickson, 1933). A similar finding was reported by Bogardus (1928), whose data are presented in Table 8.1. Here the rankings of a number of ethnic groups

Table 8.1

The way various types of Americans evaluate ethnic groups on the Bogardus social-distance scale[a]

White businessmen and schoolteachers	Blacks	Jews
1. English	1. Black	1. Jew
2. French	2. French	2. English
3. German	3. Spanish	3. French
4. Spanish	4. English	4. German
5. Italian	5. Mexican	5. Spanish
6. Jew	6. Hindu	6. Italian
7. Greek	7. Japanese	7. Mexican
8. Mexican	8. German	8. Japanese
9. Chinese	9. Italian	9. Turk
10. Japanese	10. Chinese	10. Greek
11. Black	11. Jew	11. Chinese
12. Hindu	12. Greek	12. Hindu
13. Turk	13. Turk	13. Black

[a] Adapted from Bogardus (1928).

by three American-born subpopulations—white (or "WASP") businessmen and schoolteachers, blacks, and Jews—are compared. Except for the rankings of their own group, all three subpopulations show a remarkably similar pattern of opinion regarding various ethnic groups. It seems you do not have to be a WASP to acquire the stereotypes of your culture.

To sum up, all of us grow up in cultures and subcultures in which certain stereotypical pictures of social groups are maintained. These stereotypes are especially strong in the case of minority out-groups and follow predictable patterns depending on whether the group in question is socially and economically marginal or relatively successful in competing within the majority culture. Such stereotypes are often contradictory, showing clearly that they are not the prime basis of prejudice but rather serve as the justification for it. Moreover, negative stereotypes tend to create a vicious cycle in which certain things are believed about specific groups, these beliefs causing expectations that prejudice helps to fulfill.

PEER-GROUP PRESSURE

In the Deep South, where slavery had its greatest penetration, resistance to full equality for blacks has been longest and strongest. This is not to say that racist attitudes are uncommon elsewhere in the country or that all southerners share them, but state government officials in the Deep South have been least inhibited in expressing themselves in open and florid language on the subject of school desegregation. One cannot, therefore, dismiss the evident regional differences of social climate with respect to antiblack sentiment.

Social psychologist Thomas Pettigrew (1961) has reviewed some of the evidence of such regional differences in racism and other patterns of prejudice. For example, in one study of anti-Semitism, two consecutive public opinion polls (Roper, 1946; 1947) reveal that the South, along with the Far West, manifests the least anti-Semitic prejudice of any region of the United States. And in another study (Knapp, 1944) of over 1,000 war rumors, in the South anti-Semitic stories of seditious acts and conspiracies were found in only 3 percent of the total instances, while they constituted 9 percent of the rumors for the country as a whole. The situation is different when the focus is on the black, with 8.5 percent of the southern war rumors centered on blacks, while the corresponding percentage for the country as a whole was only 3 percent. Also consistent with these observations is the finding (Prothro, 1952) that two-fifths of a white adult sample in Louisiana expressed quite favorable attitudes toward Jews but the same people expressed unfavorable attitudes toward blacks.

Studies of prejudice as a personality trait (Pettigrew, 1959) reveal no differences in degree of prejudice as a general matter between southerners and residents of other regions. The bigotry of the South is merely different in pattern; it has more legal and institutional support, as well as a different prime target than in other parts of the country, being directed largely at the black. This means that in the South the pervading social norms concerning prejudice have their own characteristics, and the social pressures tend to require expression of prejudice and acts of discrimination toward blacks. Those white southerners who are not antiblack have traditionally been stamped as deviant when they have dared to express their feelings.

Social norms concerning prejudice vary from region to region and from group to group, and such norms exert on the individual very real *pressures* to conform in word and deed. If he functions within a group whose attitudes are strongly antiblack or anti-Semitic, he is under great pressure to act accordingly, since to be deviant is to invite criticism and risk hostility, loss of prestige, ostracism, and sometimes worse. Although the pioneering research on conformity pressure (discussed in Chapter 4) was not done in the context of prejudice and discrimination, it has a close and obvious application to these problems.

Pettigrew (1961) suggests that there are many people in the South whose conformity to the social norm of antiblack sentiment is only skin deep. They are so enmeshed in a web of social and economic pressures that they are unable to openly disavow such traditional sentiments. Pettigrew calls such persons "latent liberals," because when the climate of prejudice in which they live alters they will not resist such change. He believes that too little attention has been paid to such latent liberals and that knowledge of their problems and empathy with them in their plight might contribute to improving the southern psychological climate (see Note 8.1).

Note 8.1

One way to get a feel for how psychologists design research studies would be for the reader to try to imagine a way of testing Pettigrew's notion (1961) of the "latent liberal." Presumably, in the presence of southern bigots such persons would express antiblack attitudes to which they were not really strongly committed, but if the economic and social pressures conducive to expressing such sentiments were reduced significantly, the latent liberals should show a positive shift in attitude.

If Pettigrew is right, how might latent liberals be distinguished from more dedicated bigots? What are some of the social conditions under which they would be expected to show a favorable shift in expressed attitudes toward blacks? How might such conditions be varied, either in naturalistic field settings or in laboratory experimental mockups, and what control observations should be made and why? See if you can figure out a way of researching this idea and perhaps of developing it further. As you do so, you will find yourself engaged in the kind of analysis that underlies most successful psychological research.

GROUP COMPETITION AND CONFLICT

In some societies, there is little opportunity to advance or change one's status in life. All is arranged in advance and determined by birth. In other societies, however, such as our own, the person can move upward or downward in the world, economically, socially, and educationally, depending on his own efforts, or good and bad fortune. And as a result of such mobility, there is always a strong possibility that one's lot in life may change, either for the better or for the worse. Where there is a high degree of vertical mobility, competition among individuals and groups is intensified. Such a fluid condition of life increases the likelihood that competing out-groups will be seen as potential or actual enemies. This is a state of affairs which can fuel prejudice.

Economic factors in racial prejudice

Following the Civil War, the newly emancipated blacks' rights as American citizens were pushed farther and farther back by systematic disenfranchisement, segregation statutes (passed in every southern state by 1907), and erection of economic and social barriers wherever they lived. Many of the former slaves had been skilled workers (carpenters, bricklayers, and blacksmiths). But after 1865, pursuit of such trades put the black man in competition with the white, and whites fought hard to protect their status. On the plantations, former slaves had no choice but to become sharecroppers, whose share of the crop was small indeed after rent and cost of credit were deducted. Each successive census after 1865 showed a decline in the proportion of skilled black workers.

Antiblack feeling and destructive acts mounted during the Reconstruction period. From 1880 to 1890, lynchings and violent intimidation of blacks were very common, and Jim Crow laws enforcing segregation proliferated. Efforts to promulgate liberal, biracial policies failed in the face of white-supremacist economic, political, and ideological pressures. By the end of the nineteenth century, the blacks' lot was disenfranchisement and official segregation in the South, second-class citizenship and unofficial segregation in the North. Everywhere blacks were exploited economically. And sporadic outbreaks of racist violence (often by hooded groups of the Ku Klux Klan) were part of a pattern of coercion designed to keep blacks "in their place."

In 1900, almost 90 percent of the black population lived in the South, mainly in rural areas. Northerners could still look askance at white racism in the South and view themselves as above such ugliness. But as more and more blacks migrated from the South to northern and western cities, competition-based discrimination spread. By 1960, the percentage of blacks living in the South had shrunk to 60 percent, with most of the remaining 40 percent concentrated in 12 large cities of the North or West. High population density made blacks far more visible as a social force, and with the transplantation came increased intergroup conflict over housing, schools, and occupational status. Many black migrants from rural parts of the South found themselves stranded in northern cities without employment. New York City's black population rose from 1.1

million in 1940 to two and a half times that in 1960. Los Angeles County had 75,000 blacks in 1940, and 464,000 in 1960, a sixfold rise. As many blacks lacked suitable training for industrial jobs and were also subject to discrimination in hiring, high unemployment and its negative social consequences were all but inevitable (Figure 8.3), along with much racial bitterness and conflict.

In the mid-1960s efforts were made to increase the number of skilled blacks in both the blue- and white-collar work community. "Affirmative action programs" were initiated in

Figure 8.3   One man's frame of reference. (Drawing by Handelsman; © 1972 by The New Yorker Magazine, Inc.)

"I can remember this neighborhood before it became uninhabitable."

Note 8.2

Reference in the text to economic pressures as a way of explaining growing anti-immigrant feeling in the United States and elsewhere warrants some further comment about the psychological side of the matter. There have been many similar economic interpretations of social behavior, including prejudice and hostility. For example, it has been shown that the frequency of lynching in the United States is strongly correlated with the price of cotton per acre in the South; lynchings increased in periods when economic conditions were deteriorating (Raper, 1933; Hovland and Sears, 1940; Mintz, 1946).

This explanation assumes that there is a psychological link between economic troubles in the society and pressures on people which lead them to perceive the presence of blacks, Jews, immigrants, or other minority out-groups as the cause of the trouble and hence to feel hostility toward them. Although the presumed link might seem reasonable in general, the psychologist must ask whether it can be demonstrated in any given person. Economics deals with populations at large, while psychology deals with individuals. Not everyone will be economically harmed when the overall economy (or, say, the price of cotton) is down, and some persons may even profit from such a state of affairs. And not every person who is unemployed or underpaid will necessarily blame his troubles on out-group minorities. Since many will tend to see these "outsiders" as dangerous competitors, the economic explanation is warranted and useful. But it is still necessary to supplement the economic explanation with the precise psychological factors that lead some individuals to change their attitudes toward out-group minorities or suddenly to manifest latent hostility. The reader may have trouble understanding this point, but it is necessary to recognize that different *levels of analysis* are involved in broad-scale economic interpretations and specific psychological appraisals. This point applies to many fields that overlap with psychology in their approach to human problems and yet function on different analytic levels. (See also the discussion in the Prologue of the uniqueness of psychology and the consideration in Chapter 7 of the relations between individual aggression and war.)

hiring, and efforts were made to provide added educational slots for blacks and other minority out-groups. However, such programs provoked considerable fear and often downright hostility among certain parts of the labor force, since in a period of job scarcity white-held jobs seemed threatened. This hostility fueled attacks on "quota systems" in which hiring or promotion is partly based on ethnicity. (Similar problems have arisen recently in the case of affirmative action programs designed to increase the number of women in higher job categories.) Such programs are perceived by members of the majority in-group as a personal threat, leading to an increase in intergroup hostility and prejudice. This reaction was probably a major factor in the conservative political shift of numerous blue-collar workers (and others), who in the presidential election of 1968 turned out in large numbers for George Wallace and in 1972 defected from the Democratic party and its candidate, George McGovern. In the latter campaign, the Democratic candidate represented himself as a friend of deprived minorities and a supporter of strong action programs, while the Republican candidate, Richard Nixon, criticized quota systems in hiring practices and supported maintenance of the status quo. The issue was an extremely emotional one all over the country, and one that no doubt helped Nixon to gain his resounding electoral victory.

Hostility arising from economic competition between members of two ethnic groups is commonly *perceived* by the individuals involved as a racial (or religious) matter, drawing upon the psychological fund of prejudice that has previously existed and often fueling it further. But the degree of hostile competitiveness is not the same for all individuals: some may feel quite vulnerable; others, quite secure in their positions. The important determinant of intergroup hostility is therefore not how things really are, but how they seem to be. Existing prejudices and personal insecurity often "program" the individual's reactions, building up a sense of threat from others that may be entirely unrealistic. Of course, once mutual fear and hostility escalate, imagination soon becomes reality (as we saw in Chapter 7).

Economic factors in religious prejudice

You will recall from the earlier discussion of Shakespeare's portrayal of Shylock that economic factors played a large role in the anti-Semitism of Renaissance Europe. Numerous comparable instances may be found in modern times.

In the eighteenth and early nineteenth centuries, the vast economic opportunities available in the United States made it possible to absorb all immigrants, including the relatively small number of Jews, without much trouble. There were only about 230,000 Jews in the United States in 1880. But with the growth of large-scale industry toward the end of the century, the earlier American ideal of a highly mobile society and wide-open economic competition began to give way. Economic power tended to concentrate more and more into huge corporations and trusts, and a more rigid class structure (and increased status consciousness) emerged. In a society with a growing class orientation, discriminatory actions barring Jews from hotels, resorts, and residential areas began to occur with increasing frequency.

At the same time, an upsurge in European anti-Semitism also gave tremendous impetus to immigration by Jews to the United States. From 1881 to 1914, nearly two million Jews fled eastern Europe (mainly from Russia and Poland, where a series of violent pogroms took place) and came to the United States. In an expanding economy they were, in the main, easily absorbed, and this mass immigration was at first seen as providing a cheap source of labor. By 1900, however, many frontiers were closed and economic expansion had ebbed, making it more difficult to absorb new immigrants. Agitation built up to have unrestricted immigration stopped. This agitation had at first concentrated on Chinese immigration but soon grew in strength and scope and was extended to Jews and other eastern European groups. In a period of increasing economic strains, small businessmen felt more and more threatened, and it was easy to turn their hostility toward new immigrants. Americans acquired a ready-made European-based tradition of prejudice (see, however, Note 8.2, page 350).

A purported plot by "International Jewry" to overthrow governments and to conquer the world (called the *Protocols of the Elders of Zion*) was "discovered" in Russia in 1902. These *Protocols* were a forgery, but they were circulated widely (Figure 8.4).* In 1920, auto magnate Henry Ford published a series of articles about them in his *Dearborn Independent* (see margin, page 352), a paper with a circulation of 700,000. He later became convinced that the *Protocols* were bogus and publicly apologized. But growing anti-Semitism helped power the rewriting of United States immigration laws in 1921 and 1924 in such a way as to sharply reduce immigration of eastern European Jews relative to that of more favored ethnic groups.

*The Standard Jewish Encyclopedia gives this publication date (although the document presumably had been circulating in czarist official circles at the close of the nineteenth century) and indicates that the account was actually clumsily plagiarized from a satire on Napoleon III, written by a non-Jewish journalist, M. Joly, *Dialogue aux enfers entre Machiavel et Montesquieu* (Brussels, 1865). The bogus *Protocols* were introduced into western Europe by Russian emigrés in 1919. Despite the fact that they were demonstrated to be false as early as 1921, they remained in widespread circulation and later played an important part in Nazi propaganda, disseminated by the high-powered "big-lie" machine of Dr. Joseph Goebbels.

In all parts of the world the words "Liberty, Equality, and Fraternity" have brought whole legions into our ranks through our blind agents, carrying our banners with delight. Meanwhile these words were worms which ruined the prosperity of the Goys [gentiles], everywhere destroying peace, quiet, and solidarity, undermining all the foundations of their states. . . .

[This] *aided our triumph,* for it also gave us, among other things, the opportunity to grasp the trump card, the abolition of privileges; in other words, the very essence of the aristocracy of the Goys, which was the only protection of peoples and countries against us.

On the ruins of natural and hereditary aristocracy is our intellectual class—the money aristocracy. We have established this new aristocracy on the qualification of wealth, which is dependent upon us, and also upon science, which is promoted by our wise men. Our triumph was also made easier because, through our connections with people who were indispensable to us, we always played upon the most sensitive chords of the human mind, namely, greed, and the insatiable selfish desires of man. Each of these human weaknesses taken separately is capable of killing initiative and of placing the will of the people at the disposal of the buyer of their activities. . . .

There is one great force in the hands of modern states which arouses thought movements among the people. That is the press. . . . *Through it we have attained influence, while remaining in the background. Thanks to the press, we have gathered gold in our hands, although we had to take it from rivers of blood and tears.*

But it cost us the sacrifice of many of our own people. Every sacrifice on our part is worth a thousand Goys before God. [From *The protocols of the meetings of the learned elders of Zion* (trans. from the Russian by V. E. Marsden), pp. 16–18. Chicago, Ill.: Patriotic Publishing Co., 1934]

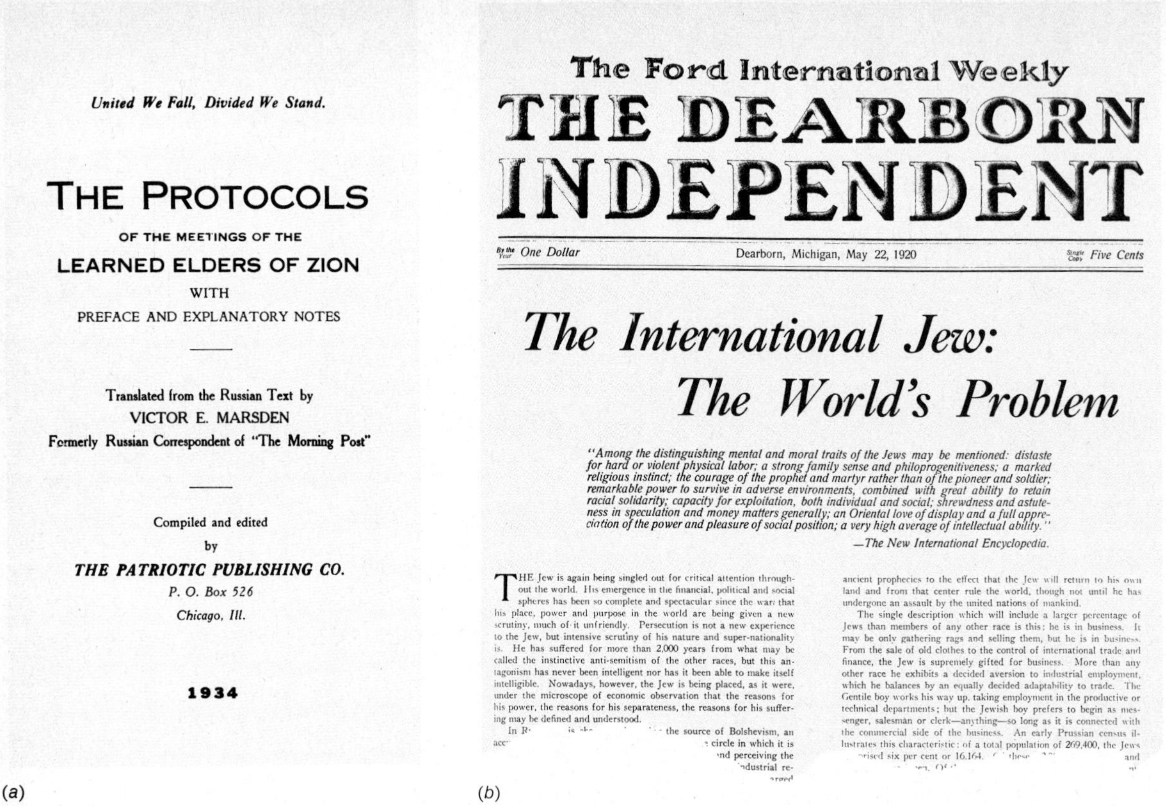

(a)

(b)

Figure 8.4 (a) *Title page of one of many editions of the bogus "Protocols," published in Chicago.* (b) *Henry Ford's* Dearborn Independent, *May 22, 1920: "The Jew is the world's enigma. Poor in his masses, he yet controls the world's finances." (Library of Congress)*

The single description which will include a larger percentage of Jews than members of any other race is this: he is in business. It may be only gathering rags and selling them, but he is in business. From the sale of old clothes to the control of international trade and finance, the Jew is supremely gifted for business. More than any other race he exhibits a decided aversion to industrial employment, which he balances by an equally decided adaptability to trade. . . . [From The Dearborn Independent, May 22, 1920, p. 1]

During the great depression of the early 1930s, economic and social conditions deteriorated around the world. The model of Nazism in Germany was copied by protofascist groups in many countries. According to Strong (1941), only five anti-Semitic organizations were founded in the United States between 1915 and 1932, nine were organized in 1933, but 105 emerged between 1934 and 1939, during the growth of Adolf Hitler's power in Europe. Although the political use of anti-Semitism in America never grew to the proportions it reached elsewhere, it did begin to show up in the 1930s at the highest levels of government. Rogow (1968, p. 348) points out that ". . . in the 1930's it was still possible for avowed anti-Semites to appear before congressional committees in opposition to the appointment of a Supreme Court Justice solely on the grounds that he was a Jew." The Jews were attacked publicly by two Congressmen, Representative Louis T.

McFadden and Senator Theodore Bilbo. However, the most prominent and influential voice of bigotry was that of Father Charles Coughlin, who, during the years between 1938 and 1942, preached to millions of Americans weekly through his radio broadcasts and newspaper. More than one hundred frankly anti-Semitic organizations were highly active and influential in the United States, although their importance seems to have dwindled after the outbreak of World War II. A major poet, Ezra Pound, gained notoriety by his obsessive concern with the evil of "usury," and during the war he broadcast in English from fascist Italy. While Franklin D. Roosevelt was President, administration policies were sometimes attacked by identification of them with Jewish advisers. Similar attacks have been directed against Presidents Truman, Eisenhower, and Kennedy.

During the depression, Jews faced many extralegal barriers to employment as white-collar workers, in business, in attempting entrance into colleges, graduate schools, and the professions. Often the only way to get a job for some Jews was to conceal their ethnic identity. A large proportion of private colleges and universities restricted Jewish admission, sometimes quite explicitly, and many still do unofficially. After World War II, such barriers receded sharply, though they have remained in various places, institutions, and fields. Surveys in the mid-1950s (Dean, 1955) suggest that Jews actually were being excluded from relatively few economic activities, the major exceptions being in certain segments of heavy industry and in the upper echelons of financial institutions (notably in the insurance business).

Again, one must remember that the problems of Jews and blacks are emphasized here as prototypical examples of what could be said about any other out-group minority similarly situated. We have only to look at the recent fate of Asians (from the Indian subcontinent) who have been expelled without recompense from Uganda, where they have lived for two or three generations, for the openly stated reason that they were too successful there economically and tended to control too much of the country's commerce. Many have been stripped of their citizenship and property. The expulsion was decreed by a modern-style military dictator who has expressed open admiration for Adolf Hitler (see the margin).

It is also noteworthy that minority out-groups often practice the same kind of conflict-based prejudice toward groups even further "out" that compete with them in hard times. Thus, German Jews arriving in North America during the depression as escapees from Hitler were often treated negatively by Jews already here, since the former entered into competition with them and endangered their rather precarious economic and social toehold. The fact that these German Jews

The real tragedy of Uganda is not the Asian problem, for that is Britain's tragedy rather than Uganda's. The real tragedy is that President Amin has been able in a very short time to unleash pent-up racist feelings among the public which observers of the Ugandan scene had thought were dead and gone. These racist feelings have provided the military government of Uganda with a base for popularity which it badly lacked and needed. But they will not solve any of the problems Uganda is faced with.

The Asians have been odd-men-out in East Africa. They are hated because they are thought to be industrious, wealthy, clannish; because they do not mix with Africans; because they cheat and bribe to advance their business; because they are smarter than Africans; because they are different; because they are Asian. But they will soon be gone from the Ugandan scene. The African will remain, and it is only then that the full scope of the Ugandan tragedy will be realized.

Already a number of prominent Ugandan Africans have disappeared. The former Chief of Staff in the Obote Government and one-time Uganda High Commissioner to Ghana, Brigadier Opoloto, has not been heard of for months. The Chief Justice, Mr. Kiwanuka, is gone. So is the vice chancellor of the country's only university. Disappearance as announced by the Government of Uganda is a euphemism for all kinds of things, including murder at the hands of soldiers. Because of the pervading insecurity and terror most of Uganda's intellectuals would dearly like to leave the country if they could do so without arousing the suspicions and anger of the trigger-happy army.

The long-term prospect for the country is bleak. Economically the current Asian crisis is disastrous for Uganda. The xenophobia which President Amin has aroused among average Ugandans is bound to boomerang, with painful consequences for everyone. That is the real tragedy of Uganda. [From H. Ng'weno, *The New York Times,* Nov. 9, 1972, p. 47]

were often better educated and of higher class standing than the predominantly Russian group already here did not help. The point is that group conflict is a social condition that commonly fuels prejudice, and this tendency is built into human social relations rather than being a property solely of any one group or nation.

Allport (1954, p. 227) has observed that prejudice is frequently intensified when the minority or out-group is large or densely packed rather than small or well-dispersed: "A single Japanese or Mexican child in a school room is likely to be a pet. But let a score move in, and they will certainly be set off from the remainder of the children, and in all probability be regarded as a threat." By the same token, the greatest antiblack prejudice exists where black density is greatest. It was, for example, slight in England before World War II, but has grown considerably to become a major feature of national politics with the immigration of large numbers of blacks from the West Indies and colored peoples from other parts of the British Commonwealth during the postwar period (Richmond, 1950). Here again we see an interesting link between population factors and social problems.

The case of women

What has been said above about economic and other forms of competition as fueling prejudice also applies to the efforts of women to change their traditional social and occupational roles away from the historically obligatory pattern of wife, mother, and homemaker. As in the case of the black, the effort at fighting sex discrimination in hiring and promotion also takes the form of affirmative action programs. In fact, protagonists of women's rights often draw an analogy, overdrawn I think in the light of the facts, between the plight of women and blacks, expressing this in the phrase "woman as nigger."

During the great depression of the 1930s, efforts by women to work outside the home commonly led to hostility on the part of men who were having trouble finding work. In our own times, to the extent that women move toward careers instead of or alongside of marriage, they enter into competition with men in general, and often with their husbands in particular. There are likely to be problems in respect to level of salary and in decision making as to whether the family is to live where the husband can find the most suitable work or where the wife can find an attractive job. In effect, with the female entry into occupational and career lines, the married couple no longer can count on a prescribed complementary division of labor, the husband having his affixed chores and the wife her different ones, and there is more potential for direct conflict between them in the roles that they wish to play. Such a situation increases tensions between the sexes not only because of the male's defense of what used to be his prerogatives, but because male and female must now compete for the same rights and privileges.

Among the most militant of women's leaders there has, in fact, been a tendency to maximize the potential conflict and hostility between the sexes, probably polarizing men and women on the issues of women's rights far more than should be necessary. Recently Susan Artandi (1972, p. 565) has noted this and made a plea for rational and temperate treatment of women's serious social aspirations:

It is a pity that the Women's Liberation Movement took the direction it did and acquired an image with which "liberated" as well as "unliberated" women quite frequently cannot identify. Rightly or wrongly, in the mind of the public "Women's Lib" tends to represent a group of sexually frustrated women trying to take revenge on men, whom they secretly admire but are unable to attract.

This image is a liability to the cause of women. Discrimination against women is a fact and a severe problem. Women's rights involve more significant matters than questions like who should wash the dishes. These are essentially private problems and should remain a matter of choice for the individual. What are important are such "public" problems as legal rights, equal pay for equal work, and protection against discrimination in getting jobs or promotions. . . .

Such basic rights for women as equal pay for equal work and equal opportunity in hiring and promotion are relatively explicit, although not necessarily clear-cut in every situation. Much more difficult to pin down are the subtle "put-downs" that men engage in when faced with women in professional or occupational environments. The intensity of the "put downs" seems to increase in direct proportion with the competence of the woman colleague involved.

Biological differences are also commonly cited by "male chauvinists" to justify the role of women in our society. Because women are obviously different from men physically (not only sexually, but in physical stature and strength), it is assumed that their traditional roles have been decreed by biology and not by lifelong socialization. It has been argued, for example, that women are less able to do what men do because menstrual activity leaves them periodically indisposed, both physically and psychologically. Similarly, the argument is often raised that the "confinement" of women in pregnancy and childbirth has made women somehow less suitable for executive career roles or in political leadership.

Indeed, the theme that "biology is destiny" is treated seriously in some scholarly discussions of women's role. It has been argued (Bardwick, 1971) that female physiology is overwhelmingly important in determining the motivational and

You know it's become almost impossible to talk accurately about relations between men and women because the whole thing has become so ideological. Everything fits into the ideological slots, and I don't think men and women are telling the truth any more. . . .

The young housewife with three little kids is not doing something inferior to her husband; she's doing something different. It was her choice and her own doing—and what's wrong with it?

If there are a lot of young housewives around that are bored, then they tend to reinforce each other. What lies at the bottom of such complaints is that life is very hard. What I object to is this notion that women have nothing to do with their own difficulties. Women are trying to get the moral credit for being a minority, when they simply aren't. They are equating their movement with the black movement, and I think it's just unholy for middle-class American women to equate themselves with blacks and say that they have been oppressed by society.

It's the undergraduate girls in the best Ivy League colleges who are saying that they have been discriminated against, and it's just a way of saying "Take it easy on me."

I suspect somebody who gets up all the time and talks about dirty diapers is not someone who is speaking from real experience. Motherhood has been reduced to a series of dirty jobs. There's nothing about the fun of it. And I pity the next generation of little children. [Midge Decter, as quoted by Deirdre Carmody, A critic offers views on women's lib. The New York Times, March 21, 1973, p. 47]

emotional components of women's personality, her intellectual functioning and style of life, and that new or alternative roles must be worked out by women around innate, biologically based needs. There are serious flaws in this argument, however (see Weisstein, 1971). Much of the evidence comes from animal studies in which attention has been focused on a few primate species where humanlike differences in sex role are found, while those primates in which marked differences are not found are ignored. Moreover, in most of the research observations on hormonal differences there is no dependable evidence whatever that they have any bearing on the execution of complex social and occupational roles in human society. It has not been demonstrated that innate physiological differences between men and women have significant bearing on the social roles they play. On the other hand, we saw earlier (Chapter 4) that conditioning and socialization have an important effect upon patterns of behavior, sexual and otherwise.

By the same token, and without any better evidence, some militant women's liberation leaders have argued (on the same grounds of inherent differences between male and female) that the world would be far more peaceful if women were in charge of nations instead of men, again suggesting a spurious biological basis for female gentleness and wisdom. Clearly, history has shown that women in authority can be as tough—and sometimes as violent—as men (Figure 8.5). There is simply not a shred of solid evidence that women are

"Woman's work is never done."

Figure 8.5   Prime Ministers Gandhi and Meir having a coffee klatch: one cartoonist's view of the theory that if liberated women ran the world instead of men, there would be universal peace. What do you think? (Drawing by Graysmith; © 1971 Chronicle Publishing Co.)

biologically either less or more able than men to play any important leadership role in the modern world. Any difference in physical strength is of little consequence in a technological-industrial world where mental agility and stamina are at a premium. Many women have these in abundance. Actually, the biological argument tends to be a rationalization for what has already been established in the way of male-female social roles, just as it is also used to justify the depressed social position of blacks. This is another example of the misleading use of biological concepts to justify given social patterns.

DISRUPTIVE EFFECTS OF SOCIAL CHANGE

As was noted in Chapter 5 rapid change may have a disrupting effect on society and the lives of people living within it. The existing social order is threatened, and this disruption intensifies intergroup suspicion and hostility. Minority outgroups are most vulnerable. During the collapse of Rome, attacks on the Christians became more common. Similarly, toward the end of the Middle Ages, when church authority was being challenged and the black plague was killing a third or more of the population, witch hunts and burnings at the stake became a familiar occurrence, wreaking havoc particularly among the mentally ill, who were victimized because they were unable to defend themselves. Their mere presence further frightened the already terrified populace (Figure 8.6).

Allport (1954, p. 224) summarizes this principle:

In times of calamities, such as flood, famine, or fire, all manner of superstitions and dread flourish, among them legends that minority groups are responsible for the disaster. For the forest fires that ravaged Maine in 1947, many citizens blamed the communists. Communists in Czechoslovakia returned the compliment in 1950 and blamed the failure of the potato crop on Americans who "released swarms of potato bugs" in that country. Whenever anxiety increases, accompanied by a loss of predictability in life, people tend to define their deteriorated situations in terms of scapegoats.

During the middle of the fourteenth century, within a two-year period in Europe, nearly 350 Jewish communities were exterminated, acts rationalized on the grounds that Jews were in league with the devil and had poisoned all the wells. This charge was connected with the black plague, which was extremely devastating and frightening. There was need for a scapegoat. The Jews evidently were less often struck down by the "Black Death," perhaps because of their rigidly prescribed dietary code and cleanliness, and many towns in the path of

(a)

(b)

(c)

The Wonders of the Invisible World:

Being an Account of the

TRYALS

OF

Several Witches,

Lately Excuted in

NEW-ENGLAND:

And of several remarkable.Curiosities therein Occurring.

Together with,

I. Observations upon the Nature, the Number, and the Operations of the Devils.

II. A short Narrative of a late outrage committed by a knot of Witches in Swede-Land, very much resembling, and so far explaining, that under which New-England has laboured.

III. Some Councels directing a due Improvement of the Terrible things lately done by the unusual and amazing Range of Evil-Spirits in New-England.

IV. A brief Discourse upon those Temptations which are the more ordinary Devices of Satan.

By COTTON MATHER.

Published by the Special Command of his EXCELLENCY the Governour of the Province of the Massachusetts-Bay in New-England.

Printed first, at Boston in New-England; and Reprinted at London, for John Dunton, at the Raven in the Poultry. 1693.

Figure 8.6 Two woodcuts, 1475: (a) Torture of Jews accused by the Holy Inquisition of heresy and practice of black magic. (b) Condemned heretics are carted away to be burned at the stake. (c) Title page of Cotton Mather's famous account of supposed witchcraft in New England that culminated in the hysterical witch hunt and execution of 20 people in Salem, Massachusetts, in 1692. Mather was a leading Puritan minister and prominent literary figure, son of the president of Harvard College. (Reproduced from Devils, Demons, Death and Damnation, *by Ernst and Johanna Lehner; © 1971 Dover Publications, Inc.)*

the plague attacked the Jews as potential well poisoners even before the plague struck.

There is one type of social crisis which sometimes seems to lessen rather than increase intergroup hostility, namely, periods when the whole society or nation is in great jeopardy from a common foe. Under these severe conditions, groups normally antagonistic to each other may lay aside their hostilities and come together to deal with the common enemy to forge, at least temporarily, a sense of unity and common purpose. That this is not always the case, however, is well illustrated by the Vietnam War, which rather than unifying the United States, produced great ruptures in what had been, at least on the surface, a relatively smoothly functioning social system. (Another exception is Russia during World War I. The disasters of that war only hastened the Bolshevik Revolution.)

Failure of United States government policy in Indo-China to unify the people may have arisen in part from the fact that many Americans were never convinced of the legitimacy of or necessity for the war. They felt no dire external threat. As a consequence, deep internal divisions developed, exacerbating ethnic, political, and social antagonisms. The reader should recognize that the key here is the degree of popular perception of great external danger; war is no antidote to disunity and intergroup hostility unless the foe is believed to menace the nation's very survival. Although it can under certain circumstances serve to unite people in a common cause, war can also divide them and intensify their antagonisms.

ASSIMILATION VERSUS MAINTENANCE OF GROUP IDENTITY

We saw in Chapter 4 that individuals are pressured to conform to the group's norms and values, and to preserve their independence individuals and subgroups must struggle against such pressure. Cultures usually press more or less openly for uniformity in language, custom, ways of thinking, and even religion, sometimes at pain of death or severe punishment. Under societal conditions in which the value of uniformity is strong, ethnic minorities are under great pressure to lose their identity and assimilate to the majority culture; under societal conditions favoring diversity (or *pluralism*), such pressures are weaker, though they are always present in subtle ways. Groups with distinctive traditions or characteristics must struggle with this conflict between maintenance of their own unique identity and assimilation to the larger culture.

The case of the Jews

Consider the example of the Jews during the nearly 2,000 years in which they have lived scattered in the Western world. In pagan Rome, under Emperor Hadrian (117–138 A.D.), there were edicts banning the study of Talmudic law, and scholars were not allowed to hold classes. On the other hand, Caracalla (211–217 A.D.) gave the Jews full Roman citizenship, and the religious nature of Judaism was later recognized formally, enabling Jews to practice their faith and live at peace, though not to proselytize, a practice, interestingly, they have never since embraced. The modern phase of anti-Semitism, in which religious doctrines played a vital part, began in 312 A.D. with the conversion to Christianity of Emperor Constantine, who soon made Christianity the official religion of the Roman Empire.

Severe anti-Semitic restrictions and oppressions were common throughout much of Europe during the Middle Ages, wherever the Holy Roman Church held sway. Christians were forbidden to convert to Judaism under penalty of death, and intermarriage was also declared a crime. At the same time, Jews were encouraged, sometimes forced, to convert to Christianity. Social interchange between Christians and Jews was closely regulated. Jews were often denied citizenship and excluded from any position of authority. The construction of synagogues was frequently banned.

Jewish life and culture nevertheless managed to survive in several parts of medieval Europe, North Africa, and Asia Minor, particularly in Italy, France, Visigothic Spain, and Byzantium, usually under marginal political, economic, and social conditions. More often than not, Jews were in the position of unwelcome aliens. It is often assumed that the constant pressure to which they were exposed as a group gave them a sense of ethnic solidarity against persecution. However, solidarity is not a necessary consequence of external pressures, since some groups collapse under such pressures. Thus, it is not really clear what it was in the mystical-ethical-religious tradition of Judaism that made such cultural survival possible.

Later, with the rise of Protestantism, the new sects were hardly more tolerant of outsiders than the Roman Catholics were before them. In 1543, after becoming convinced that the Jews would by and large not convert to Christianity, Martin Luther (cited in Rogow, 1968) wrote:

> What then shall we Christians do with this damned rejected race of Jews? . . . Let me give you my honest advice. First, their synagogues or churches should be set on fire. . . . Secondly, their homes should likewise be broken down and destroyed. . . . Thirdly, they should be deprived of their prayer books. . . . Fourthly, their rabbis must be forbidden under threat of death to teach any more. . . . Fifthly, passport and traveling privileges should be absolutely forbidden. . . . Sixthly, they ought to be stopped from usury. . . . Seventhly, let the young and strong Jews and Jewesses be given the flail, the ax, the hoe, the spade, the distaff, and spindle, and let them earn their bread by the sweat of their noses. . . . Let us drive them out of the country for all time. . . .

Much later, in the nineteenth century, although official anti-Semitism lessened in western Europe, it remained unabated in the Russian Empire. Although Jews had been prevented from crossing the Russian borders, Russian imperial expansion had taken over areas of eastern Europe in which millions of Jews lived. This area became known as the Pale of Settlement. Here their rights were again limited, their mobility restricted, and they were seriously discriminated against in other ways by official decree. For example, Czar Nicholas I in 1827 decreed that although Jews could receive none of the privileges of citizenship, they had an obligation for military service double that of any others, that is, a period of 25 years, and strenuous efforts were made to force them to convert to Christianity. To this end they were limited to eating pork (a food forbidden according to the Mosaic code) for long periods and compelled to perform Christian rites. (The reader will recall that conversion to Christianity was also part of the punishment meted out by the Venetian court to Shylock, a penalty portrayed as eminently just and sound. Conversion was also demanded, under threat of the Inquisition, in fifteenth-century Spain.) Describing the Russian pattern of anti-Semitism, Parkes (1939, pp. 82–83) wrote:

Down to the end of Tsardom she [Russia] remained determined to exclude this unwanted mass from penetration into the old provinces of Russia. A new kind of ghetto was created in the form of a series of provinces along the western frontier in which the Jews were compelled to live, and even within these provinces their rights of settlement and choice of occupation were severely restricted. Outside of these provinces selected categories of Jews might reside, visit certain fairs, and, provided they did not exceed a small proportion of the total enrollment, study at the universities. . . . [The Pale of Settlement] contained more than a half of the Jewish population of the world.

Conditions in the Pale, always oppressive, deteriorated markedly during the Russo-Japanese War, which ended in a disastrous collapse of the czarist forces and led to the unsuccessful Revolution of 1905. It is thought that dissemination of the fake *Protocols of the Elders of Zion,* discussed earlier, was part of a czarist attempt to deflect public wrath from the inept government and lay blame for the military debacle on "International Jewry" and its plots. Bloody pogroms (notably at Kishinev, Moldavia, in 1905) hastened the mass emigration of Jews to America.

The "melting pot"

A similar conflict between pressure for assimilation and the need to maintain group identity has existed in the United States among most ethnic groups, perhaps even more strikingly because this country is so much more of a "melting pot" of diverse ethnic and racial groups than most. Immigrants came to a land in which the cultural tradition was one of assimilation, and the main port of entry, New York City, was a place where foreigners ultimately were expected to lose their ethnic identity and become "Americans." The "melting" process seems to have involved several stages and diverse routes. It has been suggested that there is a strong tendency for the diverse ethnic groups in the United States to assimilate into four main "ethnoid segments," namely, white Protestant, Roman Catholic, "colored," and Jewish, although all four segments still press toward assimilation to the dominant white Protestant milieu (A. Lee, 1951).

It was once widely assumed that full assimilation was both inevitable and desirable. Second- and third-generation children manifested impatience whenever they saw evidence in their parents of "old country" ways, any ideas, values, customs, speech patterns and accents, gestures, and other qual-

(a)

(b)

Figure 8.7 The Lower East Side, New York City, at the height of mass immigration from eastern Europe: (a) Orchard Street, 1898. (b) Tenement room, 1910. (a: The Byron Collection; b: Jacob A. Riis Collection—both from Museum of the City of New York)

ities that marked the older generation as coming from an alien culture. During the height of mass immigration, there were especially strong efforts to get children in the public schools to unlearn "old" ethnic speech habits and to acquire instead the "proper" way to speak American English. On the other hand, many immigrants resisted such assimilation or felt regret at the progressive loss of their ethnic traditions.

It has become increasingly obvious that, in spite of the prevalence of the "melting pot" idea (Figure 8.7), ethnic groups in the United States have to a surprising degree retained their identity, and there are some cities where sharp lines of cleavage continue to exist between the Irish, Italian, Polish, and other ethnic communities. Such distinctions are recognized by local and national politicians who make concerted efforts to capture the "ethnic" vote. Although there has been some assimilation by such groups, this has not, as once anticipated, abolished ethnic in-group and out-group conflicts, or the prejudice associated with them. Everywhere one looks in the world, such conflict exists, sometimes even leading to open warfare (as in Northern Ireland, Bangladesh, Nigeria, or the Middle East).

The case of American blacks

The dilemma of assimilation versus maintenance of ethnic identity extends also to the black American who is torn between the wish to become a full-fledged part of the dominant white Protestant culture and the strong recent pressures of many blacks toward complete separatism and the strengthening of their Afro-American identity. To date, the several attempts at governmental desegregation have not been particularly effective, and in a society where color still serves widely as a barrier to social interaction the need for a strong sense of black ethnic identity remains. The black American is learning to view his blackness (and with it his entire cultural heritage) as a virtue to be preserved and admired.

Life of the black man in America today cannot be properly understood without reference to this struggle to find his own ethnic identity. The key historical event in this case is slavery. The slave trade is what brought most blacks to the United States, and from the outset it strongly conditioned the attitudes of white Americans and black Americans alike. The history of slavery itself offers an appalling episode of human exploitation and brutality. This ugliness of the human heart did not begin with the American version, and it is instructive to realize that slavery as a worldwide institution is as old as earliest antiquity, having been practiced extensively, for example, in ancient China, Egypt, Greece, and Rome. Although slave capture had been traditional in African tribal warfare, onset of the massive slave trade to the Americas in the sixteenth century wreaked havoc with patterns of life in Africa (see the margin). This victimization and dehumanization continued for 350 years and trade in men, women, and children was still practiced in the American South up to the Civil War, not much more than a century ago.

Consider the psychological effects of slavery on the individual. A slave was transported from his homeland far across the ocean, usually in chains and under terribly crowded conditions (Figure 8.8). Roughly two-thirds of the slaves perished on the way. Those who arrived had first to be "broken in" or "seasoned" to the slave system. Each became the personal property of his owner. He was systematically stripped of any link with his past, any sense of personal identity, even of all family ties or tradition. Within a few generations much of his cultural heritage, his language, religion, and folklore, even his origins and history, had vanished under the pressure of the slave system. The American slave was not protected, as was the feudal serf of Europe or even the South American peon, against the excesses of absolute power. Regardless of whether a slave was treated well or ill on any given plantation, his only real reason for being was his owner's profit; he was chattel, private property (like our autos and household appliances) to be used as his master saw fit.

Economic forces were of primary importance in the rise of the slavery system in America. As Gunnar Myrdal (1944) has pointed out, in the early days of slavery tobacco, rice, and indigo crops barely managed to support the plantation economy, and the future of the slavery system was in doubt. And at that time, even in the first two decades of the nineteenth century, the abolitionist movement (against slavery) was as strong in the South as it was in the North. However, the emergence of cotton as a great money crop, facilitated by the invention of the cotton gin, made large-scale cotton plantations profitable. In 1794, in the year before the cotton gin was patented, only 500,000 pounds of cotton were exported to Europe; however, 10 years later 40 million pounds were exported; and by 1850, the figure had risen to over one billion pounds (Figure 8.9). Cotton was "King." The commitment to slavery was thus renewed and belief in its necessity for the economic well-being of the South was solidified until it could no longer be shaken except by a major cataclysm, the Civil War. And much later, long after slavery had been abolished, cheap indentured labor was still being imported from China, Japan, and Mexico on "contract."

The many justifications provided for slavery did not of course stress these economic factors, but were rationalizations that slavery was quite compatible with democracy and the Bible, that it was biologically natural, that the Negro was subhuman anyway. Similar rationales about Aryan racial su-

REMARKS

ON THE

METHODS of PROCURING SLAVES

WITH A SHORT ACCOUNT OF THEIR

TREATMENT in the WEST-INDIES, &c.

THE respectable and increasing numbers of those, who, from motives of Humanity, have concurred in rejecting the produce of West-Indian Slavery, cannot but afford a subject of the sincerest joy to every friend of mankind. Even those who from motives of Interest still favor or engage in the Trade, have been obliged to be silent upon the injustice of first procuring the Negroes, and have not had the hardiness to excuse or palliate the horrors of MIDDLE PASSAGE: but still they assert that the Slaves meet with in the West-Indies... lances their previous ... e tol a state of f... ... m, and

HAVING now described the state of the plantation, it will be proper to say a few words on that of the IN and OUT-DOOR Slaves.

THE IN-DOOR Slaves are allowed to ... and fed, and less worked, than the ... however of being constantly ... caprice of their Masters an ... ... o wretched, that ... ... e field: the o ...

(a)

(b)

(c)

(d)

(e)

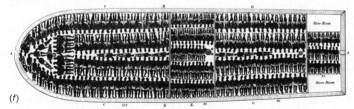

(f)

Figure 8.8 Transport of slaves in the eighteenth century: (a) Yoking of captured slaves for march to ports. (b) Mouthpiece and necklace, with hooks, to prevent escape when pursued in woods. (c) Leg bolts. (d) Dealer places his red-hot brand on purchased "property." (e) Punishment. (f) The hellish "middle passage" across the ocean. (a-e: Rare Book Division, New York Public Library, Astor, Lenox and Tilden Foundations; f: Schomburg Center for Research in Black Culture, New York Public Library, Astor, Lenox and Tilden Foundations)

periority were offered by Hitler and his cohorts for their systematic extermination of Slavs, Jews, Gypsies, and others. As a matter of fact, one of the most common ways to justify mistreatment of people is to dehumanize them. (We shall examine the various racist "biological" arguments shortly.)

Stanley Elkins (1959, 1961) has pointed up the features of slavery in the United States that made it particularly destructive to the human personality, even after legal emancipation during the Civil War. He contrasts the North American brand of slavery with the Latin American variety. Physical

Figure 8.9 When "King Cotton" reigned: (a) A day's work ended in the antebellum South. (b) Not much appears to have changed some 60 years later, in this painting of sharecroppers on a Mississippi plantation, 1906. (c) Sketch of slaves dancing to music, drawn from life by Lewis Miller in Lynchburg, Virginia, 1853. (a: Drawing by Matt Morgan; b: Library of Congress; c: Virginia State Library)

conditions in the Caribbean islands and parts of South America like Brazil and the Guianas might have been a bit worse, and treatment of the slave as an individual was perhaps more severe than in North America. But, says Elkins, in the Latin American case the issue was only physical cruelty to man, while in North America the slave was treated legally, morally, and psychologically as a creature who was not even human. Slaves in Latin America could buy their own freedom and could hold property and work for themselves part of the time, thus mitigating some of the demoralization and dehumanization produced by servitude. If he performed some meritorious service or if he had been severely mistreated, a slave might even be freed by an official. He could celebrate an anniversary or marriage in the planter's family. In short, he was not totally stripped of his sense of self and was still capable of choosing, within limited alternatives, how he might conduct his life, and he could thus feel some responsibility for his choices. In contrast, the North American slave was in marked danger of losing what little sense of personal identity he might have retained after his separation from his ethnic roots, and thus he was much more dehumanized by the practices of slavery. Therefore, when the institution was legally abolished in countries like Brazil, the social transition was smoother and more an extension of existing patterns, whereas in North America emancipation was an abrupt reversal to which adjustment was particularly difficult and without precedent.

This past has left the North American black without a clear social identity. He has not been assimilated into the white culture and ethos, and he must struggle to find a sense of self in which he can feel proud and independent.

The "double bind" for ethnic out-groups

All such struggles for ethnic identity tend to create a double bind, a situation with no easy solution for the minority out-group. On the one hand, the dominant majority resists efforts at assimilation; but when members of the minority group respond by attempting to retain and reinforce their own self-image (language or dialect, culture, religion, life style, behavior, and dress) they are pressured to submerge their uniqueness and be more like the dominant group.* As Allport (1954, p. 240) has noted in a brilliant passage, the dominant group is thus saying:

"We don't want you to be like us, but you must not be different." What is the minority to do? Negroes are blamed for being ignorant and also for seeking an education to raise their status; Jews are criticized . . . for being seclusive and for being intrusive. The Afrikaner wants total *apartheid* but is reluctant to give the Bantu people

---

*In modern Soviet Russia, Jews are prevented from practicing fully their religion, and yet their identity cards specify that they are of the Jewish "nationality." They are not allowed to emigrate to Israel in any substantial numbers. Recently when there seemed to be some relaxation of this restriction, a brutally high emigration tax was imposed, rationalized on the premise that each person owed the state what it cost to educate him. Russian Jews are thus pressed to lose their *religious* identity but forced to retain their *ethnic* identity in a society where they feel increasingly unwelcome.

the territory and political independence that alone would make total *apartheid* possible. Immigrants to America have found themselves abused both for maintaining their cultures and for pressing for assimilation. Minorities are damned if they seek assimilation, damned if they don't.

The foregoing discussion has tended to look at the question of assimilation versus pluralism only from the point of view of the minorities. But the majority too is constantly undergoing some degree of assimilation by adopting aspects of the minority cultures. For instance, numerous expressions from black "hip" talk and Yiddish have entered American colloquial speech; black music and Jewish humor are vital components of American life. Culture is a continually changing thing. And although each ethnically plural society, with its own special combinations of groups and influences, will handle the amalgam in different ways, the polarity between assimilation pressures and a tendency to preserve diversity is always present. Only in a society without differentiable elements or hierarchical structure, were such a thing possible, would intergroup tensions be totally absent. Where there is social diversity, there is always fertile ground for growth of group conflict and prejudice. Man will only resolve this dilemma when he learns to appreciate the advantages of living in a world of cultural diversity, creating an environment in which people of many kinds can pull together harmoniously. This will not be at all easy.

GROUP DIFFERENCES AND PREJUDICE

Along with the societal patterns described above, certain visible characteristics of target groups also play an important role in prejudice. This aspect of prejudice is of no small importance, since those who hold prejudicial attitudes typically regard such racial or ethnic characteristics as fundamental to their negative feelings and actions.

Group visibility

It is obviously difficult to act discriminatorily against a group if its members cannot be readily identified. Thus, the *visibility* of the target group creates an important social condition for prejudice (see Note 8.3). Anything that sets a group off as distinctive helps make it a target for prejudice, be it skin color, facial features, language, speech patterns, dress, form of worship, gestures, social outlook, or style of living. Sometimes special badges have had to be worn for purposes of identification of an ethnic minority (as in the case of Jews

Note 8.3

Visibility of target groups should not be considered *the* social cause of prejudice, though of course it is a causal condition in the sense that unless a group can be easily distinguished, it cannot be isolated and attacked. Here again we see an instance of how important it is to recognize the multiple determination of psychological events, a theme developed earlier in Note 2.1. A combination of conditions is required to produce prejudice. Group visibility is certainly a factor, but this alone is not enough.

around 1200 A.D. in Spain under the Inquisition, and later in Nazi Germany).

Although Jews do not comprise a race in any biological sense of the word, there are often visible traces of their Mediterranean origins. Probably more important in making them visible as members of an out-group are ethnic habits of facial expression and gesture (body language). Some interesting research has been done on whether people can pick out Jews and non-Jews in photos (Figure 8.10). The evidence (see All-

Figure 8.10 (a) Can you pick out the Semites from other ethnic groups in this photo? If you rely on costume alone, you will be deceived. (b–f) Now that you have had practice, can you spot which are the Jews in these five photos? Answer: All are. (a: United Nations; b–f: Israel Office of Information)

(a)

(b)

(c)

(d)

(e)

(f)

port and Kramer, 1946; Lindzey and Rogolsky, 1950) suggests that to some degree at least Jews can be identified from appearance. But Allport (1954) points out that this applies to only about 55 percent of Jewish individuals in the photos, meaning that nearly half would be misclassified. There is also some contradictory evidence (Carter, 1948), but the results may depend on the mix of faces from which the selection is made as well as on the sample of people doing the selecting. Success would surely be lower were Syrian and Jewish faces intermingled, since these groups share some physical characteristics in common, than were Jewish faces mixed with those of northern Europeans. But even so, there has been sufficient genetic admixture among the Jewish people over 2,000 years of dispersal to make any photographic identification extremely difficult.

A finding even more interesting than the above is that people prejudiced toward Jews are better able to identify them from a mixture of faces of Jews and non-Jews than people who are not prejudiced, who are probably less sensitive to ethnic details. The prejudiced person pays attention to things which are of little or no consequence to someone who is unprejudiced or "color blind," so to speak, to ethnic distinctions. By the same token, many Jews tend to feel that they can tell a Jew from a non-Jew, although this ability probably depends more on cultural and behavioral characteristics than on physical ones. People of most groups can usually recognize their "own kind" by cues invisible to others.

The concept of race

Racist notions were not evident in European anti-Semitism until around the late nineteenth century, when the myth of "Aryan" racial purity and the racial inferiority of the Jew was added to traditional anti-Semitism. This racial view did not actually become important until the rise of Adolf Hitler in Germany in the 1930s. Hitler borrowed the notion of racial inferiority and superiority from nineteenth century writers, using it skillfully for political purposes in a society already disposed to support such modes of thought. The success and failure of peoples were explained in Hitler's *Mein Kampf* (1940) by "race," and quite similar notions of the importance of racial "purity" and basic inferiority of "mongrelized" peoples are still around today.

For the person prejudiced against the black, the mere presence of dark skin color instantly mobilizes a set of negative stereotypical judgments. What is interesting about this is not the obsession with skin pigmentation, which is no longer a very important genetic trait in terms of evolution (see Chapter 1), but the *rationalization* of such prejudice on the basis of widely

In opposition to [the bourgeois and the Marxist-Jewish worlds], the folkish philosophy finds the importance of mankind in its basic racial elements. In the state it sees only a means to an end and construes its end as the preservation of the racial existence of man. Thus, it by no means believes in an equality of races, but along with their difference it recognizes their higher or lesser value and feels itself obligated to promote the victory of the better and stronger, and demand the subordination of the inferior and weaker in accordance with the eternal will that dominates this universe. Thus, in principle, it serves the basic aristocratic idea of nature and believes in the validity of this law down to the last individual. [From Hitler, 1943 ed., p. 8]

believed but totally erroneous theories of race and adaptation. We shall now examine the concept of race in its scientific sense so that we can view these racist notions in perspective.

Race as a biological category

Scientists agree that only *one human species* exists, although it may come in many varieties. These are called *races*. Such subgroups of the species *Homo sapiens* probably developed because some peoples were more or less separated by geographic and cultural barriers and were therefore *reproductively isolated*. In other words, they bred only or mainly with their own group. The human biological traits that were emphasized by this inbreeding depended on the environmental conditions under which the group lived, and qualities useful for successful adaptation within a given environment were thereby emphasized. You will recall from Chapter 1 that through natural selection dark skins were especially adaptive in equatorial zones having much sunlight, while light skins were more adaptive mainly in the northern regions lacking sunshine. Such biological differences grew out of the isolation of mating groups within certain delimited areas in which environmental conditions favored some traits over others. Several other genetic processes were involved in the evolution of racial traits among isolated mating groups, but natural selection is clearly the most important.

This conception of race as a subspecies that has developed distinctive biological characteristics through inbreeding and the process of natural selection under particular environmental conditions invites us to ask four fundamental questions (Pettigrew, 1964): (1) Are there any "pure" races in the world today? (2) What is the effect of racial mixing? (3) How many races are there? (4) Most important of all, are some races "superior" to others? This last question, of course, touches at the center of the main rationalization for prejudice.

Are there any "pure" races? Geneticists believe that the same asortment of genes (hereditary units) are found in all the races of mankind. All groups of men can interbreed, hence they are of one species. Complete geographic isolation is virtually impossible today, and by and large throughout history mankind has wandered and drifted about, constantly intermingling genetically. Although a group may tend to breed within itself because of preference or social taboos, no existent group appears to have been sufficiently isolated in its mating patterns for a long enough time to have evolved a set of genes that do not overlap heavily with all other groups. Had such isolation occurred to produce a distinctive genetic group, that group would by now no longer be able to interbreed with the others and there would be two species of *Homo* extant on this planet, not one. Thus, there are no "pure" races.

Nowhere is this mixing more true than in North and South America (including the United States), which are major biological melting pots. In countries like Brazil there is a remarkable mixture of white, black, Amerindian, and (recently) Japanese stock. Even though there are stiffer social sanctions against interracial sexual relations in the United States, Caucasian genes have for a long time been spreading substantially into the nonwhite American population, and vice-versa. At first this was largely a one-way street, with white genes passing into the black population and with all mulattoes being defined as Negro. Eventually, however, as light mulattoes began to "pass" as whites, the flow also began to go from black to white. Geneticist Curt Stern (1954) has maintained, as a matter of fact, that if there were full intermingling of blacks and whites in the United States, the darker skin shades would all but disappear without any noticeable change in the color of Caucasians. This is because the black 11 or 12 percent of the nation would be "inundated by a white sea," although those who inveigh against miscegenation (racial mixing) appear generally to believe the opposite.

Genetic investigations have attempted to estimate the main genetic influences to which the American black has been exposed, using physical-anthropological evidence and blood groupings to chart the intermixtures. From this work it has been estimated that today between 22 and 29 percent of the black American gene pool (the total available assortment of genes) is non-Negroid. The usually accepted ancestral figures are that roughly 15 percent of blacks in this country had more white than black ancestors, about 25 percent had about equal number of Caucasian and Negroid ancestors, and about 32 percent had more black than white ancestors. Also, it has been stated that about a quarter of American blacks have one or more Indian forebears. (The latter figure may be too high, however, on the basis of recent serological techniques; the main point concerning Caucasian-Negro mixing of genes is not seriously challenged by geneticists.) Clearly the American black is a mixture of several genetic influences, the Caucasian background itself being an admixture of many European strains, and the Negro genes stemming from many different African peoples. This resulting mixture has led some anthropologists even to regard the American Negro as a distinctive racial grouping, different from the African Negro. Pettigrew points out, ironically, that in spite of this heterogeneity of the American blacks' ancestry, the definition of his biological identity is based on the presence of even the slightest trace of Negro genes in his background. Thus, no matter how many Caucasian genes may be present, any known trace of Negro ancestry

Blood mixture and the resultant drop in the racial level is the sole cause of the dying out of old cultures; for men do not perish as a result of lost wars, but by the loss of that force of resistance which is contained only in pure blood. All who are not of good race in this world are chaff. [From Hitler, 1943 ed., p. 43]

makes the person black, leading to the sardonic black comment that "Negro blood must be real powerful stuff if it can over-whelm any amount of white blood."

What is the effect of racial mixing? Racists have long as-sumed that there was such a thing as human racial purity, based presumably on analogies with breeding of "thor-oughbred" animals (horses, dogs, cats, and such). Racial mix-ing (or "mongrelization," as racists like to call it) is considered damaging to the "superior" strains of mankind they claim exist, since it is assumed that inferior hybrid stock will dilute superior pure stock. Actually, geneticists (Stern, 1954) widely believe that just the opposite is true. In other species cross-breeding is generally advantageous in adaptation, resulting in especially sturdy and robust specimens. And, on the contrary, continuous inbreeding within a narrowly confined group is known to maximize the incidence of maladaptive traits; for ex-ample, hemophilia (a hereditary "bleeding" disease that in-volves failure of the blood-clotting mechanism) is prevalent in European royal families, among whom intermarriage be-tween first cousins has been frequent for many generations. So much for human thoroughbreds.

There do appear to be diseases that are more common among certain racial groups than among others, and some of these have a genetic basis. For example, blacks have a higher incidence of sickle-cell anemia than do whites. This trait arose in parts of the world where malaria is common (and where more blacks live), and it turns out that sickle-cell anemia in those regions can be quite adaptive biologically when it is inherited from one parent rather than two, since then it is usually not fatal and yet provides a blood defense against malaria. However, hereditary diseases of the blood are not the prerogative of any one race, and whites too have their Achilles' heels in this regard. Whites whose geographical origin is the Mediterranean area show a high incidence of another blood disease known as thalassemia, which also provides protection against the malaria parasite. Moreover, many diseases appear to be more common in a particular racial group, such as tuberculosis in the American black, but this is largely the result of poor diet and generally bad environmental conditions. Tu-berculosis is a disease of poverty, and poverty is found in a larger proportion of blacks than of whites in our society. But whites have a greater hereditary disposition to some other diseases, such as leukemia. All this shows that the concept of "inferior stock" is not applicable in medical terms to any race. For those to whom "mongrelization" is a threat, the complex biological facts are twisted and distorted. They ignore negative genetic traits in their own group while centering on those of the rejected group.

The solution is given in the Bible (Isaiah 13:14). The Negro must be sent back to Africa, and race-mixing will automatically stop. There was a divine purpose in the Negro being brought to this land to learn, and return to help the people in his native land. I feel that millions of Negros are beginning to feel their divine call to return to their homeland, and that they, as well as Whites, will soon begin to besiege Congress for funds for a mass exodus to Africa. With repatrization [sic] accomplished, there still remains the Jew—the spurious "Chosen One."

He will continue to agitate and make trouble, but in the end he will be defeated. Why? Because it is written that the TRUE Israelite, the White Man, will triumph. [From D. K. Stacey, Race mixing is anti-Christian! National Chronicle, Dec. 21, 1972, p. 1]

How many races are there?　Anthropologists have not been able to agree on the number of *racial groups* existing in mankind for two simple reasons: (*a*) as we saw earlier, there are no pure races; (*b*) any simple classification based on one trait fails when other traits are considered. The mating patterns of thousands of years have produced a single species of man with a huge variety of overlapping subtypes rather than a small number of pure, isolated groups (see Ashley Montagu, 1964). The distinguished geneticist, Theodosius Dobzhansky (1962, p. 254) has written about the classificatory confusion as follows:

. . . skin color is obviously not the only trait in which people differ. Some people have straight hair; some have prominent and thin and others broad and flat noses, thin or thick or everted lips; some are tall and others short or pigmy; some have long, others intermediate, and still others round heads. If the variations in all these traits paralleled each other, race classification would be strengthened. But they frequently do not: for example, some people in southern India

Figure 8.11　(a) Ethiopian woman from an inland village where the inhabitants have been cut off from the rest of the country for centuries by high mountain ranges. (b) Togolese children. (c) A policewoman directs traffic in Libreville, Gabon. (d) Primary-school students in Mauritania. (e) Now that you have seen some "typical" Africans, consider the genetic mix at this baseball game in Havana, Cuba. Are you now ready to specify just what is the "Negroid" racial type? (a–d: United Nations; e: J. Alex Langley; DPI)

(a)

(b)

(c)

(d)

(e)

have very dark skin but straight or wavy hair, and the Bushmen in South Africa have peppercorn hair but yellowish skin. A race classification made on the basis of the hair shape would be different from that based on skin color or height or head shape.

Therefore, it is no surprise that there is little agreement about racial classification, the number of races ranging from three (Caucasoid, Negroid, and Mongoloid) to several dozen. All schemes of classification emphasize the existence of great overlap between the races, and there are many marginal types that do not fit neatly into any of the general categories (Figure 8.11). Race thus remains a *relative* rather than an absolute concept. This does not mean that obvious differences in distribution of human physical traits cannot be found throughout the world or that groups having a long history of relative genetic isolation do not differ in some biological characteristics. Eskimos and Australian Aborigines are easily differentiated, but they are both clearly members of the *one human race*.

What is called into question here is the utility of such subgroupings for social purposes. As Pettigrew (1964, p. 59) puts it:

"Race has been called "man's most dangerous myth." Strange, that a scientific term should develop such lethal political and social implications. Yet the darker pages of Western history relate the story: race has been employed as a popular rationalization for slavery, for colonial domination, for segregation, for gas-chamber extermination.

Race is a loose biological concept that has been distorted in the service of certain pernicious social doctrines and aims. As a biological category it has some limited measure of utility. As a concept on which to structure society it is dangerous rubbish.

Are some races "superior" to others?   The key issue, of course, is the recurrent theme of *racial superiority and inferiority*. We must address head-on the question of whether or not there are racial differences of any importance to the capacity of peoples to adapt successfully. The important arena in which this question has been debated is that of *intelligence*. The literature on this question, particularly as regards blacks and whites in the United States, is a huge one, and it is possible here only to point up a few of the highlights. The reader is urged to consult the list of suggested readings at the end of this chapter for more complete discussions.

Again and again research has shown that black Americans, on the average, score more poorly than whites on standard tests of intelligence, and it has been argued from this evidence that blacks are innately inferior to whites. Theoretically speaking, this could be the case. However, the overwhelming opinion in psychology, sociology, and anthropology is that although black Americans do more poorly than whites on intelligence tests, this is probably not the result of innate differences in ability, but rather stems from societal inequities putting blacks at a severe disadvantage in relation to whites. The arguments hinge on the following interrelated considerations: Any test comparing different groups in innate intelligence must be able to assume that such groups have had equivalent backgrounds, because intellectual functioning depends on the complex interplay of both hereditary and environmental factors. In the case of the black and white American this assumption simply cannot be made; it is clearly violated by the socioeconomic and educational circumstances of a very high percentage of blacks from babyhood onward. Thus, any observed differences in intellectual performances cannot be said to stem from differences in the "races" but could well arise from the different social conditions under which blacks and white live. It has been clearly shown in research that when blacks migrate from the rural South to the cities of the North, for example, they show regular increases in intelligence test performance with each year of their stay, and that these changes cannot readily be attributed to selective migration (that is, to the migration North of only superior blacks). Moreover, in a number of studies, northern blacks have exceeded the performance of southern whites. Thus, environmental deprivation has limited the performance of many southern whites just as it has in the case of a larger proportion of blacks. Also embarrassing to the racist assumption that differences in performance on intelligence tests signify innate differences due to race or heredity is the fact that the degree of white ancestry in the black has no bearing on his test score. Thus, among intellectually superior blacks, the proportion of their white ancestry is not higher than it is in the total black American population.

This does not mean that intelligence does not have a large hereditary component. The evidence is overwhelming that it does, just as it is also partly a product of one's life experience (see Lazarus, 1969, Chapter 8, for an elementary discussion of this). To say that there is no evidence of significant racial differences in innate adaptive potential is not to say that when two black children (or white children) come into the world they have exactly the same intellectual potential. Each individual inherits his own set of mental and physical characteristics from his forebears; experience of living teaches the child how to meet and master the conditions of his life. There are no adequate grounds for assuming that such hereditary potential differs significantly in degree, or even in kind, among the so-called races of the world.

Most tests of intelligence have been developed and standardized for use with whites and hence are most compatible with the kinds of experiences and values common to whites. A white child is thus better prepared to do well on tests of intelligence, both in his language patterns, concepts, social experience, and social motives. Conversely, a black child grows up with a set of experiences that ill fit him to handle the tasks used in tests to assess intellectual competance. In other words, some of what is measured by intelligence tests has little to do with innate ability but rather reflects patterns of thinking and reacting indigenous to the school-oriented, achievement-related social context in which many white children live.

Consider what would happen if intelligence tests were constructed to reflect the vocabulary and life experience characteristic of the black ghetto rather than of middle-class white America. Just such a set of items has been constructed by Adrian Dove, a social worker in the Watts district of Los Angeles, and is produced in part in Table 8.2. It will be in-

Table 8.2

Sample items from the intelligence test devised by Dove to emphasize the black experience[a]

1. A "Gas Head" is a person who has a
   a. Fast moving car
   b. Stable of lace
   c. "Process"
   d. Habit of stealing cars
   e. Long jail record for arson

2. If you throw the dice and 7 is showing on the top, what faces down?
   a. Seven
   b. Snake eyes
   c. Boxcars
   d. Little Joe
   e. Eleven

3. In "C. C. Rider," what does "C. C." stand for?
   a. Civil Service
   b. Church Council
   c. Country Circuit preacher
   d. Country Club
   e. Cheatin' Charlie (The Boxcar Gunsel)

4. Cheap "chitlings" (not the kind you purchase at a frozen-food counter) will taste rubbery unless they are cooked long enough. How soon can you quit cooking them to eat and enjoy?
   a. 15 minutes
   b. 2 hours
   c. 24 hours
   d. 1 week (on a low flame)
   e. 1 hour

5. "Hully Gully" came from
   a. East Oakland
   b. Fillmore
   c. Watts
   d. Harlem
   e. Motor City

6. A "handkerchief head" is
   a. A cool cat
   b. A porter
   c. An Uncle Tom
   d. A hoddi
   e. A preacher

7. "You've got to get up early in the morning if you want to . . ."
   a. Catch the worms
   b. Be healthy, wealthy, and wise
   c. Try to fool me
   d. Fare well
   e. Be the first one on the street

8. If a pimp is up tight with a woman who is on the state, what does he mean when he talks about "Mother's Day"?
   a. Second Sunday in May
   b. Third Sunday in June
   c. First of every month
   d. First and fifteenth of every month
   d. None of these

[a] From A. Dove, unpublished material. Correct answers are given upside down as follows:

1-d, 2-a, 3-c, 4-c, 5-e, 6-c, 7-e, 8-c.

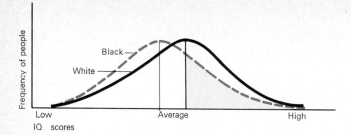

Figure 8.12 Typical I.Q. test distribution with 25 percent overlap.

structive for the reader to try to answer these multiple-choice items, especially if he is white. Unless he has intimate experience with the black setting and black slang, he will find the questions mystifying and at best will be only able to make wild guesses; those growing up within this setting will have little difficulty. (The correct answers to the items in Table 8.2 are presented at the end of the table.) Does this mean that blacks are more intelligent than whites? They certainly are better informed about their own environment and better versed in their form of colloquial English. Any conclusion as to comparative intelligence based on this test would be highly dubious, and yet precisely this sort of reasoning has predominated in interpretations of most test data in favor of whites.

Moreover, although a difference in *average* performance is usually found between black and white populations on standard intelligence (I.Q.) tests, there is usually very substantial overlap between the two groups—some blacks will score higher than most Caucasians. In Figure 8.12 a typical set of test score distributions is shown with a roughly 25 percent overlap between blacks and whites, the usual figure in much research. You will notice first that the ranges of the two distributions are the same, that is, the highest black and white scores coincide, as well as the lowest. Notice too that the shaded area represents the blacks who score higher than half of all the whites on the intelligence test (see Note 8.4).

Such a demonstration has tremendous practical implications. In a biracial school one will find many blacks and whites at the same level of ability. Also, if not segregated, some gifted black children will be right at the top of their biracial classes. Now, if you are white and meet a black, even though on the average whites have the edge over blacks in I.Q. tests (as illustrated in Figure 8.12) you will not be able to predict his intellectual competence by virtue of the fact that he is black, and all you can deduce from the available data is that he has slightly less chance statistically of being in the upper half of the population in the I.Q. rating. Except for this slight statistical disadvantage with respect to the population as a whole, the question of ability is largely an individual matter—you will not be able to make practical predictions about performance until you know a lot more about the particular person in question. As Klineberg (1963, p. 202) puts it:

> . . . lines of demarcation between groups of people, in employment, in education, in opportunities for development, based on alleged differences in averages which are essentially abstractions, do violence to the facts of individual capacities and potentialities. . . . [We] are faced with the living reality of individual human beings [not some abstract average] who have a right to the opportunity to show what they can do when they are given an equal chance.

Pettigrew (1964, p. 132) summarizes the issue as follows.

> Intelligence [and virtually every other adaptive quality of man] is a plastic product of inherited structure developed by environmental stimulation and opportunity, an alloy of endowment and experience. It can be measured and studied only by inference, through observing behavior defined as "intelligent" in terms of particular cultural content and values. Thus, the severely deprived surroundings of the average Negro child can lower his measured I.Q. in two basic ways. First, it can act to deter his actual intellectual development by presenting him with such a constricted encounter with the world that his innate potential is barely tapped. And, second, it can act to mask his actual functioning intelligence in the test situation by not preparing him culturally and motivationally for such a middle-class task.

He concludes by quoting Tuddenham (1962, pp. 499–500):

> Only a very uncritical psychologist would offer sweeping generalizations about the intellectual superiority or inferiority of particular racial or ethnic groups, despite the not very surprising fact that members of the dominant racial and cultural group in our society ordinarily score higher than others on tests of socially relevant accomplishments invented by and for members of that group.

One is often struck by the "double-think" of those who argue that there are innate psychological differences between racial groups. In many early writings on the origin of races, whites were presented as having evolved more recently than blacks, with the further inference that blacks were inferior because they were at a more "primitive" state of human development. It has also been argued that black infants exceed white infants of comparable age levels in their measured rate of development, and this is said to prove the inferior brain of the black—that is, the brain of the black child appears to reach maturity more quickly than that of the white, just as the animal brain matures faster than that of man but fails to reach the same level. Thus, "if blacks do poorly on tests, they must be inferior; if they do well [as infants], this indicates that they will be inferior later" (Klineberg, 1971, p. 125).

Note 8.4

The text discussion of the overlap between black and white intelligence test scores highlights one of the most elementary and fundamental rules of the measurement of traits, namely, that they are usually distributed in a fashion typically referred to as a *normal curve* (or normal distribution; Graph *a*). This means that a few people will have a high score, a few will have a very low score, and most others will fall somewhere near the middle. Thus, if we measure the intelligence or height of all adults, they fall into a normal curve around an average point (Graphs *b* and *c*). If we flip a hundred pennies a thousand times the number of times they will come up "heads" on each series will also be distributed in a normal curve, with an average at about 50 times (Graph *d*). If we have 500 people try to measure the length of a line to the nearest hundredth of an inch, their estimates will also be distributed around an average, with some falling above and

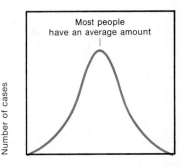

(*a*)   Amount of trait being measured

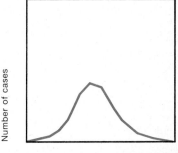

(*b*)   Intelligence quotients

others falling below (Graph *e*). If we measure aggressiveness, only a few people will be at the upper or lower extremes, and most will fall near some median level. On the accompanying graphs, the frequency is shown on the vertical axis, and the trait or event measured is shown on the horizontal axis.

In evaluating the normal distribution, we must sometimes determine whether we want to use as our middle value the *mean* (average of all measures) or *median* (the point above and below which half of the measures fall). These are not always the same value. For our purpose here, it is sufficient to recognize that the distribution of intelligence test

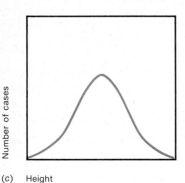

(c)   Height

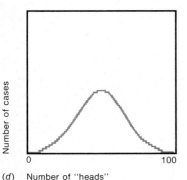

(d)   Number of "heads"

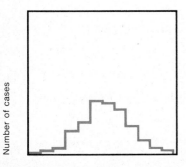

(e)   500 measures of a line

Klineberg (1971) further observes that the *Burakumin*, an outcaste population in Japan, are considered by Japanese as unclean and fit only for certain undesirable occupations (such as handling of "nightsoil"). By and large the *Burakumin* are restricted to slums or ghettos, unable to intermarry with other Japanese, and since they are of Japanese origin, form what might be called an "invisible race," that is, they are without any visible racial characteristics to distinguish them from other Japanese. Descriptions of their functioning within Japanese society sound all too much like those we have become accustomed to hear for racial minorities in America. The average intelligence score of the *Burakumin* is 16 points below that of other Japanese, and their school achievement relatively lower still. They show far more school absenteeism and truancy, and have a delinquency rate three times higher than the average Japanese (see DeVos and Wagatsuma, 1966). Here is another instance where an out-group's poor functioning is clearly related to its depressed social condition. (It would be interesting to see similar comparative studies done on the outcastes of India.)

A last word on "race"   The tragedy of the concept of race is not that it is totally without biological meaning but that it has so distorted the thinking of man about his social problems and his relations with his fellows. Anthropologist Ashley Montagu (1964, p. 26) puts this as follows:

> Whenever the term "race" is used, most people believe that something like an eternal verity has been uttered when, in fact, nothing more than evidence has been given that there are many echoes but few voices. "Race" is a word so familiar that in using it the uncritical thinker is likely to take his own private meaning for it completely for granted, never thinking at any time to question so basic an instrument of the language as the word "race."

The defects in the concept of race as it is widely used have led social scientists often to avoid the word when speaking of prejudice and to substitute the term *ethnic group*. This emphasizes the social as opposed to biological basis of in-groups and out-groups; the term adequately covers many types of groups, including Jews, blacks, Puerto Ricans, chicanos, Chinese-Americans, Amerindians, and Gypsies. In adaptational terms, such groups are distinguished not primarily by genetic or biological commonalities and differences but by shared historical and cultural backgrounds. Henceforth in this book the term *ethnicity* will be used instead of race.

Ethnicity, beliefs, and prejudice

Groups frequently differ in their systems of beliefs and their styles of thinking and acting. Each person may perceive the divergent outlook of others as a threat to his own values and way of life. Thus, divergent intellectual and life styles can contribute to prejudice.

Recently social psychologists have debated whether prejudice has more to do with ethnicity per se or with the assumed outlooks of the target groups. The question has been forcefully posed by Milton Rokeach (1960) and has led to some interesting studies of the social differences underlying prejudice. Rokeach contended that members of out-groups, such as the Jew, black, or chicano, are not really rejected because of different religion, color, or nationality but because they are appraised as alien in systems of belief and values. Investigations with college students were reported by Rokeach (1960) in which ethnicity and beliefs were pitted against each other as potential determinants of social acceptance and rejection. Subjects were asked to rate certain pairs of individuals on a nine-point scale extending the full range of likes and dislikes, as expressed by the following statements representing the extreme positive and negative attitudes: "I can't see myself being friends with such a person," and "I can very easily see myself being friends with such a person." In one study, the individuals rated were either white or black, and in another experiment they were either Jewish or Gentile; each member of the pair was described as holding different beliefs and values. Since the stimulus person varied in ethnicity as well as beliefs, it was possible to determine which of these factors was more important in reacting to a person. It was found that friendship preferences were determined primarily by correspondence in beliefs between the subject and the stimulus person (that is, *belief congruence*) rather than on ethnic grounds (either color or religion) per se. This was found to hold in both the North and South, and later studies (Smith *et al.*, 1967) have confirmed these findings.

Triandis (1961) has taken issue with Rokeach's contention, however, arguing that although it might apply when ratings are directed at the acceptability of someone as a friend, social relationships other than friendship are subject more to ethnic factors than belief congruence. As noted above, one feature of prejudice is the desire to maintain a high degree of social distance, expressed in action by excluding the negatively viewed group from one's neighborhood, as in de facto segregation. Triandis maintained that in such instances ethnicity rather than belief congruence is the more important factor. Triandis writes (exaggerating for clarity) that "people do not exclude other people from their neighborhood . . . because the other people have different belief systems, but they do exclude them because they are Negroes."

Rokeach's view supports the claim that resistance to integration arises not so much from the unwillingness of whites to live in the same community with blacks but stems from the impression, statistically correct, that most blacks tend to

scores of blacks and whites conforms to this "normal" pattern, and the differences between the groups still allow for great overlap between the scores of most individual blacks and whites. In comparing groups for some trait it is very rare that the two distributions do not overlap substantially.

It is very important to bear in mind that although groups may differ in the middle value (either the mean or median) for some trait, individuals within these groups vary considerably so that their particular position on the scale is not necessarily characterized by referring to the group's middle value. In other words, by identifying a person as black or white, man or woman, or whatever, one does not thereby position that individual around the average or median value for that group. Although a large number of people fall at or near the middle value, there is also usually wide variation around it. Therefore, although we can calculate the odds that any member of a group will fall a given distance from the middle value for that group, we cannot predict where each *particular individual* will fall along the curve. For the educator or child psychologist concerned with intelligence testing, this means that in predicting each child's potential, there is no substitute for individual evaluation, regardless of the group to which each child belongs.

be socioeconomically and educationally at a lower level than middle-class whites and that there are class differences in the manner in which people live. Middle-class families value orderly and well-kept neighborhoods, fear and resent crime and violence, and have a value system built around polite and respectful patterns of behavior. Thus, when whites reject having welfare housing built in their immediate vicinity, some are not rejecting blacks as such but are fearful of the influx of people whose patterns of behavior most middle-class whites stereotypically associate with urban slums: broken family life, social disorganization, chronic unemployment, a high incidence of violent crime, alcoholism and drug addiction, rough language and comportment in children. Although such conditions are indeed likely to be found in slums, it is invalid to generalize this image to all blacks. Whether correct or incorrect, however, such class distinctions are probably heavily implicated in resistance to integration, over and above any concerns with ethnicity. People prefer to live with like-minded, like-behaving families, and this is no doubt an important factor in the struggle of middle-class in-groups to maintain social distance from deprived out-groups. The problem of stereotyping still remains though, whether the criterion is ethnicity or social status.

The debate has recently been enlivened by two very interesting experiments, one performed by Stein *et al.* (1965) and the other by Triandis and Davis (1965). Stein and associates wanted to reconcile contradictory findings on the issue because they were inclined to see some truth in both positions. Their subjects were 23 male and 21 female white teen-agers (14 years of age) in two ninth-grade classes in California. Most came from working-class homes in a suburban industrial community. They were given mimeographed booklets by a research worker identified as from the University of California. Their interests and attitudes toward themselves, their friends, and other groups of teen-agers were surveyed, and a few months later they were asked to express their feelings toward the responses of four teen-agers who, like themselves, had answered the same questionnaire.

Actually, the subjects in the study were presented with fictitious information on how the four teen-agers they were to evaluate had answered the earlier survey, their answers having been constructed by the experimenters to be either *like* or *unlike* that of each subject. One stimulus person had presumably given responses nearly identical with those given by each subject himself, except in a few unimportant instances so as not to arouse suspicion. In the case of another stimulus person, changes were made on a number of items on which each subject had felt strongly. In this way, a picture of a stimulus person opposite in beliefs and values to each of the subjects was created. Half of the "like" stimulus persons were also identified as black and half were identified as white; similarly half of the "unlike" cases were identified as black and half white. Thus, the subjects evaluated as liked or disliked four types of stimulus persons: (1) a white person very like them in beliefs; (2) a black person very like them in beliefs; (3) a white person very unlike them in beliefs; and (4) a black person very unlike them in beliefs. Opinions were also obtained about the social distance subjects wished to maintain toward the stimulus person, that is, the extent of closeness to the stimulus person subjects would accept, from the most intimate to the least intimate. If one is willing to have a black enter one's immediate family through marriage, little social distance is maintained; on the other hand, if one is unwilling to have him in one's social club or even as a neighbor, than much social distance is maintained. Prejudice is usually presumed to be inversely related to the preferred social distance.

Stein and his co-workers (1965) confirmed Rokeach's contention about the importance of ideology for the liking or friendliness judgments, but their findings also supported Triandis's contention about the importance of ethnicity when the judgments had to do with social distance. For *liking or disliking,* when a white teen-ager (the subject) was given no information about a black teen-ager (the stimulus), he assumed that the black was unlike him and tended to reject him accordingly. If the black teen-ager (as stimulus) was described as having different beliefs, the white subject then preferred to have less contact with him than he would accept with a white having different beliefs or a black with similar beliefs. But dissimilarity of beliefs was a much greater cause of rejection than was ethnicity, even though both were influential. For *social distance,* white subjects accepted more intimacy with a person whose beliefs were similar to their own than one whose beliefs were different when ethnicity was not a consideration. However, when the more intimate forms of social contact were involved, such as the subject inviting a black person home to dinner, or agreeing to a black living in his own apartment building, or not minding if a black dated his own sister, even when the black was similar to the white subject in his beliefs, he was rejected. In sum, unfriendliness toward out-group members occurs to a large extent because such persons are perceived to be different in beliefs and values, but ethnic characteristics tend to determine the social distance maintained. Similar findings were also obtained with ninth-grade students in the Northeast, and with black and Jewish subjects evaluating the white-Gentile majority (Stein, 1966).

The point is that there are many varieties of behavior and attitude to be accounted for in prejudice, and for some of these ethnicity alone is the primary stimulus factor (Triandis and Davis, 1965). One must be skeptical of the use of single measures of prejudice, since the rules applying to each context vary somewhat. Triandis and Davis identify five factors which they see as more or less independent of each other; that is, a person may react positively to out-group members on one such basis but negatively on another. The factors include (1) formal social acceptance ("I would admire the character of . . .," or "I would cooperate in a political campaign with . . ."); (2) acceptance as a marriage partner; (3) acceptance as a friend; (4) social distance; and (5) subordination ("I would obey . . ." or "I would not treat as a subordinate . . .").

It is suggested that these different components of prejudiced attitudes and discriminatory behavior respond to varying degree of intimacy in the relationship. In the case of a relationship intermediate in intimacy, ethnicity and belief are both important; in highly intimate relationships ethnicity is more important; and in nonintimate relationships, belief congruence or divergence play a predominant role. Thus if the question about an out-group concerns falling in love or marrying, ethnic background is a major stimulus for prejudice; but if the question concerns being in the same political party or going to the same school, belief is the paramount determinant. However, some people almost always respond to others in terms of ethnicity, while others almost always respond in terms of belief, regardless of the dimension of intimacy (Triandis and Davis, 1965). The former may want to keep levels of intimacy low so as to impede any emergence of higher levels. (For instance, "Letting them go to the same school is letting them get their foot in the door—the next step will be racial mixing.")

The best conclusion seems to be that differences in belief and ethnicity are both stimuli for prejudice, depending on the nature of the relationship. Thus, Rokeach is evidently correct in implicating assumed or perceived differences in beliefs and values among groups, and Triandis is evidently correct that often ethnicity itself elicits a prejudiced or discriminatory reaction. For those concerned with social action, further knowledge about the conditions under which one or the other principles operate is clearly needed, since the effectiveness of what is done to eliminate or reduce prejudice will depend on whether it is directed at life-style or ethnic variables, and on the kind of social interaction being contemplated. (We shall consider this matter further in Chapter 9.)

CONCLUDING COMMENT

In this chapter seven societal patterns affecting prejudice were examined, including the existence of in-groups and out-groups, unfavorable stereotypes of out-groups, peer group pressures, real and imagined conflicts between groups, social change and disaster, the struggle between assimilation and maintenance of group identity, and the effect of ethnic differences. The concept of "race" was examined and replaced with the more workable social concept of ethnicity, and the respective roles of ethnicity and beliefs of target groups in affecting social preferences and prejudice were reviewed.

The key theme of the chapter was that prejudice is, in part, a product of certain institutionalized features of society and of the social circumstances under which people live. Perhaps these features make some degree of prejudice inevitable, or at least difficult to root out, although a knowledge of their role in prejudice might help in its reduction. Informed people can find better ways than prejudice to react to the pressures and frustrations of social life.

"Male chauvinism" is the current term for the attitude of men toward women seeking to live outside the traditional female occupational and role patterns (Bem and Bem, 1970). One has only to remember that women in the United States won the right to vote after much struggle a little over 50 years ago. Today there is a renewed struggle taking place about restrictions on the opportunity for women freely to choose careers, and to pursue them in place of or along side of marriage and family. In this chapter we touched on the problems that confront women who seek to change the traditional female social role.

Although most of the illustrative material of this chapter centered on anti-Semitism and white racism, and to a lesser extent on male chauvinism, the principles involved apply in some degree to many other targets of prejudice, although each particular case has its own distinctive features. Only space considerations prohibit development of each such case. There are some examples of prejudice that are more difficult to think of in terms of ethnicity, but which do fit, at least in part, within the kind of analysis made here. One example is the homosexual population, a group that has been severely stigmatized for its sexual deviancy. In consequence, most homosexuals have had to conceal this feature of their lives (as "closet homosexuals") in order to work and live within the sexually "straight" society. As noted in Chapter 4, they have often tried to "pass" as nondeviant, as have light-skinned blacks, Jews who have changed their names, people who have previously been hospitalized for mental illness, and so on, often under the pain of rejection, ostracism, or worse.

In any event, consideration of the societal aspects of prejudice explains much about the diverse nature of this phenomenon but also leaves major aspects of the problem unsettled, particularly the psychological causes and effects of prejudice within the individual. We must still explore how the victim of discrimination reacts and examine the psychological effects of prejudice on the person who engages in it. And we must examine the possibilities of eliminating prejudice through application of psychological principles. These topics are taken up in Chapter 9.

ANNOTATED LIST OF SUGGESTED READINGS

General treatments of prejudice

Allport, G. W. *The nature of prejudice.* Reading, Mass.: Addison-Wesley, 1954. A classic treatment of the subject from a psychological perspective, easy to read, though not well organized, and a bit out of date though still worth reading.

Simpson, G. E., and Yinger, J. M. *Racial and cultural minorities: An analysis of prejudice and discrimination,* 3rd ed. New York: Harper & Row, 1965. Rich, scholarly, sociologically oriented examination of prejudice, of the current status of several out-group minorities, giving the history of the problem. This is perhaps the most complete and up-to-date text treatment available, an excellent source.

Race and Genetics

Ashley Montagu, M. F. (ed.) *The concept of race.* Glencoe, Ill.: The Free Press, 1964. Series of essays by well-known anthropologists debating the nature of race as a concept.

Dobzhansky, T. *Mankind evolving: The evolution of the human species.* New Haven, Conn.: Yale Univ. Press, 1962. Outstanding review of the issues of human genetics and its implications for man as a species, with special discussions of the concept of race, by one of the most distinguished geneticists of the day. Requires careful study.

Lerner, I. M. *Heredity, evolution, and society.* San Francisco: Freeman, 1968. Lerner was an associate of Dobzhansky and has written a book covering similar ground as Dobzhansky's work (above), but for students not majoring in biology. Therefore, for nonbiological science students, this book provides an authoritative yet quite readable account of social biology and the nature of human diversity and racial strains.

Books on anti-Semitism (a small sample and nonannotated)

Graever, Isacque, and Britt, S. H. (eds.) *Jews in a gentile world.* New York: Macmillan, 1942.

Parkes, J. W. *The Jewish problem in the modern world.* London: Thornton Butterworth, 1939.

Parkes, J. W. *An enemy of the people: Antisemitism.* Middlesex, England: Penguin, 1946.

Valentin, H. *Anti-Semitism historically and critically examined.* (trans. from the Swedish by A. G. Chater). New York: Viking, 1936.

Books on white racism

Allen, V. L. Ghetto riots. *Journal of Social Issues,* 1970, **26,** entire issue.

Billingsley, A. *Black families in white America.* Englewood Cliffs, N.J.: Prentice-Hall, 1968.

Carmichael, S., and Hamilton, C. V. *Black power.* New York: Vintage, 1967.

Clark, K. B. *Dark ghetto.* New York: Harper & Row, 1965.

Cruse, H. *The crisis of the Negro intellectual.* New York: Morrow, 1967.

Epps, E. G. (ed.) Motivation and academic achievement of Negro Americans. *Journal of Social Issues,* 1969, **25,** entire issue.

Fanon, F. *The wretched of the earth.* New York: Grove Press, 1968.

Grier, W. H., and Cobbs, P. M. *Black rage.* New York: Basic Books, 1968.

Herndon, J. *The way it spozed to be.* New York: Bantam, 1969.

Jones, LeRoi. *Blues people.* New York: Morrow, 1968.

Killens, J. O. *Black man's burden.* New York: Pocket Books, 1969.

Lomax, L. E. *The Negro revolt.* New York: Signet, 1963.

Malcolm X. *Autobiography.* New York: Grove Press, 1965.

Chapter 8 looked at prejudice as a product of certain social conditions. We now examine prejudice from the point of view of the individual: the victim's reactions to it; the psychodynamic forces at work in the bigoted individual; and the personality characteristics of prejudiced and unprejudiced persons. We shall also consider various proposals and schemes aimed at eliminating prejudice and discrimination.

REACTIONS OF THE VICTIM

How do people react to being a member of a despised or rejected minority group? This is a complex question because individual reactions vary considerably depending on different circumstances of life and personality characteristics. Moreover, even a member of a dominant in-group (say, a "WASP," that is, someone white, Anglo-Saxon, and Protestant) may feel rejected and suffer psychologically as a result of his own special life circumstances. And one may belong to a minority outgroup yet manage to transcend the negative impact of prejudice. However, few people are so invulnerable as not to bear scars resulting from a continuous negative experience of feeling disparaged and socially rejected.

Feeling disparaged

Gordon Allport (1954, p. 142) has written empathically about the victim's reactions to prejudice as follows:

Ask yourself what would happen to your own personality if you heard it said over and over again that you were lazy, a simple child of nature, expected to steal, and had inferior blood. Suppose this opinion were forced on you by the majority of your fellow-citizens. And suppose nothing that you could do would change this opinion—because you happen to have black skin.

Or suppose you heard daily that you were expected to be shrewd, sharp, and successful in business, that you were not wanted in clubs and hotels, that you were expected to mingle only with Jews and then, if you did so, were roundly blamed for it. And suppose nothing that you could do would change this opinion—because you happened to be a Jew.

One's reputation, whether true or false, cannot be hammered, hammered, hammered, into one's head without doing something to one's character.

Constant disparagement works to undermine the image a person has of himself. He is made to feel deficient, lacking in the virtues usually admired in the society, even ugly. Such disparagement also makes the target individual feel isolated from the rest of society. Thus, continuing prejudice is destructive of his self-esteem and sense of security in dealing with others outside his own group. Combined with the feeling of deprivation that stems from second-class citizenship, limited employment and educational opportunities, and other social disadvantages, this chronic personal insecurity can lead to severe psychological injury. Although most members of target out-groups learn to cope with prejudice, sometimes rather successfully, overcoming the negative psychological effects of continual disparagement from childhood on presents an enormous challenge; sometimes inner resources are required beyond the individual's means. Black psychiatrists William H. Grier and Price M. Cobbs (1968) have written a passionate book about this, entitled *Black Rage.* They develop the theme

Figure 9.1   Time out for a little segregation. (© *1962 Fischetti,* New York Herald Tribune)

"Quick segregate! Here comes my father."

Figure 9.2 Hooded lynchers dealing out summary execution in D. W. Griffith's historical film Birth of a Nation, *1915. Note that the victim is played by a white actor wearing blackface. (The Museum of Modern Art/Film Stills Archive)*

that American blacks carry unusually severe psychological burdens as a result of living amid white racism (Figures 9.1 and 9.2) and illustrate this theme with clinical case histories selected from their professional practice.

In his analysis of the black American personality, Thomas Pettigrew (1964, p. 9) remarks:

For years, Negro Americans have had little else by which to judge themselves than the second-class status assigned them in America. And along with this inferior treatment, their ears have been filled with the din of white racists egotistically insisting that Caucasians are innately superior to Negroes. Consequently, many Negroes, consciously or unconsciously, accept in part these assertions of their inferiority. In addition, they accept the American emphasis on "status" and "success." But when they employ these standards for judging their own worth, their lowly positions and their relative lack of success lead to further self-disparagement. Competition with successful whites is especially threatening. Laboratory experimentation demonstrates that even when Negroes receive objective evidence of equal mental ability in an interracial situation they typically feel inadequate and respond compliantly.

American blacks, like whites, are much influenced by the family context in which they grow up: those who emerge from supportive family settings are much less vulnerable than those from disorganized and destructive family settings. (The latter are unfortunately more common in harassed minorities.) Blacks vary greatly in how they bear up under the emotional stress of prejudice, depending on the degree of inner strength

A leading Negro citizen came to a therapy session with his wife, who was suffering from a severe and intractable melancholia. She had several times seriously attempted suicide. The last attempt was particularly serious. She was angry with her husband and berated him for never opening up and exposing his feelings.

For his part, the husband remained "nice." He never raised his voice above a murmur. His wife could goad him, but he was the epitome of understanding. He was amenable to all suggestions. His manner and gestures were deliberate, studied, and noninflammatory. Everything was understated. During the course of treatment he was involved in several civil rights crises. His public life was an extension of his private one, and he used such words as "moderation" and "responsibility." His entire life was a study in passivity, in how to play at being a man without really being one.

It would be easy to write off this man as an isolated passive individual, but his whole community looks upon his career as a success story. He made it in the system to a position of influence and means. And it took an aggressive, driving, determined man to make it against the odds he faced. We must ask how much energy is required for him to conceal his drive so thoroughly. And we wonder what would happen if his controls ever failed. [From Grier and Cobbs, 1968, p. 67]

389

developed in the early years of family life. When the family structure is weak and incapable of compensating for the cultural buffeting, the black youngster is often crippled in his capacity to cope with psychosocial stress and, in consequence, may well fall prey to mental illness, drug addiction, alcoholism, crime, suicide, and the like (see Note 9.1).

Women are also becoming aware of the "put-down" inherent in their confinement to traditional social roles, especially those who resist conformity to prescribed patterns. They want women's goals to be set beyond those of becoming a wife, mother, and homemaker. Although such awareness is still concentrated in better-educated, more intellectual women, more and more young women are joining the ranks. They are pinpointing real anomalies in male-female role patterns. It is often mystifying to men who act in a courtly and attentive manner to women to find these women resentful and contemptuous of this "chivalrous" and "romantic" treatment. When they are called "male chauvinist pigs," and when sexual interest in women is treated as a typical example of feminine

Note 9.1

This observation that blacks differ among themselves in their family backgrounds, their capability of coping with disparagement, and their ability to maintain a positive self-image, points up the difference between psychological and sociological analysis. If we divide people into distinct groups, such as whites and blacks, men and women, rich and poor, educated and uneducated, middle class and lower class, and so on, we often discover that these social divisions are indeed associated with different patterns of thought and action—but only *on the average*. Classification of people according to membership in certain groups is based on the probability that such membership has an effect on their social experience. This is essentially a form of sociological analysis.

The trouble with exclusive dependence on this kind of analysis is that there are great individual variations in social experience within such groupings too. Therefore, we cannot predict with any precision how a person will react to the women's liberation movement, for example, merely by knowing whether that person is a man or a woman; nor can we tell very confidently how a person will feel about himself and the world merely

by knowing whether he is white or black. We can, however, improve our guesses about attitudes and behavior by also examining the individual psychological influences to which the person is exposed and how these work. This latter method is more characteristic of the psychological approach. In our attempts to understand people, both kinds of analysis go hand in hand. (See also Note 8.2.)

Important in this regard is the social psychological concept of the *reference group* as distinguished from the *membership group*. Categories such as the ethnic group, social class, or male and female refer to membership groups. Objectively, the individual is a member of such groups: he or she has a certain education, occupation, income, is of this or that sex, ethnic group, and so on. Subjectively, however, one's pattern of thoughts and actions may actually be more in tune with that of a group other than one's own. When someone identifies with the customs and outlooks of a group of which he is not a member, this is called his reference group. Thus, although most working-class Americans have traditionally voted the Democratic ticket and upper-class Americans have voted for Republicans in national elec-

tions, there have always been considerable numbers of individual exceptions to this sociological pattern. Particular lower-class persons may identify not with a working-class outlook, which they may reject, but with a middle- or upper-class outlook, and see themselves as upwardly mobile. A wealthy person may reject the privilege-centered and elitist values of his upper-class peers and work toward socialist causes; or a poor laborer with lower-class membership may identify with the middle-class values of achievement, hard work, and self-denial, therefore supporting political candidates who oppose welfare or other kinds of aid for the poor. And similarly, many women have personal-social identities that are closer to male patterns than to female ones, and vice-versa.

Therefore, it is certainly an overgeneralization to speak of blacks as thinking or feeling this or that, or of women as feeling disparaged, say, by males who treat them as helpless or as requiring protection. The individual's outlook and behavior depends greatly on the reference group or category with which he identifies himself, not merely on the group to which he actually belongs.

exploitation, such men fail to grasp what their female critics are trying to say (Figure 9.3).

There is a sense in which treating a woman in a courtly fashion, for example, lighting her cigarettes, holding doors for her, assisting her with packages, and behaving protectively, has a patronizing quality in the eyes of anyone with strong aspirations to be free and independent socially. Amelia Bloomer, inventor of the pantsuit, is quoted as having said, "I find it completely impossible to keep a man's attention on my talk when he's looking at my ankle." She is expressing the wish to be viewed as a person, rather than as a sex object. Women's liberationists reject that one-dimensional feminine role and aspire instead to be regarded as complex individuals with full competence to act independently and manage their own lives without the protection of the "superior" male. For such women, protectiveness helps maintain the old-fashioned stereotype of woman as helpless, vulnerable, and passive, in contrast with the portrayed image of man as strong, vigorous, dashing, and chivalrous.

This stereotyped picture of women has permitted restrictions on their behavior and discrimination in hiring and promotion in the business world, making it very difficult for them to compete in that world. Although some of the more extreme and angry rhetoric of women's lib tends to be exaggerated and counterproductive, the aspirations and frustrations from which it stems are genuine, and the rhetoric is quite clearly a way of coping with the long implicit and often explicit disparagement they see as characteristic of the traditional feminine social role.

Figure 9.3   Liberated women on the march. (Burt Glinn; Magnum)

Effect of hypersensitivity to prejudice on interpersonal relations

Sensitivity to subtle forms of disparagement is a continuing feature of social relationships between those in minority out-groups and those with whom they interact in the society at large, and this frequently puts a strain on such relationships. Special acute sensitivities develop in members of the out-group, and members of the majority in-group are often also aware of this hypersensitivity and "up-tight" about it.

Consider the experience of the black who perceives himself to be the "token Negro" at a social affair. The white host congratulates himself on being free of prejudice—displaying this by virtue of having invited a black couple to his home. This may communicate itself to the blacks not as a feeling that they are welcome as friends, but rather that they are seen as nothing but symbols. They may become conscious of a special kind of attention, which while cordial, marks them as different and makes natural social interchange very difficult.

Subtle disparagement is sensed and resented. It is laudable, of course, to try to break down racial or ethnic social barriers, and the effort is difficult to criticize, in and of itself. But the frequently clumsy efforts of whites in this sphere have been the subject of numerous biting dramatic presentations by black comedians. On the other hand, it is quite possible that members of minorities sometimes read into such situations disparaging feelings or impulses that are not even there, creating for all involved an awkward interpersonal dilemma.

Indeed, one of the most striking and troubling reactions of minorities is their hypersensitivity to ethnic insults, whether obvious or subtle, sensitivity that sometimes reaches proportions that seem truly paranoid. In the light of their frequent negative experiences with public attitudes, when members of out-groups enter a store, restaurant, hotel, school, or theater, they will often wonder uneasily whether they are about to suffer insult and humiliation. This is a barrier to normal interpersonal relations, and it is further aggravated by the fact that out-group members are prone to see in a casual remark not intended to be insulting a degrading or disparaging intent. The problem is not unique to black-white relations, but extends to all in-group and out-group interactions. The remark of a Jewish student cited by Allport (1954, p. 144) illustrates the problem:

I have encountered at first hand very few overt expressions of anti-Semitism. Nevertheless, I am always aware of its presence offstage, as it were, ready to come into the act, and I never know what will be the cue for its entrance. I am never quite free of this foreboding of a dim sense of some vaguely impending doom.

In the case of the black, Grier and Cobbs (1968, p. 161) have written:

For a black man survival in America depends in large measure on the development of a "healthy" cultural paranoia. He must maintain a high degree of suspicion toward the motives of every white man and at the same time never allow this suspicion to impair his grasp of reality. It is a demanding requirement and not everyone can manage it with grace.

Sometimes even compliments given to members of ethnic out-groups create discomfort in the listener because of their apparent insincerity. The same statement can at one time be a warm and positive expression of regard and at another time a subtle disparagement, and it is not always easy to tell which is which. A remark to a black that members of his race are exceptionally well coordinated, graceful, or gifted with a great sense of rhythm may seem unobjectionable on the surface and without any prejudicial edge; yet such an observation smacks of the hackneyed stereotype that blacks are all body and brawn but little brain. Similarly, a complimentary description of Jews as clever or sharp-witted conjures up the negative image of the sly, pushy, and mercenary Jew. The sensitive person is generally suspicious of even positive statements that are based on stereotyped imagery.

One quality which makes some positive statements appear insincere is extravagance. Since Freud, clinicians have recognized that when people have negative impulses that they consciously reject, they may prevent themselves from having to acknowledge such feelings by vigorously affirming the opposite. This defense mechanism has been called *reaction forma-tion*. In Shakespeare's *Hamlet* it is illustrated in the comment, "The lady doth protest too much, methinks" in the scene in which the player queen swears that her love is so great that once a widow she would never rewed (see the margin). Thus, poets have also sensed that whenever protestations of positive feeling are excessive and extravagant, there is reason to suspect that such statements really hide opposite, negative feelings. This principle, intuitively grasped by the sensitive person, often leads him to take excessive claims of positive regard as subtle expressions of hostility.

Our language is also rich in commonly used expressions that reflect prejudicial stereotypes. The expression "Jewing him down" refers to a bargaining process in which the seller states a given price and the customer makes a lower counter-offer; the term implies, of course, that such commercial haggling is the special province of the Jew. Actually, many business transactions are conducted in just this way. Other common examples are "the pot calling the kettle black" and "white lie." In the latter case, the black child is confronted with the disparaging thought that a good or harmless lie is white, while a bad or damaging one is black. The expression "nigger in the woodpile" clearly refers to slavery days when a black might be flushed out while hiding, an event immortalized in the English language as expressing an unexpected finding of something bad among otherwise good things.

It takes little imagination to recognize that interpersonal relations between minority out-groups and majority in-groups can be disturbed, and mutual trust eroded, in the face of these patterns of speech and behavior. Every minority out-group member has to cope with feelings of uncertainty as to whether or not he is dealing with a prejudiced person; he must also learn to handle those subtle manifestations of prejudice which the other person may not even be aware he is expressing. And if he becomes acutely hypersensitive to insult, an out-group member may be dead wrong in the inferences he draws about

Player Queen: *Each opposite that blanks the face of joy*
Meet what I would have well and it destroy.
Both here and hence pursue me lasting strife,
If, once a widow, ever I be wife!
Hamlet: *If she should break it now!*
Player King: *'Tis deeply sworn. Sweet, leave me here awhile;*
My spirits grow dull, and fain I would beguile The tedious day with sleep.
[*Sleeps*]
Player Queen: *Sleep rock thy brain; And never come mischance between us twain!*
[*Exit*]
Hamlet: *Madam, how like you this play?*
Queen Gertrude: *The lady doth protest too much, methinks.*
Hamlet: *O, but she'll keep her word.*
King Claudius: *Have you heard the argument? Is there no offence in't?*
Hamlet: *No, no, they do but jest, poison in jest; no offence i' the world.*

[From William Shakespeare, *Hamlet: Prince of Denmark*, Act III, Scene 2]

the attitudes of someone with whom he is interacting. It is probably easier for him to deal with clear, overt prejudice than with ambiguous and veiled instances (see Note 9.2).

The reader may recall from Chapter 2 the theme that behavior is not entirely governed by the objective environment (that is, the environment as it really is) but rather by the environment as it is perceived or appraised (understood and evaluated) by the person. The point in the text that the hypersensitivity of the minority person to insult may lead him to see disparagement where it does not exist illustrates this theme very well. From this standpoint, he may react to a social inter-action not as it is, or at least as it is seen by the other party to the interaction, or by observers, but as it seems to him. Often we fail to understand a person's reactions on the basis of observations of the immediate envi-ronmental context unless we also can iden-tify the personal and sometimes ideosyn-cratic past history that has "conditioned" him to see things in some special way. This approach to the way a person subjectively construes an event is called *phenomenology* (see Wann, 1964), a special variant of a philosophical viewpoint that has been adapted to psychological studies of human behavior.

Coping with prejudice

The psychological problems caused by feeling disparaged lead to the development of varied forms of defense against damage to one's self-esteem. Let us consider some of the most common forms of such defense.

Overcompensation   It has been observed that black children in integrated kindergartens frequently react to the discovery of their ethnic identity with overreactivity and special vigor, compensating, as it were, for their "handicapped" social status (Goodman, 1952). Such a reaction is common among Jewish children as well. Jews as a group have an unusually high motivation for achievement, adopting the "Protestant ethic" of hard work and self-denial in the interests of future gain. Overcompensations in early childhood are not likely to con-tinue in the absence of some mark of success, and in the lowest socioeconomic strata of black children such encouragement is rather infrequent. Often such children tend to give up the struggle and later display a declining level of achievement motivation. In contrast, black children from middle-class fami-lies are more likely to be rewarded for their efforts and so to continue their striving for excellence and achievement (see Pettigrew, 1964, pp. 30–31). This is a finding of great impor-tance to both educators and parents.

Turning inward   Another characteristic reaction of targets of prejudice is a turning in toward their own group. They seek others like themselves as allies to help support their sense of identity and to build a group-based feeling of security and mutual regard. Group cohesiveness is reinforced when it pro-vides a way of coping with disparagement. One need not be continuously on guard within one's own group.

This is one of the primary explanations of the survival of Jews as a group in spite of extreme persecution and hardship over many centuries (Figure 9.4), although it is not the whole story. In response to the external threat, Jews tended to band together, at first voluntarily, then forcibly as a result of laws restricting interaction with the rest of society. The fact that they *could* band together, through a common religion, history, and ethnic identity, was undoubtedly a major psychological resource enabling them to survive. Such group unity and cohesiveness seems to have been greatest when persecution was most severe and least when it was mild and assimilation easiest.

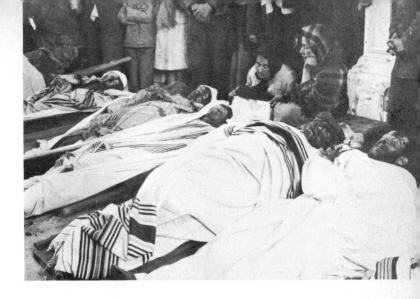

Figure 9.4 Victims of an anti-Semitic massacre (pogrom) in Zhitomir, the Ukraine, 1920. (Courtesy of YIVO Institute for Jewish Research, Inc., New York)

In turn, such group identities remain a constant irritant in the society. Refusal to assimilate (say, by religious conversion, abandonment of distinguishing group characteristics) tends to be treated, particularly by prejudiced persons, as the *cause* rather than the effect of prejudice. Thus, we saw in Chapter 8 that Jews are accused of being clannish, although in all probability this is no more true of Jews than any other ethnic group under conditions of external pressure.

A similar process has been occurring today in the American black, exhibited in efforts to affirm and strengthen black identity and consciousness. The slogan, "Black is beautiful," is an attempt to make a positive rather than negative thing of being black (Figure 9.5). The "Afro" or "natural" hair style expresses such an affirmation and symbol of groupness, opposite in style to the strenuous efforts in past decades with a hot comb and oil to eliminate the kinkiness of hair in an attempt to submerge the disparaged black identity that had been rejected by the majority culture.

For black women, an interesting dilemma has developed from the juxtaposition of two possible group identities, that of being black and that of being a woman, and stemming from problems of coping with prejudice toward each such identity. On the one hand, there is the identification with the black movement, and on the other, the aspiration of women for self-expression. These are sometimes placed in conflict, as noted by black Congresswoman Shirley Chisholm:

I have pointed out time and again that the harshest discrimination that I have encountered in the political arena is antifeminism. . . . When I first announced that I was running for the United States Congress, both males and females advised me, as they had when I ran for the New York State legislature, to go back to teaching—a woman's vocation—and leave the politics to men.

Figure 9.5 The Supremes, Diana Ross, Cindy Birdsong, and Mary Wilson, pose for photographers in London while visiting Britain for a series of singing engagements. (Wide World Photos)

There is pressure on black women to support their men in the struggle for black advancement instead of pushing their own personal aspirations. Often black women are torn between the black struggle and their own self-determination and personal growth. Thus, when the Black Unity Party of Peekskill, New York, issued a statement asking black women not to practice birth control because having children aids the black revolt against racism (see Chapter 3), some of the women replied (Haden *et al.,* 1968, p. 2):

Black women have always been told by black men that . . . we were the real niggers in this society—oppressed by whites, male and female, and the black man, too. . . . You want to use poor black women's children to gain power for yourself. You'll run the black community with your kind of black power—you on top.

Thus, turning in toward one's own group can get to be a complicated process when one is caught between two conflicting group identities, as is sometimes the case for black women who resonate to both the struggle of women and the struggle of blacks, although they are not contradictory by definition.

Assimilation Another adjustment to prejudice often found among minorities is to identify wholly with the majority culture and its attitudes (assimilation), an opposite reaction to turning in toward one's own group. Such a pattern of coping is referred to as *identification with the aggressor or oppressor.*

Without awareness that he is doing so, the rejected minority member may take on as his own the values of the powerful majority culture, seeking to insinuate himself into grace by being whatever the majority seems to demand. In this way he feels safer from attack and more worthy of appreciation. Such a transformation is not the same as the fully conscious, deliberate ingratiation of the dominant group in which the powerless person merely gives lip service to its values (see Kelman's discussion of compliance, referred to in Chapter 4). Rather, what is involved here is an identification or internalization process, an unconscious transformation of the personality, not unlike a child's internalization of its parents' values and goals.

An interesting offshoot of this tendency is the acceptance by minority members of even the prejudices of the majority culture. Thus, fully assimilated Jews may hate religious Jews and their cultural trappings. When Jewish immigrants came to the United States after others had become well established here, the newcomers were often disdained for having foreign accents and un-American ways. They reminded the assimilated Jew of his own rejected ethnic background and, feeling his own status to be threatened by their presence, he took on with a vengeance the dominant societal values, even those of anti-Semitism. Another related observation is that recent converts, for example, to the Catholic or Jewish religion, are often much more orthodox and intolerant of backsliders or casual believers than are long-standing members. Such converts validate their newly adopted status by affirming more strongly than necessary that they are what they claim to be. By being highly intolerant of others less rigorous than themselves, they seek to ensure that they will be accepted in their new role, and perhaps they also counteract any lingering inner doubts by such exaggerated affirmations.

Not only does sharing the prejudices of the majority culture allow one to feel a bond with that culture, but it also serves the function of allowing him to be the oppressor rather than the oppressed. He can then feel superior to others lower than himself in the "pecking order." Thus, we often see the tragedy of members of one oppressed minority group displaying the same kind of prejudice they decry for themselves toward another oppressed minority group. One can understand this as a distorted and often unrecognized defense of their own impaired self-esteem.

This tendency to identify with the aggressor, the dominant white world, is reflected among American blacks in the belief, now much weaker than it once was, that lighter skin meant higher status. Grier and Cobbs (1968, pp. 65–66) describe a similar tendency in their discussion of the concept of the "bad nigger":

One of the constant themes in black folklore is the "bad nigger." It seems that every community has had one or was afraid of having one. They were feared as much by blacks as by whites. In the slave legends there are tales of docile field hands suddenly going berserk. It was a common enough phenomenon to appear in writings of the times and to stimulate the erection of defenses against this violent kind of man.

Today black boys are admonished not to be a "bad nigger." No description need be offered; every black child knows what is meant. They are angry and hostile. . . . Because of his experience in this country, every black man harbors a potential bad nigger inside him. He must ignore this inner man. The bad nigger is bad because he has been required to renounce his manhood to save his life. The more one approaches the American ideal of respectability, the more this hostility must be repressed. The bad nigger is a defiant nigger, a reminder of what manhood could be.

The reader will recognize that the need to inhibit anger and defiance is part of the process of identification described in the expression *Uncle Tomism* (the term "Uncle Tom" is used derogatorily by blacks to refer to one of their own kind who has "sold out" psychologically and adopted the outlook of the white culture). Such an adjustment is, for obvious reasons, particularly anathema to those blacks who have adopted a militant approach. It would be interesting to discover just what conditions encourage identification with the aggressor rather than a strengthening of group cohesion. More research is needed on this subject.

Humor   Another way of coping with disparagement is through humor that makes light of prejudice. Thus, the Italian-American may laugh at "dago" jokes and use the derogatory term jokingly himself. In this way he shows himself to be a "regular guy" by playing the game and not being affected by it, and by playing along he deflects the most aggressive attacks. In such "hazing," the person who is greatly distressed is a more satisfying victim than one who "plays it cool." Moreover, when intergroup tension is mild, humor is probably a successful antidote; but when denigration has severe and destructive consequences, as with those minorities for whom prejudice is a life-and-death matter, it is difficult to think of it as funny. Although joking about prejudice is common among blacks, because of the depth of the problem they face such humor often has a sharp edge, frequently getting quite bitter (see the margin; Figure 9.6).

Reverse prejudice   If one is a member of a rejected outgroup, another likely form of coping with disparagement is the cultivation of retaliatory attitudes against the majority

Figure 9.6   Beatle John Lennon and his wife, Yoko Ono, meet with Dick Gregory, well-known entertainer and civil-rights activist, on a farm near Toronto, during the Lennons' 1969 peace crusade to Canada. (Wide World Photos)

[*It*] was the show at the Michigan State Penitentiary that really scared me. . . . It had been a good show—prison audiences are so hungry for entertainment. As I came off the stage, the warden introduced me to an old Negro who had been in jail for fifty years. He was an artist, and he asked me if I'd like to see his work. I did. When I saw it I got weak in the knees.

He had drawings of women, of what he thought women looked like. But every one had a man's face, a man's eyes, a man's nose, a man's jaw, a man's lips. They had long hair and they had breasts and they were wearing lipstick and dresses. But every one was really a man.

It was so weird that a man should think he was drawing a woman and he was really drawing a man. But that convict had seen only men for fifty years; those male faces were all he knew. And I talked to Lil about it and the more we talked and the more I thought about it, the more frightened I got. If you had told that old man that his drawings were all wrong he would have called you a liar and been ready to fight. And then Lil and I carried it one step further. If you were born and raised in America, and hate and fear and racial prejudice are all you've ever known, if they're all you've ever seen. . . . [From Dick Gregory (with Robert Lipsyte), *Nigger*, pp. 170–171. New York: Dutton, 1964]

in-group. This reverse form of prejudice involves hostile stereo-typing of the majority group that serves as a mirror image of its own bigotry. This response can readily escalate into angry, sometimes violent militancy. In eastern Europe, Jews leveled some choice invective against the *Goyim* (their "alien" oppressors); in the movie *Fiddler on the Roof,* mention of the Russian Tsar is followed by contemptuous spitting. When militant blacks use florid and heated rhetoric to describe "whitey" and his institutions, some of the criticism is accurate, but much of it is hyperbolic and just as stereotyped and distorted as are white-supremacist diatribes. While no social problems can be solved by such inflamed rhetoric, the under-lying impulse is understandable as a form of compensation that helps restore the victim's self-esteem.

Another example of reverse prejudice may be found in the case of some militant women's liberation leaders who bitterly attack "male chauvinist pigs" for having forced women into a subordinate social position but who then speak, act, and write intolerantly themselves about women who feel comfortable and perfectly content to stay at home in the role of wife and mother. Such intense contempt for the traditional feminine role reveals deep internal conflict as to these activists' own place in the world and their own interpersonal relations. This extreme form of reverse prejudice belies the claim that women should be autonomous in choosing how they want to live. Furthermore, this hostile approach is probably counter-productive because it threatens the majority of women who live in traditional role patterns and turns many men and women against legitimate feminist aspirations that they might otherwise support. It points up one of the correlates of ex-tremism of any kind, that it usually seeks to replace something offensive with something else that is equally offensive. No group holds a monopoly on intolerance and pigheadedness, whether it be the favored majority, the deprived minority, or any other subculture.

PSYCHODYNAMICS OF PREJUDICE

The word *psychodynamics* refers to the motivating mental and emotional forces that lead the person to act the way he does. In terms of prejudice, it concerns mainly the things that threaten a particular individual and his special ways of coping with such threat. Several psychological mechanisms have been traditionally implicated in prejudice, among the most impor-tant of which are (1) blaming others for one's troubles; (2) projection; and (3) enhancing one's self-esteem at the expense of others. None of these is unique to the bigot, and all of us have probably employed such self-protective devices at one time or another in attempting to cope with our problems. Thus, the impulse to blame others for one's problems, to identify others rather than oneself as wrongdoers, and to gain self-esteem and social esteem at the expense of others are outgrowths of universal tendencies found throughout mankind. However, for some people the circumstances of their development conspire to exaggerate these tendencies to such an extent that intense bigotry is the outcome.

Finding a scapegoat

When achievement of an important goal is blocked (that is, when we are frustrated or stymied), we typically react with efforts to find someone or something to blame. Under certain conditions, when the reasons for frustration are ambiguous or when they stem from personal inadequacies that are difficult to acknowledge, the natural tendency is to seek an explanation of the difficulty that will protect one's own self-esteem. Blaming another person or group is a handy psychological solution.

Attaching blame for our troubles is at times a highly adaptive reaction, since to cope successfully requires that we determine the actual source of difficulty before we can take corrective measures. When one is facing a clear-cut danger, such as a blizzard or flood, the most adaptive thing to do is to discover how to protect oneself against it: one can build a storm shelter, or get help to strengthen the levee, or escape to a safe place. However, when the source of the harm, be it physical or psychological, is not at all clear, the urge to find a satisfactory explanation remains strong, and in searching for something on which to blame the situation, one may readily find a *scapegoat,* a person or group on whose doorstep responsibility for the trouble can be laid. In its most healthy and adaptive form, seeking to pinpoint responsibility for a problem is a search for a valid explanation, not an alibi. But in its neurotic and prejudicial forms, the individual finds a pseudo-explanation, like blaming members of an out-group with no real justification.

An example of scapegoating occurred in the United States during the campus disturbances of the late 1960s, when the public blamed college faculties, radicals, intellectuals, and a host of other groups, often without any serious effort to establish the facts of the student unrest or understand the nature of the phenomenon. The unsettling events needed to be explained somehow, and blame had to be assigned for them. There was no trouble in finding scapegoats, although these varied with the sociopolitical outlooks of whoever was assigning the blame.

As one might expect, minority out-groups make excellent targets for scapegoating because they are usually powerless and fit long-standing negative stereotypes. Often a group that is blamed for a problem has, at least superficially, some connection with it, and this makes it easier to find (or imagine) all sorts of conspiratorial responsibility. Thus, an unemployed white worker might perceive the working black as the cause of his unemployment (see Chapter 8). This is, of course, a half truth: indeed, if there were no black workers, competition for jobs would conceivably be less; however, the main reasons for unemployment involve the state of the economy, governmental financial policy, automation, which is replacing many workers, and perhaps the worker's own marginal abilities. In actuality the black worker often suffers far more than the white worker in periods of unemployment. Thus, seizing upon blacks as scapegoats further obscures the problem and fails to deal with the real situation, the nature of which the prejudiced white does not grasp.

In the related process of *displacement,* hostility is shifted from a target that is highly threatening to one that it is safer to attack, a common phenomenon. The reader will recall from the discussion of dominance hierarchies in Chapter 6 that when an animal, say a subordinate chimpanzee, is threatened or attacked by a dominant one, the subordinate animal is forced to submit or withdraw, but in so doing he often challenges an animal below him in the hierarchy. The challenged animal in turn withdraws and acts in the same fashion toward an animal below him, and so on down the "pecking order." This behavior is also referred to as displacement (Figure 9.7). As it is seldom safe to attack targets who are powerful enough to retaliate, in human social contexts the hostility is often displaced to people who are less threatening. Frequently the object of such displacement turns out to be a vulnerable mi-

Figure 9.7   (a) Two rats attack one another after receiving electric shock. (b) When one rat is absent, the remaining rat displaces its aggression toward the doll. (Courtesy of Dr. Neal E. Miller)

(a)

(b)

nority out-group. Such an attack is safe because it is usually easy to generate mass support behind it, and the minority group is unlikely to be able to retaliate against the attackers in any significant way.

Displacement, as it operates in the context of prejudice, is well illustrated in a field experiment performed quite a few years ago by Miller and Bugelski (1948). Boys living together in a camp were required to take a long, dull examination consisting of questions by and large too difficult for them to answer. By design, the exam was made to run overtime, preventing the boys from attending bank night at the local theater, an outing to which they had looked forward with enthusiasm. Before and after the long exam, they were given a brief test in which they were asked to describe their attitudes toward Japanese and Mexicans. By comparing scores on the second test with the original one given before the frustrating exam, it was found that unfavorable attitudes toward the minority groups had sharply increased (see Note 9.3). Presumably, the anger provoked by boredom and frustration had been displaced from the appropriate target, those in authority who were responsible for the exam, to the minority groups. The study does not tell us, of course, whether or not prejudice was prolonged beyond the brief period of this frustration and whether the hostility was specific to the two minority groups involved or was simply increased in general. The experiment actually supplied the boys with ready-made targets for their

---

Note 9.3

When is a difference not a difference? This is not just a takeoff on the old joke that goes: "When is a door not a door? When it is a jar (ajar)"; it is a very fundamental statistical issue that enters into any research seeking to compare the effects of two or more conditions. In Miller and Bugelski's study (1948), for example, the experimenters found that before the frustrating examination the boys serving as subjects showed less negative attitudes toward Japanese and Mexicans than they did following it. In effect, a difference was found in their behavior under two conditions. The issue is whether that difference should be taken seriously (as one that is to be expected whenever such a comparison is made) or is merely a result of chance.

This question is vital because any time

we make a research comparison, some difference will usually be observed. Each time we do such a study, the sample of subjects will differ, and our measurements will vary, so that even though we do exactly the same things, the comparisons will each yield a quite different result. In the case of the Miller and Bugelski research, if we redo the study many times, there will be a normal distribution of differences in the average scores of prejudice around some central tendency (see Note 8.4). Sometimes the obtained difference will be large, and sometimes small, and on some occasions the results might even go in the opposite direction. A single study provides merely an estimate of the real difference. Of course, were the study done over and over again, we would have a better estimate, but this is

obviously not very practical, and there must be some other way to determine the validity of differences in results obtained.

For this reason, most research reports make use of statistical procedures to determine what is usually referred to as *statistical significance* (reliability) of the data. These procedures are based on the laws of probability, and the mathematical details need not concern us here. They involve such considerations as the magnitude of the obtained difference, the numbers of subjects (or observations) entering into the comparison, and their variability within the two conditions. In the Miller and Bugelski study, if the subjects under both conditions were extremely variable among themselves in the extent of their measured prejudice, this would make it more likely that a small difference between

hostility. There is every reason to think, however, that in real life displaced anger could contribute to the formation of prejudice itself.

The theory of displacement helps explain the German people's readiness to accept and participate in persecution of the Jews during the 1930s and throughout World War II until Germany's collapse in 1945. Adolf Hitler's propagandists made highly effective political use of scapegoatism, blaming an "international Jewish conspiracy" for all of Germany's problems that resulted from the punitive Treaty of Versailles after World War I. This peace treaty destroyed Germany's prestige and injured its vitality by imposing enormous reparation payments. The postwar era was replete with bitter frustration and economic chaos, and the German people saw in Hitler and the Nazis a chance to redress their grievances. In the process of restoring weakened national self-esteem and unifying the country against its external enemies, it became useful to blame the Jews for all past problems (Figure 9.8). Although this was quite irrational and inconsistent (Jews were condemned as Bolshevik bankers), the Germans were quick to adopt the scapegoating-displacement mechanism in the search for a way out of their plight. Linking the Jews with his political opponents, especially the Socialists and Communists, Hitler completed his climb to power. In 1932 he became Chancellor. In subsequent years, as Jews and others were imprisoned and killed, Nazi leaders accumulated huge private fortunes by

the conditions would be due to chance. Were the prejudice scores close together, however, and the obtained difference between the two conditions considerably larger than the differences within each condition (among individual subjects), there would be less likelihood that this effect was due to chance. In general, a large sample of subjects, small variation among them, and a large difference *between* conditions, all contribute to a high probability that the obtained difference is statistically significant, meaning that it would be found again and again if the study were repeated numerous times.

Usually the researcher examines differences in results (or the correlation, if that is the statistic being used) for their statistical significance, and this is expressed as a probability level. We usually accept more than five occurrences in a hundred (0.05, or 5 percent probability level) as indicating statistical significance. This means that in no more than five times in a hundred such experiments would we expect to find a certain result by chance. A 1 percent level of probability (0.01) is even more secure, since it means that only once in a hundred times would such a result occur by chance. It is much like the reasoning about probabilities in gambling. A straight flush in poker is a very rare event (far more infrequent than our 0.01 probability), but it will still happen from time to time. Similarly, whenever we find a difference in results produced by two or more research conditions, the variation might have occurred purely by chance. We must be able to show that its frequency of occurrence exceeds the level of chance if we are to place any sort of confidence in its dependability.

The reader will note that the word "significance" here is used differently than in common usage. It does not mean that a finding is important, but that it is not an accident. The measured effect may not be large; however, since it is reliable, it does represent the discovery of a condition that has some real consequence. We have thus added to our knowledge.

The important thing to remember here is that to be taken seriously any research finding involving a relationship between variables must be assessed as to its dependability (its statistical significance) and the possibility that it has occurred by chance must be weighed. That is why statistical analysis plays a key role in modern psychological research.

(a)

(b)

(c)

Figure 9.8 The swastika in America. (a) Desecration of synagogue in Williamsport, Pennsylvania. (b,c) Brownshirts picket in support of the House Un-American Activities Committee during hearings in the 1950s. (a: Wide World Photos; b,c: private collection)

holding onto the confiscated property. And the German people, bedazzled by enormous rallies in which their "Aryan" superiority was extolled, looked the other way (Figure 9.9).

Projection

In the mechanism of defense called *projection* the individual fails to recognize an unacceptable or threatening urge in himself, and to help maintain the self-defensive fiction the impulse is attributed instead to someone else. When projection occurs in the context of prejudice, the impulse is attributed to a minority out-group. Although the process is usually assumed to be unconscious, were it verbalized the reasoning involved would probably go something like this: "I am not permitted to do that (say, engage in certain sexual or aggressive acts), only inferior people (a particular minority) do it"; or "I have not done (or felt) that, they (the minority) did it, not I."

Such a mechanism has been used to explain some white racism, particularly when it has sexual overtones. It is not uncommon for a ruling majority that has been violent toward

404

a minority or that has exploited it sexually to be firmly convinced of the reverse idea that members of that minority are either violent or sexually unrestrained. MacCrone (1937) has suggested that South African whites have a great fascination with the sexual life of the "natives," conceiving of the black man as exceptionally potent sexually and the woman as particularly voluptuous. This view is combined with a morbid fear of race mixture and of rape of white women. Such a fear is strangely in excess of any real danger, however, and as such provides the tip-off to its projective nature: the fact is that virtually all interracial sexual contact in South Africa is initiated by white men, even though such contact is strongly disapproved. In this way the white ignores his own responsibility for reprehensible impulses and actions.

A similar pattern has been described by Dollard (1937) as taking place in a town in the Deep South of the United States. Here, as in South Africa, most sex contacts between blacks and whites were initiated by whites, as was most of the violence. Yet whites maintained the strong emotional conviction that blacks are violent, sexually libertine, and aggressive. Simpson and Yinger (1965, pp. 57–58) describe the psychodynamics of this in considerable detail:

Figure 9.9 Jew baiting in Nazi-occupied Poland, 1941. (Courtesy of YIVO Institute for Jewish Research, Inc., New York)

This belief is needed not only to rid many white people of a sense of guilt for having violated their own standards, but to help them resist the impulses toward violation. The Negro, a designated inferior group, symbolizes the repressed impulses that one must not admit are still motivating him. In "Southerntown" the white male is torn by a group of contradictory desires and accompanying beliefs: to maintain "race purity," to live up to the dominant moral code with regard to sex, and yet to take advantage of the relatively defenseless status of the colored population for wider sexual contact. He sees that preventing contact of Negroes with whites will help to satisfy the first desire; but he forgets that if whites initiate such contacts, the results are not different. His belief in the inferiority of the Negro helps him to satisfy the second desire or to rationalize its violation: if the inferior Negro is sexually promiscuous, I must not be; or if I make advances toward a Negro woman, it isn't really a violation of the code. This same concept of the inferiority of the Negro and belief in the strong sex urges and easy virtue of Negro women help him to satisfy the third desire. Race prejudice is a natural outcome of such a complex of mutually contradictory desires, feelings of guilt, and repressions.

One problem with this explanation is that it has tended to be overworked. It is a useful way of understanding some instances of negative stereotyping, but it is probably not a significant factor in a high proportion of prejudice, even in respect to the American black in other social contexts than the limited case described above. The trouble is that we do not have clear ideas as to when projection is centrally involved

[Black] men develop considerable hostility toward black women as the inhibiting instruments of an oppressive system. The woman has more power, more accessibility into the system, and therefore she is more feared, while at the same time envied. And it is her lot in life to suppress masculine assertiveness in her sons.

Mr. R. was a writer who presented himself for treatment in his mid-fifties. In his younger days he had enjoyed success and a certain amount of adulation in white society. Throughout the course of treatment he presented a picture of culture and refinement. His trouble was that several years earlier he had lost the spark of creativity and his writing ceased. He made frequent resolutions to resume writing, but his motivation never matched his ambition.
It developed that he was afraid to compete with white men as a writer. Whatever he wrote, his obsessional fears dictated that somewhere someone who was white had written something better. He was a defeated and despairing man when he entered treatment. He had, however, a delicious secret which he used as comfort when he was most depressed.
His face would crease with a smile when he recounted his numerous affairs as a young man. In all his life he never doubted his ability to outperform a white man sexually. He told how he had "banged many white women." He sometimes spoke of himself as a deformed man or as a cripple, but sex was the one area in which he felt completely adequate.

The mythology and folklore of black people is filled with tales of sexually prodigious men. Most boys grow up on a steady diet of folk heroes who have distinguished themselves by sexual feats. It is significant that few, if any, of these folk heroes are directing armies or commanding empires. Dreams must in some way reflect reality, and in this country the black man, until quite recently, had not been in positions of power. His wielding of power had been in the privacy of the boudoir.
[From Grier and Cobbs, 1968, pp. 63–64]

in prejudice and when it is not. In many instances it may merely be a wild extrapolation from certain phenomena seen on the psychiatrist's couch (Grier and Cobbs, 1968). Sexual fantasies and anxieties in whites are probably also encouraged by the black male's own need to affirm sexual prowess and (in recent years) the willingness of a few militant black leaders to indulge in rather overheated rhetoric (see Lester, 1968). But overworking projection as an explanation for prejudice may divert attention from some of the less exotic but more important garden-variety mechanisms of group conflict.

Enhancing self-esteem by degrading others

We live in a society stressing competition and social mobility for everyone (see Chapter 8). Where success in competition is so valued, failure poses a major threat to self-esteem, especially when it can be attributed to personal defects. A relatively unsuccessful white person can gain some measure of comfort from the belief that he is superior to a Martin Luther King, a Ralph Bunche, a Willie Mays, or a Bessie Smith, and he need not feel he is at the bottom of the pack if he considers himself better than a whole "race" of people, over 20 million strong in the United States, or even more so if he can add a host of other minorities to the list. The notion of racial inferiority thus serves as a psychological crutch for some white Americans (or Rhodesians, or South Africans, or whatever) whose self-esteem is shaky. Or, should the minority group be reasonably successful, such a person can take comfort from the conviction that they are unscrupulous and have competed unfairly. And a man with strong concerns about his own adequacy can get a great psychological boost by considering all women as inadequate and helpless, needful of his masculine protection. Believing that his wife cannot cope with a breakdown of the toilet or kitchen sink, he is delighted to show his superiority by taking over with his shop tools, or whatever. Such a man is highly threatened by a woman who can do things better than he can (say, at school or at work, in athletics or sex), and his ego is supported by a male-female role pattern that allows him to think of half the world's population as subordinate to himself.

In sum, a lifelong pattern of failure and a vulnerable ego, or momentary frustration through some setback or defeat, can produce a person who tends to denigrate others in an effort to restore his damaged self-image. His own personality defects can be forgotten when there is intense preoccupation with unfavorable stereotypes of others. The prejudiced person is usually blind to the distorted nature of his beliefs and attitudes. Because these internal psychological forces tend to operate silently, in the sense that the susceptible person cannot be aware of their existence if they are to work, prejudices derived from this mechanism are extremely resistant to direct attack by education or counterargument.

INDIVIDUAL DIFFERENCES IN PREJUDICE

Is the amount of prejudice that people manifest a consequence of the way their personalities are organized, irrespective of the sociocultural circumstances under which they live? Simpson and Yinger (1965, p. 62) phrase this question as follows: "Are there certain kinds of total personality integration that have prejudice as natural expressions, or is prejudice a specific response to specific stimuli, likely to be associated with almost any kind of personality?" The answer seems quite clearly to be the former, that there are personality traits conducive to prejudice.

First, let us examine some of the evidence. In one of the early investigations of prejudice, E. L. Hartley (1946) assessed the attitudes of college students toward nationalities and ethnic groups using the Bogardus Social Distance Scale which we have already encountered in Chapter 8 (see Table 8.1). In addition to the 32 familiar nationalities and races in his survey, he included three fictitious ethnic groups, which were referred to as "Daniereans," "Pireneans," and "Wallonians." It turned out that those students who were prejudiced against known ethnic groups, such as Jews and blacks, were also prejudiced against these nonexistent peoples. As one prejudiced student put it in a written statement, "I don't know anything about them; therefore I would exclude them from my country." In contrast, another student low in prejudice reported, "I don't know anything about them; therefore I have no prejudices against them." To the first student, any strange group seemed to be a menace; to the second, lack of information about such a group called for suspended judgment or the need to give them the benefit of the doubt. The correlation between social distance scores for the three nonexistent groups and the 32 real groups was +0.80 (where a perfect correlation is represented by +1.0; see Note 6.3). This means that when a student was prejudiced against one group he was also likely to be prejudiced against the others, even if he knew nothing about them. The correlation between negative attitudes toward blacks and Jews was +0.68; toward blacks and Catholics, +0.53; toward Catholics and Jews, +0.52; toward the nonexistent groups and communists, +0.68. These correlations indicate that there is a *general tendency* in the individual to feel or not to feel prejudice, to some extent without reference to a particular group. Allport (1954, p. 69) has stated this point as follows:

> People who dislike both Negroes and the federal administration sometimes condense their hostilities into the phrase "nigger-loving bureaucrats." The familiar expression, "Jewish international banker" reflects two fused negative attitudes—in defiance of the simple truth that remarkably few Jews are international bankers and few such bankers are Jews. In Latin America, where Catholicism is the dominant religion, one hears of a "Jewish-Protestant alliance" that threatens the world. But in lands where both anti-Catholicism and anti-Semitism are common, the result is condemnation in a single breath for the "Vatican and the Jews." The fact that scapegoats of different breeds are so often harnessed together shows that it is the *totality* of prejudice that is important rather than specific accusations against single groups.

The prejudiced person

What are the personality traits disposing one to prejudice? The typical approach to this question has been centered on traits involving a low level of self-esteem and the tendency to feel threatened, especially by people who seem different or alien. This is also consistent with the three main uses of prejudice noted earlier, namely, blaming others for one's own problems, projecting onto others one's own unacceptable qualities and impulses, and enhancing one's self-image by disparaging others. All three imply an individual with personality problems, someone who feels insecure and inadequate.

Studies along these lines have been strongly influenced by a landmark book, *The Authoritarian Personality,* written in 1950 by T. W. Adorno, Else Frenkel-Brunswik, Daniel Levinson, and Nevitt Sanford, at the University of California at Berkeley. The research program that was reported in the book began with attempts to examine anti-Semitism. At first an attitude scale was constructed to measure individual differences in anti-Semitic attitudes. Later interest broadened to prejudice in general and to the type of personality that tends to reject all out-groups as alien. The authoritarian person has an insecure or weak ego and views the world as so threatening that he must seek an "island of safety" within his own narrow sphere. Such a person generally has an inflexible system of thought, a rigid sense of right and wrong, and overpowering urges that are difficult to hold in check. A number of scales were developed in order to measure different facets of authoritarianism, including the degree of *ethnocentrism,* an exaggerated liking of one's own ethnic group and a distrust of other groups.

In the *ethnocentrism scale* subjects are asked to indicate the degree to which they agree or disagree with a number of stated

A. Jews

One trouble with Jewish businessmen is that they stick together and prevent people from having a fair chance in competition.

There is something different and strange about Jews; it's hard to tell what they are thinking and planning, and what makes them tick.

B. Negroes

Negroes have their rights, but it is best to keep them in their own districts and schools and to prevent too much contact with whites.

Most Negroes would become overbearing and disagreeable if not kept in their place.

C. Other minorities

It is only natural and right for each person to think that his family is better than any other.

Certain religious sects who refuse to salute the flag should be forced to conform to such a patriotic action or else be abolished.

D. Patriotism

The worst danger to real Americanism during the last 50 years has come from foreign ideas and agitators.

America may not be perfect, but the American Way has brought us about as close as human beings can get to a perfect society.

[From Adorno et al. (1950)]

propositions regarding Jews, blacks, and other minorities; there are also a few propositions that relate to questions of patriotism. The responses are made on a six-point scale: $+3$ indicates strong support or agreement; $+2$, moderate support; $+1$, slight support; -1, slight disagreement; -2, moderate disagreement; and -3, strong disagreement. Some of these items are shown in the margin of page 408.

Adorno *et al.* (1950) found, as did Hartley before them, that prejudice toward one minority group was strongly associated with prejudice toward other groups. In short, there is a personality trait disposing individuals to feel prejudice to any out-group.

Why should a person who agrees strongly with the statements high on the patriotism scale also believe that blacks should be kept in their place or that Jews are dangerous and provide unfair competition for non-Jews (Note 9.4)? As Allport (1954, p. 69) has noted, for the ethnocentric personality patriotism seems not to refer to loyalty to the American *creed* but has the flavor of isolationism, of distrust, of threats to security: "The person who rejects out-groups is very likely to have a narrowly conceived idea of his national in-group." The outlook is one of needing to defend against threat, of being menaced on all sides by foreigners, Jews, blacks, various religious sects, and other alien groups. A person with such an outlook is convinced that his own "kind" is better than any other. Outsiders are viewed with suspicion, and one's loyalty is directed solely to the in-group, be it one's family, ethnic group, church, or nation.

There have been many studies of the authoritarian personality, and although some variations in findings may be found among such studies, a useful summary would list the following personality traits as associated with strong prejudice: antiintellectuality; a pervading sense of pessimism, with lack of hope and confidence about the future; feelings of bitterness, doubt, and suspicion; misanthropy and querulousness; a hostile outlook verging on destructiveness; a grumbling and discontented evaluation of one's lot in life; a rigid, somewhat dogmatic style of thinking; a lack of poise and self-assurance; and a feeling that something dreadful is about to happen. With this constellation of personal problems, it is little wonder that authoritarians are so intense in their hatred and rejection of outsiders and that they "put down" others to bolster their own shaky self-esteem, blame them for their troubles or the troubles of the world, or project onto them their own guilt-provoking impulses (Figure 9.10).

Some words of caution are also in order, however. Although the correlations between prejudice toward various out-groups are high, they are by no means perfect. Thus, for

Note 9.4

The question "why" in the accompanying text discussion of the prejudiced person is a prelude to a statement of theory, an attempt to analyze the relationship among certain assessed attitudes. Allport (1954) is speculating about the psychodynamics of such prejudice, that is, how it functions within the individual and the nature of his problems and motives. The theory is, in effect, that the person is feeling threatened and is using prejudice to protect himself against this feeling. A little later we shall see a slightly different theoretical analysis proposed by Rokeach (1960). It might be useful at this point for the reader to review the discussion of theory in Note 4.4.

Figure 9.10 Women SS guards at Belsen concentration camp, one of the extermination centers where millions of men, women, and children were gassed and incinerated during World War II. (Imperial War Museum, London)

example, the correlation between anti-Semitism and anti-black feeling noted earlier in Hartley's research (1946) was +0.68, and as reported by Adorno *et al.* (1950) it was +0.74. If the correlations were perfect (1.0) there would be no need to look for situational factors to explain prejudice, since it would be determined entirely by personality. The same people would be more or less prejudiced or tolerant toward everyone regardless of the group involved. But this is not so. All groups are not hated equally by the bigot; for example, more prejudice is shown against the Jews than the Quakers or against Mexicans than against Canadians. Exclusive focus on the personality traits of the prejudiced person leads us to overlook these other very important situational factors. Numerically speaking, a correlation of 0.7 means that if you know a person is strongly prejudiced against Jews, the chances will be approximately one in two that you will be correct if you guess he will be strongly prejudiced against blacks as well. There is still plenty of room for error in the prediction, however, and we can never overlook external factors as contributors to a prejudiced reaction, as well as those within the personality (see Note 6.3).

Another problem with the conclusions of *The Authoritarian Personality* is that authoritarianism and bigotry tend to be associated theoretically with a right-wing political philosophy, while tolerance toward others is presumed to be the liberal or left-wing outlook. However, there are clearly left- as well as right-wing authoritarians, as Rokeach (1960) has argued. For Rokeach the key attribute of the prejudiced person is *dogmatism,* that is, having a closed mind about reality, organized around rigid beliefs (positive or negative) that provide a framework of intolerance toward others. Dogmatism is viewed as an attempt to defend against the threat of a complex and unpredictable world by reducing everything into neat formulas. Actually, while Adorno *et al.* (1950) were interested

410

primarily in assessing ethnocentrism as a personality *trait*, Rokeach was more interested in tapping a *process* by which people orient themselves to the world. Therefore, to him the contents of their beliefs were far less important than the formal manner in which they deal with the world around them. Although Rokeach created a scale to measure dogmatism, it was designed to be independent of whether a person was politically to the right or left or in the center; in effect, bigots of the political left, right, or center would all get the same score on his scale if they displayed similar dogmatic thought processes. This is a very important idea, and it has tended to correct one of the major defects of the ethnocentrism scale, which tends to make prejudice identical with a right-wing orientation. Bigots of all ideological complexions appear to share a sense of alienation from society, hostility, a vision of the world in conflict, and a tendency to all-or-none, black and white (dichotomous) thinking.

Many people maintain rigid systems of belief (ideological, religious, or whatever) that dominate every aspect of their lives and shape their interpretation of the world and its events. Imagine, for example, a person whose ethical system is rooted in the nineteenth-century outlook of British philosopher Herbert Spencer that since all life, human included, is engaged in a ferocious struggle for survival, only the toughest and most ruthless (the "fittest" specimens) will or *ought to* flourish.* How is such a person likely to interpret the plight of those around him who are economically and socially marginal and who cannot "make it" without some sort of continued aid (say, government welfare)? Our Spencerian, without any personal rancor, might easily regard all those who are low on the human social scale as defective or morally inadequate. In his eyes it would be immoral and foolish to support the "weak," since this practice only allows them to perpetuate themselves, when only the "fittest" should survive (Figure 9.11).

Someone who holds such views might not be threatened by or hostile to blacks or chicanos or Amerindians, per se. His way of thinking no doubt is essential to his self-image, much as the early Calvinists strove for material wealth as evidence to themselves and the world that they were the ones "chosen" for salvation. Our Spencerian might also believe quite sincerely in the "American creed" of free enterprise with equal opportunity for all under the law, but he insists that one is not "owed"

---

*This Spencerian philosophical system was an attempt to apply a somewhat simpleminded view of Darwinian biology to ethics (in Chapter 5 it was referred to as "social Darwinism"). It became very popular in Britain and America among those who sought to justify unbridled monopolistic business practices at home and imperialist expansion abroad in the late nineteenth century, and it still has some adherents in this century.

Figure 9.11 Execution scene in Terezin, Czechoslovakia. Bodies were piled into a mass grave. (Library of Congress)

a living but must wrest it through struggle. He may assert that all ethnic groups have an equal chance to succeed, that the marginal status of some ethnic minorities is not the result of persecution or discrimination but rather is proof of their moral and intellectual inferiority. In line with his tooth-and-claw philosophy of life he is strongly opposed to any remedial efforts to help such minorities or to give them a greater opportunity to compete more favorably.

Thus, not all prejudice stems from threat or frustration and attempts to bolster a wobbly self-image. Much bigotry probably derives from limited knowledge and from encapsulated belief systems or ideologies that permit one to ignore the thoughts, feelings, and harsh realities of those who are rejected and impoverished. What all prejudice has in common, however, is a tendency to think in terms of stereotypes and clichés. Our Spencerian conservative may maintain, quite sincerely, that he intends no disparagement of low-status people when he is critical of their failure to "make it" in society, but that his view is in accordance with the biological facts of life and that any other outlook reflects merely the myopia of the "bleeding heart."

The unprejudiced person

Allport (1954) has written a valuable chapter on what he calls the "tolerant personality." He suggests that tolerant people tend to be secure and lack the feeling of threat found among prejudiced people. They show greater mental flexibility, rejecting the two-valued logic of the prejudiced (the either/or outlook that regards people as of two types—strong or weak, good or bad, and so on). He makes the important point that there are two kinds of tolerance: those who behave in a tolerant way merely because it is the norm of the community in which they live; and those for whom tolerance is a well-entrenched feature of their personality. The former will show prejudice under appropriate social circumstances; the latter will not readily be swayed in their interpersonal judgments by external standards or customs and will generally not display prejudice even when it is the social norm.

As we saw earlier, all activist reformers are not necessarily unprejudiced. Some may, for example, hate the southern white as stereotypically as some whites hate blacks, making the same class error of treating all southerners as bigots. Interestingly, however, people high on the ethnocentrism scale (of Adorno *et al.*, 1950) tended to be conservative and opposed to efforts to change things; in contrast, people low in ethnocentrism (tolerant persons) tended to opt for militancy in reform (Dombrose and Levinson, 1950).

One of the traits found in tolerant personalities is their greater sensitivity to others, their ability to detect the feelings of others accurately. Scodel and Mussen (1953) did an interesting study on this. They used college students who had scored either high or low on the authoritarian scale: 27 high-scoring students were paired with 27 low-scoring students, and for 20 minutes each pair conversed separately and informally about radio, television, or the movies, whichever they preferred. Each member of the pair thus formed impressions of the other. Afterwards, each student was removed to a separate room where he was given a questionnaire to fill out as he thought the other member of the pair might do it. It was found that the high authoritarians tended to project their own prejudiced attitudes onto their partners, thus perceiving them quite inaccurately. Contrariwise, the nonauthoritarian subjects assessed their partners more accurately, clearly seeing their authoritarian attitudes or correctly assessing their tolerance. Thus, nonauthoritarian, tolerant students seemed to be better able to size up another person on brief acquaintanceship than authoritarian, intolerant ones.

Some of the other qualities associated with lack of prejudice include insight into one's own problems, the tendency to blame oneself rather than others when things go wrong, and the ability to be comfortable with ambiguity rather than needing always to have clear-cut answers. One further trait is especially interesting. Evans (1952) measured the *values* of a group of college students as well as the degree of anti-Semitic prejudice they felt. He found that the strongest interests of prejudiced students were in political, economic, religious, social, and theoretical matters, in that order, with aesthetic concerns rated lowest. In contrast, students low in anti-Semitism showed an entirely different set of values, the order from highest to lowest being aesthetic, social, religious, theoretical, economic, and political. In effect, the prejudiced individuals showed the greatest interest in power and material things and presumably viewed human transactions in terms of domination, status, hierarchy, and utilitarian considerations. Not surprisingly, therefore, minority out-groups are regarded by them as low in status, less worthy, threatening, even contemptible, to be manipulated or exploited where possible. And in spite of the importance of religion in the history of anti-Semitism, the religious value did not have any bearing on the extent of anti-Jewish prejudice in this study—it fell in the middle rank in both tolerant and prejudiced groups.

CAN PREJUDICE BE ELIMINATED?

The prevalence of prejudice and its presence in every human society known throughout history do not encourage optimism that this social ill will be easy to eliminate, but there are some grounds for hope. We cannot rely merely on good intentions, however. We need a firm psychological grasp of the dimensions of the problem if we are to improve the climate of human relations throughout the world.

As was pointed out in the introduction to Part III, prejudice is an attitude, and discrimination is negative behavior toward a particular group. The main commitment of social psychologists interested in the problem has long been aimed at elimination of prejudiced attitudes, since these have typically been regarded as the cause of negative acts toward target groups. This stems from the traditional general outlook of the social psychologist that attitudes underlie actions (although we saw in Chapter 4 that sometimes when a person engages in certain actions he undergoes a corresponding change of attitudes). For those who hold that all actions flow from attitudes, the expectation is that such attitudes will be expressed in appropriate behavior: If we feel favorably toward someone, we will want to be with that person or will show that positive feeling by smiling, evidence of pleasure, and personal warmth.

If we have negative attitudes, we will tend to express them with negative actions. Thus, if we dislike a political candidate, we are expected to vote against him at the polls. Unfortunately, as we shall see later, this convenient theoretical position is much too simplified, and it turns out that the relations between attitudes and action—in fact, between thought and action in general—are really quite complex and not yet at all well understood.

A large body of literature has developed in social psychology concerning principles of attitude formation and change and study of the social factors involved. But, as we shall see, it turns out that attitudes, particularly when they are well-entrenched and concern issues of great emotionality, can be quite resistant to change, and for our present purposes it will be fruitful to focus on this aspect of the question. We shall examine the nature of resistance to change and the problems such resistance poses in any effort to reduce or eliminate prejudice.

Resistance to attitude change

In spite of evidence that people often conform to social pressure (see Chapter 4), they also show a remarkable degree of independence in how they think and feel, even in regard to minor attitudinal questions. This is illustrated amusingly in the following vignette presented by Freedman and associates (1970, p. 290) in their discussion of the problem of influencing attitudes:

A friend of ours was in a supermarket and saw an elderly lady walk down the aisle, pushing a shopping cart in front of her. As she walked down the line of detergents, she hummed to herself the well-known Ajax commercial, "Use Ajax, the foaming cleanser," etc. Still humming, she moved unerringly to the shelf containing Babo and bought several large containers. Then she marched off, again singing the Ajax song. At first glance, this would seem to be an advertiser's dream. She heard his song, she listened to it carefully, she even liked it enough to sing it while she shopped. But at the crucial moment, she chose his chief competitor's product rather than his own. . . .

This charming story makes the point that people do not develop or change attitudes passively or automatically lose control over their own behavior simply because they are assaulted by strong persuasive pressures. Social psychologists have at times been much too sanguine about the possibilities of changing human attitudes through reeducation, but in recent years there has been a growing awareness of the complexity of the problem. If one examines the entire literature of attitude change one is impressed with the opposite idea, namely, that resistance to persuasion is often a very powerful force in human affairs. Those changes in attitudes which have been recorded in psychological research have tended to be small, superficial, and short lived, and yet the changes we would contemplate bringing about in human relations (doing away with prejudice and discrimination) are profound. Attitudes that are part of the central core of the personality, dependent on powerful defense mechanisms and interlocking belief systems, are extremely resistant to change.

Skepticism about how much our attitudes can be influenced is pointed up by some very spectacular failures. The difficulty of producing major changes in the individual even through intensive and long-term psychotherapy is one example, although there are clearly many persons for whom major changes have indeed occurred in the clinical context. Another important example is the powerful effort by the Chinese Communists during the Korean War to force captured Americans to give up their belief in American democracy and capitalism and adopt the ideology of Maoist communism. Prisoners were subjected to intensive long-term psychological and ideological pressures, which have been often referred to with the crude but graphic term "brain washing." Unlike most propaganda and advertising campaigns, there was no counterpropaganda to contend with, and the propaganda message was guaranteed to reach the intended audience. Perhaps most important of all, the power of the captors over the captives was absolute and could be used to intimidate as well as cajole or convince, a condition comparable to the parent-child relationship and ripe for the mechanism of "identification with the aggressor" (see Chapter 4). Such a situation would seem highly conducive to a change in attitudes, though not as good as the situation in which the target of propaganda is already very well-disposed toward it, perhaps because of an upheaval in his current life situation (as we saw earlier in the case of the German people's ready response to Nazi racist propaganda during a period of economic crisis; see the margin).

Contrary to original press reports implying the opposite, only an extremely small number of prisoners-of-war defected, and the indoctrination effort was very unsuccessful. As Freedman *et al.* (1970, p. 278) put it, "Practically all the American soldiers—even the uneducated, unsophisticated, tired, weak, lonely, and perhaps not strongly pro-American ones—were able to resist the Communist attempt to change their opinions." * Similarly poor results have been achieved by massive public-education campaigns to get people to use automobile seat belts, to support fluoridation of the water supply, or to

Where are the men behind the scenes of this virulent world movement? Who are the inventors of all this madness? Who transplanted this ensemble into Russia and is today making the attempt to have it prevail in other countries? The answer to these questions discloses the actual secret of our anti-Jewish policy and our uncompromising fight against Jewry; for the Bolshevic International is in reality nothing less than a Jewish International.

It was the Jew who discovered Marxism. It is the Jew who for decades past has endeavored to stir up world revolutions through the medium of Marxism. It is the Jew who is today at the head of Marxism in all countries of the world. Only in the brain of a nomad who is without nation, race and country could this satanism have been hatched, and only one possessed of a satanic malevolence could launch this revolutionary attack, for Bolshevism is nothing less than brutal materialism speculating on the baser instincts of mankind. In its fight against West European Civilization it makes use of the lowest human passions in the interests of International Jewry. [From J. Goebbels, speech delivered in Nuremberg, Germany, Sept. 13, 1935]

---

*Although the facts are still incomplete on American prisoners-of-war returning from North Vietnam, it would seem that, despite the Vietnam War's greater unpopularity, few prisoners were won over by their captors in this case either.

stop smoking or eating high-cholesterol foods. People, it would seem, are not as malleable as one might expect in face of mass-persuasion techniques.

In spite of such failures, we know that attitudes do change, sometimes quite dramatically. Thus, atheists become deeply committed to religion and vice-versa, or people are converted from one ideology to another, shifting sharply from being dedicated left-wing radicals to being equally dedicated right-wing radicals, often changing their lives around completely in the process. The movie *I Love You Alice B. Toklas,* in which Peter Sellers plays a conventional, conservative, uptight, middle-aged man who turns into a pot-using "hippie" type, is an amusing fantasy on this theme of sudden dramatic conversion. We must find out just how and why such upheavals in attitude and behavior pattern take place, as well as why minor everyday changes in attitude occur.

Reasons for the resistance   In the case of prejudice, three human characteristics stand out as particularly important in creating inertia and resistance to change.

First, as we learned in Chapter 8, prejudice is deeply embedded in the social structure, and as such it appears to many people as a normal or natural way of thinking. Such people hardly ever notice it unless it is brought to their attention. Their prejudice is so much part of them that it is invisible to them.

Second, it seems impossible to alter segregation in education and discrimination in employment and housing without changing major aspects of the social system. This provokes resistance because any such fundamental change is threatening to many people. One need only look at the struggle over school desegregation and proposals for busing of children. Such proposals seem to many to endanger the very foundations of their social system, and demagogues are quick to use the public vulnerability to such threats in combating these proposals. Change or reform is stigmatized as subversive. Thus, as it turns out, many people who would like to do away with segregation and other manifestations of prejudice oppose busing to central school complexes, not necessarily out of prejudice but out of commitment to certain aspects of the present social structure.

The ethnocentric person is even more resistant to attempts to alter the status quo than most because, as we saw, he is himself likely to be insecure and threatened, coping with the danger by seeking safety within his own group and attempting always to ward off threatening strangers. Commonly, too, the rhetoric of reformers has a way of intensifying such insecurity. Public statements by many black and white civil-rights activists are often laced with fervent moralistic pronouncements that alienate the conventionally minded. And since the bulk of minority people in this country are asking only for a fair share of what the society has to offer, their interests are not necessarily well served by calls for violence or disruption of the entire social order (Figure 9.12).

A third source of resistance is that few people acknowledge their own prejudice, either to themselves or others. We all like to think of ourselves as rational and just. We resist seeing ourselves as bigots. Our prejudices are hidden behind a fortress of ego-defense mechanisms that help to preserve a more attractive image of ourselves. This is particularly the case when powerful unconscious urges and feelings underlie the prejudice, as we saw earlier in the discussion of personality traits associated with prejudice (the authoritarian personality).

Methods of resistance   There are many devices employed by people to preserve the outlooks and attitudes to which they are committed. One of the most obvious of these hinges on the fact that no one can attend to everything in his environment. In order to perceive the world effectively, we must be selective about those things to which we pay attention (see Chapter 1). For survival, it is necessary, of course, that strong messages get through this attentional screen more readily than weak ones, since we need to be alert to external events of importance to our welfare. In reading a newspaper, we see the headline before the detailed newsprint: if the headline is written to point up something of strong emotional concern to us, we read on; otherwise we may skip it. Moreover, an eye-catching ad will be seen before a drab one.

But our personal needs, interests, and attitudes also tend to determine the things to which we pay attention. Liberals

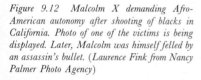

Figure 9.12   Malcolm X demanding Afro-American autonomy after shooting of blacks in California. Photo of one of the victims is being displayed. Later, Malcolm was himself felled by an assassin's bullet. (Laurence Fink from Nancy Palmer Photo Agency)

tend to read the newspaper columns and magazine articles of liberal writers, whereas conservatives prefer like-minded writers, choosing newspapers and magazines accordingly. Those who vigorously opposed the Vietnam War collected around them others who thought like them, and often their efforts to influence people were wasted on those who already agreed; this also reinforced their own attitude and gave them an exaggerated notion of the spread of similar opinions among others. In such cases, it comes as a shock to discover how many others think differently.

We often consciously avoid certain information or opinion sources because we know that they will tend to express a point of view diametrically opposed to our own. In this way, *selective attention* can be used in almost any context simply to "turn off" the displeasurable or disturbing inputs, protecting from assault the attitudes to which one is committed (see also Chapter 3). One of the earliest efforts to study how this mechanism operates was an experiment on selective learning and remembering (Levine and Murphy, 1943). Attitudes toward communism of a number of college students were assessed, and those who were either highly favorable or highly unfavorable were chosen for further study. Both types of subjects were then asked to listen to some passages, parts of which were favorable to communism, others unfavorable. Later these students were tested to find out how much they had learned and remembered of the material. Those who were initially favorable to leftist ideas appeared to remember more of the material in accord with their viewpoint, while those initially unfavorable had learned better the passages supporting their opinion.

Later research has shown that this process of selective learning and retention is actually quite complicated, depending on the strength of agreement or disagreement, the future use to which the material may be put, the presence or absence of counterarguments, the role which the person is playing in the situation, and the personality of the individual. For instance, material antithetical to one's viewpoint will be of greater interest if one knows in advance that he must use it later on in an argument or debate, or to justify himself. Recently this has been demonstrated in an experiment dealing with attitudes toward the draft (Janis and Rausch, 1970), thus bringing the earlier study into the current political context. Sixty-two Yale undergraduate students were divided into two groups, those favoring and those opposing a pledge to refuse to be drafted ("We won't go!"). After they were exposed to persuasive articles on the subject, it was found—in contrast with the results of Levine and Murphy's earlier study—that there were no differences between the pro and con groups in the learning and immediate retention of the arguments to which they were exposed.

Note 9.5

Here we see an instance of the complexity of the problem, the response to threatening communications being dictated by many factors other than simple attitudinal agreement or disagreement. Under certain conditions at least, the earlier data of Levine and Murphy (1943) notwithstanding, attention will be directed toward material with which one sharply disagrees. This does not mean, necessarily, that the original principle is wrong, but rather that it is incomplete, and we must still determine the conditions under which it holds true and those under which it does not. As always, later research has suggested how initial, oversimple notions need to be qualified. Further research often provides growing sophistication about a problem and increases our capacity to predict outcomes by discovering the conditions under which they do or do not apply.

Perhaps one difference between this recent study and the earlier one was the greater salience of the political issue in the lives of the Yale students. The draft was a serious practical matter, of great importance to them personally, not a theoretical question. Another possibility is that the climate with respect to protest had changed since the 1940s. In the recent study a marked difference was found in the interest expressed toward learning about the pro and con arguments: the men who signed the pledge expressed *less* interest in reading articles that supported their position than did the men who were not in favor of signing. It might be argued that those who signed were already overfamiliar with the supporting arguments, and furthermore it was of great adaptive value to them to study the opposing arguments, since they could expect their action (signing the pledge) to lead to great criticism and they would need to respond with an informed defense (see Note 9.5).

Another device for resisting persuasive pressure is to *refute the arguments* by marshaling points and evidence on the other side. To the extent that the opposing case is a strong one, such refutation is difficult to accomplish, yet a person sufficiently committed to his position can resort to outright rejection of the arguments and refuse to consider the matter further. Such rejection is often done by *derogating the source,* that is, by rejecting its credibility without making any effort to determine the facts.

In Chapter 4 we considered the case of Ted Kennedy's public crisis in the summer of 1969. In this instance, people maintained their high opinion of a popular public figure by dissociating the message from its source. The hero's charisma was preserved because people wanted to believe in him, and so they took what he said or did as casting no reflection on the "real man." Thus, respect for the idealized person is preserved, but his words are attributed either to others (say, his speech writers) or it is assumed that he has been taken in by unscrupulous associates. It is an interesting commentary on the stability of our attitudes and beliefs that precisely the same kind of behavior in someone else toward whom we already feel hostile would simply confirm our low opinion of him. Our hero can do no wrong by resorting to compromise and expediency, but a rejected candidate reveals his two-facedness by exactly the same acts.

One of the pioneers in the psychodynamics of attitude, Kurt Lewin (1948) introduced the expression *psychologically leaving the field* to suggest another way people sometimes cope with an intense attitudinal conflict. Unable to resolve the difficulty, the person turns it off psychologically, that is, he leaves the field, not necessarily in the physical sense of walking away but in the sense of tuning it out as one does a television program one does not like. Thus, after struggling for a long time with a conflict in which he has been deeply involved, say, between two people he loves, a person may suddenly find himself no longer involved and troubled. He is detached and free of the burden, at least for the moment. He has somehow walked out on it psychologically. He has pulled back his commitments to the conflicting forces and no longer cares, although a little earlier he was deeply caught up in it and under severe tension.

It should not be surprising that people do this, since even minor changes in beliefs and attitudes can endanger the whole cognitive system constructed with considerable struggle over one's lifetime. Hence changing certain basic attitudes may require a major and painful psychological overhaul (Rosenberg, 1960). What, for example, does a person do who has built his entire life on the ideological value of self-help and independence, who has believed that society has prospered that way, but now finds that he can no longer feed and clothe his family without public assistance? Such crises of belief and faith are sometimes shattering to people undergoing them, but they are usually the final consequence of a long period of futile struggle to prevent precisely such a crisis from taking place. A reorganization of old cognitive patterns now becomes essential if the person is not to slip into the bleakness of depression, alienation, and total despair. Most of us are probably not so vulnerable (at least usually), possibly because our ideological systems are not as tightly and inflexibly organized, or we are resilient enough to manage such conflicts. Except when such internal struggles are shared by many at a particular time of life, as in the identity crises of adolescence and youth, they usually operate in the person silently, for the most part, and may be known only to intimates or associates through unexpected eruptions of emotion, changed moods, disturbances of work habits, or troubled interpersonal relationships.

Tying the approach to the type of prejudice

One of the key implications of the foregoing discussion is that planning a campaign against prejudice requires that we differentiate among the various types of personalities and psychodynamic processes involved (see Note 9.6). In dealing with different kinds of emotional "hangups," different approaches are needed. Allport (1954) has described three key types of psychodynamics relevant to prejudice:

One type is the person whose attitudes are closely tied to his own direct experience, with some allowance for social custom. Such a person adjusts his attitudes to the prevailing social patterns without being in severe conflict with them, testing reality accurately and remaining true to his own experience. In this way he can recognize when other groups are treated unfairly and not give in to an adverse set of social norms in his treatment of these groups. He is independent

Note 9.6

The effort described here to tailor the approach to prejudice according to the person with whom we are dealing bears some further comment. One can see how close a link there often is between our practical approaches to human problems, on the one hand, and our theoretical studies of psychodynamic processes, on the other. The identification in this section of three personality types, each of which should be approached in different ways, is an application of psychodynamic concepts to the problem of prejudice.

This is not to say that the only reason for research and theory is to apply it to human problems. "Pure" scientific investigation is well justified as part of the time-honored quest for knowledge for its own sake, though often such knowledge turns out to be highly useful in unexpected ways. Of course, much scientific research is also done with practical ends in mind, though it is often difficult to know in advance just which line of research will actually turn out to be useful. The reader has probably discerned by now that this book has been built mainly around the view that much of what we learn of human psychology has relevance to mankind's problems, much more in fact than is usually suspected by the novice.

rather than a conformist. His attitudes remain largely his own rather than slavishly those of the surrounding culture. Such a person is far less likely to adopt and maintain social stereotypes, and if he does his views are subject to change by education and persuasion. Moreover, he can accept changes or reforms in the social system required to redress the imbalance against minority out-groups. He is, therefore, not subject to the constraints that lead to resistance in the other two types (described next).

The second type fits the picture of the "other-directed" man (popularized by Riesman, 1950; discussed in Chapter 5) whose standards of behavior and attitudes are shaped by and shift with the immediate social situation. Lacking a firm set of values about human relationships, he bends with every social pressure. For such a person, antiprejudice appeals that contradict the social norms under which he lives will have very little success unless they are seen as representing a growing, mass outlook. He needs the support of the community to change his ways. Such a person may respond favorably if he believes that prejudice is the antithesis of the "American creed" and that this creed is subscribed to by those whose good will and approbation he values. Protolerance appeals to this type of person must be made with full recognition of his special vulnerability to social pressure, since he is unlikely to oppose the social forces about him.

The third type, the authoritarian personality discussed earlier in this chapter, represents the group most resistant to efforts to eradicate prejudice and discrimination because for such persons prejudice serves vital psychological functions that are very well entrenched. Insecure and threatened, this type copes by scapegoating without realizing it. External pressures for change fall on deaf ears or further intensify the bigotry. Kurt Lewin (1948), in his analysis cited earlier, stressed that direct efforts to change entrenched prejudicial attitudes generally fail because they are continually buttressed by powerful, often unconscious needs, and he recommended that this type of person be helped to discover that given groups pose no threat to his status or security. To influence prejudicial attitudes, it would be necessary to deal indirectly with them by addressing the person's underlying psychodynamics. Direct attack would inevitably fail.

Reactions of the authoritarian to direct propaganda are nicely illustrated in an imaginative study by Cooper and Jahoda (1947) in which cartoons were presented depicting a character called Mr. Biggott, a highly prejudiced person who was shown in a series of situations highlighting the absurdity of his behavior toward minorities (see Figure 9.13). The cartoons were presented to both prejudiced and unprejudiced persons in an effort to evaluate their influence on attitudes. The most bigoted subjects went to remarkable lengths to avoid any identification with Mr. Biggott. Rather than feeling ridiculous themselves, they often failed to get the point of the cartoons: "What's so funny about that?" By contrast, the unprejudiced subjects readily saw the humor. These reactions point up the capacity for self-deception about one's own bigotry, effectively producing insulation against any awareness of its absurdity and ugliness and, of course, against any efforts to change one's point of view. The popular television series *All in the Family,* dealing with a bigoted character named Archie Bunker, probably generates the same sort of process in many people of this type. Its humor is not likely to be enjoyed or even understood by many of the most bigoted people, since Archie is made to look absurd in his "all-American" disparagement of blacks, Jews, Poles, Italians, his wife (the "dingbat"), and others. (As noted earlier, it is important to bear in mind that not all prejudice is based on this defense mechanism; although important, it is only one of a number of psychodynamic processes involved in prejudice.)

Figure 9.13 Mr. Biggott. (Drawing by Carl Rose; courtesy of The American Jewish Committee)

"Good heavens! It's not restricted!"

We do not know what proportion of people these three types represent. The optimist might presume that the third type constitutes a very small part of the population, while the pessimist might believe that it encompasses nearly the whole world. Nor is it a simple matter to sort people out without extensive personality study and assessment. However, the key implication of this classification is that *different strategies are needed to influence each type away from prejudice.* Any strategy which might be successful in one case is likely to fail in others.

Programs aimed at fighting prejudice

A wide variety of action programs have been created to combat prejudice, usually without regard to the varieties of people just described, and very little information is available about their comparative effectiveness (see Note 9.7). There are formal educational programs to teach children in school about different minority groups, group therapy programs to improve ethnic relations within a community, mass media presentations to examine out-group problems or to propagandize against bigotry, and political programs to pass or enforce laws against discrimination practices or to prevent segregation.

Attempts to increase social contacts between in-group and out-group members in the hope that this will make for increased friendliness are not always successful. It is becoming increasingly evident that mere contact alone can have negative as well as positive effects, depending on the *quality* of the contact. Pettigrew (1971, pp. 274–275) discusses the matter:

Many well-meaning Americans have expressed the opinion that if only blacks and whites could experience more contact with each other the nation's racial difficulties would solve themselves. Unfortunately, the case is not so simple. Africans and Europeans have more contact in the Republic of South Africa than anywhere else on the African continent, and black and white Americans have more contact in the South that in any other region of the nation; yet neither of these areas is conspicuous for its interracial harmony. It almost looks as if contact between two peoples exacerbates, rather than relieves, hostility; but this conclusion would be just as hasty and fallacious as the naive assumption that contact invariably lessens prejudice.

Increasing interaction, whether of groups or individuals, intensifies and magnifies processes already underway. Hence, more interracial contact can lead either to greater prejudice and rejection or to greater respect and acceptance, depending upon the situation in which it occurs. The basic issue, then, concerns the types of situations in which contact leads to distrust and those in which it leads to trust.

Thus, if whites see blacks socially under conditions in which the blacks have low status, or if only whites have authority and blacks are in a subordinate role, the original stereo-

---

Note 9.7

In the accompanying discussion of programs aimed at fighting prejudice, we see a pattern opposite to that described in Note 9.6 on the application of knowledge, one in which the practical attempt to intervene in the solution of man's problems provides additional and perhaps unexpected knowledge. The failures and successes of such interventions can serve as lessons in themselves from which we can gain new insights about the psychological characteristics of man.

For example, when programs designed to increase contact between blacks and whites were introduced, it was not widely suspected that mere contact by itself would not improve ethnic relationships and that the quality of such contact was of the utmost importance. When some attempts at integration failed to alter attitudes while others succeeded, a sort of field experiment was provided. With the manipulation of certain variables in the field, their effect on the attitudinal outcome could be observed, as well as the effects of other variables within the situations studied. Thus, social intervention (or social experimentation, as this is sometimes referred to disparagingly) often fails in its aims but at the same time may provide rich new sources of information about social and psychological phenomena.

In recent years there has been a tendency to be critical of social scientists because of the failure of many social engineering programs (such as those of the "Great Society" under President Lyndon B. Johnson), as if to imply that this failure represents the failure of social science itself. This is unfortunate, and a serious distortion, since most such programs have been inadequately funded and, even more important, they have not reflected the fundamental remedies social scientists have proposed. Social science cannot be held responsible for poorly constructed, half-hearted programs that were billed as offering solutions to the crime problem, poverty, racism, inadequate education, and the like. It is important not to confuse such faulty, politically inspired programs with the recommendations of social scientists when, in reality, the experts have generally been neglected in governmental planning of social engineering projects.

types are continually reinforced (Figure 9.14). To be effective, social contact must occur between people capable of modifying their attitudes, it must make possible a feeling of equality and mutual respect, and ideally it should be supported by the community at large. As Allport (1954, p. 489) puts it, "The deeper and more genuine the association, the greater its effect. While it may help somewhat to place members of different ethnic groups side by side on a job, the gain is greater if these members regard themselves as part of a *team*." Perhaps this is why the United States Army's effort to promote integration, one of the earliest such social experiments, seems to be failing. Recent reports of incidents in army camps and aboard naval vessels suggest the presence of deep conflict and hostility between whites and blacks in the armed forces. Clearly, mere contact between minority and majority groups does not eliminate and may even promote intergroup hostility under unfavorable conditions. Moreover, perhaps most important of all, the underlying social reasons for the hostility remain.

On the other side of the ledger, perhaps it would be helpful here to give a brief account of one community's efforts to deal with the problem of integration which have, thus far, been moderately successful. In 1964 the predominantly white, middle-class community of Laurelton in Queens, New York, was faced with an influx of blacks. Many of the white residents, for the most part middle-income Jewish families who had lived there for as long as 20 years, began to get nervous about the loss of their property values and what they took to be the prospects of deterioration in their schools and in the quality of their lives. (As we saw in Chapter 8, many middle-class whites believe that such changes are inevitable whenever those

The link between practical efforts to solve man's problems and scientific efforts to study the human psyche need not be just a one-way street leading from knowledge to application. On the contrary, if they are accompanied by careful and objective evaluation of the effects, practical efforts to solve human problems often provide the basis of new knowledge. Nowhere is this clearer than in clinical attempts to help persons in psychological difficulty (see Chapter 11). Many of our richest and most fruitful theories of psychodynamics have arisen out of such practical efforts.

Figure 9.14 Stepin Fetchit, in his customary screen role, purveying mint juleps to two gentlemen of quality. (Culver Pictures, Inc.)

from a lower socioeconomic class than the existing population become residents in a community.) The fear of neighborhood decline was further aggravated by "block-busting" realtors who profit by panic selling.

Some of the younger leaders of the community, sensing the probable outcome of allowing the usual course of events to take place, put into action a number of strategies designed to forestall the exodus of the long-term white residents and the consequent development of yet another black ghetto. One strategy was to provide information about blacks moving in to overcome the negative stereotypes. White Laureltonians discovered to their surprise that the black newcomers were mostly middle-class white-collar and professional families like themselves, with similar upwardly mobile values. Block busting and the steering of white clients away from the community by realtors were defeated through vigorous investigation and legal action. The tendency of banks to refuse favorable loans (called "red-lining," that is, drawing a red line on the map around a high-risk neighborhood) was fought by convincing a bank to restore conventional mortgages for the community. In addition, many white families from outside who favored living in nonsegregated communities were encouraged to move into the neighborhood. The result has been the preservation, at least for the time being, of a reasonable racial balance, with about 40 percent blacks, though the public school in the community is about 68 percent black because of busing from nearby black communities (Figure 9.15).

No one knows whether this interethnic community can be preserved as such. But as one resident put it, "If we had to select one community to find out if we can keep it stable and integrated, Laurelton would be it. If we can't do it in Laurelton, we can't do it anywhere." Nor is it clear whether or not this experience can serve as a model for other communities faced with the exodus of whites because of incoming blacks who can afford the housing of a middle-class community. It is apparent that concerted effort is required to preserve integration of this sort. If nothing had been done by the residents, Laurelton would rapidly have become all black, as has been the case in many other similar communities. Yet the success of this effort shows that integration is possible if people are willing to work for it, and it offers some hope in the face of what has been, in the main, a rather bleak picture thus far of numerous vain attempts to cope with the problem of ethnic hostility and segregation.

Attitudes versus actions

It was intimated earlier that although social psychologists have traditionally assumed that actions flow from attitudes, the relationships between attitudes and actions are considerably more complicated: there is often a substantial degree of *independence* between the two. Let us examine a few classic instances of such independence between prejudiced attitudes and behavior, and see what this implies for the elimination of prejudice and discrimination. In the 1930s, there was considerable anti-Chinese sentiment in the United States, and a social scientist by the name of R. T. LaPiere (1934) took a Chinese couple along with him on several automobile trips, taking notes about how the couple was treated (without their being aware of it). On these trips, the Chinese couple was actually denied service only once, and LaPiere adjudged the treatment they were accorded in restaurants and hotels to be above the general average in about 40 percent of the cases. Later, however, he wrote to the 250 hotels and restaurants that had been visited asking whether they would accept Chinese as guests; 128 replied, with over 90 percent of them indicating they would not serve Chinese, although they had indeed accommodated the couple. In effect, when face to face with the mixed group, the negative attitudes suggested by their later letters to LaPiere were not allowed to express themselves in discriminatory acts.

In a similar study, Kutner *et al.* (1952) visited 11 restaurants and taverns in a New York suburb with a mixed racial group. Two white girls entered first, obtained a table for three, and were then followed by a black girl. Service was neither refused nor unsatisfactory in any case. However, at a later date, a letter requesting reservations for dinner was sent to the same places that had previously been visited, containing the statement "since some guests are colored, I wonder whether you would object to their coming." Few replies were received to the letter. In follow-up phone calls, eight proprietors denied receiving the letter, and all temporized so as to avoid making the reservations or directly refused to make it. Yet the same proprietors accepted the reservations in other comparison phone calls which did not mention race. One phone call is reported (Kutner *et al.*, 1952, p. 651) as follows:

Didn't get any letter. We've got dancing after 6 P.M. (They actually don't.) Are you colored? (Yes.) I like everyone. My kitchen help are colored and they are wonderful people. But we have a certain clientele here. . . . This place is my bread and butter. Frankly, I'd rather you not come.

As Kutner and associates point out, "Discriminatory treatment is minimized when challenged in a direct face-to-face situation." In effect, when clear conflict exists between law and conscience, on the one hand, and custom and prejudice, on the other, discrimination is practiced largely in covert or in-

Figure 9.15   A white newcomer to Laurelton chats over the hedge with a neighbor who has lived in the community for 5 years. (The New York Times)

The studies by Kutner *et al.* (1952) and LaPiere (1934) illustrate, incidentally, how field studies can also be experiments, even though they take place in the natural setting rather than in the laboratory and hence are less subject to the careful control possible in the lab (see Notes 3.1 and 4.2). These studies were field experiments because the researchers manipulated a variable by comparing what happened when the mixed ethnic group actually arrived at the restaurant with the effects of a letter or phone call. In this way, an important variable condition (whether the contact was face to face or by remote communication) was isolated for study, thus making use of some of the analytic power of experimentation but also taking advantage of observations made in a natural setting. The reader might try to imagine a scenario in which comparable observations could be made in the laboratory.

direct ways but not necessarily where embarrassment might result (see Note 9.8).

Similarly, discrimination can probably be practiced even in the absence of prejudice. We do not, of course, know the private attitudes of the proprietor just quoted who expressed concern about his livelihood. It is quite possible that he may have lacked strong prejudice against blacks, but as his statement suggested feared the public reaction of his customers to having blacks served in his restaurant. This is discrimination not to disparage blacks as people, but because it is profitable, useful, or safer to do so. This is what the "silent Germans" of Hitler's day were often doing, turning their eyes from the evils of anti-Semitism because it was dangerous or inconvenient to protest. But moral issues aside, discrimination and prejudice are not always associated, although they usually are. Sometimes attitudes can be negative, but the actions positive; and sometimes attitudes can be positive, but the actions negative.

This dissociation greatly complicates the assessment of attitudes, since under certain conditions people will deny negative attitudes that they believe will put them in a bad light. Or they may act in a negative fashion with no strong hostile feelings but merely out of self-interest. Since we cannot know about attitudes except through what people do and say, any assessment of prejudice is vulnerable to errors of inference (misinterpretations) about the attitude associated with the observed behavior.

But quite as important, if the study of attitudes, including prejudicial ones, is to be useful in our understanding of discrimination against minority out-groups, then we must discover the conditions under which attitudes and behavior will be either consonant or divergent (see Wicker, 1969). Some of these conditions are likely to reside in the situation, while others in the personalities of the individuals involved. The social pressures discussed in Chapter 4 would be one example of a *situational factor*. If a person feels negatively about blacks but his peers or business superiors hold the opposite attitude, than his prejudicial views may be covered up until he is among those who agree with him. Similarly, a person may hold generally negative attitudes about a group but the behavior of a given individual in that group may strongly encourage favorable treatment toward him, thus leading to a seeming contradiction between measured attitudes and actual behavior. Thus, in LaPiere's study (1934), his Chinese companions were "skillful smilers"; they also spoke without accent and were traveling with a Caucasian: these factors probably inhibited discriminatory behavior. In the study of Kutner *et al.* (1952), the blacks were all well-dressed and well-mannered, and the black women joined white women who were already seated.

As to *personality factors,* evidence points to the important role played by other attitudes in the individual beside those he feels specifically toward the target group, as well as to competing motives which are operating in the social situation. For example, the person may feel guilty or ashamed of his negative attitude, or he may need the business even if it comes from a hated group, and so the discriminatory behavior that would follow from his prejudicial attitude may be totally or partly inhibited in the interests of these other, perhaps stronger or more salient personal motives and values. In short, many factors other than prejudice are usually operating in a social confrontation, and these too contribute to the way the person will actually behave. The relationship between attitudes and actions is therefore highly complex, and to predict discriminatory behavior requires much more information about the situational and personality factors shaping the encounter than merely the attitude of prejudice (see Note 9.9).

Recognition of this fact has led increasing numbers of social psychologists to adopt a revised position about social action designed to eliminate prejudice, namely, that the emphasis should be placed on *changing behavior* rather than changing attitudes. The assumption is that it is the negative actions toward a group that are most damaging socially and psychologically, and perhaps if actions can be changed, attitudes may shift in the long run too. To a large extent, this new approach has been brought about by the discouragement of social psychologists over the poor showing of previous attempts to significantly alter prejudicial attitudes directly. It is too early as yet to evaluate whether it is a more fruitful approach to try to force people, through laws or other manipulations of the environment, to alter their behavior toward minority outgroups. The political struggle over busing of children in the public schools to achieve racial balance illustrates how difficult the problem is and how strong is the resistance of people to changing their ways of living in the interests of social reform.

CONCLUDING COMMENT

Allport (1954) takes cognizance of the many psychological limitations imposed on both legal and educational efforts to reduce prejudice and discrimination, refusing to minimize the difficulty. But one of the virtues of his insightful treatment is that he refuses to abandon himself to total pessimism in spite of the persistence of the problems of prejudice and discrimination. He outlines a number of important principles to encourage and assist the social scientist and layman hoping for constructive developments in this arena:

Note 9.9

The accompanying text discussion makes the point that the changing of attitudes is not an easy thing to do. Social scientists concerned with prejudice still seek serviceable principles of attitude and behavior change to help reduce or eliminate prejudice and discrimination in their society. Nevertheless striking instances of such change occasionally seem to occur naturally in our society. Examining these might help us better to understand the processes involved, and at the very least they support our hope that such change can indeed occur.

One recent instance appears to be a mayoralty election in the city of Los Angeles in late May 1973, in which Thomas Bradley, a black, son of a Texas sharecropper family that had come to that city 48 years earlier in search of a better life, was elected mayor in spite of an intense campaign by incumbent Sam Yorty. Yorty's campaign was designed to arouse fear in the white community of a radical black nationalist takeover of the city government. Four years previously, Yorty had defeated Bradley following a similar type of campaign. However, this time, Yorty was soundly defeated. What made the election of Bradley remarkable as a political phenomenon is that it occurred in a city not otherwise known for liberal thought in which only about 16 percent of the population was black. Bradley succeeded in gaining almost half the white vote; he did well in liberal Jewish districts, gained a small margin among Mexican-Americans who had voted for Yorty previously, and won more than nine of every ten black votes.

There are a number of interpretations of Bradley's stunning victory, including the possible influence of the Watergate scandals which might have operated against the incumbent, an ultimate backlash of white voters against racist politics directed toward a black candidate who actually seemed to be a middle-of-the-road liberal rather than a radical, the ill-fated and humiliating attempt of Yorty to be the Democratic candidate in the last presidential election, and Bradley's considerable poise in dealing with the fear-arousing tactics of Yorty. What is perhaps most important here is the implication that a white population preferred a competent black man for their mayor to a demagogic white man who attempted to ride into office on a campaign of fear. The lesson may be that prejudicial attitudes and behavior *can* and sometimes *do* change when conditions are ripe, though it is still difficult for social scientists and social reformers to create such change when the natural social currents are running counter to it.

1. Since the problem has many sides, not one, it is wisest to eschew any single-style campaign against prejudice and discrimination but to "attack on all fronts simultaneously."

2. It is utopian (and maybe a bad idea) to expect complete assimilation of all minority groups into one ethnic grouping. We must learn to live with ethnic and ideological pluralism, and at best all we can expect is to ameliorate the social problems which come with it.

3. We should expect our efforts sometimes to have unsettling effects, since they involve attempts to change our way of doing things. Some efforts may even boomerang in the sense of stiffening opposition to changed attitudes.

4. Action tends to have better results than mere informative discussion. A person is most likely to change his attitude if he is involved in some community effort, so that his contacts with minority groups will be more realistic and natural.

5. None of the direct methods that might be employed to change attitudes are likely to work with the intense bigot in whom hostility to out-groups is deeply imbedded in his personality, fulfilling vital ego-defensive functions. The approach should always be tailored to the personality type with which one is dealing. Authoritarians are best dealt with in an authoritarian manner. If the community at large firmly rejects prejudice and discrimination, it is less likely to be displayed even by deeply committed bigots.

6. It is probably more sound to attack discrimination, that is, the negative *actions* toward a minority group, than to attack prejudicial attitudes directly. "Even if one dents the attitudes of the individual in isolation, he is still confronted by social norms that he cannot surmount. And until discrimination is weakened, conditions will not exist that permit equal-status contacts in pursuit of common objectives" (Allport, 1954, p. 509). In short, it is difficult to change attitudes without first changing the conditions that promote and sustain them. It is also wisest to concentrate on points where social change is most likely to occur (points of least resistance), as in housing and economic opportunities. And while laws about such matters may not immediately change attitudes (the old dictum that "stateways do not make folkways"), properly conceived and enforced laws might create habits and conditions favorable to eventual attitudinal change.

The key to this classic human tragedy in all societies is that mankind has yet to learn to live together successfully *in diversity*. The human race is a highly complex social organism comprising numerous in-groups and out-groups, and men are conditioned from a very young age to make narrow rather than broad identification with other men. If we raise our children with attitudes of family, religious, ethnic, and national superiority, without doubt they will do as we do and countless generations before us have done, that is, tend to flock into groups of like-minded, like-appearing, like-acting people. They will come to trust only their "blood" (family) connections, mingle socially only at "restricted" clubs, and join close-unit ethnic associations to build up their sense of security and self-esteem. In a world divided into isolated, mutually antipathetic cliques, it is easy to project onto outsiders our own anger and frustration, to see only hostile stereotypes, not human beings much like ourselves. Particularly when social systems are arranged hierarchically so that ethnic groups are pitted against one another and some dominate and exploit others, distrust and fear are inevitable. Perhaps it is in the nature of man (biologically) to compete for material things or for symbols of status. But if so we must be more realistic about man's inherent needs so that these can be gratified by the social system without provoking the worst excesses of competition and mutual destructiveness. Were there equal opportunity for all, the rich mosaic of human diversity would still remain intact, for we cannot and should not try to force everyone into the same dull mold. Each individual would be allowed to develop to his or her full potential.

I can think of no better way of ending this discussion of prejudice than with Klineberg's (1971) lofty closing statement in an examination of the current situation between blacks and whites in the United States, one that applies equally well to any group relations. He wrote:

Martin Luther King had a dream—a beautiful, eloquent dream of an American society without barriers between black and white. If he had lived, he might have brought us a little closer to its realization. The "Man of La Mancha" sang of dreaming the "impossible dream." If enough of us have the same dream, perhaps it need not be impossible.

ANNOTATED LIST OF SUGGESTED READINGS

Adorno, T. W., Frenkel-Brunswik, Else, Levinson, D. J., and Sanford, R. N. *The authoritarian personality.* New York: Harper & Row, 1950. A landmark book on the personality dynamics of prejudice, which reviews a program of research on the assessment of the prejudiced personality.

Allport, G. W. *The nature of prejudice.* Reading, Mass.: Addison-Wesley, 1954. A basic psychological analysis of prejudice, with certain chapters (notably Chapters 21–27) devoted to the personality dynamics of prejudice. It also discusses the problems encountered in attempting to eliminate prejudice and discrimination.

Brown, R. *Social psychology.* New York: The Free Press, 1965. Contains a valuable review and analysis of work on the authoritarian personality (Chapter 10).

Byrne, D. *An introduction to personality.* Englewood Cliffs, N.J.: Prentice-Hall, 1974. Contains a useful review (Chapter 4) of research on the authoritarian personality.

Pettigrew, T. F. *Racially separate or together?* New York: McGraw-Hill, 1971. A thorough, up-to-date discussion of the problem of ending segregation of the black and white communities.

Now we turn from the outer world of human problems, the ones we all encounter, and the biosocial forces influencing personality development, to the individual himself, struggling as best he can to manage the various conflicting pressures to which he is exposed. We will examine three topics: what happens when the individual is overwhelmed by pressure and can no longer cope with it, that is, when adaptation fails; how we try to help the person in trouble by diagnosis and treatment; and the question of what is successful psychological adaptation. We begin with the person in trouble (Chapter 10), proceed to assessment and therapy (Chapter 11), and end this book on the positive note of optimal adaptation (Chapter 12).

Since most of the problems of man in his world as reviewed in the last nine chapters are not new, it should come as no surprise that difficulties and even

433

[It] is not accidental that aliéné *in French and* alienado *in Spanish are older words for the psychotic, and the English "alienist" refers to a doctor who cares for the insane, the absolutely alienated person. Alienation as a sickness of the self can be considered to be the core of the psychopathology of modern man even in those forms which are less extreme than psychosis.*
[*From Fromm, 1963, p. 53*]

2

You go to a hospital and maybe once a day the doctor comes around and he stays there, maybe five minutes. He talks a little bit, but he asks you questions. Once in a while they give you a little medicine, just a bit of it. About the only thing they do is put something in your mouth and see how hot you are. The rest of the time you just lie there, but the medicine men help you all the time—they give you lots of medicine and they sing all night. They do lots of things all over your body. Every bit of your body is treated. [A Navaho Indian, quoted by J. N. Wilford, Medicine men successful where science falls short. The New York Times, *July 7, 1972]*

3

4

failure to manage them successfully have been known throughout human history. There have always been individuals who were unable to "make it" in their world, impairing the quality of life not only for themselves but for society as well. It is not possible to say with any assurance whether or not the problem of adaptive failure is greater now than in the past. The percentage of people in mental hospitals has risen since 1850, when the first census of the "asylum" population was made in the United States. Before that time no adequate records were kept. However, it is likely that much or all of this increase reflects the increasing availability of mental hospital facilities and professional workers, and the increased interest in and acceptance of mental health care in the last hundred or so years. Moreover, with the increased mobility of the population and the decline in stable family and community life, it has been increasingly difficult to care for mentally disturbed people within the home (where their presence was less likely to be publicly observed and recorded). For this reason, it cannot be determined whether the modern increase in the proportion of persons in need of mental health care reflects a growing percentage of the population actually in trouble or merely changes in public policy and better record keeping. Thus, it is not clear whether the effects of modern society—like increased industrialization, the more rapid pace of life, loss of family ties,

5

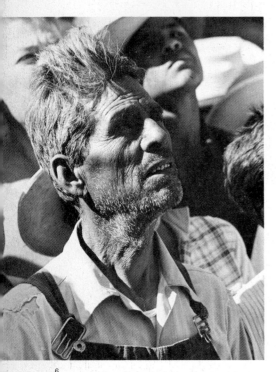

6

and growing isolation and anonymity of the individual—have brought with them increased psychological problems. Statistics on the mental-hospital population also represent just the tip of the iceberg, since the largest number of people in trouble never reach the point of hospitalization or public care, so that public records do not fully reflect the dimensions of the problem. It is enough for our purposes here to recognize that the problem of adaptive failure is a very large and important one in every modern society on which we have information, causing untold personal suffering.

Although adaptive failure has been recorded throughout history, ideas about it have changed drastically in the course of time, and it will be instructive to examine briefly how ancient and medieval man understood the problem before turning to our modern-day conceptions. Primitive man explained his troubles by reference to the actions of evil spirits or demons and of sorcerers who worked their spells through magic. Ancient man made no distinctions between mental and bodily illness and conceived of illness as the result of disturbed relationships with the supernatural world. The adaptive disturbances we now treat as mental illness were believed to be the result of a person having lost his soul, being possessed by an evil spirit, or perhaps having offended an ancestral ghost or god. The patient was responsible for his misfortune by having transgressed (knowingly or not) against the supernatural, by having broken a taboo, or by having incurred the hostility of a sorcerer or someone using the sorcerer for revenge. Natural causes were sometimes recognized—as when a bone was broken by a fall—but the root cause was thought to be an offended demon or god.

In ancient times, explanations of illness were also embedded in the religious principles and ethos of the society, but the thinking was still basically magical and demonological (see Alexander and Selesnick, 1966; Zilboorg and Henry, 1941). For example, in the Hebrew view, God was the source of both health and illness, and God's agents were precipitators of such outcomes. In *Exodus* 15:26, it is said, "For I am the Lord that healeth thee," and in *Deuteronomy* 32:39 the statement appears

7

The notion of mental illness . . . serves mainly to obscure the everyday fact that life for most people is a continuous struggle, not for biological survival, but for a "place in the sun," "peace of mind," or some other human value. . . . Our adversaries are not demons, witches, fate, or mental illness. We have no enemy whom we can fight, exorcise, or dispel by "cure." What we do have are problems in living—whether these be biologic, economic, political, or sociopsychological. [From Szasz, 1960, p. 118]

8

9

10

Revolutionary dreams

i used to dream militant
dreams of taking
over america to show
these white folks how it should be
done
i used to dream radical dreams
of blowing everyone away with my perceptive powers
of correct analysis
i even used to think i'd be the one
to stop the riot and negotiate the peace
then i awoke and dug
that if i dreamed natural
dreams of being a natural
woman doing what a woman
does when she's natural
i would have a revolution
[Nikki Giovanni, 1970]

11

"I kill and make alive; I wound and I heal." It is also written in *Deuteronomy* that, "The Lord will smite thee with madness." Such religious explanations of health and illness are also common today among many religious groups. A striking example is the Christian Science religion, which treats illness as a manifestation of wrong thinking; the cure depends not on medical science but on the spiritual purification of the person's thoughts. From such a viewpoint, health is a badge of virtue, while sickness is a sign that the person has been corrupted.

Primitive peoples living today view mental and physical disorders in essentially the same way (Frank, 1963). One may find descriptions of the treatment by the local medicine man or witch doctor of such disorders in numerous anthropological studies that illustrate the magical way of thinking about illness. In one such case, a sixty-three year old Guatemalan Indian woman evidently was suffering from what a modern American psychiatrist or clinical psychologist (the modern *shaman* or healer) would call an "agitated depression" (Gillin, 1948), the eighth such emotional crisis suffered by this woman. After diagnostic discussions with her about her trouble, the shaman attempted cure in a ceremony lasting over 24 hours and attended by numerous guests and participants. Some of the rituals in the cure involved making wax dolls of the chief evil spirit and his wife, to whom the shaman appealed for the return of the patient's soul. The patient was also massaged with whole eggs, which were believed to absorb some of the sickness, after which the eggs and other objects, including gifts for the evil spirits, were taken by the shaman to the place where the patient was said to have "lost her soul." He also pleaded with the spirits to restore her soul. Upon his return to the patient, the shaman spoke noncommital but comforting words to her, followed by altar prayers and further rituals. The patient, naked but for a small loin cloth, went outside the house and, before the audience, was sprinkled with a magic fluid while seated shivering in the cold air for about 10 minutes. Finally, she drank some of the fluid, and after the shaman reviewed the patient's eight disturbed episodes, he pronounced the cure completed. A few days later the patient seemed to observers to make a good recovery.

In pointing to the magical outlook of primitive peoples toward mental illness, one should not denigrate the shaman's therapeutic efforts or impact, since he usually strove to know his clients' personal troubles and worked hard to establish a human relationship with them. Despite his prescientific, magical outlook, almost certainly the medicine man's attentions provided the troubled person with important reassurance and support, and no doubt often helped considerably.

In the classical Greco-Roman era, especially among the intellectual elite, a striking new approach emerged in which *natural causes* came to be assigned to events that had once been ascribed to divine will or magic. The approach was increasingly rational as opposed to reli-

12

13

14

[*The*] *world as a whole is not fully urbanized, but it soon will*
be. This change in human life is so recent that even the most
urbanized countries still exhibit the rural origins of their insti-
tutions. Its full implications for man's organic and social evolu-
tion can only be surmised. [*From Davis, 1965, p. 41*]

gious, and science and medicine began to flourish. Hippocrates (460–377 B.C.), a Greek physician, maintained that the brain was the organ of intellectual activity and that mental disorder was the result of pathology of the brain. However, this tradition of science and medicine mainly went underground during the intellectual recession of the Middle Ages, when demonology returned, expressing itself frequently in the hunting down and burning of emotionally disturbed people as witches. These witch hunts lasted until the late 1600s, even in the New World, where Salem, Massachusetts, became for a time the Western capital of this mass hysteria.

Yet during this same late phase of the "Dark Ages," there were also beginnings of a new enlightened view of mental illness, along with the growing interest in art, literature, and science in general. As early as 1565, Johann Weyer, a physician, pointed out that many of the victims of witch burning, torture, and imprisonment were innocent people, whose only crime was being "insane" and whose disorder made it impossible for them to defend themselves against the charge of witchcraft. In the late eighteenth century strong movements attacking the inhuman treatment of the mentally disturbed began to get under way. French psychiatrist Philippe Pinel removed the chains from the inmates of two institutions, Bicêtre and Salpêtrière, and William Tuke in England, a Quaker, established a humane country house for the mentally disturbed called the York Retreat. In the United States, too, Dr. Benjamin Rush of Phila-

16

17

18

19

*If people wish to make a Buddha-land of this world, they
    must first cleanse their own minds. If minds are pure, sur-
roundings will be pure. If surroundings are clean and minds
    are pure, this world will be a house for Buddha.* [*Gautama
Buddha, 563–483* B.C.]

delphia (a signer of the Declaration of Independence), in the late 1700s and early 1800s made important efforts to introduce humane treatment in mental hospitals. A growing medical-scientific tradition had begun to gain strength in the field of mental disorder. We now turn in Chapter 10 to the nature of such disorder and how it is understood and dealt with today.

Illustrations: Background photo, pp. 432, 433—integrated classroom, Laurelton, New York (*The New York Times*). 1. Young man in mask (Steve Rose from Nancy Palmer Agency). 2. Mother and sick child with medicine man. 3. Kwakiutl Indians dancing to restore an eclipsed moon, British Columbia (2,3 Courtesy of The American Museum of Natural History). 4. Recreation time at an Israeli psychiatric hospital (World Health Organization photo). 5. Mother and daughter in camp for migratory fruit pickers. 6. Mexican workers at union meeting. 7. United Fruit Workers local (5,7 Paul Fusco; Magnum; 6 United Nations). 8. Youth counterculture, Big Sur, California (Roger Lubin; Jeroboam). 9. Young Adam and Eve, in a California commune (Fred Bauman from Nancy Palmer Photo Agency). 10,11. Poetess Nikki Giovanni with her son, Tommy, and a friend (photos by Jill Krementz). 12. Nigerian girl bearing up under an adult load (Louise Jefferson; Monkmeyer Press Photo Service). 13. Youngster fishing off a high cliff, in scene from Robert Flaherty's *Man of Aran* (From the Estate of Frances H. Flaherty; Museum of Modern Art/Film Stills Archive). 14. Sidewalks of New York (BIPS photo). 15. Air view of London, showing high density (Fairey Surveys Ltd.). 16. Air view of Stockholm, less dense (Rickets Allmänna Kartverk). 17. Pedestrian walkway, Stockholm (Swedish Information Service). 18. New model town of Tapiola, Finland (Consulate General of Finland, New York). 19. Tibetan refugees in India, bathing in river (Marilyn Silverstone; Magnum).

The expression *adaptive failure* is perhaps a bit strong to convey the idea of psychological difficulties in getting along in life. Most people with problems are not total failures but fall somewhere in between adequate adaptation and failure. There are, in short, many gradations and qualitative variations with respect to maladaptation, with many persons being in serious trouble psychologically for part or all of their lives, and others experiencing relatively minor difficulties. However, every degree of adaptive failure departs from an ideal of inner harmony, and the disturbed person often has difficulty in managing even his routine external affairs. We shall try here to gain some insight into what has happened in such failures.

SOME EXAMPLES OF MALADAPTATION

First, let us examine a few brief examples of serious adaptive failure.

An organic psychosis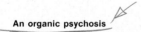

A mental patient (as described by Coleman, 1972, p. 550) had been a successful engineer and had retired some seven years prior to his hospitalization:

During the past five years he had shown a progressive loss of interest in his surroundings and during the last year had become increasingly childish. His wife and eldest son had brought him to the hospital because they felt they could no longer care for him in their home, particularly because of the grandchildren. They stated that the patient had become careless in his eating and other personal habits, was restless and prone to wandering about at night, and couldn't seem to remember anything that had happened during the day but was garrulous concerning events of his childhood and middle

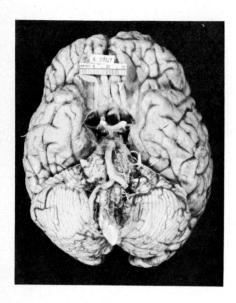

Figure 10.1   Brain changes as a result of hard-ening of the arteries, arteriosclerosis, a disease often found in elderly people suffering from mental deterioration. (Martin M. Rotker)

years. After admission to the hospital, the patient seemed to deterio-rate rapidly. He could rarely remember what had happened a few minutes before, although his memory for remote events of his child-hood remained good. When he was visited by his wife and children he did not recognize them, but mistook them for old friends, nor could he recall anything about the visit a few minutes after they had departed. The following brief conversation with the patient, which took place after he had been in the hospital for nine months, and about three months prior to his death, shows his disorientation for time and person:

DR. How are you today, Mr. _____?

PT. Oh . . . hello . . . (looks at doctor in rather puzzled way as if trying to make out who he is).

DR. Do you know where you are now?

PT. Why yes . . . I am at home. I must paint the house this summer. It has needed painting for a long time but it seems like I just keep putting it off.

DR. Can you tell me the day today?

PT. Isn't today Sunday . . . why yes, the children are coming over for dinner today. We always have dinner for the whole family on Sunday. My wife was here just a minute ago but I guess she has gone back into the kitchen.

What has gone wrong with this person's life? In this particular case the answer is that there has been damage to the tissues of the brain, the master organ of adaptation whose healthy state is critical for a coherent, integrated life. Such damage can be brought about by a head injury, infectious disease (such as syphilis), long-standing alcoholism, a stroke, a tumor, and other organic causes. Sometimes the damage is *reversible,* that is, the nerves of the brain are unable for a time to function normally, say, because of tumor-produced pressure, but surgi-cal removal of the tumor will restore the tissues to normal activity. In other cases, the damage is *irreversible;* brain tissue once destroyed does not regenerate, so permanent malfunc-tioning results. The unfortunate person in the above example is such a case. He is suffering from senility, the most common kind of an *organic psychosis.* The term psychosis refers to a severe mental disorganization. In old people degeneration of the brain cells can occur for reasons that are not yet well under-stood, perhaps impairment of blood circulation or other meta-bolic tissue changes (Figure 10.1). We are also not sure why such deterioration has occurred in this person and not in others of a similar age, but extensive brain damage is the immediate cause of his difficulties. When there has been such brain dam-age, the aged person will display impairment of intellectual activities such as learning, memory, comprehension, and judg-ment, and this will result in psychological disorientation (the person is confused about who he is and where he is).

In contrast, let us consider the following case of psychosis (P. E. Meehl, quoted by Maher, 1966, pp. 305–306):

L. W., a forty-five-year-old unmarried schoolteacher, was hospitalized following complaints by her family that she was overactive and assaultive, talked irrationally, acted peculiarly, and was generally "out of her head." Her psychotic behavior had developed only four days before admission to hospital. Having come to her parents' home from the town in which she was employed, she seemed to them to be unwell. Her complaints were largely somatic and seemed to involve a headache. A local physician prescribed sulfa drugs for her condition, but the next day grossly psychotic symptoms appeared.

She first began to mumble somewhat unclearly about having stolen or lost $100 from the school milk fund. The family went to the trouble of checking this with the school superintendent, who reported that there was no money missing. She would stand motionless for long periods merely staring vacantly into space; then would suddenly shift to a marked degree of activity. She talked vaguely about someone coming to take her away. At times she would creep around the floor on her knees with her hands outstretched, exclaiming repeatedly, "A child is born! A child is born!" (possibly a connection with the Christmas play she was directing). With considerable difficulty her parents managed to get her back into bed.

On Saturday she continued to behave peculiarly. She wandered aimlessly around the house, whined and cried a good deal, and said puzzling things. On one occasion she knelt before her mother and cried, "Mother, mother—come!" She still seemed to be under the impression that someone was coming to take her away. Various members of the immediate family remained at her bedside all that night, which on the whole was reasonably peaceful. She was able to carry on a more or less lucid conversation with her sister, although she was not very voluble and still stared for extended intervals into space.

When she awoke Sunday morning, she had a very difficult time putting on her stockings. She ate a hearty breakfast, and then at her parents' suggestion lay down for a nap. Upon awakening from this nap, she called her parents into the library, saying that she had something important to talk to them about. However, when they had come to listen, she seemed to have some sort of blocking which kept the words from coming. After manifesting this difficulty in speech, she grasped her father's hand without saying anything and squeezed it so hard that he cried out in pain. When her mother asked her what was the matter with her, she said that her stomach hurt and that she wanted a hot-water bottle for it. Upon being given the hot-water bottle, the patient began to "tear it apart." Then she suddenly became "stiff and rigid." This phenomenon alarmed the mother, who ran to the telephone saying that she was going to call the physician, whereupon the patient again became active and fought to keep her mother from the telephone. When the physician

445

arrived and decided to administer an intravenous sedative, it required the combined efforts of four people to hold the patient down. During the half hour or so before this injection took effect, the patient ran and rolled "all over the floor," bumping into furniture and grabbing at people so that it was necessary to keep objects clear of her to prevent her from injuring herself. Late that afternoon she was brought to the university hospital and admitted to the psychiatric ward.

Once in the hospital, this patient's behavior was marked by active and passive negativism. She would perform actions the opposite to those requested by the nurse. When her temperature was to be taken, she would close her mouth tightly. She would sometimes spit out the food that she had allowed to be put into her mouth, and it was necessary to catheterize her because of urinary retention. At times she would be fairly quiet and able to speak easily, but within a short time would become tense, hold her arms rigid, and two hours later have to be put into restraints because of violent activity and assaultiveness.

This person is suffering from what is usually referred to as a *functional psychosis,* that is, a severe mental disturbance that involves no evident damage to the tissues of the brain, though as we shall see later the possibility that there might well be something organically wrong, perhaps in body chemistry, is taken seriously by many professional workers. In this case, the patient is said to be suffering from *schizophrenia,* specifically of the *catatonic* variety, one of a number of psychotic behavior patterns; the symptoms are negativism, mutism, underlying mental disorders, with occasional violent states.

In the United States, schizophrenia is the mental disorder including the largest proportion of people who are considered "crazy." Such persons seem crazy to us because of a common major symptom, namely, disturbance of thought commonly leading to bizarre actions. Typical examples of such thought disturbances are delusions (false beliefs about the world—say, that the patient is President of the United States or Jesus Christ); hallucinations (seeing, hearing, smelling, tasting, or feeling things that are not there; see Figure 10.2); withdrawal from external events and retreat into inner rumination; disorganization of speech patterns (word salads, that is, a combination of rambling, incoherent, disconnected words that make no sense to the listener); and failure to follow socialized patterns in conduct and personal habits.

The *paranoid* style of thinking is one of the most interesting thought patterns to be found in mentally disturbed people. This consists of an elaborate set of delusions (false but complex, often quite logical belief systems). Two common forms are the delusion of persecution, in which the person is suspicious of being harmed, watched, poisoned, or influenced in some way, usually by some powerful force (electricity, thought waves,

So [*Don Quixote*] went on, naming many imaginary knights in each squadron; for each of whom he improvised armour, colours, devices, and mottoes, carried away by his strangely deluded imagination. . . .
Sancho Panza hung on his words and said nothing. But from time to time he turned to see if he could distinguish the knights and giants whom his master named. But, as he could not make out one of them, he said: "Sir, devil a man or a giant, or a knight your worship mentions is to be seen, for all that. At least, I can't see them. Perhaps it's all enchantment, like the apparitions last night."
"How can you say that?" replied Don Quixote. "Cannot you hear the horses neighing and the trumpets blaring and the beating of the drums?"
"The only thing that I can hear," replied Sancho, "is a great bleating of rams and ewes." And that was the truth, for the two flocks were getting near.
"It is your fear," said Don Quixote, "which prevents your seeing or hearing aright, for one of the effects of fright is to disturb the senses and make things appear as they are not. If you are so afraid, go aside a little and leave me alone, for I am sufficient on my own to ensure victory to the party to which I lend my aid."
And so saying, he spurred Rocinante, put his lance in its rest and rushed down the little slope like a thunderbolt, with Sancho shouting after him. . . . [From Miguel de Cervantes Saavedra, *The adventures of Don Quixote* (trans. by J. M. Cohen), pp. 136–137. Baltimore, Md.: Penguin, 1950]

Figure 10.2 In one of his visual hallucinations, Don Quixote sees two flocks of sheep as opposing armies and charges forward to rescue the weaker flock. (Culver Pictures, Inc.)

astrological influences, or whatever else happens to be in current vogue), and the delusion of grandeur, in which the patient believes he is some famous historical figure. The more logical and systematic the delusion, the more paranoid the patient is said to be; the more confused and inconsistent the delusion (and the "crazier" he seems to the observer), the more schizophrenic the person is said to be.

Paranoia can shade off into milder conditions in some of the people we meet in everyday life who show a generally chronic suspiciousness or grandiosity, in short, paranoid thinking patterns. Such people may believe that they are being talked about or plotted against by friends or colleagues. In milder, nonpsychotic cases (often called "paranoid personalities") the delusional system never takes hold of the personality completely. It is kept under sufficient control in ordinary social interchange so that the person does not get into too much trouble. But he is likely to be difficult to live or work with, and his suspiciousness or defensively inflated ego prevents others from being able to relate to him. Among such people are found suspicious writers or inventers who are unwilling to let anyone else see their work for fear of it being stolen; the persecuted business man or exploited scientist or engineer who views his own work as the basis of someone else's dishonest success; the extreme ideologists, reformers, prophets, and crank letter writers whose intense and single-track commitment to something or other makes life difficult for nearly everyone else with whom they come in contact. Such persons are not psychotic in the sense of being fully delusional, but their way of thinking seems parallel in many respects to the more extreme psychotic varieties of paranoia.

A clinical conversation reported by Coleman (1972, p. 276) gives us the feel of a paranoid style of thinking in a patient who is also schizophrenic. The delusional thinking is fleeting and inconsistent:

DR. What's your name?
PT. Who are you?
DR. I'm a doctor. Who are you?
PT. I can't tell you who I am.
DR. Why can't you tell me?
PT. You wouldn't believe me.
DR. What are you doing here?
PT. Well, I've been sent here to thwart the Russians. I'm the only one in the world who knows how to deal with them. They got their spies all around here though to get me, but I'm smarter than any of them.
DR. What are you going to do to thwart the Russians?
PT. I'm organizing.
DR. Whom are you going to organize?
PT. Everybody. I'm the only man in the world who can do that, but they're trying to get me. But I'm going to use my atomic bomb media to blow them up.
DR. You must be a terribly important person then.
PT. Well, of course.
DR. What do you call yourself?
PT. You used to know me as Franklin D. Roosevelt.
DR. Isn't he dead?
PT. Sure he's dead, but I'm alive.
DR. But you're Franklin D. Roosevelt?
PT. His Spirit. He, God, and I figured this out. And now I'm going to make a race of healthy people. My agents are lining them up. Say, who are you?
DR. I'm a doctor here.
PT. You don't look like a doctor. You look like a Russian to me.
DR. How can you tell a Russian from one of your agents?
PT. I read eyes. I get all my signs from eyes. I look into your eyes and get all my signs from them.

DR. Do you sometimes hear voices telling you someone is a Russian?

PT. No, I just look into eyes. I got a mirror here to look into my own eyes. I know everything that's going on. I can tell by the color, by the way it's shaped.

DR. Did you have any trouble with people before you came here?

PT. Well, only the Russians. They were trying to surround me in my neighborhood. One day they tried to drop a bomb on me from the fire escape.

DR. How could you tell it was a bomb?

PT. I just knew.

Neuroses

Neuroses are characterized by less severe distortions of reality and less marked personality and behavioral disorganization than psychoses. They might be thought of as the more "garden variety" of personal problems, shared by a large portion of people we meet and interact with in our everyday lives. *Anxiety* is one of the most frequent complaints, and it refers to a state of a vague uneasiness and the symptoms of it, such as insomnia, sweating, inability to concentrate, and other forms of "nervousness." In the more severe varieties, the person can experience a state of great alarm called *panic* and may require sedation to help relieve the intense subjective misery which temporarily crowds out all possible life satisfactions. The person is usually unable to identify the sources of his unease, or what he thinks of as the sources may shift from one time to the next, suggesting that the things to which the anxiety is attributed may not be the real source of the trouble.

A brief account of one person (from my own clinical experience) whose main complaint is attacks of anxiety will be instructive:

An eighteen-year old university freshman arrived at the campus psychological clinic a week before Christmas holiday with the complaint that he was extremely jittery and uneasy, but he had no idea why. He could not sleep, yet he felt exhausted. He could not study; when he started to read, his attention would wander. He had no appetite, and ate very little. His stomach hurt, and he trembled a great deal. He also had frightening dreams in which his mother appeared as a terrifying spectre, with large protruding eyes, and he would usually wake up in terror and soaked with sweat.

He had been on the campus for about three months, and had been fine until just before the Thanksgiving holiday, at which time he felt very much as he did now. Saturday during the Thanksgiving weekend he decided against going home and the distress disappeared, only to reappear now just before Christmas. He felt desperate, and that something terrible was going to happen.

When he was questioned about his plans for the holiday, he spoke warmly about his anticipated visit home, and brought out a letter

The grown-up patient is not a child, and to talk about the child in him, or "his" unconscious, is using a topological language which does not do justice to the complexity of the facts. The neurotic, grown-up patient is an alienated human being; he does not feel strong, he is frightened and inhibited because he does not experience himself as the subject and originator of his own acts and experiences. He is neurotic because he is alienated. In order to overcome his sense of inner emptiness and impotence, he chooses an object onto whom he projects all his own human qualities: his love, intelligence, courage, etc. By submitting to this object, he feels in touch with his own qualities; he feels strong, wise, courageous, and secure. To lose the object means danger of losing himself. [From Fromm, 1963, p. 52]

from his mother on which there was a postscript from his father. The postscript seemed to this writer to be very hostile, but the student characterized his relationship at home as pleasant and rewarding, and he extolled his closeness with his father. But as the time for going home neared, the anxiety seemed to grow worse, becoming almost unbearable. When he returned to the clinic after the holiday, he was again relaxed and no longer troubled by the previous distress. Later that spring, the same symptoms again appeared, this time evidently in connection with the end of the semester and his anticipated return home.

In the course of further discussions, it began to appear that in spite of his protestations to the contrary, the anxiety was generated by the expectation of going home and having interchange with his family. There began to emerge a picture of bitter conflict between himself and his father, in spite of the earlier statement of a benign home life. He seems to have constructed in his mind a distorted (defensive) picture of his family relationship. There was no problem in maintaining this picture while he was away at school, but as holiday time came around, the realities of the tumultuous and threatening interchanges with his mother and father to which he would soon be exposed began to crowd in on him, making the maintenance of the benign fiction increasingly difficult. Each time he struggled with what was reality in contrast to the myth he had constructed, and as he faced the ambivalence about whether to go home or stay on campus for the holiday, the anxiety whose cause he did not recognize mounted virtually to panic. At Thanksgiving the firm decision by Saturday of that weekend not to make the visit home temporarily ended the threat and calmed him. But before Christmas, and again before summer when he knew he would have to go home, the conflict again surfaced along with the anxiety. Only with the later discovery of his real feelings was he able to begin to face and cope with the problem. Ultimately the next fall he was able to make further progress, although he continued to have much anxiety in connection with visits home even though his subsequent attacks were comparatively mild and more manageable.

Just about everyone has some sort of *phobia,* an intense fear of something—of heights, confined places, snakes, animals, balloons, or what have you (Figure 10.3). The capacity to be afraid is normal and healthy in any animal, since such fear is an adaptive aspect of all animal life, a normal response to danger. What makes phobias significant and special as symptomatic of neurosis is that the fear appears to be disproportionate to the amount of real danger. When such fear is restricted to some limited and infrequently encountered feature of the environment, it may not be especially important, although it could be occasionally embarrassing. In many instances, however, it can be severely incapacitating.

Maher (1966, p. 3) gives the following brief vignette of an individual whose ability to function at his job was seriously impaired by a phobic reaction for which he sought help:

A forty-five-year-old married man came for outpatient psychiatric treatment to a private psychiatrist. He referred himself, but under some pressure from his employer, after having taken several months of sick leave. The patient was a regional sales manager for a large investment trust company, and his duties required much traveling. Some months previously he had developed strong fears of all kinds of transportation, finding it impossible to go to an airport or railroad station or get into a car without becoming anxious and nauseous. There had been no obvious incident or accident which had been related to this fear, but its onset seemed to date shortly after he had been informed that he was being considered for the position of national sales manager in the company. As his services were valued by his employers, he was given sick leave "to get over" his fears, on the presumption that they were due to overwork. As time passed with no improvement, he was asked to seek psychiatric help or be relegated to a position of less responsibility which would not require traveling. Apart from these fears, the patient had no other complaints at the time of the initial interview.

One of the current controversies about phobic reactions concerns whether or not they are the result of an isolated learning experience that can be unlearned or extinguished by counterconditioning (see Chapter 4) or, as is assumed by psychoanalytically oriented clinicians, should be regarded as

Figure 10.3 Many old-time comic movies made use of people's fears for the purposes of slapstick humor. Here we see Harold Lloyd in a perilous scene from Safety Last, *in which he plays on acrophobia—the extreme dread of heights. (The Museum of Modern Art/Film Stills Archive)*

displaced fears that express some other more deep-rooted process of which the person is unaware, perhaps a forbidden, unconscious impulse of which he is ashamed. If the latter is correct, then the phobia cannot be easily eliminated permanently without discovery of the real source of the fear; but this source presumably lies deep and inaccessible within the person. It is possible that some phobias are of the latter sort (that is, neurotic), while others have a more simple learning history and are amenable to straightforward efforts to unlearn or extinguish them. We shall consider this further in Chapter 11.

Another common neurotic pattern is called *obsessive-compulsive reaction*. This includes two sets of related patterns: (1) the person keeps thinking certain thoughts over and over (that is, he is obsessed with them), as if forced against his will to do so; (2) also seemingly against his will, he feels compelled to engage in certain ritualistic acts, such as stepping over all cracks in the sidewalk, washing his hands, or placing things (such as eating utensils) in a certain order before using them (compulsions). One is reminded here of Shakespeare's Lady Macbeth, who, after helping to kill the king in collaboration with her husband so that they could usurp the Scottish throne, compulsively keeps trying to wash the blood off her hands while crying in despair, "Out, damned spot! out" (see the margin). In severe cases of obsessive-compulsive neurosis such symptoms may be the prelude to a psychotic mental breakdown. Obsessive-compulsive symptoms shade off into milder conditions that can often be recognized in relatively healthy persons using a similar style of coping with threat, for example, the person who works compulsively and who needs to fill every moment with constructive activity (to prevent other threatening unconscious mental activity from gaining recognition) or the person who is compulsively neat, protecting himself against uncertainty by trying to arrange everything in an orderly and controlled way.

Maher (1966, p. 200) gives an example of typically obsessive-compulsive behavior in a male teen-ager:

A boy, aged seventeen years, was referred to a hospital by his parents, who had become alarmed about a gradual but marked change in his behavior over the previous six months. This patient had developed a highly elaborated ritual based upon the cardinal points of the compass. He could not sit down until he had identified the north, south, east, and west sides of the room that he had entered. When he had done so, he touched each wall in that order and then relaxed and was capable of conducting conversation on other topics. According to his parents, he would now refuse to eat his breakfast until he had been assured that food from each compass direction was on the table. Thus breakfast cereal from the North, orange juice from the South, and so forth were provided and eaten in the correct order.

Doctor: *A great perturbation in nature, to receive at once the benefit of sleep, and do the effects of watching! In this slumbery agitation, besides her walking and other actual performances, what, at any time, have you heard her say?*

Gentlewoman: *That, sir, which I will not report after her.*

Doctor: *You may to me: and 'tis most meet you should.*

Gentlewoman: *Neither to you nor any one; having no witness to confirm my speech.*

[Enter Lady Macbeth, with a taper.]

Lo you, here she comes! This is her very guise; and, upon my life, fast asleep. Observe her; stand close.

Doctor: *How came she by that light?*

Gentlewoman: *Why, it stood by her; she has light by her continually; 'tis her command.*

Doctor: *You see, her eyes are open.*

Gentlewoman: *Ay, but their sense is shut.*

Doctor: *What is it she does now? Look, how she rubs her hands.*

Gentlewoman: *It is an accustomed action with her, to seem thus washing her hands; I have known her continue in this a quarter of an hour.*

Lady Macbeth: *Yet here's a spot.*

Doctor: *Hark! she speaks: I will set down what comes from her, to satisfy my remembrance the more strongly.*

Lady M.: *Out, damned spot! out, I say! One: two: why, then, 'tis time to do't.—Hell is murky!—Fie, my lord, fie! a soldier, and afeard? What need we fear who knows it, when none can call our power to account?—Yet who would have thought the old man to have had so much blood in him.*

Doctor: *Do you mark that?*

Lady M.: *The thane of Fife had a wife: where is she now?—What, will these hands ne'er be clean?—No more o' that, my lord, no more o' that: you mar all with this starting.*

Doctor: *Go to, go to; you have known what you should not.*

Gentlewoman: *She has spoke what she should not, I am sure of that: heaven knows what she has known.*

Lady M.: *Here's the smell of the blood still: all the perfumes of Arabia will not sweeten this little hand. Oh, oh, oh!*

Doctor: *What a sigh is there! The heart is sorely charged.*

Gentlewoman: *I would not have such a heart in my bosom for the dignity of the whole body.* [From William Shakespeare, *Macbeth*, Act V, Scene 1]

Before this behavior developed the parents described the boy as extremely interested in science, and especially geography. He had large collections of books on various scientific topics and a very large library of maps that he collected voraciously. In conversation he made frequent reference to the completeness of these collections but seemed to have little interest in their content for its own sake.

Other maladaptive patterns

A wide variety of adaptive problems are commonly referred to collectively as *personality disorders*. This category includes people who seem to have acquired self-defeating patterns of reaction to social demands that readily get them into trouble. Examples are the extremely aggressive individual who flies off the handle at the slightest provocation or the utterly dependent person. To take the latter case, passive-dependent people are those for whom helplessness and indecisiveness are a way of life. Their relationships with others are manipulated so as to satisfy their need to be taken care of, protected, given direction, and provided emotional support. Such people seem incapable of relating to others in any other way. If they work with someone, the chronic theme is, "How should I do this? Is this okay? Please show me." If the other person wishes to get the job done, he often finds it simpler to do it himself, and this is precisely the way such passive-dependent persons have arranged the social situation, probably without even realizing it. If the other person grows impatient, the passive-dependent person is quite hurt, making the other feel guilty.

Another form of personality disorder involves various antisocial life styles, the most extreme form of which is frequently referred to as *psychopathic behavior*. The psychopath is usually in continuous social or legal difficulties and often manages to get himself behind bars. He displays little loyalty to others. It is not so much that he is a member of a dissident social group; he cannot sustain loyalty to dissidents either. Thus, we must distinguish here between the person who is selectively antisocial in an ideological sense and the one who lacks commitment to any social values, remaining always on the fringe of society. The following case from Maher (1966, pp. 214–215) is illustrative:

The subject was a male, forty years of age, convicted of check forgery and embezzlement. He was arrested with a young woman, aged eighteen, whom he had married bigamously some months before the arrest. She was unaware of the existence of any previous marriage; the subject had already been convicted for two previous bigamous marriages and for forty other cases of passing fraudulent checks.

Some interest attaches to the circumstances of this man's arrest. He and his "wife" had obtained employment as manager and hostess of a small restaurant in a large city. The owner of the restaurant lived in another town some distance away and had arranged to call in at the end of each week to check on progress and income. Living quarters over the restaurant were provided, plus a small salary and a small commission on the weekly total of the cash register.

At the end of one week of employment, the subject took all the money (having avoided banking it nightly as he had been instructed) and departed shortly before his employer arrived. He left a series of vulgar messages scribbled on the walls, saying that he had taken the money because the salary was "too low." He found lodgings, with his wife, a few blocks away from the restaurant and made no serious effort to escape detection. The police arrested him and his wife within a few days of the offense.

During the inquiry it emerged that he had spent the past few months cashing checks in department stores at various cities. He would make out the check and send his wife in to cash it; he commented that her genuine innocence of the fact that he had no bank account made her very effective in not arousing suspicion. He did not trouble to use a false name when signing checks or when making the bigamous marriage. Nevertheless, he was astonished at the speed with which the police discovered him.

Inquiry into the man's past history revealed that he had been well educated, attending a private school for most of his elementary and high school education. His parents were in good financial circumstances and had planned for him to enter college. Unfortunately his academic record prevented this (although on examination he proved to have distinctly superior intelligence). Failing to enter college, he was employed by an insurance company as a trainee salesman and there proceeded to do very well. He was a distinguished-looking young man and an exceptionally fluent speaker.

When it appeared that he could anticipate a successful career in the insurance business, he ran into trouble because of a failure to hand in checks that had been given him by customers to pay their initial premiums. He admitted to having cashed these checks and spent the money on a variety of small items, mainly clothes and liquor. Apparently it did not occur to him that the accounting system of the company would rapidly catch up with any embezzlement of this kind. Indeed, he described this part of his history with a note of amused indignation at the failure of the company to appreciate that he had intended to pay the money later from his own salary. No legal action was taken, but he was requested to resign from his position, and his parents made good the missing money.

At this point, World War II provided him with an opportunity to escape the tedium of civilian life, and he enlisted in the Army. His social presence and educational background were such that he was rapidly transferred to Officer Candidate School, graduating as second lieutenant and thence assigned to an infantry unit. While there was no record of any unusual difficulty at OCS, he soon ran into trouble in his operational unit for a series of minor disciplinary infractions, such as missing morning parades, being drunk on duty, and smuggling women into his quarters. These incidents earned him a series of reprimands, but more serious trouble developed when he began to cash checks in the nearby town without funds in the bank to cover them.

He was tried by the civil authority, and convicted of fraud, and sentenced to a few months' imprisonment. Simultaneously, he was court-martialed and dismissed from the Army with a dishonorable discharge. Following his release from prison, his life followed a regular pattern of finding a woman to support him, either with or without marriage. The first woman to do so was, in fact, his legal wife. She owned a small flower shop and was some ten years older than he. It was her hope that he would take over the business, and again for a time he put a good deal of energy into it. Unfortunately, he soon became involved with a woman in the neighborhood and spent many nights with her, much to his wife's distress. Finally he took a large sum of money from the safe in the store and left his wife entirely, moving in with his new sexual partner. His wife never did divorce him, apparently persisting in the belief that he had been misled by the other woman and would someday come back to her. Many subsequent affairs and offenses did nothing to shake this belief.

At the trial, where he was sentenced to five years' imprisonment, he used the traditional opportunity to speak before the sentence was passed to make a long and extremely articulate speech. He pleaded for clemency toward the young woman who was being tried with him and said that for himself, he was glad to have the opportunity to repay society for his crimes. The speech included many expressions of repentance, especially for having ruined this woman's life.

Perhaps this man wanted a quiet rest in jail.

Psychopaths are often noted for their remarkably charming, charismatic, even hypnotic personalities. They can be highly persuasive and very determined, valuable qualities in the political arena. In Chapter 9 we noted the ease with which one psychopathic type, Adolf Hitler, was able to gain a political following, take over a country, and shake the world (see Langer, 1972, in the margin).

Clinical workers also regard a host of other adaptation problems as the result of defects of personality or of the socialization process. Examples include alcoholics, drug addicts, and certain aggressive types of sexual deviates—child molesters, peeping toms, exhibitionists, sadists and masochists, rapists, and sexual psychopaths. Most such people are certainly severely troubled, but what makes this type of reaction particularly important socially and legally is the harm done to others, as in the case of crime pursued to supply the high cost of a drug habit, or the assaults on women and children by rapists and child molesters. In these cases, not only does the personality problem faced by the afflicted individual seriously foul up his own life, but it is likely to seriously injure others with whom he may come in contact.

In this brief descriptive account, there has been no attempt to cover every kind of adaptive failure recognized by clinicians. Not discussed, for example, are the *affective psychoses*, in which the most prominent pattern is depression (Figure 10.4), or certain common types of neuroses such as *conversion*

No study of Hitler would be complete without mentioning his oratory talents. His extraordinary gift for swaying large audiences has contributed, perhaps more than any other single factor, to his success and the partial realization of his dream. In order to understand the power of his appeal, we must be cognizant of the fact that for him the masses are fundamentally feminine in character. . . .
He has frequently said: "The masses are like a woman," and in Mein Kampf he writes: "The people, in an overwhelming majority, are so feminine in their nature and attitude that their activities and thoughts are motivated less by sober consideration than by feeling and sentiment." In other words, his unconscious frame of reference, when addressing a huge audience, is fundamentally that of talking to a woman.
[He] is nervous and jittery when he gets up to speak. Frequently he has difficulty in finding words with which to begin. He is trying to get the "feel" of the audience. If it "feels" favorable he starts in a rather cautious manner. His tone of voice is quite normal, and he deals with his material in a fairly objective manner. But as he proceeds his voice begins to rise and his tempo increases. If the response of the audience is good, his voice becomes louder and louder and the tempo faster and faster. By this time all objectivity has disappeared, and passion has taken complete possession of him. . . .
[A] steady stream of filth continues to pour forth until both he and the audiences are in a frenzy. When he stops he is on the verge of exhaustion. His breathing is heavy and uncontrolled, and he is wringing wet with perspiration. Many writers have commented on the sexual components in his speaking, and some have described the climax as a veritable orgasm. Heyst writes:
"In his speeches we hear the suppressed voice of passion and wooing which is taken from the language of love; he utters a cry of hate and voluptuousness, a spasm of violence and cruelty. All those tones and sounds are taken from the backstreets of the instincts; they remind us of dark impulses repressed too long."
And Hitler himself says: "Passion alone will give to him, who is chosen by her, the words that, like beats of a hammer, are able to open the doors to the heart of a people." [From Langer, 1972, pp. 203–204]

Figure 10.4. (a) Depression. (b) Edvard Munch's "The Cry." (a: Rita Freed from Nancy Palmer Photo Agency; b: National Gallery of Art, Washington, D.C., Rosenwald Collection)

hysteria and *dissociative reaction,* nor has any mention been made of *psychosomatic* or *stress disorders.* For more complete accounts, the reader is urged to read a good textbook source in abnormal psychology such as one of those listed at the end of this chapter. The remainder of this chapter is concerned with understanding adaptive failure in general, since when things go awry psychologically, no matter what form the adaptive failure may take, be it expressed as a functional psychosis, a neurosis, or whatever, all forms of maladaptation have certain important things in common.

UNDERSTANDING ADAPTIVE FAILURE

How can we begin to understand what goes wrong psychologically when a person gets into difficulty in his struggle to get along amid the often adverse conditions of life? In the introduction to Part IV it was pointed out that primitive man and medieval man ascribed mental disorder to the action of demons or sorcerers that had somehow taken possession of his soul. These were times in which magic and mysticism were the primary ways of understanding the animate and inanimate world. The most important change in outlook to emerge with the Renaissance in western Europe was a revival of the natu-

456

ralistic approach to human problems that had its origins in classical Greece and Rome but had been buried for a long time in the religious superstition, demonology, and occultism that dominated the Middle Ages. This naturalism was again applied to study of physical, biological, and social phenomena and led to the rapid growth of science. In keeping with this outlook, mental disorder was also assumed to be a natural event, capable of being investigated by scientific methods and subject to rational analysis of cause and effect.

By the eighteenth century, the Age of Enlightenment, when naturalism and rationalism predominated, two related approaches to mental disorder had emerged, both still vigorous today. One is the medical or *illness model* of mental disorder, which assumes that its sufferers are afflicted with an organic illness centered in the brain and resulting in disturbances of mind and behavior. This was a great advance in thinking over earlier demonological views because it was predicated on the idea that such disorders had causes that could be studied and understood, and it promised rational approaches to prevention and cure (Figure 10.5). From this point of view the sufferer from mental disorder is not a "possessed" person who must have the evil spirit driven out of him by violent methods (and, these failing, may be burned at the stake) but is the victim of some physical illness or malfunction of the tissues for which he is not responsible. He can be treated as a patient in the same sense as anyone suffering from a physical illness or a broken bone would be, in a humane and medically appropriate way aimed at ameliorating suffering and curing the disorder.

Figure 10.5 Dr. Philippe Pinel removing the chains from patients at Salpêtrière, an "asylum" for the insane near Paris, in the late eighteenth century. (Library, The New York Academy of Medicine)

(a)

(b)

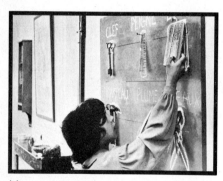

(c)

(d)

The second approach was related to the first in that it also presumed natural causes for mental disorder. However, it differed from the illness model in the assumption that those suffering from mental disorder have learned inadequate ways of coping with life. It presupposes that they have undergone damaging or stressful experiences that have impaired their ability to function. As a result of *social learning* they have acquired faulty patterns of coping with the demands of life.

An important body of work supporting this view was that of J.-M.-G. Itard (1962 ed.), a French physician of the late eighteenth century, who treated and observed the "savage of Aveyron," a wild, naked boy, about 12 years old, discovered in the woods of Aveyron, not far from Paris. He made inarticulate animal-like noises, moved on all fours, and fought with his teeth and nails. Some (like the noted psychiatrist Philippe Pinel, who was Itard's mentor) called him mentally retarded and incurable. But Itard believed that the wild child was retarded because he had been isolated from civilization at a crucial formative age, and he attempted to educate the boy during a period of 5 years. With patient effort, Itard managed to teach the child to walk and even communicate his wishes through sign language, but he never learned to say more than a few words or to care for himself (Figure 10.6). Itard's bitter disappointment was vividly expressed in his notes (margin, p. 459). Despite the apparent failure, however, many people took interest in the experiment, and the French Academy of Science pointed out that the child had really progressed a great deal from his savage state when found. Although Itard's observations could not settle the question of how much of the boy's inadequacy resulted from an inherited defect, his report stimulated later efforts to educate the mentally retarded, and it did point up the importance of social interaction in human learning at every stage of development. This was an early example of the social learning model.

Let us examine each of these broad approaches, the illness model and the social learning model, in greater detail.

Figure 10.6   Jean Pierre Cargol portrays The Wild Child, in the fine film of that name directed by François Truffaut. (a) Before being discovered, the boy lived in an animal-like state in the woods of Aveyron. (b) Under Dr. Itard's painstaking care, a new world of experience slowly opened up. (c) Although he never learned to speak, the wild boy did learn to place objects onto drawings of them, and eventually to associate words (both written and heard) with those objects. (d) At first the "savage" displayed a very narrow range of emotions, but with time he became very attached to Itard and his housekeeper. Here we see the first time that he ever cried. (©1970, United Artists Corporation, all rights reserved; The Museum of Modern Art/Film Stills Archive)

The illness model

As noted above, the illness model rests on the assumption that defects in the neural tissues, especially of the brain, or in the biochemical activities of these tissues, lie at the root of psychological problems and adaptive failure. Such a view is obviously well-founded in certain types of mental disorder, such as the case of senile psychosis with which this chapter began, though it is more difficult to support in other types, such as neuroses, personality disorders, and functional psychoses. It is also part of a larger idea, namely, that our biological makeup not only causes, or at least affects, mental disorder, but it also helps shape our personalities. The problem is to show this influence, to document its limitations as against the role of social experience, and to detail how the influence works. We shall now examine two sources of influence, genetic factors and physical constitution, though the focus is placed specifically on disturbances of adaptation rather than on the larger issue of personality in general.

Genetic factors Is there evidence linking hereditary influences to mental disorder? A positive answer to this question has been offered by Franz Kallman (1953, 1956). He pioneered use of one of the best research methods for studying the question, the method of *concordance*, which makes use of pairs of identical twins, fraternal twins, and siblings. Identical twins have exactly similar genetic makeup since they arise from a single fertilized egg (by a kind of embryological accident in which the fertilized egg divides into two, thus creating two individuals having identical genes—the carriers of heredity). Such twins are referred to as *monozygotic*, meaning coming from a single (mono) egg. Fraternal or *dizygotic* twins result from the fertilization of two different eggs by two separate sperm, and the resulting embryos then grow in the womb simultaneously. Obviously, they will have as much but no more genetic similarity than ordinary siblings (brothers or sisters), though of course they develop in closer spatial and temporal proximity. The concordance method is an excellent way of assessing hereditary effects because it allows comparison of the similarities and differences in adaptation of many sets of twins and other siblings whose genetic makeup will either be identical or merely related in the usual familial way. By this method, we can evaluate the chances that if one member of a pair has a particular illness the other will have it too.

Kallman (1953) has applied this research method to various mental illnesses and presented data suggesting a very high hereditary component in these illnesses: the concordance

The most brilliant and irrational expectations preceded the arrival of the Savage of Aveyron at Paris. A number of inquisitive people looked forward with delight to witnessing the boy's astonishment at the sights of the capital. On the other hand many people otherwise commendable for their insight, forgetting that human organs are by so much less flexible, and imitation made by so much more difficult, in proportion as man is removed from society and from his infancy, believed that the education of this child would only be a question of some months, and that he would soon be able to give the most interesting information about his past life. In place of all this what do we see? A disgustingly dirty child affected with spasmodic movements and often convulsions who swayed back and forth ceaselessly like certain animals in the menagerie, who bit and scratched those who opposed him, who showed no sort of affection for those who attended him; and who was in short, indifferent to everything and attentive to nothing. . . .

His eyes were unsteady, expressionless, wandering vaguely from one object to another without resting on anybody; they were so little experienced in other ways and so little trained by the sense of touch, that they never distinguished an object in relief from one in a picture. His organ of hearing was equally insensible to the loudest noises and to the most touching music. His voice was reduced to a state of complete muteness and only a uniform guttural sound escaped him. His sense of smell was so uncultivated that he was equally indifferent to the odor of perfumes and to the fetid exhalation of the dirt with which his bed was filled. Finally, the organ of touch was restricted to the mechanical function of the grasping of objects. . . . In a word, his whole life was a completely animal existence. . . .

All his habits bore the mark of a wandering and solitary life. He had an insurmountable aversion to society and to its customs, to our clothing, our furniture, to living in houses and to the preparation of our food. There was a profound indifference to the objects of our pleasures and of our fictitious needs, there was still in his present state, in spite of his new needs and dawning affections, so intense a passion for the freedom of the fields that during a short sojourn at Montmorency he would certainly have escaped into the forest had not the most rigid precautions been taken. . . . [From Itard, 1962 ed.]

459

Table 10.1

Kallman's data on concordance rates for various disorders[a,b]

Types of psychosis	Half sibs	Full sibs	Fraternal twins	Identical twins
Schizophrenia	7.1	14.2	14.5	86.2
Manic-depressive	16.7	23.0	26.3	95.7
Involutional	4.5	6.9	6.9	60.9

[a] The table entries give the percentages of pairs of relatives having the disorder during their lifetime depending upon degree of genetic relationship to the disturbed person.
[b] From Kallman (1953, p. 124, Fig. 36).

Concordance

rates were very high for identical twins compared with fraternal twins and other siblings. Some of these data are portrayed in Table 10.1, showing the concordance rates for three mental illnesses—schizophrenia, manic-depressive psychosis, and involutional psychosis (depression at the menopause). Similar findings have been reported by a number of other researchers using the same basic method.

These data provide evidence of the existence of a genetic component in mental illness. However, there are some problems in the use of the concordance method that temper somewhat the conclusion about the extent of hereditary influence in mental disorder. First, the diagnosis of the disorder (say, schizophrenia) could have been greatly biased by the enthusiasm of the investigator and the vagueness with which the symptoms in the nonhospitalized twin were diagnosed and reported. Kallman first located twins where one was known to be hospitalized and then searched for the other twin to determine that twin's status also. Since he knew the fate of one of the twins, he may well have been inclined to see the same symptoms of pathology in the other. Unfortunately, there is not much precision in diagnosis of mental disorder, even when very careful and unbiased methods are used.

Furthermore, the psychological environments of identical twins may well have been more alike than those of the fraternal twins, thus adding an unknown environmental component to the hereditary influences of interest. Families tend to play up the similarities of identical twins, often dressing them alike, and people expect of them more similar patterns of conduct than in other siblings. Identical twins are often very emotionally attached to one another, which also causes them to develop along similar psychological lines. Although in some cases the twins were described as having lived apart, this separation did not usually start until about 15 years of age. All this makes estimating the true extent of the hereditary influence rather difficult. For these reasons, there has been much debate about such evidence of the hereditary factor in mental disorder.

In the most carefully controlled study using the concordance method, by Gottesman and Shields (1966), these methodological problems were overcome or reduced. Additionally, special effort was made to determine whether the concordance rates varied with the severity of the mental disorder. Even in the most severe cases, the concordance rates were substantially lower than those reported by most of the other investigators, especially Kallman. However, the rate was still about 42 percent for identical twins and only 9 percent for fraternal twins. For cases where the disorder was mild the concordance differences, while evident, were considerably smaller. In any case, these findings strongly suggest that there *is* indeed a genetic component in severe mental disturbance.

No one has yet identified the nature of the defect which could be passed from parent to child, although there have been a number of as yet unproven hypotheses about this. Few writers believe that the disorder itself is directly inherited, as is Huntington's chorea (a degenerative disease of the nervous system that is genetically transmitted). A more promising idea is that some unknown factor is inherited that disposes the person to mental disorder, that is, makes him more vulnerable to the damaging or stressful conditions of life which bring it on. Thus, even people possessing the disposition should not be expected to develop the disorder if the damaging conditions conducive to schizophrenia (or other mental disorders) do not prevail (see Meehl, 1962). An analogy may be drawn here with tuberculosis, which also seems to have genetic components (some individuals and groups are less resistant than others). However, to develop the disease one must also be infected by the tuberculosis bacillus. If a person lacks a strong, genetically based resistance to tuberculosis, he will still not get the disease if he never encounters the causative agent. In the case of mental disorder too, the circumstances of life, such as diet and general physical condition, are important factors.

Physical constitution   How might mental functioning be influenced by our physical constitution? There are two main ways, direct and indirect. First, diseases or physical defects in certain tissues can *directly* impair the ability of the individual to manage his affairs. We saw a good example of this in the case of senility with which the chapter opened. Another example is the mentally retarded person whose limited intelligence greatly impairs his capacity to get along independently.

Biochemical examples are just as easy to find as neurological ones. Consider the hormone insulin, which is produced by certain cells of the pancreas, an organ known also for its role in digestion. Insulin has the function of removing sugar from the blood and storing it in the liver until it is needed. Sugar is vital to the function of all cells of the body, particularly of the muscles and brain. To be without sugar in the brain is like being without oxygen; metabolism cannot take place and the cells fail to function and may die. Some people suffer from a disease (a tumor of the pancreas) resulting in an excessive production of insulin. As excessive amounts of insulin are released into the blood, sugar is withdrawn from it and the brain and muscle cells are starved for sugar (hypoglycemia). The result can be very serious for normal adaptive behavior. The person becomes disoriented, sees double, may experience convulsions, and in more severe cases loses consciousness suddenly. The effect is usually self-limiting, that is, sufficient sugar ultimately is again liberated into the blood and the symptoms of the attack disappear, only to return once more when there is too much insulin in the blood. However, the brain cells may be permanently damaged if the disorder is not corrected or if sufficient sugar is not applied artificially to overcome the difficulty. Imagine what might happen to a person so afflicted who is driving a car, making critical decisions at work, or just relating to other people in the course of the day's activities. Because the disorder is difficult to diagnose correctly, it is probable that some of its victims are sent off to psychiatric hospitals because of mental effects that are mistakenly taken to be symptoms of psychosis. All this can be produced by a tiny tumor no larger than a matchhead. This is a dramatic example of a bodily disease with profound *direct* effects on mental functioning.

A somewhat more complicated pattern is found in disorders produced by psychological stress, disorders which further impair the individual's ability to perform the normal tasks of life. Intestinal colitis is one disease in which acute tension and anxiety play a large role. In this disease the patient suffers from persistent and sometimes severe diarrhea, often leading to ulceration and bleeding of a portion of the large intestine (the colon). He may also have difficulty in gaining nourishment and suffer from dehydration (insufficient fluid in the body). In monkeys, protracted psychological stress has produced death in several weeks from severe ulceration of the stomach and intestines (Brady *et al.,* 1958). It is believed that certain people develop the symptoms of colitis under great stress because their intestines are especially vulnerable, while others develop stomach ulcers, or high blood pressure, or whatever, depending on which organ system is most vulnerable (Figure 10.7). The causal chain is complicated: the disorder arises first from life pressures that produce psychological stress;

this, in turn, triggers "emergency" somatic (bodily) reactions typically associated with aroused emotional states; and if stress is prolonged, continuation of these reactions can result in tissue damage (Selyé, 1956). Such damage may seriously disrupt other somatic (and also mental) processes. Bodily malfunction produced by chronic or severe stress thus has a *direct* effect on a person's adaptive activities. He must either alter his way of life to reduce the stress or must learn to cope with problems better so that stress is less severe and less chronic; people who can do neither of these things find it hard to manage the important tasks of living.

Physical constitution can also influence adaptive behavior *indirectly*. Many physical traits are highly desirable socially

Figure 10.7   Psychophysiology of peptic ulcer. Nervous tension and emotional stress are known to be key factors in excessive production of gastric juices; these highly acidic juices eat away at the lining of the stomach and duodenum, producing a break, or ulcer. (a) The nerves and organs mainly involved in development of peptic ulcers. (b) Areas of ulceration in stomachs of monkeys who receive frequent hypothalamic stimulation by means of implanted electrodes. Of 19 monkeys so treated, eight showed increased restlessness, irritability, higher gastric secretion—and ulcerative changes. (c) Results of human studies indicating that strong feelings of resentment triggered increased acid production and stomach bleeding. [a: From Coleman, 1972; b: J. D. French et al., Psychosomatic Medicine, *1957,* **19,** *209–220; c: S. Wolf and H. G. Wolff,* Scope, *1946,* **2,** *4–9 (courtesy, The Upjohn Company, Kalamazoo, Mich.)]*

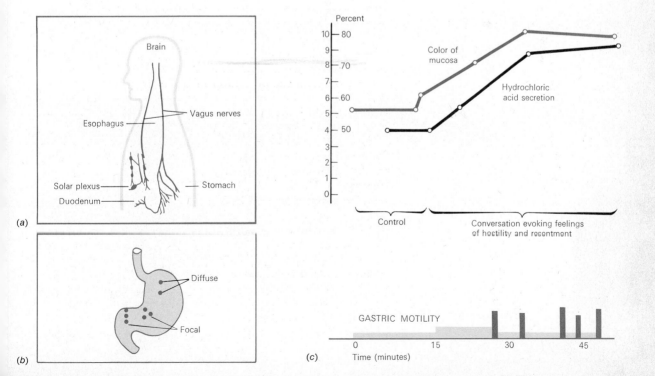

and give the possessor a history of positive experiences favorable to the growth of self-esteem and social effectiveness. Large size and physical strength in males are examples. Intelligence in both men and women is another. An agreeable physical appearance is still another. The strong, well-coordinated child can compete successfully in physical contests and is able to impose his will on other children; conversely, a puny, sickly child is likely to be a loser in the competitive social world. A bright child can succeed easily in school, effectively size up social situations, be better in touch with the adult world, and get a favorable reaction from it; a duller child is left out of things much of the time, and even when he is physically strong, he is often the butt of ridicule. A beautiful girl is an early first choice in dating and in marriage opportunities; she is usually the object of admiration and family pride. A less attractive girl must find what acceptance she can and must achieve fulfillment through quite different routes than one who is beautiful. As a child matures, his or her sense of identity and self-confidence are likely to be influenced indirectly by a variety of such physical characteristics (Figure 10.8). The effect is indirect because it operates through the social impact of such constitutional traits; this, in turn, feeds back to him, shapes his perception of himself, and affects the social role he tries to play. Although a person can often transcend social handicaps produced by an unfavorable physical characteristic and grow as a result of overcoming them into an effective and self-confident individual, they add to his burdens and can stunt or warp his psychological development and self-image (see Note 10.1).

Critique of the illness model   The illness model works very well for many mental disorders clearly involving brain damage or biochemical disturbances that affect the brain. However, it seems woefully inadequate and is often quite misleading when we are dealing with the garden variety of human problems, especially the neuroses and personality disorders, and probably the functional psychoses too.

On the basis of the evidence, it seems very unlikely that a person is necessarily suffering from a somatic disease when he is plagued by unreasonable or exaggerated fears, fritters away much of his energy in useless compulsive ritual, has continuing difficulty in his relationships with others or in achieving sexual orgasm, is angry much of the time, feels severely depressed about his life, or is inordinately suspicious of others. Although sometimes these difficulties may be the consequence of, say, a hormonal defect or a brain tumor, most of the time medicine can find *no evidence* of physiological disease. Instead, there is frequently ample evidence of a current crisis in the person's life, or a history of such crises in the past.

Note 10.1

Here we see another instance of the principle of interaction discussed in Notes 2.1 and 7.5. In this case, the effect of physical constitution in personality development depends on social factors, for example, how others react to intellectual brightness or dullness, or to physical beauty or ugliness. Thus, the impact of constitution on personality is moderated by social standards and cultural values of the community in which each individual lives. Most physical factors influencing us psychologically do not operate alone, but interact with numerous other factors. This is what makes it so difficult to pin down the conditions that shape our personalities. In general, it is rare that any isolated event will have a decisive influence on the psyche. As each personality develops, it is modified by a host of interacting influences.

Figure 10.8   An example of acromegaly, a physical condition that can easily have detrimental psychological effects. (Robert F. Escamilla, M.D.)

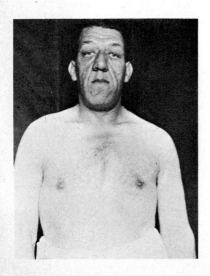

As a matter of fact, when such a person seeks professional help, by and large he is treated not by physical means but by psychotherapy; he talks about his troubles and tries to gain an understanding of how he has gotten into the bind he is in, or he is taught (often through conditioning procedures) to relinquish undesirable and ineffective forms of behavior and to acquire more serviceable ones instead. And when he is treated medically, it is likely to be with tranquilizing drugs or stimulants that are palliatives for his distress rather than a cure for some basic physiological malfunction. Thus, the most typical forms of treatment tacitly acknowledge that there is no illness, per se, but rather a failure to have learned adequate ways of managing the problems of life. (More will be said of the treatment of adaptive failure in Chapter 11.)

We must also avoid too much emphasis on labels of discrete *disease entities*, such as schizophrenia, paranoia, or obsessive-compulsive neurosis, although these are the traditional ways of referring to various problems of maladaptation. These labels create the illusion that we are dealing with a definite illness, just as one would normally speak of infectious diseases such as tuberculosis, or disorders of the adrenal glands, pancreas, or whatever. The reason for this reluctance is that such clear-cut entities simply do not exist as such. For example, schizophrenia is hardly a single disease entity, but a set of disturbed behavior patterns which may be quite variable from person to person and whose causes are not well understood. The label "schizophrenia" does not imply any definite cause or causes, as does the label "tuberculosis," or any one definite and distinctive treatment, as in the surgical removal of a tumor. Thus, to act as though such patterns of behavior are symptoms of a disease is to overstate the analogy between most psychological troubles and the medical model of a discrete illness (Note 10.2). Maher (1966, p. 23) puts it as follows:

. . . the criteria which are invoked when . . . a diagnosis of schizophrenia [is made] do not refer to bodily malfunctioning—they refer to certain kinds of behavior. The *diagnosis* of schizophrenia is not a matter of inferring the nature of some bodily state of the patient; it is a matter of describing his overt behavior. In the present state of knowledge it is not possible to give a clear answer to the question of a biological basis for this kind of behavior. Thus in the dictionary sense of the word (as a condition of the body or of some part or organ of the body, in which its functions are disturbed or deranged—*Oxford Universal Dictionary*, 1955), we do not know if schizophrenia should be called a disease.

Arguments against the illness model have been particularly well articulated in the recent writings of many clinicians (for instance, see Szasz, 1960; Adams, 1964), although opposition to this trend is still vigorously expressed by others (for

Note 10.2

If one is not justified in treating schizophrenia and other categories of mental disorder as disease entities, clinical workers have cause to be dissatisfied with the traditional system of diagnostic classification. Looking at the patterns of behavior and the complaints of mental patients, one can indeed find many varieties of symptom patterns. Some of these have been described earlier in this chapter, for example, organic psychosis, schizophrenia and its subcategories, neuroses, and personality disorders. The reader may have noticed that I did not emphasize these different diagnostic categories in giving case examples. One reason is that such categories do not point to clear-cut causes for each type of condition, or to a program of treatment specific to each. The diagnostic categories are largely *descriptive*, that is, they group many patients together under a single label on the basis of shared patterns of behavior and symptoms. Although such description is in itself useful, it does not necessarily help us understand what actually is happening to the person internally (his or her *psychodynamics*). It also tends to make such descriptive categories too important, so that we come to treat them as if they really had significance as names of disease entities in the usual medical sense. *Neurosis* and *pneumonia* are not comparable terms: we know just what causes pneumonia, and its treatment is generally agreed upon.

Moreover, the descriptive categories of "mental illness" are not as easily distinguished one from the other as they should be in any good classification scheme. Thus, although research (Schmidt and Fonda, 1956) has shown that clinicians can agree pretty well (about 80 percent of the time) about whether the patient falls into the broadest categories, that is, whether he is suffering from an organic condition, a personality disorder, or is psychotic, when the judgment must be narrowed into more refined subcategories, such as the type of personality disorder or the specific schizophrenic condition, disagreements are quite common. In short, clinicians vary widely in the diagnostic labels they apply to the same patients. One reason for this is that pure examples of each so-called type are rare, and most patients show mixtures of behavioral symptoms that often fall between two (or more) categories or display an ambiguous pattern. The examples given earlier in this chapter are more or less unambiguous cases, selected because they show classically defined clinical patterns. However, the average patient is unlikely to present such a clear symptomatic picture.

The diagnostic classificatory scheme in widest use today is that of the American Psychiatric Association (1952), although there is an international version that is slightly modified. The APA classificatory scheme originated with the medically oriented German psychiatrist Emil Kraepelin in the late 1800s, and although his original categories have undergone modification, it remains the backbone of the present system. All mental disorders are divided into two main groups, organic and functional. The functional disorders consist of six subdivisions: (1) mental retardation; (2) psychoses; (3) psychophysiological (psychosomatic or stress) disorders; (4) psychoneuroses; (5) personality disorders; and (6) transient situational personality disorders (disturbances produced by severe life stresses such as military combat and major environmental disasters such as floods or earthquakes).

Why does this system of classification and diagnosis continue to be used by clinical workers in spite of its unreliability and its failure to provide dependable orientation as to cause and treatment? One answer is that it does help us in a sketchy way to identify the main symptoms of the patient, and professionals have become very familiar with this traditional descriptive shorthand. Another is that no one has as yet come up with a better way of ordering things, one more in keeping with the causative conditions. In other words, the present classification system reflects our ignorance of the psychodynamics of most mental disorders, and we can expect that ultimately it will give way to better schemes as our understanding deepens. The problems of diagnostic classification have been scrutinized thoroughly by Zigler and Phillips (1961).

Perhaps the reader will now grasp the reason for my reluctance to provide a more formal and detailed account of the traditionally recognized "types" of adaptive failure. It is less important to be able to label and describe all of the "classical" symptoms of schizophrenia, or of each neurosis that is recognized, than to be aware of the issues of psychodynamics and treatment facing professionals who deal with people in trouble.

example, Ausubel, 1961). There is growing dissatisfaction with this model of adaptive failure, which means that more and more psychological troubles are being viewed as poorly learned or faulty patterns of coping with the tough problems of living. Unfortunately from this social learning viewpoint, the traditional terms "mental disorder," "mental illness," "psychopathology," and such, all connote a physiological disease rather than a social learning disability for which reeducation or better socialization is required. However, such terms are so ingrained in our language that it is difficult to talk about adaptive difficulties or failures without relying on the medical vocabulary of the illness model.

The social learning model

There are, of course, many theories of how people learn inadequate ways of adapting to the social conditions of their lives, and it is not possible here to try to review them all. One of the most common ways of thinking about the problem is that the conflicts and stresses to which people are exposed, especially in their formative years, often impede learning of healthy modes of adaptation (Lazarus, 1966), and this is the perspective that will be adopted here.

Stress The concept of stress describes a particular kind of commerce between the individual and his environment, one in which strong external demands are made upon a person against which he must mobilize his resources; or strong internal needs are aroused requiring mobilization of resources to gratify them. One example would be a child exposed to new situations, say, going to school for the first time. Impending surgery, or an important examination, or a dental visit are all common situations of stress (Figure 10.9). The need to gain the approval of others and to be successful are examples of stresses originating within the person. Stress can be very minor, as when weak demands are imposed on the individual that are well within his capacity, or when the needs to be gratified are relatively unimportant. However, when their importance to the person's welfare are very great, the stakes are increased and hence the stress potential. It is under such conditions of powerful external demand or internal need that we begin to see evidence of strong emotional reactions—anger, fear, anxiety, grief, guilt, shame, frustration, and depression, to name some of the most important stress-related emotions.

When the adaptive problem for the person is minor, he can ordinarily cope with it, in effect, he can engage in cool and effective problem solving. However, when the stakes in any commerce between the environment and the person grow great, the situation changes from simple problem solving to

Figure 10.9 W. C. Fields is ready to go to work on his anxious patient, in The Dentist, *Mack Sennett's hilarious comedy short, Paramount, 1932. (Culver Pictures, Inc.)*

one of major stress; more desperate efforts to cope may be brought in and the person reacts in a highly emotional way. Lacking adequate resources for securing the situation, he may have to fall back on inadequate forms of coping that have harmful consequences. Moreover, the strong emotions he experiences in such a stress situation may interfere with his adaptive activity, as when a person is highly anxious about an examination he is taking and finds himself reading and rereading the questions without understanding them because his mind is so preoccupied with the threatening consequences of failure. Children who grow up under severe stress often develop maladaptive solutions to their problems, and patterns thus acquired during the important early phases of personality development are frequently drawn upon later in life, with similar maladaptive results.

Conflict In conflict situations, the individual is faced with two contradictory demands or urges, and he cannot satisfy one without thwarting the other. For example, a soldier about to enter into combat knows that he is exposing himself to great danger; at the same time he is unable to adopt the simple solution of running away to avoid the danger, either because he cannot opt for that choice without undergoing equally dreaded punishment (imprisonment or social disgrace) or because he accepts the values requiring that he do his duty and face the danger (Grinker and Spiegel, 1945). There is a strong conflict between two powerful forces, the demand that he fight for his country and the fear that he might be killed.

There are many kinds of conflict: between two internal needs (say, simultaneous feelings of love and hate toward a

I was always embarrassed by the words sacred, glorious, and sacrifice and the expression in vain. We had . . . read them, on proclamations that were slapped up by bill-posters over other proclamations, now for a long time, and I had seen nothing sacred, and the things that were glorious had no glory and the sacrifices were like the stock-yards at Chicago if nothing was done with the meat except to bury it. There were many words that you could not stand to hear. . . . Abstract words such as glory, honor, courage, or hallow were obscene. . . . [Lt. Henry, in Ernest Hemingway's novel of World War I, A farewell to arms, p. 196. New York: Scribner's, 1929]

parent); between an internal need (say, a sexual urge) and an external demand (proscriptions against the sexual activity); and between two incompatible external demands (an expectation that an adolescent will become independent of his parents, yet pressure that he remain tied to his parents financially and emotionally). In these and other common kinds of conflict, you can see that the person is caught in an irresolvable dilemma: one of two strong needs must be thwarted to gratify the other. Sometimes the conflict is so great that it is easier to give up both rather than make a very difficult or impossible choice between them.

Strong conflicts of this type are important because they inevitably create major stress, and being so difficult to resolve they push the person toward maladaptive solutions. Sometimes the stress is so severe as to lock the person into total inaction. He is psychologically paralyzed. (Such cases, dubbed "battle fatigue" or "shell shock," are common among troops exposed to long periods of heavy combat conditions.) As we shall soon see, the critical factor here is the way in which the person copes with stress. As was noted earlier, maladaptive patterns of coping are probably acquired early in life when one's ways of thinking and reacting are being formed, and even though inadequate they often persist throughout life (Figure 10.10).

Coping with stress   The term *coping* has become an everyday part of our vocabulary, and a pharmaceutical company has even used the name "Cope" for a patent medicine. In modern psychological parlance, the term usually refers to the

Figure 10.10 One situation, but two reactions. (Drawing by J. J. Dunleavy)

"Win a few, lose a few!"

manner in which we try to handle stressful experiences, *whether or not the expedients we employ are effective.* Included within the concept are three related but separate functions: (1) elimination of threat; (2) control of disturbing emotions; and (3) gratification or inhibition of strong impulses. Thus, as in our everyday language, the word tends to cover a host of adaptation-relevant psychological activities. Much can be learned about the coping process by observation of normal people under unusual and extreme conditions. For example, researchers have studied the reactions of graduate students anticipating a crucial oral examination that would determine whether they could continue their doctoral studies or be forced to terminate their education (Mechanic, 1962). As we might expect, these students reported marked anxiety and other kinds of distress during the period during which they prepared for the exam. To cope with the threat of failure they expended much energy seeking information from other students about what to study and how to evaluate their prospects, often judged from supposed attitudes manifested by the faculty toward them. Often they would seize irrationally upon the slightest evidence suggesting they were not well regarded and would react with irrational alarm. A casually made brusk remark might be taken as evidence of a negative opinion and result in severe depression; or a book might be selected for reading merely because of an ill-founded rumor that one of the faculty had said it was the best source of information. As the examination approached, symptoms of stress disorders such as stomach trouble, sleeplessness, and fatigue became more prominent, and use of sleeping pills and tranquilizers became frequent.

Similar studies have been made of the reactions of other people under severe stress: parents of children dying of leukemia; patients who have suffered a severe heart attack; people awaiting surgery or dental injections; men anticipating their first parachute jump; victims of paralytic polio. Such research makes possible the careful analysis of the positive and negative consequences of stress and permits us to gain insight into coping processes, the conditions influencing them, and their outcomes. Not only are such extreme situations important in their own right because they are frequently encountered in life, but they also throw light on coping mechanisms and yield a better understanding of mental disorders in which the causal stressful conditions may not be readily apparent. Since there may be either remarkable personal growth in the wake of situations of crisis or great damage to the person's adaptive capacities, we need to discover just what internal and external factors favor one or the other outcome. Such knowledge is as yet quite fragmentary.

Stress is an inevitable part of life, and hence a key difference between people in trouble and those who are psychologically healthy lies in their modes of coping with it. Observations of individual differences in reactions to being severely burned offer a good example (Hamburg *et al.,* 1953, pp. 2–3):

When a psychiatric observer enters a ward in which there are a number of severely burned patients, all in the acute phase (covered with bandages, receiving transfusions, and so on), he is likely to be impressed by the varieties of behavior evident. One patient is crying, moaning, complaining, demanding that more be done for him; another appears completely comfortable and unconcerned; another appears intensely preoccupied and seems to make very little contact with the observer; still another appears sad and troubled but friendly, responding with a weak smile to any approach made to him; and so it goes, from one bed to the next . . . although the injuries are quite comparable. . . .

Such patients are coping with the problem in various ways, some seeking to achieve sympathy and relief, some refusing help, some denying the severity of the disability or its life-threatening nature, some finding scapegoats and feeling intense anger towards others not so afflicted, and so on. Obviously, people vary widely in their reactions to stress, and we shall now examine some of these mechanisms from the aspect of mental disorder or health.

The defense mechanism

One of the cornerstones of modern clinical theory and practice is the assumption that mental disorders typically involve the use of certain reality-distorting forms of coping, usually called "defenses," or "defense mechanisms." They are benign interpretations of threatening or harmful (stressful) events and are therefore a device for self-deception. Yet nearly everyone uses them at some time or other, especially in situations in which there is little or nothing that can be done concretely to remove the threat.

Clinicians have tended to assume that reality distortions are less frequent in psychologically healthy people than in neurotic ones. This is probably true, yet a case could also be made that sometimes such devices are vital in assisting us to live through serious personal crises, at least until we have gained the ability to make more realistic evaluations and take more adaptive actions. But very little is known as yet about the effects of such defenses or about the conditions under which they are either damaging or constructive.

Ironically, family and friends often encourage reality-distorting defenses rather than realistic appraisals and useful actions. Sometimes, in an effort to prevent the loved one's distress and to provide reassurance, those around him may make his plight worse rather than better. A telling example comes from a study of the reactions of relatives of children with terminal cancer (Friedman *et al.,* 1963, p. 618):

> Typically, the children's grandparents tended to be less accepting of the diagnosis than the parents, with more distant relatives and friends challenging reality even more frequently. The tendency for the degree of reality-distortion to increase with the remoteness of the source from the immediate family almost made it appear that some of the parents were surrounded by "concentric circles of disbelief." Friends and relatives would question the parents as to whether the doctors were *sure* of the diagnosis and prognosis, and might suggest that the parents seek additional medical opinion. Comments would be made that the ill child, especially if he was in remission [a temporary improvement], could not possibly have leukemia as he looked too well or did not have the "right symptoms." Individuals cured of "leukemia" would be cited, and in a few cases faith healers and pseudomedical practitioners were recommended.

Although parents generally perceived most of these statements and suggestions as attempts to "cheer us up and give us hope," they found themselves in the uncomfortable position of having to "defend" their child's diagnosis and prognosis [future prospects], sometimes experiencing the feeling that others thought they were therefore "condemning" their own child. Thus, the parents were not allowed to express any feelings of hopelessness, yet . . . they were paradoxically expected to appear grief-stricken.

One sees here that the social context often encourages self-deception. Even medical personnel tend to give optimistic statements to people with terminal illnesses, giving rise to what some have referred to as the hospital "conspiracy" not to tell the patient he is dying.

In the examples just given, the self-deception has to do with threatening external events. However, reality-distorting defenses are also directed at events stemming from within, impulses, thoughts, and feelings which the individual dares not acknowledge because they violate his own internal values and standards. In Freudian psychoanalytic writing, important examples of such threatening impulses include erotic impulses directed at a parent and hostile impulses directed at loved ones. These latter are especially threatening and difficult to acknowledge because they confront the person with an unresolvable dilemma—he feels dependent upon the loved one, but at the same time he feels hostility because these feelings threaten his autonomy. Freud thought that all strong human relationships were characterized by such *ambivalence* and involved conflicting feelings ranging from love to hate. However, the hateful impulses must be tightly controlled or suppressed lest they impair the needed love relationship.

One way of managing such ambivalence is to refuse to acknowledge the hate, even when it is aroused by the other person's actions. In the parent-child version of such conflict,

People cannot flee from their impulses as they can from a storm or a snake. Accordingly, they must rely on intrapsychic maneuvers or operations by means of which they may block any and all discharge of the threatening impulses. These operations usually entail denying conscious representation to ideas, affects and other impulses associated with the threatening impulses, as well as blocking discharge of the threatening impulses themselves. . . .

The operations by which impulses and their representations are blocked from expression in consciousness and action are known as defenses. Defenses differ from controlling or regulating ego-functions in that the latter are relatively autonomous, conflict-free functions facilitating the discharge of impulses, even in partial, modulated or indirect form. In contrast, defenses ultimately are desperate, thoroughgoing, uncompromising attempts to "eliminate" the rejected, threatening impulses and their representations. Of course, a defensive operation may fail partially or totally, in which case more or less discharge and conscious awareness of the rejected impulse result along with more or less anxiety. [From Schafer, 1954, p. 161]

Note 10.3

Since a defense mechanism is defined as a form of self-deception, how then do we infer when such a process is taking place? After all, the individual himself cannot tell us about it since by definition he is not aware of any distortion of reality.

There are three main cues by which an observer can discern the functioning of a defense mechanism. First, such a mechanism may be suspected when the individual's reaction is very much out of line with the stimulus conditions to which he is exposed. For example, he has been sharply attacked and insulted and yet reports nevertheless that the attack did not bother him at all (he may claim not to have perceived it as such, that he is not angry). Or he has been told that he has a terminal illness, or that he is in danger of losing his job, and gives no evidence of concern. The marked discrepancy between the reaction and that which would normally be expected leads us to question the genuineness of the reaction. In these above illustrations, we suspect that the person is engaged in a self-defensive process that we can call denial.

Second, we suspect a defensive process when the person is inconsistent in speaking of his impulses or feelings in some situation. For example, at first he reports only feelings of love and fondness for another person who is significant in his life, say a parent, sibling, or spouse, but later on he lets it slip momentarily that he feels hateful or negative toward that person; still later, he seems to have forgotten his previous admission of negative feeling and returns to a presentation of only positive feelings and is offended at the suggestion that negative ones are also present. The contradictory pattern of what he says suggests that he is harboring negative feelings that he is having difficulty acknowledging to others and perhaps even to himself. The contradiction, like a "Freudian slip" (see Chapter 12), has possibly revealed a conflict that is being handled by a defensive process. Another form of this kind of discrepancy is excessive concern about someone, extravagant protestations of affection and of interest in the person's welfare that are not backed up by genuine acts. The excessiveness of the claim seems to belie its validity (see the discussion of *reaction formation* in the text).

the child learns to do this by internalizing parental proscriptions against antisocial urges (see Chapter 4) and forbidding them to himself. He controls them by inhibiting them and refusing to acknowledge their existence (repression). If they seem not to be there, then he need not feel anxious or guilty about them. He has adapted by deceiving himself, by employing defense mechanisms (see, however, Note 10.3).

Defense mechanisms involve a variety of ways of thinking about threatening impulses or external dangers, all of which circumvent anxiety: one can deny the impulse or danger, take an attitude of detachment toward it, project it onto someone else, repress any knowledge of it, and so on. The terms for the most common defenses—denial, reaction formation, repression, intellectualization, projection—each designate different mental processes whereby the sense of danger is removed from one's mind.

In the case of *denial,* the individual refuses to acknowledge a danger or a threatening impulse by asserting that it simply does not exist. He says "I am not angry," or "I am not dying of cancer." Akin to denial is *reaction formation,* in which the person goes one step further, claiming not only that he is not angry, say, but what is more that he has only the most positive or loving feelings toward the person toward whom he really feels hostile. Often this defensive distortion is marked by the unwarranted intensity with which it is asserted.

Repression, considered by Freud to be the principal psychological defense, is the refusal to recognize an impulse, thought, or feeling by the very effective device of not allowing any reference to it to enter awareness. It remains entirely unconscious. Whereas in denial the person actually acknowledges the possibility of anger by denying it, in repression the very idea of anger is expelled from the mind, along with any related suggestive thoughts.

Intellectualization is the process of protecting oneself against threats by detachment from them. Love and hate, for example, can be dangerous emotions, but they can be controlled if one remains detached and analytical about people. By analyzing all one's personal relationships intellectually, one rarely risks the disturbed feelings that might arise from involvement in them. Both in medicine and in war, people often protect themselves from the distress of seeing death and suffering through the intellectualizing process of depersonalizing the victims, that is, by gaining psychological distance from them (see Chapter 7). We can usually accept the death of those whom we do not know personally more easily than that of our own friends and loved ones.

Projection consists of refusing to acknowledge an unacceptable or threatening impulse in oneself but attributing it to someone else instead. In this way, we need not take responsibility for a thought, feeling, or impulse; rather, the anger, say, or the erotic feeling, can be blamed on the other person. We have already touched upon projection in Chapter 9 in the discussion of the psychodynamics of prejudice, particularly with respect to the process of scapegoating.

Why are defenses often maladaptive?   There are two main reasons why the defense mechanisms just discussed can be faulty ways of coping with stress. First, denial of reality requires that much effort be expended to maintain the fiction against all evidence to the contrary. The individual must keep his attention away from the contradictory evidence or work hard to rationalize it or reinterpret it, and he must also make his behavior conform to the defensive interpretation so that the fiction remains believable. For example, if he denies his anger, he must also behave nonangrily, even lovingly, in word and deed, covering up as much as possible any subtle gestures that might be indicative of anger. Psychoanalyst Otto Fenichel (1945) has used the colorful expression "silent internal tasks" to refer to such inner defensive struggles, which seem to consume the energy of the person who is in neurotic conflict. He must tax too many of his resources on defense to be able productively to attack the other tasks of life.

Furthermore, distortion of reality, if it is successful, means that the individual will incorrectly interpret his circumstances, and to the extent that he acts on this misinterpretation he is likely to make erroneous decisions. For the defense mechanism to work the person must be unaware of its operation in himself and the ideas or impulses being distorted. Defenses are *unconscious processes*. Thus, the person who considers his spouse to be solely responsible for their marital failure protects himself from recognizing his own personal defects but cannot take the necessary steps to help straighten things out because he does not perceive the truth. A student who blames the professor or the institution for his academic difficulties when they are not at fault, thereby covering up his own deficiencies, will in consequence make the wrong decisions educationally and occupationally.

There are some important qualifications to the presumption that defenses are by definition pathological, that is, necessarily associated with adaptive failure. For one thing, there are times when nothing can actually be done to change the course of events in one's life, as when one has a terminal illness or when a job interview has been botched up. In such instances it may be useful to become convinced that the job was not worth having, or it might be the only way a person can hold together in the face of imminent death, say, by pursuing the fiction that his illness is not imminently fatal. Defenses seem to be very widely employed by people, even

Third, inconsistencies between what the person says about his impulses and feelings and how he acts may also signify such a conflict. The person says he has only positive feelings toward someone, or he denies negative ones, or he reports that a damaging experience does not bother him, but his behavior gives evidence of quite a different emotional reaction. He insists, for example, that he is not angry, but as he does so he pounds the table, turns red, or half snarls as he denies the anger. Or, he states that he is unafraid, or perhaps even that he relishes an upcoming experience, but as it approaches his face ashens, his blood pressure is heightened, and his palms become sweaty. Or, while he reports positive interest and affection for someone, he appears to act in an irritated fashion toward that person, or in a way that is surely going to do some injury.

Note that all three of these cues to defensive activity have in common that they involve evidence of some kind of contradiction or discrepancy—between two statements, between statements and the situational context, or between statements and actions. This discrepancy is the key to the inference of self-deception.

The attentive reader will have sensed a methodological problem here. A defense, by definition, means that the person is unaware of his distortion of reality, at least part of the time, or else the process of self-deception cannot succeed. But we have already seen elsewhere how difficult it is to be sure that someone is really unaware of what he is doing psychologically. Another simpler way of interpreting these same instances of inconsistency is to postulate that the person is seeking consciously to avoid putting himself in a bad light, that he knows full well what he is doing and is unwilling to admit it. This would be a very different process from the forms of self-deception discussed above. The term often used to refer to the manner of presenting oneself in only a positive light is *defensiveness*, and this tendency is very strong in some people and under certain conditions. A person who is being defensive in this sense will refuse to admit to socially unacceptable behavior. Although it makes great intuitive and theoretical sense, one of the limitations of the concept of a self-deceptive defense mechanism is the difficulty of distinguishing between it and defensiveness. However, close observation of a subject often reveals important differences between conscious deception of others (defensive lying) and unconscious self-deception. This differentiation often depends on the psychologist's keen intuition. There are no fool-proof tests. (For a discussion of lie-detection tests, see Note 11.1.)

Though a powerful idea, the defense mechanism has been mainly a descriptive concept. That is, it describes certain hypothetical events presumably taking place in the person's mind, but we do not yet know the precise conditions under which the process is turned on or off, or just what its consequences are for the individual. We need to know more about which personality type uses given forms of defense, the conditions under which they occur, and the past events in the individual's life that establish this mode of coping. Thus, the defense mechanism remains a key research problem in the study of human behavior.

by quite effective people, and it is not a sound position automatically to consign them to the realm of pathology. It is not always certain that living by illusions is necessarily maladaptive or undesirable. Thus, what seems to be important is not the use of reality distorting defenses as such, but when and how they are used, and to what extent the person relies on them in coping with his problems.

Defense and mental disorder. It is often assumed that each mental disorder is distinguished by its own special form of coping (Schafer, 1954; Shapiro, 1965). This is an important idea, and we shall now consider a few examples.

Earlier a form of neurosis referred to as obsessive-compulsive disorder was described. The sufferer's thoughts are filled with ideas which seem alien to him—say, that he has done some evil deed or that others dislike him (obsessions). In this kind of disturbance the person may also feel compelled to engage in peculiar and alien rituals, such as repeatedly washing his hands, stepping over cracks in the sidewalk, arranging objects on his desk in a particular fashion (compulsions). Psychoanalytic writers have interpreted these symptoms as efforts to keep the world predictable and manageable, to approach it with detached, intellectual mastery, and thus to keep under control threatening unconscious impulses that the person cannot manage or accept.

David Shapiro (1965, p. 28) cites examples of the obsessive-compulsive manner of thinking that are illuminating here: Obsessive people ". . . may listen to a recording with the keenest interest in, and attention to, the quality of the equipment, the technical features of the record, and the like, but meanwhile hardly hear . . . the music." In my own research (Speisman, Lazarus, and colleagues, 1964), I have seen people display this defense of intellectual detachment in watching with calmness distressing film scenes of mutilation and commenting casually afterwards, not on the suffering of the victims, but on the quality of the camera work. Another example, related to compulsivity, may again be taken from Shapiro (1965, p. 31): ". . . there is the compulsive patient who spends all day intensively cleaning and recleaning the house or the . . . patient who spends vast amounts of time carefully collecting and transcribing to index cards data on all the schools and colleges he can locate with the dim justification of some day attending 'the best.'" Such a person fills in the hours with emotionally neutral activities, trying to control his thoughts, presumably to keep out unpredictable, unmanageable, and excessively threatening ones.

Compared with this highly intellectualized and over-controlled way of coping, the hysterical neurotic displays a strikingly different pattern, theoretically linked to repression

(a)

as the dominant defense. Instead of seeking to manage threat-ening events by keeping tabs on them and remaining detached from them, the hysterical person represses such material, keep-ing it out of consciousness so that its existence need not be acknowledged. This leads to great naiveté about the world, often expressed as astonishment when unacceptable or ugly things come to the surface. Unlike the overcontrolled obses-sive-compulsive type, the hysteric is likely to be highly emo-tional but unable to acknowledge the problems and impulses underlying them. It is as if he is saying, "I have symptoms, but no problems." Shapiro (1965, p. 122) gives an example of a thirty-year old female patient who ". . . has periodic stormy, hysterical outbursts of anger directed principally at her husband." On one occasion, she is astonished that he tells her that he cannot put up with it. "He really means it," she says in amazement and adds, "But I don't really mean the things I say."

(b)

Each of the major types of functional mental disorder is thought to have its own particular form of defensive pattern. Psychoanalytic theory, for example, assumes that schizo-phrenics regress to very childish ways of coping (Figure 10.11), withdrawing from social involvements because they are terri-bly threatened by other people; the depressive perceives his situation as hopeless and responds as though in grief to the loss of his esteem with the outlook of helplessness characteristic of the dependent child; the paranoid projects his own danger-ous impulses onto others, like the small child who perceives all strangers as menacing; and so on (see Fenichel, 1945).

(c)

Figure 10.11 An example of regression. (a) Photo of young woman of 17 who came from a very unstable family background. She had first showed symptoms of disturbance at the age of 4, when her parents began to quarrel violently. When she was 7 her mother refused further sexual relations with her father, but the girl continued to sleep in his bed until she was 13. Suspecting that the girl was being incestuously seduced, the mother obtained legal custody of her and moved with her to a separate home. The girl resented the separation from her father, quarreled with her mother, and became a disciplinary problem at school. When she was 17, she insisted on visiting her father and found him living with a girl "in questionable circumstances." A violent scene ensued, and again her mother took her home against her wishes. After this she refused to attend school and became sullen and withdrawn. In her mother's absence she went on destructive rampages in the house, and on one of these forays found the photograph (b) of herself at the age of 5. Using this as a model, she cut her hair to a baby bob and began to affect the facial expression and posture of the pictured child, as shown in photo (c). She became infantile and untidy, and no longer controlled her urine. She "appeared to have regressed to a relatively desirable period in life antedating disruptive jealousies and other conflicts; moreover she acted out this regression in unconsciously determined but strikingly symbolic patterns. . . ."
(From Jules H. Masserman, Principles of dynamic psychiatry, *Plate I. Philadelphia: Saunders, 1961. Photos and data courtesy of Drs. John Romano and Richard Renneker)*

Although it is quite difficult to verify such hypotheses about the mechanisms underlying various kinds of disorder, the symptoms of adaptive failure can be seen as expressions of immature forms of coping.

Balance of forces between stress and coping

Throughout the foregoing discussion of the social learning model of adaptive failure it has been suggested that some people develop mental disorders because they have learned faulty modes of coping with stress. Such a statement, however, raises a question that is difficult to answer from the vantage point of our present knowledge, namely, "Can the person who has succumbed to mental disorder be said to have experienced more severe stress in his life than the one who remains reasonably healthy?" Those who have studied this question have had difficulty answering it affirmatively. Again and again one finds individuals of high adaptive competence who have seemingly undergone very stressful childhoods. Such persons seem somehow to have transcended an unfavorable social atmosphere and hard childhood and instead of being traumatized or stunted by them have evidently grown stronger and more effective. How can we reconcile this apparent paradox?

The best theoretical answer seems to be that stress traumatizes (damages) the personality when it is imposed on an individual lacking sufficient resources to cope with it but facilitates growth when the individual has sufficient resources to draw upon. In the latter case, since the stressful demands tax but do not overwhelm the person's resources, they mobilize an intense struggle to overcome the difficulties. He comes out of the struggle with a renewed sense of his own capability. He has tried new ways of adapting, brought his best to bear upon the crisis, and having succeeded, has gained in inner strength. In contrast, the person who is traumatized by stress because he has had no experience in coping with it is likely to feel even more vulnerable in the future (Figure 10.12). All of us have experienced multiple crises in our lives, and whether these aided us in learning to mobilize ourselves for the future, weakened us, or overwhelmed us depended on the extent to which we were able to draw upon sufficient internal resources to master the situation.

It is not easy to predict just when a given stressful experience will be overpowering for an individual or well within his capacity to handle: a parental divorce, a debilitating illness or injury, a physical handicap, a death in the family, a separation, a defeat in school, a sexual or aggressive assault by a parent or guardian—any of these may or may not traumatize a developing child. Nor can we predict the effects of later

Figure 10.12   A special form of deprivation. (Drawing by Handelsman; reproduced by permission of Punch)

"I suppose you meant well, daddy, but you never gave me things I really needed, like poverty."

positive experiences in mitigating earlier trauma: for example, the same child who is discouraged by early failure in his study of mathematics may later find language and literature studies easy and so come to think of himself as competent. The rules by which such complicated patterns operate are still far from clear. In any event, what goes wrong in the case of mental disorder cannot be explained merely by reference to stress but must be understood in terms of a *balance of forces.* In the maladapted person, that equilibrium has clearly gone awry.

Although no two persons have the same history, we can learn much from examining what individuals have in common—their social milieu. In the current world arena we can observe the process by which people struggle with the same problems of living and, in fact, choose common ways of coping with these problems. And we need not go to the mental hospital or psychiatric clinic to do so. All we need do is look around us. We are living in a time when there is great social unrest, evidenced by constant violence, strident protest, frenzied hatred between ethnic groups, political and economic upheavals, and general alienation from traditional values. These are symptoms of chronic social stress. The main characteristic of such symptoms, as opposed to those we see in individuals in hospitals, is that the collective forms of coping mark a struggle with problems shared widely by many people at the same time. Such problems strike at all age groups, but they are particularly significant in adolescence, when the transition to adulthood and the establishment of personal identity is being accomplished (Erikson, 1950). It will therefore be instructive to consider first some of the collective sources of stress in our present society, and next some of the collective, often maladaptive, ways people are coping with such stress.

Collective sources of stress

A number of hypotheses about current stresses on today's youth have been presented by various observers of the modern scene. Let us examine a few of the major hypotheses.

Imminent destruction of the world   The prospect of atomic destruction is one of the most frequently given explanations for current unrest among the young. One version of this position may be found in the writing of research psychiatrist Robert Jay Lifton (1970), whose first well-known work was based on observations of Japanese reactions to the atomic bomb dropped on Hiroshima in 1945. Lifton was strongly influenced by the awful effects of this cataclysm on its victims, and he, like others, has come subsequently to see "The Bomb" as the main element underlying the social malaise of post-1945 generations. He suggests that man's continuing and universal need is somehow to feel a sense of continuity in the face of the inevitability of biological death. The threat of atomic holocaust has made difficult or even impossible any of the usual ways (religious, mystical, philosophical) by which man has historically achieved this feeling. Particularly destructive, suggests Lifton, is the difficulty of relating oneself to past and future in the face of the prospect of having some idiotic or malicious psychopath (a Dr. Strangelove) press his finger on the button that could wipe out the world. Constantly living under this shadow, modern man is left without any faith in the future and life is deprived of all sense of meaning. He loses his feeling of trust in the grand order of nature and the world: even death at the hands of a mysterious or avenging god could be fitted into a meaningful cosmology, but it is meaningless, says Lifton, to face annihilation as nothing but a stupid accident. "The fear of individual death has been engulfed by a greater dread—of the end of everything" (Lifton, 1970, p. 108).

The dread of atomic holocaust seems to have reached its peak in the 1950s, and although the danger of nuclear war is still an important threat, other anxieties seem to have moved into prominence more recently. One of the new apocalyptic concerns is overpopulation (Chapter 3). Another is worldwide pollution of the environment. With these twin dangers, the earth is made increasingly uninhabitable for all living organisms by the growing and insatiable need of man for goods and space and by his failure to find ways of governing himself in the interests of the world in general as opposed to his own individual or group self-interest. The newer concerns about overpopulation and pollution continue essentially the basic nightmarish theme inherent in the threat of the bomb, of man and his machines running amok and wrecking the world. Added to this is a thought latent in the atomic threat, that even if one does not die in the catastrophe, life will hardly be worth living in its wake (Figure 10.13).

Prolongation of youth   Until recent times, no society in the history of man could afford to keep its youth in school until adulthood. Only half a century ago it was necessary to pass child-labor laws to free children below 16 years of age from economic exploitation: in the past most children worked, often 10 or more hours a day, 6 days a week, and often they were working full-time by as early as 10 years of age. Today, an increasing proportion of youth in the United States and elsewhere in the Western world remain in school until their early twenties, and many much longer. This prolongation of the period in which young people remain in school, dependent on their elders and not making an economic contribution to society, may be a mixed blessing, delaying the process whereby young people achieve a sense of adult identity and respon-

(a)

(b)

sibility. In an essay entitled *Obsolete Youth*, Bruno Bettelheim has attempted to explain social unrest among the young by emphasizing this enforced prolongation of marginality and dependency in youth owing to the increasing demand for extension of formal education past high school into college (and even into graduate school). Bettelheim (1969, pp. 9, 11, 16, 35) conceives the common denominator in student unrest during the last decade or so as follows:

[Society] keeps the next generation too long in a state of dependency; too long, in terms of mature responsibility and a striving for independence, of a sense of place that one has personally striven for and won. . . .

My thesis is that more than anything else it is the seeming vacuum to which we graduate so many of our young in the modern industrial society, which so convinces them that ours is a society that cannot make sense. . . . Their anxiety is not (as they claim) about an impending atomic war. It is not that society has no future. Their existential anxiety is that *they* have no future in a society that does not need them to go on existing.

Campus rebellion seems to offer youth a chance to short-cut the time of empty waiting and to prove themselves real adults. This can be seen from the fact that most rebellious students, on both sides of the Atlantic, are either undergraduates or those studying in the social sciences and humanities. There are precious few militants among students of medicine, chemistry, engineering, the natural sciences. To dismiss this as self-selection would be oversimplifying. It is true that those who come to the university and who are already deeply dissatisfied with themselves and society tend to study psychology, political science, philosophy, sociology. Such students even choose psychology in the hope that to study it will add to self-knowledge (which it can) and will solve their psychological problems (which it cannot). Feeling lost in themselves, they also feel lost with others and come to think that by studying society they will feel more at home in the world, and hence with themselves. But when the study of these and related subjects fails to solve their inner difficulties, or the various problems they have in relating to others, they come to hate the university whose teaching disappoints them. They are convinced that the teaching is "irrelevant"—as indeed it is when it comes to solving deep-seated emotional problems of long standing, because it was never designed to that end.

In short, by prolonging a childish, dependent, and uncertain marginal role in life, society has also delayed the emergence of more responsible adult forms of conduct. Such youths have been called "dangling men" or "marginal men." Lipset (1970, p. 680) writes, "They are in transition between being dependent on their families for income, status, and security and taking up their own roles in jobs and families." Leon Eisenberg (1970) uses the expression "the prolongation of adolescence" for this. He notes that there has been a marked historical trend toward the lowering of the mean age at which puberty occurs: the age of menarche (the first menses) in girls has been getting earlier by four months per decade in western Europe since 1930 (no one knows exactly why). Therefore, the present-day deferment of the time when young men or women take on adult social roles operates counter to the historical trend of earlier attainment of biological maturity.

The concept of "youth" is a relatively recent notion. Philip Aries (1962) has written an account of the nature of childhood over many centuries of human social existence. He points out that the idea of childhood as a separate stage of human development did not even exist in the Middle Ages and is really a modern conception. Before modern times, the child was usually assimilated into the adult world by apprenticeship without the assumption that any or much formal education was needed. Kenneth Kenniston (1965, 1968) adds that the concept of adolescence is actually a twentieth-century idea. Moreover, with so many young people now going to college rather than to work, Kenniston believes the ground has been laid for the emergence of a new stage of *postadolescent* psychological development. But this prolongation of adolescence poses new problems not evident in past eras; these problems are intensified in a time of general social unrest and even contribute to that unrest.

Disillusionment and alienation   In the normal course of personality development, an individual is said to internalize (make a part of himself) aspects of the physical and social world which seem to him salient, reliable, and consistent. This internalization helps him to form a psychological system that permits him to mobilize his actions, feelings, strivings, values, and beliefs. Criminologist Nathan Adler (1968, 1970) has proposed that many of the institutions, values, and rituals of

Poll data from *Congressional Quarterly*, July 28, 1973 and August 4, 1973; *The New York Times*, August 15, 1973:

Gallup poll (1973)

(a) Do you approve or disapprove the way Nixon is handling his job as President?

	Approve	Disapprove	No opinion
June 22–25	45%	45%	10%
July 6–9	40%	49%	11%
August 3–6	31%	67%	2%

(b) Should President Nixon be compelled to leave office?

	Yes	No	No opinion
June 22–25	18%	71%	11%
July 6–9	25%	62%	13%

(c) Which of the following do you believe?

June 22–25	Yes
1. Nixon planned the Watergate "bugging"	8%
2. Nixon did not plan the Watergate "bugging" but knew about it beforehand	27%
3. Nixon found out about the "bugging" afterward and tried to cover it up	36%
4. Nixon had no knowledge and spoke up as soon as he knew	17%
5. No opinion or not heard about it	12%

our society have been crumbling, at least ideologically, for a substantial segment of the young (see also discussion of the generation gap in Chapter 5). When this happens, the roles into which young people must fit seem to lose their salience and holding power, the world's behavior ceases to appear reliable and responsive, and there are few commitments to which the young can turn. In trying to maintain their orientation and struggling against the threat to their sense of identity, a new framework must be sought outside the context of the traditional social environment. The result is a flight from both past and future and an attempt to live only in the immediate present; an inability to tolerate any controls or delays of gratification; a feeling of complete alienation from "establishment" rules and patterns of authority, which are felt to be hypocritical; and a general rejection of society's conventions through irreverent attitudes, passive resistance, and finally outright rebellion (see Note 10.4).

This is a description of *social alienation*. Durkheim (1951) called it "anomie," a syndrome arising typically during the breakdown of traditional institutionalized patterns and values. An alienated person has lost his bearings, his frame of reference, and thus feels threatened. He is therefore psychologically isolated from the traditional social world in which he lives. The concrete issues which create this despairing state of mind in today's America are many—increasing automation and unemployment, decay of cities and ruin of the natural envi-

Harris poll (1972–1973)

(d) Do you think the Watergate episode is a very serious question involving the honesty of the White House or do you think it is mostly politics?

	Serious	Mostly politics	Not sure
Oct. 1972	26%	62%	12%
April 1973	36%	48%	16%
May 1973	40%	52%	8%
June 1973	47%	43%	10%

(e) If it is proved that President Nixon ordered the coverup of White House involvement in Watergate after Republican agents were caught there, do you think he should resign or not?

	Yes	No	Not sure
June 14–18	46%	40%	14%
July 18–22	44%	45%	11%

(f) In view of what has happened in the Watergate affair, do you think President Nixon should resign as President or not?

	Yes	No	Not sure
May	14%	75%	11%
July	22%	66%	12%

Note 10.4

In the summer of 1973, the confidence of the American public in the integrity of its government was badly shaken by the Watergate scandal and disclosures of lawbreaking by officials of the "law-and-order" Nixon administration and reelection committee. Disclosed were apparent political use by the White House of governmental agencies against American citizens, outright lying to the public on issues of the utmost national gravity, corrupt electioneering practices, and felonies such as stealing, breaking and entering, and electronic eavesdropping. These political events had such a large impact on public confidence (already shaken in the wake of the Johnson administration's "credibility gap") that they must be included here in a discussion of disillusionment and alienation.

A great many writers have tackled the problem of Watergate, but it was perhaps best summed up in a column by historian Barbara W. Tuchman in *The New York Times*

of August 7, 1973 (p. 35):"There will be no end to the revelations of misconduct because misconduct was the standard operating procedure. . . . What we are dealing with here is fundamental immorality." She continues, "[Even if,] as is conceivable, the proof [that Nixon was implicated in the Watergate affair and its coverup] fails, we will be left with a Government too compromised ever to be trusted and too damaged to recover authority. . . . Worse, we will have demonstrated for the benefit of Mr. Nixon's successors what measure of cynicism and what deprivation of their liberties the American people are ready to tolerate. From there the slide into dictatorship is easy."

Statements such as this reflected only one view, of course, perhaps a very common one, but they did not tell us accurately about the public "state of mind." Public opinion polls are the technical devices to get at this, and the pollsters were active during the period of the Senate hearings during the

spring and summer of 1973. A few examples of poll data are tabulated here in the margins, and these indicate an erosion of public confidence in the Nixon administration, as well as some interesting contradictions.

In the Gallup poll of June 22–25 (question c), 71 percent of those polled believed that President Nixon was involved in either illegal or improper activity; yet as of July 6–9 (b) only 25 percent thought that he should be compelled to leave office. This discrepancy might have depended on the perceived nature of Nixon's involvement, as was suggested by the Harris poll data (e and f). The percentage of people who disapproved of the way Nixon was performing (a) rose in the same period from 45% to 67%.

The extent to which polls reveal clearly the mental state of the public is always very uncertain, partly because the way a question is asked makes a great deal of difference,

(continued on p. 482)

and partly because the questions are generally very simple while the reasons and patterns of thought underlying the answers are extremely varied and complex. For example, voting for a man is a yes-or-no matter: *why* one does so, and how one feels about it, is another thing. Patterns of questions, and the contradictions among the results, can be more revealing than a single question. The psychological considerations that undoubtedly underlie poll data are probably more interesting and important than the actual percentages themselves.

There was probably far more real confusion in peoples' minds about what the revelations of misdoings in office in 1972 meant than was then realized. In addition, some of the data indicate tendencies toward blind faith in authority figures or in a social system. Having to acknowledge that one is living under a corrupt leadership or political system is itself threatening. As we saw in Chapter 4, people try to hold on to their basic beliefs and resist seeing them destroyed. This leads to inhibition against expression of disapproval of the Chief Executive. There were during Watergate also fears of deep division within the country, of anarchy, and even of an abrupt change in leadership. In 1945, when President Roosevelt died, before the end of World War II, large numbers of people felt suddenly abandoned and exposed; they felt leaderless (fatherless?) without the man who had guided the country for 12 years through severe crises.

For many, Watergate created a serious crisis of belief, a major source of cognitive dissonance that had to be resolved in some way. The form of the solution varied somewhat from person to person, and group to group. Thus, in the poll data on Watergate we can see repeated some of the same psychological processes we saw in Chapter 4 among the supporters of Senator Edward M. Kennedy following the Chappaquiddick incident. Many Kennedy supporters then believed that the Senator had done something reprehensible and yet still perceived him to be an upstanding man, no less worthy of political support. In this connection, Sindlinger and Co. of Swarthmore, Pa. (reportedly a favorite pollster of the White House) asked a sample of people (July 20–27) two questions: (1) "Between Watergate and Chappaquiddick, in your opinion, which concerns you most?"; and (2) "Which action do you yourself feel is more morally reprehensible—which is worse—the drowning of Mary Jo Kopechne at Chappaquiddick or the bugging of the Democratic National Committee?" To the first question, 40 percent felt Chappaquiddick was the greater concern, while 37 percent said Watergate. To the second, 44 percent said Chappaquiddick,

ronment, loneliness and estrangement from the family, the effects of the long war in Southeast Asia on confidence in government authority, and, in general, the huge gap between the American dream and American reality. To youths perceiving things this way (and it remains a question why some do and others do not) the golden promises and soaring rhetoric of our national leaders seem hollow—and the best dreams of our people all seem betrayed (Figure 10.14).

One should not get the impression from this that distress, disillusionment, and alienation are limited to youth. Below is a remarkable newspaper article written by Art Hoppe, a gifted satirist who occasionally writes a straight column expressing the thoughts and feelings of a sensitive and intelligent man directly. His column in the *San Francisco Chronicle* of March 1, 1971, gives an artistic, clinically accurate picture of a person's struggle against the forces of alienation:

The radio this morning said the allied invasion of Laos had bogged down. Without thinking, I nodded and said, "Good."

And having said it, I realized the bitter truth: Now I root against my own country.

This is how far we have come in this hated and endless war. This is the nadir I have reached in this winter of my discontent. This is how close I border on treason:

Now I root against my own country.

How frighteningly sad this is. My generation was raised to love our country and we loved it unthinkingly. We licked Hitler and Tojo and Mussolini. Those were our shining hours. Those were our days of faith.

They were evil; we were good. They told lies; we spoke the truth. Our cause was just, our purposes noble, and in victory we were magnanimous. What a wonderful country we were! I loved it so.

But now, having descended down the tortuous, lying, brutalizing years of this bloody war, I have come to the dank and lightless bottom of the well: I have come to root against the country that once I blindly loved.

* * *

I can rationalize it. I can say that if the invasion of Laos succeeds, the chimera of victory will dance once again before our eyes—leading us once again into more years of mindless slaughter. Thus, I can say, I hope the invasion fails.

But it is more than that. It is that I have come to hate my country's role in Vietnam.

I hate the massacres, the body counts, the free-fire zones, the napalming of civilians, the poisoning of rice crops. I hate being part of My Lai. I hate the fact that we have now dropped more explosives on these scrawny Asian peasants than we did on all our enemies in World War II.

And I hate my leaders who, over the years, have conscripted our young men and sent them there to kill or be killed in a senseless cause simply because they can find no honorable way out—no honorable way out for them.

I don't root for the enemy. I doubt they are any better than we. I don't give a damn any more who wins the war. But because I hate what my country is doing in Vietnam, I emotionally and often irrationally hope that it fails.

*   *   *

It is a terrible thing to root against your own country. If I were alone, it wouldn't matter. But I don't think I am alone. I think many Americans must feel these same sickening emotions I feel. I think they share my guilt. I think they share my rage.

If this is true, we must end this war now—in defeat, if necessary. We must end it because all of Southeast Asia is not worth the hatred, shame, guilt and rage that is tearing Americans apart. We must end it not for those among our young who have come to hate America, but for those who somehow manage to love it still.

I doubt that I can ever again love my country in that unthinking way I did when I was young. Perhaps this is a good thing.

But I would hope the day will come when I can once again believe what my country says and once again approve of what it does. I want to have faith once again in the justness of my country's causes and the nobleness of its ideals.

What I want so very much is to be able once again to root for my own, my native land.

This newspaper column is singularly instructive about human psychological conflict because it so clearly points up the painful struggle that goes on in a person striving to maintain his bearings, his feeling of belonging, his positive ideals, in the face of destructive and disillusioning social forces. It is instructive also about a point that has often been overlooked, that even mature, successful people are vulnerable to events that threaten their ideals. It should be even less surprising that the emerging, tender identity of many youths should be severely tested by such powerful negative forces.

    Youth as a stage of life   Another approach to the problem emphasizes either the *personality patterns* leading to alienation, protest, activism, and other psychological manifestations of unrest or the unique attributes of young people, rather than

and 34 percent said Watergate. Note that, as posed, the second question makes it sound almost as though Kennedy drowned the girl deliberately, and of all the alleged White House misdeeds, only the comparatively minor bugging episode was selected for comparison. This seems to rig the results so that those who were inclined to believe the worst of Kennedy and the best of Nixon were really permitted only one comfortable answer.

None could say for sure where these revelations of misconduct and amorality in high places would take America politically or socially. Nevertheless, the political events we have been discussing surely have had extremely profound effects psychologically upon large numbers of Americans, affecting their confidence in their government and society. This in turn could be very relevant to the future of American democracy and its ability to function, especially when it comes to the capacity of the public to unite behind its government in seeking solutions to major problems confronting the nation and the world. And silently, behind all the superficial attempts to plumb the public mind, countless persons like you and me are struggling individually to accommodate themselves to these frightening events. The central theme of Part IV of this book is precisely this personal struggle to achieve a sense of identity and to prevent feelings of alienation and apathy. Indeed, this individual achievement may be the most important human psychological task of all.

Figure 10.14 Students clash with police during antiwar demonstration at Columbia University, New York, April 1972. (Wide World Photos)

Call me Ishmael. Some years ago—never mind how long precisely—having little or no money in my purse, and nothing particular to interest me on shore, I thought I would sail about a little and see the watery part of the world. It is a way I have of driving off the spleen and regulating the circulation. Whenever I find myself growing grim about the mouth; whenever I find myself involuntarily pausing before coffin warehouses, and bringing up the rear of every funeral I meet; and especially whenever my hypos get such an upper hand of me, that it requires a strong moral principle to prevent me from deliberately stepping into the street, and methodically knocking people's hats off—then, I account it high time to get to sea as soon as I can. [From Herman Melville, Moby Dick, p. 1. New York: 1851]

the external social environment. Such analyses look inside the person for explanations of social unrest rather than to the outside conditions, though surely both are important.

In addition to recognizing the importance of the prolongation of the marginal role of youth (a situational factor), the main thrust of Bettleheim's (1969) approach to current unrest is that young people are particularly vulnerable to disturbance because of the unstable nature of their still-developing personalities. Adolescent development is commonly a period of turmoil and instability, emotional extremes, hyper-energy, and egocentricity. Bettleheim cites as illustration Herman Melville's tale of *Moby Dick* (1851) and the struggle of Ishmael to gain an identity. Ishmael, a young man in crisis, is pressured toward senseless violence and self-destruction, which may be avoided only by "dropping out," escaping his humdrum existence on land and going to sea on a whaling ship (see the margin). In Romain Rolland's *Jean Christophe* (1904–1912), adolescence is presented as a time of rebellion in which there is no room for halfway measures. Everything is rejected, the good as well as the bad aspects of both the father and the establishment. Bettleheim (1969, pp. 2–3) also sees much similarity between the more violent students of today and the reactions of German university students in pre-Hitler days:

Then, as now, we see the same lumping together of all facets and institutions of society into one defamatory image. This is meant to symbolize a reality so monolithic that it becomes out of the question to improve one or another part of it at a time. No need, then, for any reasonable assessment of differing merits for all the many and so different features of "the establishment"—or in Nazi terminology, *"das System."* Having decided *a priori* that no improvement is possible, it follows that the only thing left is to bring down the whole system. With society so rotten, it can neither reform itself nor be reformed, but can only be born again through violent revolution. Goering's "When somebody mentions culture (or appeals to reason) I reach for my revolver" reappears today in the Black Panther slogan, "1968—The Year of the Pig, the Death of the Ballot, the Birth of the Bullet." And Tom Hayden gives it symbolic expression when he ends an impassioned appeal for revolution by going off stage to return brandishing a rifle.

A study of student unrest and activism has recently been made by philosopher Lewis S. Feuer (1969), whose book *The conflict of generations* examines modern student movements in historical perspective, including such movements in Prussia and other parts of Germany in the crises of 1817 and 1848, in Bosnia just before Austrian Archduke Franz Ferdinand was assassinated there to trigger World War I (1914), in Russia prior to the Revolution of 1917, and in several countries of modern Asia, notably Japan. Feuer sees student turmoil in Freudian terms as a reflection of unconscious hatred of the father, an adolescent "emotional rebellion" in which disillusionment with and rejection of the parental values are always elements. Such youth movements are also a sign of "sickness, a malady in society," arising when there has been a breakdown of social values and institutions. In such times youth feels particularly oppressed, and their unconscious resentment of their fathers (and the oedipal wish to replace them) breaks out and is mobilized by leaders who themselves are often angry and frustrated. Feuer assumes that there are common features in all youth protest movements, and argues that they are powered, not by immediate social problems, which tend to be the excuses or rationalizations for protest, but by ever-present unconscious emotional forces. In consequence, they tend to be self-destructive and incapable of producing lasting and desirable social change. Protest also offers some excitement in what is otherwise a rather boring, highly constrained college life to all but the most dedicated (Figure 10.15).

A more favorable interpretation of youthful political involvement might be that young people also have the greatest stake in the future, and activism is a far more mature involvement in society than traditional collegiate fun and games, even if both serve a similar function of self-expression. It is unlikely that any one principle entirely explains the present social malaise or the many variations among individuals and groups in the way it is manifested. How to explain, for example, the special distress of young blacks, Amerindians, chicanos, and Puerto Ricans? We would be better advised to recognize multiple reasons for the problems of youth, and try to understand the role and interplay of each.

Figure 10.15 Bra burning at a youth festival. (Steve Rose from Nancy Palmer Photo Agency)

Collective forms of coping

Under conditions of social unrest, large numbers of people show collectively what might be called "crisis behavior," the disturbed reactions accompanying such disorder. Even in stable times, stress or crisis behavior can be observed in individuals experiencing personal catastrophe, such as serious illness, loss of a loved one, economic setbacks, or interpersonal conflict (as in divorce or social rejection). The basic difference between crisis behavior on the individual level and on the social level is that in the former the crisis depends on critical events in a single person's life, whereas in the latter such events are happening to many people at the same time so that mass psychology plays a part.

There are, of course, not one but many ways of dealing with crisis. When crises are shared by many, interpreted similarly, and coped with in a common way, a sense of social

What have the results of the recent student uprisings and black riots [of the 1960s] been? At best they have focused attention on the social problems. To the extent that such a focus results in a movement toward problem solution they have been successful. On the other hand, such action has aroused the antagonism of those opposed to social change and thus polarized the positions of persons for and against such social changes, forcing those in the middle to choose sides. Even though attention to needed social change may have been accomplished, it has been done at considerable expense to those wishing change. The violation of other social norms, particularly those involving the destruction of property and life, has aroused such revulsion in the population as a whole that further social advance may be hindered. Indeed, the arousal of forces that resist change may be so great that the needed corrective action will not occur. Repressive measures, the opposite of the corrective measures desired by the activists, may take place instead. Needed social change may actually be inhibited. Such social change, does not reveal the personal loss suffered by those immediately affected by the persons who choose a path of violent destruction, black and white alike. This is another tragic consequence of violence. Even beyond such personal losses, individuals participating in the riots hurt their own people. Black persons have destroyed their own living areas. Student rioters have destroyed their own universities. [From Fairweather, 1972, p. 4]

movement and community cohesion is created. There arises an *ésprit de corps,* an ideological unity of purpose. When an individual youth rebels against his parents' standards or way of life, there is no great stir (except in those immediately involved), but when thousands or tens of thousands of youths from all over the country embark on drug "trips" or leave home for hippie pads or communal living, the problem becomes highly visible and a strong public reaction develops. We can apply some of what we know about individual coping to crisis behavior on the larger social scale because many of the patterns are quite similar.

Withdrawal into the hippie or bohemian "counterculture," widespread use of illegal drugs, violent protest and revolutionary activity, abandonment of a career orientation for full-time political struggle, all can be viewed as shared attempts at coping with crisis in a troubled social system. Similarly, severe retaliation against students and universities by people in authority and their supporters also represents a collective response to social crisis by those who share a different evaluation of the situation.

Student protest and unrest in the 1960s was responded to with anger and alarm by many middle-aged blue-collar and white-collar workers (the so-called silent majority), whose economic progress had been rather marginal since the labor reforms of the 1930s and who were struggling in a time of soaring inflation to keep their heads above water. Such groups were normally suspicious of intellectuals; when they saw university riots on television by what they took to be spoiled, affluent student "brats" (whose lot they felt was so much better than their own), this fueled their sense of frustration and resentment (Blinzen, 1970). Their perception of social events of their time was quite opposite to that of the protestors, and subsequent "backlash" against students and college faculties represented a form of coping with a sense of deeply felt threat.

Such people coped by strongly reaffirming the threatened traditional values and vehemently denying those grievances of which the alienated youth complained. It is not surprising that the older generation is more likely to opt for resistance to change; it has already found its identity within the traditional patterns. On the other hand, the younger generation has the greatest need to find new bases of stability when the established structure seems shaky. Under conditions of social unrest, it is difficult to anchor oneself to what is viewed as likely to pass out of existence.

Merton (1949) has also analyzed social unrest in terms of coping with threat. He describes five modes of adaptation: (1) An individual or group may use *approved institutional* means, as in the behavior of the "organizational man" described by Whyte (1956); see Chapter 5. (2) He may employ *innovational* or *illicit* means, such as the "robber baron" of early American capitalism or the criminal. (3) He may adopt the *ritualistic* mode, accepting rigid institutionalized means despite not gaining the normally accepted cultural goals; thus, the poor but honest farmer or shopkeeper cannot achieve satisfactory economic ends but stubbornly perseveres in what was once the accepted means to such ends, namely, commitment to hard work and honesty. (4) *Retreatist* solutions involve rejection of both the means and ends and withdrawal from the struggle, as in the case of the social dropout (a hippie or beatnik). (5) Finally, the mode of *rebellion* may involve new ideological goals, rejection of all socially accepted means and substitution of radical ones (Maoism, Castro-like revolution), in effect, mounting an attack on the status quo (as by riots, terrorism, and organized revolutionary activity). Thus, one can observe a variety of ways of collective coping with social crisis, each with its own mystique, its own causes, and its own consequences. Such manifestations of social unrest cannot be lumped into a single category, except by treating them all as mass reactions to threat or crisis.

An example: drugs and the cult of immediacy

Adler (1968, 1970) has tried to show that many of the phenomena of social unrest among today's youth, for example, development of a drug culture and an orientation to life based upon immediate gratification, appear remarkably similar to what happened in other transitional historical periods—during the decline and fall of the Roman Empire, during the European Renaissance, just following the Napoleonic Wars, and so on. Consider the period following the Revolution of 1830 in France. The Revolution of 1830 left in its wake widespread disillusion and despair, a repudiation of conventional ideas. The young people were part of a war generation, having been born during the worst of the Napoleonic era and living their formative years in an atmosphere of military disasters and impending doom. Their parents were weary of war, disgusted with tyranny, and despairing of the future. The young felt that before a better life could be created, first everything belonging to the past had to be destroyed. They saw their fathers as having worked too hard and reaped nothing; they did not share the older generation's goal of earning a steady livelihood. Reason to them was folly; it had led nowhere. They felt the ideals of the Enlightenment and the French Revolution had been betrayed. They rejected the new establishment and turned to cultivation of the exotic and eccentric, the erotic and occult, and they provoked society by scandalous speech and actions.

Adler (1970, pp. 435–436) gives a vivid picture of the "now" generation of 1832, based on a description by Enid Starkie (1954):

The Hippies of that day were known as *"les Bouzingos."* The word means noisy, undisciplined, extravagant, and was an epithet this group proudly wore, pledged with their obscene songs to fight the philistines. They saw themselves as a camp of Tartars who used skulls as drinking vessels and danced wildly and nakedly in the streets or sat naked in their gardens to outrage the neighborhood. Gerard de Nerval, drinking from a skull, said it was his father's skull. This group cultivated a black humor similar to our contemporary underground press and they were obsessed with sadism, rape, and lycanthropy [assumption of the characteristics of a werewolf through magic]. . . .

Gautier, in his "History of Romanticism" describes these men with their hair brushed up from the sides into a high peak to simulate the flame of genius. In place of a waist coat, they wore black velvet lapels and black flowing tie. Or they dressed like Spanish grandees, or in Cossack boots, or in bright blue frock-coats with gold buttons like those worn by an Indian Maharaja. Or they wore sweeping light blue coats lined with pale pink and fastened by pearl buttons as large as our half dollar. The leader of the group, the poet Petrus Borel, wore a red waistcoat "the color of Polish blood," a wide brimmed hat with velvet doublet and pale green trousers with black velvet stripes down the side seams.

They played at dandyism, nudism, Satanism; they used [the drugs] datuine, stramonine, belladonna, atropine to dilate their pupils and to achieve a look of strange fixity. They assumed roles either of intense passion or of impassivity and detached coolness. One can only imagine the outrage of the new, earnest moneymakers and manufacturers on their way to the counting house and their despair at what their sons were doing. . . .

Adler argues that the social scene in France of the 1830s might serve as a prototype for that of a substantial part of American youth today. Did we not know he was describing Paris in the 1830s, we might have assumed that he was taking us on a tour of the Haight-Ashbury section of San Francisco, Telegraph Avenue in Berkeley, or Greenwich Village East in New York City. Adler (1970, pp. 436–437) continues:

Today, the young dress in the colorful costumes nostalgic for the popular myths of their childhood TV viewing. Rock and roll music reaches for the same goals of the *Galope Infernal* of the Paris of 1830. Ken Kesey organizes his merry pranksters to outrage the philistines just as Petrus Borel did. A popular song today says that kicks are getting harder to find. In reaching for kicks this generation has turned to the traditional devices of the occult and the exotic, of polymorphous perversity, as well as to the use of hallucinogenic drugs.

In the 1970s, all about us we see manifestations of a similar effort to cope and find meaning in a period of social turmoil. Drugs are but one example. Another is the current resurgence of interest in the mystical, the occult, and in meditation, creativity, peak experiences, yoga, and other special states of consciousness. There is a strong desire to get beneath the outer covering, the veneer of human relationship that has left the person feeling isolated and alone, and to approach the "inner emotional self."

The variations in ideological fashion here are absolutely fascinating. In Sigmund Freud's heyday, culture was seen as providing necessary constraints against man's destructive animal nature, although it was also believed that Victorian society had overdone its controls to the point of total repression; today the youth movement has swung far over in the other direction and venerates extreme egocentric freedom of action and "doing one's own thing." Believers in "encounter group" psychology, both lay and professional, seek a richer emotional sense of being alive; they are convinced that social constraints smother them and shackle and distort their humanity.

We must, in any event, not lose sight of the major theme of this discussion—that social unrest is a manifestation of collectively experienced crises and of forms of coping with them that are shared by many in the society. Such a view is quite at variance with the idea that psychological troubles constitute an "illness," a strictly somatic disorder. Moreover, by taking this stance, one does not necessarily consign protest or activism to the realm of "disorder" or "illness." It does not help us to understand these patterns to label them as "sick." Rather, they are perfectly natural human responses to crisis, though some forms of coping are more in tune with reality, or more effective, or have better adaptive outcomes than others, just as is the case with individual processes of coping.

CONCLUDING COMMENT

In thinking about adaptive failure we must always remember the biosocial nature of man, recognizing that the way an individual manages his life, for good or ill, is a product both of his biological makeup and the social forces to which he is exposed. There is an unfortunate tendency to adopt an either/or stance about the causes and mechanisms of adaptive failure, and in contrasting the illness and social learning models above it is easy to create the impression that these are contradictory theories about adaptive failure or success. Some failures are undoubtedly a product mainly of disease in the

Western psychology knows the mind as the mental functioning of a psyche. It is the "mentality" of an individual. An impersonal Universal Mind is still to be met with in the sphere of philosophy, where it seems to be a relic of the original human "soul." This picture of our Western outlook may seem a little drastic, but I do not think it is far from the truth. At all events, something of the kind presents itself as soon as we are confronted with the Eastern mentality. In the East, mind is a cosmic factor, the very essence of existence; while in the West we have just begun to understand that it is the essential condition of cognition, and hence of the cognitive existence of the world. There is no conflict between religion and science in the East, because no science is there based upon the passion for facts, and no religion upon mere faith; there is religious cognition and cognitive religion. With us, man is incommensurably small and the grace of God is everything; but in the East man is God and he redeems himself. The gods of Tibetan Buddhism belong to the sphere of illusory separateness and mind-created projections, and yet they exist; but so far as we are concerned an illusion remains an illusion, and thus is nothing at all. It is a paradox, yet nevertheless true, that with us a thought has no proper reality; we treat it as if it were a nothingness. Even though the thought be true in itself, we hold that it exists only by virtue of certain facts which it is said to formulate. We can produce a most devastating fact like the hydrogen bomb with the help of this ever-changing phantasmagoria of virtually non-existent thoughts, but it seems wholly absurd to us that one could ever establish the reality of thought itself. [From Jung, 1954, p. xxxiii]

physiological sense, whereas others are best understood and dealt with in terms of social experience. But it is largely a matter of where the major emphasis is placed in any given instance when we seek a working model. Some day, when we know more than we do now, it will be possible to say with greater precision how biological and social influences interact in affecting individual adaptive struggles.

In this chapter we have considered a human problem, one as old as mankind itself, namely, the failure of individuals to cope successfully with the stress of living and to find inner harmony, and we have examined some of the ways in which such failure might be understood. Clearly, the problem of alienation and maladaptation is a serious one in our times. In Chapter 11 we shall look at various ways by which psychologists seek to understand the individual in trouble and to help him to understand himself or change his reactions.

ANNOTATED LIST OF SUGGESTED READINGS

History of outlooks toward mental illness

Alexander, F. G., and Selesnick, S. T. *The history of psychiatry.* New York: Harper & Row, 1966. A fascinating historical review of the progression from demonology to naturalism and its implications for modern psychiatry.

Frank, J. D. *Persuasion and healing.* New York: Shocken Books, 1963. Examines parallels between the modern psychotherapist and the ancient and contemporary shaman or medicine man.

Genetic and constitutional factors in mental disorder

Maher, B. A. *Principles of psychopathology.* New York: McGraw-Hill, 1966, chap. 13, pp. 328–358. Basic text about mental disorder, with an excellent review of hereditary and constitutional hypotheses and evidence.

Stress, coping, and defense

Freud, Anna. *The ego and the mechanisms of defense.* New York: International Universities Press, 1946. Systematic account, from a Freudian standpoint, of the defense mechanisms. Although technical, it is quite readable.

Lazarus, R. S. *Patterns of adjustment and human effectiveness.* New York: McGraw-Hill, 1969. A basic textbook treating the problems of adaptation, stress, and coping and the factors that influence them.

Shapiro, D. *Neurotic styles.* New York: Basic Books, 1965. Fascinating discussion from a Freudian point of view of the ways of thinking characteristic of various neurotic types.

Psychopathology

Cashdan, S. *Abnormal psychology.* Englewood Cliffs, N.J.: Prentice-Hall, Inc., 1971. A brief, readable text.

Coleman, J. C. *Abnormal psychology and modern life,* 4th ed. Glenview, Ill.: Scott, Foresman, 1972. The most elaborate and extensive text on the varieties of mental disorder, providing an understanding of their psychodynamics and of modern approaches to treatment; lengthy, but well worth exploring.

Martin, B. *Abnormal psychology.* Glenview, Ill: Scott, Foresman, 1973. A short text written from a conditioning and behavioral point of view.

Stone, A. A., and Stone, Sue S. *The abnormal personality through literature.* Englewood Cliffs, N.J.: Prentice-Hall, 1966. A compilation of fictional descriptions of the various kinds of mental disorder found in the works of great figures of literature. The descriptions illustrate a close relationship between intuitive artistic contributions of gifted writers who accurately observe the foibles of mankind and the scientific outlook of personality psychology.

In the previous chapter we were concerned with adaptive failure, a human problem of great poignancy because of the great suffering experienced by those who struggle with limited or no success to manage their lives in the face of stress. As with man's external troubles explored in earlier chapters, such severe personal problems cry for solution. We want to help the many people whose lives have gone wrong and to prevent similar trouble in those just starting out in life. In this chapter we shall see how psychologists try to meet this challenge.

It is a basic tenet of psychology that each of us is a distinct individual whose exact conditions of life are not identical to those of anyone else. Therefore, before help can be offered in any individual case, not only a general understanding of personality, or of given types of personality, is required, but also a knowledge of the forces operating in the specific case at hand. This assessment is often not an easy one and, as noted in the Prologue, calls for a combination of science and art. Because the scientific side of psychology is still in its formative stage, there are numerous theoretical differences among therapists, and many methods of treatment must be regarded as tentative rather than firm and absolute. Our procedures are in constant need of evaluation and revision, with the ultimate aim of providing more effective diagnostic and therapeutic techniques. Such questions of assessment and treatment will be considered on the following pages.

ASSESSMENT OF PERSONALITY

Most of us try to assess the personalities of others, explicitly or implicitly, in our ordinary day-to-day relationships. In appraising other people with whom we come in contact, we are constantly applying our own experience and view of

491

human behavior. There are four main differences between this commonsense or lay psychologizing and the scientific assessment of personality. First, the psychologist has at his disposal whatever reliable knowledge is available about what makes people tick, including hard facts that support or debunk commonsense notions about psychodynamics. Second, the professional goes about the task of assessment for the purpose of doing something constructive in a systematic rather than a casual way. Third, he has at his disposal certain technical devices for assessment that can overcome some of the limitations imposed by infrequent and short-lived contact with the stranger who is his client. Whereas a wife, for example, comes to know her husband intimately by being with him for many hours a day and in many settings during an extended relationship, the psychological worker must gain his knowledge of the individual rather quickly and in somewhat limited contexts. Fourth, the professional can be more detached in his efforts to know the person in trouble, since he does not have a personal stake in what is happening. Therefore, he is likely to be more objective in his appraisal of the situation than is a close relative or intimate friend.

We can begin to get an idea of the task of clinical assessment by looking first at a few examples of diagnostic reports written about hospitalized patients.

The first example is of a patient who had sought to be hospitalized on the basis of a personality problem. In consequence, a clinical evaluation was requested. The following psychological report was written on the basis of this assessment (Tallent, 1963, pp. 218–219):

The central and prominent theme of this man's life is belligerence and rebelliousness. This negativeness has contributed to turning his marriage into a stormy affair and his job into an arena of bitter dispute. Thus the two most vital areas of his life, family and career, now are sources of heavy situational stress.

Although Mr. O is capable of dispensing rancor in many directions, the primary focus of discharge is against authority figures. The origin of this attitude seems to be in the early father-son relationship with the former being seen as unreasonable, not understanding, and over-demanding. In response to this situation the patient has become a great self-justifier and links his rebelliousness with a belief of almost pious self-righteousness. This is true even where his rebelliousness takes the form of flouting conventionality.

Mr. O feels very anxious and tense at times, sometimes unsuccessful and unhappy, not only because of the stress at home and work, but because of a basic conflict in his personal needs. Stemming from his early home life is an ambition for achievement and the need to be conforming, but an even deeper need causes him to secretly yearn for passivity and to wish to overthrow the values which are a part of him but which he does not want. Accordingly, merely fulfilling the role of a responsible male member of our society is a primary source of stress for him. If he could resolve the conflict one way or the other he would feel more comfortable.

His oppositional tendencies are a continuing source of guilt for him, and there is reason to suspect that he precipitates conflict with others so that they will retaliate, punish him and thus relieve some of the guilt. If so, this maneuver is not adequately successful for it does not sufficiently relieve deep doubts which he has about his personal adequacy. These are most readily observed in his need to present himself as a superior person.

This same type of compensating maneuver is seen in his marital infidelity. His basic sense of maleness is not strong, and he is unsure of his adequacy here, hence a need to demonstrate that he is a man. Such activity, of course, is also an expression of hostility against his wife and rebellion against his family standards. He probably would not have difficulty in justifying this kind of behavior. Thus, his pervasive negative feelings cause him to feel that others also feel obliquely toward him. He is on the defensive, feels abused, jealous and suspicious. It is very likely that at one level or another he is suspect of his wife's fidelity.

This is an intellectually bright person (his current I.Q. is 118) and he has a certain amount of appreciation of his difficulties. He recognizes that he is an openly hostile person and that this causes him trouble, but he also believes that he is "right." He therefore is not able to use his intelligence adequately in relating to others. It is easy to visualize his interpersonal conflicts as severe and ugly, since under stress he becomes impulsive, his judgment tends to give way seriously, and he cannot fairly see the other person's point of view.

Psychodiagnostically, this patient has all the earmarks of an anxiety reaction which is precipitated or aggravated by a known stress. There are important paranoid trends, but the basic respect for reality is good and there are no disturbances of the thought processes. No psychotic process is seen.

The personality conflicts which this person has should be amenable to a degree of resolution through individual insight-giving therapy of a moderately deep level, but his stay at the hospital might not be long enough to permit adequate time to reach this objective. In the short run relief in the form of symptomatic tension reduction might be of value, but his adjustment can be nothing but poor on returning to his home and work environments.

On the basis of this evaluation, hospitalization was considered inappropriate, since he was not regarded as psychotic. Presumably he could be better helped as an outpatient.

The second example is of a man who was hospitalized because he drank too much, and a clinical assessment was sought in order to get to the root of the problem, in effect, to find out what sort of person he was and what might be done for him (Tallent, 1963, pp. 221–222):

This patient's dominant orientation to life is characterized by a childlike passivity and dependency, with marked inadequacy in coping with the everyday stresses of life.

Mr. Q has never really gotten into the competitive stream of life, but, without full awareness that he is doing so, inwardly wishes to be taken care of. Superficially he subscribes to the belief that a man should be responsible and productive, but his passive needs are stronger and he can readily rationalize his shortcomings. Thus he can work for only a few months at a time, then becomes unhappy and "exhausted" and finds relief in drink. He sees himself as physically weak, not having recovered from illnesses while in service, namely malaria, jungle rash and prickly heat. Similarly, he would like to get married for the dependency gratification this might offer (his dependency needs are much more insistent than his sexual needs), but has not sought out a mate because a girl friend married another man 20 years ago and he has not yet gotten over it.

Mr. Q's mode of adjustment is fairly adequate except where he is required to come to grips with life physically or mentally, to put out any form of sustained effort. This is so because of his passive needs, but also because of defects in his intellectual functioning. Though of average endowment (current I.Q.: 98), he is very naive about life and about himself, and he is unconcerned either with the world of real everyday living or with the poor quality of his own thinking which so easily makes it possible for him to deceive himself. Beyond this, he is remarkably unsure of himself and any external pressures to make him function responsibly would only lead to indecisiveness, tension, and no doubt drinking.

Psychodiagnostically, this patient would appear to be a case of alcoholism in association with a personality disorder. The latter is probably classifiable as Inadequate Personality, but a reliable social history (the patient is not regarded as a reliable source of information about himself) could help to establish whether this is correct. It is not felt that psychotherapy can provide any real benefits, but there is a possibility that he might be helped by associating actively with Alcoholics Anonymous.

Each of these clinical assessments depicts an individual struggling unsuccessfully with the management of his life. Let us try to understand in general terms the basis for the statements about a person's psychodynamics that are made in such clinical assessments. We shall examine the various sources of psychological information, some questions of methodology, and techniques of assessment.

Sources of information

What do we look at in making an assessment of personality? As noted earlier, we cannot know directly what is going on inside the person,* his needs, thoughts, perceptions, feelings, conflicts, and internal struggles; we must draw inferences from what we can observe. We can watch how the person acts, listen carefully to what he says, but we cannot "see" beneath the

*Indeed, the word "person" derives from the Latin *persona*, the actor's mask, hence the role he plays. "Personality" in modern usage, however, is not a role but the psychological structures and processes within the individual that interact in the various roles he plays in life.

mask of personality. To help us in constructing a picture of the psychodynamics of any given individual, three sources of information (about his reactions) are generally available: observation of his actions; the content of verbal reports (which can be regarded as a form of action); and measurement of certain physiological reactions.

The person's actions   Any act can have at the same time two somewhat different qualities, namely, an instrumental value and a style. We speak interpretively of an action as *instrumental* when it is oriented toward achieving some result: say, eating; achieving success; gaining approval; escaping or avoiding danger; harming someone who is hated or at whom one is angry; or being affectionate to someone in response to love. This instrumental quality is a very important property of action, since it is from such goal-oriented activity that we draw inferences about the person's motivations.

Thus, if a student spends most of his time studying, we may infer a high motivation for learning or academic achievement, or to avoid academic failure, since he has chosen this activity in preference to many others. This activity is thus instrumental in achieving a personal goal. On the other hand, if he spends most of his time in social activity, we are likely to view him as more concerned with human fellowship (affiliation) than with academic achievement. Thus, we can observe the direction of a person's activities, and to the extent that his choice of action is consistent for many situations or stable over a long period we can infer a motivational trait from this direction. Though this is but one element in a complex network of traits, we are on the way to assessing his personality or finding out what makes him tick.

Of course, such an inference is as yet based on very limited information and is therefore suspect. In judging the student who studies a great deal we may well be giving too much weight to surface behavior taken out of context. Actually he might prefer to engage in more social activities but is too shy and socially awkward to feel effective or comfortable in company; hence he withdraws into a commitment toward something else in which he can excel—academic achievement. Similarly, the student who devotes himself largely to social fellowship may actually feel himself blocked from esteem and success, which he really wants, because he considers himself intellectually incapable of attaining them or lacks the self-control to study regularly. Such contradictory cases show how complicated is the task of judging what goes on inside a person from the way he acts. Much more information is needed to increase the accuracy of our assessments. It is precisely such complexities that make personality assessment so demanding and challenging. The responsible clinician or personologist must be wary of dogmatic pronouncements about people.

[*The terms*] person *and* personality *are not identical . . . ; the second is more restricted. A person is an individual human organism. He has not only a personality (a distinctive and characteristic pattern of traits) but also a physique, an anatomy, a physiology, a social role, and a status; he expresses and transmits a culture, performs such operations as spending and investing to keep an economy going, and, in short, is the concrete embodiment of that grand generalization, man. The psychology of personality is only one of the sciences relevant to persons, the principal subject matter of all the behavioral, social, and medical sciences. A person is so complex and many-layered that many disciplines can be brought to bear on the physiochemical, fleshly, ideological, spiritual, or other aspects of his being. The student of personality must know something about all these aspects of persons, for they affect the patterns of behavior, which are his special concern. . . .* [From R. Holt, in Janis *et al.,* 1969, p. 580]

The *style* of an action refers to the various ways it can be performed without altering its capacity to produce the intended results. We can, for example, move slowly or quickly, use expansive or inhibited gestures, write with a weak or strong pressure on the pen. We can use language that is simple and direct to express an idea or language that is complex, literary, or subtle to say the same thing.

The scientific basis for making inferences about underlying mental events from styles or expressive acts is clearest in the field of emotions. Charles Darwin (1873) maintained that certain stylistic features of behavior were expressive of particular emotional states in a given species of animal. An angry cat arches its back in a particular way and hisses, but when frightened its body posture and general comportment look quite different. Similarly, an angry dog will snarl and bare its teeth but when frightened will crouch or slink and its hair along the line of its back may stand up. As was seen in Chapter 6, there is much evidence that each animal species has a characteristic way of showing the intention to challenge and drive off a competitor or to submit in defeat and thus terminate the conflict (see the photos in the introduction to Part II; also Figure 6.10). In man, certain gestures and facial expressions are also tied to particular emotional states, but here the situation is considerably more complex. Washburn and Hamburg (1968) have pointed out that in man the communication of threat and other emotional states has shifted considerably from special bodily structures for that purpose that exist in monkeys and apes (Figure 11.1) to the hands, the face, and especially to language, the primary basis of social communication. But there no doubt remain some residuals of our evolutionary link to earlier primates in the way we express rage (by snarling, brandishing fists, bellowing), or pleasure (grinning, laughing), or affection (kissing, hugging).

Evidence that certain facial expressions may be universal in man under particular emotional states, even transcending cultural pressures to conceal or modify them, has been recently provided in cross-cultural research (see Ekman, 1971). Ekman, the present author, and several associates, made a comparison of the facial responses of Japanese and American students to several stressful and neutral motion picture scenes. While they watched the movies, their facial expressions were filmed without their being aware of it. Then the films of the facial activities of both cultural groups were shown to other Japanese and American students, who had the task of judging whether the facial expressions had been made in response to the neutral or stressful scenes and to evaluate the emotions being experienced. The results showed that Japanese and American judges could detect with reasonable accuracy which type of movie, stressful or neutral, was being responded to, and they were

Figure 11.1 Temper tantrum in a young gorilla. (R. Van Nostrand from National Audubon Society)

as accurate with foreigners as with their countrymen. To some extent also they could successfully judge the intensity of the emotion being experienced by the viewer (as compared to self-reported ratings which the subjects watching the movie had filled out).

These findings strongly suggest that certain facial movements expressive of emotion are pancultural, that is, they may be universal in mankind, and that people of sharply different cultures can often decode these expressions. This refutes the widespread notion among Westerners that Orientals are "inscrutable" or stoical in emotional expression. It is still true, however, that in certain social contexts (for example, when one person talks with another), various cultures prescribe somewhat different modes of facial expression of such emotions as sadness, anger, and anxiety. But there also appears to be evidence of biologically determined patterns of expression that transcend these cultural variations.

Such styles of acting are often observed to be consistent in a particular person. This is what provides the wonderful sense of recognition when a mimic succeeds in capturing the essence of a public figure (Figure 11.2). The person he has imitated is recognizable in *style* of speaking, hand gestures, facial and body movements, and other mannerisms. With actress Bette Davis, some of these features include holding a cigarette and whipping it about in circles, certain exaggerated body movements, pursed lips in speaking, and clipped speech.

Figure 11.2 Impressionist Jim Bailey: (a) as Judy Garland; (b) as himself. (Photos courtesy of Jim Bailey)

(a)

(b)

With President Richard Nixon, so often imitated by impressionist David Frye, some of the key stylistic elements are an ingenuous smile, certain emphatic hand gestures, and the repeated use of a few phrases ("Let me make this perfectly clear").

The significance of such styles does not come from our amusement at seeing them mimicked, of course, but from the fact that style is a clue to the person's thoughts and feelings and how he copes with his threats and conflicts, in short, to some of the important psychodynamic qualities of personality. When the style of an act is viewed in this sense, it is often referred to as an expressive act, that is, the behavior is considered to be expressive of some inner psychological event. It reflects a motive that the person may not be aware of or does not want known, a quality that is "leaked," like a slip of the tongue, inadvertently revealing something of the inner life. A style may have first emerged as a goal-oriented or instrumental act. With constant repetition the style becomes a habit, still resembling the earlier act but with the original goals faded from view so that the person no longer can recognize its adaptive origins.

What is so funny about the Frye imitation of the habitual presidential statement, "Let me make this perfectly clear"? This expression is not only characteristic and hence recognizable but also highly suggestive to many observers. Nixon seems to be trying to tell us that we are now receiving the unvarnished truth, no fooling around, no bones about it, that he is being just as straight and candid as he can be. If you are a Nixon supporter, this little habit probably seems endearing and human. Who hasn't said, "Now listen here, I really mean it" or "I want to be quite candid with you" in order to disarm someone or suppress his disbelief? To the Nixon critic, however, the statement seems to "protest too much," to be selling bunk under the label of truth. From this point of view the statement appears in character with the unflattering appellation "tricky Dick." The public amusement at the foible thus comes from being in on the deception, of having caught a high public figure "in the act." The style is believed inadvertently to reveal the man's underlying attitudes. We are always monitoring the stylistic aspects of other people's actions and speech and, whether correctly or incorrectly, interpreting them, since intuitively we all know that what someone professes is not necessarily what goes on underneath.

Research on the expressive and hence communicative value of human styles of acting in social situations can be illustrated by a study (Rosenfeld, 1966) in which female students were asked to seek another student's approval in a social interchange; their gestures were compared during the interchange with those of other female students asked to avoid approval. Approval seekers used more smiling and gesticulation than approval avoiders. In still other studies (Mehrabian and Wiener, 1966), positive attitudes toward others were observed to be inadvertently communicated by the use of simple and immediate verbal expressions such as "You feel. . ." thus and so, while critical and hostile attitudes were communicated by complex, distant, and nonimmediate language such as "You people feel. . .". Out-group minority members often intuitively sense the hostility or disparagement that may be expressed by impersonal styles of address like "You people. . .".

We have a great deal of evidence that styles of acting do reveal important qualities of the personality, including emotional reactions and ways of coping with impulses, threats, and frustrations. Most of us have intuitively learned to "read" these patterns, or at least we act on what we think the other person is thinking and feeling as revealed to us, even when we are sometimes wrong in our inferences. Often, though, our hunches are quite sound. It is likely that people differ in their skills in sensing such inner meanings. Scientists have not yet discovered all the details of the code and how it works, although research is beginning to reveal some of the rules. The idea that some styles of acting are expressive of underlying psychodynamics seems to be a valid one if we can learn to translate them accurately. The psychologist tries to do just this in his diagnostic evaluations of the person in trouble made with the purpose of giving the most suitable and effective form of treatment.

The content of verbal reports   From a commonsense standpoint, the easiest way to determine an individual's feelings, motives, or thoughts is to question the subject himself. Unlike other animals, man is capable of introspection (search into his own private mental world), and he can communicate the results verbally to someone else.

However, just as there are problems with the accuracy of inferences about mental events from observation of behavior, so verbal reports are also subject to significant sources of error. The person may be unwilling to talk candidly about his innermost thoughts. ("Why should I tell someone things that might place me in a bad light?") Certainly the motives for honest self-revelation are also likely to be quite weak when the investigator is merely engaged in "cold," disinterested research rather than being concerned with the person's welfare. Although most people like to talk about themselves, they are also frequently reluctant to do so when what they tell goes beyond the surface, especially when this is a source of shame or embarrassment.

Another source of error is limited self-understanding on the part of most subjects and their incapacity to verbalize about what is happening. Many of the important events of our lives occurred when we were children, before we could adequately comprehend and label what was happening to us. Moreover, as the reader will recall (Chapter 10), self-deceptive defense mechanisms help us preserve certain important fictions about ourselves. When someone goes to a professional therapist to get help with his problems, not only is he usually unable at the outset to grasp exactly what is troubling him, but without realizing it he constructs a protective screen to shield himself from the truth. Thus, even when he seems to want urgently to cooperate with the therapist, he is giving a distorted picture. The therapist must ultimately see through this protective screen in order to understand the patient and provide effective assistance.

Very early in his psychoanalytic writings, Sigmund Freud described this protective screen, which he called *resistance* (to be discussed later in this chapter). The therapist must "listen with the third ear." He must take what the client says with a grain of salt while remaining alert to unintended signals expressive of the person's hidden conflicts and defenses. Some of the things the person reports are unreliable or distorted; almost always his report is incomplete: ways must be found to ferret out the whole story, especially the most important things which the person cannot talk about. In doing this, contradictions between what the person reports and his actions and life patterns provide valuable clues about such hidden or unrevealed material. As long as the clinician maintains the proper skepticism and seeks other behavioral evidence to supplement this verbal information, what the person tells him can serve as an enormously valuable source of psychological information.

Physiological reactions Another way to gauge internal psychological events is to measure certain physiological changes that are linked to strong emotions. We all know that an individual may grow pale in fear or suddenly become flushed in anger or embarrassment. There are also other less obvious bodily changes that may be measured. As noted in Chapter 10 in connection with stress disorders, when we experience strong emotion automatic biological mechanisms produce profound physiological effects throughout the body. We have all been aware of some of these: our heart rate rises dramatically, along with our blood pressure, and we may sense this as a pounding in our chest; our respiration grows more rapid and often irregular; and so on.

In some emotional states (such as "stage fright"), the salivary glands reduce their secretion of fluids and the mouth becomes dry, making it difficult to talk; in certain other states there is an increased flow of saliva, and one may even drool.

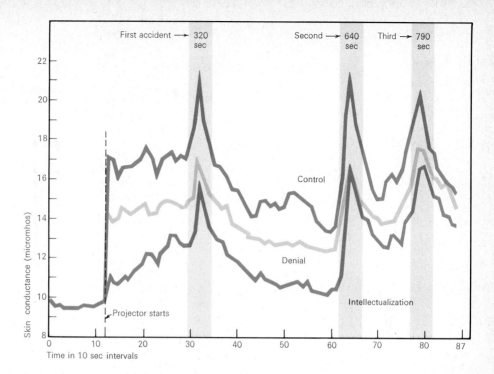

Figure 11.3 Effects of experimental treatment (statements either of denial or of intellectualization) on skin conductance measured while subjects watched a film showing stressful accidents. Note that the control group reacted much more strongly than did either of the other two groups. (From Lazarus et al., 1965)

When one is very anxious, sweat glands are often activated, and beads of perspiration may stand out on our foreheads or collect on our palms. All of these physiological changes are the result of activity of the autonomic nervous system and the endocrine (hormone-secreting) glands. These mechanisms are found in many other animals and are important in adaptation because they increase the organism's physiological resources in times of emergency. Many of the changes are quite visible to casual observation. Some cannot be detected without sensitive electrophysiological instruments or by the careful assay of endocrine gland secretions (in the blood and urine).

In recent years research psychologists have employed such measurements in order to study the effects of emotional stimuli on people. This is illustrated in the diagram in Figure 11.3. An experiment was conducted in which subjects watched a disturbing motion picture that depicted three bloody accidents in a woodworking shop (Lazarus et al., 1965). Changes in the electrical conductivity of the skin (one of the conveniently measured physiological reactions occurring in emotional states) were continuously monitored while the subjects watched the film, and it can be seen that each one of the accident scenes produced a large peak in skin conductance. Some of the subjects were prepared in advance by statements that the accidents had never really occurred but were staged to look as if they had (denial). Another group was approached

501

Note 11.1

The principle that physiological changes can supplement verbal statements as sources of information about emotional activity is used in *lie-detection tests*. These involve simultaneously recording several bodily reactions, such as changes in the electrical resistance of the skin, heart rate, blood pressure, or rate and amplitude of breathing, while the person answers questions about which truthful answers are sought. Since these physiological reactions are markedly affected by subtle changes in emotional state, such measurements can often give away a liar. One of the technical problems of lie detection is to distinguish between the person who is guilty and one who is merely frightened. The guilty person will usually respond emotionally to a key or charged question, or one on which he lies, but will not react to one that is neutral in implication.

The logic of lie detection is quite sound. However, its application is not very dependable and, in consequence, it is not admissable as legal evidence. A clever person can confuse the examiner, say, by thinking about emotional things during neutral questions, or by breathing deeply or tensing so as to produce an uninterpretable record. Some persons are extremely reactive and show marked reactions to nearly all questions, which foils the lie-detection test. Others are nonresponsive emotionally or physiologically and do not reveal anything significant.

Going back to the point that physiological reactions can be used to supplement verbal reports in making psychodynamic inferences, the conclusion is that bodily states are not infallible sources of information about a person's mental state, any more than is what the person says, although they can be quite useful as cross checks. There are many nonpsychological reasons why physiological changes might occur, such as physical activity, fever, or changes in external temperature or humidity, and to assume that a physiological reaction reveals an emotional state requires that these other, nonpsychological sources of reaction be ruled out.

The best way to look at this matter is that inferences about psychodynamics are always very tenuous and hence we need all the information we can get to have much confidence in them. Any single source of

with a highly detached statement concerned only with an intellectual analysis of the social relationships occurring between the various characters portrayed in the film (*intellectualization*). A third group received only a brief statement that they were going to watch some accidents (*control*). In Figure 11.3 you can see that both the denial and intellectualization statements sharply reduced the emotional impact of the film compared with the control condition. The statements had altered the threat value of the film events by changing the way in which these events were appraised by the subjects. Here one can see the way in which the monitoring of the physiological changes connected with emotion makes possible the study of ways of controlling or reducing emotional reactions under conditions of psychological stress. Subjects may report low levels of emotional activity even when their measured physiological reactions indicate considerable stress, thus making such physiological measurement a very useful supplement to introspective verbal reports about mental events (Note 11.1).

In order to make reliable inferences about the psychodynamics of a person in trouble (or, for that matter, about anyone), the diverse sources of information discussed here must be available. The clinician is not usually in a position to observe the subject day in and day out. The necessary information must be obtained, therefore, by getting him to perform naturally, so to speak, while being observed, whether this be in the clinician's office or in his home setting. He must be made to act, or report his actions, or someone else must make such reports (say, a parent, teacher, or spouse). Much of personality assessment consists of devising techniques for doing this and of evaluating the inferences about psychodynamics derived from them. But there are a number of methodological issues that must be understood before such techniques can be discussed properly.

Methodological issues in assessment

Whether we observe the person in his natural setting or contrive some test situation to assess his personality, two considerations must be uppermost: (1) We must make accurate observations, utilizing as fully as possible the various sources of information (be they actions, verbal reports, or physiological measurements). (2) We are never only interested in what happens in the particular setting in which the observations are obtained; rather, our purpose is to be able to generalize to other settings and occasions, especially those of daily importance in the subject's life. Three of the four special concepts to be considered next, namely, standardization, reliability, and validity, are designed to help insure both accuracy of description and legitimate generalization of our assessments (Tyler,

1971). The fourth concept, that of situational influences, adds an important qualification in our attempts to predict how people will act and react.

Standardization If we want to say that a person is bright or dull, motivated strongly or weakly toward the goal of achievement, highly inhibited or impulsive, or for that matter possessed of any quality or combination of qualities, we must compare him against some standard or norm. For meaningful description of any person, differences and similarities with other persons, real or mythical, must be noted. Thus, when we say that Jim is inhibited, we are suggesting one of two things—either that he is more inhibited than most other men or that he is more inhibited now than in the past. The former statement involves an *interindividual* comparison or standard (comparing one person with others), while the latter involves an *intraindividual* comparison (comparison of his personality in various contexts). Without inter- or intraindividual standards we can express little that is very meaningful about anyone. We cannot indicate how fearful he is or how confident, how psychologically healthy or maladapted, how calm or angry. Thus, every assessment technique requires normative or standardization data revealing how different classes of people respond in various contexts.

Reliability One of the most fundamental assessment questions is "How reliable are the observations we have made?" This refers to two separate but related matters, namely, the representativeness of the observations and the extent to which there is agreement among different observers.

Suppose we want to describe the personality of a particular person in his natural life situation. How do we do it? Were we to watch him continuously, the mass of observations would be overwhelming. For example, it required a 435-page book for one group of psychologists to record in some detail what a seven-year-old boy did in one day (see Barker and Wright, 1951). If one attempted to do this for one whole lifetime on film or paper, there would not be room enough to store the information in a large library. It should therefore be quite obvious that in assessment the observational events must be very selectively sampled. This poses the question of whether or not the events sampled and the behavior observed are truly *representative* of the person. Perhaps we have chosen to observe him on a day when he is out of sorts, tired, threatened by an imminent crisis, or whatever. We are then likely to come up with judgments that are not at all representative of the way the subject reacts in most contexts, especially in those in which we are interested because they relate to his psychological difficulties.

information, be it what the person tells us, what he does, or his bodily reactions, is highly vulnerable to error. In combination, two or more sources are likely to be far more reliable; moreover, they increase the opportunities to observe contradictions, say, between verbal reports and physiological changes, from which defense mechanisms and defensiveness are often inferred (see Note 10.3).

Representativeness goes to the heart of our ability to generalize about how a person will react in other situations or occasions, say, how he will respond to some clinical treatment. If his usual patterns are poorly reflected by the observations, then we can have no confidence in having obtained the basis for a "true" estimate of the traits being assessed, and any predictions about how he will react later, or in a different context, will have little validity.

As to the second kind of reliability, namely, *observer agreement,* if two or more observers cannot agree about what they have seen, we can have no confidence in what they have reported. Disagreements among observers can arise for a variety of reasons. Observers may emphasize different aspects of a complex behavioral event, or they may remember it differently later. Furthermore, although there may be high agreement on the description of what happened, each may interpret it differently. For example, all observers of a two-person interaction might agree that one of the persons under study reacted with anger; but one observer may view the anger as an uncalled-for act revealing a hostile personality, while another observer sees the same expression of anger as defensiveness in a person who is vulnerable and threatened and who has been treated with insensitivity.

Some of these sources of disagreement can be overcome or at least minimized by making the observer's task simpler. But when all is said and done, if carefully trained observers or judges cannot agree about the events they have observed, no sound assessment is possible. For this reason, the psychologist must demonstrate reasonable observer agreement if his inferences and assessment are to be taken seriously.

Validity   If we make a general statement about someone, say, that he is impulsive, self-controlled, or motivated for approval, we must have solid evidence supporting it. The term employed to refer to how much confidence we can have in this evidence is *validity*. As applied to an assessment technique, the term means that the technique accurately measures what it is supposed to measure.

The simplest test for validity establishes whether or not some specific type of behavior can be predicted from another already known kind of behavior; this is often called *criterion-related validity*. For example, we may want to predict how well someone will do in college (the criterion). One of the best predictors of this criterion is how well he did in high school. Thus, the validity of high school grades as a predictor of college grades may be tested by correlating one with the other, that is, by determining the statistical relationship between the two sets of grades. If the high school students with high grades tend to some given extent (the index of correlation) to be those with high grades in college, then the high school grades are a *valid* measure of grades in college to that extent (Note 11.2).

A valid *assessment measure* in the sense of criterion-related validity is one that permits the prediction of another form of behavior, and the *degree of validity* is the amount of accuracy with which this prediction can be made. If our interest is mainly in the practical value of such predictions, then we may not care whether or not we can explain the reason for the correlation. The situation is different, however, when we are concerned with the way certain personality traits work. In most cases, such personality traits do not have a one-to-one relationship with any single bit of behavior; but an inference may be drawn about an underlying process or trait that ties together a pattern of many kinds of behavior. For example, we may infer that a given person is highly intelligent even though he cannot remember names of people to whom he has just been introduced and seems forgetful and impractical. His intelligence is not manifest in any simple way in all situations and tasks. In assessment we are usually trying to construct an idea of the person's traits from what we observe, such traits being inferred properties of the person rather than some observable performance (such as getting good grades in school). Nevertheless, it is still necessary to demonstrate that the inferences are valid, and this calls for a somewhat more complex approach than in the simple criterion-related validity test just discussed. The term usually employed by psychologists for this is *construct validity*.

To establish construct validity, we make some "if . . . then" types of statements about the trait in question. That is, "if" on the basis of what is observed the person is said to have some given trait, "then" certain other things are expected. These other things may include certain events in the person's past that are believed to produce such a trait, or certain other behavior patterns that ought to be demonstrable in people with that trait. At this point an investigator can make further observations to see if these "other things" do indeed follow, as the theory predicts.

An instance of such investigation involves a test scale devised by personality psychologist Harrison Gough (1960) to measure degree of socialization. (A highly socialized person has internalized the values and norms of his society; poor socialization is often related to psychopathic behavior, as described in Chapter 10.) The test covers certain social attitudes and ways of responding having to do with whether or not the person behaves in accordance with social expectations. Here are some examples: "Before I do something I try to consider how my friends will react to it." "I often think about how I look and what impression I am making upon others." "I find it easy to 'drop' or 'break with' a friend." "I have often

Note 11.2

Here again we come upon the concept of correlation, whose meaning, you will recall, was discussed in Note 6.3, and the problems of interpreting correlations in causal terms in Notes 5.1, 6.4, and 7.3. The concept of validity will be much easier to grasp if you also understand the meaning of correlation.

gone against my parents wishes." "If the pay were right I would like to travel with a circus or carnival." When a person answers "yes" to the first two items and "no" to the others, this pattern indicates someone who is highly socialized.

Now if this interpretation of the person's pattern of answers is sound, then a subject with a high-socialization score ought to behave conventionally, while one with a low score should transgress social norms frequently and behave antisocially. In one study of the construct validity of the socialization scale (Gough, 1960), something quite like this was found: people who had been judged by others to be "good citizens" scored high on the scale; delinquents, disciplinary problems, felons, and residents of the county jail scored low. These and other research findings suggest that the trait being assessed by the test could legitimately be termed "degree of socialization." Although the trait itself cannot be observed directly, its presence or absence (or its strength) can be reasonably inferred from a person's pattern of answers, and such an inference permits us to make fairly accurate predictions as to his future acts. Since so much of what is said about a person consists of inferences or interpretations about personality, construct validity is a very fundamental assessment concept.

Situational influences   It must be obvious by now that much of our behavior is governed by the social situation (as documented in Chapter 4), and to ignore this is to overstate the role of personality factors in an individual's efforts to adapt to his world. Thus, when we observe a person in psychological trouble and try to understand what is happening, our assessment must take into account his life situation and the situational contexts in which his problems appear most acute. A proper account of his psychodynamics should thus include such information as the impact of his family, the kinds of people who readily arouse his anger or his suspicions, what brings on feelings of depression, in what context did his ulcers become inflamed, and so on. An understanding of the individual requires more than a mere catalog of stable personality traits; it also requires an analysis of the ways in which he responds to the various changing features of his social milieu. It is inability to carry on successful commerce with a variable environment that marks all cases of adaptive failure.

Clinical assessment is not magic crystal-ball gazing but rather a scientifically based approach to description and prediction. Psychologists can never predict exactly how a person will react in the future, because not being clairvoyant they cannot know the circumstances to which he will be exposed. But as our diagnostic techniques become more refined, it should be increasingly possible to say that, given a particular set of circumstances (this or that treatment), the person may be expected to react in a specific way. We are still a long way from this important goal.

Techniques of assessment

Three of the most important techniques used in clinical assessment and in personality research in general are the *life history*, the *interview*, and the *psychological test*. These are described briefly below.

The life history   The personality of an adult does not spring into being full blown but is the product of the lifelong interplay of biological factors and social experience. A life history is, then, nothing more than a chronology of the person's psychological development, usually focusing on those events which are regarded as most important in explaining that development. In the case of someone in trouble, the focus is placed on the events that contributed to the difficulty.

Typically the life history is obtained through interviews with the subject, although other members of the family may be called upon and objective information from family records, schools, hospitals, or records of military service may be used to supplement the account if available. Since the life history is usually based on reports by the person himself, or by his family and friends, there is always a question about the validity of the information being presented. People forget details of the past, and furthermore their account is colored by their own biases and efforts to present themselves in a particular light. Much of the information provided by the family is also distorted by such biases and errors in recall. Still, even when there is major distortion of events and relationships, a professional can usually discern a great deal about the developmental process from the way past events are filtered through the person's eyes. To discover, say, that a subject views his father as unfeeling and unsympathetic is as important as to know the actual truth about the father's attitudes.

As with any effort to examine the countless happenings in the lives of people, only a limited sample of them can be reviewed. This means that a clear decision must be made about the types of events to be included in such a history. Two considerations influence this decision: (1) The subject naturally tends to emphasize those events in his life which most stand out in his memory. (2) The psychologist's conception of personality development will play a key role in the choice. Professionals approaching the task from varying theoretical viewpoints will emphasize different features of the history and put different constructions on what is recounted.

Since Freudian psychoanalysts, for example, believe that the first three years of life are of particular importance in personality development, they often make special efforts to obtain this type of early material. Psychotherapists of other schools might not consider it worthwhile to explore that early period of life unless it comes up naturally. Thus theories help influence what we look for in a life history and serve as guides (or blinders) to investigation.

The interview   Undoubtedly the most widely used technique of assessment is the interview and, as we just saw, even the life history is obtained typically through use of interview procedures. The interview is flexible, allowing the psychologist to tailor his questions or reactions to what has been said. Not only does it permit examination of how the person himself sees and reports his experiences and reactions, but such verbal reports are supplemented also by behavioral reactions that can be observed while the person tells his story or responds to inquiries from the interviewer. This behavior can be observed as a check on what is being said: for example, slips of the tongue may reveal otherwise hidden intentions; expression of emotion can suggest a depth of feeling toward certain thoughts or wishes; gestures and facial expressions may imply conflict; emphasis (or deemphasis) on certain events can reveal characteristic styles of coping such as denial, detachment, or paranoid suspiciousness, on which inferences about characteristic modes of defense are founded (see Chapter 10). The two-person, face-to-face interview thus makes it possible for the psychologist to be right on the spot and to detect such behavioral cues at the same time that he is hearing the introspective self-report. On the other hand, the very flexibility of the interview increases the methodological problems related to the reliability and validity of the observations, as noted earlier.

The psychological test   The test is a way of studying behavior under relatively standardized conditions, avoiding some of the problems just mentioned. In theory, the test is an attempt to control or exclude all sorts of irrelevant influences that creep into every assessment situation. By using a standardized format and questions, the test is therefore analogous to a laboratory experiment designed to study the influence of a few limited variables and exclude irrelevant ones. Actually such exclusion is only relative, since the tester is bound to introduce some of his own personality into the testing situation, as has been shown frequently (see Sarason, 1954). In fact, there are certain situations, for example, intelligence testing in children, where the active role of the examiner is desirable and critical to performance; he must be highly skillful in reassuring and encouraging the nervous child so that he will perform up to his capacities. Despite these reservations, the psychological test still has the advantage of being a much better controlled means of obtaining personal data than any other technique.

There are many kinds of tests and no attempt will be made to review them all here. It will be worthwhile though to give a few examples of two types of tests, structured and unstructured.

Structured tests generally consist of questionnaires with multiple-choice answers, such as *yes, no,* or *cannot say.* These tests are called structured because the task and the possible responses are unambiguous; there is no problem of observer agreement, since the examiner can score them simply by recording the frequency of each type of answer.

One of the best-known personality questionnaires is the *Minnesota Multiphasic Personality Inventory* (MMPI; Hathaway and McKinley, 1943), which was designed to distinguish among people with various types of adaptive failure. There are subscales (groups of questions) measuring tendencies toward schizophrenia, paranoia, depression, hysteria, obsessive-compulsive disorder, and other disturbances. Some examples of items from this complex test are given in Table 11.1. Another highly respected personality questionnaire is the *California Psychological Inventory* (CPI; Gough, 1957), which includes the socialization scale mentioned earlier in connection with

Table 11.1

Some sample items from the Minnesota Multiphasic Personality Inventory (MMPI)[a]

Some items contributing to a score for hypochondriasis (morbid concern about health, with delusions of physical illness)

- T   There seems to be a fullness in my head or nose most of the time.
- T   Parts of my body often have feelings like burning, tingling, crawling, or like "going to sleep."
- F   I have had no difficulty in starting or holding my bowel movement.

Some items contributing to a score of psychasthenia (obsessive-compulsive disorders)

- T   I usually have to stop and think before I act even in trifling matters.
- T   I have a habit of counting things that are not important, such as bulbs on electric signs, and so forth.
- F   I have no dread of going into a room by myself where other people have already gathered and are talking.

Some items contributing to a score for paranoia

- T   I believe I am being followed.
- T   Most people inwardly dislike putting themselves out to help other people.
- F   I have no enemies who really wish to harm me.

[a] Items labeled T and F are those which, when answered true or false as indicated, contribute to a positive score in a particular diagnostic category. From Hathaway and McKinley (1943).

Table 11.2

Some sample items from the California Psychological Inventory (CPI)[a]

Some items contributing to a score for self-control

F A person needs to "show off" a little now and then.
F I am often said to be hotheaded.
F Sometimes I feel like smashing things.

Some items contributing to a score for self-acceptance

F When in a group of people I usually do what the others want rather than make suggestions.
T My daily life is full of things that keep me interested.
F It is hard for me to start a conversation with strangers.

Some items contributing to a score for achievement by means of conformity

F When I was going to school I played hooky quite often.
F When someone does me a wrong I feel I should pay him back if I can, just for the principle of the thing.
T There is something wrong with a person who can't take orders without getting angry or resentful.

[a] Items labeled T and F are those which, when answered true or false as indicated, contribute to a positive score on a particular trait. From Gough (1957) by permission of Consulting Psychologists' Press, Inc., Palo Alto, California.

the concept of construct validity. While the MMPI is oriented entirely toward psychopathology, the CPI focuses on the personality traits of "normal" populations. Some examples of CPI items are shown in Table 11.2.

At one time, when questionnaires first began to appear, they were regarded as the outstanding and most objective approach to assessment. They proliferated until the 1940s, when critical doubts began to be raised about the validity of such tests. They were clearly oversold, and reality set in with widespread disillusionment. During the 1940s, there was a wave of interest in depth psychology, stimulated by Freudian theory. In consequence, *unstructured tests* took the spotlight and were widely regarded as the new key to assessing depth aspects of personality.

Personality tests are called unstructured when they involve presentation to the person of an ambiguous stimulus situation (that is, without structure, or with limited or minimal structure) to be interpreted. They are known also as *projective* tests because of their association with the Freudian defense mechanism of projection, in which an unacceptable impulse is attributed to someone else and hence denied in oneself. This concept of projection, however, has been broadened by making it refer to the process of attributing to someone or something qualities that it does not necessarily have. Thus one interprets an ambiguous stimulus by "projecting" one's thoughts, feelings, and conflicts into that stimulus, since it does not have precisely defined properties of its own (see also discussion of stimulus ambiguity and perception in Chapter 2). In any case, in unstructured tests a wide latitude is permitted (and encouraged) in the response, the stimulus materials being inkblots, drawings, photos of people in unclear situations—in effect, any type of ambiguous material. The person must draw on his own personal and unique experience to interpret the stimulus, and in doing so he reveals some of his distinctive inner qualities, for example, his motives, outlook, and modes of coping.

Among the most widely known and used unstructured tests are the Rorschach Inkblot Test, the Thematic Apperception Test, and sentence-completion tests of which there are many versions. Hermann Rorschach was a Swiss psychiatrist who experimented extensively with the responses of patients to inkblots. In doing so, he developed a standard set of ten stimulus inkblots (Rorschach, 1942). The technique was brought to the United States during the late 1930s. In this test, the subject is shown the ten inkblots, one at a time, and asked to say what they look like, resemble, or might be. The psychologist's interpretation is based on what the subject has seen (animals, people, events, or whatever), its location in the inkblot, shape, color, whether people and animals are seen in motion or as stationary, and the extent to which the things seen are built up or organized out of separate parts or details. Such interpretations are related to much accumulated clinical and research information about how various kinds of people have previously performed the same task (Figure 11.4).

Although the blots are ambiguous and could look like many different things or events, there is some structure too, so that one finds certain common responses as well as highly

Figure 11.4 A Rorschach inkblot. Try writing down everything you see here. Now compare your responses with those of friends. You will be surprised at the diversity of images seen. The pictures that we project into this inkblot can give valuable clues to our thoughts and emotions. (From Rorschach, 1942)

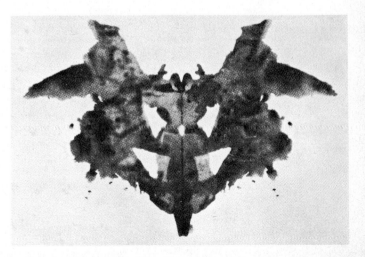

unusual responses, and it is possible to evaluate the extent to which the subject departs from more common responses to the stimulus or hews conventionally to them. This quality in the testing situation is analogous to reality testing in life, a process that seems to be impaired in seriously disturbed mental patients. In this sense, the Rorschach Inkblot Test is thought to be a microcosm of reality, suggesting how the person copes with the larger world in which he lives.

Among the most important clues to personality is the style with which the task of interpreting the inkblots is tackled. The same object may be seen in qualitatively different ways by two subjects. For example, both may see a butterfly, a common response to one of the inkblot cards, but one person adds the comment, "How beautiful," while the other adds the qualification, "If I stretch my imagination I guess it could look like a butterfly." Such stylistic differences are thought to be associated with different characteristic ways of coping with conflict and threat. The former comment would be expected in people tending toward a Pollyannaish, denial type of defensive style, while the latter is illustrative of a detached, intellectualized mode of defense (see Chapter 10). As with any assessment-based interpretation of personality, a most important problem with the Rorschach Test is the construct validity of the inferences derived from the performance, and a very large, complex, and controversial literature has grown up dealing with validity of the standard Rorschach interpretations.

The Thematic Apperception Test (TAT) originated by Christiana Morgan and Henry A. Murray (1935), consists of 20 ambiguous pictures, most of them showing people in various settings and relationships (Figure 11.5). The person is asked to create a dramatic story about each, to imagine what the people are thinking and feeling, the events leading up to the situation depicted, and the outcome of the situation. Although the TAT pictures are quite ambiguous, like the Rorschach there are some stimulus constraints on what is seen. Some pictures suggest a father and a son, a mother and son, a married couple, people in distress, in short, people in common roles, conceived as struggling with common human problems, conflicts, and dilemmas. Yet there is also considerable diversity in what is seen and in the story themes, thus revealing some of the emotional problems, preoccupations, and ways of dealing with them in the person being studied. The basic principles of the TAT have also been adapted to many specific assessment purposes. One of the best-known adaptations is a special set of pictures used by David C. McClelland and his colleagues (1953) for assessing degree of achievement motivation based on the story themes they stimulate.

The sentence-completion test consists of a set of incomplete sentences, or sentence stems, which the person being

Figure 11.5 A picture from the Thematic Apperception Test. What is the story that goes along with this picture? Let your imagination run wild. Now try the picture on several other people. The results should be quite varied. Psychologists systematize such answers for purposes of study and appraisal of human personality. (From Henry A. Murray, Thematic Apperception Test; ©*1943, Harvard University Press)*

assessed is asked to fill in. There are many forms, few of them well standardized. The stem may be highly ambiguous, as in the example, "I feel _____," or it may be highly suggestive of certain thoughts or impulses, as in the example, "I get angry when _____." Thus, the person who fills in many such ambiguous items with answers like "I feel *angry*" appears to have a proclivity for angry thoughts. Presumably in that person anger is a strong impulse that expresses itself without much provocation. On the other hand, the person who responds to the second type of item by "I hate *to get caught in the rain without my umbrella*" seems to reveal conflict over the inhibition of hostility; he has gone out of his way to deny it or to turn the suggested emotional meaning into a bland cliché.

Here too a key consideration about which there has been much debate concerns the construct validity of such psychodynamic interpretations from sentence-completion test data. The problems of validity are complicated because of the multiple influences underlying any kind of behavior and the fact that one is dealing with unseen or inferred psychological states and processes, calling for sophisticated theory, elaborate tests of construct validity, and great ingenuity on the part of investigators generating the behavioral observations following from the constructs.

These tests represent various efforts to get people to display behavior patterns from which their fundamental personality traits can be inferred and which significantly show how they act and react in their real-life settings. As yet such devices remain promising beginnings rather than proven ways of assessing personality on which we can rely with confidence. Difficult as it is to assess accurately even a single personality trait, it is even more difficult to construct a valid portrait of the "whole" person.

THERAPY

There are two basic reasons for personality assessment. One is that it helps us to discover something about human behavior, the ways people are constructed psychologically, and how we come to be what we are. The second reason is primarily practical, namely, we study people in order to know how best to help them when things go wrong. Ultimately, we seek also to find ways to prevent people from getting into psychological difficulty in the first place.

The aim of surefire treatment through exact knowledge is at the present time more an ideal than a reality. Although assessment does indeed help us in making many clinical decisions—whether a person is likely to try suicide as a solution

Note 11.3

The reader will recall that this point about the diagnostic classification of mental disorder was made earlier in Note 10.2. There it was said that the various types of illness were distinguished primarily on the basis of behavioral symptoms, not on causal or treatment considerations. This means that merely labeling a patient as a particular kind of neurotic or psychotic is not particularly useful for prescribing a program of treatment. Clinicians think of accurate diagnosis not merely as sticking a label on a patient in this way, but as a search for the past and present sources of his troubles. It is important to discover just what has disrupted his characteristic ways of coping. Nevertheless, although such psychodynamic diagnosis can be useful in therapy, it is unfortunately still true today that the overall plan of treatment is often not greatly influenced by it, and many therapists who have specialized in one type of approach will use it regardless of whom they are treating. This is one of the worst results of lack of cross fertilization among the diverse disciplines on whose knowledge effective treatment depends.

to his problems, whether he is suffering from brain damage or a learned disturbance of social living, whether his problem is likely to be short-lived or chronic, whether his complaints are easy to resolve by short-term reeducation or reflect a serious underlying difficulty that requires long-term depth treatment—by and large treatment currently available is somewhat limited in its possibilities. Unlike physical medicine, where the diagnosis largely determines the treatment, special drugs or hormones, specific surgery, or whatever, treatment for adaptive failure tends to be much less attuned to specific ailments. The result is that clinical diagnosis has been far less important in psychologically oriented treatment than it ought to be, and therapists tend to gain most of their understanding of the patient as the treatment proceeds. Thus, therapy looks quite similar whether the person is an obsessive-compulsive neurotic, phobic, depressed, or mildly psychotic. Undoubtedly this is a product of our ignorance, and increasingly there is recognition that treatment must vary with the condition (Note 11.3).

For some persons treatment can be oriented modestly toward removal of a symptom that is troublesome or incapacitating, as in the case of a specific fear or phobia, or certain sexual problems such as male impotence (inability to have a penile erection) or female frigidity or lack of sexual climax. It may be that aside from such symptoms of stress the person is managing to get along adequately. The main difficulty may be inability to handle an immediate crisis related to separation or loss, retirement, a specific interpersonal tangle, physical illness, and the like, problems not requiring a lengthy and ambitious analysis or a major overhaul of life pattern.

In other instances, however, the problem must be construed in quite different terms. The individual may be experiencing feelings of isolation or alienation and the absence of meaning and commitment in his life. He requires a profound reorientation of his outlook and life style if he is to obtain some measure of inner well-being. This latter goal of treatment is far more ambitious than that of tiding the person over an immediate crisis that is presumed to be largely situational and short-lived.

Finally, there is the goal of reaching a severely incapacitated mental patient (such as the regressed schizophrenic) whose mode of living is so inadequate that he cannot get along independently without hospitalization or continuing care. There may be long-standing incapacitation suggestive of a profound problem. For such a person one may have to settle for the rather modest goal of getting him to accept limited human relationships without extreme fear of treachery. Evidence of even a small degree of trust may be regarded as a therapeutic triumph, however limited it is.

When we think of treatment it is important to recognize

the large variety of problems for which people need help and the variations in severity of maladaptive conditions. In sum, treatment is not one thing, but many, varying in goal and specific tactics depending on the nature of the problem, both the conception held by the therapist about the psychodynamics of the disorder and his viewpoint about the best way of tackling it therapeutically. Adaptive failure and its treatment must not be oversimplified in our wish to obtain handy answers. Indeed, it has taken a major part of a disturbed person's lifetime to produce many of the psychological problems from which he suffers, and it would be naive to imagine that most such problems can be swept away by the wave of a wand or a procedure as simple as administering a pill, a swift kick, or a few learning sessions.

We shall now briefly review present approaches to the treatment of adaptive failure. Three main types of approach may be distinguished, namely, physical (medical) treatment, nonphysical psychotherapeutic methods, and those which focus on the social environment.

Physical approaches to therapy

If one takes the position that adaptive failure is the result of tissue malfunctioning or defects, the logical approach to its treatment is to be sought in physical medicine. One of the earliest such treatments (during the 1930s) made use of the pancreatic hormone *insulin* to produce a temporary coma by withdrawing sugar from the brain cells. Although this insulin shock therapy is no longer widely used, it is still employed on a limited scale with schizophrenic patients (see Horowitz, 1959), usually in combination with psychotherapy. Another physical treatment that has mostly gone out of vogue, though it has not disappeared, is *psychosurgery* (Freeman, 1959). This involves the destruction of some brain tissue, most often by cutting the neural connections between the frontal lobes of the brain (where the cognitive centers involved in anticipation of the future are located) and lower (autonomic) brain centers. Another physical approach that is still widely used is *electroshock* treatment (Kalinowsky, 1959), which involves producing a pseudoepileptic convulsion by means of an electric current applied to the head (Figure 11.6; see also Note 11.4).

Public awareness of electroshock therapy was heightened during the American presidential election campaign of 1972, when it was revealed that the Democratic vice presidential candidate, Senator Thomas Eagleton of Missouri, had recently undergone a series of such shock treatments to counter episodes of mild depression. The subsequent political furor led to withdrawal of his candidacy. Such treatment is not uncommon for severe depression. It is also readily employed for relatively

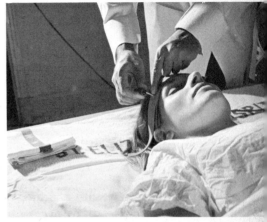

(a)

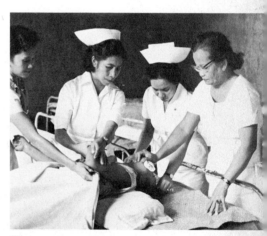

(b)

Figure 11.6 (a) Electroshock therapy. (b) Administration of muscle relaxant before shock treatment. (a: National Institutes of Health; b: World Health Organization/Photo by Eric Schwab)

minor mental problems (like mild depression) in a few parts of the country (including the Midwest) but usually only for severe conditions in other sections (such as the East), hence the public uneasiness at the disclosure. During a treatment series, shock is typically administered three or four times a week, often in a physician's office, and some patients may be given hundreds of shocks over the years. There has been and still is much controversy over the effectiveness of this treatment, and it has less support today than in past decades; some concern has been voiced over possible brain damage with frequent use. However, the treatment seems to be well-established to shorten episodes of depression in large numbers of mental hospitals in spite of uncertainty generally about its overall utility (Kalinowsky, 1959).

Clearly the most widespread modern physical treatment,

Note 11.4

It is worth observing that psychodynamically oriented professionals, both in psychiatry and clinical psychology, often feel considerable concern if not distaste for the three physical approaches to treatment mentioned thus far, namely, insulin shock, psychosurgery, and electroshock. The reasons for this are a combination of grave doubts that these therapeutic methods are normally helpful, belief that there is no adequate rationale for them even if they do help some persons, and—lastly and most important—concern that they sometimes can do irreparable harm to the brain of the patient. Insulin was dropped from most treatment centers because it is extremely dangerous, producing a coma that is the result of withdrawal of sugar from the brain cells. The patient must be watched carefully, and there is no guarantee that a few administrations might not produce irreversible damage. Similarly, psychosurgery involves permanent destruction of important brain tissues, and in the worst instances this "treatment" can create vegetablelike men and women, perhaps now lacking severe anxiety, but also lacking an intact mind. Even in modified versions of this type of operation in which damage is quite restricted, there is something disturbing about destruction of brain tissue in an effort to cure symptoms without getting at the person's fundamental problems. Such a procedure should surely not be employed unless all other hope has been lost, a conservatism that unfortunately is rare among enthusiasts of any procedure. Finally, electroshock too

has its potentials for brain damage, though this risk is relatively small if the procedure is not overdone. In general, the violence of these procedures argues for rejecting them for milder methods wherever possible, and indeed this has led to their gradual curtailment or elimination at the most advanced medical centers, especially where mental disorder is regarded as a problem of living rather than a physiological or structural anomaly of the brain.

Though many professionals advocate eliminating them; it is difficult to say whether or not all surgical procedures on the brain for treatment of behavioral problems should be ruled out. Such procedures are used, for example, to relieve intractable pain, to curb the tremor effects of Parkinson's disease (used until the recent development of the drug L-dopa), and to suppress uncontrollable rage and violence. Consider, for example, the following case reported by Sweet *et al.* (1969):

A generally reserved 34 year old man reported episodes of violence about once a week. Frequently they would be initiated by a petty remark made by his wife after which he would work himself into a fury and then physically beat and injure his wife and children. In an attempt to solve his problem he went to three different psychiatrists for a period of seven years, all to no avail. He was finally given EEG [electroencephalogram] tests which revealed abnormal electrical activity in the temporal lobes. When antiseizure

drugs failed, he volunteered for . . . surgery. Banks of electrodes were surgically implanted bilaterally into the medial and lateral nuclei of the amygdala [a portion of the subcortical brain]. Electrical stimulation through one of the electrodes in the medial area caused the patient to declare that he "felt" one of his fits coming on. Similar stimulation just 4 mm. lateral in another electrode caused the patient to completely relax and exclaim, "I feel like I'm floating on a cloud." By regular stimulation about once a day in the lateral amygdala, favorable moods continued and seizures were avoided. When such continued treatment became impractical, small portions of the medial amygdala were electrically lesioned [destroyed] with high levels of electrical current. Following this, the patient returned to normal life and experienced no further attacks.

It is certainly quite possible that some severe behavioral disturbances involving uncontrollable violence are caused in part by brain tumors. The tragic case of Charles J. Whitman points this up dramatically. Whitman was a student at the University of Texas and a former altar boy and Eagle scout. On July 31, 1966, he wrote the following letter (cited in Sweet *et al.*, 1969):

I don't really understand myself these days. I am supposed to be an average, reasonable and intelligent young man. However, lately (I can't recall when it started) I have been a victim of many unusual and irrational

particularly with psychotic patients, is administration of *drugs* (commonly referred to as chemotherapy). Sedative drugs such as bromides and barbiturates have had a long history in psychiatric usage. There are newer drugs, however, and many bromides and barbiturates which are addicting have been all but abandoned. Despite initial grave misgivings about their use, drugs have clearly changed for the better the atmosphere of mental hospitals where they are in use. They have produced earlier discharge of many patients, have made it possible for many to function in their family and community setting in spite of continuing severe problems, have made hospital wards far more tranquil and pleasant, eliminated the need for most forms of physical restraint (such as straitjackets), and made locked wards obsolete. However, such drugs are only palliatives, not cures, alleviating symptoms such as anxiety and

thoughts. These thoughts constantly recur, and it requires a tremendous mental effort to concentrate on useful and progressive tasks. In March when my parents made a physical break I noticed a great deal of stress. I consulted a Dr. [C_____] at the University Health Center and asked him to recommend someone that I could consult with about some psychiatric disorders I felt I had. I talked with a Doctor once for about two hours and tried to convey to him my fears that I felt overcome by overwhelming violent impulses. After one session I never saw the Doctor again, and since then I have been fighting my mental turmoil alone, and seemingly to no avail. After my death I wish that an autopsy would be performed on me to see if there is any visible physical disorder. I have had some tremendous headaches in the past and have consumed two large bottles of Excedrin in the past three months.

It was after much thought that I decided to kill my wife, Kathy, tonight after I pick her up from work. . . . I love her dearly, and she has been a fine wife to me as any man could ever hope to have. I cannot rationally pinpoint any specific reason for doing this. I don't know whether it is selfishness, or if I don't want her to have to face the embarrassment my actions would surely cause her. At this time, though, the prominent reason in my mind is that I truly do not consider this world worth living in, and am prepared to die, and I do not want to leave her to suffer alone in it. I intend to kill her as painlessly as possible. . . .

That same night, Whitman killed his mother and his wife. Then, on the morning of August 1st, he stationed himself on the observation platform of a tower at the University campus and killed 14 people and wounded 24 others using a hunting rifle with a telescopic sight. Police ultimately broke into the barricaded tower and shot Whitman to death. In an autopsy, a malignant brain tumor was found in the area of his amygdala, a brain structure that appears to regulate the onset and termination of rage.

If we examine Whitman's social history we can find previous violent outbursts and a family history conducive to aggressive disturbances. For example, his father was said to have been an occasional wife beater, and Whitman too had a history of attacking his wife and others when provoked. He was court-martialed from the service for insubordination and fighting. Was the brain tumor responsible for Whitman's murderous frenzy? We cannot say for sure, but it is highly probable that it played an important if not key role. In keeping with this theory is the observation that the earlier recorded aggressive incidents date mostly from his early adulthood when it is possible the tumor had already begun to grow. Whitman's letter is particularly interesting and poignant because it suggests a man who has been struggling to cope with severe internal turmoil and what became an overpowering urge to kill.

Noting that this case illustrates the possibility of organic brain disorder as the basis of disturbed and destructive behavior does not, of course, imply that all or most such behavior has such a cause, or that such disturbances should be routinely treated physically rather than behaviorally. On the contrary, this could be the relatively rare rather than usual case. Still, instances such as this should make us wary of an either/or approach to treatment. We cannot discard the search for neural and biochemical factors that could disturb psychological functioning, nor for advanced physical treatments when such factors have been implicated.

The problem here is that brain surgery is being used and advocated today even where there is no solid evidence that there is any brain pathology, or even that any particular portion of the brain is tied to the behavioral disturbances. Moreover, one of the most disturbing features of such treatment is that although the patient himself may consent to the surgery, or even seem to want it, when the treatment is given to someone who is imprisoned or hospitalized by court order and his release is tied to the treatment, there is grave doubt that he is freely giving his consent to the procedure. Refusal would obviously mean that he must remain in the institution indefinitely. The issue at this moment is very controversial and confused, and there is mixed feeling about outlawing such operations completely since they might offer hope for some persons and there is always the possibility that advances in knowledge about the brain and behavior will justify the treatment (see Holden, 1973).

disturbed thinking, but not encouraging patients to come to grips with their problems.

There are three main kinds of drugs used with mental patients: the antipsychotics or major tranquilizers; the sedatives or minor tranquilizers; and the antidepressants. The antipsychotics (notably, reserpine and chlorpromazine) are used to calm the psychotic patient. Hoch (1959, p. 1549) notes that no one can say at present how they work:

> A great deal of exploration has been going on in the last few years to elucidate the action of the tranquilizing drugs, but we still are not able to state how they influence mental disorders. The clinical-action radius [the type of patient to be treated and the behavioral effects] of the tranquilizing drugs is fairly well known. What we do not know is how they influence central-nervous-system function and where. Clinical observations indicate that they relieve excitation and tension and make a person more calm. Therefore, they have a sedative action but lack some of the features of sedatives such as barbiturates. The tranquilizing drugs usually do not interfere with consciousness and do not produce sleep, even when given in high doses, as in the case with barbiturates. The tranquilizing drugs have no uniform action on the psyche. Not all functions are reduced, but many . . . symptoms in a mental disorder, such as hallucinations, delusions, etc., are influenced to a considerable degree. Emotional overcharge is also reduced. The tranquilizing drugs, as far as we know today, suppress symptoms, but they do not eliminate the basic structure of the psychosis. In many patients the symptoms can return rather quickly, even after successful treatment and when the drugs have been withdrawn.

The sedatives or minor tranquilizer drugs (notably, meprobamate, chlordiazepoxide, and diazepam, whose familiar trade names are Miltown, Librium, and Valium) seem to reduce anxiety and tension and are commonly used in neurotic and psychosomatic disturbances. Also in this class are the very dangerous barbiturates, including phenobarbital and Seconal, the latter being widely used to induce sleep, or in the illegal drug market to induce pleasant, drowsy, euphoric feelings. Their danger lies in the fact that like morphine and heroin they are highly addictive, and in fact generate a very serious withdrawal problem (severe reaction to the cessation of drug intake), capable of producing death. As in the case of the major tranquilizing drugs, they are palliatives rather than cures, though they can be used along with psychotherapy to calm the patient until he learns to come to grips with his problems.

Finally, the *antidepressants,* like imipramine (trade name, Tofranil), have been used mainly with depressions as "mood elevators," though they have some other uses too. Stimulants might also be included in this category, such as the amphetamines (Dexedrine and Benzedrine), whose effects are sought outside proscribed medical use to prolong wakefulness, to tide people over difficult periods when they need more "pep," and to create a euphoric "high." However, the very harmful and addictive effects of these drugs, and the fact that their use is generally followed by a severe letdown, have given them a very bad reputation. This well-deserved reputation is reflected by the phrase "speed kills," meaning both fast driving and injection of amphetamine ("speed") into the veins for a fast high. Continued use of amphetamines produces very destructive effects on the nervous system.

Some clinicians have had high hopes that drugs would ultimately cure people of the most serious mental disorders, but as yet this is an article of faith rather than a reality. Part of the present difficulty is that there is as yet no established connection between any hypothesized organic malfunction and the drugs being used to treat mental patients. Chemotherapy as presently practiced is not like the use of drugs to combat a tumor or even of antibiotic medicines to rout a bacterial infection that has overcome the body's resistance; rather, it is the use of a chemical whose neural effects are scarcely understood to treat a disturbance whose basis is equally obscure. The search for a tissue defect in adaptive failure (especially psychoses) goes on: were it found, one could confidently expect successful physical treatments to follow. There is always the hope that new chemotherapeutic agents will be discovered that will help to overcome, or at least reduce, the pathological conditions accompanying adaptive failure.

My own hunch is that this can only happen where a clear organic illness is implicated in the adaptive failure, and that for the most part such failures stem from destructive social experiences and the consequent learning of faulty modes of coping with stress (see Chapter 10). But one cannot reject out of hand the possibility that organic causes and physical treatments will ultimately be found. Moreover, on the basis of what little is known at present about the causes of psychotic disorders, a condescending attitude toward psychopharmacological research is not really warranted. If we are wise we will keep an open mind at this juncture and hope that ultimately someone will come up with the right answers.

Psychotherapeutic approaches

Therapy is a general term for the treatment of pathology of any kind; *psychotherapy* refers to attempts by a variety of behavioral means to help those who are having trouble managing their lives. Such attempts include repeated conversations between the therapist and the patient, and (as in behavior therapy) use of special procedures designed to help him acquire new and more adequate ways of dealing with troubling situa-

Just as psychology is beginning to enjoy its place in the sun, I find myself recommending that we work to cultivate skepticism and criticism in our recent benefactors, the media. They must be aware of the fact that we have not the slightest notion of why euphoria follows in the echoes of . . . stimulation [of a portion of the brain] or why certain drugs have their psychological consequences. Indeed, we cannot offer a plausible explanation for the ubiquitous influences of the Law of Effect. The greatest danger is that the public will think we know what we are doing instead of appreciating the experimental nature of our enterprise. Recognizing that it is experimental, society will be able to determine the extent to which it wishes to participate. [From Robinson, 1973, pp. 132–133]

tions. The lay person typically does not differentiate between the terms "psychotherapy" and "psychoanalysis." However, psychoanalysis originated with Freud and involves a specialized therapeutic technique as well as a particular theory of personality. (This theoretical aspect of the Freudian approach will be considered in Chapter 12.)

Although psychotherapy is not one approach but many, one feature which distinguishes psychotherapy from ordinary conversations and relationships between intimates, friends, and acquaintances is that the professional therapist uses some sort of systematic theory about human problems and their treatment, and he also usually brings professional expertise and training into the therapeutic situation. Another feature is that the therapist does whatever he believes will help the patient cope with his problems more effectively, rather than what will make the therapeutic relationship seem more comfortable or pleasant, or what will protect and enhance his own self-esteem. For example, he will not usually respond to verbal attack by the patient with a counterattack, but will try to aid the patient in understanding the reasons for his actions or in controlling them. Nonprofessionals certainly can and do help other people, and they may sometimes be highly sensitive to another person's plight and know how to respond to it. In the long run, however, what seems to be needed in a therapist, in combination with a desire to help and natural sensitivity, are a set of tried and true skills and techniques and much necessary knowledge of human behavior.

As Jerome Frank (1973, p. 22) points out, "The current psychotherapeutic scene is a bewildering panorama of schools and methods, practitioners with all sorts of backgrounds, and patients with an enormous variety of woes and ills. Religious-mystical leaders coexist with Freud's followers, whose tradition is still powerful, if not dominant. No single therapy holds a monopoly. Paraprofessionals, subprofessionals, and nonprofessionals, some with no training at all, compete with orthodox psychologists. Even leaderless, self-help groups proliferate."

We cannot review the many different schools of psychotherapy that exist (Ford and Urban, 1963). Some of the variations are fundamental, and others turn on relatively minor disagreements in emphasis and procedure. However, we shall examine and distinguish between two main streams of thought and therapeutic strategy, the depth therapies, on the one hand, and the behavior therapies on the other.

Depth therapies   The basic concepts and strategies of the depth therapies owe their existence to Freud and to a group of men (including Carl Jung, Otto Rank, Alfred Adler, and others) working and studying with him, some of whom later went their own ways and developed their own strategies and systems of thought (see Chapter 12). We can best understand depth therapy by looking at Freudian psychoanalysis and then considering what is common to all the derivative branches.

Freud got into psychology because he and other neurologists of his time saw patients who had symptoms that seemed to indicate neurological disorders but that on examination turned out not to stem from genuine neural disease. A patient might display anesthesia (loss of sensation), for example, in the entire hand (sometimes termed "glove anesthesia" because it is as if the whole hand is covered by an anesthetizing glove). Since the loss of sensation did not conform to the known distribution of nerves in the hand, something else was evidently responsible for the anesthesia. Interested in this puzzle, Freud spent some time studying in Paris with J. M. Charcot, a prominent French neurologist. Charcot had demonstrated that the neurological symptoms could be made to disappear under hypnosis. On the basis of such observations Freud surmised that some psychological process of which the patient was unaware was responsible for the symptoms. The problem was to discover its nature and so he experimented further with hypnosis in the treatment of "hysterical" symptoms (Breuer and Freud, 1895; see 1957 ed.). Ultimately he abandoned hypnosis and began systematically to use a strategy he called *free association*, in which the patient was encouraged to say whatever came into his mind in an effort to uncover the sources of his symptoms, which Freud believed were forgotten or repressed memories and impulses. Over the subsequent years of such experimentation with neurotic patients, Freud evolved a set of psychotherapeutic strategies for the exploration and treatment of neurotic disorders and also a theory about their underlying mechanisms.

Freudians rely on five main strategic principles:

1. The therapist avoids leading the patient, especially early in the therapy, but tries to get him to talk freely about whatever comes to his mind. Otherwise what will emerge will tend to be a product of the therapist's bias and interests rather than what is vital to the patient. This is sometimes called the principle of *minimal activity*. Since there are many things the patient will talk about that the therapist does not consider fruitful or important, or about which the therapist wishes the patient to clarify, he may have to direct the patient from time to time, but this is done by careful and subtle means. For example, he may ask in a general way, "Tell me some more about that," or "I don't quite understand."

2. The therapist creates rapport with the patient by showing that he is attentive, that he understands, that he is *following the patient*. He may paraphrase what the patient says, give signals that he has heard what the patient has said, or by summing-up occasionally.

Identifying data

The patient is a woman in her early forties, married, who has been in analysis almost seven years at the time of this dream. She came to analysis because of chronic depression, incomplete sexual satisfaction, and other general complaints. The analysis is about to terminate by mutual agreement. The analytic results have not been fully satisfactory, especially due to severe, obsessional character resistance. But progress has been made, and the patient has experienced many positive and negative transference feelings vis à vis the analyst. The dream is reported near the beginning of an hour.

Patient *I had a dream last night. I was going up a ladder. First it was an easy ladder—wide open. The interpretation is obvious. As I got further up the ladder it was enclosed in a tubing—like the water tower in the town where I grew up. It had a tubular structure for safety, but it was harder to get through, harder to get from the inside to the outside. I identify it with my home town. In the dream the steps were banging. There were not two but only one metal hook. I didn't know if I made it to the outside or not. That has to do with the analysis. There should have been two metal hooks. Why didn't they get it fixed? With another hook it would have cost $138. Maybe $138 to get it fixed. I couldn't understand why they wouldn't fix it.*

I probably thought of the dream because I was just talking about you. I had a conversation with Jim, a business associate. I was even comfortable talking to him about the analysis. That would be an achievement! It was a good conversation.

The hook. Just one last step—meaning the day I walk out of here. Even the last step was a bit treacherous, because you had to walk outside. Incidentally I used to love to climb to the top of the water tower, which other people were scared to do. Its disturbing to me that explanations of dreams are not more obvious. That one wasn't until I began talking about it here.

Analyst *Could reaching the top—climbing to the top—have some other meaning?*

Patient *Nothing that comes to me immediately. Oh, it could be just like having an orgasm. I don't think so. It seems more the other. The parallel is there however. It seems like the stairs represent the climb. It has been a long and dangerous one. It seems like the completion of analysis. The other one—it doesn't seem to be.*

3. There is a selective *emphasis on feelings* expressed by the patient rather than on intellectual analysis. It is in the area of emotions that the patient is troubled, and he needs to find out about them and explore them fully.

4. The therapist gives *acceptance and support* and avoids a tone of criticism. Often the patient will be afraid to confide in his family, friends, or associates, who he feels are all too willing to offer advice, criticize, or express shock at his most private thoughts and impulses. It is precisely this ordinarily censored material that needs to be uncovered and examined, and the Freudian therapist will not do anything to inhibit the patient from bringing up and looking at even the most "shocking" thoughts and feelings.

5. The therapist makes use of *interpretations* that attempt to put what is said in a new light for the patient. Interpretations are rarely introduced by the Freudian therapist early in the therapeutic process, partly because the patient is likely to resist them and partly because the therapist is not confident about their validity at the outset. As therapy proceeds, however, interpretations are made occasionally, first in a gingerly fashion, then more freely as the patient comes to accept them. If the patient has said that it bothers him when other people get ahead, for example, the therapist may simply reflect the statement without interpretation by saying, "I see," or "You are troubled when others are successful," or he can paraphrase in a more interpretive manner, such as, "You resent other people's success." The patient has not actually said he is resentful, but the therapist thinks such a meaning is implicit and he draws it to the patient's attention.

Freud also made an extensive study of his patients' dreams, and modern psychoanalysts often use dreams as the starting points for free association by the patient and subsequent interpretations. In Freudian thought the dream is an expression of a person's unconscious conflicts and wishes. In sleep the person is less vigilant in defending against unacceptable, repressed impulses and feelings, and the dream therefore provides important clues about what is hidden. However, because recognition of this hidden material is threatening and anxiety-provoking, the real meaning of the dream is likely to be disguised or expressed in symbolic form. The task is to unravel the real meanings, which means the symbolic content of the dream must be analyzed and interpreted. As we saw in Note 7.2, some symbols may be universal in man or in people of the same culture, while others are probably idiosyncratic to the individual and based on his own personal experience. Therefore, most interpretations given by Freudian analysts are derived from the associations of the patient to the reported dream content, although the analyst also brings to bear his previous clinical experience and insights derived from his own analysis. A dream and its interpretation is given in the margin (pages 522–524).

We must now consider several processes that Freud thought were important in the course of therapy. These include catharsis, resistance, transference, and working through. Some of these principles are found in all depth therapy, while others are deemphasized or ignored in some modern variants.

Catharsis refers to the expression in word or act of previously unrecognized feelings and impulses; it represents a kind of release or purging of the system. People have long recognized that it often helps to verbalize and act out feelings that have been bottled up. Freud thought that there would be tension and distress if they remained unexpressed and that many repressed impulses continued to have an influence throughout life. Therefore, he regarded catharsis as a primary agent of therapy. For one thing, the therapy clearly cannot proceed if the patient does not uncover the real feelings and impulses that lie behind his troubles. For another, this very release can produce some relief for the patient and also encourages further the process of self-discovery and insight.

As might be anticipated, the patient comes to therapy with an incorrect conception of himself and his problems or symptoms. This erroneous idea is a product of self-deceptive defense mechanisms (see Chapter 10) that protect him from painful awareness of the real nature of his problems. In his early work with neurotic patients Freud was, in fact, very impressed by the paradox that though patients come voluntarily for help, they nonetheless avoided facing their real problems for as long as possible. This process of self-protection in therapy, Freud called *resistance*. The therapist must help the patient to give up these long-established self-protective mechanisms and expose himself to the painful truth that he has hitherto been unable to face so that he can grow psychologically. Of all the stages in psychoanalysis, this overcoming of resistance is perhaps the most dramatic and important, and it is universally recognized by all depth therapies.

The most potent therapeutic force enabling the patient to uncover the truth is the emotional relationship established with the therapist, a relationship called by Freud the *transference*. While his deepest feelings are being examined during the long period of intensive therapy, the patient develops a charged relationship with his analyst. Freud had at first wondered at the surprisingly intense feelings expressed by patients toward him. Patients developed erotic fantasies about him, or showed resentment or jealousy of his interest in other patients. Patients became preoccupied with pleasing the analyst or behaved as though they were wholly dependent on him for guidance. Patients also expressed strong anger and resentment toward him.

Analyst *It happens that climbing stairs is an exceedingly common symbol of intercourse.*

Patient *I can't argue with that.*

Analyst *The question is, does it apply in this dream?*

Patient *It seems there was a woman up there who lived there. She had a room, or a house.*

Analyst *Who was the woman? Someone who had made it to the top?*

Patient *I don't know.*

Analyst *Is it you, when you make it up there?*

Patient *No. It was someone disinterested. That second hook—they wouldn't fix it. 138 bucks was too much.*

Analyst *Why that figure?*

Patient *I bought groceries yesterday for $37—actually $37.50.*

Analyst *Just like in the dream. How did you feel shopping?*

Patient *It wore me out. I got 2 slips and a bra first—not quite the right size. Then about the groceries. I bought too much. I argued with myself. Then I was embarrassed by meeting someone whom I knew in the store. Its hard to know what to buy. Here I could buy all I want. I feel like Mother Earth. I wish I could grow my own vegetables. So what do I think of the $37.50? I wish I could go to the store once a week and spend $50. I don't mind. I'm delighted to get large amounts of groceries. In the dream the woman didn't have $138.*

Analyst *Who was she?*

Patient *The woman in the dream was my size and looked quite young. I think of myself as looking young. The $100 part of it: I was appalled when I called up for a fairly minor plumbing repair. It came to $99. I like to round things off. I'm not convinced the $100 was right to spend. I don't like to spend money wrong.*

Analyst *So you were misled by the repairman.*

Patient *So there's the $100. And $38 makes $138. The woman in the store is like my mother—trying not to be extravagant.*

Analyst *Is the thought in the dream about the large cost of the analysis?*

Patient *I thought you would bring that up.*

Analyst *So the thought was there anyway in your mind.*

Patient *I did think it but it didn't seem to be the point.*

Analyst *But the $100, rounded off $99, referred in reality to being misled by the repairman. It came back in the dream related to the analysis.*

Patient *Well, maybe. I had a thought of maybe keeping a toehold in here. But no—there was no thought of saving money. [Here the session ended.]*

Analyst's comment *In spite of her disclaimer at the end, the dream probably did* reflect her feelings of extravagance about the cost of analysis and clearly was concerned with the ending of the analysis. Also, pretty obviously she was feeling "misled" by the plumbing repairman (me) about not getting fully satisfactory results for a large cost. Particularly interesting in this dream is the analysis of the $138, a condensation of several real numbers in her external life. Freud's dream specimens have similar examples. [Private communication, 1973]

To Freud, this emotional pattern seemed to be a reenactment of the child-parent relationship with its intense love, jealousy, and hate. He believed too that this relationship in the adult was facilitated by the patient's infantile needs and by the therapist's minimal activity. By being minimally active, the therapist is therefore less obtrusive as a person, leaving room for the patient to project onto the therapist qualities he had experienced in his own parents, to relive with the therapist childhood relationships.

Not all his patients displayed transference, and Freud proposed that certain kinds of neurotics (like hysterics and obsessive compulsives) displayed the capacity for intense emotional attachments, while others (notably, schizophrenics and psychopaths) lacked this capacity. In short, only the "transference neuroses" were believed by Freud to be capable of being treated by psychoanalytic therapy because only such types of patients could develop the transference relationship in therapy.

Why is the transference relationship thought to be essential in Freudian analysis? It is considered to have two vital functions: (1) it provides information about the patient's early relationships with his parents and allows him to relive or reenact them in therapy; (2) the analyst makes use of the transference to help motivate the patient to go through the threatening process of self-exposure and to support him in this. To tolerate being stripped of his defenses, the patient needs to want very much to please the therapist and he needs to be protected and supported. Ultimately, he must come to see his emotional relationship with the analyst as a part of his childhood self rather than as an adult reality. In order to terminate therapy he must give up the infantile relationship of his own accord, accept himself for what he is, and move ahead to consolidate what he has learned about his neurotic modes of living and to replace these with more adult and effective ones.

For the patient to move away from his dependence on the therapeutic relationship requires not merely insight into his neurotic mechanisms but also the application of what he has learned inside the therapeutic office to his everyday life situation. This is the last step in the therapeutic process, usually referred to as *working through*. He must learn new ways of dealing with his conflicts and apply them in situations that previously had incapacitated him or produced neurotic symptoms. In successful analysis, the person begins to see old and repeated traumatic situations in a new light. He now learns to handle such situations with less distress.

Earlier it was noted that there are diverse forms of depth therapy, the Freudian approach being the main progenitor of most of the others. Yet Freudian psychoanalysis has certain

conceptual features that distinguish it from most other therapies. Consider, for example, how Freudian analysis is usually
practiced tactically. In the orthodox Freudian treatment, the
patient is seen intensively (four or five times a week for a
fifty-minute hour) with the therapy typically extending over
a period of a few years (or more). The patient does most of
the talking, especially during the early stages, and lies on a
couch with the therapist sitting behind him out of the line
of sight. Dreams are typically used to throw light on the
patient's psychodynamics; evidences of the transference relationship are looked for and welcomed when they appear, and
these are employed in the attempts to understand the patient.
When the patient ultimately leaves therapy, it is recognized
that he may want to return for a time at a later date to work
through additional problems.

In contrast, other depth approaches are often designed
to be less intensive, with visits occurring once a week, say, and
the treatment may not be expected to extend beyond several
months. The patient typically sits face-to-face with the therapist, and the level of activity (talking) of the therapist may
be much greater. Such details are not trivial because they often
alter the basic nature of the relationship between therapist and
patient. Thus, transference in short-term depth therapies is
relatively unimportant, and the focus of attention in such
therapies is likely to be on the individual's present problems
and how they are being dealt with rather than on childhood
experiences to which Freudians give major attention.

Most depth therapists today are outside of the strictly
orthodox Freudian school of thought. The garden-variety versions of psychotherapy represent a kind of loose amalgam of
Freudian and post-Freudian ideas, strategies, and tactics.
Thus, depth therapists usually make use of the notions of
defense mechanism and resistance, but only some concern
themselves with transference, though many still regard the
relationship between therapist and patient to be an important
consideration in treatment.

There is almost no adequate way to survey the manifold
variations in modern psychotherapeutic practice and in the
psychodynamic ideas of practitioners. Nevertheless, most share
a common conception of neurosis and of its treatment, a conception quite different from that of behavior therapists, as we
shall see shortly. It will be useful here to sum up with a broad
statement of this joint conception of the depth therapies that
are closest to the Freudian origins we have been considering:
In depth therapy, the therapist does many things to facilitate
the process of self-discovery, including listening, giving reassurance, sympathetically responding to distress, reflecting back
to the patient (repeating) in different words some of the
thoughts and feelings he has expressed, temporizing, seeking

Client *I felt absolutely up-tight yesterday. I had that old paranoid feeling for which they hospitalized me before I came to you.*

Therapist *You found it necessary to distort reality again.*

Client *I really wanted to hurt you . . . I felt you were manipulating me again and you have to cut it out!*

Therapist *I seemed to be your enemy.*

Client *I can't live up to your standards for me. I could never be a Jungian analyst. You're like my mother in some ways.*

Therapist *Paranoia is a good cop out.*

Client *I can't believe in myself. It just won't work. I'm condemned to be nothing.*

Therapist *Somebody always sold you short.*

Client *Yes. She wanted something. I did it. But it was never any good. But my brother couldn't do anything wrong.*

Therapist *You wanted her approval so badly.*

Client *Yes. But pain always and invariably followed . . . oh, the humiliation and depression!*

Therapist *You're afraid I'll do the same to you. Lead you down the wrong path again as she did.*

Client *I can't trust anybody. You seem to be OK but how do I know? But I guess I have to trust somebody. I do admire you.*

[From Burton, 1972, p. 90]

clarification, giving advice, and interpreting what the patient has said. The interchange presented in the margin (from Burton, 1972) provides examples of a therapist's interpretations of what the patient (referred to as client) has said.

The person with a neurosis has a set of conscious life goals, attitudes, and self-conceptions, and he assumes that these guide his actions and reactions. However, beneath the surface lie another set of goals, attitudes, and self-images of which he is unaware or at best only dimly aware. They derive from immature, self-centered, and irrational childhood impulses that are no longer appropriate to adult life but remain active, still operating silently and guiding his feelings and actions. Thus, the neurotic individual cannot be the person he consciously wishes to be because at the same time he unconsciously is driven to be a different kind of person, to do things that are compatible with these childhood residuals, and he dare not acknowledge to himself the existence of this other inner life because it threatens him. He feels constantly torn, and his decisions are often futile because they are predicated on an incorrect assessment of what he is and wants. The unconscious childish urges are, instead, dealt with by reality-distorting defense mechanisms that help preserve the conscious fiction. This inner struggle is revealed to be taking place in neurotic symptoms such as affective distress (anxiety, depression), ineffective functioning in his job or in his relationships with other persons of importance to him, strange and unexplained behavior, and various psychosomatic ailments. These symptoms are often what bring him to seek professional help, and typically he sees them not as the result of inner

"Oedipus, Shmedipus, Doctor . . . so long as he loves his mother."

Figure 11.7 In psychotherapy a family consultation is sometimes enlightening. (Drawing by J. J. Dunleavy)

turmoil but as medical problems for which he needs treatment. If it were possible, he would rather have the symptoms excised as in surgery rather than confront the real underlying problems, but the depth-oriented therapist assumes that easy solutions are impossible and that the neurotic person must discover the nature of the "hidden agenda" in order to overcome it and learn new, more effective, and satisfying ways of managing his life (Figure 11.7).

It should be fairly obvious that this form of treatment is suited only to a particular kind of troubled person, basically one suffering from a neurosis (as defined above and in Chapter 10). Moreover, to participate in this kind of therapy requires a person of substantial intelligence, one who is capable of sustained verbal discussion and analysis of his problems, willing to accept the idea that internal defects rather than external matters over which he has no control are to a considerable extent responsible for his troubles, and one who, despite his neurotic difficulties and defenses, is capable of judging reality reasonably well (Figure 11.8). This set of personal requirements eliminates (or at least poses major difficulties for) many troubled persons. Thus, depth therapy is poorly suited to the unsocialized psychopath and other troubled personality types that seem refractory to establishing the emotional relationship (transference) important to such therapy or that lack ability to tolerate frustration and delay. Similarly, schizophrenic and paranoid patients are usually not able to participate very effectively in this type of treatment, particularly those who are seriously disturbed, fragile, or withdrawn from human psychological contact.

One of the more recent variants of depth therapy is the *humanistic-existential* approach in which the emphasis is placed on the person's *quest for meaning in life* in contrast with the Freudian focus on the person's infantile sexual and aggressive conflicts. Whether in the context of group or individual therapy, the humanistic-existential movement emphasizes the following ideas and values: (1) The therapist should have a high regard for the patient's subjective experiences, which are seen as valid phenomena in their own right rather than as disguised manifestations of his unconscious (hence "real") feelings and thoughts. (2) The overarching problem is the patient's need to discern meaning in his life and this is bound up in his feelings about death. Such concerns about meaning are part of the fabric of human existence and not necessarily derivative of repressed biological urges. (3) The personality contains within it the possibilities of courage and creativity as well as violence and cruelty, or dependency and passivity, and these positive urges need to be released and cultivated for successful living. (4) The patient and therapist are more nearly equals, whatever the respective degrees of expertise, since both have to reconcile

Figure 11.8   Not all problems have solutions. (Drawing by Mal Hancock; © Washington Star Syndicate, Inc.)

themselves to nearly insurmountable problems of existence. (5) The therapist as a real person is more potent for the patient in therapy than his "transference" image as a parent, and so the therapist should be willing to accept and share with the patient his real feelings about him. And (6) the therapist should be willing to "let the patient be," accepting all aspects of his being, including his freedom to choose how to live and even to resist the therapist and the treatment (Shaffer and Galinsky, in press).

The humanistic-existential approach tends to emphasize the importance of existence itself, that is, the *uniquely human situation as it is experienced* by the person himself. His troubles are seen as the result of the breakdown of traditional values, the alienation of people from the social systems in which they live, and their depersonalization or loss of the capacity to act in the highest traditions of which human beings are capable (see also Chapter 5). This breakdown leads to a condition of meaninglessness, or of the reaching for meaning which somehow fails. As Rollo May (1967, p. 41) has put it, "Neurotic anxiety . . . consists of the shrinking of consciousness, the blocking off of awareness; and when it is prolonged it leads to a feeling of depersonalization and apathy. Anxiety is losing the sense of one's self in relation to the objects of the world." The goal of therapy then becomes reversing the narrowing or closing of consciousness that has occurred under the ordinary pressures and threats of living, of opening up the self to new awareness and to the possibilities inherent in life.

There are many versions of the humanistic-existentially oriented therapy, distinguished by the distinctive writings of its various protagonists, each with his own specific emphases and special techniques. One version, for example, is identified with Victor Frankl (1965), who writes (1965, p. ix–x): "Man lives in three dimensions: the somatic, the mental, and the spiritual. The spiritual dimension cannot be ignored, for it is what makes us human. To be concerned about the meaning of life is not necessarily a sign of disease or of neurosis. It may be; but then again, spiritual agony may have very little connection with a disease of the psyche. The proper diagnosis can be made only by someone who can see the spiritual side of man." Another variant of this outlook is *Gestalt therapy* developed by Frederick Perls (1967, 1969). Gestalt means the "whole," and the idea of the therapy is the unity of both mind and body, and the integration of thought, feeling, and action. The therapy aims at increasing the awareness of the person of his self and the parts of himself and the world that have been blocked out of consciousness by his fears and the avoidance of that which he cannot master. The therapy is generally used in a group setting, but the focus is nevertheless on the individual. He must confront his feelings and conflicts in the group, and discover that the world does not fall apart when he gets "angry, sexy, joyous or mournful" (Figure 11.9).

Although psychoanalysis and many of its later variants originally began with the individual in trouble and proceeded in the clinician's office in a one-to-one relationship, there is nothing in the general approach demanding that treatment be limited to a single person at a time. In the 1930s and thereafter there were growing numbers of experiments with *group therapy.* Today there is great interest in treatment in the group setting. Groups have a number of advantages over the single patient–therapist pattern. First, the problems of troubled individuals usually center on interpersonal relationships. What better way could there be for the person to confront his difficulties with other people than in a group setting where he can discover how he responds to others and how they respond to him? The therapist too can see the person in action, rather than having to depend on what he reports about interpersonal relationships. Furthermore, there is something reassuring as well as enlightening in coming to realize that others have problems similar to one's own. The group members can also give support to the individual, which may mean more from a fellow sufferer than when it comes from a therapist who gives it for professional reasons.

It will be instructive to look at one example of a typical group therapy session conducted from the humanistic-existential point of view (Shaffer and Galinsky, in press). This fictitious group (which the writers constructed from their own experience for illustrative purposes) consists of four men and three women and the therapist. It is heterogeneous in age, vocation, and other qualities. The group has met for two-and-a-half years with Dr. R., the therapist, five of them having

Figure 11.9   An encounter group letting off steam. (Mimi Forsyth from Monkmeyer Press Photo Service)

been steady members for the entire time, and two having joined it during the previous ten months. The excerpt of the session goes as follows (Shaffer and Galinsky, in press, Chapter 5):

The group begins without any structuring from Dr. R., who is silent. Ruth, a "hippie"-type girl in her early twenties, is talking about the fact that Bob, the man with whom she is living, is probably having an affair with her best friend, Terry. She knows he is attracted to Terry, and each of them has recently, in talking to her about the other, made some ambiguous and erotically-tinged remarks. Ruth doesn't know what to do about this; she is annoyed with herself for being jealous, for she knows that whatever Bob has going with Terry is a purely "physical" thing, and he made it clear to her when they decided to live together that he did not feel sexually bound by conventional notions of a monogamous relationship. Yet she feels hurt at times, and betrayed by Terry; then at other times, she feels that she is being old-fashioned, that it is obviously just a sex thing for Terry, who is basically interested in another, unavailable man.

Mort, a brunette man in his middle thirties, razzes her; he says: That's right, Ruthie; Bob just has too much love in him to share with just one woman; besides, you love both of them so much this is really just an act of generosity on your part—you're giving two people you love to one another!

Ruth reacts with a slight giggle, and continues to discuss the problem. Mort continues to bait her. Felicia interrupts at this point, saying that it makes her uncomfortable to see the way Mort is baiting Ruth and the way she allows him to do it.

Ruth interrupts, saying: But what difference does it make?; I'm used to Mort's sarcasm—besides I'm worried about Bob, not Mort. Felicia says: Yes, but you take the same crap from both of them. Mort joins in, saying: Yes, she's so goddamned dumb with those rose-colored glasses on; doesn't she know what the world is like? Boy she really asks for it.

Ralph then joins in for a moment: She may ask for it, Mort—but I notice you're always there firstest with the mostest to give it to her.

Felicia says in a quiet voice: Ruth isn't happy until she has something to make her really miserable.

Ruth then says: Would everyone stop talking about me as though I weren't here?!

Felicia expresses pleasure at Ruth's ability to speak up. Dr. R. then wonders when Felicia is going to start talking up for herself. Felicia at first reacts with defensiveness and confusion, saying: I *am* speaking up.

Dr. R. replies: Yes, but on behalf of Ruth, which is your usual way of participating. Perhaps this is partly your way of testing out what you're learning as a social-work student. Look, it's okay with me, I *like* having a co-therapist, but I find myself wishing that you'd find a way to take as well as give; sometimes I sense that underneath that competent, supportive exterior there's a needy, bewildered little girl looking for comfort.

Felicia responds: Yes, I know what you mean, and there are day-to-day problems that I could bring up and at times would like to bring up; but they always seem so insignificant alongside what the others introduce; I guess I'm not ready yet.

Dr. R. replies: Ok—I just thought I'd give you a little nudge.

For a few moments everyone is silent. Dr. R. asks the group members what they are experiencing. Alice speaks up and says she was thinking about Ruth's problem, and wondering why Ruth was suddenly quiet. Ruth speaks up, saying: I felt criticized by Al in a way—when he pointed out how rarely Felicia brought up her problems, I thought maybe he was also saying that I do the opposite—always take up the group's time.

Dr. R.: No, Ruth, I don't feel that way; I feel you have the right to ask for as much from the group as you can.

Ruth: Well, anyway, I don't know what to do about Bob. I guess I should just wait and let this affair between him and Terry blow over—that is, if there *is* an affair; probably if I wasn't so insecure I'd just accept it for what it is.

Nelson: I don't know Ruth—I could see being plenty jealous. I know I would be if Harriet (i.e. his current girlfriend) was making it with some guy.

Mort, with heavy-handed sarcasm, says: But Nelson, you're so square, so bourgeoisie; you have this monogamy hang-up; Ruthie's emancipated; both she and Bob have complete sexual freedom—the only difference between them being that he's free to exercise his while she isn't; besides, she's supposed to understand that he loves her more than any other woman he screws because he's living with her—so what does she have to be worried about?

Ruth answers Mort: I'm not sure that the idea you ridicule is so crazy, Mort; Bob is a very unusual guy—he's able to love more than one woman at once, and he's made it clear that in many ways I'm very special to him—that's why I get annoyed with myself for being jealous.

Mort becomes angrier and raises his voice, shouting at Ruth: Bob has one helluva good deal with you because you're so fucking blind; he can ball anybody he wants and still be welcomed home by your bleeding heart!

Ralph says: Lay off her, Morty—do you want to help her or destroy her? Ruth then says to Ralph: I don't mind his tone—I just want to figure out if he's right.

Dr. R. says: Mort and Ralph are both pointing out the same thing to you, Ruth; how you, with almost no awareness, allow others to abuse you. Mort tries to show you how you get it from Bob, and Ralph how you get it from Mort.

Ruth asks: But if Mort is right, how is he abusing me?!

Alice answers: By talking to you with contempt!

Ruth says: I think he feels that's the only way he can get through to me; and if he's right—if I *am* being naive with Bob—I want to find out; I don't care *how* I find out.

Dr. R. says: Ruth, you keep so busy figuring out what is right and what is fair that you don't instinctively notice that Bob and Mort don't give two damns about whether or not they hurt you; but what impresses me is the irritation and impatience that I am getting to feel—for a second just now I had the strong impulse to whiplash you verbally, to tell you how masochistic and thick you are—something similar to Mort; so my hunch is that you have a need to provoke people's anger.

Ruth, seemingly bewildered, asks: But why would I want to provoke you? Dr. R. replies: I feel you continuing in the same vein; the innocent young girl, with a perplexed, almost eager expression on your face, still trying to figure it all out.

Ruth asks: But what's wrong with that? Aren't I supposed to discover the reasons for what I do?

Dr. R. answers Ruth: Again I'm finding myself starting to become irritated; until you get in touch with what you're feeling right now I don't think we're going to get anywhere.

Ruth is quiet for a minute, while the rest of the group seem attentive. Then she says; I don't know—I guess I feel sad more than anything else, and somehow inadequate; I feel like you're all mad at me, and like you're probably right to be, but I can't figure out just why—mainly that I'm being stupid about something; if I could only figure it out, then I could stop doing it and you'd all stop being so impatient with me.

Dr. R. intervenes: So you mainly are aware of our anger with you—not yours with us, right? Ruth answers in the affirmative. Dr. R. says: And what you're mainly aware of is your intense need to reason it all out, so you can find a way to get us to stop being irritated with you.

Ruth says: That's right; and this feels like the story of my life; since I was very young I somehow was doing things wrong enough for my mother to get very mad at me—but somehow I could never be sure why.

At this point Felicia speaks up and says: I can understand that feeling; it's like: I'll be any way you want, so long as you love me. Mort then speaks up, saying: That's very good, Felicia, very empathic. I think we should give you A+ in Casework Methods II for that particular remark.

Alice quickly says: You know, Mort, when you get nasty like that I really feel like killing you. Mort is silent, and no one talks for a minute. Alice suddenly says: So why don't you turn your hostility on me?—I'm waiting—my heart is pounding. Mort asks her what she means. She answers: I mean that when I say something like what I just said I expect to get some of your venom, and I imagine some of it would reach its mark and really get to me; so when I don't get it—like Felicia and Ruth seem to—I wonder why am I so lucky?; when will my turn come?—and then I resent being so damned afraid of you.

Mort comments: There you all go again; because I say what I think and remind people of the kind of crap that passes for brilliant insight around here and don't play your love-in game, I become some kind of hostile monster who everybody is terrified of.

Dr. R. breaks in, saying: Maybe if you allowed yourself to believe that people could be very scared of you you'd have to start getting in touch with your own terror. Mort responds: Gee, Doc, you're getting more profound than Felicia—are the two of you in some sort of competition?!

Dr. R. says: Mort, level with me—do you believe the group when they say they're afraid of you? Mort answers: No. Dr. R. rejoins: Well, I don't know how to convince you that they do; I know that

I'm feeling it right now—as I often do when I start to tangle with you.

Mort says to him: You're just saying that to make your theoretical point. Dr. R. answers: Bull shit!—I don't tell you I'm feeling something if I'm not! Mort asks him: But what are you scared of? Dr. R.: Probably of what you'll do if your rage gets great enough; I don't feel it right now, but I remember asking myself that same question last session—what *am* I afraid of in you?—and my immediate fantasy was of your going really berserk and wrecking the office—but *completely* wrecking it, and of us standing by helplessly letting you do it.

Mort says to him: I still have the feeling you're putting me on. Dr. R. replies: But isn't that your mistrust of everyone?—who does level with you completely as far as you're concerned? Mort answers: I don't know for sure—I'm never sure. Dr. R. says: My guess is that if you had to admit that others are terrified, you might have to begin wondering why you never get frightened; you're very comfortable with your anger, but you don't let yourself know anxiety or fear.

Dr. R. then adds: By the way, Mort, I think my fear of your physical destructiveness is irrational, and probably has something to do with some uncomfortableness I still have with my own anger. But I also know that Alice's feeling of being intimidated by you is real.

At this point Mort doesn't say anything; he seems a bit red in the face, as though caught off guard. After a few seconds, Felicia says to Dr. R.: I don't think you should have told him your fantasy—it probably will make Mort that much more afraid of his rage. And it sounds a bit pat to me—a little like Mort was saying—that you were over-playing the part of the "for-real," experiential therapist—letting us know just where you "are at" with everything.

Dr. R. says: Well, Felicia, I invite you to become your own kind of therapist in your own style real soon—I sure as hell don't have a monopoly on technique; I do know that I felt quite genuine in saying what I did to Mort, and that it also felt great to hear you criticize me like that just now.

Felicia says: I can't imagine ever feeling that way about somebody's criticism of me. Dr. R. rejoins: Well, I didn't get there overnight; I can remember in my earlier days not liking it one bit when my patients had something negative to say about me—or anybody else for that matter, but I was a rather different person then.

And so the session continues. . . . [Interaction] in the present situation remains reasonably lively, and by the end of the meeting all participants have spoken up spontaneously, although a few have been considerably more active than others. While analysts remain silent for periods as long as seven or eight minutes in the psychoanalytic group, Dr. R., our existential-experiential therapist, is more active; for example, from the beginning of the session from which we drew an illustrative segment, to its end, the longest interval of silence that he allowed himself was about four minutes.

There are many variations of group therapy, ranging from the relatively limited type of encounter (limited because it meets on only one or at most a few occasions) to relatively stable groups that meet regularly over a long period of time. Some group therapy programs are also specifically oriented to certain social contexts, for example, the troubled family. In *family group therapy,* the therapist meets simultaneously with the husband, wife, and children. An important premise of this type of therapy is that the problems of each individual are inextricably tangled up with those of the other family members, in other words, with the family as a social unit. The therapist can observe and point out to the members of the family how they interact as they confront each other during the therapy session.

Behavior therapies   There has always been dissatisfaction with the depth approaches on the part of some psychologists, partly on ideological and partly on practical grounds. On the ideological score, speculations about unconscious processes have seemed to these psychologists to be impossible to prove, a kind of mythology rather than a scientific approach to influencing human behavior. Many of the goals of the depth therapies seem intangible, as in the idea of struggling for meaning in life. On the practical side, such psychologists find little hard evidence that the depth therapies work consistently in solving psychological problems. Moreover, the person in trouble comes for help with certain complaints or symptoms that interfere with his comfort or effectiveness, such as concrete fears, inability to participate adequately in love making, inability to control undesirable impulses and poor self-discipline (say, inability to quit smoking), specific social inadequacies in the presence of certain others, and so on. You will recall that in the depth therapies such symptoms are not regarded as the "real" problem, and the person is often encouraged into a long-term and ambiguous therapeutic situation that emphasizes hidden neurotic agendas rather than focusing directly on the immediate trouble. Thus, behavior therapy arose as a protest against the depth theories of neurosis and their resulting tactics of therapy (see also Ullmann and Krasner, 1969).

To understand this, one needs to recognize that the key distinction between the depth therapies and the behavior therapies lies in their respective conceptions of the person's troubles. The tactics of therapy follow more or less from these conceptions. For the behavior therapist, the symptom does not necessarily symbolize some deeper problem; it *is* the problem. Since the symptom is a bad habit of living and coping that was acquired through learning, it can be unlearned or extinguished by somehow reversing the original learning process, in effect, by using the same principles of learning that brought it into being in the first place.

We saw in Chapter 4 that there were a number of ways

How does a "psychology of behavior control" differ from the science of psychology? The differences are subtle, but important. A science of psychology seeks to determine the lawful relationships in behavior. The orientation of a "psychology of behavior control" is that these lawful relationships are to be used to deliberately influence, control, or change behavior. This implies a manipulator or controller, and with it an ethical and value system of the controller. As we learn more about human behavior it is increasingly obvious that it is controllable by various techniques. Does this mean that we, as psychologists, researchers, or even therapists, at this point could modify somebody's behavior in any way we wanted? The answer is no, primarily because research into the techniques of control thus far is at the elementary stage. Science moves at a very rapid pace, however, and now is the time to concern ourselves with this problem before basic knowledge about the techniques overwhelms us. . . . [From Krasner, 1962, p. 500]

in which learning takes place (for example, classical and operant conditioning). If one follows this reasoning into the context of behavior therapy, then there will also be a number of methods of unlearning or extinction of maladaptive behavior patterns, depending on the nature of the problem. And since one learns such patterns as a result of certain environmental contingencies (like patterns of reward and punishment), great attention must be given to such contingencies in the unlearning and relearning process.

Thus, the main emphasis in all behavior therapy is on manipulation of environmental conditions to influence the patient's behavior. As Krasner (1963, p. 601) puts it:

> The key concepts in this . . . approach to psychotherapy are social reinforcement and behavior control. Social reinforcement refers to the use and manipulation of environmental stimuli to reward preselected classes of behavior in such a way as to increase the probability of their recurring. Psychotherapy is viewed as a lawful influence process within the broader context of studies of behavior controls, studies which investigate the conditions that change behavior.

Behavior therapists sometimes employ a technique of systematic reward or *response shaping* (see Skinner's operant conditioning in Chapter 4) to encourage behavior that is desired. This is illustrated in the following brief case description (Wolf *et al.*, 1964):

> A 3-year old autistic [extremely withdrawn and disturbed] boy lacked normal verbal and social behavior. He did not eat properly, engaged in self-destructive behavior such as banging his head and scratching his face, and manifesting ungovernable tantrums. He had recently had a cataract operation, and required glasses for the development of normal vision. He refused to wear his glasses, however, and broke pair after pair.
> The technique of shaping was decided upon to counteract the problems of glasses. Initially, the boy was trained to expect a bit of candy or fruit at the sound of a toy noisemaker. Then training was begun with empty eyeglass frames. First the boy was reinforced with the candy or fruit for picking them up, then for holding them, then for carrying them around, then for bringing the frames closer to his eyes, and then for putting the empty frames on his head at any angle. Through successive approximations, he finally learned to wear his glasses up to twelve hours a day.

In a book devoted to "behavior modification," that is, influencing the behavior of others by systematic reward and punishment, Mehrabian (1970) provides other illustrations of such principles of systematic reward in everyday interpersonal relations. In one such example, a girl is having trouble with her boyfriend because of subtle ways in which she is communicating possessiveness toward him. The girl, Amy, describes the situation as follows:

The problem situation results from possessiveness between my boyfriend and me. There are times, for example, when he wants to go drinking with the guys. This in itself is fine, but if I haven't seen him in quite awhile, or have something special I would like to do with him at the same time, I get rather upset. If I try to pretend I don't mind, he can see through it. If I really don't care, he acts as if he expects me to be mad, and I start wondering why I'm not. I guess the problem is that I am pretty possessive, more so than he is.

Mehrabian comments about this situation in behavior modification terms:

Amy's possessiveness is more a positive reinforcement for her boyfriend (i.e., making him feel important and needed) than a negative one (i.e., giving him a cramped or restricted feeling). Thus, he continues to expect her to act displeased and upset when he wants to do something which doesn't involve her. Faced with this expectation, she finds herself in the awkward position of communicating possessiveness even when she doesn't really feel it. Her possessiveness is thus both negatively and positively reinforcing for her, as it is for him. One reason for the perpetuation of this problem may be that acting possessive is the primary way in which Amy communicates affection and love for her boyfriend. Thus, one avenue of change might be for her to seek other ways to reinforce him positively. Consider the following communications: "I don't want you to go out because I love you," [or] "I don't want you to go out," [or] "I love you." The first is undesirable, whereas either of the latter two could be appropriate since they do not tie "love" to "restriction." She could learn, then, to separate her communications of love from those of demand and restriction. If her communications of love and affection were frequent enough, he might no longer need or expect her to communicate possessiveness. Further, having been assured of her feelings in this way, he might be more willing to comply with her demanding or restricting requests when they do occur.

So far so good. The above illustrations have the special feature of either (1) involving children in the process of development where there is yet considerable plasticity in behavior, so that changing the environmental contingencies (as in the case of the autistic child) can have an effect on later behavior, or (2) helping an adult (the girl and her boyfriend) to recognize what he or she is doing interpersonally so that he or she can learn to act differently. Large numbers of psychological problems are of this order, and relatively simple forms of relearning ought to be possible that should aid the person to be more effective socially without elaborate and lengthy therapy. Many examples fit more or less well into the operant-conditioning pattern (discussed in Chapter 4), so that once a

Chicken plays baseball

A coin-operated game known as BatBird, enabling a trained chicken in a cage to play baseball against a human contestant, was patented this week for Animal Behavior Enterprises, Inc., Hot Springs National Park, Ark. Grant Evans, Billy Joe Petty and Robert E. Bailey were granted Patent 3,727,740. When a light signal shines, the chicken bats by pulling a plastic loop with its bill and gets a reward of grain. The human player bats by pressing a button outside the cage. [From The New York Times]

desired response is made, it can be stamped in or shaped by manipulation of rewards and punishments. However, the problems that depth therapists refer to as neurotic (or worse) are often of a different order, involving many forms of anxiety-related behavior that severely handicaps them in living. Consider the illustration in Chapter 4 (p. 153) of the child with the fear of furry animals. There are two parts to the problem: First, fear is learned (conditioned) of things (the furry animal) that hold little or no actual danger. Researchers have shown that fear and anxiety are readily conditionable to almost any object (see Dollard and Miller, 1950). Second, the person (as in the child in the above example) also learns to avoid the fearful object. He has acquired what behavior therapists refer to as a *conditioned avoidance response*. It is retained more or less permanently because the individual always withdraws at the first indication of the presence of the painful object or situation (as in a phobia), so he never has an opportunity to find out whether or not the painful consequences of that situation will materialize. In other words, because he automatically acts to prevent confrontation with the object, the maladaptive habit (the conditioned avoidance reaction) is never extinguished.

Now think of all the problems of adaptation (symptoms if you like) that such a pattern of faulty learning might produce: A person is afraid to fly in airplanes, and hence his whole world is restricted thereby. Or he will not speak up in class, or give professional talks, because public speaking frightens him, and he has learned to cope with this by avoidance. He drinks himself nightly into a stupor to avoid the apprehensive or depressive thoughts or responsibilities that plague him. He avoids intimate and potentially satisfying involvements with other people because they threaten him in one way or another. He fails in love making by not being able to maintain an erection because physical intimacy threatens him, and his mode of coping with the fear is to avoid being aroused. In the female counterpart, fear makes it impossible for her to enjoy sexual foreplay or to have an orgasm (sexual climax).

On the assumption that such symptoms need not imply a deeper, unconscious psychological problem, the task of treatment in such cases from the behavior therapy standpoint is to enable the person to perform the desired act without the conditioned anxiety which leads to various kinds of avoidance. This is not easy, but there are a number of ways used by behavior therapists to accomplish this difficult task.

One is called *systematic desensitization* (Wolpe, 1969). Its aim is to extinguish the anxiety reaction and its associated avoidance by supporting the desired response with nothing but positive or rewarding experience. Let us consider an example using the symptom of male sexual inadequacy. Systematic desensitization therapy involves three steps. First, the person is trained systematically to relax over several sessions. Second, the therapist must construct for the patient a hierarchy of anxiety-inducing situations. By means of diagnostic interviews, the therapist finds that no anxiety is produced when the person only sits in a classroom with males and females; there is an ascending order of anxiety in the following sequence: in situations of talking to a girl, especially a sexy or provocative one, touching a girl on the hand, touching her on the knee, touching her on the breasts, kissing her, caressing her in the genital area, being caressed by her, undressing in her presence, and engaging in further steps toward sexual intercourse. Such a hierarchy is individually constructed for each patient, since this might not be the order of anxiety production for another person with a similar problem. Third, the actual process of desensitization is accomplished by getting the patient to relax in a comfortable chair with his eyes closed, while the therapist describes the first scene to him, asking him to imagine himself experiencing it. The first scene is the most neutral one and if the person remains relaxed, the therapist proceeds to the next most anxiety-producing image, and so on until the patient experiences noticeable anxiety, in which case the session is terminated. Thus, in the view of Wolpe the anxiety can be extinguished little by little, this process of extinction being facilitated by maintaining the patient as much as possible in a relaxed state. Eventually over many such sessions the patient may be able to imagine even sexual intercourse without anxiety, or without as much anxiety as previously, so that there is less chance of failure in subsequent encounters with love making.

It is important to recognize that to be effective, such treatment must be carried over by the patient (generalized) to the real-life situations in which the problem occurs; just as in depth therapy, the insights gained in treatment must also be utilized outside the therapist's office to be effective. For many psychologists, such learning can only be understood in cognitive terms, that is, as involving the discovery by the patient that the troubling situation does not hold the dangers he had originally come to expect. There is much theoretical debate among clinicians about the process of extinction and relearning taking place in such procedures, debate that revolves around issues touched upon briefly in the discussion of learning in Chapter 4.

Quite a different behavior therapy approach is called *implosive therapy* (Stampfl and Levis, 1967). Here the problem of extinguishing the link between anxiety, conditioned avoidance, and some particular situation is handled by mounting a massive flood of anxiety produced by a strong stimulus in a safe and supportive setting. When harm is not forthcoming, the stimulus will lose its power—permitting extinction of the damaging avoidance behavior. Like systematic desensitization, the theoretical objective is to overcome the inadequate mode of coping with anxiety by teaching the patient that what is dreaded will not happen. However, instead of using relaxation to minimize or circumvent the anxiety, the therapeutic strategy is to create the anxiety, but under supportive conditions that serve to lower its potency to paralyze adaptive behavior. In still other approaches, emphasis is placed on teaching the person interpersonal skills that he lacks, such as responding effectively to an insult. To the extent that a person's ability to cope is strengthened, situations that have ordinarily been highly threatening need no longer be so. They no longer must lead to paralysis and subsequent avoidance.

Another behavior therapy technique, *aversion therapy,* is designed for problems such as alcoholism, the termination of smoking, overeating, drug dependence, or gambling, all of which are thought to be various kinds of "temptations" that the individual has not been able to control. The basic strategy of aversion therapy is to punish the undesirable behavior. In one version, used with alcoholics, a drug (Antabuse) is given which produces nausea whenever the person takes a drink. Incidentally, it is this form of approach that inspired Alex's treatment in *A Clockwork Orange,* the dystopian novel and film discussed in Chapter 5. Alex is made to feel nausea every time he has the impulse toward aggressive violence or sex, presumably through a conditioning procedure involving a nausea-producing drug. Anthony Burgess, author of *A Clockwork Orange,* clearly disapproves of such conditioning procedures. Similar ideologically based disapproval has been directed at real-life attempts in experimental prison programs in California and elsewhere to treat prisoners by aversive techniques. In Chapter 5 we have already considered some of the issues surrounding such "control" of human behavior by conditioning and other procedures.

Does psychotherapy work?   There continues to be considerable controversy over the effectiveness of psychotherapy, both the depth and behavior approaches, which means that the evidence about their effectiveness is equivocal. The evidence is meager because therapists, particularly depth therapists, have tended not to assess the outcomes of their treatments. Those in professional practice are seldom in a good position to do systematic evaluations (and besides, it is easier to assume they are helping people than to check whether this is so). But the main reason is that making adequate evaluation requires elaborate research and is really quite difficult and complex (see Stollack *et al.,* 1966). The difficulties fall into three major categories:

1. In the case of depth therapies it is difficult to specify

If the advent of a powerful science of behavior causes trouble, it will not be because science itself is inimical to human welfare but because older conceptions have not yielded easily or gracefully. We expect resistance to new techniques of control from those who have heavy investments in the old, but we have no reason to help them preserve a series of principles that are not ends in themselves but rather outmoded means to an end. What is needed is a new conception of human behavior which is compatible with the implications of a scientific analysis. All men control and are controlled. The question of government in the broadest possible sense is not how freedom is to be preserved but what kinds of control are to be used and to what ends. . . . [From B. F. Skinner, in Rogers and Skinner, 1956, p. 508]

I believe that in Skinner's . . . writings, there is a serious underestimation of the problem of power. To hope that the power which is being made available by the behavioral sciences will be exercised by the scientists, or by a benevolent group, seems to me a hope little supported by either recent or distant history. It seems far more likely that behavioral scientists, holding their present attitudes, will be in the position of the German rocket scientists specializing in guided missiles. First they worked devotedly for Hitler to destroy the U.S.S.R. and the United States. Now, depending on who captured them, they work devotedly for the U.S.S.R. in the interest of destroying the United States, or devotedly for the United States in the interest of destroying the U.S.S.R. If behavioral scientists are concerned solely with advancing their science, it seems most probable that they will serve the purposes of whatever individual or group has the power. [From C. R. Rogers, in Rogers and Skinner, 1956, p. 511]

what therapists are actually doing with a patient, making comparison difficult. Psychoanalysts talk a great deal *about* what is happening in therapy but seldom provide detailed recorded interview material to show exactly what is said at various junctures. How then can we gauge the effectiveness of their procedures when these remain general and vague rather than specific?

2. The goals set for patients are likely to be quite variable, and as I have intimated earlier, they may even vary among different therapeutic approaches, as between depth therapies and behavior therapies. In one instance, the therapeutic goal may be very modest, say, to tide the patient over a temporary crisis; in another, it will be to have the patient comprehend his entire life style and its origins in childhood, and perhaps to revamp that style quite extensively; in still another, all that is sought is the disappearance of a single symptom, say, a limited fear or a bad habit such as smoking or drinking. Moreover, we cannot meaningfully compare therapy in a mildly neurotic person with that in a highly disturbed psychotic. Some types of problems may be more difficult to treat by certain tactics than others. Thus, adequate research on the effectiveness of psychotherapy and of different therapeutic approaches requires some degree of matching of the type and severity of the patient's problem, the patient's intelligence and ability to verbalize, and a host of other factors that could be influential in the outcome. This calls for a complex research design that has seldom if ever been employed in therapy research for obvious reasons of cost, time, and opportunity.

3. The evaluation of the effectiveness of psychotherapy also requires an ability to assess personality change accurately so that patients before therapy can be compared with themselves after therapy. Although a complex technology of personality assessment exists, it is far from adequate for precise measurement of the many criteria of adaptive failure and mental health that we would need to consider. Thus, aside from the simplest criterion of the disappearance of a particular symptom, our present ability to assess the changes that might be brought about by therapy is still quite primitive, restricting major research efforts.

What about the comparative merits of depth therapies and behavior therapies? A simple comparison is meaningless because their goals and types of problems are usually so different. The former usually set the more ambitious goal of producing major transformations of the person's life style, while the latter seek mainly to change certain specific types of behavior that have been judged by the person and those with whom he interacts as undesirable. Another complicating consideration concerns the definition of neurosis and its application to the sorts of patients seen by depth therapists and behavior therapists. One might argue that what the behavior therapist calls a phobia is not a phobia in the sense used by depth therapists. It is quite possible that some patients display symptoms that cannot be readily eliminated by the usual behavior therapy tactics of habit extinction and relearning because, as the depth therapists claim, the symptom is not the real problem. Thus, some patients might profit more from insight therapy, while others will do better by concentrating on the symptom as the problem. Because behavior therapy arose in opposition to the existing therapeutic outlook, its protagonists have tended to mount much rhetoric against the depth approaches; and only recently, in the light of their growing accomplishments and place in psychology, have some behavior therapists begun to tone down the attack, to begin to examine the theoretical bases for their own therapeutic strategies, and to recognize the psychological complexity of the problems of people in trouble.

There are those who question whether any form of therapy can be shown to be really successful in correcting the personal problems built over a lifetime of damaging social experiences (Figure 11.10), while others are much too sanguine about the capacity of psychotherapy to "cure" the more serious adaptive failures. However, it is likely that many people obtain considerable help from a wide variety of approaches, although the rules about how this works are not well understood, nor is the research data on which to base positive statements very impressive.

It would appear that only a small proportion of people needing help receive it. Surveys have shown that about 14 percent of those needing help seek it (Frank, 1973), and this is not the result of a scarcity of professionals but has more to do with the disposition on the part of individuals. Of those who do seek help, about 42 percent go to clergymen, 29 percent to physicians, 10 percent to social agencies, leaving only 19 percent (of the total 14 percent of the population) who go to psychiatrists or psychologists. Thus, a very small and highly select group among those with personal problems are ever seen by psychotherapists.

Furthermore, all forms of psychotherapy appear to claim roughly the same rates of success, though the objective data on this are quite inadequate. In spite of arguments about which methods are better, no professional approach has gone out of existence because its protagonists were persuaded they were less effective than any other approach. Practitioners of all varieties report successes with patients who had not been helped by competing systems of treatment. Frank suggests one possible exception, namely, that persons with phobias may do better with behavior therapy than with depth therapy, but he also states that such patients account for less than 3 percent of those seeking psychotherapy in England and the United States. In any case, patients showing the greatest improvement

Figure 11.10   The hard bite of reality. (Drawing by Mal Hancock; © Washington Star Syndicate, Inc.)

Table 11.3

Contrasts between depth therapy
and behavior therapy[a]

Psychodynamic approach	Behavioral approach
Intrapsychic processes emphasized	Intrapsychic processes deemphasized
Symptoms seen as consequence of intra-psychic conflict	Intrapychic conflicts denied; symptom seen as the problem
Behavior change seen as secondary to intrapsychic change	Focus on behavior change
Therapist approaches symptoms indirectly	Therapist deals with symptoms directly
Patient-therapist relationship emphasized	Patient-therapist relationship deemphasized
Therapy tends to be long term (often several years)	Therapy tends to be short term
Techniques subordinate to patient-therapist relationship	Techniques seen as primary
Outcome evaluated in terms of total functioning	Outcome evaluated in terms of specific behavior change
Based on psycho-analytic or psycho-dynamic principles	Based on learning-theory principles
Addressed to broad range of psychological and behavioral mal-adaptations	Addressed to specific behavioral problems, for example, phobias
Patient's ability to be articulate important	Patient's ability to be articulate of less importance
Not claimed to be highly efficient	Claimed to be highly efficient
Degree and quality of outcome depend on evaluator's viewpoint	Degree and quality of outcome depend on evaluator's viewpoint

[a] From H. H. Strupp, *Psychotherapy*, p. 6. Morristown, N.J.: General Learning Press (pamphlet).

regardless of their problem or the form of therapy they receive seem to share certain characteristics in common. They have good integration or ego-strength (that is, they normally manage their affairs adequately and can see their problems realistically), they have complaints that seem linked to identifiable environmental stresses, can readily express their feelings and problems, relate well to others, and have a strong desire to get treatment. We clearly need to know much more than we do about the factors in treatment as they relate to various kinds of psychological difficulties, and what can be done with the person who is not now treated or treatable by presently available psychotherapeutic methods (Table 11.3).

There will continue to be claim and counterclaim, attack and defense, mainly rhetoric, until clinicians of all theoretical persuasions recognize the urgent need to evaluate what they are doing with scientific precision. There is no panacea in the treatment of adaptive failure, and because our lives are so tangled up in complex and often destructive social conditions, there will probably never be one.

Social approaches

The approaches discussed above have generally taken place in a therapist's office, far removed from the social setting of the client's life—his family, neighborhood, or work environment; they are all predicated on the principle that the troubled person has somehow missed out on the acquisition of sound ways of coping with life. That is, the focus is mainly on the person himself, how he feels, what he needs, his sources of distress, and the ways he has acquired of managing his life. Although such a principle is reasonable, it is only a half-truth. The problem lies not only within the person but also in his social environment, and if this is so, then treatment could also be directed at changing that environment. Let us examine three approaches that involve some kind of direct intervention: putting the person in a mental hospital; providing him with community mental health services; and seeking through direct action to change his social scene.

Hospitalization   One of the oldest approaches to adaptive failure is to remove people in psychological trouble from their homes and communities and place them in mental institutions. Until recent times, the mental institution was essentially a jail (hardly an "asylum") where mental patients were kept away from the "normal" community. They were not patients in the medical sense, but inmates, "loonies," crazy or "possessed" people, and often were sources of amusement for spectators who paid for the privilege of gawking at and making fun of them (Figure 11.11). Even today mentally disturbed persons

Figure 11.11 The original Bedlam, in London, depicted by William Hogarth in 1735: "The rattling chains with Terror hear, behold Death grappling with Despair." (The Metropolitan Museum of Art, Harris Brisbane Dick Fund, 1932)

are a source of fear and superstition for much of the public. The modern, medical grounds for putting such persons in mental institutions were to provide them with treatment, keep them safe and protected against themselves, and to remove them temporarily from the social setting with which they had failed to cope (like a rest cure or change of scene). However, this is often merely rationalization of society's hostility and need to get them out of sight, as is evidenced by the terrible institutional conditions under which they have typically been

543

A psychiatric label has a life and an influence of its own. Once the impression has been formed that the patient is schizophrenic, the expectation is that he will continue to be schizophrenic. When a sufficient amount of time has passed, during which the patient has done nothing bizarre, he is considered to be in remission and available for discharge. But the label endures beyond discharge, with the unconfirmed expectation that he will behave as a schizophrenic again. Such labels, conferred by mental health professionals, are as influential on the patient as they are on his relatives and friends, and it should not surprise anyone that the diagnosis acts on all of them as a self-fulfilling prophecy. Eventually, the patient himself accepts the diagnosis, with all of its surplus meanings and expectations, and behaves accordingly. [From Rosenhan, 1973, pp. 253–254]

made to live and the absence of much if any actual treatment (see Goffman, 1961).

The large mental institution seems to be on the way out today for two main reasons: (1) It has become clear that merely giving custodial care or a modicum of treatment in an impersonal, understaffed, overcrowded institutional setting is not very therapeutic. If the troubled person stays long in that setting (say a year), it becomes increasingly unlikely that he will ever leave. In this so-called hospitalization syndrome, he is seen and comes to see himself as a sick person and learns to play that role. He loses track of his loved ones if there are any, loses his social and work skills, and comes to prefer the role of chronic, dependent hospital patient to having to face his problems outside on his own. (2) The success of tranquilizing and other drugs in reducing the most severely disturbed behavior patterns of mental patients has made hospitalization less necessary than it once seemed. The new emphasis is to get the patient out of the mental institution as quickly as possible and to keep him home. There is still, however, a large population of chronic mental patients (many of them senile) who must be cared for in institutions since they cannot care for themselves and there is no one in their family who can do so (Figure 11.12).

For those institutions that remain, as a result of drugs there has also been a shift away from locked wards and restraints upon the freedom of the patient, and in their place the patients are encouraged to take responsibility for their behavior and to participate in decisions about their treatment. This began with the concept that the institution should be a "therapeutic community" (Jones, 1953). It is a social system like any other, and all its activities should be as therapeutic or constructively helpful to the patients as possible in order to get them back to their families and community settings as quickly as possible before the "hospitalization syndrome" sets in. In the therapeutic community, all of the institution personnel are considered important in the treatment of the patient, and they are taught to view the patient as a human being who merits courtesy and consideration despite his mental disorder.

One of the most difficult problems of the patient who is leaving the institution is his transition back to the community, where he may be treated with suspicion, rejected socially, and ridiculed. Provisions must be made to assist the patient during and after his transition to deal with problems and setbacks that may occur, and even before he leaves the institution, to prepare him as much as possible for the insensitive treatment he must expect from a prejudiced public. In some communities halfway houses have been established in which the patient can live while he returns to work to facilitate his

(a)

(b)

Figure 11.12 (a) *Psychiatric ward of a hospital in Central Africa.* (b) *An Asian mental hospital.* (a,b: *World Health Organization/Photos by Paul Almasy and Eric Schwab*)

ultimate return to full living in the community. These halfway houses are typically staffed by lay persons and are operated by the patients themselves.

In spite of these advances in handling people in serious mental difficulty, however, little but custodial care is still all that is available in mental hospitals throughout much of the country, and the mental patient is still widely regarded as a pariah. The wisdom and ultimate savings inherent in investing in rehabilitation of ex-patients still eludes much of our society, as it does also in the case of ex-criminals.

Community mental health services For some time there has been a growing consensus among American clinicians that the person in trouble is better helped within his own community,

545

rather than by being placed in an institution far removed from home. The passage of the Community Mental Health Services Centers Act in 1963 provided federal funds for the creation of mental health centers in local communities, and over 400 of them have been established. Ideally they provide the following services: some short-term hospital care; day or night partial hospitalization for persons able to come home either evenings or mornings; outpatient therapy while the patient lives at home and goes about his normal activities; emergency care around the clock when someone in the community appears to need it; and professional consultation and education available to members of the community who seek it. Thus, a parent worried about a sex or disciplinary problem with a child can get help or advice from a professional by contacting the local center. Groups of people in the community can attend lectures and seminars on mental health topics. An individual or family experiencing a momentary crisis can call in and get help. A person who needs limited hospitalization can receive it while not being uprooted from home and family, or job. And in the event a patient needs brief hospitalization, this can be obtained in a more flexible manner than before.

Although there has been disagreement about how this plan for providing mental health services at the local level has worked, it is clearly a better idea than has ever been in operation previously, and the extent to which it can fulfill its ideal goals depends heavily upon the imagination and flexibility of the professionals staffing the centers (and the funds available to them). The chief complaints about such centers have been that they reach only a small proportion of the people who need them and that they have operated in too traditional a psychiatric fashion, with the patient coming to the office of the professional in the center, rather than the staff going out into the community and functioning as consultants in the social settings in which most people live and work. Moreover, there is no longer much sense of community in our metropolitan centers.

Several important new trends in community treatment programs are developing and are sometimes linked or integrated with the mental health centers. One is the establishment of *crisis intervention centers* to which people can come for help with problems before they escalate into more serious mental disturbances. Their therapeutic focus is placed mainly on the immediate problem or crisis in the person or family and not on long-term psychotherapy. In some instances, the therapist can even see the family in its own home setting, helping both to clarify what is happening and to mobilize the support of other family members. Such centers may operate telephone "hot lines," with someone continually manning the telephone to receive calls from persons feeling desperately lonely, as though they are about to fall apart, or considering suicide. *Suicide prevention centers* have been springing up in many communities and are discovering that even a sympathetic nonprofessional with only limited experience and training can be helpful in easing the distress of the caller and reducing the possibilities of a suicidal attempt. It is a good sign that the person has telephoned rather than attempted suicide, since this is typically a "cry for help" at a time of despair, a plea for someone to be concerned when there are no others to care or when the person feels deserted by his loved ones. He may announce that he has just swallowed a lethal dose of sleeping pills, and his life often may be saved if the hot line monitor manages to obtain his name and address.

The increasing use of *paraprofessionals*—who, while lacking the intensive and extensive training of the psychiatrist, clinical psychologist, and social worker, nevertheless can provide important therapeutic services—is an important development in mental health care. Housewives, teachers, clergymen, nurses, college students, and policemen can be trained in therapy with delinquent children, mental patients, adolescents with drug problems, and many other people in trouble (Cowen *et al.,* 1967; Matarazzo, 1971; Rioch *et al.,* 1963).

Another development is the realization, slow as yet to mature, that just as the community mental health center is designed to bring help closer to the local community, so professional workers can go even further in this direction by providing their services in the very settings where people live and work rather than in an office building downtown. Clinicians can and do, for example, serve as *consultants* in the classroom and school (school psychologists), and on request observe children interacting on the spot. They are thus in a position to offer suggestions not only about handling emotional problems in individual children, but about the entire social format of the class or school. Although community mental health means going out into the social community to offer the benefits of what is known about human adaptation and maladaptation, the extent to which professionals have done this is still exceedingly limited, partly because the financial and institutional arrangements have not yet been made to facilitate such a role, and partly because most professionals were not trained in this fashion. Nevertheless, much more of this is likely in the future.

Social action   One of the major responsibilities of clinicians is to translate what is known about psychological development into evaluation of the social conditions that tend to breed maladaptation and into coherent and practical recommendations about the design of better human environments. In the United States, with the tradition of the free marketplace

Note 11.5

The reader's attention is called to Notes 9.5 and 9.6, in which social action as an application of knowledge and social action as a source of knowledge were discussed. That discussion is just as relevant here in our consideration of people on the margins of society who cannot find a suitable place.

and individualism, we have been slow to recognize the importance of "social engineering," the systematic design of social and physical environments. As the problems produced by industrialization and technology (like overpopulation and pollution) continue to mount, and the economic and social gap between the rich and the poor widens in many parts of the world, pressures for an increased government role in our lives will also grow. In other countries, such as Sweden, there is a much stronger tradition of social engineering.

The breeding grounds for much adaptive failure lie, in part, in disordered social institutions, in slums that keep producing a high percentage of social derelicts, in disrupted family life, in schools that grind down the self-image of inadequate or marginally adequate children, in the social isolation of the aged and handicapped that facilitates their senile deterioration, forcing them to live out the remainder of their lives in a more or less vegetative state in old-age homes or mental hospitals. From this point of view, the best route toward the treatment and prevention of adaptive failure lies in changing many social patterns to make them less destructive and more capable of gratifying man's needs (Note 11.5).

Although our science has not advanced far enough to make it possible to specify with assurance the social conditions under which children can grow up and live successfully, and social engineering on the large scale is undoubtedly impractical at present, there are many more modest social settings to which the psychologist can address himself with some hope of having an impact. One example may be found in the area of aging, particularly in the context of government efforts at urban renewal. Usually when old buildings are torn down and the residents transferred to new quarters, old people are severely displaced and the new arrangements are typically even less adequate to their needs than were the old slums, making their conditions of life worse, not better (Birren, 1964, 1970).

More than half the people in the United States over 65 years of age are poor, and so they have little choice about their living conditions. Like anyone else, they dislike their inadequate housing, but they also have other, more important needs which are seldom considered when their old housing is razed and new housing is provided. The elderly need to live in familiar surroundings, so that even the act of moving is threatening to them. They also need privacy, but still want easy contact with others. They are easily discouraged by physical obstacles that would not faze younger people—for example, the high steps of a bus, or having to cross wide, busy streets. Thus, even when such services are available, aged persons do without banks, doctors, repair services, dentists, shops, or parks because they lack the energy and mobility to use them. Because of this the elderly should live with all their necessities located within a small area. They find an older neighborhood with clustered small shops and narrow streets easier to live in than a high-rise building with shopping and other services located far away. Ordinary housing that might be quite suitable and even ideal for the young will not do for the old and may even handicap them further in maintaining necessary social contacts and activity. Behavioral and social scientists should clearly be involved in planning the goals and patterns of living for the aged, a form of social engineering in which psychology could play an important role aimed at improving the possibilities for adaptive success and minimizing adaptive failure. Attention in such social engineering is on the kind of environment required by persons with certain specifiable characteristics, and it is aimed at improving the fit between the person and his environment by modifying the latter (rather than the former).

CONCLUDING COMMENT

There are many concerned professional workers who think that not enough is known about the conditions producing adaptive failure and healthy adaptation to make definite recommendations about social institutions, or about how children should be raised and taught in school, or whatever. For them the major task of psychology is first to obtain the solid facts and principles on which to base practical efforts at assessment and treatment, or to engage in preventive efforts. There is perhaps much truth in this position. However, human problems and efforts at their solution simply cannot wait until all the data are available. Although many of us should be busy at trying to obtain such knowledge, there is, nonetheless, no higher calling than to do one's best with the resources one has at hand, while at the same time being sensitive to the existence of many alternative notions about the reasons for adaptive failure and the conditions promoting successful adaptation. Faced with monumental and widespread human problems, we can do too little to feel satisfied. The best strategy is to recognize the challenge that remains, in seeking both to understand the whys and wherefores of adaptive failure, so that tangible therapeutic help can be given, and to make knowledgeable recommendations for social changes that will improve the chances that subsequent generations will achieve the good life.

In Chapter 12 we shall conclude on the positive note of examining that quest for the good life.

There was an excellent example of the probabilistic control exerted by a verbal stimulus at a recent symposium at Yale University organized to discuss "Beyond Freedom and Dignity." On the second evening, several students brought in a large banner reading "Remember the Air War," which they hung from the balcony. It could not be seen by many in the audience, but it confronted the five panelists on the platform throughout the evening. It had a predictable effect: Everyone of us mentioned the war in Vietnam at some point in his discussion and the last speaker, Sir Dennis Brogan, put aside his manuscript and spoke only of the war.

That was good behavioral engineering. We should learn to live with it. [From B. F. Skinner, Freedom and dignity revisited. *The New York Times,* August 11, 1972]

General discussions of assessment

Lazarus, R. S. *Patterns of adjustment and human effectiveness,* Chapter 10. New York: McGraw-Hill, 1969. Review of major considerations in psychological assessment.

Megargee, E. I. (ed.) *Research in clinical assessment.* New York: Harper & Row, 1966. Professional level series of articles covering research issues.

Tyler, Leona E. *Tests and measurements,* 2nd ed. Englewood Cliffs, N.J.: Prentice-Hall, 1971. Brief textbook devoted to psychological testing.

General discussions of psychotherapy

Burton, A. *Interpersonal psychotherapy.* Englewood Cliffs, N.J.: Prentice-Hall, 1972. A brief primer of depth psychotherapy that is not unrepresentative of professional practice patterns today.

Colby, K. M. *A primer for psychotherapists.* New York: Ronald Press, 1951. Similar in scope to Burton, but from a slightly different point of view.

Coleman, J. C. *Abnormal psychology and modern life.* Glenview, Ill.: Scott, Foresman, 1972. Although mainly a textbook about adaptive failure, this book also has an excellent and up-to-date coverage of therapy.

Ford, D. H., and Urban, H. B. *Systems of psychotherapy.* New York: Wiley, 1963. Major attempt to review and analyze the theory and general tactics of many schools of psychotherapy, such as the Freudian and Adlerian systems, also presenting their theoretical approaches to personality in general.

Shaffer, J., and Galinsky, M.D. *Models of social interaction and group therapy.* Englewood Cliffs, N.J.: Prentice-Hall, in press. The most thorough review to date of the major theories and practices of group therapy, with comparative analyses of each.

Ullmann, L. P., and Krasner, L. *A psychological approach to abnormal behavior.* Englewood Cliffs, N.J.: Prentice-Hall, 1969. Though mainly a look at abnormal behavior from a behavioral point of view, this text also provides a picture of behavior therapy.

If hour after hour as a psychiatrist or clinical psychologist you observed or heard about every possible form of personality distress imaginable and every symptom of adaptive failure, you would soon begin to doubt that anyone could be managing life adequately. No doubt you would be impressed if you ran into a happy person without such troubles, though you might doubt what you observed on the surface, and you might have trouble recognizing a mentally healthy person if you saw one. The simplest way you would have of defining health would be as the absence of illness as evidenced by symptoms. If there were no symptoms, the person was okay. This is the way most professionals regarded the matter up to the early 1950s.

This outlook is typified in a study by Roy R. Grinker (1962), a distinguished research psychiatrist, who made one of the earliest systematic attempts actually to look at people lacking incapacitating psychological troubles. Sixty-five male students from a small YMCA training college in Chicago were selected for such study in the late 1950s. They were carefully screened so as to include only those without evidence of crippling mental handicaps. They were the sons of families whose incomes averaged $6,000 per year, the fathers occupying such jobs as janitor, truck driver, street repairer, watchman, farmer, and school teacher. They came from all over the United States and Canada, but were mainly from the Midwest. As a group they were slightly above average in intelligence and were obtaining slightly better than C grades during their first year in a college whose average grade was C+. They were studied carefully by a series of interviews and the use of other assessment devices. The traditional outlook of most professional workers of the day toward mental health is nicely revealed in the following amusing comment made by Grinker (1962, pp. 405–406):

The impact of these interviews on me was startling! Here was a type of young man I had not met before in my role as a psychiatrist and rarely in my personal life. On the surface they were free from psychotic, neurotic, or disabling personality traits. It seemed that I had encountered some mentally "healthy" men who presented a unique opportunity [for] study.

Perhaps this experience could serve as a tentative definition of "mental health"—its startling impact on a psychiatrist who has devoted most of his professional life to working with people who complain unhappily, suffer from disabling symptoms, and behave self-destructively. Three years after my preliminary shock and after this peculiar population was systematically studied, I came across the following reassuring sentence written by Henry Murray: "Were an analyst to be confronted by that much heralded but still missing specimen—the normal man—he would be struck dumb, for one, through lack of appropriate ideas."

As Grinker describes them, these students were not persons likely to be seen by a psychiatrist. Although they did not display a complete absence of psychopathology, some being suspicious, unhappy, withdrawn, fearful, compulsive, and the like, by and large they were comfortable psychologically and none was seriously impaired by these problems. In school, they procrastinated in studying and crammed for exams, as is common throughout the country, but they usually passed their courses. They were active in sports and enjoyed themselves, felt generally favorable about themselves, and had positive hopes for the future, though they had little ambition for great social or economic gain, being generally content with modest and undistinguished expectations. Their relationships with parents, other relatives, teachers, and friends were warm. They were not particularly visible people in the sense that they made no splash nor achieved any notoriety. Grinker called them "homoclites," that is, "normal, healthy, ordinary, just plain guys." He was impressed with the differences between these persons and those typically seen in a psychiatrist's office, particularly in their lack of ambition and the absence of major dissatisfaction. He summed up their attitudes thus (Grinker, 1962, p. 446): "We lived in a nice house, our clothes were good, we always had enough to eat. True we had an old car, but it ran. Why did [we] need to earn more? A job you like is better than one you don't even if it pays more." Perhaps most interesting of all are Grinker's comments (1962, p. 446) about this bland and self-satisfied set of attitudes:

I often described my subject population to various local and professional groups characterized by driving social upwardmobile or prestige-seeking people, who, although outwardly serene, were consumed with never-satisfied ambitions. The invariable comment was "those boys are sick, they have no ambition." In the broadest sense to "do the best I can" (a common outlook of this sample) seems to be a true ambition.

One gets a somewhat different image of mental health if he uses as his model the Mercury astronauts, the first seven men in the space program, who became American heroes in the 1960s (Figure 12.1). As part of that program their biological responses to space flight were studied, but there were also some modest efforts at psychological study (Korchin and Ruff, 1964; Ruff and Korchin, 1964). The image one gets of these men from such psychological study is that above all they were highly competent and resistant to stress, at least to the stresses involved in training and space flight, which required absorption of much highly technical information, and the need to make rapid but accurate decisions under pressure and to function well despite ever-present physical dangers.

The Mercury astronauts were generally ambitious men with a strong early commitment to their jet pilot careers and later to the space program. They appeared to know who they were and where they were going. They were self-confident and self-controlled men, a confidence and control that seemed to

Figure 12.1 The Mercury astronauts: front row, left to right—Walter M. Schirra, Jr., Donald K. Slayton, John H. Glenn, Jr., and Scott Carpenter; back row—Alan B. Shepard, Jr., Virgil I. Grissom, and L. Gordon Cooper. (NASA)

Note 12.1

In the studies of Grinker (1962) and Korchin and Ruff (1964), we are again dealing with a problem discussed earlier in Note 4.5, namely, the *representativeness* of samples used in psychological research. The students observed at the YMCA college in Chicago are a distinctive population, as are the Mercury astronauts or the people who on principle opposed the Vietnam War and the draft. In such research, no attempt is being made to examine mental health, however it is defined, as it is found in the population at large. Grinker, for example, started with some ideas about mental health, and a population was selected that expressed these characteristics. Thus, because Grinker used interviews to screen out all students at the college who had traditional psychiatric symptoms, he cannot say anything about most students at such a college or students in general, but only about a particular sample, limited by the selection procedures he established. Such research cannot tell us, therefore, how widely the traits observed in these samples are distributed in the population at large, and how they operate in different contexts.

grow out of a family context in which their lives had always flowed rather smoothly, with few critical choices, crises, or major setbacks. This smooth-flowing quality of their lives began in the well-organized families in which they grew up, families which had considerable solidarity and were affluent and well integrated into the town or community in which they were situated. All seven of the astronauts were Protestant, had been active in sports and outdoor living, educated in public schools, had achieved college degrees in engineering, and were married and had children when selected for the program. Like the blander, more ordinary and contented group studied by Grinker, these hard-driving men present still another image of mental health, though we have rather superficial information about their innermost thoughts, fantasies, and feelings. Perhaps because of their public position and the superficiality of the psychological examination of their psychodynamics, they tend to be viewed stereotypically as "all-American boys" rather than as real persons with ordinary human problems.

Let us look at one further contrasting image of mental health, one usually not regarded as such because it is built of turmoil, struggle, and rebelliousness rather than inner harmony or harmony with the social environment. Consider the youths who as part of the civil rights movement of the early 1960s chanced injury, ostracism, and death (some were actually killed) by going into the Deep South to challenge Jim Crow laws and to help register blacks to vote. And what of many youths who refused to be inducted into the military service during the height of the Indochina War? Their protest was a principled one, based on the refusal to accept what they viewed as unjust and evil. Their lives have seemed anything but free of troubles. Some have chosen to go to prison rather than participate in the war. Women like Joan Baez, the popular folksinger, and Jane Fonda, the actress, put their careers on the line by continuing publicly to protest the war during the saturation bombings of Hanoi and Haiphong in late 1972 (Figure 12.2). Or what of the Air Force pilot of B-52 bombers who refused to fly any more such missions because the goals did not justify the continued mass destruction and killing? Or the army doctor who refused to train Green Beret medics because he felt they were using and withholding medicine militarily in Indochina? (See Note 12.1.)

Are these protesters to be viewed as alienated youths or as those who display strong commitment to a high set of human values by acting out their convictions (see Kenniston, 1965, 1968)? Certainly not all draft resisters and military deserters are motivated by idealism. But some belong to that select group of people throughout history who have in conscience stood up and opposed what they deeply felt were evils of society. They were often troubled people. By what reasoning, then, can they be thought of as mentally healthy? From the traditional professional standpoint, are they not to be seen as maladapted in terms of accepted societal standards of behavior? One influential writer, Frank Barron (1963, p. 144), in attempting a rebuttal of this traditional position, has made some persuasive observations about rebelliousness that deserve serious reflection in our attempts to define mental health:

The first and most obvious consideration in the relationship of rebelliousness to morality and psychological health is one which by now has passed from iconoclastic protest to virtual stereotype. None-theless, it should not be disregarded. It is simply this: rebellion-resistance to acculturation, refusal to "adjust," adamant insistence on the importance of the self and of individuality is very often the mark of healthy character. If the rules deprive you of some part of yourself, then it is better to be unruly. The socially disapproved expression of this is delinquency, and most delinquency certainly is just plain confusion or blind and harmful striking out at the wrong enemy; but some delinquency has affirmation behind it, and we should not be too hasty in giving a bad name to what gives us a bad time. The great givers to humanity often have proud refusal

Figure 12.2 Joan Baez, American folk singer, heads a column of Easter peace marchers in Essen, West Germany, a city that was virtually obliterated by Allied saturation bombing during World War II. (Wide World Photos)

in their souls, and they are aroused to wrath at the shoddy, the meretricious, and the unjust, which society seems to produce in appalling volume. Society is tough in its way, and it's no wonder that those who fight it tooth and nail are "tough guys." I think that much of the research and of the social action in relation to delinquency would be wiser if it recognized the potential value of the wayward characters who make its business for it. A person who is neither shy nor rebellious in his youth is not likely to be worth a farthing to himself nor to anyone else in the years of his physical maturity.

Considerable dissatisfaction over the tradition, reflected in Grinker's conception of mental health, of regarding successful adaptation as the obverse of adaptive failure began to emerge in the 1950s. The basic sources of dissatisfaction were twofold:

First, to venerate the absence of signs of conflict is to make an ideal of the attainment of harmony with the social environment, whatever it is. Such a person is a "contented cow," comfortably adjusted regardless of what the world around him is like. From this standpoint, a psychologically healthy person living under the Nazi Reich would have had to be cooperative with or at least comfortable with the evil aims and deeds of his nation's leaders. By the same token, one could question whether mental health in today's world implies equanimity about social evils such as racism, widespread poverty amid affluence, persistent militarism and resort to violence, or worldwide failure to act effectively to meet the environmental crisis of overpopulation and pollution. To be outraged at the social inequities and hypocrisies of a very imperfect society means also that the person must display some of the traditional signs of stress, since he certainly is not in harmony with the world in which he lives. In the traditional view such signs mark the person as "maladjusted."

Furthermore, to emphasize merely the absence of troubles, or to view psychotherapy merely as the simple unlearning of bad habits and the relearning of more serviceable ones, seems to reduce complex human achievements such as love, altruism, humanism, and maturity to the status of quickie acquisitions. Successful living is an achievement of a lifetime, hewn out of conflict and disappointment, arrived at through courage, wisdom, struggle, and persistence, and it demeans this achievement to think of it solely in negative terms as the absence of trouble or disturbed symptoms rather than in terms of positive striving and accomplishment.

In the early 1950s there began a reexamination of the traditional approach (Riesman, 1950; Jahoda, 1950, 1958), and a new intellectual movement arose oriented to the idea of positive mental health. As was pointed out in Chapter 10 in the discussion of the illness model, the terms "mental illness"

Psychology does not produce nuclear warheads, nor does it produce the apocalyptic birds which may take them to a selected target, but psychology is concerned with human decisions. . . . The greatest power in the world is the power of rational decision. Atomic physics deals with the release of great forces, but answers to ethical questions may be the decisive ones for the future of humanity. [From Creegan, 1958, pp. 272–275]

and "mental health" often distort our understanding of a person's difficulties in adapting to life's demands. The reader may have noticed that in this chapter I have so far avoided the expression "the healthy personality" in the light of my conviction about this. However, it will now be necessary to use this undesirable term because the authors of most important theoretical treatments of the topic of successful adaptation use it and it is well engrained in our vocabulary. Besides, it will be easier to spell out the reasons why the term is unfortunate after we have examined the existing ideas about it.

Things are obviously getting complicated. Where then do we stand? How have psychologists attempted to define mental health? Our task now is to examine what writers since Sigmund Freud have thought about the ideal of the "good life," of successful human adaptation, and then to try to put these ideas into perspective. There have been many such attempts, varying considerably in outlook as one might expect, although there are also some common themes too. To make sense out of this question we must begin at the modern beginnings, which means that we must start with Freud's analysis of personality and use this as our intellectual base of operations, a sort of launching pad, when considering some of the other outlooks.

THE FREUDIAN VIEW

As we saw in Chapter 11, Sigmund Freud has had a major influence on our ideas about the treatment of psychopathology. His views have also tended to dominate the field of mental health—either directly, by providing many widely used concepts, or indirectly, by stimulating dissident viewpoints that can be seen as counterpoints to Freudian thought. Over the years, Freud's views have also been subject to much criticism and attack, and some psychologists will regret the emphasis they are given here. In spite of divergent assessments of his ideas, it is important to review Freud, since it is virtually impossible to make good sense of the varying points of view about mental health without some grounding in psychoanalytic theory. It would be unthinkable for the student to approach psychology for the first time without meaningful contact with the Freudian theory of how the mind works.

Freud's conception of personality

All living things, and any machine such as a television set or automobile engine, are constructed of parts that move or do things. In the case of the automobile engine, there are pistons which move up and down within the cylinder walls as a gas-air mixture explodes, and this provides the energy to turn the wheels. To understand how a car works it is essential to understand these crucial parts of the engine and how they act in relation to each other. So it is with human personality, which has parts (or, as they are usually termed, *structures*), and things which it does (called *functions*), such as maintaining various kinds of commerce with the environment oriented toward survival and achieving ends that go beyond survival (see Chapters 1 and 2). There is a third consideration in personality which applies to living organisms more than machines, namely, how the system got to be the way it is (called *development*). Therefore, to present Freud's basic ideas about personality requires that we understand how he conceived its structure, dynamics, and development. Only then will his (and other) views of the nature of mental health be meaningful, since any judgment of psychological well-being is essentially an evaluation of how well the personality system is operating in its commerce with the outer world.

Personality structure   Freud (1949, 1961) conceived of the personality as having three substructures, the *id, ego,* and *super-ego.* At one time he believed that these literally were located in certain specific portions of the brain, but this idea had to be dropped on the basis of neurophysiological evidence. These substructures are now thought of as convenient ways of thinking about the various facets of the personality rather than as actual neural centers.

The *id* is the most primitive part of the personality, consisting of the innate drives or instincts passed down to man from his animal ancestors. In the infant, these drive energies are quite diffuse and undirected, since the personality does not yet have much structure and organization. But soon separate drives are differentiated. According to Freud, the main drives of interest for the formation of personality are the *life instincts* and the *death instincts.* In the former the most important is the sexual drive (*libido*), though there are other life-preserving drives such as hunger and thirst, to name the most obvious. They are called life instincts because their operation helps preserve the individual and the species. Aggression was seen by Freud as stemming from the death instincts and as a temporary turning outward of the self-destructive impulses. Actually, many psychoanalytically oriented writers today reject the notion of a death instinct and believe that aggression can be better explained as a consequence of the frustration of life instincts or a response to threat (see Chapter 6). Freud thought that it is mainly the way the sexual drive operates that determines the health of the personality system. This is because most other self-preservative drives such as hunger and thirst are not ringed with social taboos so as to produce intense inner conflict. Were it not for such taboos, found in virtually all human societies in some form or other, perhaps sexual activity might not be so important as a cause of maladaptation, rather than being the basic causative factor in neurosis.

The *ego* is the executive agency of the personality. It is concerned with the control and screening of unconscious impulses arising from the id: when they are positive, it seeks to maximize their chances of being gratified; when they are negative and self-destructive, it seeks to minimize the danger of harm to the system that such impulses might generate. In short, the major function of the ego is monitoring the continuous biological and psychological commerce between the individual and the environment; to do this effectively, it must evaluate the objective nature of reality (what is going on internally, and the current state of the environment). Therefore, cognitive activity such as perception, learning, and thinking are major ego activities. While the drives of the id activate and give the personality system initial direction, the question of which drives will be expressed, as well as how and when, is controlled through the activities of the ego.

The *superego* is the mental representation in the person of the moral values of the society as assimilated from, communicated, and enforced by his parents or by persons serving as substitutes for them. Through socialization these become an integral part of the personality of the growing child, and they guide how he acts and feels about his actions. Freud was one of the earliest writers to argue that man's conscience (another term for superego) is not God-given, but arises from social experience, formed anew in each developing child through the normal struggle of being reared within the family and as part of the adaptive process of identification with the parent (see Chapter 4).

In Freud's early writing, not only was the personality seen as divided into these three interacting realms, the id, ego, and superego, but it was also further separated into conscious, preconscious, and unconscious portions. To emphasize the then revolutionary idea that most of mental life was unconscious, Freud used the striking metaphor of the iceberg (Figure 12.3), which floats mostly below the surface with only the smallest part being visible. The id was said to be entirely below the surface; the superego was mostly below, but with small portions above the surface; and the ego was positioned mainly between the id and the outer world, with some of its activities below the surface but a considerable portion above. The preconscious portion (of the ego and the superego) comprised mental activities that are usually below the level of ordinary awareness but which can be brought to the surface with some effort or when signalled by some environmental event.

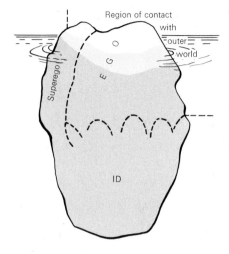

Figure 12.3 Freud's iceberg metaphor illustrates the relationship of personality structures (id, ego, and superego) to consciousness: the unshaded area is conscious; the lightly shaded area is preconscious; the darker area is unconscious. (From W. Healy, Augusta F. Bronner, and Anna Mae Bowers, The structure and meaning of psychoanalysis, *p. 56. New York: Knopf, 1930)*

In later writings, Freud recognized the logical defects in this approach, which conceived of the unconscious as a place in the mind, and he modified his reasoning about this while not discarding the notions of conscious and unconscious. In his revised conception, conscious and unconscious became *qualities* of mental events rather than physical subdivisions, making it possible to say that any mental event, an impulse, thought or feeling, say of guilt, could be conscious or unconscious (or perhaps preconscious). Although this conception is more in keeping with the sophisticated logic of modern scientific psychology, it remains somewhat controversial because we can never be sure that when a person fails to report something about his mental life it is necessarily outside of his awareness. The reader will recall discussion of this unresolved issue in the Prologue and in Chapter 11.

The general idea that mental activities may not be recognized by the person is not in itself so difficult for critics to accept. Many of us have casually responded to something without seeming to be aware of the process, as when we automatically change the tempo of our dancing when the musical tempo changes. We make many left and right turns at decision points while driving over a familiar route, stopping and starting at signals, yet at the end of the trip are not able to remember that we have performed all these complicated tasks because they have been automatized and our mind was intent on other things. On the other hand, the idea that some mental activity is inaccessible or unconscious because of the screening operation of a defense mechanism such as repression (Chapter 11) is a far more complicated and controversial one. This requires that we accept the notion that there are conflicting spheres or zones in the mind, ego activities that stand guard against our becoming aware of threatening id impulses. For such a concept to be scientifically adequate requires that the theorist ultimately do what has not yet been fully accomplished, namely, to set forth the rules and observable conditions under which an impulse will be kept out of awareness or allowed entrance. One possible rule, proposed initially by Freud, would be that when anxiety or guilt generated by the impulse rises above a certain level, it will trigger the defense mechanism. Thus, the idea of depth in psychology implies different levels of mental activity—a surface level which the person knows about, and a deeper level which is often in conflict with the conscious mind, especially in the neuroses. In speaking of defense we have shifted focus to the topic of personality dynamics.

Personality dynamics   What did Freud consider the main rules of operation of the personality system? The key idea is that everything the person does is built on the principle of

[Why] do so many people dream of flying? Psychoanalysis answers this question by stating that to fly or to be a bird in the dream is nothing but a concealment of another wish, to the recognition of which we are led by more than one linguistic or real bridge. When the inquisitive child is told that a big bird like the stork brings the little children, when the ancients have formed the phallus winged, when the popular designation of the sexual activity of man is expressed in German by the word "to bird" (vögeln), when the male member is directly called l'uccello (bird) by the Italians, all these facts are only small fragments from a large collection which teaches us that the wish to be able to fly signifies in the dream nothing but the longing for the ability of sexual accomplishment. This is an early infantile wish.

tension-reduction, which Freud (1925, 1961) called the "pleasure principle." The innate drives of the id are energy forces requiring discharge. For example, the sexual drive must be expressed or else there is tension and distress; such discharge can be automatic, as when the body's natural processes remove the mounting tension through sexual orgasm or climax. Freud thought that all such excitations from innate drives must be discharged to prevent dangerous and distressing tension, much like the way pressure in a steam boiler builds until the point of explosion unless there are valves to allow the pressure to dissipate. Freud theorized that such discharge or tension reduction results in feelings of pleasure.

However, the proper discharge of most innate drives requires an external object. To satisfy the libido, we need another person, preferably of the opposite sex; and to make discharge maximally gratifying we require a love object, someone who will respond to our love. But many forms of tension reduction run afoul of social taboos. In many cultures the adolescent must defer sexual gratification until the society says it is appropriate, say, in socially sanctioned marriage or in some other way as prescribed by custom. Not to obey these sanctions exposes the person to internal conflict or actual danger, and thus the impulse created by the innate drive must be controlled. This function is performed either by the ego, specifically those mental activities which regulate what we do in the interests of practicality, or the superego, which regulates our behavior in keeping with our internalized moral sense.

All this means that as a child matures and is expected to respond to social demands, another principle of psychodynamics must take precedence over the pleasure principle, one predicated on self-control and self-preservation in the face of conflicting social and internal pressures. Freud called this the *reality principle*. The main thrust of life is still to discharge innate drives successfully, but now counterforces are at work to prevent the undisciplined expression of impulses that are environmentally dangerous (Figure 12.4). The overriding principle of human activity is still tension reduction—all activity being oriented toward this—but such behavior must be accommodated to pressures imposed by the outer world. This may require delay or inhibition of pleasure. The importance of delay is illustrated even in erotic activities, for love making can have deeper and more lasting worth when there is a prolonged period of foreplay in which sexual climax is deferred until both man and woman are fully stimulated. Impulse control is required to prevent the sexual act from being prematurely completed.

Such modification and transformation of innate drives is of the utmost importance in the Freudian system of thought about healthy adaptation to the real world. In this view, neu-

When the grownup recalls his childhood, it appears to him as a joyful time, in which one is happy for the moment and looks to the future without any wishes; it is for this reason that he envies children. But the children themselves, if they could inform us about it, would probably give us different reports. It seems that childhood is not that blissful idyl into which we later distort it, that, on the contrary, children are lashed through the years of childhood by the wish to become big, and to imitate the grown-ups. This wish instigates all their playing. If in the course of their sexual investigation children feel that the grown-up knows something wonderful concerning the mysterious and yet so important realm that they are prohibited from knowing or doing, they are seized with a violent wish to know it, and dream of it in the form of flying. . . .

By admitting that he entertained a special personal relation to the problem of flying since his childhood, Leonardo confirms what we must assume from the investigation of children of our own times, namely, that his childhood investigation was directed to sexual matters. At least this one problem escaped the repression which later estranged him from sexuality. From childhood until the age of perfect intellectual maturity this subject, slightly varied, continued to hold his interest, and it is quite possible that he was as little successful in the attainment of his cherished art in the primary sexual sense as in the mechanical, that both wishes were denied to him.

As a matter of fact, the great Leonardo remained infantile in some ways throughout his whole life; it is said that all great men must retain something of the infantile. As a grown-up he still continued playing, which sometimes made him appear strange and incomprehensible to his contemporaries. . . . [He] constructed the most artistic mechanical toys for court festivities and receptions. . . . [From Freud, 1947 ed., pp. 102–104]

Figure 12.4 The perfect audience. (Courtesy, The Register and Tribune Syndicate, Inc.)

ENGLAND
Reading

"And I can safely say without fear of contradiction . . ."

rosis arises from the failure adequately to discharge powerful human drives in a satisfactory way. The failure arises initially because the society seeks control over and blocks many of man's natural impulses in order to preserve itself. Thus, for Freud, the fundamental basis of conflict lies in the struggle between the primitive, animal side of man and the complex requirements of social living (discussed in Chapter 5). An effective ego is capable of managing the primitive impulses without stifling them. Adaptive failure arises for two main reasons: either the ego is strong enough to control impulses but too weak and vulnerable to manage them in any way other than by overcontrol, that is, by suppressing them altogether as in self-deceptive defense mechanisms; or the ego is so weak that it is dominated by the id, that is, by innate drives. To oversimplify a bit, perhaps, the former describes the neurotic personality; the latter, one with such personality disorders as psychopathic behavior. Freud asserted that without external social control, man would be a monster (Mr. Hyde rather than Dr. Jekyll). On the other hand, when social control gets out of hand and becomes repressive, as it was in the Victorian world that Freud knew, it leads frequently to warped patterns of neurotic living. The world has of course changed markedly in its attitude to sexuality since Freud's heyday, partly because of his influence no doubt.

In Freud's theory (1938, 1953), the term *personality dynamics* refers to the ways in which internal conflicts are resolved and external social forces are accommodated. When this task is handled badly, the result is neurosis or psychosis; when it is handled well, the outcome is mental health.

Since everyone must deal with such inner struggles, we can frequently observe the expression of conflict in the form of slips of the tongue ("Freudian slips"), unaccountable lapses in memory, fantasies, dreams, and many neurotic symptoms. These expressions reveal the active impulses and countervailing social forces, and the way the ego, through its regulating devices (like defense mechanisms), is handling the conflict. An illustration will help make this process more clear. Consider, the following Freudian slip, which expresses a conflict between two opposing intentions, one of which is unconscious (Freud, 1963, pp. 35, 62–63):

We are told that a lady who was well known for her energy remarked on one occasion: "My husband asked his doctor what diet he ought to follow; but the doctor told him he had no need to diet: he could eat and drink about what *I* want. . ."

What we have before us are corrections, additions or continuations, by means of which a second purpose makes itself felt alongside of the first. . . . "My husband can eat and drink what *he* wants. But, as you know, I don't put up with wanting anything at all, so he can eat and drink what *I* want." [Italics added.]

Dreams and nightmares, according to Freud, are expressive of unconscious mental activity which is kept out of awareness by an alert ego during wakefulness but which slips through the "censorship" screen during the relaxation of sleep, though in a somewhat disguised form (this process of disguise is called the "dream work"). That is why dreams so often seem confused and irrational (see Chapter 11). In Freud's view dreams are also fulfilled wishes (Freud, 1963), but this view of dreams has been modified in more recent formulations by other students of dream activity. For example, Breger (1967) maintains that a dream is an attempt by the psyche to cope during sleep with unconscious and unresolved problems, rather than necessarily expressing, as Freud thought, the fulfillment of impulses or wishes. There seems to have been little advance in our understanding of the psychodynamics of dreaming since Freud, and relatively little research, although we know much more now about the physiological state of sleep under which dreams occur (Dement and Kleitman, 1957) and there has been a renewed interest in levels of unconsciousness during trances and sleep in recent years (Tart, 1969).

Personality development   Before we can fully appreciate Freud's conception of mental health one more step remains, namely, to consider how a drive- or id-dominated infant comes to be an adult with fully developed ego activity; we shall now consider some of the pitfalls he may experience on this tortuous developmental route. Freud's focus was on a series of sexual stages through which the child passes; he tried to plot the course of psychosexual development, which he proposed starts at birth and sets the pattern for pathology or mental health (Freud, 1933b, 1949).

At the very start of infancy, there is at first a brief diffuse erotic condition in which no special set of tissues have sexual significance (a period called by Freud, "polymorphous perverse"). With the advent of the *oral stage*, which begins shortly after birth and proceeds during most of the first year of life, the child's mouth becomes differentiated as the focus of sensual pleasure. Not only does the child satisfy its hunger through the mouth, but sucking and other manipulations of the area are the major source of enjoyment and discharge of tension. In a sense, the mouth is therefore the first "organ" of sexuality.

Think about what Freud was trying to do in this analysis. He was trying to understand the origins of some of the problems his patients brought to him. Some of them were very dependent and passive, very "oral"; perhaps their behavior heavily emphasized the mouth, they were constantly sucking things or biting their nails, they had a drinking problem, or they were strongly oriented to oral copulation. He asked himself where a person could have acquired such behavior patterns and decided that similar activities are typical (and normal) in the very young child who sucks at the breast or bottle nipple, or on a pacifier. He concluded that if a person somehow never outgrows these tendencies, they may carry over into adult life. The mouth is the child's first major avenue of interchange with his environment. He examines the world with his mouth, so to speak, sucking the nipple, his thumb, rubber toys, putting things in his mouth and spitting them out, biting on them, and so on. He is comforted by this activity and seems to enjoy it, and he responds with distress if it is interrupted. His psychological relationships with people are also affected by this oral interchange. The mother gives nourishment or withholds it. The child takes or rejects. The manner in which the mother plays her part signifies the response of the environment to the child, the nature of external reality. It can be harsh and destructive or warm and nurturant, dependable or undependable, a source of gratification or of pain. Since oral activity involves the act of receiving, its major psychological counterpart is therefore the tendency passively to accept help or sustenance from others.

As Erik Erikson (1963) has put it in his important exten-

sions of Freudian thought, the key issue of orality is trusting or mistrusting others (Figure 12.5). When things go wrong at the oral stage of psychosexual development, two things can happen: (1) the child can develop excessively trusting or even passive-dependent attitudes in which the environment is expected to maintain him; or (2) he can develop an attitude of suspicion and distrust of others because the mother is inconstant, unreliable, or hostile in her nurturing activities. If the child acquires trust, he will be disposed to think of others accordingly, and he may be on his way to healthy psychological development. A great deal depends, of course, on what happens in the later critical transitions. If he does not acquire autonomy at a further stage of development, then this infantile trust may develop into a stultifying optimism ("I will be taken care of somehow"). This attitude will undermine any later efforts to make his way in the world independently. On the other hand, if the child feels unfulfilled and continually sees others with mistrust, he is also headed toward pathological development. In any event, the initial oral transactions with the world begin to lay down the patterns of trust or mistrust that will become stable features of the person's outlook toward others in later life.

During roughly the second and third years of life, there is a shift away from "orality" and toward the anal region. At this time, the expulsion and retention of feces becomes a focus for erotically pleasing experience. This is the *anal stage*. The anus now becomes the prime "organ" of sexuality, and

(a)

*Figure 12.5
baby's experien
the bases for at
life. (b) Dr. Er
Monkmeyer Pre
W. W. Norton*

(b)

*Figure
tionsh
just p
(Dra*

(a)

(b)

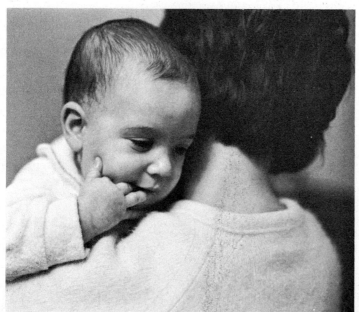

Act 1: "Just one more spoon
for mommy . . ."

ct 2: "Don't tell me you can't . . .
ou're not really trying . . ."

*12.6   In some mother-infant rela-
*s, the oral stage and the anal stage are
*rt of one long struggle for dominance.
ng by J. J. Dunleavy)

the child develops new kinds of transactions with the environment that have important ramifications for his personality
(Figure 12.6).

On the psychological side the central issue is the parental
handling of bowel activity (toilet training) and the reactions
of the child to this social pressure. The parent as a representative of the culture has certain attitudes of his or her own
toward feces (interest, disgust). The child perceives these and
struggles with the escalating problem of gratifying his own
biological drives and the demands of his parents. In the process, the child's expectations and attitudes about discipline are
being forged, and he must also begin to come to terms with
problems posed by his growing opposition and hostility toward
his parental socializers. Erikson (1963, p. 251) puts it this way:

> Muscular [anal] maturation sets the stage for experimentation
> with two simultaneous sets of social modalities: holding on and
> letting go. As is the case with all of these modalities, their basic
> conflicts can lead in the end to either hostile or benign expectations
> and attitudes. Thus, to hold can become a destructive and cruel
> retaining or restraining, and it can become a pattern of care: to have
> and to hold. To let go, too, can turn into an inimical letting loose
> of destructive forces, or it can become a relaxed "to let pass" and
> "to let be."

In Erikson's language, the social attitudes emerging from the
anal stage are those of healthy autonomy, on the one hand,
and pathological shame and self-doubt, on the other. The child
can struggle obstinately against the rules, or he can accept the
pressure and learn to manage himself and events in accordance
with these rules. An adequate reaction to this struggle permits
him to be effective and yet does not hamper his freedom and
initiative. In effect, an autonomous yet self-controlled individual is the healthy outcome of the struggle, while the pathological outcome is resistance and obstinacy, a sense of shame over
impulses, and feelings of doubt about his bodily activity and
social relations.

The *phallic stage* begins to emerge during around the
third and fourth years. At this time the genital organs (penis
and vaginal area) now take over as the main locus of sexual
activity. Needless to say, in Freud's time the claim that children engaged in sexual activity was very shocking, led to much
social criticism and required considerable courage on Freud's
part to pursue his analyses. Freud (1933a) was impressed with
the importance of this stage by some observations by a father
of a 5-year-old boy whom he called Little Hans. The father
was a layman sympathetic to Freud's ideas, and he was concerned with his son's intense fear of horses. Although it would
be unheard of today to do so, Freud encouraged the father
to treat his own child, in occasional consultation with Freud,

and this led to some important clinical observations which contributed to Freud's theory.

The father observed manifestations of a sexual interest on the part of the boy in his mother. For example, Little Hans greatly enjoyed getting into bed with his mother. He and his mother would hug and caress each other, and the boy would ask her to touch his penis because it was great fun. Little Hans also had sexual fantasies about his mother and some of his playmates while he played with his penis. Freud reports one incident of this sort as reported to him by Little Hans' father (Freud, 1933a, p. 32):

I put my finger to my widdler just a very little. I saw Mummy quite naked in her chemise, and she let me see her widdler. I showed Grete, my Grete [a female playmate], what Mummy was doing, and showed her my widdler. Then I took my hand away from widdler quick . . . the chemise was so short that I saw her widdler.

Freud also recounts that Little Hans evidently enjoyed being together with his mother in the bathroom when she went to the toilet. According to the father, the boy's mother stated that "He goes on pestering me till I let him." The boy also talked about fantasies that he would marry his mother some day (a not uncommon attitude in young boys) and that they would have children. He displayed behavior that Freud interpreted as hostility toward and jealousy of his father, such as roughhousing with him, defying attempts to keep him out of his mother's bed, and wishing that his father would die so that he could have his mother all to himself. This reinforced Freud's growing impression that the major conflict of the phallic stage of psychosexual development was the family triangle. The choice of an external object of love is the critical psychological issue to be resolved in the context of the family triangle.

Very early in his formulation of psychoanalytic theory, Freud had also worked clinically with a female neurotic patient who reported a sexual assault by her father; similar experiences were reported again and again by other women with hysterical neurotic symptoms. At first Freud thought that he had stumbled upon the cause of hysteria, but it seemed very unlikely to him that a physical sexual approach by the girl's father (incest) would be experienced in so many families. In a creative insight, Freud ultimately came to the conclusion that such reports did not reflect actual events but instead represented fantasies or wish fulfillments.

These observations, along with his knowledge of Greek mythology, led Freud to evolve the concept of the Oedipus and Electra complexes as the essence of the family drama. These terms derive from the names of male and female dramatic personages in two classic tragedies, which are based on

Figure 12.7 Orestes, son of the murdered King Agamemnon, about to slay his mother, Clytemnestra, in revenge. (From The House of Atreus, *John Lewin's translation-adaptation of the* Oresteia *of Aeschylus; directed by Sir Tyrone Guthrie; designed by Tanya Moiseiwitsch; Len Cariou plays Orestes and Douglas Campbell is Clytemnestra in this powerful 1967 production of The Guthrie Theatre in Minneapolis)*

Electra: *Yet hear this last cry, father; look on us as we sit*
Here at your tomb; have pity on your own flesh and blood,
Male and female, through whom alone your race will live.
Orestes: *We are the seed of Pelops; let us not be blotted out.*
You are dead—and yet not dead: still you can live in us.
Electra: *Children preserve alive a dead man's name and fame.*
They are like corks that hold the fisherman's net, and keep
His knotted lines from sinking to the ocean bed.
Orestes: *Our pleas are for your sake. Hear, then, and save yourself.*
Chorus: *Come! You have spoken liberally to discharge all duty,*
Honouring the grave a hard fate left unwept. But now,

ancient Greek legends. Freud theorized that boys of every culture experience the *Oedipus complex** during the phallic stage of psychosexual development; this involves erotic feelings for the mother and hostility toward the father-competitor. Girls were believed by Freud to struggle with a parallel version of the family triangle, often called the *Electra complex,*† in which the father is the love object and the mother the competitor toward whom hostile impulses are generated (Figure 12.7).

The psychosexual conflict of the phallic period is ultimately resolved when the child gives up the opposite-sexed parent as a love object and substitutes a nonparental love object outside the immediate family. This is made necessary in every culture by taboos against incest (sexual relations between sisters and brothers, fathers and daughters, mothers and sons, and other close relatives) that Freud saw as the universal social solution to the destructive primitive mating patterns and intense competitive urges which man has acquired from lower animals. Freud, an avid reader of the literature of ancient myths and legends and of accounts of tribal customs, believed that such taboos prevented murderous strife between fathers and sons and between brothers. Such conflict is recounted in the biblical story of Cain and Abel, or in the Greek myth in which Cronus ate his sons so that they could not grow up to threaten him until one son, Zeus, who had been hidden away until he could grow to manhood, succeeds in attacking him with a scythe and castrating him. Because of the universal taboo against incest, sons were forced to renounce their mothers as sexual objects, and daughters their fathers, thus avoiding murderous competition within the family. Freud proposed that these incestuous urges were retained on an unconscious level (repressed) and that the family triangle was the most important psychosexual crisis that had to be resolved by each person in his or her progress from childhood to adulthood.

The permanent resolution of the family triangle does not actually occur until young adulthood, although the seeds of such resolution are laid within the first three years of life. In the meantime, another stage of psychosexual development, the *latency period,* emerges at about the age of five and continues until puberty. The boy who experiences strongly erotic feelings toward his mother, as in the illustration of Little Hans above, also experiences anxiety because his jealous feelings toward the

*Oedipus slays his father, the king of Thebes, not knowing who he is. Later he saves Thebes by answering the riddle of the Sphinx, a monster who has been plaguing the city (see the Prologue, page 3). The Sphinx is destroyed and Oedipus, now a hero, marries the queen, Jocasta, unaware that she is his mother.
†Electra goads her brother Orestes into killing their mother, Queen Clytemnestra, in revenge for the murder of their father, King Agamemnon.

father seem to place him in jeopardy. He fears that his father will retaliate, specifically by cutting off his penis, the offending organ (castration anxiety). Little girls feel that they have already been deprived of their penis. One temporary solution is for the child to repress his or her erotic and hostile impulses. This occurs during the latency period. It can be observed that girls and boys often seem indifferent and even hostile to each other during this period. By repressing the offending erotic impulses, they are freed of the severe anxiety they have been experiencing over the prospects of castration (in the case of boys) or further punishment by the mother-competitor (in the case of girls). It is at this time too that the major steps in the development of conscience (the superego) take place through the child's identification with the parent of the same sex and the internalization of the moral values of that parent (see Chapter 4).

Erotic concerns reappear strongly in adolescence with the upsurge of physical development and glandular maturation at puberty. The latency period then is ended, and the family triangle emerges once again in full strength, breaking through the earlier repression. It is terminated only when the boy gives up his mother as an erotic love object and freely chooses a girl outside the family. He is then able to retain an affectionate though sexually neutral relationship with his mother, while perhaps making friends with his father, thereby achieving his own independent male identity free of the earlier dependency on his parents' nurturance and support. The girl goes through a comparable process of choosing a new male love object, desexualizing her earlier relationship with the father and eliminating the competitive struggle with the mother. This resolution, if accomplished adequately, is the final step, the *genital stage,* in psychosexual development.

Value of Freudian theory

Seen in its totality, Freudian theory, of which only the broad outlines have been given above, is a very remarkable and comprehensive achievement. This is because it encompasses so many diverse aspects of human personality within a self-consistent framework. Freud introduced a useful personality typology—the oral personality, the anal personality, the phallic personality, and the genital personality. Let us take the first two as illustrations. The psychological traits connected with the oral or the anal stage may be emphasized and retained throughout the person's life as a result of either overindulgence or underindulgence at those stages, producing what Freud called *fixation* at one of the pregenital stages. If the child is overindulged during the oral period and the transition to the next stage does not go well, he may continue thereafter

Seeing your will is bent on action, lose no
   time;
Swiftly to work, and prove the favour of
   Heaven.
Orestes: *I will.*
And yet, it is not idle or dilatory to ask
What made her send forth these libations?
   Why so late
Must she show scruple for a wrong no care
   can cure? . . .
Chorus: *I can tell, son; I was there. It was
   dreams, nightwalking terrors,*
*That frightened the godless woman and
   made her send these gifts.*
Orestes: *Did you ask what the dream was?
   Can you describe it clearly?*
Chorus: *She told us herself. She dreamt that
   she gave birth to a snake.*
Orestes: *What followed? Or was that all? Tell
   me the point of it.*
Chorus: *She wrapped it in shawls and lulled
   it to rest like a little child.*
Orestes: *Surely this new-born monster
   needed food—what food?*
Chorus: *She herself, in her dream, gave it
   her breast to suck.*
Orestes: *Her nipple surely was wounded by
   its loathsome fang?*
Chorus: *Yes; with her milk the creature drew
   forth clots of blood.*
Orestes: *This dream was sent. It came from
   her husband, Agamemnon.*
Chorus: *She screamed out in her sleep, and
   woke in a fit of trembling;*
*And through the palace many lamps, that the
   dark had dimmed,*
*Flared up to reassure her. Immediately she
   sends*
*Libations, hoping to purge this poison at its
   source.*
Orestes: *I pray, then, to this earth that holds
   my father's bones,*
*That the dream's meaning may be thus ful-
   filled in me.*
As I interpret, point by point it fits. Listen:
First, if this snake came forth from the same
   place as I,
And, as though human, was then wrapped
   in infant-clothes,
Its gaping mouth clutching the breast that
   once fed me;
If it then mingled the sweet milk with curds
   of blood,
And made her shriek with terror—why, it
   means that she
Who nursed this obscene beast must die by
   violence;
I must transmute my nature, be viperous in
   heart and act!
The dream commands it: I am her destined
   murderer.

[From Aeschylus, *The Oresteian trilogy* (trans. by P. Vellacott), pp. 121–123. Baltimore, Md.: Penguin, 1956]

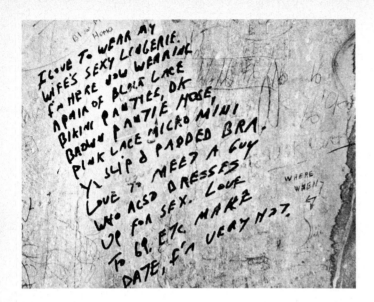

Figure 12.8 An example of anal graffiti (or "latrinalia"), an anonymous underground form of literary expression that is an apt subject for serious psychological study. (Joel Gordon)

The couching of genital affairs in anal terms is paralleled by the whole concept of dirty words in American culture. Dirty jokes, for example, are largely genital, not anal in content. Yet jokes about sex are called "dirty jokes." One reason why genitality is considered to be "dirty" may be guilt by association. The organs concerned are recognized and identified first as producers of urine, that is, as producers of dirt. Later it is discovered that the sexual act is performed by the same dirt-producing instrument. This situation has been summed up by Yeats in his poem "Crazy Jane Talks With the Bishop" when he wrote: "But Love has pitched his mansion in the place of excrement." Here is dirt by association. . . .

For those who may be skeptical of the theory that the psychological motivation for writing latrinalia is related to an infantile desire to play with feces and to artistically smear it around, I would ask only that they offer an alternative theory. For those who doubt that the greater interest on the part of males in latrinalia is related to anal creativity stemming from pregnancy envy, I would ask the same. It is all too easy to elicit destructive criticism. We know that latrinalia exists. What we want to know is why it exists and what function it serves. One day when we have more information about the writers of latrinalia (and perhaps psychological projective tests administered to such writers) and when we have better cross-cultural data, we may be better able to confirm or revise the present attempt to answer the questions. [From Dundes, 1966, pp. 103–104]

to function in oral, self-indulgent ways, thus avoiding the potential trauma connected with being weaned. Or if frustrated (underindulged) in his oral gratification, he may continue to seek the oral gratification of which he was deprived. In so doing he may suck his thumb long after orality should have disappeared or, more importantly, manipulate every social situations so as to obtain succorance from others, perhaps remaining passive-dependent in his interpersonal relationships. Similarly, if the developmental difficulty had centered on the anal period, the child's transition to the phallic stage may be inhibited, and he will continue thereafter to display anal traits, such as stinginess, obstinacy, and meticulousness, thus repeating over and over throughout his life the earlier struggles over his bowel function.

The forms which such oral and anal traits take depend on the attitudes that developed in his relationship with his parents. In orality the alternatives are either trust and reliance in others or mistrust and aggressive suspicion. In anality, obsessive concern with being neat, orderly, clean, and socially proper, on the one hand, or being aggressive and obstinate in rejection of all authority, on the other, are retained in later interpersonal relationships.

Even in normal development we see carry-overs of the pregenital oral and anal stages. Evidence of orality is found in sexual foreplay involving kissing and mouth-genital sexual activity. Anality is revealed in sexual interest in the anal portion of the body, in the ubiquitous anal grafitti found on toilet walls everywhere in the world (see the margin; Dundes, 1966), and in anal ("dirty") jokes or numerous expressions such as "up your ass" (Figure 12.8). There are also interesting cases of misers who have been hoarding cash all their lives but who have squandered money on solid gold toilet seats! (Gold symbolizes feces in Freudian terms as of course does all money.) In its most extreme form, anality becomes the clinical phenomenon of coprophilia, the marked interest in excrement and its use to stimulate sexual excitement.

Other explanations of psychosexual development can no doubt be constructed. However, we have little else in the way of theory that is so rich in its ability to integrate clinical observations, particularly the more exotic normal, neurotic, and psychotic phenomena. This can only be appreciated by reading case material and by examining the raw fantasies expressed by most people in therapy. Against such material much of the usual academic personality theory seems sterile and pallid. In literature we have the imaginary, but not unreal, flow of Leopold Bloom's subjective experience after breakfast as written by James Joyce in his novel *Ulysses* (1961 ed.). In the excerpt presented in the margin, Mr. Bloom's stream of consciousness starts with a reverie stimulated by a letter from his daughter Milly that mentions the attentions some young men are giving her. In this passage, author Joyce connects sex with orality and anality, especially the latter. The desire to defecate flows out of Mr. Bloom's sexual reverie, and is erotic itself in its sensate imagery of resisting and yielding. Of course, Joyce was familiar with psychoanalytic theory, which was very much in the news while he was writing his novel, first published in Paris in 1922. His stream-of-consciousness technique owes much to Freudian "free association."

Freud explained the symptoms of neuroses and psychoses as the result of *regression* to a psychosexual stage of functioning at which there had been major fixation, say at the oral or anal level. Later in life when a person is exposed to major stress and is unable to cope with the adult crisis, he will manage to cope in the way suitable to the earlier, pregenital stage. It is as if there has been a flight from a problem that cannot be managed at a more adult level to an earlier level that is less threatening or demanding. Psychosis involves a serious regression to a very early stage of psychosexual development, for instance, the oral stage in the case of schizophrenia.

This helps make the Freudian analysis of personality development and adaptive failure very thoroughgoing because it encompasses many diverse facets of development and dynamics within the same system: consideration of the type of impulse (to take in at the oral stage, to expel or hold back at the anal, and erotic feelings toward the parent at the phallic); the mode of defense or coping (say, repression or intellectualization); and the symptoms of neurosis or psychosis. It is assumed that at each psychosexual stage, the modes of

---

Seaside girls. Torn envelope. Hands stuck in his trouser's pockets. . . . singing.

> *Those girls, those girls,*
> *Those lovely seaside girls*

Milly too. Young kisses: the first. . . . Mrs. Marion (Bloom). Reading lying back now, counting the strands of her hair, smiling, braiding.
  A soft qualm regret, flowed down his backbone, increasing. Will happen, yes. Prevent. Useless: can't move. Girl's sweet tight lips. Will happen too. He felt the flowing qualm spread over him. Useless to move now. Lips kissed, kissing, kissed. Full gluey women's lips.

  . . .

  The cat, having cleaned all her fur . . . stalked to the door. . . . Wants to go out. . . .
  He felt heavy, full: then a gentle loosening of his bowels. He stood up. . . .
  A paper. He liked to read at stool. Hope no ape comes knocking just as I'm.
  He kicked open the crazy door of the jakes. . . . The king was in his counting house. . . .
  Asquat on the cukstool he folded out his paper turning its pages over on his bared knees. . . . No great hurry. Keep it a bit. . . .
  Quietly he read, restraining himself, the first column and, yielding but resisting, began the second. Midway, his last resistance yielding, he allowed his bowels to ease themselves quietly as he read, reading still patiently. . . . Hope it's not too big bring on piles again. No, just right. So. Ah! . . . He reads on, seated calm above his own rising smell. [From James Joyce, *Ulysses*, pp. 67–69. New York: Modern Library, 1961 ed.]

Jymes wishes to hear from wearers of abandoned female costumes, gratefully received, wadmel jumper, rather full pair of culottes and onthergarmenteries, to start city life together. His jymes is out of job, would sit and write. He has lately commited one of the then commandments but she will now assist. Superior built, domestic, regular layer. Also got the boot. He appreciates it. Copies. ABORTISEMENT. [From James Joyce, *Finnegans wake*, p. 181. New York: Viking, 1939; see also W. Y. Tindall, *James Joyce: His way of interpreting the modern world.* New York: Scribner's, 1950]

thinking characteristic of the child will differ. Therefore, if major difficulties arise at any given stage, the way in which the child is likely to cope will be determined by the repertoire of coping mechanisms and ways of thinking characteristic of that stage, and this in turn will determine the symptoms of psychopathology. It is little wonder that this analysis has had such a major impact on clinical thought, although these logical virtues do not guarantee validity of the analysis. The theory must be evaluated as to how it accords with the facts, based on observations still being made, and how useful it is in getting us to further knowledge.

Criticisms of Freudian theory

Freud's theory of personality has been criticized on a variety of grounds, with varying complaints leveled at one or another portion of the total system. Thus, of all the portions, the psychosexual theory has been the most controversial. Indeed, a large literature has grown up on criticisms and answers to them. Below are some of the main problems that have been identified in Freudian thought.

1. People are usually mixtures of many influences, so that clinically one does not usually see pure types such as the hysteric, paranoid, or obsessive-compulsive. By the same token, there is little hard evidence that a given type of crisis occurring at a particular period in life is necessarily associated with a given form of defense or pattern of neurotic symptoms. Although in practice a Freudian therapist is likely to look for an oedipal conflict in a case of conversion hysteria, an anal conflict in an obsessive-aggressive patient, or a conflict of orality (dependency and trust) in a schizophrenic, the pattern in any given case is likely to be very mixed and confused, and the clinician must remain flexible in the way he integrates the evidence. The theoretical system just sketched out, though an extraordinary conceptual tour de force, is a bit too neat in the face of all the confusion of observation and divergent data. It is a theory, and like all theories it is only an *idealized approximation of reality,* one that will probably give way to new conceptualizations as we learn more. One has to say at present that the psychosexual theory is one of several formulations of human psychological development, none of which are yet conclusively established by solid clinical or experimental evidence.

2. Less attention has been given in Freudian writings to the *modes of thinking* characteristic of the various stages than to the biological (instinctual) urges which the child and the society must manage. While Freudians focus on the motives or, more correctly, the instinctual drives powering the child's functioning, as well as the emotions (like anxiety, anger, de-

pression) which accompany their blockage or frustration, they have not spelled out too well the modes of thinking characteristics of the various stages of development. Thus, although in life thinking and feeling are intimately connected in any reaction, Freud has given us a system of formal development mainly centered on the latter.

Recall if you will Jean Piaget's theory of cognitive development reviewed in Chapter 2. Piaget's focus was exclusively placed on how conceptual thought develops out of sensorimotor thought, though like Freud he approached the problem from the standpoint of the stages through which an individual passes. But Piaget concerns himself little with the motivational and emotional processes of life or their consequences for adaptive success and failure. On the other hand, Freud centered his attention on the motivational and emotional aspects of mental life and on the things that can go wrong, and he gave less attention to the cognitive or intellectual, though he did not ignore these completely since they were primary activities of the ego. Later psychoanalytic theorists (see Hartmann, 1958, 1964; Holt, 1967), often called "ego psychologists," have given more attention to the cognitive sphere.

3. We do not know enough about the *conditions under which fixation and regression* occur or under which people learn to cope with their problems or fail in their adaptive efforts. Knowledge of such details is needed in order to make sound recommendations about child rearing as well as the prevention and treatment of mental disorder.

4. One of the earliest criticisms of Freud's psychosexual theory was that it emphasized too strongly a *biological view* of man's psychological development. For Freud, whose medical training was in neurology, the psychosexual stages were thought to be guided largely by biological forces unfolding in essentially the same sequence regardless of the culture to which the person was exposed. The developmental pattern could be blocked or interfered with by traumatic events, even distorted in pathological directions, but its normal and proper pattern and direction was thought to be universal (often referred to as "epigenetic"), as is development of the embryo. The direction and sequence had the status of a biological law. Variations in personality had to be understood mainly through the manner in which the parents, representing the culture, responded to the child at each successive stage. In the 1930s and 1940s much research was done on the psychological effects of various child-rearing practices: breast versus bottle feeding; early or late weaning; rigid versus relaxed toilet training; the handling of masturbation; and so on. Many of these studies were in response to Freud's psychosexual theory.

Numerous writers, however, have challenged the idea that orality, anality, or the problems of the phallic stage are the result of biological pressures. These writers, often psycho-analysts who had originally worked with Freud or at least had been strongly influenced by Freudian thought, argued either that the psychosexual stages were mythical (or less important than Freud saw them to be) or that they were the product of particular social experiences rather than of biological disposisions. These critics have been called neo-Freudians.

5. Still other critics point out that in the main Freud and later psychoanalytic writers have tended to base their analyses of man's mental activity too much on patients who were suffering from adaptive failure rather than on persons whose functioning was adequate or even outstanding. The *unrepresentativeness* of the sample of persons seen by depth-oriented therapists is a natural outgrowth of the fact they build their clinical evidence out of observations of people in trouble who come to them for help. Freud believed that one could extrapolate from such clinical evidence to the normal person, and to some extent this was probably correct, but in doing so he may have overstated the importance of certain tendencies in neurotic patients that are less signficant in the healthy person. Since we have few intensive studies of healthy people, it is difficult to say whether the processes seen in patients are typical and central or atypical and secondary in importance.

6. In obtaining the clinical observations on which the theory is based, the clinician-theorist is a lone observer whose observations are to some extent subject to his own biases. There is usually no one available to check the *objectivity of the conclusions,* or even the observations on which they are based, particularly when the interviews on which the conclusions are based are not recorded on tape or by film (see the discussion of reliability in Chapter 11). Thus, Freudian theory, for all its fascination and seeming sensibility, always carries this disturbing question: To what extent are these data a reflection of one man's (or one group's, the Freudians) biased observation and interpretation? And because of the nature of the theory, depending as it does on subjective inferences about inner mental events, it has proven very difficult to test in empirical studies.

7. Another criticism of Freud's analysis of personality development is that it *overemphasized the sexual drive.* In a masterful critique, Robert White (1960) argued that even more important than sexuality for personality development is what he calls the drive of "effectance," that is, wanting to have an effect on the environment, to make a ripple, so to speak. White believes this is just as innate as any bodily drive such as sex, hunger, or thirst. Competence develops because babies also have the need to understand and manipulate the environment, and they will do so without reference to these other drives. About this White writes (1960, p. 102):

(a)

(b)

Figure 12.9 (a) The struggle for competence—with the spoon. (b) Jean Piaget, that keen observer of children (see Chapter 2), would no doubt agree with Robert White's critique of the overemphasis on sexual drive in Freudian theory of personality development. (a: Censer; Monkmeyer Press Photo Service; b: Jean-Pierre Landenberg; courtesy of Dr. Jean Piaget)

The theory that we learn what helps us to reduce our viscerogenic [innate] drives will not stand up if we stop to consider the whole range of what a child must learn in order to deal effectively with his surroundings. He has much to learn about visual forms, about grasping and letting go, about the coordination of hand and eye. He must work out the difficult problem of the constancy of objects. . . . He must learn many facts about his world, building up a cognitive map that will afford guidance and structure for his behavior. It is not hard to see the biological advantage of an arrangement whereby these many learnings can get underway before they are needed as instruments for drive reduction or for safety. An animal that has thoroughly explored its environment stands a better chance of escaping from a sudden enemy or satisfying a gnawing hunger than one that merely dozes in the sun when its homeostatic crises are past. Seen in this light, the many hours that infants and children spend in play are by no means wasted or merely recuperative in nature. Play may be fun, but it is also a serious business in childhood. During these hours the child steadily builds up his competence in dealing with the environment.

White proceeds to document his critique with a reanalysis of the various periods of psychosexual development, oral, anal, and phallic. In discussing the oral period, for instance, White points out that although much of the child's behavior is centered about the mouth, and although he takes a great deal of pleasure in sucking, feeding, mouthing, and receiving things through his mouth, he displays a lot of other behavior that does not fit well into the idea of direct oral gratification (Figure 12.9). White states this as follows (1960, p. 110):

For one thing there are clear signs that additional entertainment is desired during a meal. The utensils are investigated, the behavior of spilled food is explored, toys are played with throughout the feeding. Gesell suggests that at one year of age a toy in each hand is the only guarantee that a meal will be completed without housekeeping disaster. A similar situation prevails during the bath, when water toys are needed and when the germ of scientific interest may express itself by "dabbling water onto the floor from the washcloth." More important, however, is the infant's growing enthusiasm for the doctrine of "do it yourself". . . . Around one year there is likely to occur what . . . [is called] . . . "the battle of the spoon," the moment "when the baby grabs the spoon from the mother's hand and tries to feed itself." From Gesell's painstaking description of the spoon's "hazardous journey" from dish to mouth we can be sure that the child is not motivated at this point by increased oral gratification. He gets more food by letting mother do it, but by doing it himself he gets more of another kind of satisfaction—a feeling of efficacy, and perhaps already a growth of the sense of competence.

Freud's ideas on mental health

Having examined the essentials of the Freudian theory of personality and its development, we are now in a position to consider how Freud and other psychoanalytic spokesmen regard the healthy personality, and then turn to other viewpoints which either rest in part on Freud's thinking (the neo-Freudians) or use it as a counterpoint for proposing contrasting outlooks. Actually, Freud never wrote much about the healthy personality, as such, although he did of course make some oblique comments about it, and other Freudian thinkers such as Erik Erikson have given special attention to this question, building their analysis out of the Freudian theory of psychopathology.

It is said that Freud was once asked what a normal person should be able to do that a neurotic could not, and he is supposed to have replied, *"Lieben und arbeiten"* ("Love and work"). This epigrammatic statement has meant different things to different writers. The main point, however, is that a healthy person is capable of making a balanced commitment to both love and work, while a neurotic cannot.

For the Freudian, the epitome of health is expressed in the concept of the "genital character" (Abraham, 1949; Jones, 1942), which is the culmination of the series of earlier, more immature stages of psychosexual development that we considered earlier. Here, psychosexual maturity involves not only the actual somatic component of sexual activity, the pleasurable stimulation of erogenous (readily excitable) zones, but also the adult attitudes a person has toward such sexual activity and the mature relations which he or she has with the beloved.

The healthy person is one who has passed successfully through each of the earlier stages on his way to mature genital

I am reminded at this joyous little juncture of when we lived in Jersey City, back when I was still very much my mother's papoose, still very much a sniffer of her body perfumes and a total slave to her kugel and grieben and ruggelech—there was a suicide in our building. A fifteen-year-old boy named Ronald Nimkin, who had been crowned by the women in the building "José Iturbi the Second," hanged himself from the shower head in his bathroom. "With those golden hands!" the women wailed, referring of course to his piano playing—"With that talent!" Followed by, "You couldn't look for a boy more in love with his mother than Ronald!" [From Philip Roth, Portnoy's Complaint, pp. 96–97. New York: Random House, 1969]

sexuality. At the immature phallic stage the quality of his relationships is demanding, selfish, and tumultous. If he (or she) remains hung-up at the phallic stage he will be unable to abandon his original (oedipal) attachment to his mother (or the girl, to her father). He will find it hard to form adult heterosexual love relationships, and if he gets married, he may still be more responsive to his mother than to his wife. The mother-son theme has long been popular in American literature, both serious and comic. Philip Roth's *Portnoy's Complaint* is a hilarious example (see p. 576). Likewise, the girl still in the throes of the Electra complex will find no one who can compare with her father as an object of admiration and love.

In Freud's system, then, to achieve balance and psychological health the person must pass beyond the phallic stage with its conflicts to the mature genital stage. Such a person has a strong controlling ego; he has the capacity and the will to moderate his impulses and to discharge or gratify these impulses successfully in socially acceptable ways. He is not tyrannized over by his animal urges, yet he is capable of releasing and enjoying them when appropriate. In short, he is rational in thought and action yet capable of freedom of expression and deep emotion. A person with such an ego is in full command of himself, with the power and flexibility either to suppress feelings or let them go, and he is not threatened by his emotions. Thus, along with rationality, the healthy person in the Freudian scheme is also capable of richer emotional experience than the neurotic person, whose weak ego is constantly struggling to keep control of threatening infantile urges (see Note 12.2).

The notion that the healthy personality is capable of acknowledging, accepting, and using impulses rather than being threatened by them is quite important, as we shall see, in many views of mental health. It is the basic conceptual underpinning of the idea in modern therapy and encounter groups that to manage his life effectively a person needs to get in touch with his inner feelings, those that are most often suppressed in ordinary social intercourse. Barron (1963, pp. 223–224) has expressed this theme beautifully in the following passage on human creativity:

The effectively original person may be characterized above all by an ability to regress very far *for the moment* while being able quite rapidly to return to a high degree of rationality, bringing with him the fruits of his regression to primitive and fantastic modes of thought. . . . Perhaps when the cortex is most efficient, or intelligence greatest, the ego realizes that it *can afford to allow regression—* because it can correct itself. A basic confidence in one's ability to discern reality accurately would thus facilitate the use of the powers of imagination.

In such an individual there might therefore occur some transitory

Note 12.2

One of the important implications of Freud's view about sexuality is that disturbances of sexual activity need not necessarily be regarded as a primary problem but rather as a symptom of an interpersonal difficulty. Sexual problems such as impotence and frigidity are indeed sources of frustration and contribute to marital difficulties. Homosexuality is linked to numerous other interpersonal problems: fear based on parental injunctions and social taboos, lack of interpersonal trust, absence of affection in childhood, disturbed parental identification, failure to resolve oedipal difficulties, and so on. Heterosexual problems often point to something else even more fundamental, namely, inability to establish intimacy with someone, a problem that presumably enters into every area of human relationships.

It has been found that monkeys who have been deprived of normal mothering and of peer contacts and peer play later fail to achieve successful copulation (Harlow, 1971). It is not merely their sexual activity that has been impaired, but the entire pattern of their social and affectional relationships. Similarly, in men and women, sexual activity is part of a much broader range of human behavior that we group under the sweeping (and oft-misused) term "love." When the ability to love is disturbed, this will frequently express itself in disturbance of sexuality.

Notice that from this standpoint the treatment of such difficulties might have to go beyond concern merely with technique, a view that runs counter to the present-day preoccupation with "how-to-do-it" manuals on sexual activity. This is not to say that such manuals have no utility for those with the normal capacity to love, but rather that they often suggest that sex is merely a skill rather than also being an intimate human relationship. This relationship requires sensitive awareness of another person's feelings and needs, desire to provide pleasure to another, and capacity to immerse oneself in the sexual experience. Of all the things two people do together, none is dependent on a broader constellation of human involvement than is sex. It can, therefore, be regarded as the bellwether of an individual's psychic health.

phenomena of the sort that in truly pathological form are characteristic of the very weak ego (such as hallucinations, sense of oneness with the universe, visions, mystical beliefs, superstitions . . .). But in the highly creative individual the basis for these phenomena is precisely the opposite of their basis in mentally ill individuals. . . . Thus, the creative genius may be at once naive and knowledgeable, being at home equally to primitive symbolism and to rigorous logic. He is both more primitive and more cultured, more destructive and more constructive, occasionally crazier and yet adamantly saner, than the average person.

The quality of the sexual experience was, for Freud, one clinical sign of health or pathology, since he presumed that neuroticism crippled the ability to function adequately in sex. Genital love refers not merely to its sensual side, although that is certainly part of it, but also to its altruistic side. Healthy genital love for Freud also meant generosity in the relationship, intimacy, mutual trust, and gratification. At the same time, the healthy personality is also capable of involving himself in productive contributions to the community, giving meaning to life and providing a sense of personal worth. Such work should not be all-consuming, however. Balanced expression, in short, is given to both libido and labor. Psychopathology, for Freud, was thus the opposite of health, that is, a crippled capacity to love and work.

In extending and elaborating the Freudian analysis of psychosexual development, Erikson did not quarrel with Freud's basic analysis, but he pointed out another major psychological task of life during adolescence and youth, namely, to determine who one is biologically and socially, to establish and consolidate a mature social role, to define one's *ego identity* in the world. Erikson (1951, p. 9) wrote (italics added):

The central problem [of adolescence] is the establishment of a sense of self-identity. The identity the adolescent seeks to clarify is *who he is,* what his role in society is to be. Is he a child or is he an adult? Does he have it in him to be someday a husband and father? What is he to be as a worker and an earner of money? Can he feel self-confident in spite of the fact that his race or religious or national background makes him a person some people look down upon? Overall, will he be a success or a failure? By reason of these questions adolescents are sometimes morbidly preoccupied with how they appear in the eyes of others as compared with their own conception of themselves, and with how they can make the rules and skills learned earlier jibe with what is currently in style. . . .

The danger of this developmental period is self-diffusion. As Biff puts it in *Death of a Salesman,* "I just can't take hold. I can't take hold of some kind of life." A boy or girl can scarcely help feeling somewhat diffuse when the body changes in size and shape so rapidly, when genital maturity floods body and imagination with forbidden desires, when adult life lies ahead with such a diversity of conflicting possibilities and choices.

Every young person must one day grapple with the issue of who and what he is. LSD [lysergic acid diethylamide] offers some the illusion of choice in the discovery of truth. For the college student free of parents for perhaps the first time, LSD suggests a quick chemical answer to this quest for identity. LSD may appeal to the user for other reasons. Its use is illegal, secretive, "in," and antiadult. The movement has its own language to distinguish the "ins" from the "outs" and to bar those over thirty from initiation into its secret rites.

The acid scene is one in which the user can "freak freely" either alone or with fellow cultists. While "making or digging the scene" he feels for perhaps the first time in his life a sense of true belonging and acceptance by others. He has achieved the ultimate in snobbery, a feeling of superiority, and the freedom to express prejudice—the world is nicely divided into two camps, one containing the square majority and the other peopled by the hip minority. [From McNeil, 1967, p. 118]

Erikson also proposed further stages beyond the genital that the person must reach to be a psychologically healthy person, these following closely on the heels of the struggle for ego identity. One is to accept and be capable of "intimacy" with another person; another is willingness to invest oneself in the continuity of human life by being ready to take responsibility, say, for the well-being of one's children, or of one's students, or of posterity in the abstract; Erikson called this stage "generativity."

In this way Erikson, essentially a Freudian in approach, has provided a list of qualities or traits to index pathological personality patterns, on the one hand, and healthy ones, on the other. On the pathological side, there are possible unhealthy outcomes at each stage of psychosexual development: mistrust (oral), shame and doubt (anal), guilt (phallic), and three others of youth and early adulthood—confusion as to role, lack of personal intimacy, and excessive selfishness. On the side of health, the developmental sequence is as follows: trust (oral), autonomy (anal), initiative (phallic), and later ego identity, intimacy, and generativity.

THE NEO-FREUDIANS

In the early days of psychoanalysis, in Vienna before World War I, Freud collected around him a small group of men of various professional backgrounds, who were interested in his theory of personality and who not only participated in discussions about this but also made significant contributions to psychoanalytic principles. Among these men were Carl Jung, Otto Rank, and Alfred Adler, each of whom later became critical of certain of Freud's views and separated from the group to evolve theories of their own.

To this list of dissidents from orthodox psychoanalytic thought were later added others who had been originally trained in psychoanalysis but who evolved theoretical variations of their own. These latter include Karen Horney and Erich Fromm. Although these neo-Freudian theories vary greatly in detail and vocabulary, they also have certain things in common. All depart from the Freudian emphasis on biological universals, and instead regard social forces as paramount in psychological development. Thus, these views have generally deemphasized the sexual aspects of development considered so basic by Freud.

Jung (1953), an influential Swiss psychiatrist, pointed out that around middle age the individual is no longer governed to the same extent by imperious sexual and aggressive drives but increasingly seeks to find a measure of meaning in his life,

The extraverted tendency of the West and the introverted tendency of the East have one important purpose in common: both make desperate efforts to conquer the mere naturalness of life. It is the assertion of mind over matter, the opus contra naturam, a symptom of the youthfulness of man, still delighting in the use of the most powerful weapon ever devised by nature: the conscious mind. The afternoon of humanity, in a distant future, may yet evolve a different ideal. In time, even conquest will cease to be the dream. [From Jung, 1954, p. xlix]

Figure 12.10   Dr. Erich Fromm. (Bender, New York; courtesy of Doubleday & Company)

Figure 12.11   Power of the mass. (a) Adolf Hitler being hailed by giant throngs at Tempelhof Airport, Berlin, where he delivered a speech on Germany's National Labor Day, May 1, 1935. (b) One of the gigantic Nuremberg Nazi Party rallies; the spectacular lighting effects were dubbed a "cathedral of ice." (c) A crowd of 200,000 gathers for the Jesus Music Festival, part of Explo 72, held in Dallas, Texas. (a,c: Wide World Photos; b: copyright by Zeitgeschichtliches Bildarchiv; Heinrich Hoffman)

to determine his place in the cosmos, and to deal with the problem of death. Jung felt that Freud failed to recognize the importance of this and many other issues in the psychological concerns of the mature person and that he also overemphasized the importance of the first few years of life at the expense of the continuing quest for meaning and harmony throughout life.

Adler, a Viennese physician, emphasized, on the other hand, the helplessness of the child and the consequent tendency to compensate for this neurotically by striving for power (see Ansbacher and Ansbacher, 1956). He also introduced a new idea, which others have since developed, that man has an inherent tendency to seek perfection in the union with others; that social feeling (kinship with others, love rather than competition, cooperativeness and unselfishness) is a basic human quality whose pursuit, in place of the neurotic striving for power, is the only way man can achieve psychic health.

Despite these and other variations, the primary theme shared by neo-Freudians is that the problems of human adaptation arise from the relationship each person has with the social environment. For this reason they are often designated as socially rather than biologically oriented personality theorists. One of the major neo-Freudians is Erich Fromm, who has written extensively and whose ideas epitomize this point of view. We will let his views illustrate the neo-Freudian approach instead of presenting a welter of closely related modes of thought that might easily confuse the unfamiliar reader.

Fromm received his doctorate at Heidelberg University

(a)

(b)

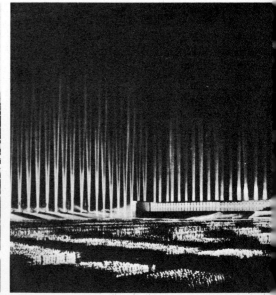

in 1922 and was initially trained in Freudian psychoanalysis in Europe, later practicing in Chicago, where he came to lecture. He then established a psychoanalytic practice in New York, and ultimately became head of the Mexican Psychoanalytic Institute in Mexico City, where he remains today (Figure 12.10). His earliest well-known book, *Escape from Freedom* (1941), clearly deviated from the Freudian biological, psychosexual emphasis by focusing on the role of society in shaping personality development. Here, Fromm maintained that the child grows apart from his family as he develops, and as such becomes less dependent and more capable of expressing his own individuality. This movement toward individuality and freedom, however, also confronts each of us with a basic dilemma: as we lose some of our dependence on others and learn to stand alone, we feel increasingly exposed, isolated, and lonely. Thus, the new-found independence is frightening as well as potentially gratifying, a conflict that Fromm regarded as distinctively human. One way that many people have of avoiding this sense of isolation and loneliness is an "escape from freedom," a submission to absolute authority. Such a solution has been common throughout history: men have sought to avoid accepting the fact of their relative insignificance in the cosmos by total subjection of their will to an all-powerful deity. Such a solution, says Fromm, has not been altogether satisfactory because religious commitments tend to become formalistic, lose their conviction, and ultimately fail to provide the security that is craved (Figure 12.11). Another solution is submission to a totalitarian state, as when in the

(c)

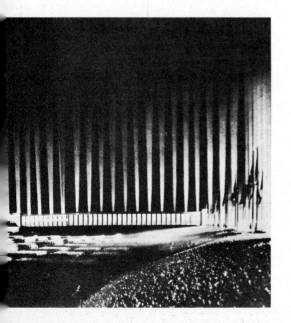

Alienation of thought is not different from alienation of the heart. Often one believes he has thought through someting, that his idea is the result of his own thinking activity; the fact is that he has transferred his brain to the idols of public opinion, the newspapers, the government or a political leader. He believes that they express his thoughts while in reality he accepts their thoughts as his own, because he has chosen them as his idols, his gods of wisdom and knowledge. Precisely for this reason he is dependent on his idols and incapable of giving up his worship. He is their slave because he has deposited his brain with them. [From Fromm, 1963, p. 55]

economic crisis of the 1930s the German people accepted a Fuehrer and in effect subjected themselves to him.

In Fromm's view, no society has ever been evolved by man that provides adequate means of resolving the fundamental conflict between man's need for security and his need to be an individual. In authoritarian societies, man can feel more or less secure in conformity to the rules and standards, but he thereby loses his individuality. In democracies, there is only the *illusion* of individuality and freedom, since enormous social pressures to conform tend to destroy the individual's spontaneity and uniqueness. Man needs to create a new form of society that enables him to fulfill both these needs. Only then will he realize his full potential and develop into a truly integrated personality.

In later writings (1947, 1955) Fromm continued this theme. Unlike Freud, he did not consider animal instincts to be of primary importance, but instead regarded social needs as paramount in shaping man's life. These give man his distinctly human nature (as distinguished from animal nature). Among the most important human needs were the following: the need to *belong*, that is, to feel a part of the group; the need for *transcendance*, in effect, to become a creative person who rises above his animal nature; the need for *identity*, to feel oneself a unique individual; the need for a *frame of reference*, a stable and consistent way of perceiving and understanding the world in which one lives. In his recent writings Fromm has remained optimistic that a society will ultimately be achieved in which all these requirements can be fulfilled and in which the seemingly contradictory needs both to belong and to be independent are successfully integrated.

For Fromm, the psychologically healthy person is free to pursue his human nature rather than shrinking from it, and as such he maintains his individuality rather than conforming to social pressure; he is productive in his way of life, using his creative powers to make a constructive contribution to the society in which he lives as long as that society is itself a sane or constructive one. Societies that are authoritarian or repressive render it difficult or even impossible for people living within them to be fully human, in these terms, and therefore such societies lead to pathological results. While Freud had assumed that society most often served as a constructive force in controlling man's animal nature, a force that incidentally could not be avoided or transcended except through modification (or "sublimation") of the animal instincts, Fromm sees society as often at fault when man's behavior turns in pathological directions. If children are permitted to grow up in an atmosphere where they can express their humanity creatively and fully, they can move toward a world where cooperation and love, rather than hate and violence, predominate. How this can be arranged, of course, is still a totally unresolved question. In any event, says Fromm (1956), everyone of us, each in his own small sphere, should learn to practice the art of loving.

OTHER APPROACHES TO MENTAL WELL-BEING

There are a number of other approaches to mental health that draw upon many of the seminal ideas originating with Freud and the neo-Freudians but which do not regard it as merely the opposite of pathology. Rather, they emphasize mental health as a singular positive achievement leading to a number of desirable personality traits, some of which were not emphasized by Freud and his followers, or by the neo-Freudians. The writings of Marie Jahoda (1950, 1958) represent one influential example. Jahoda, without attempting to develop a distinctive theory of personality, presented a valuable summation of major criteria of health that is, in the main, a distillate of the best general ideas of depth psychology.

For Jahoda, one of the major hallmarks of the healthy personality is a *positive and realistic outlook toward oneself,* as opposed to a negative and distorted self-image; such a person has accessibility to his own inner life and is not afraid of his impulses. He has an *accurate perception* of external reality even when he is in conflict with the cultural values of the society in which he lives. The healthy person is *capable of continuous growth and development* and moves throughout his life toward the fuller actualization of his potentialities as an individual. Instead of being stuck in childish modes of thought and reaction, he reaches out for new experience and utilizes this experience in his growth. The healthy person displays a *harmonious balance of psychological* forces rather than an exaggerated emphasis on a single quality. He is integrated rather than fractionated, with a consistent outlook on life and a clear sense of ethical direction. Such a person is *autonomous* rather than conformist, and he is not afraid of standing out from the crowd. And, finally, the healthy person is *competent* to cope with his environment.

Notice that in this characterization of mental health some of the traits clearly arise directly from Freudian modes of thought, for example, the goals of seeing oneself and one's impulses clearly, of discerning external reality accurately, and of being integrated rather than at war with oneself. Other qualities, such as positive self-regard, continuous development, and competence to master the environment, while not inconsistent with Freudian ideas, represent somewhat new emphases. The focus on continuous personal growth and openness to experience seems more in keeping with Fromm's lines of thought, as well as of the humanistic-existential movement (see Chapter 11). The emphasis on competence resonates well with Robert White's critique (1960) of Freud, discussed earlier. Thus, in defining mental health Jahoda brings together a number of diverse values derived from several theoretical perspectives about personality dynamics. Her formulation has the virtue of spelling out specific criteria of health more explicitly than previous writers have done, although it is not often clear how these criteria are expressed in concrete behavior and patterns of living.

Overlapping substantially with Jahoda's portrait of the healthy personality are a set of criteria described by Abraham Maslow (1968, 1970), although he has added some other qualities to the list (Figure 12.12). Maslow's analysis of the healthy personality is part of a more general view in which the primary motivating force is "growth" and "self-actualization": he proposed that a person is willing to experience pain to achieve self-actualization or fulfillment because the urge to grow is very strong in all of us. Thus, although the adolescent may feel apprehensive about leaving the protection of the parental home and venturing forth on his own, he nevertheless exhibits a strong urge to seek independence and autonomy. Rather than remaining secure in a child's role, given half a chance he will strive toward self-actualization. Of course, the precise way this is accomplished varies depending on his resources and circumstances.

An interesting feature of Maslow's thinking is the assumption that certain needs are more primitive than others in that they have to do with survival and are shared by all animals, while others seem to have emerged only in higher animals, late in the course of evolution. Physiological needs such as hunger, thirst, and sex, for example, are fundamental and predominate over all others; that is, they are more vital and must be gratified. Needs for security are next in urgency, followed by needs for love, esteem, and finally the highest need is for self-actualization, that is, the realization of one's own individual potential. These latter are less critical for survival, more fragile, and more easily suppressed. There is thus a "hierarchy of needs," ascending from those involving vital physiological requirements to those related to psychological well-being and artistic self-expression. It is only the latter which express the unique qualities of man and which are often suppressed by destructive social environments that keep him in a continual state of insecurity and deprivation.

For Maslow then, mental health is synonymous with self-actualization, and he recognized the need to specify more clearly the traits expressing or defining it. Through biographical material he picked out a number of well-known

Figure 12.12   Dr. Abraham H. Maslow. (Courtesy of Bertha G. Maslow)

public and historical figures as well as contemporaries whom he felt represented self-actualizers. He evaluated their lives, their use of their talents, and the absence of what he regarded as pathological trends. Some of the well-known figures he chose as self-actualizers included Abraham Lincoln, Thomas Jefferson, Henry David Thoreau, Ludwig van Beethoven, Walt Whitman, Albert Einstein, Eleanor Roosevelt, and William James. After he made a study of their lives, Maslow tried to draw up a composite picture of their personalities, emerging with a list of traits characterizing self-actualizing people. The list was a mixture of his own preferences and values as expressed in people he admired:

1. Efficient perception of reality and comfortable relations with it
2. Acceptance of other people, of oneself, and of nature, for what they are
3. Spontaneity in one's inner life, thoughts, impulses
4. Being problem-centered rather than self-centered
5. Having the quality of detachment and the need for privacy
6. Achieving autonomy and independence from the culture and environment in which one lives
7. Freshness of appreciation; the ability to enjoy and appreciate things throughout life in new rather than stereotyped ways
8. Capacity to have profound mystical or spiritual experiences, although not necessarily of a religious nature
9. Identification with mankind, with sympathy and affection for people (what Alfred Adler called "social feeling")
10. Capacity for deeply emotional and intimate relationships with another (or others)
11. Having democratic (rather than authoritarian) values and attitudes
12. Being unconfused about the distinction between ends and means
13. Having a sense of humor that is philosophical rather than hostile
14. Creativity
15. Capacity to resist pressures to conform to the culture

A brief examination of this list shows that items 1, 2, 4, 6, 9, 10, and 15 are essentially contained within Jahoda's criteria, although the exact terms used are sometimes different. In the main Jahoda's and Maslow's views of psychological health have a great deal in common, and they overlap also with those of some writers touched on earlier.

In the years before his death in 1970, Maslow had also become extremely interested in what he called "peak experi-

As I lay with my head in your lap, camerado,
The confession I made I resume, what I said to you and the open air I resume,
I know I am restless and make others so,
I know my words are weapons full of danger, full of death,
For I confront peace, security, and all the settled laws, to unsettle them,
I am more resolute because all have denied me than I could ever have been had all accepted me,
I heed not and have never heeded either experience, cautions, majorities, nor ridicule,
And the threat of what is call'd hell is little or nothing to me,
And the lure of what is call'd heaven is little or nothing to me;
Dear camerado! I confess I have urged you onward with me, and still urge you, without the least idea what is our destination,
Or whether we shall be victorious, or utterly quell'd and defeated.

[From Walt Whitman, *Leaves of grass*, pp. 363–364. New York: Modern Library, 1921]

Monticello Jan. 8. [1825]

Dear Sir
It is long since I have written to you. This proceeds from the difficulty of writing with my crippled wrists, and from an unwillingness to add to your inconveniences of either reading by the eyes, or writing by the hands of others. The account I receive of your physical situation afflicts me sincerely. But if body or mind was one of them to give way, it is a great comfort that it is the mind which remains whole, and that it's vigor, and that of memory, continues firm. Your hearing too is good as I am told. In this you have the advantage of me. The dullness of mine makes me lose much of the conversation of the world, and much a stranger to what is passing in it. Acquiescence is the only pillow, altho' not always a soft one. . . . I am comforted and protected from other solicitudes by the cares of our University [the new University of Virginia]. In some departments of science we believed Europe to be in advance before us, and thought it would advance ourselves were we to draw thence instructors

in these branches, and thus to improve our science, as we have done our manufactures, by borrowed skill. . . .

I have lately been reading the most extraordinary of all books, and at the same time the most demonstrative by numerous and unequivocal facts. It is Flourens' Experiments on the functions of the Nervous system, in vertebrated animals. He takes out the cerebrum compleatly, leaving the cerebellum and other parts of the system uninjured. The animal loses all it's senses of hearing, seeing, feeling, smelling, tasting, is totally deprived of will, intelligence, memory, perception etc. yet lives for months in perfect health, with all it's powers of motion, but without moving but on external excitement, starving even on a pile of grain unless crammed down it's throat; in a state, in short, of the most absolute stupidity. He takes the cerebellum out of others, leaving the cerebrum untouched. The animal retains all it's senses, faculties and understanding, but loses the power of regulated motion, and exhibits all the symptoms of drunkenness. While he makes incisions in the cerebrum and cerebellum, lengthwise and crosswise which heal and get well, a puncture in the medulla elongata is instant death, and many other most interesting things, too long for a letter. Cabanis had proved, from the anatomical structure of certain portions of the human frame, that they might be capable of receiving from the Creator the faculty of thinking. Flourens proves that the cerebrum is the thinking organ, and that life and health may continue, and the animal be entirely without thought, if deprived of that organ. I wish to see what the spiritualists will say to this. Whether, in this state, the soul remains in the body deprived of it's essence of thought, or whether it leaves it as in death, and where it goes? His memoirs and experiments have been reported on with approbation by a committee of the Institute, composed of Cuvier, Bertholet, Dumeril, Portal and Pinel. But all this you and I shall know, when we meet again in another place, and at no distant period. In the mean time, that the revived powers of your frame, and the Anodyne of philosophy may preserve you from all suffering, is my sincere and affectionate prayer.   [T.J.]

[Letter from Thomas Jefferson, age 82, to John Adams, age 90, in *The Adams–Jefferson Letters* (L. J. Cappon, ed.), pp. 605–606. Chapel Hill, N.C.: Univ. of North Carolina Press, 1959; both men died the following year on the same day, July 4, 1826, the fiftieth anniversary of the Declaration of Independence]

ences," immediate, short-lived, and effortless moments of exhilaration in which the person feels a strong sense of well-being, fulfillment, and perfection. He sought to pin down the nature of such experiences through intensive interviews. Maslow believed that self-actualizing persons had peak experiences more frequently and more intensely than others. He also referred to his general style of thinking about the self-actualizing process as "humanistic psychology," and he displayed in his later writings a very strong interest in creativity as a central feature of the healthy personality.

Perhaps more than any other recent writer, Maslow has been identified with an "inspirational" view of the creative mental life. However, in a provocative address he delivered in 1968, Maslow showed some irritation with the tendency to treat creativity as the antithesis of disciplined effort, and he felt constrained to correct this erroneous impression. He wrote that there was an unfortunate tendency ". . . to deify the one side of the creative process, the enthusiastic, the great insight, the illumination, the good idea, the moment in the middle of the night when you get the great inspiration, and of underplaying the two years of hard and sweaty labor that then is necessary to make anything useful out of the bright idea." He added (Maslow, 1968; published, 1972):

In simple terms of time, bright ideas really take a small proportion of our time. Most of our time is spent on hard work. My impression is that our students don't know this. It may be that these dead cats have been brought to my door more because my students so frequently identify with me, because I have written about peak-experiences and inspirations and so on, that they feel that this is the only way to live. Life without daily or hourly peak-experiences, that's no life, so that they can't do work that is boring.

Some student tells me, "No, I don't want to do that because I don't enjoy it," and then I get purple in the face and fly up in a rage—"Damn it, you do it, or I'll fire you"—and he thinks I am betraying my own principles. I think also that in making a more measured and balanced picture of creativeness, we workers with creativity have to be responsible for the impressions we make on other people. Apparently one impression that we are making on them is that creativeness consists of lightning striking you on the head in one great glorious moment. The fact that the people who create are good workers . . . tends to be lost.

Writers such as Maslow and Fromm view man as a creature who is born not only with animal instincts that get him into trouble but also with fundamental positive drives that would be evident if the external social conditions of life permitted their expression. Man is described as having within him a *force for growth* that propels him to the realization of positive qualities such as altruism, love, ethics, empathy, and independence. While Freud saw altruistic love as a transformation of animal instinct, Maslow saw it as an innate drive, albeit a somewhat weak one. In a very real sense, therefore, Freud's image of man and Maslow's image are quite contrary: Freud saw man as a potentially dangerous animal who had to be controlled by social forces: to Maslow (and Fromm), man is a fundamentally good being whose inherent humanity is thwarted by a destructive society (see Note 12.3).

Another unfortunate tendency of the Freudian theory is to dichotomize man and evolutionarily simpler but related forms of life. Results of current research in ethology imply that nonhuman primates show rudimentary forms of some of the positive social tendencies we value most in man. Recall, if you will, the observations that baboons and chimpanzees have a highly complex social life and evidently form highly emotional attachments to each other, which, when broken by death or separation, lead to very humanlike grief reactions (discussed in Chapters 1 and 6). From this standpoint, man's tendencies to form attachments and to live in cooperative social groups depend as much on his biological heritage as his more destructive tendencies of aggression and defense. Maslow acknowledges this implicitly in his approach to human needs, which he sees as arranged hierarchically from fundamental physiological needs to the higher ones that are especially well developed in man as a species. The lesson in this is that we should not limit our conception of man's biological heritage to the "bad" animal instincts emphasized by Freud, but we need to recognize that both desirable *and* undesirable human tendencies are outgrowths of the evolutionary process.

Anyway, it can be seen that these later writers have moved quite far from the view that equates mental health with inner quietude and harmony. The emphasis tends in the direction of independence, emotional peaks, and even a degree of turmoil. This is not the "contented cow" type by any means. Nowhere, for example, does Maslow point to the absence of bodily stress symptoms or anxiety as evidence of mental health. The focus is on positive qualities rather than on the absence of the negative, although Maslow is not as explicit about this as is Frank Barron, quoted earlier in this chapter, who suggests that mental health can also include being in conflict and pain arising from an active struggle to change a destructive or dehumanizing environment.

In his own observational studies Barron (1963) examined clinically 80 male graduate students, mostly doctoral candidates in the sciences at the University of California at Berkeley, and using the judgments of professors in the students' major department as the criterion of soundness, had them studied further by a staff of professional assessment psychologists over a several-day period.

Note 12.3

When these seemingly opposing views of Freud versus Maslow and Fromm are stated in the extreme, that is, that man is either inherently bad or inherently good, they seem highly naive in assuming that one or two overriding motives (tension-reduction versus force-for-growth) could account for the enormous diversity observed in man's life styles. Freud is really at his best not when he is emphasizing the overriding influence of the pleasure principle, but when he recognizes the multiple and conflicting forces operating in everything we do. Similarly, when Fromm or Maslow acknowledge the multiple possibilities and routes for self-actualization, the pitfalls of a simplistic analysis are more likely to be avoided.

One of the major defects of the force-for-growth analyses of writers such as Fromm and Maslow is that they are extremely vague about how particular personality outcomes can be produced by the social conditions of life operating in accordance with their principles. Their writings often seem more in the nature of philosophical treatises on man, albeit provocative and appealing ones, rather than scientific theories about how children should be reared to produce healthy and happy adults. Much more precision is needed in our knowledge of human development, especially in the area of emotional maturation.

The traits that were found most consistently related to "personal soundness" (Barron's term) as conceived by the professors and psychologists were effectiveness and organization in working toward goals, correct perception of reality, sound character and integrity in the ethical sense, and smooth interpersonal adjustment. But as one might expect from Barron's emphasis on creativity, struggle against injustice, and rebelliousness, many of the subjects in his study whom he saw as sound also displayed periods of personal alienation, emotional disturbance, and even rather odd patterns of behavior that could easily be considered psychopathological.

This willingness to consider as healthy those who show many of the symptoms of neurotic conflict is explained by Barron (1963, pp. 64–65):

The conclusion to which the assessment staff has come is that psychopathology is always with us, and that soundness is *a way of reacting to problems, not an absence of them.* The transformation of pathological trends into distinctive character assets and the minimization of their effects through compensatory overdevelopment of other traits are both marks of "sound" reaction to personal difficulties. At times, indeed, the handling of psychopathology may be so skillful and the masking of pathological motivations so subtle that the individual's soundness may be considerably overrated. There is no doubt that some of our apparently "balanced" subjects were balanced quite precariously, and that their stability was more semblance than fact. It is possible to mistake for soundness what is actually rigidity based on a sort of paralysis of affect engendered by a fear of instinctual drives. These cases of pseudosoundness were probably few, however. . . . The existence of psychopathology in even the quite sound individuals has been emphasized here partly by way of counteracting the sort of trite determinism with which so many clinical studies seem to conclude: broken homes leading to delinquency; psychosis in the parents being passed on, through whatever mechanism, to the offspring; unloving mothers rearing hateful children; catastrophe breeding catastrophe. Undoubtedly such correlations exist in nature, and they were, indeed, found in our own investigation; but considerable variance remains unaccounted for. What we should like to suggest here is that within the population of subjects of ordinary physical and psychological integrity, soundness is by no means exclusively determined by circumstances but may be considered in the nature of an unintended—and perhaps largely unconscious—personal achievement. Our high soundness subjects are beset, like all other persons, by fears, unrealizable desires, self-condemned hates, and tensions difficult to resolve. They are *sound* largely because they bear with their anxieties, hew to a stable course, and maintain some sense of the ultimate worthwhileness of their lives.

Here then is a very different picture of psychological health from that expressed by those who see it as the absence of symptoms of adaptive struggle. Its positive value is the striving for integrity rather than the achievement of harmony and

(a)

(b)

(c)

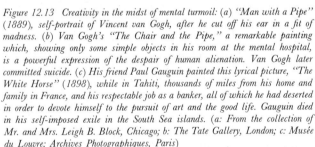

Figure 12.13 Creativity in the midst of mental turmoil: (a) "Man with a Pipe" (1889), self-portrait of Vincent van Gogh, after he cut off his ear in a fit of madness. (b) Van Gogh's "The Chair and the Pipe," a remarkable painting which, showing only some simple objects in his room at the mental hospital, is a powerful expression of the despair of human alienation. Van Gogh later committed suicide. (c) His friend Paul Gauguin painted this lyrical picture, "The White Horse" (1898), while in Tahiti, thousands of miles from his home and family in France, and his respectable job as a banker, all of which he had deserted in order to devote himself to the pursuit of art and the good life. Gauguin died in his self-imposed exile in the South Sea islands. (a: From the collection of Mr. and Mrs. Leigh B. Block, Chicago; b: The Tate Gallery, London; c: Musée du Louvre; Archives Photographiques, Paris)

peace. High on the hierarchy of values are creativity, unity of inner direction, and a continual struggle to cope with contradictions and social ills. People are flawed rather than ideal (Figure 12.13). An individual possessing such traits would be far less likely than a conformist to be popular and well-received, since such struggle frequently produces abrasiveness in human relations. A person of this type is perhaps the modern equivalent of Goethe's Faust, who failed to achieve earthly happiness but through continuous struggle finally achieved salvation in spite of his contract with Mephistopheles.

You will notice that in these diverse though overlapping conceptions of the person who is functioning adequately or well, mental health is not seen as merely a collection of independent or unrelated traits, but frequently is treated as indivisible, each of the traits being smoothly integrated into a unified system. Each part must work harmoniously and effectively with every other part, as in a smoothly functioning machine. Mental well-being from this standpoint requires the integration of the diverse substructures comprising the personality (the id, ego, and superego), whereas in pathology the diverse parts are in conflict. The ideally healthy person is said to show this integration in *every* realm of psychological functioning rather than exhibiting health in some areas and pathology in others.

In thinking about this, it is helpful to imagine two kinds of organic disease—one having little to do with the overall functioning of the body, the other being crucial to it. Consider, say, a minor skin disease compared with a serious metabolic disorder. If one goes to a physician with the former and is given an overall examination, the doctor may report that the patient is fundamentally very healthy and prescribe an ointment or some other minor therapy. The isolated skin condition has little or no impact on the functioning of the rest of the biological system. That is why we call it minor. In this sense, physical health is not a unitary concept, since we can speak of the person as healthy in general although there is sickness in respect to the isolated skin malady.

On the other hand, should the skin ailment prove to be cancer, the conclusion would have to be quite different, since this disease endangers the viability of the whole biological system. Or in the case of a metabolic disorder, such as an insulin-secreting tumor of the pancreas, it simply cannot be thought of in isolation from the rest of the biological system. It influences the thought processes, mood, operation of muscle cells, digestion, endocrine gland activity—just about everything that the person does is tangled up with it, even though the disorder may be produced by a small tumor. In this case, the operation of one organ system interacts with or invades that of many others.

In the sphere of mental health, the question can be raised whether it might not be possible for a person to have highly accurate perception of reality, say, and still be unable to relate adequately to others; a person might display a high degree of autonomy yet define reality idiosyncratically and badly.

Thus, failure in one area of mental health would not necessarily preclude success in another, and only the very rare person would be "perfectly" healthy in the optimal sense of having no psychological disturbances of any kind. This is precisely the position vigorously espoused by some (see Smith, 1961), who argue that mental health is not a unitary concept or process at all, but merely a rubric—a topic for study—involving a collection of diverse personality traits representing things we value in people. Each such trait may well be partly or completely independent of every other one, having its own developmental history and being fashioned from quite different biological forces and social experiences. Thus, resistance to the development of mental disorder under stress may have little or no bearing on traits such as spontaneity, acceptance of others, and creativity, or vice versa, and cultivating one will not necessarily increase the likelihood of having the others. If we want to encourage interpersonal competence or good discernment of reality, we must discover the conditions of life promoting (or retarding) such qualities and build these conditions into (or exclude them from) our childrearing and educational processes.

HEALTH AND VIRTUE

Now we come to the sticky problem just barely touched on at the beginning of this chapter, the problem that makes the term "mental health" misleading and undesirable in spite of our penchant for thinking of successful adaptation as healthy and unsuccessful adaptation as pathological. One reason why the term healthy is a bad one has already been discussed at length in Chapter 11, that is, that the word means the opposite of illness, and the illness model for evaluating the adequacy of psychological adaptation often simply does not square with what is wrong with the person. The illness–health polarity connotes the idea that there is an invariant biological law making one form of adaptation healthy and another form unhealthy. We can then even use the word "sick" as a form of put-down or disparagement ("He's sick!").

However, there is another powerful argument against the use of such imagery, namely, that any definition of health and pathology is inextricably tangled up with personal values, of judgments of what is good and bad, desirable and undesirable. But science can only tell us what *is,* not what should be.

Every writer about health and pathology either implicitly or explicitly identifies accurate discernment of reality as a key feature of the healthy personality. On the other hand, it is conceivable that certain illusions about life may also be

(a)

(b)

(c)

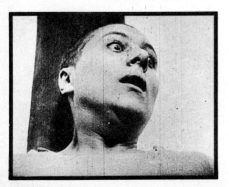

(d)

indispensable for a desirable state of mind. Such a view, heretical in a sense, is often expressed by great poets and dramatists. For example, Eugene O'Neill's play *The Iceman Cometh* has the theme that life is intolerable without illusion. Alfred Adler has suggested that human plans and actions are, to a large extent, built on an edifice of self-deception, which he referred to as "fictional finalism." Man lives by many useful and attractive fictions, such as "All men are created equal," "Honesty is the best policy," or "Evil will be punished." And most religious and political ideologies are built largely on some form of grand mystique.

Psychologists have tended to think of unrealistic perceptions as the result of "defense mechanisms" that protect the person from having to acknowledge the unacknowledgeable. In their research with dying patients, Hackett and Weisman (1964) have noted a marked tendency for terminal cancer patients and critically ill coronary patients to deny that they are near death. However such patients very often display what the authors call "middle knowledge" of the truth, that is, they somehow sense that their hopeful outlook (and that of their relatives and friends or the medical staff treating them) is not an accurate appraisal. Still it seems that they need to retain some hope for the future, and the illusion is in that sense a useful adaptation. The importance of maintaining hope in the face of bleak circumstances has been increasingly emphasized by psychologists in recent years (see Stotland, 1969).

Furthermore, what is regarded as pathological in one culture may be viewed as normal or even healthy in another. In some primitive societies, persons who hallucinate and display other "crazy" behaviors are revered as gods, angels, or messengers of gods, since they are "obviously" possessed by some powerful superhuman force. Joan of Arc in France was regarded as such a person by many, although to the politicians and church leaders of her time she also posed a political threat to their power, a theme which George Bernard Shaw developed brilliantly in his play *Saint Joan.* Danish film director Carl Dreyer depicted the same theme in cinematic terms (Figure 12.14). In other societies (as we saw in Chapter 10), such persons were considered to be possessed by evil demons rather than by benign gods or spirits; in consequence the demons had to be exorcised by cutting a hole in the skull to let them out or by other ceremonious exorcisms and punitive procedures (as in the play *The Dybbuk*, by S. Ansky). In our own culture,

Figure 12.14 Stills from Carl Dreyer's La Passion de Jean d'Arc *(1927), a monumental film of the silent era: (a) The interrogator. (b) Joan, being readied for execution. (c) The way to the stake. (d) Immolation. (Danish Film Museum)*

such behavior can be certified as "insane" (a legal term for psychosis), and the person may then be incarcerated in a hospital out of harm's way—and out of the way of those whom he has disturbed or offended. We see that from one point of view a person may be regarded as sound, while from another vantage point he may be judged unsound.

There is also a long-standing impression in psychiatric circles that such ailments as ulcers, headaches, or high blood pressure are expressions of stress paid for silently and internally instead of being expressed outwardly toward others. The individual with chronic anger directed towards his friends or associates is quickly rejected for this antisocial conduct and may be regarded as disturbed. On the other hand, the presence of an ulcer may make him simply "a member of the club" (of suffering executives, say). Is a person who gets along well with others but kills himself with alcohol or cigarettes in better shape (less "sick") than one who shows his "nervousness" in more socially obnoxious forms, such as in facial ticks (involuntary grimacing), sweaty palms, stammering, impatience with others, or foolish self-deceptions? Such questions cannot, of course, be answered without choosing certain values about what is more or less desirable or undesirable. Thus, even in the area of evident symptoms of psychopathology, our judgments depend on values that cannot be provided entirely by science.

The term *adjustment* in psychology has tended to incorporate pseudoscientific acceptance of current societal values, and in the 1950s social scientists began to search for better means of evaluation. The replacements (like Maslow's and Jahoda's lists of criteria), however, were still incorporated within the medical view of mental health, with the connotation that they were not merely new values of human virtue and goodness but that they somehow had the authority of *scientific pronouncement*. The term "mental health" suggested that these criteria were not a matter of the personal philosophies of their protagonists, but that they carried the weight of biological law. One can believe in love, creativity, and independence without having to have scientific support. But by placing these values within a scientific frame, we somehow assume that the question is settled, that mental health is adequately defined—despite the differences of opinion found among peoples and cultures. In short, the implication of the term is that being healthy is more than merely being well-behaved or virtuous, when in reality that is all it is.

Any well-designed effort to define positive mental health must provide criteria of health and pathology that transcend cultural variations. Such criteria should apply equally well whether one is dealing with a middle- or lower-class American, an Eskimo, African, South Sea islander, Christian, Jew, Mo-

Rabbi [*exorcising the spirit that has taken possession of a young girl*]: Dybbuk! Soul of one who has left the world in which we live! In the name and with the power of a holy community of Jews, I Azrael, son of Itzele, order you to depart out of the body of the maiden, Leah, daughter of Channah, and in departing, to do no injury either to her or to any other living being. If you do not obey me, I shall proceed against you with malediction and anathema, to the limit of my powers, and with the utmost might of my uplifted arm. But if you do as I command you, then I shall bend all my strength to drive away the fiends and evil spirits that surround you, and keep you safe from them. [From S. Ansky, *The Dybbuk*, Act III]

hammedan, or Hindu. Gross mental disorder does not pose so much of a problem in this regard; there is little debate that the thought disturbances of a schizophrenic patient (see Chapter 10) is a pathological state, clearly inimical to the "good life." The difficulties grow, however, as one approaches the milder forms of trouble or enters the arena of positive mental health. On what grounds can one say that autonomy, creativity, self-awareness, commitment to productive labor, competence, and altruism (as opposed to excess egoism) are healthy or good? We have to recognize that the justification is simply that we prefer these values, that they will produce what we believe to be desirable outcomes in human affairs.

What agreement about such values there is among various psychologists, and there is quite a lot, derives in large measure from their common cultural heritage. Such writers come from the Judeo-Christian Western world and are members of the educated, technologically oriented middle class. The criteria might be quite different if most of them emerged from Asian or African cultures. Thus, for example, the idea of competence is largely Western in theme, reflecting our commitment to the effective struggle for control over the environment, our striving to transform events in accordance with our material needs. We of this tradition feel distressed and deeply frustrated when things go against us, as in illness or death. In Western culture a physician is offended by death, since it suggests that he has failed in the mastery of medicine. Such a view is in contrast with the Eastern ideal of acceptance of the inevitable, of resignation, of accommodation to the environment. Buddhists are not so quick to reject the idea that psychological health consists of harmonious adjustment to the environment, the image of a reed that bends with the wind rather than an oak that stands up to it. Buddhist writings have much influenced the Japanese view of death, as we see in the haiku poem in the margin. Note also the extracts from the Buddhist scriptures. What might a Western psychiatrist say to this viewpoint? Yet Eastern teachings are not always out of step with what a Freudian, say, might regard as reasonable or acceptable. For example, also in Buddha's teachings is found the following: "Just as the pure and fragrant lotus grows out of the mud of a swamp rather than out of the clean loam of an upland field, so from the muck of worldly passions springs the pure enlightenment of Buddhahood. . . ." Here in this statement is a conception of harmony and enlightenment (the strong, integrated ego) arising, as Freud, Fromm, and Maslow might agree, from the struggles between the libido and a repressive world. In any case, the issue is clearly one of diverse subjective values rather than scientific objectivity.

Nowhere is the issue of human values more evident than in the way we are likely to see healthy sexual functioning in

The wind blows,
    the grass bends.

To worry in anticipation or to cherish regret for the past is like cutting reeds that wither in a day.
The secret of health for both mind and body is not to mourn for the past, not to worry about the future, not to anticipate the future, but to live the present moment wisely and earnestly.
Do not dwell in the past, do not dream of the future, concentrate the mind on the present moment. [From *The teachings of Buddha*, p. 171. Tokyo: Bukkyo Dendo Kyokai, 1966]

both men and women. Recall, for example, that for Freud and other writers cited in this chapter, healthy sex is not to be divorced from altruistic love. The value question here is indicated by the fact that what is said is that sex *should* not be divorced from altruistic love. I have never seen a respected text on mental health or adjustment that did not imply the need to link sex with love, an ideal fostered by concepts of romantic love that originated as an important cultural force in the Middle Ages, as expressed in the chivalric legends of King Arthur and the Knights of the Round Table of the twelfth century. This view ultimately revolutionarized marriage as a social institution by gradually leading to the elimination of arranged marriages and their replacement by the theme of marriage based on love. We have come to believe, in effect, that the best and most cherished sexual activity is tied to love.

But does this mean that sex unrelated to love is not desirable or healthy? It is an interesting question, not readily answerable on the basis of fact, but only on the basis of values and beliefs handed down to us as eternal verities as if they were biological laws. Yet there has been emerging in our society a new value, at least one that if not new has rarely been admitted openly and widely among otherwise "solid" citizens, and this is that although love for one's partner may enhance the experience of sex, be good for family life if it is sustained, and be moral in a biblical sense, it is not an essential feature. In fact, the romantic outlook can create social, sexual, and emotional prisons for persons who are joined legally but unhappily in marriage, and this is reflected in the extraordinarily high divorce rate. From this latter standpoint, it is the person who requires a loving relationship for sexual activity that has the hangup, and not the other way around. To be human is also to want erotic activity, to be capable of erotic stimulation and of freely participating in it when the spirit so moves.

The reader should not misunderstand. I have not claimed that the ideal of romantic love which links sex and love is bad, or a poor value for an individual or a society to pursue, although I have acknowledged that it can also create problems. On the contrary, I am raising an issue, pointing to a value that, without being labeled as such, has crept into our notion of successful adaptation by linking it with the medical idea of health as opposed to illness, thus making it seem unassailable. At the opposite side of the argument, one sees purely mechanical sex, as Alex participates in it in *A Clockwork Orange* (see Chapter 5), or as it is experienced by women who live by prostitution.

What is the answer? There is none that science can give; science is morally neutral, although scientists may choose to study or not to study certain things on moral grounds. The

Night fell . . . and [Geraint and Enid] came to a castle at the head of the valley where Geraint asked for lodging.
"Right welcome shall you be," said the lord of the castle, whose name was Sir Oringle of Limors, "and your fair lady also: there was surely never a fairer seen than she."
After the banquet Geraint sat moodily apart, for his heart was still sore on account of Enid's cruel and thoughtless words [earlier]. She sat alone also, not knowing how to win back Geraint's love, for she feared greatly that she had lost it for ever by her folly. And as she sat thus, Sir Oringle came and sat beside her:
"Fair damsel," he said, "surely the journey with yonder dolorous knight is none of your seeking?"
"I would rather journey with him than with any other," answered Enid.
"Be counselled by me," went on Sir Oringle. "Leave this man and dwell always with me. All my earldom shall be yours, and all the good things that you shall wish for—the jewels, the fair robes, servants and handmaidens."
"That will I not, by Heaven!" cried Enid. "My faith is pledged to yonder man, and never shall I prove inconstant to him." [From *King Arthur and his Knights of the Round Table* (retold out of the old romances by R. L. Green), pp. 157–158. Baltimore, Md.: Penguin, 1953]

only thing the scientist can do is to study the consequences of the divergent values so that when he chooses he can do so in the most informed way possible. Had we all the necessary evidence, we could certainly judge whether sex unconnected with love produces beneficial or harmful consequences. But the choice is ours, and that depends on the life values we regard most positively or most negatively. Each of us will have his own answer, or at least will seek one, probably on the basis of his own ideological predilections and upbringing and the extent to which he resonates with traditional cultural values.

In any case, the conclusion is this: Although modern professional psychologists do not use the terms "goodness" and "virtue" when they write about positive mental health, they are making essentially that type of evaluation but clothing it in pseudoscientific terminology. Research cannot choose these values for us.

IMPACT OF THE CIRCUMSTANCES OF LIFE

There is a widespread tendency to think of successful adaptation as a trait that operates independently of the circumstances under which the individual lives. In effect, one is saying that there are sound people and there are troubled or disturbed people, and that is that. Of course, it is true that some people do seem to manage to cope better than others under a wide range of conditions. But this view overstates the role of personality somewhat and understates the importance of external conditions under which people must live. A person's life situation, both in the formative years and in adulthood,

Figure 12.15   The mysterious will to live, in the face of horrendous physical conditions, is all that saved these starving people while countless others died. (a) Slave laborers in Buchenwald Concentration Camp, near Jena, Germany, when U.S. troops freed them in April 1945. (b) Scene inside the hut where victims of typhus were housed in Belsen Concentration Camp. (a: U.S. Army photo; b: Imperial War Museum, London)

(a)   (b)

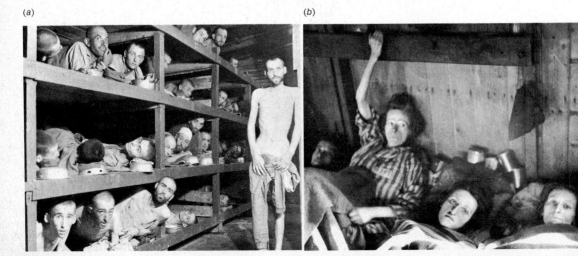

may have an overriding impact on his adaptation. Not everyone has the same opportunity to display successful adaptation.

Obviously traits such as autonomy, trust in others, identification with mankind, or having a philosophical sense of humor do not flourish in a highly destructive environment, say, a concentration camp (Figure 12.15) or under the condition of slavery! It might be objected here that most people today do not live in such extreme hardship. However, marked variations certainly do exist in the favorability of people's circumstances, depending upon the socioeconomic strata to which they belong; obviously some people have a far better chance to display positive adaptive outcomes than others. Criteria such as autonomy, identification with mankind, or a philosophical sense of humor make no sense when seen in the context of severe poverty and deprivation—for those undernourished and undereducated people who are a significant percentage of the world's population.

Consider the divergent conditions and styles of life of two young men, described in recent newspaper accounts, illustrating the complex interplay between environmental forces and personality. The first, let us call him Dan, is a teen-ager growing up under rural conditions in a well-organized and well-adapted family; he attends high school, helps out on the family farm, and plays football. The second youth, John, is incarcerated in the highly destructive setting of a penal institution.

Dan is a 16-year-old soft-spoken farmboy from a town of 468 persons in an upper midwestern state. He lives on a 1,400-acre farm that produces an income of about $17,000 a year for a family consisting of mother, father, and four sons by dint of disciplined, cooperative hard work by all. In the summer, Dan arises at 5 A.M., drives his car 12 miles to the local high school, and by 5:50 A.M. is on the football field, where he is striving to make the team by practicing 2 hours at a stretch. Following this he showers, has a bite to eat, and then returns home to help his father and cousins bale straw, stacking over 300 dusty 50-pound bales on wagons, while his mother works on four daily loads of wash and serves lunch at noon. Toward the end of the day, Dan works on his last chores, feeding the pigs before he has an early dinner, and is back on the football field by 6 P.M. At home around 8:30 he works on his car, tosses a football around with his brothers, or telephones his girl friend, getting to bed usually around 11. On Friday nights he and his girlfriend see a movie in the town 13 miles to the north, or they sip a soda in his home town. He is a high school junior getting average grades, has no desire to attend college, and assumes that he and his brothers will inherit the land and stick to farming. He relishes this because he dislikes the idea of someone telling him what to

Fiddi Angermeyer is fourteen years old. He has big hands and feet like his father and uncles. His toes lie in straight lines and are widespread, because most of his lifetime he has been shoeless. . . .

For Fiddi, growing up in the Galápagos has involved growing up in the little European settlement at Academy Bay. . . . But in islands where boys his own age are scarce and where the waters are so prolific and the skies so full of bird life, it also involves animals, and they figure in his life as humans do. . . .

There are the porpoises, leaping toward your boat from all quarters of the sea, their brotherhood telepathized to you, it seems, as soon as you see them at a distance. . . .

There are mornings before the sun has risen, when the water is calm and its most delicate blue, the horizon vague, the far sky and water pastel pink and blue, everything out of focus but your boat, a dark point and soft splashing in the unrealness, when suddenly many points and splashings—porpoises, making for you in their morning joy and pride at early waking and dawn fishing, racing to reach you.

For a boy with a long gaff, porpoises are most interesting when they have reached the boat and are pacing it, swimming easily ahead. Lying on the bowsprit he can lean down and scratch them, if his gaff is long enough, or

he can just watch them. Sometimes they are twelve to fourteen deep the deepest one just a light blue shape in the deep blue water but the higher ones so close that he can watch their eyes when they roll sideways slightly to look up at him. . . .

Lying on the bowsprit he [becomes] conscious of their talk. At first it seems a high whistling in the rigging and he forgets it. But it is their voices, and when he realizes it, it fills his head. It's a disembodied sound, existing someplace above the water, seeming not to come from it. It's louder and clearer to a boy than to someone older. Its pitch is so high that the oldest men on board can't hear it at all.

That fall Fiddi was going to Massachusetts, where he would go to school. In the Galápagos we worried about how he would make out in so strange a place. Fiddi had spent his every waking minute under the equator learning things, but they were not things you need to know in Boston. . . . He used words that might not be acceptable to Massachusetts boys, words like "lovely." Once, when we were hunting for a hawk's nest high on the side of a worn crater, . . . Fiddi stopped to watch the hawks above, and said, "It would be lovely to fly like that. I wish I could do it. But I would be satisfied to have a balsa glider and sail down just to the headland." I hoped that the desire would be familiar enough to Massachusetts boys for them to tolerate its expression.

But I worried about Fiddi. I saw him in a railroad station in that strange country, colder than he had ever been . . . before, his Lincolnesque hands and feet inadequately covered, maybe—and then I remembered what had happened to Lincoln in Illinois, and to Darwin in the Galápagos, to Gauguin in Tahiti, to Thoreau at Walden. I remembered the place Fiddi had been, and what had happened to Crazy Horse in the Dakotas, to Buddha under the bo tree, to Mohammed and Jesus in the desert; and I realized, no need to worry about him, best to watch out for him. [From Brower, 1970, pp. 100–127]

do, and he also finds city life unpleasant. On visiting Duluth, in northern Minnesota, he found it a "mad place," where "the people are all over you. . . ."

In contrast, John is 19, a former college student who was arrested 2 years ago for the first time after a drug raid at an eastern state university, along with some two score others. The indictment charged him with twice selling marijuana. He was visiting his brother on the West Coast at the time of the indictment, and he returned home and surrendered himself to the authorities. Although the other youths with whom he was charged pleaded guilty and were given mostly suspended or light sentences, John was sentenced to a 7- to 15-year term in the state penitentiary for drug peddling. It has been a terrible and bewildering time for him. He claims that he was not regularly dealing in marijuana, and that the two sales on which he was charged were a favor for a friend, the amount of each sale being $10. Since the sales occurred before the penal code was changed, he was tried under the old law which provided a mandatory minimum sentence of 7 years for trafficking in drugs, and apparently the judge had no choice under the law. John notes sardonically that one of the men he has met in prison was caught with 800 pounds of marijuana and received a sentence of 5 years.

Now he is the first student in a special correspondence program to obtain an Associate of Arts degree in a community college, and is in the top 2 or 3 percent of the students. He hopes either to obtain executive clemency or barring that to find a way to obtain his bachelor's degree in prison. Under the circumstances he is coping rather well, though he talks about his dilemma with irony, and states that "I'd like to do something on the level. There's so much foulness going on in government, somebody's got to do something about it."

That the prognosis for these two boys is very different cannot be doubted. This is undoubtedly in part a product of their different circumstances of life, although Dan's more naive outlook could also be a product of his younger age. Consider, however, how these two youths might cope with unexpected later stresses. They will certainly move in different worlds as a result of their divergent outlooks and aspirations, levels of sophistication and education, family and social supports, economic opportunities, and so on. The pattern of their adaptation must be different, because on the basis of experience and personality each chooses a different setting in which to live, avoiding those contexts which he cannot handle and seeking those that harmonize with his own dispositions and resources.

Can we attempt to predict their later adaptations to problems of life? To try to make a comparison without reference to the circumstances with which they will have to cope is to look at only half the story. What would happen if they were both forced to contend with the same sets of demands, as they might in the army, in a social disaster such as widespread unemployment, or a personal disaster such as a handicapping physical injury or illness or loss of a loved one? It is quite likely that their different dispositions and personal resources would lead to divergent modes of adaptation. But each young man might make a satisfactory adjustment in his own way. The problem, of course, is to discover the qualities that favor an adaptive outcome in each individual, even if they lead to the good life by means of quite divergent routes.

We must thus be cautious about defining successful adaptation as an enduring trait of personality without reference to the circumstances under which a person lives. We might better ask: How is the person coping with the particular circumstances of his life from the vantage point of his own developmental history? We must then sometimes regard the individual who displays various symptoms of maladaptation as relatively successful in the sense that he is coping as best he can with rather unfavorable circumstances (Figure 12.16). From such a standpoint, absolute standards of mental health seem meaningless. Moreover, the ideal human values expressed by writers such as Maslow seem suitable mainly for those who have secure access to the elemental life conditions capable of fostering them. In this view, one can agree with Erich Fromm that certain forms of society are so structured as to make it difficult or impossible for man to fulfill the highest human values. Maslow also recognized this in his notion that man's best qualities cannot be realized when his most primitive needs remained ungratified. We do not yet understand fully the factors that lead one individual to transcend his environment and another to be victimized by it.

CONCLUDING COMMENT

In a sense we are back at where we began—with a variant of the ecological view that man and his environment are interdependent. We also started out with the environmental stressors to which people must adapt, and now have ended up with the focus on the individual himself, his adapting personality. Man as a being cannot be understood divorced from his environment, and the clash between his nature and that environment determines the outcome we call successful adaptation or adaptive failure. For this reason, the "good life," in all its varied meanings, is only an ideal; but realistically we can strive for optimal functioning, however we conceive of this, under the life conditions we must face. We are, in short, concerned with finding the most suitable match between the

Figure 12.16   The economic view of happiness. (Drawing by Mal Hancock; © *Washington Star Syndicate, Inc.)*

Humanizing the earth . . . implies much more than transforming the wilderness into agricultural lands, pleasure grounds, and healthy areas suitable for the growth of civilization. It also means preserving the kinds of wilderness where man can experience mysteries transcending his daily life, and also recapture direct awareness of the cosmic forces from which he emerged. It is obvious, however, that man spends his daily life not in the wilderness but in environments that he creates—in a man-made nature. . . . [By] using scientific knowledge and ecological wisdom we can manage the earth so as to create environments which are ecologically stable, economically profitable, esthetically rewarding, and favorable to the continued growth of civilization. [From Dubos, 1973, p. 772]

two units, the environment and the person, to maximize some psychological outcome that goes well beyond mere survival. In struggling to attain what he believes to be the best fit between himself and his environment, man is constantly changing himself, and at the same time changing his environment, and the effort to understand and influence this process will go on as long as the outcome of the struggle is less than we desire, in short, as long as perfection in life is not attained. As much as anything else, understanding this struggle is what psychology is all about.

In a cemetery at Burlington, Vt., is a tombstone with this inscription: "She lived with her husband 50 years and died in the confident hope of a better life."

ANNOTATED LIST OF SUGGESTED READINGS

Accounts of Freudian theory

Brenner, C. *An elementary textbook of psychoanalysis.* New York: International Universities Press, 1955. (Paperback by Doubleday Anchor Books). Well written, and slightly longer than the works of Hall and Holzman below, it is an authoritative traditional exposition of psychoanalysis.

Erikson, E. H. *Childhood and society,* 2nd ed., especially Chapter 7. New York: Norton, 1963. Erikson is close to the Freudian view, yet has expanded the psychosexual theory and given it a more social caste. His writings are well-worth exploring in their own right.

Hall, C. A. *A primer of Freudian psychology.* New York: World Publishing, 1954. (Paperback edition, Mentor Books.) The shortest and cheapest of the brief treatments of Freud, naturally less complete and with less perspective, but adequate for a first look.

Freud, S. *An outline of psychoanalysis.* New York: Norton, 1949. (First German ed., 1940.) Freud's own attempt to write a simplified and comprehensive treatment of his own system. Useful especially for getting the flavor of Freud's prose and emphasis. On the other hand, the reader who has carefully gone over the past three chapters might find something like Freud's *The interpretation of dreams* and *The psychopathology of everyday life* especially rewarding (see References).

Holzman, P. S. *Psychoanalysis and psychopathology.* New York: McGraw-Hill, 1970 (paper). An excellent brief treatment of Freudian theory, with some clinical illustrations and a historical approach that reveals the changes in Freud's thinking over the years, giving it a sense of incompleteness, tentativeness, and growth.

Neo-Freudian theory

Fromm, E. *Escape from freedom.* New York: Holt, Rinehart & Winston, 1941.

Fromm, E. *Man for himself.* New York: Holt, Rinehart & Winston, 1947.

Fromm, E. *The sane society.* New York: Holt, Rinehart & Winston, 1955. There are many variations on neo-Freudian theory, but the one emphasized here is that of Fromm. These three books show the evolution of Fromm's thought over the years.

The reader who wishes a broader review and analysis of psychoanalytic and related forms of thought might look into a compact book by Robert T. Hogan entitled *Personality theories,* Englewood Cliffs, N.J.: Prentice-Hall, in press. Another comparative source is Hall, C. S., and Lindzey, G. *Theories of personality.* New York: Wiley, 1957.

Other writings on mental health

Barron, F. *Creativity and psychological health.* Princeton, N.J.: Van Nostrand, 1963. Analysis and research on the topic from a psychoanalytic frame of reference, but with Barron's own special emphasis on creativity and personal struggle.

Jahoda, Marie. *Current concepts of positive mental health.* New York: Basic Books, 1958. One of the major early analyses of the case for a positive approach to mental health, with detailed elaborations of the major criteria cited in this chapter.

Smith, M. B. *Social psychology and human values: Selected essays.* Chicago: Aldine, 1969. Very valuable discussions by a social psychologist of the problem of values and the nature of mental health, with special emphasis on competence as a key criterion. Chapters 9 through 15 are particularly relevant to the topics discussed here.

This book has focused on man's troubles, but we must not forget the more positive side of his existence as well. In spite of his problems, *Homo sapiens* is clearly a magnificent biological species that has survived remarkably well, at least up to now. He has created complex and remarkable civilizations to provide for his diverse biological and social needs, some reaching unparalleled heights of knowledge, technology, creativity, and artistic expression. Side by side with his self-centeredness and frequent outbursts of destructiveness, he has also frequently displayed empathy with and concern for his fellow man. Especially for those with whom he has close ties, he has shown himself capable of extraordinary loyalty and self-sacrifice. Moreover, despite all criticism, it is clear that among the societies of the world, the peoples of the United States and of the British Commonwealth have done rather well. The Anglo-American constitutional tradition, with its Magna Carta and Bill of Rights, has produced a more open and free society than most, has distributed wealth more widely than most, and expresses, at least in its stated values, some very high ideals.

Nevertheless, the theme implicit in this book is that things have not yet worked out well for a large proportion of mankind (or for a substantial portion of our own citizenry). It would take a very self-satisfied person to believe that all is well with the world merely because his own life is secure and satisfying. How, for example, can anyone be totally sanguine about world society, and our own, when over 200 billion dollars are annually spent by the world's nations on armaments (this estimate does not include police and militias to protect society from within). This almost unimaginable wealth, poured out in preparation for warfare, is eloquent expression of the widespread fear and distrust in which all of mankind lives today. Furthermore, the very superpowers that devote the bulk of this treasure to their military preparedness seem the most insecure and feel that they do not have sufficient resources to provide adequately for their substantial numbers of poor, their indigent aged (who in affluent America make up from one-half to two-thirds of older people), their neglected youth, and the physically and mentally ill. Indeed, in the present period of economic strains, we seem to be turning away entirely from the important task of developing a humane and rational set of social priorities.

Although it is always dangerous to make predictions about the future, it is safe to assume that the great problems of mankind will still be with us during our lifetime. We can expect continuing growth in world population, and even in the United States (where the rate of growth has recently been declining) there will be continuing pollution of the environment as man's technology continues to expand by leaps and bounds. With the tapering off of the Indochina War and the beginnings of détente between the West and East, it is possible that mankind will not be plagued with large-scale warfare, at least for a while. But massive armaments and war

601

preparation will still plague us, and "limited" international violence (as in the Middle East) seems unlikely to abate. It is also safe to predict that human prejudices are unlikely to vanish in the foreseeable future, especially in the absence of genuine efforts to do something effective about them by going after some of their sources. And in a stressful world a distressingly high proportion of people will continue to suffer some form of maladaptation or alienation.

We can also be sure that psychological research, theory, and practice will remain at the heart of efforts to understand these classic and modern human difficulties in the hopes of finding ways of resolving them. It is the individual who is the ultimate locus of these problems, who is poignantly caught up in the conflicts between biological and social forces, who suffers from deterioration of the quality of life, from war, prejudice, alienation, and psychological malaise.

When the individual is in trouble, he is either out of step with his own psychophysiology, with his society, or both. And the alleviation (treatment) of his ills can occur on three different levels: (1) we can seek to change the nature of man as a species, though this has generally been assumed to be presently beyond our control; (2) we can try to change the social system; (3) we can try to change the individual, either physiologically or psychologically, through therapy of some kind. All such solutions are designed to improve the fit between the individual and his psychophysiological makeup or between the individual and the social conditions under which he lives.

Because this book has been problem oriented and has dealt with topics that arouse concern and emotion in most of us, and because there is scant knowledge and a myriad of diverging opinions, it has also been much more personal than most psychology textbooks. The nature of the problems tackled have sometimes inevitably forced us into areas of political and social controversy. As author, I have tried as much as possible to avoid this and to give as balanced a presentation of controversial issues as is possible. But in those issues that are intimately related to questions of social action or inaction, it is, as we all know, impossible to be

totally free of ideological bias (as discussed in Note 5.2), and on many occasions I could not shy away from a personal slant or observation. Moreover, one's personal outlook is an important determinant of the choice of material. Only in a book dealing with issues utterly irrelevant to important human concerns can one be without some emotional commitment, though it is helpful to be aware of such bias and to let it be obvious to others.

Over and above the real conflicting interests involved in human problems, two unfortunate tendencies inevitably get in the way of allowing us to find solutions. First, there is a tendency to line up on one or the other side of social issues along strictly ideological lines, from which vantage point we automatically accept or reject various proposed solutions. And when we are strongly committed to an ideology, our passions are easily aroused, whether it be in Northern Ireland, the Middle East, or right in our own backyard. James Reston has noted in discussing the political arena, "It is a common habit of most people to proclaim great principles when it suits their purposes, and evade or ignore them when it doesn't."

We can learn from history that extremists in power do not ultimately change things for the better for most people but only produce a change in status for a few. Solutions based on ideological extremes rarely can be successfully imposed for long. For one thing, they are usually oversimple; for another, they invariably traduce the rights and concerns of the other side, with much subsequent suffering. Successful solutions involving mankind usually require compromises in which the loser is not wiped out but shares in the solution with dignity. For example, the United States seems to have learned a lesson from the disaster of the destructive Versailles treaty after World War I that spawned Hitlerism and World War II, as evidenced by wiser treatment of Germany and Japan after the latter war. Neither world peace nor betterment of the lot of mankind can be forcibly achieved by simplistic one-dimensional answers for multidimensional problems.

We thus need to bring back into respectability the principle of compromise, in which everyone wins by losing a little. If there is only one "right" way, and only those believing in it are regarded as good or deserving while all the others are "evil," there must be continuous fear and strife. We also must learn to allow the other fellow to save face, and to treat all people with dignity if not with affection. This might indeed be a more practical aim than "love thy neighbor," since he may *not* be lovable (at least in your eyes); yet compromise, cordiality, and cooperation will permit both of you to live rather than just one.

Solutions to large-order problems are rarely possible in the abstract, and our efforts are best directed to specific problems occurring in certain places, under given circumstances, and in particular kinds of people. One of the problems with extreme ideological solutions is that they are general philosophies which fail to take into account such details. Thus, social action oriented to one group is rarely suitable for other groups whose problems and needs differ greatly. One example of this given in the text was of the environmental problems of the aged. Providing for them in the same way that one might provide for younger people can have the effect of worsening things rather than bettering them. If there is one thing we should have learned in psychological study, it is that groups and individuals differ in important ways, and what is good for one is not necessarily good for another.

This insight applies particularly well to the great dilemmas of man discussed throughout this book. Threats to the environment, aggression and war, prejudice, alienation, these are very broad and abstract problems, and although guidelines are often helpful, we do better in applying our knowledge to particular instances where we can specify the details of the biological, social, and psychological forces that are operating. Abstract crises seem incapable of solution, but specific and concrete issues often can be resolved. In fact, this is the way of science, which tries to dissect a problem into its component parts.

Really workable solutions, if they can be found, will probably call for considerably more psychosocial and psychobiological knowledge than we now have about the nature of man and how each individual can best realize his or her full potentialities. We will require increased sophistication in helping people to accept and use new ideas and to cushion themselves from the threats and stresses that go along with change. More understanding of the human psyche is needed—not cold, unfeeling, power-oriented knowledge devoted to the domination of others, but knowledge predicated on an ethical concern for the fate of individuals. Salvation does not lie with those who desire to help mankind in the abstract but who do not care how many individuals are destroyed in the process. Perhaps the answers will be a long time in coming, but seeking them is one of the most worthwhile challenges to which educated people can commit themselves.

To close this book on a note of optimism, perhaps it might be helpful to think of mankind as in its adolescence, for surely there is a shortage of mature wisdom in the conduct of human affairs. This is how humorist Art Hoppe whimsically portrays man, as a youth, still evolving or becoming, and since an occasional laugh helps us to see things in perspective, let us conclude with one of Hoppe's amusing columns (*San Francisco Chronicle,* March 18, 1973):

SCENE: The Heavenly Real Estate Office. The Landlord is rummaging through a bin marked, "Morning Stars." His business agent, Mr. Gabriel, enters, his golden trumpet under his arm.

* * *

THE LANDLORD: A half-dozen of my loveliest Morning Stars would be perfect for my new Galaxy 13-603A. Hmmm, what about this one? Or this one or . . .
GABRIEL: Excuse me, Sir. But I think I've discovered the fatal error in your property management techniques concerning that planet, Earth.
THE LANDLORD: My beloved little blue-green jewel? What now, Gabriel?
GABRIEL: Well, you know how the tenants have been mucking up the place, dumping their garbage everywhere, burning napalm holes in the carpeted forests, gouging . . .
THE LANDLORD (frowning): We've been through all that. What's this error you're talking about?
GABRIEL (grimly): The error, Sir, is that you've leased the property to a bunch of adolescents.

THE LANDLORD: Adolescents, Gabriel?

GABRIEL: Yes, Sir. Look at the mess they're making. Typical adolescent behavior.

THE LANDLORD (sighing): Well, I will admit that even I can't get an adolescent to clean up his room.

GABRIEL: And their attitude toward sex . . .

THE LANDLORD: Sex, Gabriel, is a Me-given pleasure.

GABRIEL: I know, Sir. But no matter what their age, they're now obsessed by it. Pornographic books and movies, wife-swapping, mass orgies. They seldom talk about anything else. They all act as though they'd just reached puberty and were discovering sex for the first time.

THE LANDLORD: Hmmm, that does sound somewhat juvenile.

GABRIEL: Oh, that's not all, Sir. Take any middle-aged businessman. What interests him? Talking on the telephone, gossiping, drugs such as tranquilizers and alcohol, spending money, the newest style in clothes, the latest model cars . . . Who does he sound like to you, Sir?

THE LANDLORD (grudgingly): A high school boy.

GABRIEL: Exactly, Sir. and look at the way they now wage war—always in "self-defense." Precisely like teen-aged gangs defending their territory. Really, Sir!

THE LANDLORD (musingly): I remember back a million years or so when they went around with clubs, releasing their infantile aggressions on each other.

GABRIEL (nodding): And you excused them, Sir, because they were only babies.

THE LANDLORD: And then, for thousands of years, they behaved childishly, taking what they could by force, practicing deceit, having tantrums . . .

GABRIEL: And you said they were only children. But now they're adolescents, Sir—messy, sex-obsessed, fad-conscious, rebellious adolescents who don't care a whit about keeping up the property. The very worst kind of tenants. (He raises his golden trumpet.) Shall I sound the eviction notice now, Sir?

THE LANDLORD (waving a hand): No, no, Gabriel. After all, you can't judge adolescents by what they are.

GABRIEL: For Your sakes, Sir! How do you judge them then?

THE LANDLORD (smiling gently): By what they will become, Gabriel. By what they will become.

References

PROLOGUE

Bettelheim, B. *Obsolete youth: Towards a psychogram of adolescent rebellion.* San Francisco, Calif.: San Francisco Press, 1969.

Conklin, H. C. The relation of the Hanunoo culture to the plant world. Unpublished doctoral dissertation, Yale University, 1954. Cited in J. Wallace. *Psychology: A social science.* Philadelphia: Saunders, 1971.

Cotton, H. A. The etiology and treatment of the so-called functional psychoses. *American Journal of Psychiatry,* 1922, **2,** 157–210.

Deese, J. *Psychology as science and art.* New York: Harcourt Brace Jovanovich, 1972.

Evans-Pritchard, E. E. *The Nuer.* New York: Oxford Univ. Press (Clarendon), 1940.

Kopeloff, N., and Cheney, C. O. Studies in focal infection: Its presence and elimination in the functional psychoses. *American Journal of Psychiatry,* 1922, **2,** 139–156.

Skinner, B. F. *The behavior of organisms.* New York: Appleton-Century-Crofts, 1938.

Skinner, B. F. *Walden Two.* New York: Macmillan, 1961.

Skinner, B. F. *Beyond freedom and dignity.* New York: Knopf, 1971.

Whorf, B. L. The relation of habitual thought and behavior to language. In *Language, culture and personality* (L. Spier, A. I. Hallowell, and S. S. Newman, eds.). Salt Lake City: Univ. of Utah Press, 1960. (Originally published, Menasha, Wisconsin: Sapir Memorial Publication Fund.)

Yeats, W. B. Sophocles' King Oedipus. Translated for the modern stage in *The Collected Plays of W. B. Yeats,* pp. 323–324. New York: Macmillan, 1953.

INTRODUCTION TO PART ONE

Benedict, Ruth. The sense of symbolism. In *An anthropologist at work* (M. Mead, ed.), p. 113. Boston: Houghton Mifflin, 1959.

Elkin, A. P. *The Australian Aborigines,* p. 170. Garden City, N.Y.: Doubleday (Natural History Library), 1964.

Mirsky, Jeannette. The Eskimo of Greenland. In *Cooperation and competition among primitive people* (M. Mead, ed.), pp. 51–85. Boston: Beacon Press, 1961.

Paul, Jacqueline. *Japan quest,* p. 3. Rutland, Vt., and Tokyo: Tuttle, 1962.

Rapoport, A. *House form and culture,* p. 11. Englewood Cliffs, N.J.: Prentice-Hall, 1969.

Washburn, S. L., and DeVore, I. The social life of baboons. *Scientific American,* 1961, **204** (6), 62–71.

CHAPTER ONE

Amos, W. H. Teeming life of a pond. *National Geographic,* 1970, **138,** 274–298.

Aquinas, St. Thomas. *On the governance of rulers* (trans. by Gerald B. Phelan). New York: Sheed and Ward, 1938.

Ashley Montagu, M. F. *The human revolution.* Cleveland: World, 1965.

Baker, P. T. Human adaptation to high altitude. *Science,* 1969, **163,** 1149–1156.

Bowlby, J. *Attachment and loss,* Vol. 1. New York: Basic Books, 1969.

Cowgill, Ursula M. The people of York: 1538–1812. *Scientific American,* 1970, **222,** 104–112.

Craik, K. H. The comprehension of the everyday physical environment. Reprinted in *Environmental psychology: Man in his physical setting* (H. M. Proshansky, W. H. Ittelson, and L. G. Rivlin, eds.), pp. 646–658. New York: Basic Books, 1970a.

Craik, K. H. Environmental psychology. In *New directions in psychology* (K. H. Craik *et al.,* eds), Vol. 4, pp. 1–122. New York: Holt, Rinehart & Winston, 1970b.

Darwin, C. *The origin of species.* London: Murray, 1859; New York: New American Library–Mentor Book, 1958 (paper).

Day, M. *Guide to fossil man.* New York: World, 1965.

Delgado, J. M. R. *Physical control of the mind.* New York: Harper & Row, 1969.

Dexter, E. G. *Weather influences.* New York: Macmillan, 1904.

Dubos, R. J. *Man adapting.* New Haven, Conn.: Yale Univ. Press, 1965.

Ford, Amasa B. Casualties of our time. *Science,* 1970, **167,** 256–263.

Gilbert, G. M. *Personality dynamics: A biosocial approach.* New York: Harper & Row, 1970.

Klausner, S. Z. *On man in his environment.* San Francisco: Jossey-Bass, 1971.

Lasker, G. W. Human biological adaptability. *Science,* 1969, **166,** 1480–1486.

Lerner, I. M. *Heredity, evolution and society.* San Francisco: Freeman, 1968.

Linton, R. *The tree of culture.* New York: Knopf, 1955.

Loomis, W. F. Rickets. *Scientific American,* 1970, **223** (6), 77–91.

Lorenz, K. Z. *King Solomon's ring.* New York: Thomas Y. Crowell, 1953 (paper).

Lucretius. *On the nature of things,* Book I. (Trans. by H. A. J. Munro, in *Great Books of the Western world,* R. M. Hutchins, ed.) Chicago: Encyclopedia Britannica, 1952.

McAlester, A. L. *The history of life.* Englewood Cliffs, N.J.: Prentice-Hall, 1968.

Magoun, H. W. *The waking brain,* 2nd ed. Springfield, Ill.: Charles C Thomas, 1963.

Marshack, A. *The roots of civilization.* New York: McGraw-Hill, 1972.

Matthiessen, P. *The tree where man was born.* New York: Dutton, 1972.

Oberle, M. W. Lead poisoning: A preventable childhood disease of the slums. *Science,* 1969, **165,** 991–992.

Odum, E. P. *Ecology.* New York: Holt, Rinehart & Winston, 1963.

Penfield, W., and Rasmussen, T. *The cerebral cortex of man.* New York: Macmillan, 1950.

Porter, E., and Brower, K. *Galápagos: The flow of wildness,* 2 vols. New York: Sierra Club–Ballantine Books, 1970 (paper).

Proshansky, H. M., Ittelson, W. H., and Rivlin, L. G. (eds.) *Environmental psychology: Man in his physical setting.* New York: Basic Books, 1970.

Stebbins, G. L. *Processes of organic evolution.* Englewood Cliffs, N.J.: Prentice-Hall, 1966.

van Lawick-Goodall, Jane. *In the shadow of man.* New York: Dell, 1971 (paper).

Washburn, S. L., and DeVore, I. The social life of baboons. *Scientific American,* 1961, **204** (6), 62–71.

Wells, H. G., Huxley, J. S., and Wells, G. P. *The science of life.* Garden City, New York: Doubleday, 1938.

Whiting, J. W. M. Effects of climate on certain cultural practices. In *Explorations in cultural anthropology: Essays in honor of George Murdock* (W. H. Goodenough, ed.), pp. 511–544. New York: McGraw-Hill, 1964.

Woodruff, C. E. *Effects of tropical light on white men.* New York: Rebman, 1905.

Wooldridge, D. E. *The machinery of the brain.* New York: McGraw-Hill, 1963 (paper).

CHAPTER TWO

Adelson, J., and O'Neil, R. P. Growth of political ideas in adolescence: The sense of community. *Journal of Personality and Social Psychology,* 1966, **4,** 295–306.

Benedict, Ruth. Psychological types in the cultures of the Southwest. In *Proceedings of the 23rd International Congress of Americanists,* pp. 527–581. New York: 1930. Reprinted in *An anthropologist at work* (M. Mead, ed.), pp. 248–261. Boston: Houghton Mifflin, 1959.

Benedict, Ruth. *Patterns of culture.*

New York: New American Library, 1934.

Bourke, J. G. The medicine men of the Apache. *U.S. Bureau of American Ethnology, 9th Annual Report, 1887–1888.* Washington, D.C.: 1892.

Bruner, J. S., and Postman, L. On the perception of incongruity: A paradigm. *Journal of Personality,* 1949, **18,** 206–223.

Carmichael, L. A., Hogan, H. P., and Walter, A. A. An experimental study of the effect of language on the reproduction of visually perceived form. *Journal of Experimental Psychology,* 1932, **15,** 73–86.

Duncker, K. The influence of past experience upon perceptual properties. *American Journal of Psychology,* 1939, **52,** 255–265.

Froman, R. *Science, art, and visual illusions.* New York: Simon and Schuster, 1970 (paper).

Furth, H. G. *Piaget and knowledge.* Englewood Cliffs, N. J.: Prentice-Hall, 1969.

Furth, H. G. *Piaget for teachers.* Englewood Cliffs, N.J.: Prentice-Hall, 1970.

Gibson, Eleanor J., and Walk, R. D. The "visual cliff." *Scientific American,* 1960, **202,** 64–71.

Gibson, J. J. *The senses considered as perceptual systems.* Boston: Houghton Mifflin, 1966.

Gillin, J. The balance of threat and security in Mesoamerica: San Carlos. In *Personalities and cultures: Readings in psychological anthropology* (R. Hunt, ed.), pp. 139–149. Garden City, N.Y.: The Natural History Press, 1967.

Ginsburg, H., and Opper, Sylvia. *Piaget's theory of intellectual development.* Englewood Cliffs, N.J.: Prentice-Hall, 1969.

Itoh, T., and Futagawa, Y. *The elegant Japanese house: Traditional sukiya architecture.* New York and Tokyo: Walker/Weatherhill, 1969.

Koffka, K. *Principles of gestalt psychology.* London: Kegan Paul, 1935.

Lazarus, R. S., Eriksen, C. W., and Fonda, C. P. Personality dynamics and auditory perceptual recognition. *Journal of Personality,* 1951, **19,** 471–482.

Lewis, O. The culture of poverty. *Scientific American,* 1966, **215** (4), 19–25.

Loomis, W. F. Rickets. *Scientific American,* 1970, **223** (6), 77–91.

Morris, C. *Paths of life.* New York: Harper and Row, 1942.

Piaget, J. *The origins of intelligence in children.* New York: International Universities Press, 1952.

Piaget, J. *Logic and psychology.* New York: Basic Books, 1957.

Rapoport, A. *House form and culture.* Englewood Cliffs, N.J.: Prentice-Hall, 1969.

Rotter, J. B. Generalized expectancies for internal versus external control of reinforcement. *Psychological Monographs: General and Applied,* 1966, **80** (Whole No. 609).

Senden, M. V. *Space and sight: The perception of space and shape in the congenitally blind before and after operation* (trans. by P. Heath). New York: The Free Press, 1960.

Sims, J. H., and Baumann, D. D. The tornado threat: Coping styles of the North and South. *Science,* 1972, **176,** 1386–1392.

van Lawick–Goodall, Jane. *In the shadow of man.* New York: Dell, 1971 (paper).

Vernon, M. D. *The psychology of perception.* Middlesex, England: Penguin Books, 1962 (paper).

White, L., Jr. The historical roots of our ecological crisis. *Science,* 1967, **155,** 1203–1307.

Witkin, H. A., Lewis, Helen B., Machover, Karen, Meissner, P. B., and Wapner, S. *Personality through perception.* New York: Harper & Row, 1954.

CHAPTER THREE

Bem, D. *Beliefs, attitudes, and human affairs.* Belmont, Calif.: Brooks/Cole, 1970

Buckout, R. Toward a two-child norm: Changing family planning attitudes. *American Psychologist,* 1972, **27,** 16–26.

Calhoun, J. B. Population density and social pathology. *Scientific American,* 1962, **209,** 139–148.

Carson, Rachel. *Silent spring.* New York: Crest Books, 1962 (paper).

Christian, J. J., and Davis, D. E. Endocrines, behavior, and population. *Science,* 1964, **146,** 1550–1560.

Deevey, E. S., Jr. The human population: with biographical sketch. *Scientific American,* 1960, **203,** 48, 194–198.

Ehrlich, P. R. *The population bomb.* New York: Ballantine Books, 1968.

Ehrlich, P. R. Eco-catastrophe. *Ramparts Magazine,* September 1969, pp. 1–5.

Fawcett, J. T. *Psychology and population.* New York: The Population Council, 1970.

Feldman, R. E. Response to compatriot and foreigner who seek assistance. *Journal of Personality and Social Psychology,* 1968, **10,** 202–214.

Ford, Amasa B. Casualties of our time. *Science,* 1970, **167,** 256–263.

Galle, O. R., Gove, W. R., and McPherson, J. M. Population density and pathology: What are the relations for man? *Science,* 1972, **176,** 23–30.

Hardin, G. (ed.) *Population, evolution and birth control.* San Francisco, Calif.: Freeman, 1969.

Johnson, H. How pollution is killing a dream. *San Francisco Chronicle,* February 16, 1970, p. 8.

Klepinger, B. D. *Population size: Its effects on behavior and stress-responsive physiological systems.* (Doctoral dissertation, Indiana Univ.) Ann Arbor, Mich.: Univ. of Michigan Microfilms, 1969, No. 69-4769. (Cited by Fawcett, 1970.)

Langer, W. L. Checks on population growth. *Scientific American,* 1972, **226,** 92–99.

Latané, B., and Darley, J. M. Bystander "apathy." In *Psychology: adapted readings* (J. Kagan, M. M. Haith, and Catherine Caldwell, eds.) New York: Harcourt Brace Jovanovich, 1969a.

Latané, B., and Darley, J. M. Bystander "apathy." *American Scientist,* 1969b, **57,** 244–268.

Latané, B., and Darley, J. M. *The unresponsive bystander.* New York: Appleton-Century-Crofts, 1970.

Lerner, I. M. *Heredity, evolution, and society.* San Francisco: Freeman, 1968.

Malthus, T. R. An essay on the principle of population. In *Population evolution and birth control* (G. Hardin, ed.), pp. 4–16. San Francisco, Calif.: Freeman, 1964 (first published in 1798).

Milgram, S. The familiar stranger: An aspect of urban anonymity. *APA Division 8 Newsletter,* July 1972, p. 1.

Neel, J. V. Lessons from a "primitive" people. *Science,* 1970, **170,** 815–822.

Pohlman, E. H. *Psychology of birth planning.* Cambridge, Mass.: Schenkman, 1969.

Rainwater, L. *And the poor get children.* Chicago: Quadrangle Books, 1960.

Rainwater, L. *Family design.* Chicago: Aldine, 1965.

Stokols, D. On the distinction between density and crowding: Some implications for future research. *Psychological Review,* 1972, **79,** 275–277.

Thiessen, D. D. Role of physical injury in the physiological effects of population density in mice. *Journal of Comparative and Physiological Psychology,* 1966, **62,** 322–324.

United Nations Association, National Policy Panel on World Population. *World population: A challenge to the United Nations and its systems of agencies.* New York: May 1969.

Van Tienhoven, A., Eisner, T., and Rosenblatt, F. Education and the population explosion. *Bioscience,* 1971, **21,** 16–21.

Wallace, B. *Essays in social biology,* Vol. 1: *People, their needs, environment, ecology.* Englewood Cliffs, N.J.: Prentice-Hall, 1972.

Westoff, C. F., and Bumpass, L. The revolution in birth control practices of U.S. Roman Catholics. *Science,* 1973, **179,** 41–44.

Wynne-Edwards, V. C. Self-regulating systems in populations of animals. *Science,* 1965, **147,** 1543–1548.

Zimbardo, P. G. The human choice: Individuation, reason, and order versus deindividuation, impulse, and chaos. In *Nebraska Symposium on Motivation* (W. J. Arnold and D. Levine, eds.), pp. 237–307. Lincoln, Nebr.: Univ. of Nebraska Press, 1969.

CHAPTER FOUR

Asch, S. E. Effects of group pressure upon the modification and distortion of judgments. In *Readings in social psychology* (G. E. Swanson, T. M. Newcomb, and

E. L. Hartley, eds.), pp. 2–11. New York: Holt, Rinehart & Winston, 1952a.

Asch, S. E. *Social psychology.* Englewood Cliffs, N.J.: Prentice-Hall, 1952b, 459–473.

Asch, S. E. Studies of independence and conformity: A minority of one against a unanimous majority. *Psychological Monographs: General and Applied,* 1956, **70** (Whole No. 416).

Bandura, A. *Aggression: A social learning analysis.* Englewood Cliffs, N.J.: Prentice-Hall, 1973.

Bandura, A., and Walters, R. *Social learning and personality development.* New York: Holt, Rinehart and Winston, 1963.

Beecher, H. K. Relationship of significance of wound to pain experienced. *Journal of the American Medical Association,* 1956, **161,** 1609–1613.

Beecher, H. K. Generalization of pain of various types and origins. *Science,* 1959, **130,** 267–268.

Beecher, H. K. Increased stress and effectiveness of placebos and "active" drugs. *Science,* 1960, **132,** 91–92.

Bem, D. *Beliefs, attitudes, and human affairs.* Belmont, Calif.: Brooks/Cole, 1970 (paper).

Benedict, Ruth. *Patterns of culture.* New York: New American Library, 1934.

Benedict, Ruth. *The chrysanthemum and the sword.* Boston: Houghton Mifflin, 1946.

Berger, P. L., and Luckmann, T. *The social construction of reality.* New York: Doubleday, 1966.

Breger, L. Conformity as a function of the ability to express hostility. *Journal of Personality,* 1963, **31,** 247–257.

Brehm, J. W., and Cohen, A. R. *Explorations in cognitive dissonance.* New York: Wiley, 1962.

Breland, K., and Breland, M. *Animal behavior.* New York: Macmillan, 1966.

Brown, R. *Social psychology,* New York: The Free Press, 1965.

Caudill, W. Observations on the cultural context of Japanese psychiatry. In *Culture and mental health* (M. K. Opler, ed.), pp. 213–242. New York: Macmillan, 1959.

Clark, K. B. The pathos of power: A psychological perspective. *American Psychologist,* 1971, **26,** 1047–1057.

Conn, L. K., and Crowne, D. P. Instigation to aggression, emotional arousal and defensive emulation. *Journal of Personality,* 1964, **32,** 163–179.

Davis, B. D. Prospects for genetic intervention in man. *Science,* 1970, **170,** 1279–1283.

Delgado, J. M. R. *Physical control of the mind.* New York: Harper & Row, 1969.

DeVos, G. A., and Hippler, A. E. Cultural psychology: Comparative studies of human behavior. In *The handbook of social psychology* (G. Lindzey and E. Aronson, eds.), 2nd ed., Vol. 4, pp. 323–417. Reading, Mass.: Addison-Wesley, 1969.

Epstein, S. Comments on Dr. Bandura's paper. In *Nebraska Symposium on Motivation* (M. R. Jones, ed.), pp. 269–272.

Lincoln, Nebr.: Univ. of Nebraska Press, 1962.

Festinger, L. *A theory of cognitive dissonance.* Evanston, Ill.: Row-Peterson, 1957.

Frankl, V. E. *Man's search for meaning: An introduction to logotherapy.* New York: Washington Square Press, 1963 (paper).

Freedman, J. L. How important is cognitive consistency? In *Theories of cognitive consistency: a source book* (R. P. Abelson et al., eds.). Chicago: Rand McNally, 1968.

Freedman, J. L., and Doob, A. N. *Deviancy: The psychology of being different.* New York: Academic Press, 1968.

Freedman, J. L., Carlsmith, J. M., and Sears, D. O. *Social psychology.* Englewood Cliffs, N.J.: Prentice-Hall, 1970.

Freud, S. *The problem of anxiety.* New York: Norton, 1936.

Freud, S. The ego and the id. In *The complete psychological works of Sigmund Freud,* Vol. 19. London: Hogarth, 1961 (first published in 1923).

Freud, S. *Civilization and its discontents.* London: Hogarth, 1968.

Fromm, E. *The sane society.* New York: Rinehart, 1955.

Glueck, S., and Glueck, Eleanor. *Unraveling juvenile delinquency.* New York: Commonwealth Fund, 1950.

Goffman, E. *Stigma.* Englewood Cliffs, N.J.: Prentice-Hall, 1963.

Goffman, E. *Relations in public.* New York: Basic Books, 1971.

Goldsen, R. K., Rosenberg, M., Williams, R. M., and Suchman, E. A. *What college students think.* Princeton, N.J.: Van Nostrand, 1960.

Hess, R. D., and Torney, J. *The development of political attitudes in children.* Chicago: Aldine, 1967.

Janis, I. L. *Victims of groupthink.* Boston: Houghton Mifflin, 1972.

Jennings, M. K., and Niemi, R. G. The transmission of political values from parent to child. *American Political Science Review,* 1968, **62,** 169–184.

Jones, Mary C. A laboratory study of fear: The case of Peter. *Pediatrics Seminar,* 1924, **31,** 308–315.

Kaplan, A. *The conduct of inquiry.* San Francisco: Chandler, 1964.

Kelman, H. C. Processes of opinion change. *Public Opinion Quarterly,* 1961, **25,** 57–58.

Lewin, K. *A dynamic theory of personality* (trans. by K. E. Zener and D. K. Adams). New York: McGraw-Hill, 1935.

Lieberman, S. The effects of changes in roles on the attitudes of room occupants. *Human Relations,* 1956, **9,** 385–402.

McCord, W., and McCord, Joan. *Psychopathy and delinquency.* New York: Grune & Stratton, 1956.

McCord, W., and McCord, Joan. The effects of parental role model on criminality. *Journal of Social Issues,* 1958, **14,** 66–75.

Mead, G. H. *Mind, self, and society.* Chicago: Univ. of Chicago Press, 1934.

Mead, Margaret. *Sex and temperament in three primitive societies.* New York: Morrow, 1935.

Mehrabian, A. *Tactics of social influence.* Englewood Cliffs, N.J.: Prentice-Hall, 1970.

Miller, N. E. Experimental studies of conflict. In *Personality and the behavior disorders* (J. McV. Hunt, ed.), Vol. I. New York: Ronald Press, 1944.

National Review. A survey of the political and religious attitudes of American college students. October 8, 1963, pp. 279–302.

Newcomb, T. M. *Personality and social change.* New York: Dryden, 1943.

Newcomb, T. M., Koenig, K. E., Flacks, R., and Warwick, D. P. *Persistence and change: Bennington College and its students after twenty-five years.* New York: Wiley, 1967.

Olds, J., and Olds, M. E. Drives, rewards, and the brain. In *New directions in psychology* (F. Barron and others, eds.), Vol. II, pp. 329–410. New York: Holt, Rinehart, & Winston, 1965.

Rank, O. *The trauma of birth.* New York: Robert Brunner, 1952.

Roethlisberger, F. J., and Dixon, W. J. *Management and the worker.* Cambridge, Mass.: Harvard Univ. Press, 1940.

Rosenberg, B. G., and Sutton-Smith, B. *Sex and identity.* New York: Holt, Rinehart & Winston, 1972.

Rosenberg, M. J. An analysis of affective-cognitive consistency. In *Attitude organization and change* (C. I. Hovland and M. J. Rosenberg, eds.), pp. 15–64. New Haven, Conn.: Yale Univ. Press, 1960.

Rotter, J. B. Generalized expectancies for internal versus external control of reinforcement. *Psychological Monographs: General and Applied,* 1966, **80** (Whole No. 609).

Schachter, S. Deviation, rejection, and communication. *Journal of Abnormal and Social Psychology,* 1951, **46,** 190–207.

Sherif, M. A study of some social factors in perception. *Archives of Psychology,* 1935, **27** (Whole No. 187).

Silverman, I. On the resolution and tolerance of cognitive inconsistency in a natural-occurring event: Attitudes and beliefs following the Senator Edward M. Kennedy incident. *Journal of Personality and Social Psychology,* 1971, **17,** 171–178.

Singer, J. L., and Opler, M. K. Contrasting patterns of fantasy and motility in Irish and Italian schizophrenics. *Journal of Abnormal and Social Psychology,* 1956, **53,** 42–47.

Skinner, B. F. *Beyond freedom and dignity.* New York: Knopf, 1971.

Tolman, E. C. Cognitive maps in rats and men. *Psychological Review,* 1948, **55,** 189–208.

Ullmann, L. P., and Krasner, L. *A psychological approach to abnormal behavior.* Englewood Cliffs, N.J.: Prentice-Hall, 1969.

Washburn, S. L. Phi Beta Kappa Lecture. University of Kansas, Lawrence, Kans., 1963.

Willems, E. P., and Rausch, H. L. (eds.)

Naturalistic viewpoints in psychological research. New York: Holt, Rinehart & Winston, 1969.

CHAPTER FIVE

Baumrind, Diana. Current patterns of parental authority. *Developmental Psychology Monographs,* 1971, **4** (Whole No. 1), Pt. 2, p. 103.

Baumrind, Diana, and Black, A. E. Socialization practices associated with dimensions of competence in preschool boys and girls. *Child Development,* 1967, **38** (2), 291–327.

Bell, D. *The end of ideology.* New York: Pantheon, 1962.

Bellamy, E. *Looking backward: 2000–1887* (J. L. Thomas, ed.) Cambridge, Mass.: Harvard Univ. Press, 1967 (originally published in 1888).

Benedict, Ruth. *The chrysanthemum and the sword.* Boston: Houghton Mifflin, 1946.

Bronfenbrenner, U. Socialization and social class through time and space. In *Readings in social psychology* (Eleanor E. Maccoby, T. M. Newcomb, and E. L. Hartley, eds.), 3rd ed. New York: Holt, Rinehart & Winston, 1958.

Brown, N. O. *Life against death: The psychoanalytical meaning of history.* New York: Vintage Books, 1959.

Burgess, A. *A clockwork orange.* New York: Ballantine Books, 1962.

Davis, A., and Havighurst, R. J. Social class and colour differences in childrearing. *American Sociological Review,* 1946, **11,** 698–710.

de Tocqueville, A. *Democracy in America.* New York: Vintage, 1954 (first published in 1835).

Dobzhansky, T. *Mankind evolving.* New Haven, Conn.: Yale Univ. Press, 1962.

Fairweather, G. M. *Social change: The challenge to survival.* Morristown, N.J.: General Learning Press, 1972.

Fletcher, J. *Situation ethics: The new morality.* Philadelphia: Westminster, 1966.

Gallup, G. Post-GOP convention survey finds voter shift to Nixon. *Gallup Opinion Index,* Rept. No. 87. Princeton, N.J.: American Institute of Public Opinion, 1972.

Gans, H. *Levittowners.* New York: Pantheon, 1967.

Grossack, M., and Gardner, H. *Man and men.* Scranton, Pa.: International Textbook, 1970 (paper).

Hersey, J. *Letter to the alumni.* New York: Knopf, 1970.

Hofstadter, R. *Social Darwinism in American thought.* Philadelphia: Univ. of Pennsylvania Press, 1944.

Hogan, R. T. The new moralities. *The Johns Hopkins Magazine,* December 1969, pp. 28–32.

Huxley, A. *Brave new world.* London: Chatto & Windus, 1932.

Huxley, A. Human potentialities. In *Science and human affairs* (R. E. Farson, ed.)

Palo Alto, Calif.: Science and Behavior Books, 1965.

Jacobs, Jane. *The death and life of great American cities.* New York: Vintage, 1961.

Johnson, W. (ed.) *Focus on the science fiction film.* Englewood Cliffs, N.J.: Prentice-Hall, 1972 (paper).

Lowenthal, L. *Literature, popular culture, and society.* Englewood Cliffs, N.J.: Prentice-Hall, 1961 (paper).

Manuel, F. Toward a psychological history of utopias. *Daedalus,* 1965, **94,** 293–322.

Marcuse, H. *Eros and civilization.* Boston: Beacon Press, 1961.

Maslow, A. H. *Toward a psychology of being,* 2nd ed. Princeton, N.J.: Van Nostrand, 1968.

Mead, Margaret. *Culture and commitment: A study of the generation gap.* Garden City, N.Y.: Natural History Press/Doubleday, 1970.

More, T. *Utopia.* London: Alsop and Fawcett, 1939 (first published in 1516).

Morris, C., and Small, L. Changes in conceptions of the good life by American college students from 1950 to 1970. *Journal of Personality and Social Psychology,* 1971, **20,** 254–260.

Orwell, G. *1984.* New York: Harcourt Brace Jovanovich, 1949.

Pastore, N. *The nature-nurture controversy.* New York: King's Crown, 1949.

Reich, C. A. *The greening of America.* New York: Random House, 1970.

Riesman, D. *The lonely crowd.* New York: Doubleday, 1950.

Sears, R. R., Maccoby, Eleanor E., and Levin, H. *Patterns of child rearing.* New York: Harper & Row, 1957.

Skinner, B. F. *Walden two.* New York: Macmillan, 1961.

Stendler, Celia B. Sixty years of child training practices. *Journal of Pediatrics,* 1950, **36,** 122–134.

Toffler, A. *Future shock.* New York: Random House, 1970.

Tompkins, S. S. Affect and the psychology of knowledge. In *Affect, cognition, and personality* (S. Tompkins and C. E. Izard, eds.), pp. 72–97. New York: Springer, 1965.

Whyte, W. H., Jr. *The organization man.* New York: Doubleday, 1956.

Wolfenstein, Martha. Trends in infant care. *American Journal of Orthopsychiatry,* 1953, **23,** 120–130.

INTRODUCTION TO PART TWO

Benedict, Ruth. The uses of cannibalism. In *An anthropologist at work* (M. Mead, ed.), pp. 44–48. Boston: Houghton Mifflin, 1959.

Freud, S. *Civilization, war and death* (J. Rickman, ed.), p. 80. London: Hogarth Press, 1968.

Liddell Hart, B. H. *The revolution in*

warfare. New Haven, Conn.: Yale Univ. Press, 1947.

Matthiessen, P. *The tree where man was born.* New York: Dutton, 1972.

Scott, J. P. Biology and human aggression. *American Journal of Orthopsychiatry,* 1970, **40,** 569–577.

Teleki, G. The omnivorous chimpanzee. *Scientific American,* 1973, **228** (1), 32–42.

Watanabe, S. Nuclear hematology: Based on experience with atomic explosions. In *Nuclear hematology* (E. Szirmai, ed.), pp. 485–537. New York: Academic Press, 1965.

CHAPTER SIX

Ardrey, R. *The territorial imperative.* New York: Atheneum, 1966.

Ashley Montagu, M. F. (ed.) *Man and aggression.* New York: Oxford Univ. Press, 1968.

Azrin, N. Pain and aggression. *Psychology Today,* 1967, **1,** 27–33.

Bandura, A. *Aggression: A social learning analysis.* Englewood Cliffs, N.J.: Prentice-Hall, 1973.

Beach, F. A. The descent of instinct. *Psychological Review,* 1955, **62,** 401–410.

Benedict, Ruth. *Patterns of culture.* Boston: Houghton Mifflin, 1934.

Benedict, Ruth. *An anthropologist at work* (M. Mead, ed.), p. 113. Boston: Houghton Mifflin. 1959.

Berkowitz, L. *Aggression: A social psychological analysis.* New York: McGraw-Hill, 1962a.

Berkowitz, L. Impulse, aggression and the gun. *Psychology Today,* 1962b, **2,** 19–22.

Calhoun, J. B. Mortality and movement of brown rats (*Rattus norvegicus*) in artificially supersaturated populations. *Journal of Wildlife Management,* 1948, **12,** 167–172.

Calhoun, J. B. The study of wild animals under controlled conditions. *Annals of the New York Academy of Sciences,* 1950, **51,** 1113–1122.

Cannon, W. B. *The wisdom of the body,* 2nd ed. New York: Norton, 1939.

Carpenter, C. R. Sexual behavior of free-ranging rhesus monkeys. *Journal of Comparative Psychology,* 1942, **33,** 113–142.

Carpenter, C. R. *Naturalistic behavior of nonhuman primates.* University Park, Pa.: Pennsylvania State Univ. Press, 1964.

Carpenter, C. R. In *War: The anthropology of armed conflict and aggression* (M. Fried, M. Harris, and R. Murphy, eds.), p. 54. Garden City, N.Y.: The Natural History Press, 1968.

Chagnon, N. Yanomamo social organization and warfare. In *War: The anthropology of armed conflict and aggression* (M. Fried, M. Harris, and R. Murphy, eds.), pp. 109–159. Garden City, N.Y.: The Natural History Press, 1968a.

Chagnon, N. *Yanomamö: The fierce*

people. New York: Harcourt Brace Jovanovich, 1968b.

Clark, G., and Birch, H. G. Hormonal modifications of social behavior. I. The effect of sex-hormone administration on the social status of a male castrate chimpanzee. *Psychosomatic Medicine,* 1945, **7**, 321–329.

Clark, G., and Birch, H. G. Hormonal modification of social behavior. II. The sex effects of sex-hormone administration on the social dominance status of the female-castrate chimpanzee. *Psychosomatic Medicine,* 1946, **8**, 320–331.

DeVore, I. (ed.) *Primate behavior.* New York: Holt, Rinehart & Winston, 1965.

Dollard, J., Doob, L., Miller, N. E., Mowrer, O. H., and Sears, R. R. *Frustration and aggression.* New Haven, Conn.: Yale Univ. Press, 1939.

Durbin, E. J. M., and Bowlby, J. *Personal aggressiveness and war.* New York: Columbia Univ. Press, 1939.

Eibl-Eibesfeldt, I. Ontogenetic and maturational studies of aggressive behavior. In *Brain function,* Vol. V: *Aggression and defense* (C. D. Clemente and D. B. Lindsley, eds.), pp. 57–94. Los Angeles: Univ. of California Press, 1967.

Eibl-Eibesfeldt, I. *Ethology: The biology of behavior* (trans. by E. Klinghammer). New York: Holt, Rinehart & Winston, 1970.

Evans-Pritchard, E. E. *Nuer religion.* New York: Oxford Univ. Press (Clarendon), 1956.

Fenichel, O. *The psychoanalytic theory of neurosis.* New York: Norton, 1945.

Frank, J. D. *Sanity and survival: Psychological aspects of war and peace.* New York: Random House, 1967.

Freeman, D. Human aggression in anthropological perspective. In *The natural history of aggression* (J. D. Carthy and J. J. Ebling, eds.), pp. 109–119. New York: Academic Press, 1964.

Freud, S. *New introductory lectures in psychoanalysis.* New York: Norton, 1933 (first German ed., 1933).

Freud, S. *Civilization and its discontents* (trans. by Joan Riviere). London: Hogarth, 1957 (first publ. 1930; first German ed., 1920); also reprinted in *Civilization, war and death* (J. Rickman, ed.), pp. 26–81. London: Hogarth Press, 1968.

Freud, S. Why war? A letter to Albert Einstein. In *The collected papers of Sigmund Freud* (Ernest Jones, ed.), Vol. 5, Chap. 25. New York: Basic Books, 1959; also in the *Standard edition of the complete psychological works of Sigmund Freud* (trans. by James Strachey), Vol. 22. London: Hogarth Press, 1953; reprinted in *Civilization, war and death* (J. Rickman, ed.), pp. 82–97. London: Hogarth Press, 1968.

Fromm, E. *The sane society.* New York: Holt, Rinehart & Winston, 1955.

Goldman, I. The Ifugao of the Philippine Islands. In *Cooperation and competition among primitive people* (M. Mead, ed.), pp. 153–179. Boston: Beacon Press, 1961a.

Goldman, I. The Kwakiutl Indians of Vancouver Island. In *Cooperation and competition among primitive people* (M. Mead, ed.), pp. 180–209. Boston: Beacon Press, 1961b.

Hebb, D. O. On the nature of fear. *Psychological Review,* 1946, **53**, 259–276.

Leakey, L. S. B. Development of aggression as a factor in early human and pre-human evolution. In *Brain function,* Vol. V: *Aggression and defense* (C. D. Clemente and D. B. Lindsley, eds.), pp. 1–33. Los Angeles: Univ. of California Press, 1967.

Lehrman, D. S. The reproductive behavior of ring doves. *Scientific American,* 1964, **211** (5), 48–54.

Lorenz, K. *King Solomon's ring.* New York: Thomas Y. Crowell, 1953.

Lorenz, K. Ritualized fighting. In *The natural history of aggression* (J. D. Carthy and J. J. Ebling, eds.), pp. 39–50. New York: Academic Press, 1964.

Lorenz, K. *On aggression.* New York: Harcourt Brace Jovanovich, 1966.

McClelland, D. C. *The achieving society.* Princeton, N.J.: Van Nostrand, 1961.

McDougall, W. *An introduction to social psychology,* 13th ed. Boston: Luce, 1918.

Maddi, S. R., and Costa, P. T. *Humanism in personality: Allport, Maslow, and Murray.* Chicago: Aldine, 1972.

Marshack, A. *The roots of civilization.* New York: McGraw-Hill, 1972.

Maslow, A. H. Deprivation, threat, and frustration. *Psychological Review,* 1941, **48**, 364–366.

Maslow, A. H. Conflict, frustration, and the theory of threat. *Journal of Abnormal and Social Psychology,* 1943, **38**, 81–86.

Maslow, A. H. *Toward a psychology of being,* 2nd ed. Princeton, N.J.: Van Nostrand, 1968.

Mathews, L. H. Overt fighting in mammals. In *The natural history of aggression* (J. D. Carthy and J. J. Ebling, eds.), pp. 23–32. New York: Academic Press, 1964.

Mead, M. (ed.) *Cooperation and competition among primitive people.* Boston: Beacon Press, 1961.

Menninger, K. *Love against hate.* New York: Harcourt Brace Jovanovich, 1942.

Miller, N. E. Theory and experiment relating psychoanalytic displacement to stimulus-response generalization. *Journal of Abnormal and Social Psychology,* 1948, **43**, 155–178.

Moyer, K. W. Kinds of aggression and their physiological basis. Report No. 67-12, Carnegie-Mellon Univ., Pittsburgh, Pa., 1967.

Norbeck, E. African rituals of conflict. *American Anthropologist,* 1963, **65**, 1254–1279.

Orwell, G. *Animal farm.* New York: Harcourt Brace Jovanovich, 1954.

Pastore, N. The role of arbitrariness in the frustration-aggression hypothesis. *Journal of Abnormal and Social Psychology,* 1952, **47**, 728–731.

Persky, H., Smith, K. D., and Basu, G. K. Relation of psychologic measures of aggression and hostility to testosterone production in man. *Psychosomatic Medicine,* 1971, **33**, 265–277.

Reik, T. *Myth and guilt.* New York: Braziller, 1957.

Rosenzweig, S. An outline of frustration theory. In *Personality and the behavior disorders* (J. McV. Hunt, ed.) New York: Ronald Press, 1944.

Rothballer, A. B. Aggression, defense and neurohumors. In *Brain function,* Vol. V: *Aggression and defense* (C. D. Clemente and D. B. Lindsley, eds.), pp. 135–170. Los Angeles: Univ. of California Press, 1967.

Sargent, S. S. Reactions to frustration—a critique and hypothesis. *Psychological Review,* 1948, **55**, 108–114.

Schaller, G. B. *Year of the gorilla.* Chicago: Univ. of Chicago Press, 1964.

Schlesinger, A., Jr. *Violence: America in the sixties.* New York: Signet Books, 1968 (paper).

Scott, J. P. *Aggression.* Chicago: Univ. of Chicago Press, 1958.

Seward, J. P. Aggressive behavior in the rat. III. The role of frustration. *Journal of Comparative Psychology,* 1945, **38**, 225–238.

Southwick, C. H. Aggression among nonhuman primates. *Module in anthropology.* Reading, Mass.: Addison-Wesley, 1972.

Storr, A. *Human aggression.* New York: Atheneum, 1968.

Teleki, G. The omnivorous chimpanzee. *Scientific American,* 1973, **228** (1), 33–42.

Tinbergen, N. *The study of instincts.* New York: Oxford Univ. Press, 1951.

Tracey, H. *Chopi musicians: Their music, poetry and instruments.* New York: Oxford Univ. Press, 1948.

van Lawick–Goodall, Jane. *In the shadow of man.* New York: Dell, 1971 (paper).

Vayda, A. P. Hypotheses about functions of war. In *War: The anthropology of armed conflict and aggression* (M. Fried, M. Harris, and R. Murphy, eds.), pp. 85–91. Garden City, N.Y.: The Natural History Press, 1968.

Waelder, R. *Basic theory of psychoanalysis.* New York: International Universities Press, 1960.

Washburn, S. L. Speculations on the inter-relations of the history of tools and biological evolution. In *The evolution of man's capacity for culture* (J. N. Spuhler, ed.). Detroit, Mich.: Wayne State Univ. Press, 1959.

Washburn, S. L., and DeVore, I. The social life of baboons. *Scientific American,* 1961, **204** (6), 62–71.

Washburn, S. L., and Hamburg, D. A. Aggressive behavior in Old World monkeys and apes. In *Primates: Studies in adaptation and variability* (P. C. Jay, ed.). New York: Holt, Rinehart & Winston, 1968.

Wilson, A. P., and Boelkins, R. C. Evidence for seasonal variation in aggressive behavior by *Macaca mulatta. Animal Behavior,* 1970, **18,** 719–724.

CHAPTER SEVEN

Abrahams, R. D., and Dundes, A. On elephantasy and elephanticide. *Psychoanalytic Review,* 1969, **56,** 226–241.

Alexander, F. G., and Selesnick, S. T. *The history of psychiatry.* New York: Harper & Row, 1966.

Allport, G. W. *The nature of prejudice.* Reading, Mass.: Addison–Wesley, 1954.

Andreski, S. Origins of war. In *The natural history of aggression* (J. D. Carthy and J. J. Ebling, eds.), pp. 129–136. New York: Academic Press, 1964.

Bandura, A. *Aggression: A social learning analysis.* Englewood Cliffs, N.J.: Prentice-Hall, 1973.

Berkowitz, L. *Aggression: A social psychological analysis.* New York: McGraw-Hill, 1962.

Berkowitz, L. Impulse, aggression and the gun. *Psychology Today,* September 1968, pp. 19–22.

Berkowitz, L., and Green, R. G. Film violence and the cue properties of available targets. *Journal of Personality and Social Psychology,* 1966, **3,** 525–530.

Berne, E. *Games people play.* New York: Grove Press, 1964.

Breger, L. Conformity as a function of the ability to express hostility. *Journal of Personality,* 1963, **31,** 247–257.

Breger, L. *From instinct to identity.* Englewood Cliffs, N.J.: Prentice-Hall, 1973.

Brown, R. *Words and things: An introduction to language.* Glencoe, Ill.: The Free Press, 1958.

Burnstein, E., and Worchel, P. Arbitrariness of frustration and its consequences for aggression in a social situation. *Journal of Personality,* 1962, **30,** 528–540.

Cohen, A. R. Social norms, arbitrariness of frustration, and status of the agent of frustration-aggression hypothesis. *Journal of Abnormal and Social Psychology,* 1955, **51,** 222–226.

Cohen, N. *Warrant for genocide.* London: Eyre & Spottiswoode, 1967.

Conn, L. K., and Crowne, D. P. Instigation to aggression, emotional arousal and defensive emulation. *Journal of Personality,* 1964, **32,** 163–179.

Daniels, D. N., Gilula, M. F., and Ochberg, F. M. (eds.) *Violence and the struggle for existence.* Boston: Little, Brown, 1970.

Dundes, A. On the psychology of legend. In *American folk legend: A symposium* (W. D. Hand, ed.), pp. 21–36. Berkeley, Calif.: Univ. of California Press, 1971.

Eibl-Eibesfeldt, I. Ontogenetic and maturational studies of aggressive behavior. In *Brain function,* Vol. V: *Aggression and defense* (C. D. Clemente and D. B. Lindsley, eds.), pp. 57–94. Los Angeles: Univ. of California Press, 1967.

Epstein, S., and Taylor, S. P. Instigation to aggression as a function of degree of defeat and perceived aggressive intent of the opponent. *Journal of Personality,* 1967, **35,** 265–289.

Erikson, E. H. *Childhood and society.* New York: Norton, 1950.

Eron, L. D. Relationship to TV viewing habits and aggressive behavior in children. *Journal of Abnormal and Social Psychology,* 1963, **67,** 193–196.

Eron, L. D., Huesmann, L. R., Lefkowitz, M. M., and Walder, L. O. Does television violence cause aggression? *American Psychologist,* 1972, **27,** 253–263.

Fanon, F. *Black skin, white masks.* New York: Grove Press, 1967.

Feshbach, S., and Singer, R. D. *Television and aggression.* San Francisco: Jossey-Bass, 1971.

Frank, J. D. *Sanity and survival: Psychological aspects of war and peace.* New York: Random House, 1967.

Fried, M. Social change and personality character. In *Personality and social systems* (N. J. Smelser and W. T. Smelser, eds.), 2nd ed., pp. 368–392. New York: Wiley, 1970.

Fried, M., Harris, M., and Murphy, R. (eds.) *War: The anthropology of armed conflict and aggression.* Garden City, N.Y.: The Natural History Press, 1968.

Fromm, E. *The sane society.* New York: Holt, Rinehart & Winston, 1955.

Fromm, E. *The art of loving.* New York: Harper & Row, 1956.

Gladstone, A. The conception of the enemy. *Journal of Conflict Resolution,* 1959, **3,** 132–137.

Gordon, J. E., and Cohn, Faye. Effect of fantasy arousal of affiliation drive on doll play aggression. *Journal of Abnormal and Social Psychology,* 1963, **66,** 301–307.

Graham, H. D., and Gurr, F. R. (eds.) *Violence in America: Report of the National Commission on the Causes and Prevention of Violence.* New York: Signet Books–New American Library, 1969 (paper).

Graham, F. K., Charwat, W. A., Honig, A. S., and Weltz, P. C. Aggression as a function of the attack and the attacker. *Journal of Abnormal and Social Psychology,* 1951, **46,** 512–520.

Hallowell, A. I. Aggression in Saulteaux society. *Psychiatry,* 1940, **3,** 395–407.

Himmelweit, Hilde T., Oppenheim, A. N., and Vince, Pamela. *Television and the child.* New York: Oxford Univ. Press, 1958.

Jung, C. G. Symbol formation. In *The Collected Works of C. G. Jung* (Sir Herbert Read, M. Fordham, and G. Adler, eds.; trans. by R. F. C. Hull), Vol. 8, pp. 45–61. New York: Pantheon, 1960; also found in G. Lindzey and C. S. Hall (eds.) *Theories of personality: Primary sources and research,* pp. 77–85. New York: Wiley, 1965.

Kelley, H. H. Communication on experimentally created hierarchies. *Human Relations,* 1951, **4,** 39–56.

Kruger, Alice. Direct and substitute

modes of tension-reduction in terms of developmental level: An experimental analysis of the Rorschach Test. Doctoral dissertation, Clark University, Worcester, Massachusetts, 1954.

Kuo, A. Y. The genesis of the cat's response to the rat. *Journal of Comparative Psychology,* 1930, **2,** 1–35.

Laski, Margharita. The hostile world. From *The world of children.* London: Paul Hamlyn, 1966.

Liddell Hart, B. H. *The revolution in warfare.* New Haven, Conn.: Yale Univ. Press, 1947.

Livson, N., and Mussen, P. H. The relaxation of ego-control to overt aggression and dependency. *Journal of Abnormal and Social Psychology,* 1957, **55,** 66–71.

Lorenz, K. *On aggression.* New York: Harcourt Brace Jovanovich, 1966.

MacLeish, K., and Launois, J. Stone age cavemen of Mindanao. *National Geographic,* 1972, **142,** 219–249.

Maslow, A. H. Synergy in the society and the individual. *Journal of Individual Psychology,* 1964, **20,** 153–164.

Maslow, A. H. Self-actualization and beyond. In *Challenges of humanistic psychology* (J. Bugental, ed.). New York: McGraw-Hill, 1967.

Maslow, A. H. *Toward a psychology of being,* 2nd ed. Princeton: Van Nostrand, 1968.

Mead, Margaret. Alternatives to war. In *War: The anthropology of armed conflict and aggression* (M. Fried, M. Harris, and R. Murphy, eds.), pp. 215–228. New York: The Natural History Press, 1968.

Megargee, E. I., and Hokanson, J. E. (eds.) *The dynamics of aggression.* New York: Harper & Row, 1970.

Menninger, K. *Love against hate.* New York: Harcourt Brace Jovanovich, 1942.

Milgram, S. Some conditions of obedience and disobedience to authority. *Human Relations,* 1965a, **18,** 57–75.

Milgram, S. Liberating effects of group pressure. *Journal of Personality and Social Psychology,* 1965b, **1,** 127–134.

Miller, N. E. Theory and experiment relating psychoanalytic displacement to stimulus-response generalization. *Journal of Abnormal and Social Psychology,* 1948, **43,** 155–178.

Mirsky, Jeannette. The Eskimo of Greenland. In *Cooperation and competition among primitive people* (M. Mead, ed.), pp. 51–86. Boston: Beacon Press, 1961.

Misch, R. C. The relationship of motoric inhibition to developmental level and ideational functioning: An analysis by means of the Rorschach Test. Doctoral dissertation, Clark University, Worcester, Massachusetts, 1954.

Mishkin, B. The Maori of New Zealand. In *Cooperation and competition among primitive people* (M. Mead, ed.), pp. 428–457. Boston: Beacon Press, 1961.

Opton, E. M., Jr. It never happened and besides they deserved it. In *Sanctions for evil* (N. Sanford and C. Comstock, eds.), pp. 49–70. San Francisco: Jossey-Bass, 1971.

Parker, T., and Allerton, R. *The courage of his convictions.* London: Hutchinson, 1962.

Pike, L. O. *A history of crime in England,* 2 vols. London: Smith, Elder, 1873, 1876.

Pruitt, D. G., and Snyder, R. C. (eds.) *Theory and research on the causes of war.* Englewood Cliffs, N.J.: Prentice-Hall, 1969.

Richardson, L. F. *Statistics of deadly quarrels.* London: Stevens, 1960.

Rose, T. (ed.). *Violence in America.* New York: Vintage Books, 1969 (paper).

Rotter, J. B. Generalized expectancies for internal versus external control of reinforcement. *Psychological Monographs: General and Applied,* 1966, **80** (Whole No. 609).

Sanford, R. N., and Comstock, C. (eds.) *Sanctions for evil.* San Francisco: Jossey-Bass, 1971.

Schlesinger, A., Jr. *Violence: America in the sixties.* New York: Signet Books, 1968 (paper).

Schramm, V., Lyle, J., and Parker, E. B. *Television in the lives of our children.* Stanford, Calif.: Stanford Univ. Press, 1961.

Scott, J. P. *Aggression.* Chicago: Univ. of Chicago Press, 1958.

Scott, J. P. Hostility and aggression in animals. In *Roots of behavior* (E. L. Bliss, ed.), pp. 167–178. New York: Harper & Row, 1962.

Seward, J. P. Aggressive behavior in the rat. IV. Submission as determined by conditioning, extinction, and disuse. *Journal of Comparative Psychology,* 1946, **39,** 51–76.

Short, J. F., and Wolfgang, M. E. (eds.) Collective violence. *The Annals of the American Academy of Political and Social Science,* 1970, **391** (entire issue).

Stagner, R. Personality dynamics and social conflict. *Journal of Social Issues,* 1961, **17,** 28–44.

Storr, A. *Human aggression.* New York: Atheneum, 1968.

Thibaut, J., and Riecken, H. Authoritarianism, status, and the communication of aggression. *Human Relations,* 1955, **8,** 95–120.

Toch, H. *Violent men.* Chicago: Aldine, 1969.

Toch, H. The social psychology of violence. In *The dynamics of aggression* (E. I. Megargee and J. E. Hokanson, eds.), pp. 160–169. New York: Harper & Row, 1970. (Condensed from an invited address delivered to Division 8 of the American Psychological Association, September 1966.)

Vonnegut, K., Jr. *Mother night.* New York: Avon, 1967 (paper).

Walker, T. A. *A history of the law of nations,* Vol. I: *From the earliest times to the peace of Westphalia, 1848.* New York: Cambridge Univ. Press, 1899.

Wertham, F. C. *Seduction of the inno-*

cent. New York: Holt, Rinehart & Winston, 1954.

Whittlesey, D. *German strategy of world conquest.* New York: Farrar & Rinehart, 1942.

Wolfgang, M., and Ferracuti, F. *The subculture of violence: Toward an integrated theory of criminology.* London: Tavistock, 1967.

Wright, G. A study of war. In *International Encyclopedia of the social sciences* (D. L. Sills, ed.), pp. 453–467. New York: Macmillan, 1968.

Zawodny, J. K. (ed.) *Man and international relations,* Vol. I: *Conflict.* San Francisco: Chandler, 1966.

INTRODUCTION TO PART THREE

Hitler, A. *Mein Kampf.* Boston: Houghton Mifflin, 1943.

Hunt, J. McV. Black genes—white environment. *Transaction,* June 1969, pp. 238–248.

CHAPTER EIGHT

Adorno, T. W., Frenkel-Brunswik, Else, Levinson, D. J., and Sanford, R. N. *The authoritarian personality.* New York: Harper & Row, 1950.

Allport, G. W. *The nature of prejudice.* Reading, Mass.: Addison-Wesley, 1954.

Allport, G. W., and Kramer, B. M. Some roots of prejudice. *Journal of Psychology,* 1946, **22,** 16ff.

Artandi, Susan. Misrepresented by "women's lib." *Science,* 1972, **178,** 565.

Ashley Montagu, M. F. (ed.) *The concept of race,* pp. 12–28. Glencoe, Ill.: The Free Press, 1964.

Bardwick, J. M. *Psychology of women.* New York: Harper & Row, 1971.

Bem, Sandra L., and Bem, D. J. Case study of a nonconscious ideology: Training a woman to know her place. In Bem, D. J. *Beliefs, attitudes, and human affairs.* Belmont, Calif.: Brooks/Cole, 1970.

Bettelheim, B., and Janowitz, M. *Dynamics of prejudice: A psychological and sociological study of veterans.* New York: Harper & Row, 1950.

Bogardus, E. S. *Immigration and race attitudes.* Boston: Heath, 1928.

Brigham, J. C. Ethnic stereotypes. *Psychological Bulletin,* 1971, **76,** 15–38.

Broverman, Inge K., Vogel, Susan R., Broverman, D. M., Clarkson, F. E., and Rosenkrantz, P. S. Sex-role stereotypes: A current appraisal. *Journal of Social Issues,* 1972, **28,** 59–78.

Carter, L. F. The identification of racial membership. *Journal of Abnormal and Social Psychology,* 1948, **43,** 279–286.

Dean, J. P. Patterns of socialization and association between Jews and non-Jews. *Jewish Social Studies,* 1955, **17,** 247–268.

DeVos, G., and Wagatsuma, H. (eds.) *Japan's invisible race.* Berkeley and Los Angeles: Univ. of California Press, 1966.

Dobzhansky, T. *Mankind evolving.* New Haven, Conn.: Yale Univ. Press, 1962.

Elkins, S. *Slavery: A problem in American institutional and intellectual life.* Chicago: Univ. of Chicago Press, 1959.

Elkins, S. Slavery and personality. In *Studying personality cross-culturally* (B. Kaplan, ed.), pp. 243–270. New York: Harper & Row, 1961.

Gilbert, G. M. Stereotype persistence and change among college students. *Journal of Abnormal and Social Psychology,* 1951, **46,** 245–254.

Hitler, A. *Mein Kampf.* Boston: Houghton Mifflin, 1943.

Hovland, C. I., and Sears, R. R. Minor studies in aggression: VI. Correlation of lynchings with economic indices. *Journal of Psychology,* 1940, **9,** 301–310.

Karlins, M., Coffman, T. L., and Walters, G. On the fading of social stereotypes: Studies of three generations of college students. *Journal of Personality and Social Psychology,* 1969, **13,** 1–16.

Katz, D., and Braly, K. W. Racial stereotypes of 100 college students. *Journal of Abnormal and Social Psychology,* 1933, **28,** 280–290.

Klineberg, O. Negro-white differences in intelligence test performance: A new look at an old problem. *American Psychologist,* 1963, **18,** 198–203.

Klineberg, O. Black and white in international perspective. *American Psychologist,* 1971, **26,** 119–128.

Knapp, R. H. A psychology of rumor. *Public Opinion Quarterly,* 1944, **8,** 22–37.

Lazarus, R. S. *Patterns of adjustment and human effectiveness,* Chap. 8. New York: McGraw-Hill, 1969.

Lee, A. MacC. Sociological insights into American culture and personality. *Journal of Social Issues,* 1951, **7,** 7–14.

Lindzey, G., and Rogolsky, S. Prejudice and identification of minority group membership. *Journal of Abnormal and Social Psychology,* 1950, **45,** 37–53.

Maykovich, M. K. Stereotypes and racial images—white, black and yellow. *Human relations,* 1972, **25,** 101–120.

Mintz, A. A re-examination of correlations between lynchings and economic indices. *Journal of Abnormal and Social Psychology,* 1946, **41,** 154–160.

Myrdal, G. *An American dilemma: The Negro problem and modern democracy,* 2 vols. New York: Harper & Row, 1944.

Parkes, J. W. *The Jewish problem in the modern world.* London: Thornton Butterworth, 1939.

Pettigrew, T. F. Regional differences in anti-Negro prejudice. *Journal of Abnormal and Social Psychology,* 1959, **59,** 28–36.

Pettigrew, T. F. Social psychology and desegregation research. *American Psychologist,* 1961, **16,** 105–112.

Pettigrew, T. F. *A profile of the Negro American.* Princeton, N.J.: Van Nostrand, 1964.

Prothro, E. T. Ethnocentrism and anti-Negro attitudes in the Deep South. *Journal of Abnormal and Social Psychology,* 1952, **47,** 105–108.

Raper, A. F. *The tragedy of lynching.* Chapel Hill, N.C.: Univ. of North Carolina Press, 1933.

Richmond, A. M. Economic insecurity and stereotypes as factors in colour prejudice. *Sociological Review,* 1950, **42,** 147–170.

Rogow, A. A. Anti-Semitism. In *International Encyclopedia of the Social Sciences,* Vol. 1, pp. 345–349. New York: Macmillan (The Free Press), 1968.

Rokeach, M. (ed.) *The open and the closed mind.* New York: Basic Books, 1960.

Rokeach, M., Smith, Patricia, W., and Evans, R. I. Two kinds of prejudice or one? In *The open and closed mind* (M. Rokeach, ed.), pp. 132–168. New York: Basic Books, 1960.

Roper, E. United States anti-Semitics. *Fortune,* 1946, **33,** 257–260.

Roper, E. United States anti-Semitics. *Fortune,* 1947, **36,** 5–10.

Simpson, G. E., and Yinger, J. M. *Racial and cultural minorities: An analysis of prejudice and discrimination,* 3rd ed. New York: Harper & Row, 1965.

Smith, Carole R., Williams, L., and Willis, R. H. Race, sex, and belief as determinants of friendship acceptance. *Journal of Personality and Social Psychology,* 1967, **5,** 127–137.

Stein, D. D. The influence of belief systems on interpersonal preference: A validation study of Rokeach's theory of prejudice. *Psychological Monographs,* 1966, **80** (Whole No. 616), 1–29.

Stein, D. D., Hardyck, Jane A., and Smith, M. B. Race and belief—An open and shut case. *Journal of Personality and Social Psychology,* 1965, **1,** 281–289.

Stern, C. The biology of the Negro. *Scientific American,* 1954, **191,** 81–85.

Strong, D. S. *Organized anti-Semitism in America.* Washington, D.C.: American Council on Public Affairs, 1941.

Triandis, H. C. A note on Rokeach's theory of prejudice. *Journal of Abnormal and Social Psychology,* 1961, **62,** 184–186.

Triandis, H. C., and Davis, E. E. Race and belief as determinants of behavioral intentions. *Journal of Personality and Social Psychology,* 1965, **2,** 715–725.

Tuddenham, R. D. The nature and measurement of intelligence. In *Psychology in the making* (L. Postman, ed.), pp. 499–500. New York: Knopf, 1962.

Weisstein, N. Psychology constructs the female. In *Roles women play* (M. H. Garskof, ed.). Belmont, Calif.: Brooks/Cole, 1971.

Zeligs, Ruth, and Hendrickson, G. Racial attitudes of 200 sixth-grade children. *Sociology and Social Research,* 1933, **18,** 26–36.

CHAPTER NINE

Adorno, T. W., Frenkel-Brunswik, Else, Levinson, D. J., and Sanford, R. N. *The authoritarian personality.* New York: Harper & Row, 1950.

Allport, G. W. *The nature of prejudice.* Reading, Mass.: Addison-Wesley, 1954.

Cooper, E., and Jahoda, Marie. The evasion of propaganda: How prejudiced people respond to anti-prejudice propaganda. *Journal of Psychology,* 1947, **23,** 15–25.

Dollard, J. *Caste and class in a southern town.* New Haven, Conn.: Yale Univ. Press, 1937.

Dombrose, L. A., and Levinson, D. J. Ideological "militancy" and "pacifism" in democratic individuals. *Journal of Social Psychology,* 1950, **32,** 101–113.

Evans, R. I. Personal values as factors in anti-Semitism. *Journal of Abnormal and Social Psychology,* 1952, **47,** 749–756.

Freedman, J. L., Carlsmith, J. M., and Sears, D. O. *Social psychology.* Englewood Cliffs, N.J.: Prentice-Hall, 1970.

Goodman, Mary E. *Race awareness in young children.* Cambridge, Mass.: Addison–Wesley, 1952.

Grier, W. H., and Cobbs, P. M. *Black rage.* New York: Basic Books, 1968.

Haden, P., Rudolph, S., Hoyt, J., Lew, R., Hoyt, C., and Robinson, P. The sisters reply. In *Poor black women.* Boston: New England Free Press, 1968.

Hartley, E. L. *Problems in prejudice.* New York: King's Crown Press, 1946.

Janis, I. L., and Rausch, C. N. Selective interest in communications that could arouse decisional conflict: A field study of participants in the draft resistance movement. *Journal of Personality and Social Psychology,* 1970, **14,** 46–54.

Klineberg, O. Black and white in international perspective. *American Psychologist,* 1971, **26,** 119–128.

Kutner, B., Wilkins, Carol, and Yarrow, P. R. Verbal attitudes and overt behavior involving racial prejudice. *Journal of Abnormal and Social Psychology,* 1952, **47,** 649–652.

Langer, W. C. *The mind of Adolf Hitler.* New York: Basic Books, 1972.

LaPiere, R. T. Attitudes versus actions. *Social Forces,* 1934, **13,** 230–237.

Lester, I. *Look out whitey! Black power's gon' get your mama!* New York: Grove Press, 1968.

Levine, J. M., and Murphy, G. The learning and forgetting of controversial material. *Journal of Abnormal and Social Psychology,* 1943, **38,** 507–517.

Lewin, K. *Resolving social conflicts: Selected papers on group dynamics* (Gertrude W. Lewin, ed.). New York: Harper & Row, 1948.

MacCrone, I. D. *Race attitudes in South Africa.* New York: Oxford Univ. Press, 1937.

Miller, N. E. Theory and experiment relating psychoanalytic displacement in stimulus-response generalization. *Journal of Abnormal and Social Psychology,* 1948, **43,** 155–178.

Miller, N. E., and Bugelski, R. Minor studies of aggression: II. The influence of frustrations imposed by the in-group on attitudes expressed toward out-groups. *Journal of Psychology,* 1948, **25,** 437–442.

Pettigrew, T. F. *A profile of the Negro American.* Princeton, N.J.: Van Nostrand, 1964.

Pettigrew, T. F. *Racially separate or together?* New York: McGraw-Hill, 1971.

Riesman, D. *The lonely crowd: A study of the changing American character.* New Haven, Conn.: Yale Univ. Press, 1950.

Rokeach, M. (ed.) *The open and the closed mind.* New York: Basic Books, 1960.

Rosenberg, M. J. An analysis of affective-cognitive consistency. In *Attitude organization and change* (C. I. Hovland and M. J. Rosenberg, eds.), pp. 15–64. New Haven, Conn.: Yale Univ. Press, 1960.

Scodel, A., and Mussen, P. Social perceptions of authoritarians and non-authoritarians. *Journal of Abnormal and Social Psychology,* 1953, **48,** 181–184.

Simpson, G. E., and Yinger, J. M. *Racial and cultural minorities: An analysis of prejudice and discrimination,* 3rd ed. New York: Harper & Row, 1965.

Wann, T. W. (ed.) *Behaviorism and phenomenology.* Chicago: Univ. of Chicago Press, 1964.

Wicker, A. W. Attitudes versus actions: The relationship of verbal and overt behavioral responses to attitude objects. *Journal of Social Issues,* 1969, **25,** 41–78.

INTRODUCTION TO PART FOUR

Alexander, F. G., and Selesnick, S. T. *The history of psychiatry.* New York: Harper & Row, 1966.

Davis, K. The urbanization of the human population. *Scientific American,* 1965, **213** (3), 41–53.

Frank, J. D. *Persuasion and healing.* New York: Schocken, 1963.

Fromm, E. *Beyond the chains of illusion.* New York: Simon and Schuster, 1963.

Gillin, J. Magical fright. *Psychiatry,* 1948, **11,** 387–400.

Giovanni, Nikki. Revolutionary dreams. Poem in *Re:creation.* New York: Broadside, 1970.

Szasz, T. S. The myth of mental illness. *American Psychologist,* 1960, **15,** 113–118.

Zilboorg, G., with Henry, G. W. *A history of medical psychology.* New York: Norton, 1941.

CHAPTER TEN

Adams, H. B. Mental illness: Or interpersonal behavior. *American Psychologist,* 1964, **19,** 191–197.

Adler, N. The antinomian personality: The hippie character type. *Psychiatry,* 1968, **31,** 325–338.

Adler, N. Kicks, drugs and politics. *Psychoanalytic Review,* 1970, **57,** 432–441.

Alexander, F. G., and Selesnick, S. T. *The history of psychiatry.* New York: Harper & Row, 1966.

American Psychiatric Association. *Diagnostic and statistical manual: Mental disorders*. Washington, D.C.: Am. Psychiatric Assoc. Mental Hospital Service, 1952.

Aries, P. *Centuries of childhood: A social history of family life* (trans. from the French by R. Baldick). New York: Vintage Books, 1962.

Ausubel, D. P. Personality disorder is disease. *American Psychologist*, 1961, **16**, 69–74.

Bettelheim, B. *Obsolete youth: Towards a psychogram of adolescent rebellion*. San Francisco: San Francisco Press, 1969.

Blinzen, P. *Whitetown, U.S.A.* New York: Random House, 1970.

Brady, J. V., Porter, R. W., Conrad, D. G., and Mason, J. W. Avoidance behavior and the development of gastroduodenal ulcers. *Journal of Experimental Analysis of Behavior*, 1958, **1**, 69–72.

Cashdan, S. *Abnormal psychology*. Englewood Cliffs, N.J.: Prentice-Hall, 1971.

Coleman, J. C. (with W. E. Broen, Jr.) *Abnormal psychology and modern life*, 4th ed. Chicago: Scott, Foresman, 1972.

Durkheim, E. *Suicide*. New York: The Free Press, 1951.

Eisenberg, L. Student unrest: Sources and consequences. *Science*, 1970, **167**, 1688–1692.

Erikson, E. H. *Childhood and society*. New York: Norton, 1950.

Fairweather, G. M. *Social change: The challenge to survival*. Morristown, N.J.: General Learning Press, 1972.

Fenichel, O. *The psychoanalytic theory of neurosis*. New York: Norton, 1945.

Feuer, L. S. *The conflict of generations: The character and significance of student movements*. New York: Basic Books, 1969.

Frank, J. D. *Persuasion and healing*. New York: Schocken Books, 1963.

Freud, Anna. *The ego and the mechanisms of defense*. New York: International Universities Press, 1946.

Friedman, S. B., Chodoff, P., Mason, J. W., and Hamburg, D. A. Behavioral observations on parents anticipating the death of a child. *Pediatrics*, 1963, **32**, 610–625.

Fromm, E. *Beyond the chains of illusion*. New York: Simon and Schuster, 1963.

Gillin, J. Magical fright. *Psychiatry*, 1948, **11**, 387–400.

Gottesman, I. I., and Shields, J. Schizophrenia in twins: 16 years' consecutive admissions to a psychiatric clinic. *British Journal of Psychiatry*, 1966, **112**, 809–818.

Grinker, R. R., and Spiegel, J. P. *Men under stress*. New York: McGraw-Hill, 1945.

Hamburg, D. A., Hamburg, Beatrix, and deGoza, S. Adaptive problems and mechanisms in severely burned patients. *Psychiatry*, 1953, **16**, 1–20.

Healy, W., Bronner, Augusta F., and Bowers, Anna Mae. *The structure and meaning of psychoanalysis*. New York: Knopf, 1930.

Itard, J.-M.-G. *The wild boy of Aveyron*
(trans. by G. Humphrey and M. Humphrey). New York: Appleton-Century-Crofts, 1962.

Jung, C. G. Psychological commentary. In *The Tibetan book of the great liberation* (W. Y. Evans-Wentz, ed.), pp. xxix–lxiv. New York: Oxford Univ. Press, 1954.

Kallman, F. J. *Heredity in health and mental disorder*. New York: Norton, 1953.

Kallman, F. J. The genetics of human behavior. *American Journal of Psychiatry*, 1956, **113**, 496–501.

Kenniston, K. *The uncommitted: Alienated youth in American society*. New York: Delta (Dell), 1965.

Kenniston, K. *The young radicals: Notes on committed youth*. New York: Harcourt Brace Jovanovich, 1968.

Langer, W. C. *The mind of Adolf Hitler*. New York: Basic Books, 1972.

Lazarus, R. S. *Psychological stress and the coping process*. New York: McGraw-Hill, 1966.

Lazarus, R. S. *Patterns of adjustment and human effectiveness*. New York: McGraw-Hill, 1969.

Lifton, R. J. The politics of immortality: A conversation between Robert J. Lifton and T. George Harris. *Psychology Today*, November 1970.

Lipset, S. M. American student activism in comparative perspective. *American Psychologist*, 1970, **25**, 675–693.

Maher, B. A. *Principles of psychopathology*, Chap. 13, pp. 328–358. New York: McGraw-Hill, 1966.

Mechanic, D. *Students under stress*. New York: The Free Press, 1962.

Meehl, P. E. Schizotaxia, schizotypy, schizophrenia. *American Psychologist*, 1962, **17**, 827–838.

Melville, H. *Moby Dick*. New York: 1851; Modern Library ed., 1950.

Merton, R. K. *Social theory and social structure*. New York: The Free Press, 1949.

Reik, T. *Myth and guilt*. New York: Braziller, 1957.

Rolland, R. *Jean Christophe*, 10 vols. Paris: 1904–1912; English trans. available in Modern Library edition.

Schafer, R. *Psychoanalytic interpretation in Rorschach testing*. New York: Grune & Stratton, 1954.

Schmidt, H. O., and Fonda, C. P. The reliability of psychiatric diagnosis: A new look. *Journal of Abnormal and Social Psychology*, 1956, **52**, 262–267.

Selye, H. *The stress of life*. New York: McGraw-Hill, 1956 (paper).

Shapiro, D. *Neurotic styles*. New York: Basic Books, 1965.

Speisman, J. C., Lazarus, R. S., Mordkoff, A. M., and Davison, L. Experimental reduction of stress based on ego-defense theory. *Journal of Abnormal and Social Psychology*, 1964, **68**, 367–380.

Starkie, E. *Petrus Borel*. London: Faber & Faber, 1954.

Stone, A. A., and Stone, Sue S. *The abnormal personality through literature*. Englewood Cliffs, N.J.: Prentice-Hall, 1966.

Szasz, T. S. The myth of mental illness. *American Psychologist*, 1960, **15**, 113–118.
Thompson, W. R. Behavior genetics. In *McGraw-Hill Yearbook of Science and Technology*, pp. 27–35. New York: McGraw-Hill, 1965.

Whyte, W. H., Jr. *The organization man*. New York: Doubleday, 1956.

Zigler, E., and Phillips, L. Psychiatric diagnosis and symptomatology. *Journal of Abnormal and Social Psychology*, 1961, **63**, 69–75.

Zilboorg, G., with Henry, G. W. *A history of medical psychology*. New York: Norton, 1941.

CHAPTER ELEVEN

Barker, R. G., and Wright, H. F. *One boy's day*. New York: Harper & Row, 1951.

Birren, J. E. *Psychology of aging*. Englewood Cliffs, N.J.: Prentice-Hall, 1964.

Birren, J. E. The abuse of the urban aged. *Psychology Today*, 1970, **3** (March), 36–38, 76.

Breuer, J., and Freud, S. *Studies on hysteria* (J. Strachey, trans. and ed.) New York: Basic Books, 1957 (first German ed., 1895).

Burton, A. *Interpersonal psychotherapy*. Englewood Cliffs, N.J.: Prentice-Hall, 1972.

Colby, K. M. *A primer for psychotherapists*. New York: Ronald, 1951.

Cowen, E. L., Gardner, E. A., and Zax, M. (eds.) *Emergent approaches to mental health problems*. New York: Appleton-Century-Crofts, 1967.

Darwin, C. *Expression of the emotions in man and animals*. New York: Appleton, 1873 (reprinted by Appleton-Century-Crofts).

Dollard, J., and Miller, N. E. *Personality and psychotherapy*. New York: McGraw-Hill, 1950.

Ekman, P. Universals and cultural differences in facial expressions of emotion. In *Nebraska Symposium on Motivation* (J. K. Cole, ed.), pp. 207–283. Lincoln, Neb.: Univ. of Nebraska Press, 1971.

Ford, D. H., and Urban, H. B. *Systems of psychotherapy*. New York: Wiley, 1963.

Frank, J. D. The demoralized mind. *Psychology Today*, 1973, **6** (April), 22, 26, 28, 31, 100–101.

Frankl, V. E. *The doctor and the soul*. New York: Bantam Books, 1965 (paper).

Freeman, W. Psychosurgery. In *American handbook of psychiatry* (S. Arieti, ed.), Vol. II, pp. 1521–1540. New York: Basic Books, 1959.

Freud, S. *Standard edition*, Vols. 4 and 5: *The interpretation of dreams*. London: Hogarth Press, 1953 (first German ed., 1900).

Goffman, E. *Asylums*. New York: Doubleday, 1961.

Gough, H. G. *Manual for the California Psychological Inventory*. Palo Alto, Calif.: Consulting Psychologists' Press, 1957.

Gough, H. G. Theory and measurement of socialization. *Journal of Consulting Psychology*, 1960, **24**, 23–30.

Hathaway, S. R., and McKinley, J. C. *The Minnesota Multiphasic Personality Inventory*, rev. ed. Minneapolis: Univ. of Minnesota Press, 1943.

Hoch, P. H. Drug therapy. In *American handbook of psychiatry* (S. Arieti, ed.), Vol. II, pp. 1541–1551. New York: Basic Books, 1959.

Holden, C. Psychosurgery: Legitimate therapy or laundered lobotomy? *Science*, 1973, **179**, 1109–1112.

Horowitz, W. A. Insulin shock therapy. In *American handbook of psychiatry* (S. Arieti, ed.), Vol. II, pp. 1485–1498. New York: Basic Books, 1959.

Janis, I., Mahl, G. F., Kagan, J., and Holt, R. R. *Personality: Dynamics, development, and assessment.* New York: Harcourt Brace Jovanovich, 1969.

Jones, M. *The therapeutic community.* New York: Basic Books, 1953.

Kalinowsky, L. B. Convulsive shock treatment. In *American handbook of psychiatry* (S. Arieti, ed.), Vol. II, pp. 1499–1520. New York: Basic Books, 1959.

Krasner, L. Behavior control and social responsibility. *American Psychologist*, 1962, **17**, 199–204.

Krasner, L. Reinforcement, verbal behavior and psychotherapy. *American Journal of Orthopsychiatry*, 1963, **33**, 601–613.

Lazarus, R. S., Opton, E. M., Jr., Nomikos, M. S., and Rankin, N. O. The principle of short-circuiting of threat: Further evidence. *Journal of Personality*, 1965, **33**, 622–635.

McClelland, D. C., Atkinson, J. W., Clark, R. A., and Lowell, E. L. *The achievement motive.* New York: Appleton-Century-Crofts, 1953.

Matarazzo, J. D. Some national developments in the utilization of nontraditional mental health manpower. *American Psychologist*, 1971, **26**, 363–372.

May, R. *Psychology and the human dilemma.* Princeton, N.J.: Van Nostrand, 1967.

Mehrabian, A. *Tactics of social influence.* Englewood Cliffs, N.J.: Prentice-Hall, 1970 (paper).

Mehrabian, A., and Wiener, M. Nonimmediacy between communicator and object of communication in a verbal message: Application to the inference of attitudes. *Journal of Consulting Psychology*, 1966, **30**, 420–425.

Morgan, Christiana D., and Murray, H. A. A method for investigating fantasies: The Thematic Apperception Test. *Archives of Neurology and Psychiatry*, 1935, **34**, 289–306.

Perls, F. Group vs. individual therapy. *ETC*, 1967, **34**, 306–312.

Perls, F. S. *Gestalt therapy verbatim.* Lafayette, Calif.: Real People Press, 1969.

Rioch, Margaret J., Elkes, C., Flint, A. A., Usdansky, B. S., Newman, R. G., and Silber, E. National Institute of Mental Health pilot study in training mental health counselors. *American Journal of Orthopsychiatry*, 1963, **33**, 678–689.

Robinson, D. N. Therapies: A clear and present danger. *American Psychologist*, 1973, **28**, 129–133.

Rogers, C. R., and Skinner, B. F. Some issues concerning the control of human behavior: A symposium. *Science*, 1956, **124**, 1057–1066.

Rorschach, H. *Psychodiagnostics* (trans. by P. Lemkau and B. Kronenberg). New York: Grune & Stratton, 1942.

Rosenfeld, H. M. Instrumental affiliative functions of facial and gestural expressions. *Journal of Personality and Social Psychology*, 1966, **4**, 65–72.

Rosenhan, D. L. On being sane in insane places. *Science*, 1973, **179**, 250–258.

Sarason, S. B. *The clinical interaction: with special reference to the Rorschach.* New York: Harper & Row, 1954.

Shaffer, J., and Galinsky, M. D. *Models of group therapy and social interaction.* Englewood Cliffs, N.J.: Prentice-Hall, in press.

Stampfl, T. G., and Levis, D. J. Essentials of implosive therapy: A learning-theory-based psychodynamic behavioral therapy. *Journal of Abnormal Psychology*, 1967, **72**, 496–503.

Stollak, G. E., Guerney, B. G., Jr., and Rothberg, M. *Psychotherapy research: Selected readings.* Chicago: Rand McNally, 1966 (paper).

Sweet, W. H., Ervin, F., and Mark, V. H. The relationship of violent behavior to focal cerebral disease. In *Aggressive behavior* (S. Garattini and E. Sigg, eds.). New York: Wiley, 1969.

Tallent, M. *Clinical psychological consultation.* Englewood Cliffs, N.J.: Prentice-Hall, 1963.

Tyler, Leona E. *Tests and measurements*, 2nd ed. Englewood Cliffs, N.J.: Prentice-Hall, 1971.

Ullmann, L. P., and Krasner, L. *A psychological approach to abnormal behavior.* Englewood Cliffs, N.J.: Prentice-Hall, 1969.

Washburn, S. L., and Hamburg, D. A. Aggressive behavior in Old World monkeys and apes. In *Primates: Studies in adaptation and variability* (Phyllis C. Jay, ed.), pp. 458–478. New York: Holt, Rinehart & Winston, 1968.

Wolf, M., Risley, T., and Mees, H. Application of operant conditioning procedures to the behavior problems of an autistic child. *Behavior Research and Therapy*, 1964, **1**, 305–312.

Wolpe, J. *The practice of behavior therapy.* New York: Pergamon, 1969.

CHAPTER TWELVE

Abraham, K. *Selected papers on psychoanalysis*, Chap. 25. London: Hogarth, 1949.

Ansbacher, H. L., and Ansbacher, Rowena, R. (eds.) *The individual-psychology of Alfred Adler.* New York: Basic Books, 1956.

Barron, F. *Creativity and psychological health.* Princeton, N.J.: Van Nostrand, 1963.

Breger, L. Functions of dreams. *Journal of Abnormal Psychology Monographs*, **72** (No. 5, Whole No. 641), 1967.

Brower, K. Galápagos sketches. In Porter, E., and Brower, K. *Galápagos: The flow of wildness*, Vol. 2, pp. 93–160. New York: Sierra Club–Ballantine Books, 1970 (paper).

Creegan, R. F. Concerning professional ethics. *American Psychologist*, 1958, **13**, 272–275.

Dement, W., and Kleitman, N. Cyclic variations in the EEG during sleep and their relation to eye movements, body motility, and learning. *EEG Clinical Neurophysiology*, 1957, **9**, 637–690.

Dubos, R. J. Humanizing the earth. *Science*, 1973, **179**, 769–772.

Dundes, A. Here I sit—A study of American latrinalia. *Kroeber Anthropological Society Papers*, 1966, **34**, 91–105.

Erikson, E. H. A healthy personality for every child: A fact finding report: A digest. In *Midcentury White House Conference on Children and Youth*, pp. 8–25. Raleigh, N.C.: Health Publications Institute, 1951.

Erikson, E. H. *Childhood and society*, 2nd ed. New York: Norton, 1963.

Freud, S. Instincts and their vicissitudes. In *Collected papers*, Vol. 4, pp. 60–83. London: Hogarth Press, 1925 (first German ed., 1918).

Freud, S. Analysis of a phobia in a five-year old boy. In *Collected papers*, Vol. 3, pp. 149–296. London: Hogarth Press, 1933a (first published in German, 1909).

Freud, S. *New introductory lectures on psychoanalysis.* New York: Norton, 1933b (first German edition, 1933).

Freud, S. The psychopathology of everyday life. In *The basic writings of Sigmund Freud* (A. A. Brill, ed.). New York: Random House, 1938 (first German edition, 1904).

Freud, S. *Leonardo da Vinci: A study in psychosexuality* (trans. by A. A. Brill). New York: Random House, 1947.

Freud, S. *An outline of psychoanalysis.* New York: Norton, 1949 (first German edition, 1940).

Freud, S. *Standard edition*, Vols. 4 and 5: *The interpretation of dreams.* London: Hogarth Press, 1953 (first German edition, 1900).

Freud, S. *The complete psychological works of Sigmund Freud*, Vol. 21: *The ego and the id* (trans. by J. Strachey in collaboration with Anna Freud). London: Hogarth Press, 1961.

Freud, S. *Standard edition*, Vols. 15 and 16: *Introductory lectures on psychoanalysis.* London: Hogarth Press, 1963 (first German edition, 1916–1917).

Fromm, E. *Escape from freedom.* New York: Holt, Rinehart & Winston, 1941.

Fromm, E. *Man for himself.* New York: Holt, Rinehart & Winston, 1947.

Fromm, E. *The sane society.* New York: Holt, Rinehart & Winston, 1955.

Fromm, E. *The art of loving.* New York: Harper & Row, 1956.

Fromm, E. *Beyond the chains of illu-*

sion. New York: Simon and Schuster, 1963.

Grinker, R. R. "Mentally healthy" young males (homoclites). *Archives of General Psychiatry,* 1962, **6,** 405–453.

Hackett, T. P., and Weisman, A. D. Reactions to the imminence of death. In *The threat of impending disaster* (G. H. Grosser, H. Wechsler, and M. Greenblatt, eds.), pp. 300–311. Cambridge, Mass.: M.I.T. Press, 1964.

Harlow, H. F. *Learning to love.* San Francisco: Albion, 1971.

Hartmann, H. *Ego psychology and the problem of adaptation.* New York: International Universities Press, 1958.

Hartmann, H. *Essays on ego psychology.* New York: International Universities Press, 1964.

Holt, R. R. (ed.) *Motives and thought: Psychoanalytic essays in honor of David Rapaport.* New York: International Universities Press, 1967.

Jahoda, Marie. Toward a social psychology of mental health. In *Symposium on the healthy personality* (M. J. E. Senn, ed.), pp. 211–230. New York: Josia Macy, Jr. Foundation, 1950.

Jahoda, Marie. *Current concepts of positive mental health.* New York: Basic Books, 1958.

Jones, E. The concept of a normal mind. *International Journal of Psychoanalysis,* 1942, **23,** 1–8.

Joyce, J. *Ulysses.* New York: Modern Library, 1961 (first publ.: Paris, 1922).

Jung, C. G. Two essays on analytical psychology. In *Collected works of C. G. Jung,* Vol. 7. New York: Pantheon Books, 1953.

Jung, C. G. Psychological commentary. In *The Tibetan book of the great liberation* (W. Y. Evans-Wentz, ed.), pp. xxix–xliv. New York: Oxford Univ. Press, 1954.

Kenniston, K. *The uncommitted: Alienated youth in American society.* New York: Delta (Dell), Inc., 1965.

Kenniston, K. *The young radicals: Notes on committed youth.* New York: Harcourt Brace Jovanovich, 1968.

Korchin, S. J., and Ruff, G. E. Personality characteristics of the Mercury astronauts. In *The threat of impending disaster* (G. H. Grosser, H. Wechsler, and M. Greenblatt, eds.), pp. 197–207. Cambridge, Mass.: M.I.T. Press, 1964.

McNeil, E. B. Where did you go on your trip? In *The quiet furies: Man and disorder,* p. 116. Englewood Cliffs, N.J.: Prentice-Hall, 1967.

Maslow, A. H. A holistic approach to creativity. In *A climate for creativity: Reports of the Seventh National Research Conference on Creativity,* 1968 (C. W. Taylor, ed.). New York: Pergamon Press, 1972.

Maslow, A. H. *Toward a psychology of being,* 2nd ed. Princeton, N.J.: Van Nostrand, 1968.

Maslow, A. H. *Motivation and personality,* rev. ed. New York: Harper & Row, 1970.

Riesman, D. *The lonely crowd: A study of the changing American character.* New Haven, Conn.: Yale Univ. Press, 1950.

Roth, P. *Portnoy's complaint.* New York: Random House, 1969.

Ruff, G. E., and Korchin, S. J. Psychological responses of the Mercury astronauts to stress. In *The threat of impending disaster* (G. H. Grosser, H. Wechsler, and M. Greenblatt, eds.), pp. 208–220. Cambridge, Mass.: M.I.T. Press, 1964.

Smith, M. B. "Mental health" reconsidered. *American Psychologist,* 1961, **16,** 299–306.

Stotland, E. *The psychology of hope.* San Francisco: Jossey-Bass, 1969.

Tart, C. T. (ed.) *Altered states of consciousness.* New York: Wiley, 1969.

White, R. W. Competence and the psychosexual stages of development. In *Nebraska Symposium on Motivation* (M. R. Jones, ed.), pp. 97–141. Lincoln, Nebr.: Univ. of Nebraska Press, 1960.

Glossary

Adaptation *In biology:* A species' capacity to survive, modes of survival, or degree of success in surviving by propagating and coping with its environment. *In psychology:* An individual's (as opposed to species') capacity to survive, his modes of surviving, or his degree of success in surviving; more generally, the term is concerned with thriving physically and psychologically, as a person or animal struggles to cope with its environment; alternative term, *adjustment.*

Affect Subjective, feeling component of an emotional state, along with the related thoughts and ideas.

Aggression *In man:* Effort to harm or injure another individual (or object); the importance of the actual intention of the aggressor in this definition is controversial (pp. 214–226). *Intraspecies:* Fighting, or threats of fighting, among members of the same species (pp. 256–263). *Interspecies:* Attacks by one animal on another of a different species, most often for the purpose of predation (killing for food) or defense (pp. 251–255).

Alienation Lack of a positive relationship with one's society, group, or other people in general (pp. 433; 480–489); sometimes called *anomie.*

Altruism Doing positively regarded things without self-serving motives, as in altruistic love, in which the welfare of the loved one is uppermost (p. 578).

Ambivalence Simultaneous presence of contradictory attitudes toward the same person; as when that person is both loved and hated or feared.

Anthropology Scientific discipline which studies human societies, their variations, origins, and evolution: *physical anthropology* is concerned with anatomical differences among men (past and present) and their evolution; *social* or *cultural anthropology,* with social institutions.

Apollonian Life outlook resembling that of the Greek god Apollo, venerating order, harmony, and moderation in all things (pp. 78–81; compare *Dionysian*).

Assertiveness Competitive, mastery-centered behavior which does not necessarily imply anger, aggression, or hostility (p. 216).

Assessment Systematic attempts to specify and perhaps measure personality traits and psychodynamic characteristics of an individual, usually in the interests of creating a complete psychological portrait. Psychodiagnosis is a form of assessment employed in the clinical context of adaptive failure (pp. 491–494).

Assimilation Submerging one's own identity or that of a social group in the

values and behavior patterns of the larger culture (see *Internalization;* also pp. 359, 361–363, 367–368, 396–398). As used by Piaget, modifying oneself to fit the demands of the environment (pp. 63–64).

Attitude Tendency to react evaluatively (either positively or negatively) to some person, situation, idea, or object (pp. 328, 163–164).

Carnivore Meat-eating animal. (Man is an *omnivore,* that is, he eats meat or vegetable food, "omni" meaning everything.)

Catharsis Discharge of tension resulting from blocked or inhibited drives whose energy would otherwise tend to build up and ultimately express itself in pathological disturbances (pp. 234–235, 273–274).

Cognition Mental activity involving perception (knowing), thinking, learning, remembering, problem solving, or decision making.

Complex (as in *Oedipus complex*) Cluster of emotionally laden attitudes, desires, impulses, or memories which direct behavior without the individual being aware of them or their origins.

Compliance Superficial adoption of an outlook, attitude, or action merely to gain approval or acceptance (pp. 160–163; compare *Internalization* and *Conformity*).

Compulsion Persistent, seemingly alien impulse to engage in some act or ritual; failure to perform it results in marked distress or anxiety (pp. 452–455).

Conditioning Learning process by which responses are tied to stimuli or other responses, as in *classical conditioning* and *operant conditioning* (pp. 150–154).

Conformity Responding to social pressure by acting or thinking in the same way as the group (pp. 130–139).

Control group In research, comparing the effects of two or more conditions, the "control" not subject to the influence of the conditions whose effects are being studied (p. 10; Note 1.1, p. 31).

Coping Ways by which a person or animal attempts (successfully or unsuccessfully) to master or manage environmental demands, conflicts, stressful events, and emotional reactions (see *Defense mechanisms;* also Note 2.1, pp. 74–75; pp. 468–477).

Correlation Relationship between two variables or measures, commonly expressed quantitatively as a numerical index (pp. 258–261).

Creativity Achieving (or the process of achieving) novel and useful insights in thought or in any field of human endeavor (pp. 577–578, 585–586).

Defense mechanisms Various methods of coping with threat in which the

person deceives himself about the truth (pp. 470–474).

Dehumanization Conceiving of or treating others as less than human, hence unworthy of concern and decent treatment, or forcing them to be so through destructive institutions or social experience. Also, a way of protecting oneself against the guilt and distress experienced following destructive or indifferent behavior toward others (pp. 302–304, 207–208).

Delusion Belief system that contradicts reality and is maintained in spite of all efforts at rational persuasion or contradictory evidence (pp. 446–449).

Demography Scientific discipline specializing in the dynamics and prediction of population size, density, and distribution.

Denial Defense mechanism in which a person protects himself against a threatening thought or impulse by denying its existence in word and action (p. 472).

Dionysian Life outlook resembling that of the Greek god Dionysus, emphasizing conflict and struggle, sensuousness, frenzy, and the attempt to attain uncommon, ecstatic modes of experience (pp. 78–81; compare *Apollonian*).

Discrimination Negative acts directed against the target of prejudice (pp. 325, 426–429).

Disparagement Belittling, demeaning, or "putting down" another person or group (pp. 387–391).

Displacement Shifting a behavioral impulse, attitude, or feeling (say, anger) from one object or person to another, usually because directing it toward the original object is dangerous or guilt provoking (pp. 264, 309–310, 400–404).

Disposition Inferred tendency or propensity to act or react in certain ways under suitable conditions, as in the disposition to be anxious or to use the defense mechanism of denial.

Dogmatism Closed system of thinking, organized about rigid beliefs and polar opposites, as in the tendency to think evaluatively and oversimply about people as good and bad, strong or weak, or whatever (pp. 410–411).

Dominance hierarchy Organization of social ranks among a given group of animals or people; also called *pecking order* (pp. 110–111, 256–257).

Drive State of tension or arousal, based on deprivation of needs, which triggers behavior potentially capable of drive reduction or cessation of the tension: some drives are largely innate and based on tissue deprivation, as in hunger and thirst, or on neurological activity in the brain, as in curiosity; others are largely learned, as

616

in anxiety. When a drive becomes connected through learning and cognitive activity to some form of adaptive behavior, we tend to speak of a *motive* or *goal* (Note 3.2, pp. 116–118).

Ecology Scientific discipline which studies the interrelationships between living organisms and their natural environments.

Ego identity A clear sense of who and what one is as a person in relation to the social and biological world (p. 578).

Electra complex Freudian concept referring to a girl's sexual interest in and desires toward her father (pp. 160, 567–569).

Emotion Complex state of arousal produced by any commerce between a person or animal and his environment that is perceived as important to his welfare; in man the state is characterized by certain subjectively experienced affects (such as fear, anger, guilt, joy), internal physiological disturbances, and motor actions or impulses to act in certain ways (say, flee or attack).

Endocrine glands Group of (ductless) glands, secreting hormones directly into the blood stream, that are powerful in affecting physiological functioning and behavior.

Equilibrium Preset level or balance of physiological activity maintained either by automatic or behavioral regulatory processes; for example, maintenance of body temperature or blood sugar; achieved by the process of *homeostasis* (pp. 111, 230).

Ethnic group Subgroup within a society that shares, or is treated as sharing, a distinctive racial or cultural background, often with its own language, outlook, and behavioral patterns, or residuals of these.

Ethnocentrism Exaggerated appreciation of one's own ethnic group, family, caste, religious sect, or nation, and a simultaneous dislike and distrust of other groups (pp. 408–409).

Ethology Scientific discipline that focuses on animals and animal behavior in their natural habitats.

Existential Model of man, influenced strongly by the philosophy of *existentialism,* emphasizing the importance of experience, of being, and of man's search for fulfillment.

Extinction Process by which a conditioned response is eliminated, that is, the conditioned stimulus no longer triggers the response (pp. 152–153).

Family triangle (or *family romance*) Charming expression for the Oedipus and Electra complexes, involving the erotically tinged three-way relationship among boy-father-mother or girl-mother-father (pp. 566–569).

Feedback Any response-produced changes in the environment that return (feed back) to the organism and, when perceived, affect subsequent reactions. Used in slightly different but interrelated ways in physiology, ecology, the sciences dealing with social behavior, and in the

psychology of learning through reward and punishment—as, *feedback* from the effects of behavior (pp. 36–37, 50–51, 148–149).

Frustration Either the circumstances which thwart or interfere with goal-directed activity or the state of annoyance or distress stemming from such interference (pp. 243–246).

Homeostasis (see *Equilibrium;* also pp. 111, 230).

Hormones Biochemical secretions (of the *endocrine glands*) that influence bodily states and behavior and are distributed throughout the body through the blood stream.

Hostility An aggressive attitude or disposition maintained over a fairly long time or indefinitely; distinguished from *aggression,* which is a fleeting, specific act, and *anger,* which is a temporary, specific emotion.

Humanistic psychology Outlook that emphasizes a positive, respectful, and hopeful attitude toward man in contrast with the idea of man as a mere animal mechanism shaped and pulled by external events.

Identification The process in which one takes on the values and patterns of conduct of others (say, parents) by unconscious modeling and makes their characteristics a part of one self (see the related term *Internalization;* also pp. 159–163).

Ideology As used in this text, coordinated body of ideas and beliefs about human life and culture that may be characteristic of an individual, group, or culture, and which shapes feelings and reactions; the term has somewhat different meanings among various social sciences (similar to *Outlook,* which see).

Innate Inborn, hereditary component of a physiological or behavioral trait. Thus, innate drive refers to impulses that arise from the inherited neural and hormonal structure of the person or animal, as in hunger or sex.

Instinct Species-specific, inborn tendency to display a particular complex reaction to some special pattern of stimulation (pp. 228–229; Note 6.1, pp. 224–225).

Intellectualization Defense mechanism in which the person distances or insulates himself from disturbing emotions through detached analytic forms of thought (p. 472).

Interaction Way one causal variable modifies the influence of another on an observable effect or outcome (Note 2.1, pp. 74–75).

Internalization Making an external (environmental) value or demand a part of oneself (see also *Identification;* and pp. 481, 159–163).

Intrapsychic Inferred internal psychological processes; for example, conflict between two motives or impulses, presumably taking place *within* the person's mind.

Mechanism Synonym for *process;* the way a psychological event works; in effect,

the rules of interplay of its variables (see also *Defense mechanisms*).

Modeling Acquiring psychological traits through observation and imitation of another person (pp. 159–163).

Motive Inferred internal state which pushes behavior toward some particular kind of activity or goal; closely related to *Drive* (which see; also Note 3.2, pp. 116–118).

Natural selection Key principle of Darwin's theory of evolution stating that any organism that has characteristics which aid its successful adaptation to the environment in which it lives will have a better chance of surviving; hence, within the species, these adaptive characteristics will be naturally selected over less useful or maladaptive ones; also expressed as "survival of the fittest" (pp. 35–36).

Neurosis Emotional disturbance of living, often producing subjective distress and self-defeating behavior that involves maladaptive use of reality-distorting defense mechanisms (pp. 449–453; 526–527).

Obsession Persistent and unbidden thoughts which the person recognizes as irrational and alien but which he cannot seem to control (pp. 452–453).

Oedipus complex Freudian concept referring to the boy's sexual interest in and desires toward his mother (pp. 160, 567–569).

Outlook Rather broad set of interrelated attitudes and beliefs about some aspect of life (see also *Ideology*).

Paranoid thinking Characterized in mild forms by unreasonable suspiciousness; in more severe instances, by delusions of grandeur and persecution (pp. 446–449).

Personality Broad concept emphasizing the organization of inferred psychological characteristics that influence a person's reactions to environmental events and distinguish one person from another (p. 495, margin).

Phobia Persistent fear which is disproportionate to any real danger and whose origin may be hidden to the person (pp. 450–452).

Phylogeny Evolutionary development of types of organisms or species (adj., *phylogenetic*); usually distinguished from *ontogeny,* that is, the course of development of any individual organism within a species.

Pluralism Diverse pattern of life styles and ways of thinking, feeling, and acting in a society or social group (p. 193).

Predation Hunting and killing of animals (prey) for food; thought to involve quite different mechanisms than other forms of aggression, such as territorial or competitive aggression between members of the same species (pp. 216–219; 251–255).

Prejudice Tendency to think well or ill of a person, group, or idea without basis in actual fact or experience (see *Attitude;* also pp. 325, 328).

Projection Attributing one's own thoughts, impulses, and feelings to some other person or object; when this is employed to prevent having to acknowledge alien characteristics in oneself, it is regarded as a *defense mechanism* (pp. 404–406, 472–473, 510–511).

Psychiatry Medical discipline whose major concern is understanding and treating adaptive disturbances.

Psychoanalysis A theory of personality originated by Sigmund Freud and modified by neo-Freudians; also the psychotherapeutic strategy that has evolved alongside of the theory, having its own particular rationale and tactics (pp. 520–527, 556–576).

Psychodynamics Any psychological mechanisms inferred to help explain the reactions of individuals and of people in general.

Psychology Broad, diverse discipline concerned with understanding all facets of human behavior and mental activity. In the case of psychologists committed to diagnosing and treating adaptive disturbances, functions overlap almost completely with those of *psychiatry,* though many psychologists are also involved in research studies, while psychiatrists generally concentrate on medical concerns.

Psychopath Type of personality disorder in which the individual appears to be stunted in moral development and is unable to relate to and show loyalty to others; synonym, *antisocial personality;* sometimes the term *sociopath* is also used synonymously, though these terms may be distinguished on the basis of supposed causal antecedents and mechanisms (pp. 453–455).

Psychosexual Fusion of biological sexuality with cognitive activity and social relations as emphasized by Freud in his theory of psychological development (pp. 564–569).

Psychosis Most severe class of adaptive failure, characterized by poor contact with reality, and disorganized, disturbed behavior; frequently requires hospital care (pp. 443–449).

Psychosomatic disorder (see *Stress disorder*).

Rationalization Defense mechanism in which a person finds plausible or acceptable reasons to justify an action or intention, rather than acknowledging the unflattering or threatening truth (pp. 122–123, 375).

Reaction formation Defense mechanism in which an unacceptable thought, impulse, or feeling, say, hate, is replaced with exaggerated manifestations of its opposite, love (pp. 393, 472).

Regression Coping with overwhelming stress by returning to earlier, sometimes childish modes of reacting (p. 475).

Releasing stimulus (or *releaser*) Environmental stimulus that elicits some innate (instinctual) behavior or behavior pattern (pp. 239–243).

Repression Defense mechanism in which threatening or otherwise unacceptable impulses or ideas are blocked from consciousness; regarded by Freud as the primary defense (p. 472).

Response Reaction, consisting of overt acts, subjective feelings and thoughts, or physiological changes, elicited by a given stimulus.

Sadomasochism Obtaining gratification through the production of pain or suffering in another (*sadism*), or by being subjected to pain or suffering (*masochism*), or both; for some, sexual gratification is impossible without such pain, or is sharply enhanced by it (pp. 158, 269).

Scapegoating Blaming (or attacking) an undeserving person or group for a frustrating problem instead of the real sources of the trouble, usually because the latter cannot safely be blamed or attacked; a form of *displacement* (pp. 309–310).

Schizophrenia Psychosis taking many variant forms (like paranoid or catatonic), usually involving disturbances of thought, severe social withdrawal, and in some cases hallucinations and delusions (pp. 445–449).

Socialization Shaping of the individual's patterns of behavior and personality as a result of the influence of the social environment (pp. 148–170).

Social mobility Movement up or down in the social hierarchy of status or class as a result of what the person does (p. 266).

Social role Behavior that is expected of a person (or that he expects of himself) in a particular social position; all people play many roles (father, husband, professor, colleague, etc.); *sex role* refers to instances in which one's sex is a determinant of social behavior (pp. 150–151, 162–164).

Sociology Scientific discipline which deals with human social organization, how it is formed, and how various social institutions operate.

Stereotype Generalized idea about the characteristics of people of a given social group (ethnic, racial, political, socioeconomic, or whatever); usually involves assignment of false or overgeneralized characteristics, and all or most individuals belonging to that group are assumed to possess these characteristics (pp. 337, 338–346).

Stimulus Objectively describable event, occurring within the organism or in the environment, which elicits a response (reaction).

Stress *Physiological:* Important commerce between an organism and its environment which, by requiring major physiological adaptations, can be injurious to tissues, especially if prolonged or excessive (pp. 462–463). *Psychological:* Important commerce between an organism and its environment which, by being psychologically demanding, challenging, or threatening, requires special efforts by the organism if it is to cope (pp. 466–470).

Stress disorder Tissue injury or disturbance resulting from prolonged or severe stress (pp. 466–470).

Subculture Distinctive social group with its own values and behavior patterns that are preserved in the midst of a larger and more complex cultural entity (p. 297).

Sublimation Freudian psychological mechanism in which blocked sexual (and aggressive) energy is partly channeled into substitute activities that are socially and personally acceptable; *substitution* is a more general term without the energy ("boiler analogy") connotations.

Syndrome Organized pattern of symptoms representing the typical picture of a disorder.

Territoriality Tendency of many animal species to establish, control, and defend a piece of ground, feeding site, potential mates, or the young against incursions by members of the same and other species (pp. 110, 257, 267–268).

Theory Analytic, speculative model or cognitive map designed to explain relationships observed among variables; usually involves certain assumptions and reference to unobservable structures and processes or mechanisms (Note 4.4, pp. 156–157).

Transaction Commerce or interchange between a person (or animal) and his environment; the emphasis is on the entire relationship, rather than on either party to the action alone.

Unconscious Absence of awareness about impulses, wishes, motives, feelings, attitudes, beliefs, ideas, or any other psychological event, as a result of limitations in verbal labels, inattentiveness, lack of memory, or the action of defense mechanisms (pp. 6–7, 473–474).

Violence Usually refers to physical harm done to a person, animal, or object, although some writers extend the meaning to more subtle forms of damage, such as to a person's reputation or sense of wellbeing, or to include the threat of harm (pp. 219–221).

AUTHOR INDEX

Numbers in italic are those pages on which references appear.

A

Abelson, R. P., *607*
Abraham, K., 576, *614*
Abrahams, R. D., 288, *610*
Adams, D. K., *607*
Adams, H. B., 465, *612*
Adelson, J., 69, *605*
Adler, A. (*see* Ansbacher, H. L., and Ansbacher, R. R.)
Adler, G., *610*
Adler, H., 480-481, 487-488, *612*
Adorno, T. W., 343, 408-410, 413, *431, 611, 612*
Aeschylus, 568-569
Alexander, F. G., 305, 436, *490, 610, 612*
Allen, V. L., 386
Allerton, R., 297, *611*
Allport, G. W., 321, 336, 343-344, 354, 357, 367-368, *386*, 387-388, 392, 408, 413, 421, 425, 429-430, *431, 610, 611, 612*
Amos, W. H., 26-27, *605*
Andreski, S., 316, *610*
Ansbacher, H. L., 580, *614*
Ansbacher, R. R., 580, *614*
Ansky, S., 592-593
Aquinas, St. Thomas, 31, 35, *605*
Ardrey, R., 265, 268, *276, 608*
Aries, P., 480, *613*
Arieti, S., *613, 614*
Arnold, W. J., *606*
Aronson, E., *607*
Artandi, S., 355, *611*
Asch, S. E., 130-133, 139-140, 162, 170, 300, *606, 607*
Ashley Montagu, M. F., 46, 267, *276*, 374, 380, *386, 605, 608, 611*
Atkinson, J. W., 512, *614*
Ausubel, D. P., 466, *613*
Azrin, N., 246, 310, *608*

B

Baker, P. T., 53, *605*
Baldick, R., *613*
Bandura, A., 149, 159, 269, 316, *607, 608, 610*
Bardwick, J., 355-356, *611*
Barker, R. G., 503, *613*
Barron, F., 555, 577-578, 587-589, *600, 607, 614*
Basu, G. K., 258-260, *609*
Baumann, D. D., 83, *606*
Baumrind, D., 191, *608*
Beach, F. A., 249, *276, 608*
Beecher, H. K., 136-137, *607*
Bell, D., 196-198, *608*
Bellamy, E., 207, *608*
Bem, D. J., 115, 138, 150, 163, 171, *172*, 342, 385, *606, 607, 611*
Bem, S. L., *611*
Benedict, R., 15, 78-81, 145-146, 202-203, 220, 236, 254, 318-319, *605, 607, 608*
Berger, P. L., 128-129, *607*

Berkowitz, L., 245, *276*, 289-290, 292-294, *323, 608, 610*
Berne, E., 282-283, *610*
Bernstein, L., *297*
Bettelheim, B., 12, 341, 479-480, 484, *605, 611, 613*
Billingsley, A., 386
Birch, H. G., 258, *608*
Birren, J. E., 548, *613*
Black, A. E., 191, *608*
Blinzen, P., 486, *613*
Bliss, E. L., *611*
Boelkins, R. C., 258, *609*
Bogardus, E. S., 345-346, *611*
Bourke, J. G., 80, *606*
Bowers, A. M., 559, *613*
Bowlby, J., 51, 245, *605, 609*
Brady, J. V., 462, *613*
Braly, K. W., 341, *611*
Breger, L., 143-144, 277, 312, 563, *607, 610, 614*
Brehm, J. W., 163-164, *607*
Breland, K., 137, *607*
Breland, M., 137, *607*
Brenner, C., *600*
Breuer, J., 521, *613*
Brigham, J. C., 338, *611*
Brill, A. A., *614*
Britt, S. H., 386
Bronfenbrenner, U., 191-192, *608*
Bronner, A. F., 559, *613*
Broverman, D. M., 342, *611*
Broverman, I. K., 342, *611*
Brower, K., 36, 597-598, *605, 614*
Brown, N. O., 211, *608*
Brown, R., 159, *172, 431, 607, 610*
Bruner, J. S., 76-77, *606*
Buckley, W. F., Jr., 137-138
Buckout, R., 120, *606*
Buddha, 59, 211, 442, 594
Bugelski, R., 402, *612*
Bugental, J., *610*
Bumpass, L., 118, *606*
Burgess, A., 204, 207, 539, *608*
Burnstein, E., 284-286, *610*
Burton, A., 526, 550, *613*
Byrne, D., *431*

C

Caldwell, C., *606*
Calhoun, J. B., 103-104, 256-257, 260, *606, 608*
Cannon, W. B., 230, *608*
Carlsmith, J. M., 134, *172*, 415-416, *607, 612*
Carmichael, L. A., 73-75, *606*
Carmichael, S., *386*
Carpenter, C. R., 258, *608*
Carson, R., 95, *606*
Carter, L. F., 370, *611*
Cashdan, S., *490, 613*
Caudill, W., 145-146, *607*
Cavanaugh, E. B., 463
Cervantes (Cervantes Saavedra, M. de), *446*
Chagnon, N., 268, *608*
Charwat, W. A., 305, *610*
Cheney, C. O., 10, *605*
Cheyne, J. A., *88*

Chodoff, P., 471, *613*
Christian, J. J., 103, 111, *606*
Clark, G., 258, *609*
Clark, K. B., 171, *386, 607*
Clark, Lord Kenneth, 201-202
Clark, R. A., 512, *614*
Clarkson, F. E., 342, *611*
Clemente, C. D., *276, 609, 610*
Cobbs, P. M., 386, 388-389, 392, 397-398, 406, *612*
Coffman, T. L., 341, *611*
Cohen, A. R., 163-164, 305, *607, 610*
Cohen, J. M., *446*
Cohen, N., 304, *610*
Cohn, F., 313-314, *610*
Colby, K. M., *550, 613*
Cole, J. K., *613*
Coleman, J. C., 443-444, 448-449, 463, *490, 550, 613*
Comstock, C., 302, *323, 610, 611*
Conklin, H. C., 6, *605*
Conn, L. K., 143, 312-313, *607, 610*
Conrad, D. G., 462, *613*
Cooper, E., 422-423, *612*
Costa, P. T., 234, *609*
Cotton, H. A., 10, 132, *605*
Cowen, E. L., 547, *613*
Cowgill, U. M., 55, *605*
Craik, K. H., 30, *88, 605*
Creegan, R. F., 556, *614*
Crowne, D. P., 143, 312-313, *607, 610*
Cruse, H., *386*

D

Daniels, D. H., *610*
Darley, J. M., 136, 106-109, *606*
Darwin, C., 26, 28, 35-36, 109, 229-230, 496, *605, 613*
Davis, A., 191, *608*
Davis, B. D., 171, *607*
Davis, D. E., 103, 111, *606*
Davis, E. E., 382-384, *612*
Davis, K., 440, *612*
Davis, M., 310
Davison, L. A., 474, *613*
Day, M., 46, *605*
Dean, J. P., 353, *611*
Deese, J. E., 8, *605*
Deevey, E. S., Jr., 92-93, *606*
de Goza, S., 470, *613*
Delgado, J. M. R., 51, 171, *605, 607*
Dement, W., 563, *614*
de Tocqueville, A., 193, *608*
DeVore, I., 17-18, 48, 257, 260, 263, *605, 609*
De Vos, G., 171, 380, *607, 611*
Dexter, E. G., 31, *605*
Dixon, W. J., 132-133, *607*
Dobzhansky, T., 173, 374-375, *386, 608, 611*
Dollard, J., 243-245, 405, 537, *608, 612, 613*
Dombrose, L. A., 413, *612*
Doob, A. N., 141, *607*
Doob, L., 243-245, *608*
Dubos, R. J., 56, 599, *605, 614*
Dundes, A., 570-571, *610, 614*
Durbin, E. J. M., 245, *608*
Durkheim, E., 481, *613*

SUBJECT INDEX

Acknowledgments

EXTRACTS AND TABLES

p. 2: Fifteen-line verse selection (chorus part) from *Sophocles' King Oedipus,* in COLLECTED PLAYS of William Butler Yeats. Copyright 1934, 1952 by Macmillan Publishing Co., Inc. Reprinted by permission of Macmillan Publishing Co., Inc., New York, and Mr. M. B. Yeats, The Macmillan Company of London and Basingstoke, and The Macmillan Company of Canada.

pp. 15, 78, 220, 236, 254: Extracts from AN ANTHROPOLOGIST AT WORK: *Writings of Ruth Benedict* by Margaret Mead. Houghton Mifflin, Boston. © 1959 by Margaret Mead. Used with kind permission of Margaret Mead.

pp. 21, 249, 274, 294-295, 321: Extracts from COOPERATION AND COMPETITION AMONG PRIMITIVE PEOPLE, edited by Margaret Mead. Beacon Press, Boston. © 1961 by Margaret Mead. Used with kind permission of Margaret Mead.

pp. 48-49, Table 1.2: From S. L. Washburn and I. DeVore, The social life of baboons. *Scientific American,* 1961, Vol. 204 (6), pp. 62-71. © 1961 by Scientific American, Inc. All rights reserved.

p. 99, Table 3.1: From Bruce Wallace, PEOPLE, THEIR NEEDS, ENVIRONMENT, ECOLOGY: *Essays in Social Biology,* Volume 1 © 1972 by Prentice-Hall, Inc., Englewood Cliffs, N.J. Reprinted by permission of the publisher.

pp. 100, 104, 120, 125, 256-257, 353, 355, 434, and 549: Extracts from *The New York Times* of November 14, 1972, September 19, 1972, July 7, 1972, August 11, 1972, March 21, 1973, November 9, 1972, January 17, 1973, January 21, 1972, and January 31, 1973 © 1972, 1973 by The New York Times Company. Reprinted by permission.

pp. 103-104: Newspaper article by Tom Huth of May 9, 1971, Copyright, Washington Post. Reprinted with permission of Los Angeles Times/Washington Post News Service.

pp. 124, 187: Extracts from CULTURE AND COMMITMENT: *A study of the generation gap* by Margaret Mead. Natural History Press/Doubleday, Garden City, N.Y. © 1970 by Margaret Mead. Used with kind permission of Margaret Mead.

pp. 128, 129: Excerpts from THE SOCIAL CONSTRUCTION OF REALITY by Peter L. Berger and Thomas Luckmann. Copyright © 1966 by Peter L. Berger and Thomas Luckmann. Reprinted by permission of Doubleday & Company, Inc.

p. 131, Table 4.1: From "Effects of group pressure upon the modification and distortion of judgments" by Solomon E. Asch; data first reported in *Groups, Leadership and Men,* edited by H. Guetzkow. © 1951 by Carnegie Press; © 1963 by Russell & Russell. Reprinted by permission.

pp. 160, 226, 231: Extracts reprinted from *Civilization and Its Discontents* by Sigmund Freud. Translated from the German, edited by James Strachey. By permission of W. W. Norton & Company, Inc., New York. Copyright © 1961 by James Strachey. Acknowledgment is also made to Sigmund Freud Copyrights Ltd., The Institute of Psycho-Analysis, and The Hogarth Press Ltd., London, for permission to quote from this work in Volume XXI of THE STANDARD EDITION OF THE COMPLETE PSYCHOLOGICAL WORKS OF SIGMUND FREUD, revised and edited by James Strachey.

pp. 184-185, 482-483, 603-604: Columns by Arthur Hoppe in the *San Francisco Chronicle* of November 9, 1970, March 1, 1971, and March 18, 1973. Copyright 1970, 1971, 1973 Chronicle Publishing Company; reprinted by permission.

pp. 185, 486: Extracts from George W. Fairweather, SOCIAL CHANGE: THE CHALLENGE TO SURVIVAL, pp. 4, 7 (Morristown, N.J.: General Learning Press) © 1972 General Learning Corporation. Reprinted by permission.

p. 196: Words and music of the song "Little Boxes" by Malvina Reynolds, © copyright 1962 by Schroder Music Co. (ASCAP). Used by permission.

pp. 204-205: Extract from the filmscript of *Things to Come* by H. G. Wells © 1935. Reprinted by permission of the Estate of H. G. Wells.

pp. 223, 316, 317: Excerpts from B. H. Liddell Hart, THE REVOLUTION IN WARFARE, Yale University Press, New Haven, Conn., 1947. Copyright, 1947, by B. H. Liddell Hart. Reprinted by permission of A. Watkins, Inc., New York, and David Higham Associates, London.

pp. 264-265: Extract from Jane van Lawick–Goodall, IN THE SHADOW OF MAN copyright © 1971 by Hugo and Jane van Lawick–Goodall. Reprinted by kind permission of the publishers, Houghton Mifflin Company, Boston, and William Collins Sons & Company Ltd., London.

p. 275: Excerpt from NJAL'S SAGA, translated by Magnus Magnusson and Hermann Pálsson (Penguin Classics 1960). Copyright © Magnus Magnusson and Hermann Pálsson, 1960. Reprinted by permission.

p. 292, Table 7.1: From Leonard D. Eron, *Journal of Abnormal and Social Psychology,* 1963, Vol. 67, pp. 193-196. Copyright 1963 by the American Psychological Association. Reprinted by permission.

pp. 303-304: Extract from Ross Stagner, Personality dynamics and social conflict. *Journal of Social Issues,* 1961, Vol. 17, pp. 28-44. Reprinted by permission of *Journal of Social Issues* and the author.

pp. 308-309: Extract from James Joyce's story "Counterparts" in *Dubliners.* All rights reserved. Reprinted by permission of The Viking Press, Inc., New York, and The Society of Authors as the literary representative of the Estate of James Joyce, Jonathan Cape Ltd., London, and the Executors of the James Joyce Estate.

p. 312: Excerpt from D. P. Crowne and D. Marlowe, THE APPROVAL MOTIVE, pp. 23-24. John Wiley & Sons, Inc., New York, 1964. Reprinted by permission of the publisher.

pp. 336, 343, 344, 357, 367-368, 387-388, 392, 408: Excerpts reprinted by special permission from G. W. Allport, THE NATURE OF PREJUDICE, 1954, Addison-Wesley, Reading, Mass.

pp. 341, 343-344, 405: Excerpts from G. E. Simpson and J. M. Yinger, RACIAL AND CULTURAL MINORITIES: *An Analysis of Prejudice and Discrimination,* 1965 edition, by kind permission of Harper & Row Publishers Inc., New York. (A 1972 edition is now available.)

pp. 375, 379, 389: Excerpts from A PROFILE OF THE NEGRO AMERICAN by T. Pettigrew © 1964 by Litton Educational Publishing, Inc. Reprinted by permission of Van Nostrand Reinhold Company.

pp. 389, 398, 392, 406: Excerpted from Chapter 4 of BLACK RAGE, by William H. Grier and Price M. Cobbs, © 1968 by William H. Grier and Price M. Cobbs, Basic Books, Inc., Publishers, New York, and Jonathan Cape Ltd., London.

p. 408: Excerpt from T. W. Adorno, Else Frenkel-Brunswik, D. J. Levinson, and R. N. Sanford, THE AUTHORITARIAN PERSONALITY, 1950, reprinted by kind permission of Harper & Row Publishers Inc., New York.

p. 438: The poem "Revolutionary Dreams" by Nikki Giovanni, from her book RE-CREATION, published by Broadside, New York. Copyright 1970 by Nikki Giovanni. Reprinted by permission.

pp. 443-444, 448-449: Excerpts from ABNORMAL PSYCHOLOGY AND MODERN LIFE, Fourth Edition, by James C. Coleman. Copyright © 1972 by Scott, Foresman and Company. Reprinted by permission of the publisher.

pp. 445-446: Extract by Paul E. Meehl, from *Case Histories in Clinical and Abnormal Psychology,* edited by Arthur Burton and Robert E. Harris, p. 71. Harper & Row Publishers Inc., 1947. Reprinted by permission of the publisher.

pp. 451, 452-453, 453-455, 465: From PRINCIPLES OF PSYCHOPATHOLOGY by B. A. Maher. Copyright © 1966 McGraw-Hill, Inc. Used with permission of McGraw-Hill Book Company.

p. 455: Excerpt from Chapter 5 of THE MIND OF ADOLF HITLER, by Walter C. Langer, © 1972 by Basic Books, Inc., Publishers, New York, and Martin Secker & Warburg Ltd., London. Reprinted by permission of the publishers.

p. 460, Table 10.1: Reprinted from *Heredity in Health and Mental Disorders* by Franz J. Kallmann. By permission of W. W. Norton & Company, Inc. Copyright © 1953 by W. W. Norton & Company, Inc.

pp. 478-480, 484: Excerpts from Bruno Bettelheim, *Obsolete Youth,* San Francisco Press, Inc., San Francisco, 1970. Used by permission. (Originally based on an essay in *Encounter,* this reprint is available as a 50¢ paperback.)

p. 480: Poll data from the American Institute of Public Opinion (The Gallup Poll, 1973). Used by permission.

p. 481: Poll data from The Harris Survey, © 1972-1973 Chicago Tribune Co. Used by permission.

p. 488: Excerpt from Nathan Adler, "Kicks, drugs and politics." Reprinted from THE PSYCHOANALYTIC REVIEW, Vol. 57, No. 3, 1970, through the courtesy of the Editors and the Publisher, National Psychological Association for Psychoanalysis, New York, N.Y.

p. 489, 579: Extracts by C. G. Jung from THE COLLECTED WORKS OF C. G. JUNG, edited by G. Adler, M. Fordham, H. Read, and W. McGuire, translated by R. F. C. Hull, Bollingen Series XX, Vol. II, *Psychology and Religion: West and East,* "Psychological Commentary on 'Tibetan Book of the Great Liberation,'" (copyright © 1958 by Bollingen Foundation and © 1969 by Princeton University Press). Used by permission.

pp. 492-494: Excerpts from Norman Tallent, *Clinical Psychological Consultation,* Prentice-Hall, Inc., Englewood Cliffs, N.J.,

1963. Reprinted by kind permission of the author.

p. 509, Table 11.1: The Minnesota Multiphasic Personality Inventory (MMPI). Reproduced by permission. Copyright 1943, renewed 1970 by the University of Minnesota. Published by The Psychological Corporation, New York, N.Y. All rights reserved.

p. 510, Table 11.2: From H. G. Gough, *Manual for the California Psychological Inventory,* Consulting Psychologists Press, Inc., Palo Alto, Calif., 1957. Reprinted by permission of the publisher.

p. 518: Excerpt from P. H. Hoch, "Drug therapy," Chapter 77 of AMERICAN HANDBOOK OF PSYCHIATRY, Volume II, edited by Silvano Arieti, © 1959 by Basic Books, Inc., Publishers, New York. Reprinted by permission.

pp. 530-533: Excerpt from John B. P. Shaffer and M. David Galinsky, GROUP THERAPY AND HUMAN RELATIONS TRAINING, © 1974 by Prentice-Hall, Inc., Englewood Cliffs, N.J. Used by permission of the publisher.

p. 535: Extract from M. Wolf, T. Risley, and H. Mees, Application of operant conditioning procedures to the behavior problems of an autistic child. *Behavior Research and Therapy,* 1964, Vol. 1, pp. 305-312. Reprinted with the permission of Microform International Marketing Corporation, exclusive copyright licensee of Pergamon Press journal backfile.

p. 536: Excerpt from Albert Mehrabian, TACTICS OF SOCIAL INFLUENCE, © 1970 by Prentice-Hall, Inc., Englewood Cliffs, N.J. Used by permission of the publisher.

p. 539: Excerpts from C. R. Rogers and B. F. Skinner, Some issues concerning the control of human behavior. *Science,* Vol. 124, pp. 1057-1066, 30 November 1956. Reprinted by kind permission of *Science* and the authors.

p. 542, Table 11.3: From Hans H. Strupp, PSYCHOTHERAPY, p. 6 (Morristown, N.J.: General Learning Press) © 1972 General Learning Corporation. Used by permission of the publisher.

pp. 555-556, 577-578, 588: Excerpts from CREATIVITY & PSYCHOLOGICAL HEALTH by F. Barron, © 1963. Reprinted by permission of D. Van Nostrand Company.

pp. 560-561: Extract from Sigmund Freud, LEONARDO DA VINCI: *A Study in Psychosexuality,* translated by A. A. Brill. Copyright 1916 and renewed 1944 by A. A. Brill. Reprinted by permission of Random House, Inc., New York, and Routledge and Kegan Paul Ltd., London.

pp. 568-569: Excerpt from Aeschylus, THE ORESTEIAN TRILOGY, translated by Philip Vellacott (Penguin Classics 1956). Copyright © Philip Vellacott, 1956. Reprinted by permission of Penguin Books.

pp. 575-576: Excerpts from R. W. White, Competence and the psychosexual stages of development. Reprinted from NEBRASKA SYMPOSIUM ON MOTIVATION, 1960, edited by Marshall R. Jones, by permission of the University of Nebraska Press. Copyright © 1960 by the University of Nebraska Press.

pp. 597-598: Extract from "Galápagos

sketches," pp. 100-127 of GALAPAGOS: *The Flow of Wildness,* Vol. II (paper) by Eliot Porter, edited by Kenneth Brower. Copyright © 1970 by the Sierra Club & Ballantine Books. Used with permission.

ILLUSTRATIONS

Cover and title page (p. ii): Face of the Sphinx. Courtesy of the Egyptian State Tourist Administration.

p. 2: Douglas Campbell as King Oedipus, in a scene from *Oedipus Rex* of Sophocles, as presented at the Stratford Shakespearean Festival, Stratford, Ontario, Canada, in 1955. Directed by Tyrone Guthrie; designed by Tanya Moiseiwitsch; music by Cedric Thorpe Davie. By permission of Douglas Campbell and Actors' Equity Association.

p. 25: Alaskan Eskimo wooden mask with features of man and seal. Courtesy of The American Museum of Natural History.

p. 57: Wooden mask from Huastec, Mexico. Courtesy of The American Museum of Natural History.

p. 73, Figure 2.12: From L. A. Carmichael, H. P. Hogan, and A. A. Walter, An experimental study of the effect of language on the reproduction of visually perceived form. *Journal of Experimental Psychology,* 1932, Volume 15, pp. 73-86. Copyright 1932 by the American Psychological Association. Reprinted by permission.

p. 89: Figure (flute top) from the Sepik area of New Guinea. Courtesy of The American Museum of Natural History.

p. 127: Alaskan Eskimo seal effigy mask, 10 inches high, made of weathered driftwood. Courtesy of The American Museum of Natural History.

p. 173: Kwakiutl Las'laxa mask, from the Pacific Northwest Coast of North America. Courtesy of The American Museum of Natural History.

p. 227: Lelolalal mask for Leo'laxa ceremony, with mouthpiece and skull, from the Pacific Northwest Coast of North America. Courtesy of The American Museum of Natural History.

p. 227: Mask from Tabar, New Ireland, in the South Pacific. Courtesy of The American Museum of Natural History.

p. 335: Ife bronze head from Nigeria. Courtesy of The American Museum of Natural History.

p. 387: Mask made of raffia, burlap, and wood from Bapende, Zaire (the former Congo). Courtesy of The American Museum of Natural History.

p. 443: Pascola dancer's mask from Yaque, Mexico. Courtesy of The American Museum of Natural History.

p. 491: Akujo (demon) mask of the classical Japanese Noh theater, dating from the late sixteenth century. Courtesy of the Oyama Shrine, Kanazawa, Japan.

p. 551: Statue of Tutankhamen, the pharaoh who reigned over Egypt in the fourteenth century B.C. Courtesy of the Egyptian State Tourist Administration. Photo by C. Zachary.

By failing to invest in real psychological rehabilitation of people in prison, we commit increasing numbers of men and women to lives of desperation and crime in which they become predators upon the rest of society. Punitive ideologies that blame economically marginal groups such as slum dwellers, the aged, and the educationally deprived for their plight may well alienate large numbers of people, increase the likelihood of crime, and endanger the security of the rest of society. As a final example, recently the governor of California vetoed a bill which would have eliminated the requirement that public school children obtain parental consent before learning about venereal disease. Insofar as this makes it more difficult to teach the causes of such disease to schoolchildren, at a time of rampaging incidence of venereal disease that is reaching epidemic proportions, such action to preserve the traditional attitude toward sex probably increases the dangers to the physical well-being of our youth. It is always a matter of judgment, of course, as to whether a given course of action will threaten or enhance public security and well-being, but the argument that physical survival can be endangered by ideologically based decisions is unassailable.

Sometimes ethical values must take precedence over survival values, however. Survival as a biological principle is ethically neutral—the biologically fittest survive, while those lacking adaptability perish. If we blindly applied this principle of natural selection to the problem of air pollution, there is little doubt that the biological laws of survival would take over. Were we not to clean up the air (it would be cheaper not to), then numerous people would grow sick and many would die; the problem of overpopulation would be alleviated. Those with weaker lungs would succumb to respiratory diseases (this is evidently already happening in the case of emphysema), and others with tougher lungs would survive. Eventually, after many generations, evolutionary changes in man's lungs probably would produce a new breed for whom pollution might no longer pose a significant problem. But in the process, we would be callously casting aside all humanitarian values that make life worthwhile. "Our best interests" are often divided between values of sheer physical survival (for the individual, for the group, or for the nation) and maintenance of important cultural or ethical standards. Such standards are uniquely important to man, who lives by symbols that are both endearing and provoking. Our cultural values guide us in seeking long-range improvements in the human condition. Culture itself has evolved, via the transmission and preservation of useful ideas (in literature, history, science, philosophy, art), from generation to generation.

Although I have been saying here that cultural factors are important in the way man handles his life and the physical

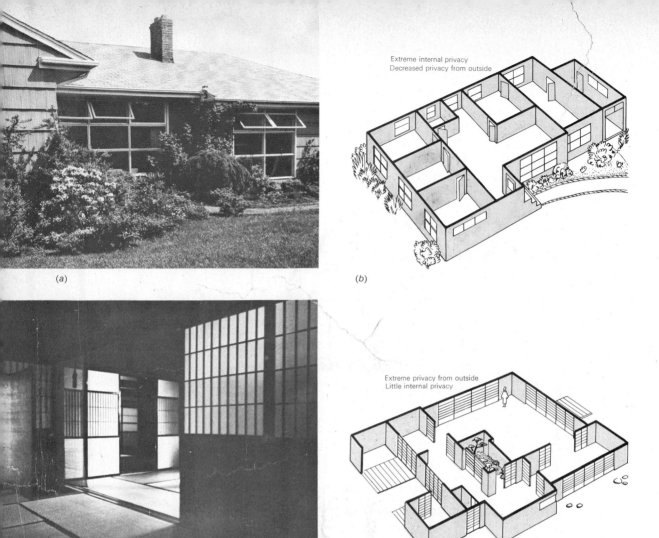

(a)

(b) Extreme internal privacy
Decreased privacy from outside

(c)

(d) Extreme privacy from outside
Little internal privacy

Figure 2.17 Privacy realms: effect of cultural factors upon house design. (a,b) The American house has many windows and is subdivided into several rooms. There is maximum internal privacy and less privacy from the outside. (c,d) The Japanese house turns a blank façade of high fences, walls, or closed screens to the outside world; but inside there is little concern about privacy and people can hear each other through the paper screens, which may often be left open for ventilation so that the whole house can be seen through. Thus there is maximum privacy from the outside and little internal privacy. (a: Felix Cooper; c: Hiroshi Hosono, Foreign Correspondents' Club, Tokyo)

world in which he lives, I seem to be hedging on whether they are more important or less important than survival factors. The question is not very meaningful in the abstract, since sometimes cultural factors will transcend biological ones and at other times be dwarfed by them. Biologists and cultural anthropologists generally weigh these factors as one would expect them to from their respective vantage points. For example, in a fascinating book on the kinds of houses built in different parts of the world, Amos Rapoport (1969) considers culture as the primary force in house design, and climate and geography as merely secondary modifiers. The physical setting provides mainly the possibilities, but the choice of style and materials reflects cultural taboos, customs, and tradition.